INSIDERS' GUIDE

NC'S Southern Coast & Wilmington

by

Linda Grattafiori

Gwynne Moore

Published and Marketed by:
By The Sea Publications, Inc.
P.O. Box 4368
Wilmington, NC 28406
(910) 763-8464

The Insiders' Guide®
is an imprint of
The Globe Pequot Press

•

TENTH EDITION
1st printing

•

Copyright ©2003
by By The Sea Publications, Inc.

•

Printed in the United States
of America

•

Publications from The Insiders' Guide®
series are available at special discounts
for bulk purchases for sales promotions,
premiums or fundraisings. Special
editions, including personalized covers,
can be created in large quantities for
special needs. For more information,
please write to
By The Sea Publications, P.O. Box 4368
Wilmington, NC 28406
or call (800) 955-1860

Large cover photos front & back: NC Travel & Tourism
Small photos courtesy Jay Tervo

By The Sea Publications, Inc.

President/Publisher

Jay Tervo

Sales and Marketing

Rosemarie Gabriele

Tom Jones

Heather Roberts

Sharron Swann

Director of Client Services

Leslie MacDonald

Administrative Manager

Susan Sims

Art Director

Matt Shortell

Project Editor

Molly Harrison

Graphic Artist

Stephanie Wills

Preface

Welcome to the tenth edition of *The Insiders Guide® to North Carolina's Southern Coast and Wilmington*. We think you'll find this book to be the most reliable and comprehensive collection of facts and tips and advice available for the southern coastal region extending from Topsail Island to the South Carolina border.

Inside this book you'll find recommendations on where to hear a symphony, charter a dive boat or shop for antiques. You'll find out where to rent a Jet-Ski, study yoga, buy original art, avoid traffic snarls, volunteer your time for a good cause, store your boat, locate emergency medical care or repair your bike. Those relocating here will find the chapters on Real Estate, Retirement, Health Care, Commerce and Industry and Schools and Child Care invaluable.

For this edition we've added a new chapter on Wedding Planning, due to an increasing number of couples choosing to say their vows on the southern coast. This chapter will help brides and grooms with finding musicians, caterers, locations, photographers and all of the other necessary service providers that make for a great wedding day.

This guide is not merely a checklist of things to do or places to go. Rather, it is designed to give you a sense of the character of the region and its offerings. We've tried to include information that will prove useful not only to short-term visitors, but also to newcomers who plan to stay. Even longtime residents and natives may gain new perspectives and histories about the people, places and events that have shaped this coastal area.

Keep in mind that you'll also find us on the Internet at www.insiders.com. There you can view each and every chapter in this book, investigate other locales in The Insiders' Guide series and e-mail us your questions and comments. We'd love to hear from you.

See you on the beach!

About the Authors

Linda Grattafiori

Linda Carol Grattafiori loves people and the arts and finds the written word the most satisfying form of expressing creativity. After living in Wilmington 30 years and freelance writing more than half that time, her first year with *The Insider's Guide* has taught her more about her "hometown" and herself than she thought imaginable. Linda also writes for *Encore Magazine* and has written for various regional publications including the *Wilmington Morning Star*, *Our State Magazine*, and her alma mater's *Campus Communique* at UNCW.

Gwynne Moore

Gwynne Moore is president of Blue World Press, a writing, editing and publishing company. A Duke University graduate, born and raised in New York, she is a former resident of Wisconsin, South Carolina, Georgia and Ohio. Gwynne has lived in Carolina Beach for seven years. Prior to becoming a permanent resident, she vacationed often in this area and has traveled extensively throughout the South with her husband, Terry.

Gwynne has written two regular columns for the *Carolina Beach Island Gazette*: "The Yankee Transplant," with information and opinion for non-Southerners who have moved to the South and "A Few French Fries Short...," a popular he-says, she-says humor piece she and her husband write together. Other local publications where her writing has appeared include the *Wilmington Morning Star*, *Greater Wilmington Business Journal*, *Scene* magazine and *Wilma!*, Wilmington's magazine for women.

During nearly 10 years as Director of Community Relations for a 400-bed hospital in Ohio, Gwynne published a monthly news magazine, annual reports, press releases and a variety of brochures. A Registered Nurse, she's self-published tips booklets, a Patient Teaching Kit, and educational materials.

About the Contributors

Terry Moore

Terry Moore, who finally realized that writing is far better than working, comes from a sales and marketing career in the steel industry. He says that his wife, Gwynne, "one of the big deal authors," has said it all — as she usually does — in far more words than he would have used. We might add that Terry's hobby, ever since he was in high school, has been humor writing. In addition to co-writing with Gwynne a humor column, "A Few French Fries Short...", for a local newspaper, he also co-writes with Gwynne a humor column called "Wilma & Fred" for a new women's magazine, *Wilma!* He also does a bit of business writing for *Greater Wilmington Business Journal*, and, after all that arduous exertion, he collapses in front of the TV or in the pool.

Jeanne Nociti

Jeanne Nociti has been a Topsail Area resident since 1993; however, her career in tourism dates back to the early 1980s when she was the Executive Director of The Seminole Area Chamber of Commerce in Seminole, Florida. Jeanne brought her love of chamber and tourism work to Topsail where she served for seven years as the Executive Director of the Greater Topsail Area Chamber of Commerce and Tourism. During this time, she was active in Pender County's efforts to develop a Tourism Development Authority and presently serves as the Authority's chairman. Always interested in writing, Jeanne has, in addition to *The Insiders Guide*, used her tourism experiences to write newspaper articles, create brochures and write editorial for tourism websites.

Rebecca Pierre

Rebecca Pierre has been a resident of Oak Island since 1992. Her writing experience, prior to moving from Pennsylvania, consisted mostly of business writing including: package labeling, job descriptions and procedures, personnel, volunteer and resident newsletters, personnel and volunteer handbooks, employee surveys, and a weekly column on volunteerism in a local daily newspaper. Rebecca began freelance writing after she moved to Oak Island. Her experience writing award-winning poetry brings discipline, an economy of words and vivid descriptions to her work.

Wildlife-watching is a wonderful pastime on the southern coast.

Acknowledgments

Gwynne

This has been great fun..... thanks to our esteemed publisher Jay Tervo, the terrific staff at By The Sea Publications, our awesome editor Molly Harrison, my inspirational, talented co-author, Linda Grattafiori, and highly capable, professional contributing writers Jeanne Nociti and Rebecca Pierre. With their help, I've grown another foot or two as a writer and I've benefited tremendously from our collegial relationship. Most of all, I thank my husband Terry whose writing and editing expertise have been invaluable to me, not to mention his love, support and sense of humor. Together we visited a variety of establishments, found places we didn't know existed and met a lot of really, really interesting folks. Just being part of such a first-class publication is rewarding in itself, so I feel particularly fortunate to have also gained new friends, new insights, new knowledge and new experiences. Learning about North Carolina's southern coast and Wilmington has been fascinating. All the people and places I've encountered while preparing my chapters have reinforced my feeling that this very special corner of the world is where I want to spend forever.

Linda

"What an amazing learning experience producing the 10th edition of Insiders' Guide continues to be! When our publisher Jay Tervo first came to my house with his daughter Caroline to download the Insiders' software, he assured me that he would come back to tutor "as many times as it took." It only took three times! Jay's patience is a match for Job's. Without his encouragement and that of our supportive editor Molly Harrison, this work would not sing. Former Insiders' writer Deb Daniel wrote some fine key notes and I hope I embellished the melody. Deep heart notes go to friend Penelope Morningstar who gave generous consults on the new wedding chapter. All of the staff at Insiders' are warm and helpful, especially my new life-long friend and co-author Gwynne Moore. She will always sit in the first chair of my orchestra. When all of these wonderful people are at home, I look at the pictures of my grandchildren Madison and Logan and my daughters Carol and Licia, who bless my life and keep my writer's spirit high."

VISIT US TODAY!
www.insiders.com

Table of Contents

Directory of Maps

Nothing beats a day on the water.

Photo: Jay Tervo

Wilmington And The Cape Fear Coast

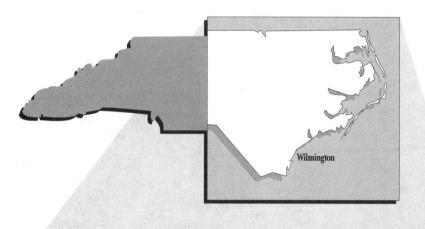

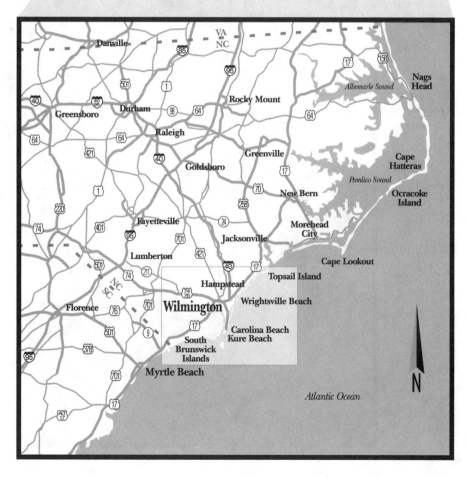

Topsail Island To Calabash

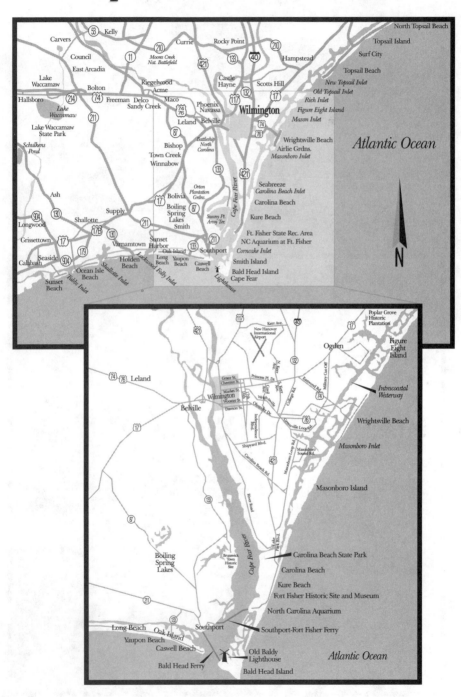

Downtown Wilmington

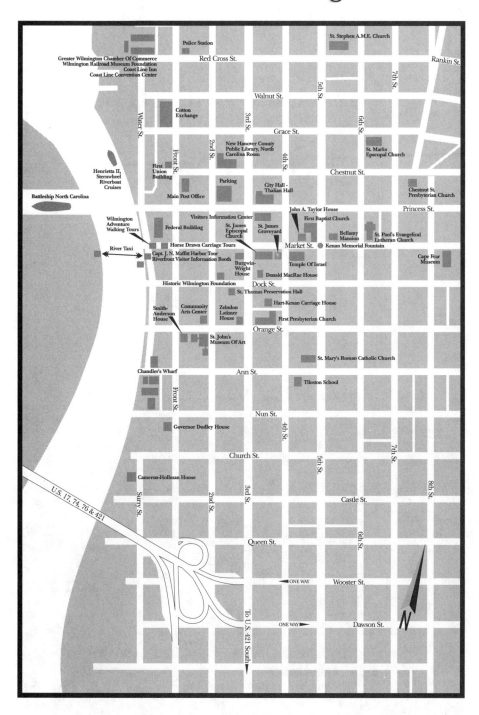

Unwrap The Perfect Rental Package.

Great Cars, Low Rates, Free Pick-up.

Pick Enterprise. We'll pick you up.®
1 800 rent-a-car

Pick-up subject to certain restrictions.

Getting Here, Getting Around

Tourists and newcomers to North Carolina's southern coast will find it relatively easy to get around in the area, which consists of four coastal counties: New Hanover, Pender, Brunswick and Onslow. The city of Wilmington makes up most of New Hanover County, geographically the second smallest but among the fastest growing of North Carolina's 100 counties. Wilmington's population is around 91,000 and New Hanover County's is about 160,000.

Pender County, bordering New Hanover county on the north, includes the southern half of Topsail Island (Surf City and Topsail Beach), Figure Eight Island (private), Hampstead and Burgaw. Primarily rural, Pender County was founded in 1875 and is the state's fifth largest county in area.

The northern half of Topsail Island is in Onslow County, which includes the coastal towns of Swansboro, Holly Ridge and Sneads Ferry. The City of Jacksonville, Camp Lejune Marine Base and Hammocks Beach State Park on Bear Island (accessible only by boat or ferry) are also in Onslow County.

Brunswick County, across the Cape Fear River to the west of New Hanover County, is quite unique in that its beaches face the Atlantic Ocean to the south. These beaches, on barrier islands between the ocean and the Intracoastal Waterway, stretch from the South Carolina border to the historic fishing village of Southport. Bald Head Island is approximately four miles from Southport at the mouth of the Cape Fear River where it meets the ocean. Bald Head Island can be reached only boat or the Bald Head Island Ferry, which does not ferry vehicles.

To help you find your way around the Cape Fear area, a variety of maps are available at various locations. *The Guide Map*, published by the Cape Fear Coast Convention & Visitors Bureau, 24 N. Third Street, (910) 341-4030 or (800) 222-4757, is good for the downtown Wilmington riverfront and historic district and includes information on attractions outside the city. A wide variety of other maps and brochures for the Cape Fear area is also available at the Wilmington Chamber of Commerce at 1 Estell Lee Place (just north of the Best Western Coast Line Inn at the west end of Nutt Street), (910) 762-2611. The Chamber of Commerce has extensive relocation data, community maps, a newcomer's guide and helpful information for students coming to our local colleges and universities. The Oak Island Recreation Center has maps of Oak Island, and the Visitor Center in Southport can help you with maps of that area.

Getting Here by Land

Roadways

Although Wilmington lacks a freeway system (part of its relaxed charm, perhaps), navigating through the area is fairly easy. Many streets and

LOOK FOR:
- Ground
  Transportation
  Roadways
  Buses
  Bike Routes
  Trolley
  Taxis/Limos
  Car Rentals
- Ferries
- Air
  Transportation

CLOSEUP
- The Days of
  Ballrooms and
  Beach Cars

roads are being widened and improved to handle the increasing traffic flow of tourists and new residents.

Martin Luther King Parkway Jr., on the north side of town, runs from Eastwood Road to N. 23rd Street. Eventually, the Parkway will extend to downtown, where it will link with U.S. Highway 17 from the west and will serve as a bypass for traffic from both the north and the west headed for the beaches.

Eastwood Road (U.S. Highway 74) is the only access to Wrightsville Beach. Market Street (U.S. Highways 17 and 74) is the main east-west route to and from downtown. Just east of College Road, Eastwood branches off to Wrightsville Beach, and Market Street continues northeast as U.S. 17 to access the northern beaches. U.S. Highway 76 from the west takes a southerly route through Wilmington along Oleander Drive, a major shopping thoroughfare, and joins Eastwood Road (U.S. 74) just before it crosses the Intracoastal Waterway and proceeds to Wrightsville Beach.

From the north, Interstate Highway 40 ends on the north side of Wilmington and becomes N.C. Highway 132, which is College Road, the main north-south route through the city. College Road continues south until it ends at U.S. Highway 421 (Carolina Beach Road), which continues south through Monkey Junction to Pleasure Island, where Carolina Beach and Kure Beach are located. U.S. 421 ends at the southern tip of Pleasure Island, the location of the state ferry to Southport.

The beaches of Brunswick County can be accessed either by taking U.S. 17 South from Wilmington and using the various feeder roads, or by taking the ferry from Fort Fisher on Pleasure Island to Southport and using N.C. Highways 133 and 211until N.C. 211 merges with U.S. 17 South.

With the opening of the final leg of I-40, access to Wilmington and the Cape Fear area from the north and northwest became much easier. From the south, the widening of U.S. 17 to four lanes has improved that access route considerably, while the widening of much of U.S. 74 has eased the trip from the west. Eventually, a U.S. Highway 17 Bypass will open allowing access from I-40 to the northeastern and southwestern beach communities without having to go through the city.

Wilmington, one of the few deep-water ports on the southeastern seaboard, is about 50 miles from the South Carolina border. We've listed a few distances and driving times below to give a feel for how easy it is to get here.

Raleigh, NC: 127 mi. — 2 hrs.
Charlotte, NC: 197 mi. — 4 hrs.
Asheville, NC: 310 mi. — 6½ hrs.
Charleston, SC: 170 mi. — 3½ hrs.
Columbia, SC: 210 mi. — 4 hrs.
Washington, DC: 375mi. — 7½ hrs.
New York, NY: 610 mi. — 12½ hrs.
Cleveland, OH: 750 mi. — 14 hrs.

Interstates and Highways

For those wanting to take a really long drive to get here, Wilmington is linked to Barstow, California, via 2,554 miles of Interstate Highway 40, the longest interstate highway in the nation.

From the south, U.S. Highway 17 roughly parallels the Atlantic Ocean shore, but is a number of miles inland, so there are no views of the ocean. If you don't have to stop in Myrtle Beach, be sure to avoid Business 17, which takes you along The Strand and through downtown — a 20-mile trip that can take forever during the tourist season. Regular U.S. 17, which once bypassed the congestion of Myrtle Beach, has become surrounded by the commercial sprawl of the town, and though slow, is much better than Business 17. On the plus side, gas prices are usually pretty good along U.S. 17 in Myrtle Beach. Calabash, off U.S. 17 on N.C. 179 just across the state line, is the home of a number of restaurants serving the famous Calabash-style seafood.

Continuing north on U.S. 17, when you reach Supply you have the option of taking N.C. 211 into Southport, a historic fishing village at the mouth of the Cape Fear River. From Southport, you can take N.C. 133 north to rejoin U.S. 17 or take the state ferry to Fort Fisher on Pleasure

Island. On U.S. 421 north of the ferry dock are Fort Fisher State Historic Site, Fort Fisher State Recreation Area and the recently expanded North Carolina Aquarium, the largest of the state aquariums.

From the west, U.S. 74 from Charlotte and Interstate 20 becoming U.S. 76 from Columbia, South Carolina, merge near Whiteville and continue toward Wilmington. They junction with U.S. 17 just west of the N.C. 133 north exit to the USS North Carolina Battleship Memorial. The majority of these roads are easy-driving four-lane highways through gently rolling countryside and coastal plains.

Metro Area Streets

Wilmington's unusual geographical configuration of being situated more or less on a tapering peninsula between the Atlantic Ocean and the Cape Fear River, results in a layout of streets that does not follow any sort of orderly pattern one might find in an inland city. Downtown Wilmington is the only part of the city where blocks are laid out in a standard north/south, east/west

Crossing water — sometimes waiting a while to do so — is a fact of life in coastal-area travel.

Photo: Jay Tervo

arrangement. As a result, getting around for the tourist or newcomer is best accomplished by following route numbers whenever possible.

Because the city has no expressway system, city streets must carry all of the traffic flow. Surprisingly, even without freeways, traffic moves fairly well except during rush hours or heavy shopping periods, and even then, only a few streets are involved in the congestion.

Traffic from the west on U.S. Highways 17, 74 and 76 enters Wilmington via the Cape Fear Memorial Bridge, a very high, platform-type lift bridge that allows large ocean-going vessels to navigate up the Cape Fear River to the industrial area north of town. From downtown, the routes split, with U.S. 17 and 74 following the main drag, Market Street, on a more or less easterly direction through the city. U.S. 76 meanders toward the ocean on Dawson Street, then Oleander Drive, Wrightsville Avenue and finally Eastwood Road as it rejoins U.S. 74 and continues into Wrightsville Beach. U.S. 17 continues in a northeasterly direction on Market Street and provides access to Figure Eight Island and the Topsail Island beaches on its way to Pender and Onslow Counties plus Jacksonville and Camp Lejeune.

Traffic from the north on I-40 flows onto College Road, N.C. Highway 132, the main north/south route through Wilmington. College Road crosses Market Street and Oleander, then ends at Monkey Junction where it joins with Carolina Beach Road, U.S. 421, coming southeast from downtown. Carolina Beach Road continues south to Pleasure Island (Carolina Beach and Kure Beach).

Not only are Market Street, Oleander Drive and College Road the most heavily traveled streets in Wilmington, they also have the greatest concentration of commercial establishments. Restaurants, strip malls and shopping centers proliferate on all three thoroughfares, with the largest mall, Westfield Independence Shoppingtown Mall, being located on Oleander Drive at Independence Boulevard. If you're heading for Wrightsville Beach, be aware that delays can occur at the drawbridge on U.S. 74 and 76 going onto Harbor Island. Once there, U.S. 74 heads to the north end of Wrightsville Beach and U.S. 76 goes to the south end.

Bike Routes

The Cape Fear area is not blessed with true independent biking and hiking paths and trails like those found in other parts of the country. The closest thing is a widened section of U.S. Highway 421 on Pleasure Island. About three feet of roadway on each side of the road is marked off and identified as a bike path for about 4½ miles from north of Kure Beach to the ferry dock at Fort Fisher. This path will eventually connect with one under construction that starts at the state boat launch area on Snow's Cut just east of Bridge Barrier Road in Carolina Beach.

A number of other bike routes using city streets and county roads have been developed, and maps for them are available, showing cyclists how to get around town on roads that match their traffic-handling skills. Roads are designated as neighborhood streets, local commuting streets, busy through-routes or touring routes. Parks, schools, public buildings and other points of interest are indicated. A complete street index is shown and a park matrix that shows the facilities available at each location is provided. To obtain Wilmington bike maps, contact the City of Wilmington, Transportation Planning Department, P.O. Box 1810, Wilmington, NC 28402; (910) 341-7888.

The River-to-Sea Bike Route stretches from Riverfront Park at the foot of Market Street in Wilmington to Wrightsville Beach, a ride of just less than 9 miles. This is a somewhat informal route used mostly by "locals" — maps are hard to find except at some Wilmington bicycle shops. (See our chapter on Sports, Fitness and Parks.)

A flat landscape and predominantly well-maintained roads make touring the coastal plain by bicycle very pleasurable. Some state-funded Bicycling Highways pass through Wilmington and along the neighboring coast. They're marked by rectangular road signs bearing a green ellipse, a bicycle icon and the route number.

INSIDERS' TIP

When driving in the City of Wilmington, please note that a number of busy intersections are monitored by cameras that automatically photograph license plates. Going through a red light will net the vehicle owner a $50 citation in the mail — and that person is required by law to pay!

The Ports of Call Route, N.C. Bike Route 3, is a 319-mile seaside excursion from the South Carolina border to the Virginia line. Approximately 110 miles of it are along the southern coast, giving access to miles of beaches and downtown Wilmington.

The Cape Fear Run, N.C. Bike Route 5, links Raleigh to Southport. This 166-mile route crosses the Cape Fear River twice and intersects the Ports of Call.

Obtain free maps and information from the North Carolina Division of Bicycle & Pedestrian Transportation, 1552 Mail Service Center, Raleigh, NC 27601-1552; (919) 733-2804. Although the maps are updated regularly, be ready to improvise when it comes to information on campgrounds and detours. Detailed information, maps and map order forms are available online at www.ncdot.org/transit/bicycle.

Brunswick County, which is essentially rural with small towns, has many biking opportunities on lesser-traveled roads through the countryside, in the towns and residential developments. In addition, there is a designated route of 32 miles from the historic fishing village of Southport to Orton Plantation and Brunswick Town historic Site. A 3-mile segment of paved shoulder bike paths has recently opened from the state ferry dock to downtown Southport. At the Oak Island Recreation Center, you can obtain a booklet of bicycle trail maps conveniently sized to fit in your pocket. In it you will find 11 maps, including text description and trail length, with names like Heron Loop, Crab Dock Loop and Scenic Walkway Loop. Bald Head Island features an eight-mile loop trail that includes Old Baldy Lighthouse. This island is accessible only by private ferry from Southport; the fare is $15 per person round trip. Primarily residential with fine beach homes, Bald Head Island has a unique maritime forest and an excellent marina. No automobiles are permitted, so golf carts and bicycles are popular modes of travel.

Pender County has no designated bicycle routes or trails, but the area is primarily rural, with many lesser-traveled roadways available for bike touring.

In Onslow County, three bicycle-touring routes are designated: Swansboro Bicentennial Bicycle Trail, Richlands Loop Bicycle Route and Jacksonville City to the Sea Route. Call (910) 347-5332 or (910) 455-1113 for information. The Swansboro Trail is a 25-mile loop that begins in Swansboro, crosses the White Oak River to Cape Carteret, then winds through the Croatan National Forest, crosses the river again and returns to Swansboro. Idyllic spots abound. The Richlands Loop can be 50 or 20 miles, depending on your preference. The route is marked by green and white bike route signs. The terrain is level, and all roads are paved. The Jacksonville trip takes you from the Jacksonville Mall to Hammock's Beach State Park. This route intersects with the Ports of Call Route. Brochures can be obtained from Onslow County Tourism or Onslow County Parks & Recreation, 1244 Onslow Pines Road, Jacksonville, NC 28540; (910) 347-5332.

If by Sea

Most boaters coming to the Cape Fear region do so via the magnificent Intracoastal Waterway (ICW), although some use that big puddle offshore, the Atlantic Ocean. Extending 3,000 miles along the Atlantic coast from Boston to Key West, the Intracoastal Waterway provides protection from the sea, along with a multitude of marinas and harbors. In North Carolina, the ICW follows a path behind a nearly continuous string of barrier islands from Virginia to South Carolina. See our chapter on Marinas and the Intracoastal Waterway for detailed information.

Getting Here by Air

Wilmington International Airport (formerly New Hanover International Airport) is the prime entry point for most people flying into the greater Wilmington area. Myrtle Beach International Airport in South Carolina is nearly the same distance from Shallotte as the Wilmington airport (about 40 miles), so visitors traveling by air to or from the Calabash and South Brunswick Islands areas might do well to check flight availability via Myrtle Beach. Those traveling to or from from Oak Island, Southport, Pleasure Island or points north will find Wilmington International Airport easier to use. Small aircraft destined for Brunswick County can use Brunswick County Airport, just outside Southport.

Airports

Wilmington International Airport
1740 Airport Blvd., Wilmington
• (910) 341-4125

Wilmington International is an entirely modern facility, complete with baby-changing areas accessible to dads. Yet it has plenty of that charm peculiar to small airports. The airport fronts 23rd Street, 2 miles north of Market Street, and, by car, is within 10 minutes of downtown Wilmington and about 20 minutes of Wrightsville Beach.

Two airlines serve the airport: Atlantic Southeast Airlines (ASA), (800) 282-3424, the Delta connection to Atlanta, and USAirways, (800) 428-4322. The number of daily flights varies with the tourist season.

Short-term parking rates are $1 per half-hour, with a maximum 24-hour charge of $10. Long-term parking costs $1 per hour, with a maximum charge of $7 per day. Fifteen minutes of free parking is available in both parking areas.

Brunswick County Airport
4019 Long Beach Rd., Southport
• (910) 457-6483

The Brunswick County Airport is a fast-growing, full-service airport located on the mainland side of the Oak Island Bridge and is especially convenient to Bald Head Island and the Southport-Oak Island area. It has a 4,000-foot paved and lighted runway, which can handle general aviation aircraft from the lightest to fairly sizable jets. The airport is in the process of widening the runway and lengthening it to 5,500 feet with the addition of a full-length parallel taxiway. It supports instrument approaches (GPS,NDB).

There are now 30 T-hangars and six commercial hangars with more planned. Services provided include: flight instruction, rental aircraft, a full-service aircraft repair facility on the field (Oak Island Aviation), and a state-of-the-art computerized fueling system. With a fuel purchase, you receive one free overnight tie-down. In addition, there is a full-time skydiving and sight seeing operator, and during the summer months banner towing along the beaches is available. The terminal houses airport operations, Eastern Aviation Air Charter Service and Enterprise Rent-A-Car. There is also a computerized weather graphics station and an Automated Weather Observation System with real-time aviation weather available at (910) 457-1710.

Myrtle Beach International Airport
1100 Jet Port Rd., Myrtle Beach
• (843) 448-1580

The Myrtle Beach International Airport is convenient for those residents or visitors in the extreme southern coastal area. It is serviced by six airlines: Atlantic Southeast Airlines (ASA) and Comair, which are part of the Delta Connection, a group of strong regional carriers that work together to give more passengers access to the Delta Air Lines network (800) 282-3424; AirTran (seasonal) (800) 247-8726; Continental Airlines (800) 525-0280; Spirit Airlines, (800) 772-7117; and USAirways, (800) 428-4322. Short-term parking rates are 75¢ for each 20 minutes; the maximum for each 24 hours is $21. Long-term parking is $2 for up to two hours, two to six hours is $4 with the maximum $8 for 24 hours. The airport's new economy parking is $1 up to one hour, each additional hour is $1, the maximum for each 24 hours is $5. Take advantage of the free shuttle bus service between the terminal and the Economy lot; buses run approximately every five to seven minutes. Added to each Long Term or Economy parking lot transaction is a $1 fee to cover increased security costs.

Air Charters, Rentals, Leasing

If you're looking for a place to charter, rent or purchase a small aircraft, you can do it here. If your plane needs servicing or refueling, you can have it done here. If you want flight instruction, you can get it here. All the companies listed below are based at Wilmington International unless otherwise noted; not all services are provided by each company, but their staffs are knowledgeable and will assist you in finding whatever you need. (See also our section on Flying in the chapter Sports, Fitness and Parks.)

Aeronautics, maintenance and service, (910) 763-4691

Air Wilmington, maintenance, service, charters, leasing, flight training, (910) 763-0146

ISO Aero Service Inc. of Wilmington, flight training, maintenance, transient services, (910) 763-8898

Eastern Aviation Inc., Brunswick County Airport, Southport, charters, (910) 457-0710

Getting Around Once You're Here

Local Buses

Wilmington Transit Authority
1110 Castle St., Wilmington
• (910) 343-0106

Wilmington Transit Authority (WTA) operates six Wilmington-area public bus lines. The adult one-way fare is 75¢. The fare is 35¢ for handicapped individuals with a Medicare card and seniors older than 65. A transfer is 10¢, or 5¢ for seniors and the handicapped. Children younger than 5 ride free when accompanied by a paying adult. Other children pay the adult fare of 75¢, unless using student tickets. UNCW students and faculty with valid IDs ride free. Drivers do not carry change, so have your exact fare ready when you board the bus.

Discount ticket books are available from any bus driver — 11 rides cost $7.50. For senior citizens, the disabled and students in grades 1 through 12 on weekdays during the school year, the 11-ride ticket books are $3.50.

Buses run from 6:30 AM until about 6:30 PM (a few routes may offer service until 7:30 or 8 PM). Buses do not run on Sundays or Thanksgiving Day, Christmas Day, New Year's Day, Memorial Day, July Fourth, Labor Day and Martin Luther King Jr. Day; some routes may have limited schedules or do not operate at all on Saturdays.

Routes include East Wilmington - Long Leaf Park (Route 1); Marketplace - UNCW (Route 2); Oleander Shopping Centers (Route 3); Eastwood Road - Cape Fear Memorial Hospital (Route 4); New Hanover Regional Medical Center - Brooklyn (Route 5); Westfield Independence and Long Leaf Malls - UNCW (Route 6). All are handicapped accessible.

The city of Wilmington offers curb-to-curb transportation called Paratransit Service or Dial-A-Ride Transportation (DART) for disabled individuals who have Americans With Disabilities (ADA) certification. Service is available Monday through Saturday from 6 AM to 6 PM. The fare is $1.50. Call at least 24 hours, but preferably four or five days, in advance. Call (910) 343-0106 and speak with the ADA contact person.

UNCW shuttle and fixed route services are free to all UNCW students and faculty who show a valid UNCW identification card (ID). Three Seahawk Shuttles (routes 7, 8, and 9) run within and around the campus area continuously Monday through Thursday from 7 AM to 9:30 PM and Friday from 7 AM to 6:30 PM. For information, call (910) 962-3178.

The Wilmington Public Transit Guide, which contains a map and a table of schedules, is available at the Visitors Information Center, 24 N. Third Street in Wilmington, and on buses. For more information call the WTA at (910) 343-0106 Monday through Friday from 8 AM to 4:30 PM PM or TDD at (910) 763-9011. Or stop by the WTA office at 1110 Castle Street, between 11th and 12th streets.

New Hanover Transportation Services
320 Chestnut St., Ste. 502, Wilmington
• (910) 341-7415

New Hanover Transportation Services (NHTS) is a coordinated human services system designed to meet the non-emergency transportation needs of the elderly, disabled and other special populations who are clients of area human services agencies. Agency funding sources determine who is eligible for transportation and the types of trips that can be provided. The "Blue Line" offers clean, courteous service using two 16-passenger minibuses to safely transport passengers to several designated locations. The cost is $2 per one-way trip or 11 tickets for $20. Passengers may transfer to Wilmington Transit Authority buses. Services are available Monday through Friday, excluding holidays. For more information, call (910) 341-7415.

Trolley

Front St. Free Trolley
Wilmington Transit Authority, 1110 Castle St., Wilmington • (910) 343-0106

A fun way to see the riverfront area and some of the shops is to take the Front Street Free Trolley in downtown Wilmington. A single trolley runs continuously from 7:30 AM to 7 PM Monday through Friday and 11 AM to 7 PM on Saturday; it doesn't have service on Sunday. Trolley stops are marked along the route, which goes along Front, Water and Second streets. You can look for the trolley to stop approximately every 10 minutes along Front Street and about every 20 minutes on Water and Second streets.

The Days of Ballrooms and Beach Cars

Before the days of gas stations and weekend traffic, the best way to get to Wrightsville Beach was the "Beach Car," the electric trolley that ran from Princess and Front streets in downtown Wilmington to what was once the biggest beach attraction south of Atlantic City: Wrightsville Beach's Lumina Pavilion.

Originally known as New Hanover Banks or Ocean View, early developers envisioned the community as the Atlantic City of the South. Somewhat less sophisticated in those days, an 1897 meeting of property owners proposed an ordinance to prohibit cattle running loose. Today, aside from restaurant fare, no trace of cattle can be found.

The trolley began operating in 1902, replacing an older railway train. The route roughly paralleled the "shell road" (now Wrightsville Avenue) and ran along today's Park Avenue, where a couple of the old station shelters still remain. Operated by the Tidewater Power Company, the trolley cars were orange with cream trim, carried 68 passengers each, and made the trip from downtown to the beach in as little as 35 minutes. Five-car trains ran during the height of the season.

In 1903, the Tidewater Power Company purchased an oceanfront lot for $10 at Station 7, the end of the line, where it built the Lumina Pavilion, named for the thousands of incandescent lights that made the building visible from far out at sea. Constructed entirely of heart pine, it was opened on June 3, 1905, and underwent two major expansions in subsequent years.

The pavilion featured a vast promenade, bowling lanes, a ladies' parlor, an upstairs restaurant and downstairs lunch service, dressing rooms, slot machines and other amusements, but the gem of the pavilion was its second-floor dance hall. The enormous dance floor accommodated hundreds of dancers, and the high-ceilinged room was festooned with bunting and flags. Some of the era's most famous orchestras and big bands played there, including Kay Kaiser, Guy Lombardo, Cab Calloway Tommy Dorsey, Paul Whiteman and Stan Kenton. (Wilmington was the biggest city in North Carolina at the time.) Curiously, a writer in 1910 recalled that opera was favored by Lumina audiences over so-called popular music of the day.

Other attractions included dance contests, beauty pageants, beach games such as sack races and water sports, and convention dances. Swimmers could rent bathing suits emblazoned with "Lumina" on the front. An especially unusual attraction was motion pictures. The owners erected a screen about 50 yards into the surf and projected silent movies that could be viewed from seating on the beach or from the promenade. The screen was moved closer when "talkies" appeared. This tradition lives on in the annual Lumina Daze celebration, which benefits the Wrightsville Beach Museum of History. (See our Annual Events chapter.)

Manners were carefully observed at the Lumina. Jacket and tie were essential. Cheek-to-cheek dancing? Unacceptable! Mrs. Bessie Martin, the Lumina's permanent chaperon, saw to that. No alcoholic beverages or rude behavior were permitted, either — Tuck Savage saw to that. Some called Tuck a "supervisor"; today we'd call him a bouncer.

Admission was free before World War I. After that, the trolley to the beach cost 35¢, which included admission to the Lumina.

The trolley line even influenced the birth of Wilmington's early suburbs — Carolina Place, Carolina Heights, Oleander, Audubon, and Winter Park grew up along the route. Then, in the 1930s, the first automobile route was built to Harbor Island. Billboards sprung up: "In a hurry? Take the Causeway." It wasn't long before the road spanned Banks Channel, and another road was paved down the length of the island in 1935. Soon the trolley became a throwback to a more sluggish era, and it declined in popularity. Its last run took place April 27, 1940. The only beach car alleged to remain today is in Annabelle's Restaurant on Oleander Drive.

The Lumina remained viable a while longer. Hot dogs and surf accessories were sold downstairs. Rock concerts were occasionally held there in the 1960s, but by the early '70s the ballroom stood perpetually dark, and in 1973 the pavilion was torn down. The Lumina lives on in many place names around the beach and, like the old Oceanic Hotel and the Harbor Island Casino, it won't be totally forgotten any time soon. The Lumina and the beach trolley are reminders that perhaps being in a hurry really isn't what the beach is all about.

The photo of the trolley here is one of 250 photos in Wrightsville Beach, A Pictorial History by the nonprofit Wrightsville Beach Preservation Society. For a copy of the book write to the society at P.O. Box 584, Wrightsville Beach, NC 28480, or call (910) 256-2569.

Also beginning to develop late in the 1800s, Carolina Beach south of Wilmington became a very popular oceanfront destination. In 1898, the Sedgeley Hall Club and the Hanover Seaside Club were established with sizable memberships. The Carolina Moon Pavilion was quite popular with visitors until its destruction by the great fire of 1940, which destroyed twenty-four businesses and three whole blocks, including the boardwalks and amusement area.

The Beach Car trolley picks up passengers outside Wilmington, c. 1915.

Photo: Cape Fear Museum

Taxicabs, Shuttle Vans and Limousines

In the areas of Wilmington, Wrightsville Beach, Carolina Beach and Kure Beach, taxis, shuttles, sedans and limos abound. Some companies provide strictly taxi service, some provide limousine, sedan or shuttle van service, and some companies provide a combination of some or all services. An asterisk (*) after the listing denotes that only taxicab service is available. Within the city, fares are uniform at $1.35 plus 20¢ per eighth mile; outside city limits, fares are a set rate depending on destination; for example, fares from the airport to downtown or the beaches are usually on a flat fee basis.

A Capital Style Limo, Sedan, Van & Bus Service, (800) 948-6170 (Raleigh)

A & K Limo Services, (910) 686-8575

Azalea Limousine Service, (910) 452-5888

*****Beach Buggy Taxi**, (910) 792-0232

*****Clay's Taxi**, (910) 793-4451

Classic Limousine, (910) 793-8843

Exquisite Limousine & Transportation Services, (910) 796-3009

Kat's Taxi, (910) 233-4702 or (910) 763-5014

Lett's Taxi and AAA Lett's Limousine Service, (910) 343-3335 or (910) 362-8888

*****Madina Taxi**, (910) 297-4812

Port City Taxi Inc., (910) 762-1165 or (910) 762-5230

Prestige Limousine Service, (910) 799-4484

*****Roadway Taxicab**, (910) 790-0350

Sandhills Transportation, (910) 798-8294 or (910) 279-5238

Security Limousine, (910) 341-5733

Tom-Kat Limousine, (910) 350-1110 or (910) 540-0569

Top Hat Limousines, (910) 262-8889

*****X-tra Cab**, (Wrightsville Beach), (910) 798-5888

*****Yellow Cab**, (910) 762-3322

*****Wilmington Transport**, (910) 579-9944

Brunswick County has no limousine service, but the following taxicab and shuttle services are available. Easy Way and Southern are primarily airport shuttle by reservation.

A & E Cab, (910) 278-9100

Calabash Cab, (910) 575-7555

Easy Way Transport Service, (910) 579-9926

Handy Taxi, (910) 443-8456

Oak Island Cab, (910) 278-6373

P & J Cab Company, 754-2860

Southern Hospitality, (910) 457-4949

In Onslow County, the following cab and limo services are available, primarily out of Jacksonville.

A - 1 Taxi, (910) 353-0365

American Cab, (910) 455-6662

Barringer Limousine Service, (910) 938-2486

Diamond Cab, (910) 455-2222

Dynamic Cab, (910) 347-5757

Yellow Cab, (910) 353-1111

Car Rentals

Along with the national chains and independent car rental services listed here, several new car dealerships also lease cars long-term.

Avis Rent A Car, Wilmington International Airport, Main Terminal, Wilmington, (910) 763-1993, (800) 831-2847

Budget Rent A Car, 1740 Airport Boulevard and 4911 Market Street, Wilmington, (910) 762-9247 or (910) 762-8910 (these numbers takes you to a central routing system that will connect you with the local rental agent), (800) 527-0700.

Enterprise Rentals, 5601-B Market Street, Wilmington, (910) 799-4042; 2642 Carolina Beach Road, Wilmington, (910) 397-9110, 1930 Castle Hayne Road, Wilmington, (910) 772-1560; 412 South College Road (910) 798-9178, (800) 736-8222

Enterprise Rent-A-Car, Brunswick County Airport, (800) 736-8222

E-Zgo Car Rental, 2403 Castle Hayne Road, Wilmington, (910) 763-1213

Hertz, Wilmington International Airport, (910) 762-1010, (800) 654-3131

National Car Rental, Wilmington International Airport, (910) 762-8000 or (910) 762-0143, (800) 227-7368

Rent-A-Wreck, 2013 North Kerr Avenue, Wilmington, (910) 452-2233

Triangle Rental, 4124 Market Street, Wilmington, (910) 251-9812

Ferries

Southport-Fort Fisher Ferry
(800) 368-8969

North Carolina's ferry system actually began in the 1920s with a private tug and barge service crossing Oregon Inlet on the Outer Banks. Other private ferries subsequently developed that were subsidized by the state during the 1930s and '40s. In the late '40s and '50s, the state began purchasing the private ferry systems, and today, North Carolina has seven ferry routes, 21 ferries and 475 employees. More than 900,000 vehicles and 2.5

million passengers are transported every year over seven bodies of water.

The Southport-Fort Fisher ferry service is not only a mode of transportation that saves miles of driving, but also one of the least expensive scenic tours. On the approximately 30-minute cruise, the ferry provides a panoramic view of the mouth of the Cape Fear River above Southport. On the Brunswick County side, huge yellow cranes mark the Military Ocean Terminal at Sunny Point, the largest distribution center in the country for military supplies. Other sights include Old Baldy, North Carolina's oldest lighthouse on Bald Head Island; Price's Creek Lighthouse, which guided Confederate blockade runners through New Inlet during the Civil War; and the Oak Island Lighthouse, the nation's brightest. (For information on tours and attractions, see our Attractions chapter.)

The Fort Fisher ferry terminal on Pleasure Island is near the southern terminus of U.S. 421 on the right. The Southport terminal is on Ferry Road, just off N.C. 211, about 3 miles north of town. During summer months, you need to get to the terminal at least 20 minutes before departure, on holiday weekends 30 minutes. This ferry is extremely popular with visitors; capacity is limited to about 38 cars.

Departure Times
* Winter only: 1/1 – 5/20 and 9/24 – 12/31
** Summer only: 5/21 – 9/23

Departs Southport	Departs Fort Fisher
5:30 AM	6:15 AM
7:00 AM	7:45 AM
7:45 AM*	8:30 AM
8:30 AM	9:15 AM
9:15 AM	10:00 AM
10:00 AM	10:45 AM
10:45 AM	11:30 AM
11:30 AM	12:15 PM
12:15 PM	1:00 PM
1:00 PM	1:45 PM
1:45 PM	2:30 PM
2:30 PM	3:15 PM
3:15 PM	4:00 PM
4:00 PM	4:45 PM
4:45 PM	5:30 PM
6:15 PM	7:00 PM
7:45 PM**	8:30 PM

Fares
Pedestrians, $1
Bicycle & Rider, $2
Motorcycles, $3
Vehicle and or combination less than 20 feet, $5
Vehicles or combinations in excess of 20 feet up to 40 feet, $10
Vehicles or combinations greater than 40 feet to 65 feet maximum, $15
Annual Pass, $100

Call in advance if ferrying larger vehicles. Rates and schedules are subject to change. For information about the Southport-Fort Fisher Ferry only, call (910) 457-6942 or (800) 368-8969. For statewide and individual ferry information call (800) BY-FERRY (293-3779) or go to the website www.ncferry.org

INSIDERS' TIP
Following severe rainstorms, flooded streets are commonplace. Deep pools of standing water and small lakes form, make driving hazardous. DO NOT drive through these bodies of water, even with four-wheel drive vehicles.

Bald Head Island Ferry
Foot of W. Ninth St., Southport
• (910) 457-5003, (800) 234-1666

The ferry between Southport and Bald Head Island is strictly for passengers. Travel on the island is by foot, bicycle or electric cart — no passenger cars are allowed. An individual round-trip ferry ticket is $15 for adults, $8 for children ages 3 through 12. Children 2 and younger ride free. In Southport, the ferry terminal is at Indigo Plantation at the foot of Ninth Street. It departs on the hour from 8 AM to 10 PM, except at noon, seven days a week. Ferries leave Bald Head Island every hour on the half-hour, except at 11:30 AM. Ferry parking in Southport costs $5 or $7 per day depending on which lot you use.

Long-Distance Bus Lines

Long-distance bus service to Wilmington is provided by **Greyhound**, (800) 231-2222, and **Carolina Trailways**, (910) 762-6625, at the Wilmington bus terminal, 201 Harnett Street between N. Third and N. Front streets. Hours are 8:30 to 11 AM, 1 to 4:30 PM and 8:30 to 9:00 PM. When phoning this location, use the Trailways number, as one agent handles both bus lines; the toll-free number for Greyhound provides helpful recorded information and centralized service but is not local.

Area Overview

The wonderful history, culture and economy of North Carolina's southern coast would not exist without the area's proximity to the water. While the ocean gets top billing in terms of geographical attractions, it was the existence of a relatively narrow river that gave rise to successful European settlement here. The Cape Fear River, a deep, often fast-moving body of water, begins at the confluence of the Haw and Deep rivers near Greensboro, meanders through Fayetteville and empties into the Atlantic Ocean 200 miles south of its source. With a compelling history and dangerous reputation, the Cape Fear River has always been a major influence on the formation and evolution of the city of Wilmington, 30 miles upstream from the ocean.

The Cape Fear River

For centuries Native Americans had this area to themselves, until European settlers came. In 1524 when Spanish explorer Giovanni da Verrazano took his French-financed expedition into an unknown river in a wild place, he ushered in a new historical period that would slowly lead to European development of the area.

Verrazano wrote glowingly of the area in his journal: "The open country rising in height above the sandy shore with many faire fields and plaines, full of mightie great woods, some very thicke and some thinne, replenished with divers sorts of trees, as pleasant and delectable to behold, as if possible to imagine."

Despite the explorer's enthusiastic description, very little happened in terms of development at that time. More than 100 years passed before European settlement, when members of the Massachusetts Bay Colony, led by William Hilton, attempted to colonize the region in 1663. Their effort failed, and the following year, a new settlement ventured into the region. A group of English settlers from Barbados, led by John Vassal, established a settlement in 1664. By 1667, that settlement was abandoned because of a disagreement with the Lords Proprietors who backed another settlement, Charles Town, farther south on the west bank of the river. That effort failed in 1667 because of hostile coastal Indians, pirates, weak supply lines, mosquitoes and other problems that drove the residents south, where they founded the City of Charleston in South Carolina. Perhaps one of the greatest reasons for failure was, ironically, the very river that sparked interest in settlement.

In 1879, settler George Davis in James Sprunt's *Chronicles of the Cape Fear River*, vividly described part of the problem with settlement caused by the river:

"Looking to the cape for the idea and reason of its name, we find that it is the southernmost point of Smith's Island — a naked, bleak elbow of sand, jutting far out into the ocean. Immediately in front of it are the Frying Pan Shoals, pushing out still farther, twenty miles, to sea. Together, they stand for warning and for woe; and together they catch the long majestic roll of the Atlantic as it sweeps through a thousand miles of grandeur and power from the Arctic toward the Gulf. It is the playground of billows and tempests, the kingdom of silence and awe, disturbed by no sound save the sea gull's shriek and the breakers' roar. Its whole aspect is suggestive, not of repose and beauty, but of desolation and terror. Imagination can not adorn it. Romance cannot hallow it. Local pride cannot soften it."

The Town of Brunswick was founded by disgruntled English settlers from South Carolina on the west bank of the river in 1726, but it withered away as more strategically located Wilmington, on the high east bank, began to prosper. In 1729, a settlement evolved where Wilmington is now located, and where river rafters would stop to trade at a place called the Dram Tree. Originally called Newton, Wilmington was subsequently founded in 1734 and incorporated in February 1740 by act of the North Carolina General Assembly.

Incorporation says something for the tenacity of successful settlers who managed to tame what was apparently a very wild place. But they understood, as do their descendants, that the river posed more opportunities than obstacles. The positioning of the City of Wilmington on a bluff created a port relatively safe from storms. And what created a challenge for early settlers would prove to be a protective barrier against outside invaders from England during the Revolutionary War and Union troops during the Civil War.

The Cape Fear River presented numerous opportunities and was a great area for trading goods such as tar, turpentine and pitch, but sailors disliked coming here, partly because they were looked down upon by the residents. In fact, by statute of the time, tavern keepers, retailers of liquor or keepers of public houses were not permitted to give credit to seamen, and seamen were not permitted to be kept, entertained or harbored by any resident longer than six hours.

Also, the waters were dangerous, and Wilmington did not and would not have sewage or drainage systems for years to come. As a result, diseases prevailed, such as small pox and malaria, and there were few doctors (the first, Armande de Rossett, did not arrive until 1735).

It was with trepidation and dread that seamen sailed into the river's waters. And that's how the river got its foreboding name.

Wilmington: The Port City

Previously called New Liverpool, New Carthage, New Town and Newton, Wilmington was eventually settled in 1729. That same year, St James Parish was founded and still exists today as St. James Episcopal Church at the corner of Third and Market streets. The name of the city was finally decided when Governor Gabriel Johnston took office. He was so excited and thankful for the prestigious appointment that he named the city after the man who gave him the job — Spencer Compton, Earl of Wilmington.

The City of Wilmington was incorporated in 1740 and continued to grow and prosper. During part of the 1700s, Wilmington also functioned six times as the seat of government for North Carolina, because at that time the Colonial Assembly moved about, usually being located where the governor lived or where the legislators met.

In keeping with its English heritage, many streets in Wilmington, such as Red Cross, Castle, Walnut, Chestnut, Princess, Market, Dock, Orange, Ann, Nunn, Queen and Church streets, are named after streets in Liverpool, England.

Wilmington flourished as a major port, shipbuilding center and producer of pine forest products. Tar, turpentine and pitch were central to the economy, and lumber from the pine forests was a lucrative economic resource. At one time, Wilmington was the site of the largest cotton exchange in the world. The waterfront bustled with steam ships crowding together to pick up or unload precious cargo.

Initial involvement in the American Revolutionary movement began for Wilmington in 1765, when the British Parliament passed the Stamp Act. Reaction and vigorous resistance were immediate and colorful, with much of the activity taking place at night and emanating from the taverns. Eventually, the Stamp Officer was intimidated into composing a letter of resignation, whereupon the residents gave him three cheers, carried him about the town on a chair and treated him to the finest liquors. Subsequently, the colonists refused to receive the stamps from the British and forced the officials to abandon the use of stamps. In 1775 residents signed a pledge supporting the Continental Congress.

The city became involved in the Revolutionary War when Loyalists battled the Patriots at Moore's Creek in February 1776. The Patriots easily won this battle, but British forces captured

AREA OVERVIEW

the city in 1781 and held it under the command of Major James Henry Craig. Later, in 1781, he was joined by General Charles Cornwallis, who stayed in the Burgwin-Wright House at the corner of Third and Market streets. Across the street, the British Cavalry occupied St. James Church, using it as a riding school. The British troops were withdrawn when Cornwallis later surrendered at Yorktown in October 1781

Following the Revolutionary War, Wilmington prospered greatly, both socially and as an important trading center. Numerous estates and plantations flourished on the outskirts, and many fine homes were built in the city. However, during the early stages of the 1800s the city floundered because of poor roads, few bridges, swamps surrounding the city, inadequate medical and sanitation facilities and navigation problems on the Cape Fear River. Soon, with the advent of steam power, railroads and navigational improvements to the river, Wilmington again began to prosper, and by 1840 was the largest city in the state. Thalian Hall, which currently houses the oldest continuously operating little theater company in the United States, was built in 1855 and has recently been restored.

During the Civil War, Wilmington was the Confederacy's most important port. Fort Fisher and the Cape Fear River were home to many blockade runners who brought materials in from the islands. Built in 1861, Fort Fisher was the last fort to fall to the Union army.

After the war, cotton, rice, peanuts, lumber and naval stores helped Wilmington regain its trading force. A sizable black middle class developed, and Wilmington became home to the state's first black lawyer and black physician. In 1866, the town officially became a city. However, by 1910 Wilmington lost its identity as the state's largest city when inland cities grew due to the development of the tobacco and textile industries.

During World War I, a thriving shipbuilding industry developed and cotton exports peaked. The Great Depression of the 1930s hit Wilmington hard and the city declined. However, World War II brought a rebirth of shipbuilding, with 243 ships being built. In 1945, the North Carolina Legislature created the State Port Authority, which enabled the transformation of the shipyards into a modern port facility. In 1947 Wilmington College was established, later becoming the University of North Carolina at Wilmington.

Over the years, much of Wilmington's growth had been facilitated by a strong railroad industry, which eventually consolidated into the Atlantic Coast Line Railroad, a major employer in the city. Unfortunately, in 1955 the Atlantic Coast Line closed their offices and moved to Jacksonville, Florida, dealing a severe blow to Wilmington. A major effort was undertaken to bring diversified industry to the area, and by 1966 Wilmington had begun to rebound and was designated an "All American City."

The famous World War II battleship, USS *North Carolina*, was brought to the city in 1961 and berthed on the west side of the river across from downtown, providing a magnificent backdrop for Wilmington's Riverfront area. During the 1970s, a strong revitalization effort began in the downtown area, which, coupled with an intense preservation undertaking in the large historical district, resulted in a revitalized and exciting central city.

In the 1980s the city saw another upswing as major companies, such as Corning Inc. and General Electric, moved in and encouraged other diverse companies, including Applied Analytical Industry and Takeda Chemical Products to call Wilmington home. Pharmaceutical Product Development became a homegrown Wilmington success story. (See our Commerce and Industry chapter.) A major film studio grew here, currently known as Screen Gems Studios, and many movies have been made in the area, earning Wilmington the nickname "Wilmywood" (see the Closeup in this chapter).

The downtown revitalization effort in the mid-1980s did much to bring Wilmington into prominence. The successes of Chandler's Wharf Shops, The Cotton Exchange and The Coastline Convention Center encouraged other establishments to set up shop. Restaurants, clothing stores, art galleries and antiques shops soon lined the streets. The flourishing nightlife adds a trendy setting to Wilmington as well with streets in the downtown area being quite safe. Throngs of tourists and residents alike stroll about until late in the evening.

Downtown Wilmington remains the historical core of the community and is still in many ways the neighborhood that defines the region. Suburbs may flourish, but there is something fascinating about the historic homes and buildings downtown, with their intimate proximity to the river. Both visitors and residents are affected by a sense of lingering ghosts. Important events happened here, in places that are still standing — places that have not been obscured by modern architecture or lost in the trends of a constantly changing American culture. Home to the county's seat of government for more than 250 years, this urban area has been on the forefront of historic changes.

The best perspective on Wilmington's rich and colorful history can be foaund at the Cape Fear Museum, 814 Market Street, (910) 341-4350, where the unique format allows visitors to walk through time in chronological order. (See our Attractions chapter.)

Wilmington in the 21st Century

Today the Wilmington area and its adjacent rural/suburban counties are experiencing substantial growth as both tourists and potential residents discover the desirability of vacationing and living in the area. An influx of retirees, many of them from the Northern states, has helped to make Wilmington a much more cosmopolitan city than one would expect in the heart of Dixie. Younger families, escaping from the stress of the larger cities and looking for a more relaxed way of living and better quality of life, also have contributed to the population surge.

One of the keys to success in any central-city area is the presence of residents — a core group of people who do not leave for the suburbs at the end of the workday. Wilmington, blessed with a beautiful Historic District that did not fall victim to either urban renewal or developers in the name of progress, has many full-time residents living in the downtown area. The Historic District continues to expand as more and more old homes are restored and occupied, and additional growth in downtown residency is occurring as condominiums and townhouses are added (see our Real Estate chapter).

Wilmington's extensive Historical District is made up of some 200 blocks and is expanding as more areas are added. Beautifully restored homes, many of them antebellum, line the shaded streets. Magnificent and stately live oaks are draped with Spanish moss and retain their leaves all year long. Azaleas and oleanders abound, and many of the homes have extensive gardens, some of which are opened to the public during the Azalea Festival in the spring, Riverfest in the fall, the History-Mystery tours at Halloween and the Old Wilmington by Candlelight in December (see

our Annual Events chapter). A leisurely walk through the Historic District is an adventure in history, and walking tours are available. For those who prefer to ride, both horse-drawn carriage and trolley tours are available, both narrated (see our Attractions chapter).

With excellent shopping, outstanding restaurants, antiques to be discovered and a view of the river wherever you go, downtown Wilmington flourishes more every year. In the past ten years, the Cape Fear River has become a second focal point of the city's booming tourist industry, vying for tourist attention with the nearby beaches. Downtown hotels, inns, shops and restaurants situated on its banks enjoy brisk business all year long, and docking space for boats is experiencing a substantial increase.

Aside from being the center of government for the city and New Hanover County, downtown Wilmington is also the center of the cultural arts scene. Thalian Hall puts on many wonderful productions, both musical and dramatic. The Community Arts Center is constantly enhancing the arts scene by offering classes and sponsoring productions for adults and children. Downtown Wilmington also hosts many art galleries, music shops and the Cape Fear Museum (see our Attractions and The Arts chapters). The popularity and charm of this area has attracted many retail stores, financial institutions and entertainment and dining establishments.

During the day, downtown Wilmington is quaint and charming, but at night it comes alive in a whole new way. Dance clubs, jazz bars, local and touring musicals, venues for rock 'n' roll, rhythm and blues and more can be found in the 55-block area of the downtown commercial district (see our Nightlife chapter). Perhaps the nicest thing about downtown Wilmington — and something that separates it from the rest of the city and nearby communities — is its pleasant and fascinating walkability. The Riverwalk, with its view of the Battleship *North Carolina* moored on the western shore, is a great place to stroll, grab a hot dog from a street vendor, listen to free music and gaze at the river. The Riverwalk is currently being extended to more than a mile in length and soon will run from north of the Coast Line Convention Center to south of Chandlers Wharf. Complete with wide patio-style areas and pocket parks with benches, the Riverwalk offers spectacular views of the river, especially at night.

Greater Wilmington and New Hanover County

With the recent annexation of an eastern suburban area, Wilmington's population increased to more than 90,000, making it the larger of the two major Wilmingtons (the other one is in Delaware). New Hanover County's population now stands at more than 168,000, reflecting an increase of 65 percent since 1980.

Overall, the city of Wilmington and the surrounding area have experienced an exceptional growth in construction. Shopping centers now boast national chains such as Target, Barnes & Noble, Wal-Mart, Lowe's, Dillard's, Sears, JC Penney and Home Depot, all of which have en-

AREA OVERVIEW

hanced the region's shopping choices considerably. Many upscale and specialty stores have also appeared throughout the area (see our Shopping chapter).

With all this new growth and the continuing popularity of the area, real estate is a lively business. "Plantations," new gated communities and new neighborhoods are developed so quickly that natives have been heard to say they occasionally get lost because of the changing landscape. However, in spite of the rapid growth, new housing in the area still remains quite affordable (see our Real Estate chapter).

Wilmington remains the educational hub of the southeastern North Carolina coast, with the University of North Carolina at Wilmington and Cape Fear Community College within its boundaries. Mount Olive College, Shaw University and Miller-Motte Business College are also in Wilmington (see our Higher Education and Research chapter).

The city holds the distinction of being the cultural center for not only this corner of the state, but also the whole North Carolina coastline. Performances by touring and home-based theater, dance and music companies enliven the local stages of Thalian Hall Center for the Performing Arts downtown and Kenan Auditorium and Trask Coliseum on the campus of UNCW. Writers, artists and musicians are evident in abundance. Louise Wells Cameron Museum of Art is a showcase of regional and international artists (see our The Arts chapter).

The film industry lends an exciting opportunity for spotting the occasional celebrity or just watching the process of making movies. Filmmaking now accounts for a significant portion of the local economy and has the potential for growth because of Wilmington's well-established film industry infrastructure. The cornerstone of the local film industry, EUE/Screen Gems Studios, is complemented by a seasoned crew base, an active regional film commission and a large talent pool. Since the first movie filmed here in 1983 (Dino DeLaurentiis' Firestarter) Wilmington has been home to more than 300 movies and six television series, including Matlock and Dawson's Creek. Stars spotted in recent years include Bruce Willis, Richard Gere, Katherine Hepburn, Alec Baldwin, Kim Basinger, Mathew Modine, Sharon Stone, Patrick Swayze, Julie Harris, John Travolta and Anthony Hopkins. Linda Lavin, Broadway star and a woman known affectionately as "Alice" from the '70s TV series, lives downtown and works closely with the Community Arts Center.

As North Carolina's principal deep-water port, the North Carolina State Port at Wilmington and some of the industrial complexes north of downtown are host to about 800 ships per year from many nations. The river currently is being dredged and deepened so that larger cargo ships and some of the cruise ships can manage to get into Wilmington.

Statistical Data

As the second smallest of the state's 100 counties, New Hanover County encompasses only 198 square miles, most of which is City of Wilmington. The county's 2002 population of 168,536 reflects a 31 percent growth from 1992 to 2002, one of the highest growth rates in the nation. Median household income for 2002 was $50,100, which is somewhat higher than the median for the state.

The largest export from the State Port is wood pulp at over a half- million tons in 2001, and the largest import in 2001 was chemicals at 437,510 tons; Korea was the largest shipping destination from the port at 138,387 tons as well as the largest shipper to the port at 147,186 tons. Current tonnage through the port alone exceeds two million tons.

The largest industrial employer in the county is General Electric, with nearly 2,000 employees making nuclear fuel assemblies and aircraft engine parts. Corning, producing optical fibers, and International Paper, which produces pulp and paperboard, are two other major industrial employers. Recent years have seen an influx of pharmaceutical companies as well. By workforce, the largest is service at 27 percent, followed closely by retail trade at 24 percent, reflecting the influence of tourism in the area. The total workforce is 89,848, of which 5,590 are directly attributable to travel and tourism, while about 10 percent of the workforce is in manufacturing.

Politically, the county has 115,210 registered voters. Of the registered voters, 46,674 are Democrat, 44,400 are Republican and 23,622 are unaffiliated. In the November 2000 election, 54 percent of the registrants voted.

Because of the Wilmington area's popularity and recent growth, educational facilities have been growing in number and reputation. The University of North Carolina at Wilmington, long a relatively dormant institution, has taken off in the past decade and is currently ranked as one of the best state universities in the South. The 661-acre campus is among the fastest-growing universities in the 16-campus UNC system. It offers degrees in more than 60 areas of concentration, including a marine sciences program that was recently ranked fifth-best in the world (see our Higher Education and Research chapter).

The public school system prides itself on innovation. With a budget of more than $162 million, the system devotes 70 percent of its monies to direct instructional costs. There are 37 schools in the New Hanover County Public School System, organized as kindergarten through 5th grades, 6th through 8th, and 9th through 12th, with an estimated 22,000 students and a student/teacher ration of 23:1 see our Schools and Child Care chapter).

With the mild climate, recreational opportunities abound in the area. Golf courses, playable year round, can be found throughout the area, with at least ten in New Hanover County and a considerable number in Brunswick County, many of which are residential golf communities. Most county and municipal parks contain baseball and soccer fields along with tennis courts. Our many miles of coastline, rivers and sounds offer a wide variety of fishing, watersports, and boating activities, and quite a few harbors, marinas and yacht clubs are available.

Wrightsville Beach

Wrightsville Beach is a special place for both the resident and the visitor and is quite unlike the commercial beaches that often come to mind when one thinks of the coast. There is no carnival atmosphere — no Ferris wheels or gaudy displays of beach merchandise (well, maybe just one that locals try hard to overlook), no bumper boats, no arcade. Instead, Wrightsville Beach is primarily an affluent residential community that has its roots in Wilmington. For nearly a century, the 5-mile-long island beach has been a retreat from the summer heat for residents of Wilmington. Many of the homes are owned by city residents whose families have maintained ownership through the decades, and that is not likely to change soon.

Wrightsville Beach was incorporated in 1899 as a resort community. The Tidewater Power Company built a trolley system from downtown to the beach, providing the only land access to the island until 1935. The company, which owned the island, was interested in development and built the Hotel Tarrymore in 1905 to attract visitors and revenue. Later named The Oceanic, this grand hotel burned down in 1934, along with most structures on the northern half of the island. Lumina, a beach pavilion, was also built by the Tidewater Power Company to attract visitors

On the site of the current Oceanic Restaurant at the south end of the beach, Lumina offered a festive place where locals gathered for swimming, dancing and outdoor movies. The building was demolished in 1973. (See the Close-up in our Getting Around chapter for more about the Lumina.)

The Carolina Yacht Club, the first large structure on the island, was built in 1856 and is the second oldest in the country, after the New York Yacht Club. Development of the beach continued steadily until 1954 when Hurricane Hazel, a monster storm, came ashore and wreaked devastation on the island's homes and buildings. Hazel also shoaled the channel between Wrightsville Beach and adjacent Shell Island.

Developers, seeing an opportunity for expansion, filled in the remaining water and joined the islands together. Today, the area is the site of the Shell Island Resort Hotel, numerous condominiums and large homes. In the aftermath of two hurricanes in 1996, the resort hotel found itself precariously close to an advancing inlet. Shell Island's condominium owners wanted to erect a seawall to save their property from the encroaching sea, but the state denied them permission to do so. North Carolina has very strict laws regarding seawalls because of their negative impact on the rest of a beach. In 2002, the inlet was dredged and moved north toward Figure Eight Island, thereby, for the time being, reducing the threat to Shell Island.

AREA OVERVIEW

Welcome to "Wilmywood"

Believe it or not, more movies are filmed each year in Wilmington than in any other American city except Los Angeles and New York. TV's long-running *Matlock* series, starring Andy Griffith, was filmed here, as were TV's *American Gothic*, many commercials, music videos and industrial films.

At the heart of this phenomenon is EUE/Screen Gems Studios, a 32-acre complex on N. 23rd Street. Some of the studio's eight sound stages — totaling more than 100,000 square feet — are among the largest in the East. And you've probably seen the backlot several times on screen, although you probably thought you were looking at the streets of New York City, New Orleans, Beirut, Detroit or Bucharest.

The spark that ignited Wilmington's steadily burning film industry came in 1983 when Stephen King's *Firestarter* was filmed at the studios, then owned by Dino DeLaurentis. Carolco Pictures (makers of the Terminator films) bought the studio in 1989, then EUE/Screen Gems in 1996. Wilmington's ideal weather, its variety of locations, accessibility to transportation and low labor costs offer the film industry an effective formula for success.

So it's not surprising so many Wilmingtonians have film experience. Local musicians performed in The Radioland Murders. Local dancers went Stomping at the Savoy. Scores of locals earn their livings as "techies." Hundreds more work as on-screen extras. At least one Wilmington city councilman may be seen in TV commercials.

State-of-the-art recording studios serving the film industry also thrive around town. It's not unusual to see major Hollywood celebrities frequenting local restaurants and clubs while they're in town for a shoot. And fees collected for film permits go toward downtown beautification projects.

Just a glance at the following sample of movies and TV shows made in and around Wilmington (the list is always growing) makes it clear why Wilmington has earned the nickname "Wilmywood":

28 Days, A Soldier's Daughter Never Cries, Black Dog, Dawson's Creek, Against Her Will: The Carrie Buck Story, Alan and Naomi, Betsy's Wedding, Billy Bathgate, Blue Velvet, Crimes of the Heart, The Crow, Dream a Little Dream, Empire, Everybody Wins, Fall Time, Golden Years, Justice and a Small Town: The Sandra Prine Story, Lolita, Margaret: A Burning Passion, The Member of the Wedding, Noble House, Out of Carolina, Raw Deal, Simple Justice, Sleeping With the Enemy, The Squeeze, A Stoning in Fulham County, To Gillian on Her 37th Birthday, Too Young the Hero, Truman Capote's One Christmas, Tune In Tomorrow, Virus, When We Were Colored, Windmills of the Gods and *Year of the Dragon*.

And who could forget *Amos & Andrew, Bad With Numbers, Cannibal Vampire Schoolgirls from Outer Space, Cyborg, Date with an Angel, The Exorcist III, Firestarter, King Kong Lives, Little Monsters, Loose Cannons, The Lost Capone, Super Mario Bros., Teenage Mutant Ninja Turtles, Teenage Mutant Ninja Turtles II: The Secret of the Ooze, Weeds* and *Weekend at Bernie's*.

Film-making on the streets of downtown Wilmington.

credit: EUE/Screen Gems Studios

Today's Wrightsville Beach is a very busy and prosperous place. Because of its popularity with both residents and tourists, there is almost no available land for sale. Visitors who fall in love with Wrightsville Beach and fantasize about owning a home on this pristine island can expect to pay, at the very least, $400,000 for a single-family home. Condominiums range in price between $250,000 and $500,000 for a one- or two-bedroom unit. The area is still a stronghold of long-term residents who summer in family homes built to catch the ocean breeze. The permanent residential population is about 3,000, but that figure swells considerably in the summer.

With a land mass of nearly a square mile, this island manages to maintain its charm despite an increasing influx of visitors. Surprisingly, brisk commercial development in the form of marinas, restaurants, the Blockade Runner Resort Hotel, the Holiday Inn Sunspree Resort and other services has not seriously changed the residential orientation of the island and its very clean beaches. Lifeguards oversee the safety of swimmers in the summer season, and the beach patrol keeps an eye on the area to make sure laws are obeyed. Alcohol and glass containers are not allowed on the beach. If you have questions, just ask one of the friendly lifeguards.

Boaters, sun worshippers, swimmers, surfers and anglers will find much to appreciate and enjoy about the setting. Public beach access points, liberally sprinkled along the shoreline, make a day in the sun a free experience for daytrippers — with the notable exception of parking. Always an issue at Wrightsville Beach, the parking situation was exacerbated by the installation of parking meters.

Insiders know the island is extremely crowded during peak summer weekends and are inclined to leave those times for visitors. On in-season weekends, visitors are wise to arrive before 9:30 AM and bring plenty of quarters for the parking meters. (A quarter buys 15 minutes.) Or you can try your luck at finding a non-metered parking space. Parking lots at area restaurants and hotels are vigilantly guarded, and residents are not inclined to allow unknown cars to occupy their driveways. Towing is very strictly enforced in no-parking zones.

Opportunities for water-related sports and entertainment are plentiful on Wrightsville Beach. Some of the most luxurious marinas along the North Carolina coast are clustered around the bridge at the Intracoastal Waterway and offer a full range of services (see our Marinas and Intracoastal Waterway chapter).

Charter boats, both power and sail, are available in abundance. Jet Ski rentals, windsurfing, parasailing, kayaking and sailing lessons are there for the asking (see our Watersports chapter). Bait, tackle, piers and more than enough advice on the best way to fish are all easy to find (see our Fishing chapter). Visitors who bring their own boats will appreciate the free boat ramp just north of the first bridge onto Harbour Island, the island between the mainland and Wrightsville Beach.

A visit to Wrightsville Beach, whether for a day or for a vacation, is bound to be a pleasant experience that will be repeated time after time. The island is wonderfully walkable, and you can find everything you need for a comfortable and memorable vacation almost any time of the year.

Figure Eight Island

Figure Eight Island, just north of Wrightsville Beach, is a private, very exclusive, oceanfront resort community. This island is, in the most extreme sense, a highly restricted residential island of 406 expensive homes. It's a favorite hideaway for stars and political bigwigs who want privacy when they're visiting the area. Former Vice President Al Gore and family, for example, have enjoyed vacationing here since 1997.

The development includes a yacht club, a marina, tennis courts and a boat ramp. The island is connected to the mainland by a causeway bridge, and a guard will let you onto the island only if you've called ahead to someone on the island, such as a friend or a real estate agent, and are on the list at the gate.

There are virtually no commercial enterprises here, just pure beautiful beaches for the vacationer looking for some R&R and peace and quiet. The celebrity orientation of the island doesn't mean regular folk can't rent homes and enjoy a private vacation. In fact, the island is very hospitable to vacationers and welcomes guests to its uncrowded shores. To contact real estate companies on or near Figure Eight Island for rental information (some of the larger Wilmington real estate companies may also handle properties on this exclusive island) see our chapter on Weekly and Long-Term Rentals.

Masonboro Island

South of Wrightsville Beach and north of Carolina Beach is Masonboro Island. Barren of any development, Masonboro Island is the last and largest pristine barrier island remaining on the southern North Carolina coast. This 8-mile-long island, with an Atlantic Ocean beach on its eastern shore and marshes on its western shore facing the Intracoastal Waterway, is accessible only by boat. If you are fortunate enough to have a shallow-draft boat, just look for a spot to put in among the reeds — probably alongside other boats — and tie a meaningful line to the shore with your anchor because, as in all areas of the Cape Fear region, the tides have wide fluctuation. If you tie up at high tide, you may have a tough job getting off the sand if you try to leave at low tide.

The island, consisting of about 5,000 acres, has about 4,300 acres of tidal salt marshes and mud flats and only about 600 acres of beach. Although parts of the island belong to private landowners, no development is allowed. Masonboro is a component of the North Carolina Coastal Reserve and the National Estuarine Research Reserve. The island is home to gray foxes, cotton rats, a variety of birds, river otters and several species of aquatic life; it is an important nesting site for the beautiful and famous loggerhead sea turtles. You can spot the island by the large number of pleasure craft clustered on the Masonboro Sound side. If you want to be alone, pass by this gathering and look for small passages farther south on the island.

Access is only limited by the draft of your boat and how easily you can push it off when you run aground. Gather your gear and hike a short way to the ocean beach, where it's a special pleasure to take a picnic and relax on the uncrowded beach. There are no facilities so be prepared to rough it. If you make the trip in the fall, be sure to take along insect repellent because the yellow flies can be extremely annoying.

Monkey Junction

At the southern end of College Road (State Route 132) where it junctions with Carolina Beach Road (US Route 421), you'll find an area that has been rife with heated controversy recently. Known for many years as Monkey Junction, this rapidly expanding area has experienced enormous growth both commercially and residentially, some of it fairly upscale. Some of the residents, especially ones more recently moving into the area, feel that the name "Monkey Junction" does not convey the image they'd like to have for their community. They prefer "Myrtle Grove," which is an area east of Monkey Junction.

Ever sensitive to the desires of their customers, the U.S. Postal Service dutifully changed the name of their postal station in the area from Monkey Junction to Myrtle Grove. However, the New Hanover County commissioners, ever sensitive to the desire of most residents of the county to preserve our historical heritage, have officially designated the area as Monkey Junction, and signs to that effect will soon be planted.

The name Monkey Junction harkens back to the 1920's when the bus to Carolina Beach stopped at this intersection and passengers were allowed to get off. An enterprising gas station nearby featured live monkeys as an attraction to draw customers. When the driver stopped, he announced, "Monkey Junction," and that's how it's been known ever since.

Carolina Beach

Carolina Beach, just 30 minutes from downtown Wilmington by car, is on a narrow slip of land between the Cape Fear River and the Atlantic Ocean. Separated from the mainland by the Intracoastal Waterway (Snow's Cut), the island is called Pleasure Island.

Established in 1857, when Joseph Winner planned the streets and lots for the 50 acres of beach property he had purchased, the island's only access then was by water. In 1866 a steamship began carrying vacationers down the Cape Fear River to Snow's Cut and a small railroad took them the rest of the way into Carolina Beach. In later years, a high-rise bridge was built over Snow's Cut connecting the island with the mainland.

Carolina Beach has undergone a dramatic transformation during the 1990s. Once considered a wild party spot, it is now a heavily residential community dedicated to creating a wholesome family environment. Recent years have seen the cultivation of improved services, pleasant land-

INSIDERS' TIP

If you're coming to the Cape Fear Coast as either a new resident or a tourist, plan on bringing only about half as many clothes as you think you'll need. The area is very relaxed and laid back, and you'll find most business and professional people are wearing sports clothes. Khaki pants and a sports shirt will get you by just about anywhere. During the lengthy warm season, shorts and a polo shirt are the uniform of the day. No black sox, though.

scaping, attention to zoning and tangible citizen action to make Carolina Beach an attractive visitor destination.

The busy central business district is centered around an active yacht basin containing a large number of charter fishing boats and large excursion boats. The nearby Boardwalk area is currently undergoing revitalization and rebuilding in conjunction with an oceanfront Courtyard by Marriott Resort Hotel scheduled for completion in 2003.

A drive through Carolina Beach reveals a pleasant 1950s-style beach town of modest cottages, increasingly more upscale single-family dwellings, and an abundance of three- and four-story condominiums. Near the center of Carolina Beach is Jubilee Park, where you'll find water slides, miniature golf courses and other activities that appeal to the kids.

The town also has a movie complex, grocery stores, drugstore, beach shops and boutiques, numerous restaurants, both upscale and simple, hardware and variety stores, an ABC store and even bait shops. The beachfront motels, including several vintage motor courts, offer a welcome blast from the past. If you were a kid during the '50s and your parents took you on vacation to the beach, this was the kind of place you probably remember. Some of the best beachfront lodging values are offered in these spots, and several new hotels and motels are in the planning stages, and a new shopping plaza opened in 2002.

Anglers love Carolina Beach. The surf promises wonderful bounty all year long, and there are plenty of tackle shops and piers as well as the opportunity to experience deep-sea fishing from the sterns of a number of charter boats berthed in the municipal yacht basin. Several annual fishing tournaments are based on the abundance of king mackerel, and you can pay a nominal entry fee for a chance to reap as much as $50,000 for the winning fish.

At the extreme northern end of the island, the beach is open only to four-wheel-drive vehicles. While there is a certain allure to driving right off the street onto the sand of this expansive space, don't do it if you are in a two-wheel-drive car. Without the right tires, it's even possible to get stuck in the sand in a four-wheel-drive vehicle.

Carolina Beach also offers one of the few state parks in the region. For a modest fee, you can camp and enjoy the wonders of nature. The Venus's flytrap, a carnivorous plant that eats insects, is abundant in the park. This plant, a relic from pre-human existence on the planet, grows naturally within a 60-mile radius of Wilmington. A sizable marina is also located in the park.

Away from the seasonal bustle at the center of the city, Carolina Beach is a quiet community of about 5,000 regular residents. That number jumps three to five times at the peak of the vacation season. The community is growing in appeal to both locals from Wilmington and newcomers from other areas for two big reasons: it isn't crowded yet and it's affordable. Many a Wilmingtonian has given Wrightsville Beach over to visitors for the summer in the past few years and turned to Carolina Beach for a quiet spot on the sand.

Kure Beach

To the south, Carolina Beach merges into the town of Kure Beach. Kure Beach (pronounced "CURE-ee") is a younger community. Development began in the 1870s when Hans Andersen Kure moved from Denmark and bought large tracts of land in the middle of the island. Apparently, things moved slowly because Kure Beach wasn't incorporated until 1947.

Today Kure Beach is overwhelmingly residential, dotted with modest cottages, new houses and a number of beach motels. Several condominium buildings cluster together in one area, but there is little in the way of tall buildings. In fact, new structures may not be built taller than 35 feet. At the center of town, a popular fishing pier extends well out over the ocean and there are several restaurants. A charming boardwalk with benches extends north along the beach and is lighted at night.

AREA OVERVIEW

Once upon a time, some of the best real estate deals could be found in Kure Beach, but today this sleepy beach town is fast growing in popularity and price. Two of the newest developments, Kure Beach Village and Beachwalk, feature homes and town homes along with tennis courts, pools and clubhouses. Prices range from $160,000 to more than $400,000, and even more for beachfront homes.

You won't find a lot of amusement park-style entertainment here, although there is an arcade. There is very little in the way of shopping. A permanent population of 1,500 residents makes for a very close community, but Kure Beach's small size should not lead visitors to think they're out in the boondocks. The town maintains its own municipal services and fire protection, and a local planner describes the community as being "like any big city, only smaller."

Kure Beach will remain small because it is completely surrounded. The Fort Fisher State Recreation Area and Historic Site are on the south side, and the U.S. Government owns the west side as part of a buffer zone for the military terminal at Sunny Point across the Cape Fear River. Carolina Beach borders the town on the north. Of course, the Atlantic Ocean forms the east border.

Fort Fisher

To the south of Kure Beach are the Fort Fisher State Historic Site and Fort Fisher State Recreation Area. The Historic Site, amidst twisted live oaks on the west side of U.S. Highway 421, was the largest of the Confederacy's earthwork fortifications during the Civil War. It fell to Union forces in 1865, cutting off the last of the Confederacy supply lines from the sea. During World War II, as an arm of Camp Davis to the north, it became an important training site for anti-aircraft and coastal artillery defenses and a large airstrip was located there. An extensive, newly expanded visitors center offers guided tours.

The Recreation Area on the east side of U.S. 421 has 4 miles of wide, unspoiled beach, a visitor center with bath house, a snack bar and restrooms (see our chapter on Sports, Parks and Fitness).

The North Carolina Aquarium at Fort Fisher, which was closed for nearly two years due to construction, has been expanded into North Carolina's largest aquarium and reopened in the spring of 2002. The aquarium has many new features and exhibits and features a huge shark tank (see our Attractions chapter).

At the southern end of U.S. 421 is the Fort Fisher-Southport Ferry, possibly the best $5 cruise in the world. See our Getting Around chapter for information about the ferry. Across the road is a public boat launch area that is popular for windsurfing, parasailing, kiteboarding, kayaking and fishing. All in all, these southernmost beaches of New Hanover County from Carolina Beach to the southern tip of Pleasure Island offer 7.5 miles of very pleasant vacationing and living.

Brunswick County

Southport

Southport is a quaint, seaside town that offers numerous restaurants, antiques shops and historic sites. Along the west side of the Cape Fear River's mouth, Southport is reachable by both ferry and scenic highway. Leaving Wilmington, take the Cape Fear Memorial Bridge and hang a fast left onto N.C. Highway 133 just off U.S. Highways 17, 74 and 76. If you miss it, you can also take N.C. Highway 87, although the N.C. 133 route is very beautiful and offers several attractions, including Orton Plantation, the Carolina Power & Light nuclear plant with its visitor center, the North Carolina Maritime Museum and Brunswick Town, site of the first European colony in the region. For information on the ferry route and schedule, see our Getting Around chapter.

The city of Southport is steeped in history. This coastal community saw the establishment of North Carolina's first fort in 1754: Fort Johnston. A small community of river pilots, fishermen and tradespeople grew up around the fort. In 1792, the town of Smithville was created. In 1808, Smithville became the county seat of Brunswick County. For the remainder of the century, the town made plans to link rail service with the existing river traffic to make the community a major southern port, and the city was renamed Southport.

The town was one of the first areas in the state to celebrate the Fourth of July and is widely regarded as the Fourth of July Capital of North Carolina. History records that in 1795, citizens gathered at Fort Johnston and observed a 13-gun military salute to the original 13 states. In 1813, a Russian warship anchored in the harbor fired a 13-gun salute, and it was on this Fourth of July that fireworks were used for the first time to close the celebration. In 1972, the Fourth of July Festival was chartered and incorporated as the official North Carolina Fourth of July Festival, and it has become a tremendously popular four-day event for residents and visitors. Southport, listed on the National Register of Historic Places, is ranked by both Rand McNally and Kiplinger as one of the most desirable places in the United States to retire. But Southport is great fun even for just a daytrip. History buffs will especially appreciate a visit to Southport for its beautiful old homes and historic cemeteries. Be sure to check out some of the better known historic spots. The Captain Thompson Home, for example, offers visitors a glimpse into the life of a Civil War blockade runner.

The literary set will enjoy a visit to the Adkins-Ruark House where Robert Ruark lived as a young boy with his grandfather. One of Ruark's novels, The Old Man and the Boy, gives readers insight into Southport life years ago.

Southport's live oak-lined streets, charming architecture, quaint shops — most notably an abundance of antiques shops — as well as year-round golf, boating and fishing create an enormously pleasant environment. This is the place for people who genuinely want to kick back and enjoy beautiful coastal scenery. With a year-round population of 2,660, there's still plenty of elbow room. If you fall head over heels for Southport and decide to make a permanent move, keep in mind that its charm also means that the town includes some of the area's most exclusive homes, with waterfront homes fetching prices of $300,000 and more.

Leave the car — parking is free — and just walk around until you discover shops, restaurants and views that please you. It's an extremely casual community that invites visitors to pause and savor a slow pace of life that is fast disappearing in nearby Wilmington.

Bald Head Island

Four miles off the coast of Southport and the mainland, at the mouth of the Cape Fear River, is the island of Bald Head. The island is easily identifiable in the distance by the wide-based Bald Head Island Lighthouse. Built in 1817 and retired in 1935, the lighthouse is cataloged as the oldest lighthouse in North Carolina.

Once a favorite hiding spot for pirates such as Blackbeard and Stede Bonnet, Bald Head Island is now an affluent residential and resort community of 215 year-round residents. It can only be reached by the island's private ferry or personal boat. The island is graciously open to the public, and the summer population can reach more than 3,000, with visitors renting vacation homes and playing golf (see our Golf chapter for course information).

It is probably safe to say this is one of the most unspoiled beach and maritime forest areas on the North Carolina coast. The island's natural beauty is protected, despite residential development as well as a few commercial amenities such as a restaurant, bed and breakfast inn, general store with deli, marina, golf course, specialty store, and golf cart and bike rental business.

The island has 14 miles of beaches, unspoiled dunes, creeks and forests. The 2,000 acres of land are surrounded by 10,000 acres of salt marshes. The owners have deeded nearby Middle Island and Bluff Island to the state and The Nature Conservancy. The Bald Head Island Conservancy, a nonprofit organization, was formed to ensure that the unique natural resources of the island are maintained and preserved.

Turtle nesting on Bald Head Island accounts for 50 percent of all turtle eggs laid in North Carolina. The Sea Turtle Program, featured on public television, protects and monitors these wonderful creatures. There is an Adopt-a-Nest Program that pairs concerned humans with turtles in an effort to protect the nest and encourage the hatchlings toward the sea. Studies in which female turtles were tagged have revealed that pregnant turtles return

INSIDERS' TIP

Don't be surprised, taken aback or startled if complete strangers strike up a conversation with you. Southerners love to chat, they're just naturally friendly and they're interested in you. This will be a welcome change from what it was like up north, and you'll soon find yourself falling into the habit.

Take a walk off the beaten path...

THE ISLANDS AND BEACHES OF BRUNSWICK COUNTY

MAKE THE MOST OF YOUR VACATION BY PLANNING TO DO NOTHING AT ALL

FOR MORE INFORMATION ON PLANNING YOUR BEACH, GOLF AND FAMILY VACATION, CONTACT THE BRUNSWICK COUNTY CHAMBER OF COMMERCE 4848 MAIN STREET SHALLOTTE, NC 28459 (800) 426-6644 (910) 754-6644 WWW.BRUNSWICKCOUNTYCHAMBER.ORG

BRUNSWICK COUNTY
CHAMBER OF COMMERCE

to the same site to lay eggs every other year. Due to the many species of birds found on the island, the Audubon Society conducts an annual count here as part of its national program.

Something quite special about the island is the absence of cars. Gasoline-powered engines, with the exception of security and maintenance vehicles, are not allowed. The residents and visitors who rent lovely homes all drive electric carts or ride bicycles. The resulting lack of noise pollution and exhaust fumes is one of the finest features of the place.

A visitor can come for the day by private ferry service from Indigo Plantation in Southport. The cost is $15 round trip. Day parking in Southport is $5 or $7 depending on the lot you choose. For a longer stay, there are many rental units on the island. The cost, compared to rental on much of the mainland, is slightly on the upper end, but so is the experience for the visitor who wants to really get away from it all in quiet style.

Despite Bald Head Island's private status, the welcome mat is always out for visitors. The lighthouse can be toured for a small fee. The well-appointed marina welcomes transients. For information on Bald Head Island's numerous amenities, call (800) 234-1666.

Oak Island

Just across the water from Bald Head Island and Southport is Oak Island, a narrow strip of land that includes the Town of Oak Island and Caswell Beach.

Caswell Beach is the site of Fort Caswell, a military stronghold that dates from 1827. Fort Caswell is now owned by the North Carolina Baptist Assembly and welcomes visitors of all denominations each year. The community has some summer homes, but the area has mostly permanent residences. The year-round population is 383, but up to 1,200 people can be staying on this part of Oak Island in the summer. Be sure to check out the Oak Island Lighthouse, which has been guiding seafarers since 1958.

As the name implies, Oak Island is famous for its beautiful live oak trees. Recreational areas include a championship golf course, 65 beach-access points, a picnic area on the Elizabeth River estuary system, a few restaurants and motels, and fishing piers. With a population of 7,000, Oak Island offers a quiet respite for a peaceful family vacation. For the most part, a visitor will enjoy renting a house for an extended vacation. In fact, vacation rental is the liveliest business here, with more than a dozen rental companies operating on Oak Island.

South Brunswick Islands

Of the three islands in the group known as the South Brunswick Islands, **Holden Beach** is the longest and the largest. Stretching 11 miles along the Atlantic Ocean, the island is a jogger's paradise. Approximately 1,200 year-round residents call Holden Beach home. Visitors will find a host of opportunities for assimilating themselves into this exceedingly quiet family community. The beach and the sea are the central attractions in this town, which prides itself on a serene quality of life.

Ocean Isle Beach is the center island, offering 8 miles of beach with a total resort experience: restaurants, specialty shops, public tennis courts, access to all watersports, and a water slide. This beach has the only high-rise hotel on the South Brunswick Islands. There is an airport that makes getting to Ocean Isle accessible by air, but don't expect to see commercial jets at this relatively small facility. Home to slightly more than 700 full-time residents, Ocean Isle welcomes visitors to a peaceful place.

Sunset Beach, described as a diminutive island gem, is only 3 miles long. Despite its size, this island experienced a 150 percent population increase between 1990 and 1997, with a current year-round population of almost 1,900 residents. Because it is reached by a one-lane pontoon bridge, making it the only island without a high-rise bridge in Brunswick County, there is sometimes a bit of a wait to get to Sunset in the high tourist season. However, the island is well-worth the wait. This bridge will probably be replaced by a high-rise someday, if the Department of Transportation has its way, but that discussion has been going on for years. Islanders like their bridge the way it is because it tends to keep traffic levels down.

Although this island is residential in character, it is a great choice for a family vacation. Some of the best bargains in vacation rentals are here, and the visitor who wants a quiet coastal place will do very well to book a house on this beach. As with all of the beaches on the southern coast,

Your place in the sun awaits.

Photo: Jay Tervo

quality golfing is available on the mainland. For fishing enthusiasts, there is a full-service pier. Sunset Beach also offers a special delight — a walk to Bird Island at low tide.

Bird Island is completely untouched by development. A walk through the shallow inlet at low tide is easy for adults as well as children. Frequently, there are informal guided tours, announced by posters attached to street markers on the beach, so it's easy to hook up with locals who are pleased to share their knowledge of the island. The environment is purely natural and deeply comforting, where people of the 20th century can experience life as it was before the development of the land. In order to keep it this way, in 2002 the state of North Carolina purchased the island and dedicated it as the state's 10th Coastal Reserve site. Through this purchase, nearly 1,300 acres of wetlands, marsh and beaches are preserved for use by endangered species including sea turtles and some species of sea birds.

Calabash

Calabash, home of the delicious Calabash Seafood, sits on the banks of the Intracoastal Waterway where restaurants abound and deep-sea fishing boats are docked, waiting to take you on the adventure of your life. Though small, with 800 year-round residents, it is abutted on the north by the town of Carolina Shores, a residential-only community.

Shallotte

The town of Shallotte serves as the hub for services for Brunswick County's beach communities. In fact, it is perhaps best-known as the commercial mecca of the county. Because of its mainland location and island proximity, Shallotte offers residents and visitors the convenience of larger-town living and services. This is the place in Brunswick County where you will find shopping malls with nationally known stores. The Brunswick County Chamber of Commerce is

headquartered in Shallotte and can provide any information you may need about the South Brunswick Islands and the inland area. The town has a year-round population of approximately 2,000.

Pender and Onslow Counties

Topsail Island and Vicinity

Topsail Island is a 26-mile-long barrier island approximately 30 minutes north of Wilmington. The island is located in both Onslow and Pender counties and consists of three towns, **North Topsail Beach**, **Surf City** and **Topsail Beach**. The two mainland towns of **Sneads Ferry** and **Holly Ridge** complete the section known as the Greater Topsail Area.

Two bridges allow access to the island — a swing bridge in Surf City and a high-rise bridge connecting Sneads Ferry to North Topsail Beach. A single main road runs parallel to the ocean along the length of this narrow island, with side streets running from the ocean to the sound or Intracoastal Waterway. In a few instances on the wider parts of the island, you will find an additional smaller street or two running parallel to the ocean. There is only one traffic light on the whole island strand.

Topsail's summer population swells up to 35,000, as compared to the 3,500 year-round residents, consisting mostly of retirees. The convenient location between the cities of Jacksonville and Wilmington makes Topsail a desirable place to live. Residents here enjoy a relatively inexpensive, quiet lifestyle on the beach.

North Topsail Beach, the northernmost town, is a residential community with oceanfront resort condominium complexes and rental cottages. With only two restaurants, a pizza shop and small convenience store, North Topsail Beach's visitors depend on Surf City or Sneads Ferry for most of their shopping and entertainment. Surf City, located on both the island and mainland, is in the center of the island. It is the commercial hub with an array of restaurants and retail establishments. A variety of vacation rental homes, condominiums and motels are also found here, along with the most year-round residents. Topsail Beach, on the southern end of the island, is accessible only through Surf City. It is a quieter area with year-round homes, rental cottages, motels and condominiums complementing a small downtown shopping area.

On the mainland, Sneads Ferry and Holly Ridge offer more choices for entertainment, dining or shopping. Sneads Ferry is a small village where shrimping and fishing are a way of life. In recent years, however, the area has continually grown and developed into a community of upscale housing developments and shopping centers along the main highways. It is also home to the only waterslide park in the area. Holly Ridge boasted a large population during World War II when Camp Davis was established as an Army coastal artillery and antiaircraft training base. The town is now a quiet place enjoyed by longtime residents who find pleasure in the friendly services of locally owned restaurants, retail stores and service businesses.

Topsail Island is a small place with a big history. From the early Indians and explorers in the 1500s to pirates, the Civil War Era, World War II and Operation Bumblebee to the present, much has been documented about the Topsail area. This history can be found in the Missiles and More Museum on Channel Boulevard in Topsail Beach.

INSIDERS' TIP

You've probably come to the Cape Fear area to relax, enjoy yourself, reduce your stress level or find a better quality of life. Remember that when you get behind the wheel. Traffic may be a little slow during rush hours, partly because we have no expressways, but it's a whole lot better than the exasperating stop and start driving for twenty minutes to move a mile you had on the Kennedy in Chicago or the Long Island Expressway in New York. Relax and go with the flow — paradise will still be here an hour from now — and tomorrow, too.

Local residents are protective of their environment. This is particularly evident in the Topsail Turtle Project and Karen Beasley Sea Turtle Rescue and Rehabilitation Center, both totally run by volunteers. Many of the volunteers locate and monitor loggerhead turtle nests until the young turtles are hatched and make their way to the sea, while others maintain the center and care for sick and injured sea turtles until they have been rehabilitated and returned to the ocean. Still others take responsibility for the Turtle Talks, where participants can learn about the turtles and how they can help protect them. A visit to the Turtle Hospital, as it is affectionately known, is a real highlight of a Topsail Island vacation.

The greater Topsail Island area is a friendly place, offering a nice balance between residents and visitors and busy and quiet times. It's a place where nature at is finest can still be enjoyed.

Area Chambers of Commerce

Chambers of commerce are great resources for gaining an understanding of the big picture in terms of a community's business, educational, entertainment and institutional flavor. Although these organizations are not generally in the tourism business, they have brochure racks filled with information of interest to the visitor, newcomer and even the longtime resident who just wants to know what's going on. Staff members are always courteous and interested in providing information to visitors.

Greater Wilmington Chamber of Commerce, 1 Estell Lee Place, Wilmington, (910) 762-2611

Pleasure Island Chamber of Commerce, 1121 North Lake Park Boulevard, Carolina Beach, (910) 458-8434

Wrightsville Beach Chamber of Commerce, P.O. Box 466, Wrightsville Beach, NC 28480, (910) 395-2965, (800) 232-2469

Greater Topsail Area Chamber of Commerce & Tourism, Treasure Coast Landing, 13775 N.C. Highway 50, Suite 101, Surf City, (910) 329-4446, (800) 626-2780

Burgaw Area Chamber of Commerce, 707-C Enterprise Drive, Burgaw, (910) 259-9817

Hampstead Chamber of Commerce, 16865 U.S. Highway 17, Hampstead, (910) 270-9642, (800) 833-2483

Southport-Oak Island Area Chamber of Commerce, 4841 Long Beach Road S.E., Southport, (910) 457-6964, (800) 457-6964

Brunswick County Chamber of Commerce, 4948 Main Street, Shallotte, (910) 754-6644, (800) 426-6644

North Brunswick County Chamber of Commerce, 151 Poole Road, Leland, (910) 383-0553

Myrtle Beach Chamber of Commerce, 1200 N. Oak Street, Myrtle Beach, (843) 626-7444; South Strand Office, 3401 U.S. 17 S. (Business), Murrells Inlet, (843) 651-1010; (800) 356-3016.

Hotels and Motels

The beach areas of the North Carolina's southern coast have been a haven for tourists for many years. Early visitors were primarily from North Carolina because the Wilmington area was difficult to access. However, with the completion of Interstate 40 and the expansion of the Wilmington airport, coupled with the rebirth of downtown Wilmington and the Historical District, this area has become a popular destination for tourists from all across the nation. As a result, the number of hotels and motels dotting the streets and coastline has nearly doubled, particularly in Wilmington at the area surrounding the intersections of S. College Road, Market Street and New Centre Drive. But even though resort hotels, efficiency apartments and simple motel lodgings truly abound, don't count on coming to town without a reservation if you're traveling on holiday weekends — even Valentine's Day!

Full-service resort and business hotels are strategically located in desirable areas such as Wilmington's riverfront, Carolina Beach and Wrightsville Beach. In smaller towns such as Surf City, Kure Beach and Oak Island, lower-priced oceanfront motels are more common. In Wilmington, the motel strip is Market Street west of College Road, and College Road itself, south of Market Street. You can find motels of every price range, from the budget Motel 6 to the pricier Wilmington Hilton.

In addition to a major new oceanfront hotel, Carolina Beach teems with cozy family-run motels concentrated within a small area — no fewer than 15 line Carolina Beach Avenue N. within a half-mile of Harper Avenue. Kure Beach offers a similar strip of pleasant older motels along Highway 421 in the center of town. In general, beach motels, especially the older ones, are known for their great locations rather than their stylish decor.

There are no hotels or motels on Bald Head Island. Daily accommodations are limited to two large bed and breakfast inns (see our Bed and Breakfasts and Small Inns chapter). Some rental homes are available for stays as short as a weekend (see our Weekly and Long-Term Vacation Rentals chapter).

No matter what type of accommodations you desire, plush or plain, city or beach, large or small, you'll be able to find a motel or hotel to satisfy your needs in the southern coast area. This chapter deals only with traditional hotel and motel accommodations. For other accommodation options, see our Bed and Breakfasts and Small Inns, Weekly and Long-Term Vacation Rentals and Camping chapters.

Wilmington

AmeriHost Inn & Suites
$-$$$ • 5600 Carolina Beach Rd., Wilmington • (910) 796-0770, (800) 961-STAY

Brand new in 2002, the 65-unit, three-story AmeriHost Inn & Suites is centrally located on U.S. Highway 421 S. in the Monkey Junction area. Just a few miles from the beaches of Pleasure Island, the Fort Fisher Historic Site, state parks and the North Carolina Aquarium, this family-

Price Code

Since prices are subject to change without notice, we provide only price guidelines based on double-occupancy, per-night rates during the summer (high season). Our codes do not reflect the 7 percent state/county and 1 to 6 percent room occupancy taxes (taxes may vary by county or municipality). Most establishments offer lower rates during the off-season. Always confirm rates and necessary amenities before reserving.

It may also be beneficial to inquire about corporate, senior citizen, AAA or long-term discounts even when such discounts are not mentioned in our descriptions. Most establishments accept major credit cards, and some accept personal checks when payment is made well in advance.

$ $75 or less
$$ $76 to $120
$$$ $121 to $150
$$$$ $151 and up

friendly hotel is a great place to put down temporary roots while visiting area attractions or playing a round or two of golf at one of the many nearby courses. Only 7 miles from UNCW and 8 miles from historic downtown Wilmington, this inn rates high on convenience. AmeriHost Inn & Suites is within walking distance of restaurants and shopping, too.

Guests can choose from standard king, double-bed and whirlpool suites, all featuring free cable TV with HBO, free local calls and free high-speed Internet access. Other in-room amenities include a coffeemaker, an iron and ironing board, a hairdryer and a safe. Some rooms have a wet bar, micro-fridge or recliner. A complimentary continental breakfast is served every morning, and guests may enjoy complimentary fresh fruit and baked cookies in the evening. Maybe you'd like to take a swim in the large indoor pool or lounge around it while watching the kids. A meeting room that accommodates up to 70 people is available also.

Comfort Inn Wilmington
$-$$ • 151 S. College Rd., Wilmington
• (910) 791-4841, (800) 221-2222

The Comfort Inn provides excellent amenities for a low price, which explains its popularity among families and business travelers alike. It is a newly remodeled, 146-room establishment midway between downtown Wilmington and the beach. Just minutes from I-40, Comfort Inn is only 1 mile from UNCW, 6 miles from Wrightsville Beach and minutes to downtown Wilmington. With more than 100 rooms with two double beds, the Comfort Inn is a great choice for company retreats, wedding par-

ties, sports teams and bus tours. Laundry and valet services, in-room coffee, free local telephone calls, an outdoor pool and complimentary guest membership to Gold's Gym (just a three-minute walk from the hotel) contribute to the Comfort Inn's value.

Deluxe continental breakfast and daily newspapers are available each morning in the lobby. Children younger than 18 stay free when sharing their parents' room. Corporate, AAA, senior citizen and group discounts are available, and all guests are entitled to a 10 percent discount at preferred local restaurants. Forgot your major toiletries? The staff provides complimentary items. Meeting rooms can accommodate up to 50 people for board meetings and conferences. Reservations may also be made through a central booking service at (800) 221-2222.

Comfort Suites of Wilmington
$-$$$ • 4721 Market St., Wilmington
• (910) 793-9300, (800) 221-2222

The Comfort Suites of Wilmington is conveniently located between scenic Wrightsville Beach and Wilmington's downtown historic district. Each of the 73 deluxe suites features iron/ironing board, hairdryer, coffee maker, microwave, refrigerator and a 27" television with extended cable and pay-per-view channels. In addition, you get free local phone calls on two line telephones with voice mail and dataports. Rooms have either two double beds or one king size bed, and both smoking and non-smoking rooms are available. The 17 first floor rooms are set up for business clients and feature high-speed Internet access.

The hotel has an indoor fitness center and a heated indoor pool. All guests are afforded a complimentary continental breakfast and a free USA Today newspaper on weekdays. There are a limited number of pet-friendly suites, so you can bring your four-legged friend with you, as long as its less than 30 pounds. Call for additional restrictions.

Courtyard by Marriott
$$ • 151 Van Campen Blvd., Wilmington
• (910) 395-8224

This 128-room hotel offers comfortable accommodations especially suited to the business traveler. Rooms include large work desks, fold-out sofas, ironing equipment, cable TV with pay Nintendo, coffee makers, dataports and voice mail. Rollaways and cribs are available, as are dry-cleaning service (except Sundays), self-service laundry facilities and a fitness center on site.

HOTELS AND MOTELS

The attractive courtyard features a pool, whirlpool spa and gazebo amid colorful landscaping. Beneath the high-peaked ceiling of the Courtyard Cafe, a moderately priced breakfast buffet (free for kids 3 and younger) is available daily from 6:30 to 10 AM weekdays and 7 to 11 AM on Saturday and Sunday. In the evenings you can relax beside the fireplace in the lounge, where drinks are served nightly from 5 to 11 PM. The hotel also has meeting and banquet space available. To reach the Courtyard by Marriott, turn right from the southbound lanes of S. College Road onto Imperial Drive, just south of the Market Street overpass; then turn right onto VanCampen Boulevard.

Fairfield Inn Wilmington
$-$$ • 306 S. College Rd., Wilmington
• (910) 392-6767, (800) 228-2800

Looking for top quality accommodations and exceptional service at reasonable rates? This is the place for you! Always clean and comfortable, Fairfield Inn's spacious guest rooms feature amenities galore. Well-lit work desks, data ports and free local calls are just what you need when you're traveling on business. The hotel also offers same-day dry cleaning Monday through Friday and 24-hour fax service. The Fairfield Inn is convenient to Corning Glass, DuPont, General Electric and UNCW, within walking distance of popular restaurants and close to shopping centers.

If you're coming to Wilmington with your family to visit or spend some time enjoying all the area has to offer, the Fairfield Inn would be perfect. Start the morning with a complimentary continental breakfast of fruits, cereal, as-

sorted breads and muffins, juice, milk and fresh coffee. Later, after a day at the North Carolina Aquarium and Historic Fort Fisher, you all will be ready to splash in the outdoor pool or watch a little cable TV in your room before dinner.

The Greentree Inn
$ • 5025 Market St., Wilmington
• (910) 799-6001

The family tradition of warmth and hospitality has graced Wilmington's Greentree Inn since its opening in 1972. The classic '70s architecture features a wrap-around balcony that allows guests direct access from car to any of the 123 rooms. Located in the midtown section of Wilmington, the Inn is conveniently situated between the beautiful sandy shores of Wrightsville Beach (6 miles) and Wilmington's downtown Historic District (4 miles).

The Greentree Inn provides excellent amenities for the price, which explains its popularity among families and business travelers alike. Boasting 123 clean and spacious rooms, Greentree features include color TV with free cable, remotes, 60 channels, free HBO, ESPN and CNN. Free local phone calls, complimentary continental breakfast, an outdoor swimming pool and sundeck are some of the services that bring back satisfied visitors season after season. A restaurant is on the property as well. The Inn offers king deluxe rooms, rooms with two queen beds or two standard beds, non-smoking rooms and disabled-accessible accommodations.

Hampton Inn Wilmington Central and Medical Park
$$-$$$ • 2320 S. 17th St., Wilmington
• (910) 796-8881

Wilmington's newest Hampton Inn is located within the Medical Park area, practically across the street from the New Hanover Regional Medical Center and just minutes from historic downtown Wilmington and area beaches. It features 85 rooms with 14 suites in an all interior property. The meeting space, which seats up to 75 people theater style, is perfect for medical conferences, corporate occasions and wedding purposes. Amenities include an outdoor swimming pool in a well landscaped setting, a fitness center on property as well as a free full membership to the Wilmington Spa Health Club just around the corner.

The Hampton Inn rooms have on-command movies, refrigerators and wet bars, coffee makers, hairdryers, irons and ironing boards. Each room also provides free high-speed Internet access, voice mail and dataport hook-ups. In addition, the Hampton Inn Medical Park offers a 50-item complimentary continental breakfast, a business center and outstanding customer service. A hospital shuttle is available to guests.

Hampton Inn Wilmington
$$ • 5107 Market St., Wilmington
• (910) 395-5045, (800) HAMPTON

Hampton Inn Midtown has 118 tastefully appointed rooms, each featuring dataports, an iron, ironing board, hairdryer, cable TV with HBO, and a coffee maker. Upgraded rooms include the King Study and rooms with microfridges. Valet laundry is available during the week. Guests receive free passes to the Spa Health Club, and there's an on-site outdoor pool that's open from April through September. The hotel offers a meeting room accommodating up to 30 people. Local phone calls are free.

Ideally located, Hampton Inn is just 4 miles from Wrightsville Beach and Wilmington's Historic Downtown — and it's less than a mile from UNCW. The hotel is within walking distance of several popular restaurants and shopping venues. Hampton Inn offers many packages for holidays, special events, shoppers and golfers; those booking ten rooms or more receive group discounts.

Hilton Wilmington Riverside
$$$-$$$$ • 301 N. Water St., Wilmington
• (910) 763-5900, (800) 445-8667

Situated on the Riverwalk, surrounded by a beautiful historic setting, the Hilton is Wilmington's largest hotel and conference center. The hotel features 274 newly renovated guest rooms, each featuring a dual-line telephone with voicemail and dataport, high-speed internet access, hairdryer, ironing equipment, coffeemaker, On-Command Movies, HBO, WebTV and Nintendo.

The Hilton's Poolside & Cabana Bar, complete with ceiling fans and palm trees, is a great place for a sunset cocktail. Spencer's is the hotel's fine restaurant serving grilled steaks, seafood and Sunday brunch. The hotel's River Club Lounge and its fitness room are both popular. With 20,000 square feet of meeting and banquet facilities, the hotel offers 19 meeting rooms, including the Grand Ballroom, accommodating from 10 to 600 people with food service.

Located in the heart of historic Wilmington, this property is convenient to more than 50 shops and restaurants, all within walking distance, and is only three miles from Wilmington International Airport.

Riverview Suites at Water Street Center
$$$ • 106 N. Water St., Wilmington
• (910) 772-9988

Riverview Suites at Water Street Center, located across the street from and operated by the Hilton, offers 65 well-appointed suites overlooking the Cape Fear River. Each suite boasts a walk-out balcony, kitchen area, washer/dryer, pull-out sofa, cable television, hair dryer, ironing equipment, coffeemaker and just about the most fantastic view in all of downtown Wilmington.

Holiday Inn Express Hotel & Suites
$$ • 160 Van Campen Blvd., Wilmington
• (910) 392-3227, (800) HOLIDAY

Exceptionally customer-focused, impeccably clean, well-maintained and tastefully decorated, this hotel provides a wide range of services and amenities. For a modest price, you can have top-notch lodging, from king and double-bed rooms to two-room executive or whirlpool suites. All rooms include cable TV with free HBO, Pay-Per-View movies, Nintendo, ironing equipment, coffee makers, voice-mail telephones and dataports. The hotel has a 24-hour internal security system with state-of-the-art hallway cameras.

Enjoy your complimentary deluxe continental breakfasts by the fireplace in the cozy living room-style lounge or while relaxing next to the outdoor pool. Hotel amenities also include an exercise room, coin-operated laundry, airport shuttle and complimentary daily newspaper. The hotel boasts a comfortably furnished executive boardroom and several meeting rooms suitable for up to 150 people; audiovisual equipment is available for rental and catering can be arranged.

Centrally located, the 131-room Holiday Inn Express Hotel & Suites is convenient to Wilmington's business districts, downtown and Wrightsville Beach. Within walking distance are major restaurants, Wal-Mart Super Center and a large shopping complex. To reach the

INSIDERS' TIP
Before entering that inviting pool, please shower or hose yourself thoroughly. Sand, soil and sunscreen are very detrimental to pool filters, liners, tiles and pumping equipment. Oily surfaces can harbor germs as well.

HOTELS AND MOTELS

HOTELS AND MOTELS

hotel, turn right from the southbound lanes of South College Road (N.C. 132) onto Imperial Drive, just south of the Market Street overpass; then turn right onto VanCampen Boulevard.

HomeStay Inn
$ • 245 Eastwood Rd., Wilmington
• (910) 793-1920

Ideally situated between I-40 and Wrightsville Beach, this 107-room establishment is just 3 miles from the beach and 10 minutes from downtown Wilmington. Since each room features a kitchen, HomeStay Inn is a great choice for nightly or long-term visits and other special needs. Other amenities include dataport hookup, cable TV (including HBO) and voice mail. The hotel features daily maid service, a conference room, a copier and fax machine that

guests can use, plus an outdoor pool, barbecue grills and a basketball court. Handicapped-accessible rooms are available. HomeStay is on Eastwood Road, which is off Market Street.

Howard Johnson Express Inn
$-$$ • 3901 Market St., Wilmington
• (910) 343-1727

This one-story, 80-unit motel offers a variety of comfortable smoking, non-smoking and handicap-accessible rooms to meet the needs of most travelers. Choose from standard rooms with king or two double beds, home office rooms with upgraded amenities or efficiencies that have kitchenettes. All have private bath, color TV with cable and free HBO, telephone and voicemail, dataport and coffee maker; many also come with a microwave and small refrig-

erator. There's no charge for local phone calls and a complimentary continental breakfast is served from 6:30 to 10 AM daily. Children up to age 16 stay free in the same room with adults. Long-term rates are available. The Howard Johnson Express Inn is located 3 miles from downtown Wilmington, 7 miles from Wrightsville Beach and 3.5 miles from Wilmington international Airport.

Jameson Inn
$$ • 5102 Dunlea Ct., Wilmington
• (910) 452-5660, (800) 526-3766

Promising "A Perfect Stay...Every Time," the Jameson Inn hospitality family believes each guest deserves a clean, comfortable, high-quality room and exceptional service. This inviting white-columned, colonial-style property has 67 rooms including doubles, kings and suites; premium rooms feature microwaves, refrigerators, coffee makers and recliners. Among the many amenities are spacious work stations, ironing equipment, free local calls, weekday newspaper, dataports, complimentary deluxe continental breakfast, 25-inch TV with cable and a movie channel. A fitness center, pool and meeting room make this hotel popular with business travelers and families alike.

Main Stay Suites
$-$$$ • 5229 Market St., Wilmington
• (910) 392-1741

New in 2003, Main Stay Suites is a well thought out, comfortable, attractive alternative to traditional transient lodging. Whether you're in town on business or on vacation, you can call this your home away from home for as long as you like. A variety of accommodations is available to meet your needs, from king single to two-bedroom suite with many choices in between. Thoroughly modern, every suite features its own central heating and air system, complete kitchen facilities, including full-size refrigerator with ice maker, two-burner electric stove, microwave, toaster, coffee maker, dishwasher, dishes, utensils pots — even dishtowels and potholders. Other in-room amenities include cable TV, phones with dataports, ironing equipment, hairdryer and shower organizer. A guest laundry is available, as are a fitness room, business center with high-speed Internet access and an enclosed courtyard complete with grills for guest use. Convenient to shopping and restaurants, Main Stay Suites is only minutes from area beaches, historic downtown and Wilmington International Airport.

HOTELS AND MOTELS

Sleep Inn
$-$$ • 5225 Market St., Wilmington • (910) 313-6665, (866) SLEEP-99

Located less than a half-mile west of the Market Street /I-40 overpass, Sleep Inn offers 104 inside-corridor rooms with either queen-size or two double beds. All rooms come complete with oversized showers, key-card security locks, cable TV, modem ports, coffee makers, irons and ironing boards. To make your stay more comfortable and pleasurable, Sleep Inn offers a fitness room and seasonal outdoor pool. A copier, fax machine and meeting room are available for guest use. A free continental breakfast is offered every morning, and hot beverages are available free all day in the lobby lounge.

The Wilmingtonian
$$-$$$$ • 101 S. Second St., Wilmington • (910) 343-1800, (800) 525-0909

The Wilmingtonian (formerly the Inn at St. Thomas Court) comprises five buildings with 40 unique suites, plus dining rooms, a non-smoking jazz bar with live entertainment, conference and meeting rooms as well as a large ballroom. The buildings, dating from 1841 to 1994, are surrounded by extensive gardens and ponds with courtyards and balconies. The famed de Rosset House, built in 1841, features sweeping views of the Cape Fear River and offers a fascinating glimpse into the past. Its six luxurious suites are historically decorated yet equipped with modern conveniences, such as gas log fireplaces, large whirlpool tubs and separate showers. The signature suite, the Cupola, offers exquisite views of the city and breathtaking sunsets. Amenities for all suites include kitchen or wet bar, refrigerator, coffeemaker, microwave, toaster and VCR.

The Wilmingtonian's dining room, located at the nearby private City Club, referred to as "the very best in gourmet dining" by Wilmington Magazine, is a great choice for corporate events and weddings and is accessible to guests of the inn. The hotel is just two blocks from the Cape Fear River and within walking distance of area restaurants, galleries, antique stores and shopping. The beaches are just a short drive away.

Wingate Inn
$-$$$ • 5126 Market St., Wilmington • (910) 395-7011, (800) 228-1000

"Built for Business" is Wingate Inn's slogan, but vacationers say it was also built for leisure. This outstanding hotel has the amenities, facilities and service every traveler requires, backed by a 100 percent satisfaction guarantee. Conveniently located to area attractions, beaches, golf, airport, shopping and historic downtown, the hotel offers an uncommon oasis of comfort where you can relax and enjoy your Wilmington experience.

Wingate Inn's oversized guest rooms, Jacuzzi Suites and Executive Suites are not only tastefully appointed and thoughtfully arranged, they're functional. Each offers separate areas for sleep and work, free high-speed Internet connection, refrigerator, microwave, hairdryer, iron, ironing board, coffeemaker and safe. Local calls are free and rooms are equipped with two phones and voice mail. The desk phone has two lines, a speaker, dataport and conference-call capabilities. The bedside phone is a 900 megahertz cordless. The 25-inch color TV offers more than 65 free cable channels, including HBO, CNN and the Weather Channel. You will be able to order a first-rate movie, play Nintendo 64 video games or go on line with Web TV from your room.

Whether you decide to lounge by the beautiful outdoor pool or take advantage of the well-equipped fitness center and spa, you're sure to find a way to relax and unwind. The complimentary business center is complete with computer, laser printer, fax and copier. There's an Executive Boardroom and a larger meeting room available for your conference requirements.

Read your complimentary morning paper or watch the news while enjoying a nutritious complimentary breakfast from the 42-item buffet. The hotel hosts a guest appreciation reception Monday through Thursday evenings, with complimentary wine, beer, soft drinks and snacks. Express check-in/check-out expedite your travel day.

Wallace

Holiday Inn Express Hotel & Suites
**$$ • 131 River Village Pl., Wallace
• (910) 285-9200**

This award-winning hotel has been the recipient of the prestigious Torch Bearer Award for two consecutive years. Ranked in the top 10 percent of hotels in the world by InterContinental Hotels Group, this impressive award is based on property condition, quality of guest service and guest satisfaction. The large stone fireplace and 18th-century art in the lobby are just the begin-

ning of the ambience offered in this facility hotel has 55 rooms and 15 suites, all with queen or two double beds. Amenities include an interior corridor, on-site laundry facilities and a full-service business center with copy, e-mail, internet, fax, PC and printer services. Groups and meetings of up to 60 people can be accommodated in the meeting room. The Mad Boar Restaurant is adjacent to the motel. The free Express Start Breakfast Bar features some of the world's best cinnamon rolls as well as the traditional breakfast offerings. For the sport enthusiast there is an on-site fitness center with state-of-the-art fitness machines; golfing and tennis facilities are close by. The Holiday Inn Express is easily accessible off I-40, Exit 285. It is 40 miles from Wilmington.

Wrightsville Beach & Vicinity

Blockade Runner Resort Hotel
$-$$$$ • 275 Waynick Blvd., Wrightsville Beach • (910) 256-2251, (800) 541-1161

Located in the heart of this beautiful barrier island, the Blockade Runner is one of the premier oceanfront resort hotels in Wrightsville Beach. Everything you need for a perfect vacation can be found within minutes of your room. When it comes to fun, this hotel has it all. At the harborside activity center, you'll find complete services for sailing, fishing, kayaking, windsurfing and diving. Several championship golf courses are nearby, and shuttle service to tennis courts is available.

Families with children ages 4 to 12 will appreciate Sandcamper's, a supervised children's program that includes indoor crafts and games, plus beach, pool and island excursions and evening activities.

The Blockade Runner's outdoor patio deck has a spectacular view overlooking manicured gardens and the waters of the Atlantic Ocean. Patio service offers casual dining featuring seafood and hamburgers. In East Restaurant at the Blockade Runner, you'll enjoy an unforgettable dining experience; don't miss sushi night in the Lobby Lounge, Friday night's fresh local seafood and lobster, the Saturday night Seafood and Prime Rib Buffet and especially the famous Sunday Jazz Brunch. Entertainment is provided in season.

All 150 room have either ocean or harbor views and some also have balconies. Each has its own refrigerator, coffeemaker, hairdryer, iron

HOTELS AND MOTELS

iron and board, and luxurious bathrobes. Other amenities include complete room service, the Gift Shop and complimentary safe-deposit boxes. For the executive traveler, the Blockade Runner's Corporate Club offers discounted room rates and meals, free local calls, incoming fax service and high-speed wireless Internet connections. Conference and banquet facilities are available. Corporate rates are offered year-round.

You'll find a complete fitness center including whirlpool and dry sauna. Looking for a massage after a long day? The hotel will schedule one for you.

Getting to and from the Blockade Runner is a breeze with a complimentary airport shuttle (reservation needed), as well as a complimentary island shuttle. The resort is conveniently located and is about 10 to 20 minutes from Interstate 40 or Highway74/76.

Carolina Temple Apartments
$$, no credit cards • 550 Waynick Blvd.,
Wrightsville Beach • (910) 256-2773

Mentioned in *Family Fun* and *Parents* magazines, Carolina Temple Apartments is the kind of beach-cottage accommodation our parents remember from their childhood. Carolina Temple Apartments consists of two historic plantation-style cottages built by the Temple family after the turn of the century. The property runs from the sound side of the island to the ocean, yet the buildings are set back like a well-kept secret. The inn was once Station 6 along the Wrightsville Beach trolley line (ask to see the old photos), and the pride with which the place is run is evident everywhere. Both buildings are classics: central hallways; spacious, breezy, wraparound porches furnished with large rockers and the occasional well-placed hammock; a high sun deck overlooking the ocean; and louvered outer doors to each of the 16 apartments. The apartments are not large but they are beautifully maintained, comprising one-, two- and three-room air-conditioned suites with private baths, ceiling fans and fully equipped kitchenettes.

The apartments are perfect for couples and families (up to six people). The decor is tropical, with luminous beach colors and Caribbean-style folk art. The dune-front patio, surrounded by palms and oleander, is a cool, shaded place to relax. There's a communal TV room with a video library for the youngsters. Rentals from June through August mostly require a one-week minimum (Sunday to Sunday), but split weeks

sometimes become available. In spring and autumn, split weeks are offered as they become available; the inn closes in winter. This is an excellent bargain relative to the area. Extras include a small soundside beach perfect for toddlers, a laundry facility, complimentary morning coffee, soundside docking facilities and cribs.

Harbor Inn
**$$$-$$$$ • 701 Causeway Dr.,
Wrightsville Beach • (910) 256-9402,
(888) 507-9402**

Situated where Banks Channel meets the Causeway Bridge, the Harbor Inn offers something for everyone. Private balconies overlooking the harbor are just the place to relax with your morning coffee to plan a day on the water or at the beach. Except for the handicapped-accessible suite which sleeps four, each tastefully appointed suite sleeps up to six people and features a fully-equipped kitchenette with microwave, mini-fridge, coffee maker and stove/oven. The living room area has a dining table and comfortable furniture enhanced by a picture-perfect water view. Other amenities include individually controlled heat and air conditioning, daily maid service, linens, kitchen utensils, pots/pans, iron and ironing board, cable TV, hair dryers and toiletries. All of the rooms are non-smoking, however smokers may use their private balcony to smoke at any time.

The Harbor Inn has a dock that can accommodate boats up to 25 feet, which makes this a very popular spot for boaters to vacation. Add to all that, a beautiful outdoor swimming pool and you have the recipe for a totally delicious experience. AAA and AARP discounts are available as well as weekly rates.

Holiday Inn SunSpree Resort
**$$-$$$$ • 1706 N. Lumina Ave.,
Wrightsville Beach • (910) 256-2231,
(877) 330-5050**

This 2002 Quality Excellence award-winning oceanfront resort hotel by Intercontinental Hotels Group has an elegant yet casual atmosphere that makes you feel relaxed and comfortable, whether you're visiting for fun, on business or attending a convention. A year-round destination spot, the seven-story Holiday Inn SunSpree Resort offers first-class amenities and impeccable service.

As you enter into the expansive oceanfront lobby, you're greeted by two blue and gold macaw parrots, one of the hotel's main attractions. An adjoining living room setting features a grand piano and fireplace. Just beyond, an inviting

terrace that extends almost the full width of the hotel offers rocking chairs, outdoor dining tables, and a fabulous view of both the ocean and pools.

In the Verandah Cafe Restaurant, you'll enjoy a variety of culinary creations for breakfast and lunchtime specials of wraps, salads, sandwiches and seafood. Southern cuisine makes dinner a delight, and on Saturdays, piano jazz enhances the ambiance. The hotel's Sunday Brunch Buffet is popular with everyone, including the locals. Children eat free from the kids' menu when accompanied by an adult hotel guest (some restrictions apply). Gabby's Lounge is ideal for that pre-dinner cocktail and appetizer or late-evening nightcap. A market/gift shop is available for those forgotten items, and there's an ATM on site as well.

What a vacation!

Photo: Jay Tervo

The resort offers a complimentary, supervised children's program for ages 4 to 12 and has a dedicated children's activity room. A video arcade, beach playground, volleyball court and fitness center with state-of-the-art equipment give you lots of ways to exercise and have fun. Five recreational pools, including one in the indoor atrium, and a poolside bar and grill outdoors means you can enjoy yourself whatever the weather. An activity desk staff person can assist you by making tee times, dinner reservations, an appointment with the onsite masseuse or suggesting other places to go and things to do.

The hotel was architecturally designed so that the majority of the hotel's 184 guestrooms have verandas with views of either the ocean or the sound marshes and the Intracoastal Waterway. Whirlpool suites or rooms are also available. All rooms have microwave, refrigerator, coffeemaker, ironing equipment, hairdryer, in-room safe, two dataport phones with voice messaging, in-room movies and Nintendo video games. A two-level covered parking deck is available for complimentary guest parking.

The hotels conference center, with 8,500 square feet of meeting/conference space, features the 4,100-square-foot Lumina Ballroom, designed after the original Lumina Pavilion dating from the early 1900s at Wrightsville Beach. An executive boardroom, smaller oceanfront meeting rooms and a business center make the hotel an ideal choice for business meetings and conventions.

Landfall Park Hampton Inn & Suites
$$-$$$$ • 1989 Eastwood Rd., Wrightsville Beach • (910) 256-9600, (877) 256-9600

This is the No. 1 ranked Hampton Inn & Suites in the world for 2001. The moment you walk into the lodge-style lobby of this property, you sense the quality. The free-standing stone chimney above a two-sided gas fireplace is surrounded by oversize rattan chairs and a plush sofa on one side and by the handsome Eagle Bar Lounge on the other.

With 90 traditional rooms and 30 apartment-style suites, the inn provides high-end amenities, complete with bell staff. It's just minutes from the beach and next door to one of the area's better restaurants, Port City Chop House. All suites feature a full kitchen with a microwave, stove, dishwasher and refrigerator. The Signature Suite provides "celebrity" accommodations, with a double-sided fireplace, entertainment center and two-person whirlpool bath. Executive one- and two-bedroom suites are en-

ticing to movie-production staff and other business travelers seeking high quality. Desk and data modem are standard.

The Landfall Park Hampton Inn serves an upscale, 18-item continental breakfast (6 to 10 AM daily) and provides valet service on weekdays. A dedicated boardroom and large meeting room (for 30 to 120 people) are suitable for corporate retreats or small receptions. Of special interest are the large kidney-shaped pool set in a lush garden landscape, a fitness room, a 24-hour suite shop, rattan rocking chairs on a colonnaded porch (a great place for breakfast) and the Gazebo Bar in summer. Landfall Park is on the mainland, less than a half-mile from the drawbridge, and one mile from the beach.

One South Lumina
$$-$$$$ • 1 South Lumina, Wrightsville Beach • (910) 256-9100, (800) 421-3255

In the heart of Wrightsville Beach, One South Lumina offers one-bedroom condominiums for nightly and weekly rentals. The condos feature a queen bed, bunk bed, living room, full kitchen, washer/dryer and private balcony. An oceanfront pool is at your disposal, and there's plenty of reserved parking. The condominiums can be rented by the night or the week; there's a three-night minimum during holidays and a two-night minimum on the weekends.

Sandpeddler Motel & Suites
$$-$$$$ • 15 Nathan St., Wrightsville Beach • (910) 256-2028, (800) 548-4245

The Sandpeddler Motel & Suites, located across the street from the Oceanic Pier & Restaurant, offers contemporary one-bedroom, one-bath condominium-style suites with a kitchenette. Each suite offers a private balcony with a great ocean view. All units sleep up to four people with one queen bed in the bedroom and a queen sleeper sofa in the living room. The Sandpeddler offers an outdoor swimming pool, laundry facilities, linen service and access to email, voice mail, a copier, a fax machine and a printer. Sandpeddler is 40 yards from the ocean and within walking distance of many shops and restaurants.

Shell Island Oceanfront Suites
$-$$$$ • 2700 N. Lumina Ave., Wrightsville Beach • (910) 256-8696, (800) 689-6765

In Wrightsville Beach, overlooking 3,000 feet of pristine white sand beaches, this family-friendly resort hotel offers 160 oceanfront suites, each with a magnificent view of the ocean. Each beautifully decorated suite can sleep up to six people and includes a bedroom, one and a half bathrooms, a separate living room, a dining area, a private balcony and a kitchenette with refrigerator, microwave, stove top, coffeemaker and blender.

Hotel amenities include an outdoor pool and indoor heated pool, hot tub, fitness room, sauna, bicycle rentals, sand volleyball court, convenience store and laundry facilities. Plenty of parking is available in a covered deck; valet service is offered during the summer season. A beautiful oceanfront restaurant and bar opened in spring 2003.

Also ideal for meetings, conventions and social gatherings, Shell Island has more than 5,000 square feet of meeting space. What better way to relax and unwind at the end of a day-long meeting than to have the beach just a few steps away? Golf packages, shopping, fine dining, riverboat cruises, ghost tours or a stroll through the historic district complement your event at Shell island. Experience the tranquility of Shell Island Oceanfront Suites, where the road ends and the beach begins.

Summer Sands Suites
$$$-$$$$ • 104 S. Lumina Ave.
Wrightsville Beach • (910) 256-4175,
(800) 336-4849

This comfortable, 32-suite efficiency motel sits in the heart of Wrightsville Beach within a short walk of restaurants, shopping, laundry facilities and the strand. Rooms are ideal for two adults and two kids. Suites feature sleeping accommodations for up to four people, with a queen-sized bed in the bedroom and queen-sized wall bed in the living room. In addition, the suites offer a kitchen, dining area and private balcony with spectacular views of the island. The outdoor pool is open in the summer. Two handicapped-accessible suites are available.

Surf Suites
$$$$ • 711 S. Lumina Ave., Wrightsville
Beach • (910) 256-2275, (877) 625-9307
for reservations

Open year round, Surf Suites offers 45 beautiful, oceanfront suites. Each unit features a separate bedroom with queen bed, private bath and full kitchen, cable TV and telephone; the living room sofa converts to a double sleeper, and there's a private oceanfront balcony. Relax

> ## INSIDERS' TIP
> Sand is a fact of life down here. We actually love and treasure it, but it can be a huge nuisance. Don't expect to go home without at least a little of the stuff in your suitcase or ground into your car's floor mats — no matter how vigorously you vacuum them!

by the oceanside outdoor pool and let Surf Suites friendly staff ensure a pleasant stay for you, your family and friends. The front desk is open 24 hours a day for your convenience and protection. Housekeeping service is provided daily. Other amenities include parking, coin laundry, private access to the beach and outdoor showers. All suites were completely renovated in spring, 2002; updates include dishwasher and dataport as well as voice mail for each unit.

Carolina Beach and Kure Beach

Astor Hotel
$-$$ • 110 Harper Blvd., Carolina Beach
• (910) 458-9081, (800) 862-7867

The Astor is centrally located on the Boardwalk in downtown Carolina Beach, literally within a block of everything you could want. Close at hand you will find restaurants, entertainment, nightlife, an amusement park, charter boats and moonlight cruises. The ocean is only a block away. The hotel features a swimming pool, an on-site lounge, a patio and a nightclub. In-room amenities include cable TV, air conditioning, refrigerators and microwaves.

Atlantic Towers
$$-$$$ • 1615 S. Lake Park Blvd., Carolina
Beach • (910) 458-8313, (800) BEACH-40

This 11-story establishment offers attractive, well-kept condominium suites with separate bedrooms and full kitchens. Each suite accommodates up to six guests. All 137 condos are oceanfront, and each has a telephone, cable TV, private balcony, an exterior terrace entrance, maid service and elevator service. The outdoor pool deck is in view of the ocean and stands beside a gazebo — a perfect place for a picnic. For cool evenings, there's an indoor heated pool in full view of the ocean. Inquire about the Club Room, which is suitable for corporate retreats, reunions and other special occasions.

Beachside Inn
$-$$ • 616 S. Lake Park Blvd., Carolina
Beach • (910) 458-5598

The family-owned Beachside Inn is in Carolina Beach. Four cozy cottages surround the outdoor pool. Twenty rooms feature color TV with

HOTELS AND MOTELS

Located just minutes from Carolina Beach, Historic Downtown Wilmington and the University of North Carolina at Wilmington

AmeriHost Inn & Suites

5600 Carolina Beach Road
Wilmington, NC 28412
(910) 796-0770 (toll free) 800-961-STAY
www.amerihostinn.com

cable, refrigerator, telephone, heating/air and microwave. Continental breakfast is included with every weekend stay. Beachside Inn combines the feel of a bed and breakfast with the privacy of a hotel. Guests are welcomed by beautiful flowers and views of Carolina Beach Lake and the Atlantic Ocean. For fishermen, Seagull Bait & Tackle is across the street and charters are nearby.

Benson's Landing
$$-$$$$ • 801 Carolina Beach Ave. N., Carolina Beach • (910) 458-5886, (800) 932-0498

At Benson's Landing, the living is easy and relaxed. Only about 150 steps to the beach and a short stroll to restaurants, shops, harbor and amusements, this cozy motel offers a comfort-

able ambiance all year round. Several types of accommodations are available to fit your family's needs, including doubles, efficiencies, one-bedroom units and two-bedroom condos, each with telephone and cable TV. Fully equipped kitchens make all but the double-bed rooms perfect for an extended stay. Guests are invited to enjoy the outdoor pool. Pets are welcome in the motel units but not in the condos. Proprietor Nick Benson, a warm and friendly host, can help you find just the right activities, such as golfing, fishing and loafing, in his little corner of "Beach Heaven."

Blue Marlin Apartments and Cottages
$$-$$$$ • 318 Ft. Fisher Blvd., Kure Beach • (910) 458-5752

A wonderful place for families and friends to relax in a newly renovated, home-like apartment or cottage, the Blue Marlin is just a few steps from the beach. You'll appreciate having your own hot water heater along with fully-equipped kitchen facilities including basic dishes and utensils, central heat and air, color cable TV, private bath and telephone. Bed linens and bath towels are furnished for your convenience. Apartments sleep from two to seven persons, depending on the unit, and the beach house sleeps five to eight. Their Bait and Tackle Shop has T-shirts, souvenirs, rafts, gifts and a small line of groceries in addition to fishing gear.

Buccaneer Motel
$-$$ • 201 Cape Fear Blvd., Carolina Beach • (910) 458-8506

This 16-room motel is in the heart of Carolina Beach across from the boardwalk and within walking distance of many shops and restaurants. Room amenities include full-sized beds, heating/air and telephones; some units have refrigerators. A swim-

Oceanfront Condos with Balconies, 1 or 2 Bedrooms, Fully Furnished, Oceanfront & Heated Enclosed Pools, Video Game Room, Conference Room

INDOOR Heated Pool, Local Calls FREE,
For FREE Brochure or Reservations:

1-800-BEACH-40

www.atlantic-towers.com

1615 S. Lake Park Blvd.
Carolina Beach, NC 28428

ming pool and Mama Mia's Italian Restaurant are on the premises.

Cabana De Mar Motel
$$-$$$$ • 31 Carolina Ave. N., Carolina Beach • (910) 458-4456, (800) 333-8499

Cabana De Mar resembles a condominium complex more than a motel. Its 76 condominium-style suites (one to three bedrooms) are small yet pleasant, with cable TV, elevator access and daily housekeeping service. Some rooms face the ocean and have modest private balconies. Streetside suites are the best value. Laundry rooms are available, but some rooms are equipped with washer/dryers. The motel is within a short walk of central Carolina Beach's attractions and restaurants.

Columbus Motel
$ -$$ • 213 Cape Fear Blvd., Carolina Beach • (910) 458-5281

If you're looking for a clean, friendly, reasonably priced family motel, this is the place for you. The Columbus Motel's quaint charm and convenient location make it especially appealing to folks who don't want to be driving all over the place to have their vacation needs met. Here you'll find comfort, a big blue pool, and old-fashioned, down-home atmosphere. Within walking distance are the beach, shopping, Boardwalk, and good places to eat. The motel offers 18 rooms on two levels, each with a view of the pool.

Courtyard by Marriott
$$$$ • 100 Charlotte St., Carolina Beach • (910) 458-2030 (800) 321-2211

Opening July 1st 2003 as the first oceanfront Courtyard in the Cape Fear resort area, this 100,000 square-foot new hotel offers traditional Courtyard features and style plus added flair and amenities for the beach. All 144 rooms, including king bed rooms with Jacuzzi baths and 18 two-room suites, face the ocean and have private balconies. In-room amenities include granite vanities, upgraded furniture and decor, refrigerators, coffee makers and dataports. Suites include the above amenities plus a separate living area with wet bar and microwave.

A luxurious focal point of the hotel is a custom designed oceanfront outdoor pool and tropical plaza featuring a sunbathing deck with direct beach access and an outdoor café. The indoor pool and spa are open year round, and an extensive exercise room and guest laundry facility are also available. Kayaks, bikes, beach chairs and umbrellas are available to rent.

The Courtyard Cafe, open for breakfast, lunch and dinner, overlooks the tropical plaza and pool, and also offers outdoor patio dining. A guest

Marketessen carries a variety of food and snack items plus gifts, clothing and sundries. A 3300 sq. ft. convention center with theatre seating can handle groups to 300, or can be used for dinner and social events for groups to 250; it can be divided into three rooms for smaller events or conventions.

Docksider Oceanfront Inn
$$-$$$$ • 202 N. Ft. Fisher Blvd., Kure Beach • (800) 383-8111

At this "nautical inn on the beach," you've a choice of 34 immaculately clean, comfortable, attractively decorated efficiency-style or standard rooms with either queen or double beds on one of three levels, many with a private porch. Half the units boast fully-equipped kitchens and dining areas, all other units have refrigerators, microwaves

and coffeemakers. Of course, you'll get color TV with more than 30 channels, telephones with dataports, radio, alarm clock and hairdryer, too. You can take a swim in the large outdoor pool and sunbathe on the oceanview deck or "sunketch" on the roof. Then take a moonlight stroll on the beach, which is just a few steps from your door. Ooooh, that does sound good, doesn't it?

Golden Sands Motel
$$ -$$$ • U.S. Hwy 421 S., Carolina Beach • (910) 458-8334

You couldn't ask for more — immaculate, comfortable, spacious and attractive accommodations with a fantastic oceanfront location. Each of the 88 tastefully decorated, bright rooms is air conditioned and has a refrigerator, phone and cable TV; most also have microwaves. A great feature is the split design offered in many of the rooms: two double beds separated by a half wall, which is just the ticket for families with children or two couples staying together. Hotel guests can choose from double, king, or efficiency-style rooms — the majority face the ocean, and all have balconies or porches. Look for an additional 64 oceanfront rooms to be added in 2004. On site is a popular seafood restaurant with tables out on the pier, where you'll also find a Tiki Bar. Golden Sands has two sparkling-blue outdoor pools and a great gift shop, too. Complimentary coffee is served in the lobby every morning starting at 6:30 AM.

Guy Johnson Motel
$$ • 235 Carolina Beach Ave. N., Carolina Beach • (910) 458-8105

Conveniently located one block from the boardwalk, next to the charter boat docks and across the street from the beach, this cozy motel has been a Carolina Beach fixture since the early 1940s and family-owned since 1960. With a variety of amenities, the rooms and apartments are a boon to families, something for which the friendly owners pride themselves. Small kitchenettes are in the majority of rooms and the others have coffeemakers, refrigerators and microwaves. Three rooms sleep up to four people. The remainder of the motel is apartments, which accommodate three to six people each. The rooms and apartments are exceptionally clean, with the staff going so far as to wash the bedspreads after each guest leaves. Other amenities include cable TV with HBO, rockers and lounge chairs on the street-side patios and a refreshing in-ground pool.

"You gonna eat the rest of that sandwich?"

Photo: Jay Tervo

Microtel Inn & Suites
$$ • 907 N. Lake Park Blvd., Carolina Beach • (910) 458-1300, (888) 771-7171

With an opening planned for June 2003, this three-story motel will have 62 attractively decorated rooms, including singles, doubles and suites with wet bar. All rooms will be accessible by inside corridor and feature microfridges. Several rooms will be handicapped accessible. Amenities include elevator, security cameras throughout, continental breakfast and swimming pool.

Nelson's Motel
$$-$$$ • 112 Ft. Fisher Blvd., Kure Beach • (910) 458-9011

In the heart of Kure Beach, just a few short steps to the ocean and fishing pier, you'll find this well-maintained, clean, attractive motel with a variety of comfortable accommodations, a pool and plenty of parking spaces. Standard rooms are furnished with two extra-long beds, full-size refrigerator, phone, color cable TV and air conditioning. Also available are a handicapped-accessible room, suites, efficiencies, two-bedroom apartments, a cottage and an oceanfront house, all with complete kitchens. A big plus is a 24-hour on-site manager; however, the office is open only from 8 AM to 11 PM. Close to the newly expanded North Carolina Aquarium at Fort Fisher and other attractions, Nelson's is open from March through Thanksgiving.

Sandstep Motel
$-$$ • 619 Carolina Beach Ave. N., Carolina Beach • (910) 458-8387, (800) 934-4076

Family owned and operated, Sandstep Motel offers peace and solitude for families and couples. It is located on the quiet end of Carolina Beach but is just a 10-minute walk from the restaurants, marina and boardwalk. The diverse motel offers five buildings and 40 rooms, with single and double occupancies plus effic-heated swimming pools, a barbecue patio with a gas grill and picnic tables, a fishpond, a breezeway and a garden swing. Pets are allowed, but be sure to let the owners — Joyce and Peter — know before you sign in. And be aware that pets are only allowed on the beach from November to February. All rooms include cable TV, a refrigerator and a coffee maker. The apartments and efficiencies have fully equipped kitchens. Children are graciously accommodated at the Sandstep. Kids younger than 12 receive a free Clark the Bear sand pail and spade. A few boogie boards are available for swimmers, and there's a fish-cleaning station for successful fishermen.

SeaWitch Motel & Cafe
$$-$$$ • 224 Carolina Beach Ave. N., Carolina Beach • (910) 458-8564

If you're looking for the ultimate in relaxation, superb dining, beach pleasures, pool and quality accommodations all in one spot, the Sea Witch is just right for you. Forget driving. From here you're only a few steps away from everything you need for an unforgettable vacation. Each of the recently renovated, comfortable rooms has air conditioning, refrigerator, microwave, dataport, 27-inch TV with cable and telephone. The motel's oceanfront location features a recreation area with pool, decks and outdoor showers. Open March through October, the Sea Witch invites you to come away and play. (See our chapter on Restaurants.)

Seven Seas Inn

$$-$$$$ • 130 Ft. Fisher Blvd., Kure Beach • (910) 458-8122

The Seven Seas is a family owned and operated inn on the oceanfront in Kure Beach. Consisting of three buildings — oceanfront, ocean view and pool view — Seven Seas has 32 clean, comfortable rooms in a variety of configurations. Large efficiencies, two-room efficiencies, interconnecting units and standard motel accommodations are roomy and equipped with twins, doubles and queen-size beds; non-smoking rooms are available. All rooms have telephones, refrigerators, cable TV with complimentary HBO, individually controlled air conditioning and heating units. Rooms can accommodate up to six people. The well-kept grounds

include fine pool facilities with two shaded gazebos, a courtyard, benches and extensive landscaping. Small children, seniors and non-swimmers will appreciate a second three-foot-deep pool with seats all around. Restaurants, shops and the popular Kure Beach Fishing Pier are within a short walk of the Inn. When entering Kure Beach by the main road from the north (U.S. 421), look for the Seven Seas Inn on the left with its many beautiful agave plants.

Tradewinds Motel

$$-$$$ • 309 S. Fort Fisher Blvd., Kure Beach • (910) 458-8742 , (800) 794-8379

Featuring oceanfront and ocean-view rooms, the family-owned Tradewinds Motel offers many amenities for your vacation pleasure. A number of different configurations are available, including singles, doubles, some with two or three separate bedrooms and a few two-bed efficiencies. All units have private baths, microwaves and refrigerators; some have full kitchens. The kid in you will enjoy the onsite pool. The closest oceanfront motel to the North Carolina Aquarium at Fort Fisher, Tradewinds is only two blocks from the Kure Beach Pier and restaurants. Tradewinds welcomes small pets.

Southport-Oak Island

Blue Water Point Marina Resort Motel

$$ • 57th Pl. and W. Beach Dr., Oak Island • (910) 278-1230, (888) 634-9005

Located on the soundside of Oak Island, this small, comfortable 28-room motel is especially convenient to boaters, while just across W. Beach Drive is a boardwalk to the beach strand. The motel offers rooms with waterway views, two double beds, showers, TVs and telephones. Various patios and sundecks provide a fine sunset view. The marina rents floating docks and boat slips with a water depth of 5 feet at mean low tide. City-owned boat ramps adjoining the marina are available to use for free. Other amenities include an adjoining restaurant and lounge (open from February 14 to November 1), a ship's store and tackle shop, boat chartering and head boat trips, plus rentals of kayaks, john boats, beach chairs and umbrellas. Free sunset cruises on the 60-foot head boat are available to motel guests.

Captain's Cove Motel

$-$$ • 6401 E. Oak Island Dr., Oak Island • (910) 278-6026

Captain's Cove, family owned and operated for 30 years, is located on the main street in

Oak Island. Rooms open out onto the central parking court and are surrounded by beautiful oak trees. All rooms contain refrigerators and coffeemakers. Microwaves are available upon request. Efficiency apartments are available in addition to the standard rooms. The great things about Captain's Cove are the quiet family atmosphere, the beach access, a pool in a sunny location and the fact that restaurants and shopping are within walking distance. Captain's Cove is small-pet friendly as well.

Driftwood Motel
$ • 604 Ocean Dr., Oak Island
• (910) 278-6114

This attractive two-story motel has an oceanfront location, an outdoor pool, laundry facilities, outdoor grills and picnic tables, plus a refrigerator, telephone and cable TV in every room, all at a reasonable cost. The second-floor verandas provide wonderful views, especially at sunset, and are equipped with deck chairs and tables for relaxing in the ocean breeze. The Driftwood offers neat, carpeted rooms, each with its own air conditioning and heat, and a full kitchen is available for all guests to share. Adjoining the kitchen is an outdoor play area for children.

Hampton Inn
$-$$$ • 5181 Southport Supply Rd.,
Southport • (910) 454-0016,
(800) HAMPTON

The Hampton Inn opened in June 2000. It is conveniently located near two shopping centers, halfway between downtown Southport and Oak Island and less than a 10-minute drive from the Brunswick County Airport. Eighty home-like guest rooms are available, containing king- or queen-sized beds, A/C, TV, coffee makers, hair dryers, data ports and voice mail. Some rooms contain a microwave and refrigerator as well. Available upon request are cribs, rollaway beds and refrigerators. Nonsmoking and handicapped-accessible rooms are available. Continental breakfast is provided and can be eaten in the well-appointed dining area. The inn offers an outdoor pool, a fitness center and a business center with free high-speed Internet access. Group rates are available, and the meeting room seats up to 40. In the Hampton Inn tradition, 100 percent satisfaction is guaranteed.

The Inn at South Harbour Village
$$$$ • 5005 O'Quinn Blvd., Southport
• (910) 454-7500, (800) 454-0815

The spectacular waterway view from the decks adjoining the nine suites in The Inn at

South Harbour Village are reason enough to stay there whether it be for a romantic getaway, a honeymoon or even a meeting. But the view inside is lovely as well. There a golden glow permeates the plush ambience of every room. All suites contain a full kitchen, two have Jacuzzis, one has a bath and a half, and one has two baths and a family room as well as a living room. Gary Albertson, Innkeeper, is a minister as well. He will coordinate your wedding and perform the ceremony in the chapel. (See our Wedding Chapter) All guests receive a free round of golf on the South Harbor Golf Course in the village; access to the pool and exercise room at the club; bicycles and complimentary deli breakfasts. Conference rooms are available. Ask about extended stays.

HOTELS AND MOTELS

Island Resort & Inn
$$-$$$ • 500 Ocean Dr., Oak Island
• (910) 278-5644

With a direct private beach access and an oceanfront deck and gazebo, Island Resort & Inn provides lovely ocean views. The inn features single rooms that include refrigerators, microwaves, coffeemakers, complimentary coffee and HBO; apartments consisting of one or two bedrooms with full kitchens including stoves, refrigerators, microwaves and dishwashers; and two oceanfront cottages. Island Resort offers a pool and a hot tub. Other amenities include a free fishing pier pass to Long Beach Pier, wedding and anniversary packages, golf packages and a 36-foot private yacht available for charter.

Ocean Crest Motel
$$ • 1417 E. Beach Dr., Oak Island
• (910) 278-3333

The owners and staff of the Ocean Crest Motel will make you feel welcome from the moment of your first contact. In fact, they are so friendly, their guests just keep coming back. Add to this the fact that, unique to Oak Island, the Ocean Crest is located right on the beach strand, not across the street, and what more could you ask? A swimming pool? They have one. A gift shop with a line of prints of Oak Island and Southport, beach towels, tropical shirts, hats, etc.? They have that too. In addition, this 62-room motel is situated adjacent to a fishing pier and a restaurant, making it an ideal spot for vacation accommodations. Especially attractive is the "stay for seven days,

pay for five" discount rate available year round.

All oceanfront and standard rooms are newly renovated, airy and bright, each equipped with a ceiling fan and colors reminiscent of the tropics. Rooms contain two double beds, air conditioning, refrigerator, color TV with expanded cable and remote, telephone with free local calls, coffeemaker and coffee. Most rooms also have a bistro-style table and chairs. Some oceanfront rooms have private balconies, others have a shared walkway, and all have the same glorious view. Handicapped-accessible rooms are available as well. The spacious oceanfront townhouse, which sleeps eight, has two bedrooms, a Jacuzzi in the master bath and is available by the week and the month.

No pets are allowed, but the Ocean Crest is a couples and family-oriented motel. They even allow wedding parties and family reunions with plenty of rooms to accommodate everyone. Golf packages and fishing charters can also be arranged.

Riverside Motel
$ • 103 W. Bay St., Southport
• (910) 457-6986

This small eight-room establishment situated on the waterfront between the Ships Chandler Restaurant and the Cape Fear Pilot Tower commands an excellent view of Southport's harbor and the mouth of the Cape Fear River where it meets the sea. Both Old Baldy and the Oak Island Lighthouse can be seen from this spot. The motel was totally renovated in 2002, and the cozy double-occupancy rooms are equipped with either two double beds or queen-sized beds, ceiling fans, microwave ovens, cable TV, refrigerators, coffeemakers, toasters and telephones (local calls are free). The rooms are small and well-kept, and the location on the Riverside in the historic district is conducive to strolls through the scenic town for meals, shopping or sightseeing.

Sea Captain Motor Lodge
$$-$$$ • 608 W. West St., Southport
• (910) 457-5263

The Sea Captain, near the Southport Marina, is the largest motel in Southport. Each of the 96 units is modern, well-kept and equipped with a refrigerator, telephone and TV. Accommodations include single motel rooms, doubles and efficiencies. An Olympic-size outdoor pool and shaded gazebo are centrally located among the lodge's four buildings. The adjoining dining facility, the Sea Captain Restaurant, is open for breakfast, lunch and dinner. The conference room accommodates 50 people.

INSIDERS' TIP

Many facilities offer beach towels as a courtesy to guests. Be sure to return them when you're done with them.

HOTELS AND MOTELS

Southwinds Motel
$-$$ • 700 Ocean Dr., Oak Island
• (910) 278-5442
Including singles, doubles and efficiency suites, the accommodations are comfortable at Southwinds, an older, well-run operation. It is ideally situated across the street from the beach strand, the Yaupon Beach Fishing Pier and two restaurants. Rooms are quaint and equipped with refrigerators, cable TV, air conditioning and a telephone. The larger accommodations have fully equipped kitchens, sleeper sofas and double beds. A cabana adjoins the heated pool, and an outdoor grill and picnic area are nearby. Ask about cottage rentals. Parking is available for boats and oversize vehicles. Truckers welcome.

South Brunswick Islands

Causeway Motel
$-$$ • 12 Causeway Dr., Ocean Isle Beach
• (910) 579-9001
The Causeway Motel has 35 very clean rooms. Each room is equipped with double beds (with the exception of the three handicapped-accessible rooms, which have twin beds), indi-vidual air conditioning and heat, telephones, refrigerators and cable TV. The outdoor pool and sun deck are close to the parking lot, and the beach only 200 yards away. This family-oriented motel is also convenient to dining and entertainment, including mini-golf and the waterslide, much of it within walking distance.

Gray Gull Motel
$ • 3263 Holden Beach Rd. S.W., Holden Beach • (910) 842-6775
This family-owned motel, the only one at Holden Beach, is very well-maintained and cour-teously run. Each of the 17 carpeted rooms has cable TV and a telephone as well as easy access to the outdoor pool and picnic tables. The Gray Gull is on the mainland side of the Intracoastal Waterway, just minutes from the beach. The office is in the hardware store next door, where anglers can also buy tackle. Cancellations re-quire 24-hour notice.

The Islander Inn
$$-$$$ • 57 W. First St., Ocean Isle Beach • (910) 575-7000, (888) 325-4753
This oceanfront family hotel offers 70 guest rooms with either an ocean or sound view. Room

Oceanfront Ocean Isle Beach

Relax in oceanfront luxury overlooking our breathtaking island beach, palm trees and lush subtropical gardens. Choose from deluxe rooms, one to three bedroom suites (complete with kitchens and livingrooms) and 4, 5 & 6 bedroom Resort Houses. Enjoy daily housekeeping, complimentary hot breakfast buffet, three pools (one indoor), whirlpool spas, exercise room, shuffleboard, bikes. The Garden Bar features light dining and mixed beverages. Golf packages on over 100 of the Carolinas' finest courses. Ask about our Free Summer Golf!

Ocean Isle Beach's Highest Rated (AAA) Accommodations!

800-334-3581

AAA — Mobil Travel Guide

The Winds **Inn & Suites**

Info@TheWinds.com   www.TheWinds.com

amenities include a double, queen or king bed, a wet bar, a refrigerator, a microwave and in-room coffee service. The Islander Inn offers daily extended continental breakfasts. There's an outdoor oceanfront pool with a sun deck and an indoor heated pool with a Jacuzzi. The Islander Inn also offers handicapped-accessible rooms. Golf packages are available. The Islander Inn has conference space that seats 55 persons for business meetings and other occasions. Inquire about AAA and AARP discounts and off-season rates.

Island Motel
$-$$ • 19 Causeway Dr., Ocean Isle Beach • (910) 579-6019

One-and-a-half blocks from the beach, the Island Motel occupies the second floor of a building and consists of 10 simple and neat double-occupancy rooms and two two-room suites. Each has air conditioning, a view of the waterway and sound, cable TV and a telephone. Boat slips with access to the Intracoastal Waterway are available to rent, as is charter boat service. The adjoining grocery-and-supply store (which carries fishing tackle and video rentals), the gas station and the Plaza Marina earn the Island Motel high marks for convenience.

Ocean Isle Inn
$$-$$$ • 37 W. First St., Ocean Isle Beach • (910) 579-0750, (800) 352-5988

The Ocean Isle Inn is sure to please the most discerning vacationer. The Inn offers oceanfront rooms with private balconies and sound-view rooms overlooking the tranquil Intracoastal Waterway. The ambiance of the South Pacific Islands permeates each room as suggested by the tiled floors, teak furniture, unique artwork and bright, vibrant colors. All rooms also include a wet bar, mini-fridge, dataport phone, hairdryer and coffee service.

Guests of the Ocean Isle Inn may relax in either of two swimming pools — one on the oceanfront and the other a heated indoor pool with an attached spa. Guests are entitled to complimentary continental breakfasts and can purchase golf packages offering a choice of play at more than 36 area courses within 10 minutes of the Ocean Isle Inn. The conference space offers quiet, off-the-beaten-path facilities for business meetings and other special occasions. Be sure to inquire about midweek Supersavers discounts during the off-season, weekly rates, and AAA and AARP discounts. Handicapped facilities and elevators are also available.

Shallotte Microtel Inn & Suites
$-$$ • 4646 East Coast Ln., Shallotte • (910) 755-6444

Strategically located in Shallotte, this brand-new, 62-room hotel provides a haven for business and vacation travelers alike. Beaches are five to eight miles away, six top golf courses are within five miles, and historic Wilmington is a short 25 mile drive away. Special dining treats await 8 miles down the road in Calabash, home of several renowned seafood restaurants.

Room amenities include dataports and free local calls, and there are non-smoking rooms. Coffee and tea service in the lobby, copy and fax service, and guest laundry on-site are some of Microtel's special features. Guests can plan their side trips over the free continental breakfast or by the outdoor pool.

The Sunset Inn
$$-$$$$ • 9 North Shore Dr., Sunset Beach
• (910) 575-1000

The Sunset Inn opened its doors to the beauty of the saltwater marsh and island life in June 2000. The honey-colored hardwood floors in the entrance and living area shine softly in the light that filters through the large white-framed windows. Here, continental breakfast is served on a lace-covered table every morning from 7:30 until 10 AM ,or you can choose to have your morning meal in the living room or in the privacy of your own suite. There are 14 suites, each with a different theme and decor. All suites have a king-sized bed, wet bar, refrigerator, love seat and private screened porch with rockers. The four grand suites each have a Jacuzzi and a shower in their private baths, while the other 10 have three-quarter showers in theirs. Come experience the quiet comfort for yourself. Special rates are available off season.

The Winds Oceanfront Inn & Suites
$$-$$$ • 310 E. First St., Ocean Isle Beach
• (910) 579-6275, (800) 334-3581

This oceanfront resort is an excellent choice for its range of accommodations and prices. Studios, mini-suites, deluxe rooms, one- and two-bedroom suites and resort houses with four, five or six bedrooms are all richly appointed and comfortable. Some of the resort houses have private, outdoor Jacuzzis, many accommodations have indoor whirlpools, and all have kitchen facilities. The grounds are beautifully landscaped with 11 varieties of palm trees, banana trees and lush flowering plants nestled among meandering boardwalks and decks. The newly renourished beach provides a wide expanse of sand for such activities as sunning, castle building or searching for seashells.

The Winds has a heated pool indoors, two outdoor pools, two outdoor Jacuzzis, an exercise room, beach bocce, shuffleboard, volleyball, bike rentals and nearby tennis. The Garden Bar Restaurant serves a light menu featuring salads, sandwiches and fresh-baked pizza and mixed beverages including margaritas and daiquiris. A complimentary hot breakfast buffet is served daily. Honeymoon and golf packages (available at more than 100 championship courses) are easily arranged. In addition, from June through August 2003, free summer golf programs are available at over two dozen courses. Some rooms are handicapped accessible. Ask about special off-season Take-A-Break packages.

Topsail Island Area

Breezeway Motel and Restaurant
$-$$ • 636 Channel Blvd., Topsail Beach
• (910) 328-7751, (800) 548-4694

This vintage, soundfront motel, with a restaurant on the premises, features amenities for the whole family, including a swimming pool, fishing pier and boat dock, all available to motel guests. The many returning guests continue to enjoy the beautiful scenery, sunsets and easy access to sandbars for swimming or shelling in the sound. The 47 rooms offer a choice of two double beds, a king bed or efficiencies, some with a refrigerator. All rooms have color cable TV and daily maid service. An ice machine and complimentary coffee are offered in the office. Breezeway is close to the Missiles and More Museum, the Turtle Rehabilitation Center, shopping and the beach. See our Restaurants chapter information about the Breezeway Restaurant.

Holiday Inn Express Hotel & Suites Topsail Island Area
$-$$ • 1565 N.C. Hwy. 210, Sneads Ferry
• (910) 327-8282, (800) 465-4329

Opened in 2000, this hotel received the newcomer of the year award in 2001. Hotel amenities include a large outdoor pool and a great room with a fireplace with wonderful scenic views of North Shore Golf Course Country Club and the Intracoastal Waterway. In-room amenities include coffeemakers, irons and ironing boards, hairdryers, two-line speaker phones with dataports, and color televisions. Out of a total of 68 rooms, there are 15 suites with king-size beds and pull-out sofas, refrigerators and microwave ovens. Some rooms have whirlpool tubs. Guests can enjoy a free deluxe continental breakfast bar featuring fresh fruit, cereals, pastries and assorted breads. Located on the golf course, this hotel is just a short drive over the high-rise bridge to North Topsail Beach. Seasonal rates apply. AAA and AARP discounts and government rates are available as well as wedding and golf packages and group rates. The hotel has an elevator, is ADA compliant and is open year round.

Island Inn
$-$$ • 302 North Shore Dr., Surf City
• (910) 328-2341 (800) 573-2566

The Island Inn, directly across from the beach, has a private beach access and includes an oceanfront deck and chaise lounges on the beach. Accommodations include 20 motel rooms, each with a refrigerator, microwave and coffeemaker, plus a

three-bedroom, two-bath oceanfront house, and two-bedroom, one-bath apartments. There is a pool on the premises. Island Inn is located within two blocks of downtown Surf City restaurants and shopping and the fishing pier.

Jolly Roger Inn
$-$$$ • 803 Ocean Blvd., Topsail Beach • (910) 328-4616 (800) 633-3196

Oceanfront, on the same premises as the Jolly Roger fishing pier and centrally located in downtown Topsail Beach — what more could a vacationer want? The Jolly Roger Inn has 65 rooms that include bedrooms, efficiencies and suites, some with a kitchen. Open year-round, the inn offers daily, weekly and seasonal rates.

Sea Star Inn
$-$$$ • 2108 N. New River Dr., Surf City • (910) 328-5191, (800) 343-0087

Whether your choice is golf, kayaking, canoeing or scuba diving, the Sea Star Inn has a package vacation for you. This friendly, newly decorated motel welcomes new and returning guests year after year. The beach is just across the back yard, so it is conveniently located for fishing or swimming in the Atlantic. If the ocean isn't your choice for swimming, try the Sea Star's pool. Every room has a refrigerator, cable TV and in-room phone with direct calling. Some units have a completely furnished kitchen and microwave oven. Ask Kim or Sharon about special weekend activities planned for added vacation fun. Open year round and pet friendly, the Sea Star caters to families and couples.

HOTELS AND MOTELS

Sea Vista Motel
$-$$ • 1521 Ocean Blvd., Topsail Beach • (910) 328-2171, (800) 732-8478

Guests, many of them who return regularly, are considered friends at the Sea Vista Motel. New managers William and Maura Johnson have continued the tradition of friendly service at this oceanfront motel that features large rooms, full-size appliances, cable TV, balconies and individually controlled air conditioning. In a quiet location, it's still within easy walking distance of the Topsail Sound Fishing Pier and Marina and Latitude 34 restaurant. Individual rooms are privately owned, so decor and furnishings vary. There are 17 rooms with refrigerator and microwave, eight efficiencies, five mini-efficiencies and two apartments. Golf packages, romantic getaways and family reunions are some of the services offered. Discounts apply for seniors and seven-day stays, and children younger than 12 stay free. Pets are allowed with a $20 surcharge.

St. Regis Resort
$$$-$$$$ • 2000 New River Inlet Rd., North Topsail Beach • (910) 328-4975, (800) 682-4882

This vacation resort offers condominium units with one to three bedrooms, all with two full baths, both oceanfront and oceanview. Each unit is individually owned and is tastefully furnished. In addition to clean, uncrowded beaches, you'll find a fitness center, a sauna, steam showers, tennis courts, shuffleboard, and indoor and outdoor pools with a Jacuzzi. A small convenience store and pizza restaurant are on the premises. It's open year round.

Surfside Motel
$$ • 124 N. Shore Dr., Surf City • (910) 328-4099, (877) 404-9162

Surf City's only oceanfront motel is conveniently located downtown within walking distance of restaurants, shopping and the fishing pier. The large deck is a great place to relax, enjoy the sun and listen to the soothing sounds of the ocean. The seven oceanfront rooms have microwaves and refrigerators. All rooms have cable TV, heat and air conditioning.

Tiffany's Motel
$-$$ • 1502 N. New River Dr, Surf City • (910) 328-1397, (800) 758-3818

Mention pride in ownership, and Tiffany's immediately comes to mind. Owners Bob and Ann Smith continually work to upgrade this property, last season adding a new section to bring their total to 28 rooms. This year, two new pools are being added. All rooms have a refrigerator and microwave, and the new rooms also have coffeemakers and hairdryers. The delightful gathering room has hosted weddings as well as groups such as the Moose and Elks, who bring their families for vacations at the beach. The pool and deck are a great place to relax and forget your cares. There are two wheelchair-accessible rooms with handicapped showers and bathroom rails. Tiffany's offers special weekly rates, five-night packages and group rates.

The Topsail Motel
$$-$$$ • 1195 N. Anderson Blvd., Topsail Beach • (910) 328-3381, (800) 726-1795

Located directly on the ocean in Topsail Beach, just south of Surf City, the Topsail Motel has 30 oceanfront units with air-conditioning and cable TV. Room choices range from singles to kings, all with refrigerators and microwaves. For the larger family, there is a three-bed, two-room efficiency. A special honeymoon room is offered. Private porches and open decks overlook the ocean. The Topsail Motel is open from March 1 through October 31.

Villa Capriani Resort
$$$$ • 790 New River Inlet Rd., N. Topsail Beach • (910) 328-1900, (800) 934-2400

Relax in this beautiful oceanfront resort complex with the Atlantic Ocean at your door. Villas include one-, two- and three-bedroom units, either oceanfront or oceanview. A picturesque multilevel courtyard features several swimming pools and a whirlpool. Tanning decks and a cabana offer a spectacular view of the ocean. Paliotti's at the Villa is an onsite restaurant serving fresh seafood and Italian dishes. It's open year round.

Bed and Breakfasts and Small Inns

Even though we've entered the third millennium, technology has yet to produce a machine allowing us to travel backwards in time, back to the days of horse-drawn carriages, sitting on the porch, sipping mint juleps and watching passersby. Until technology catches up with our yen for bygone days, there are always bed and breakfasts or small inns to quench our thirst for romance and escapism. Despite, or maybe because of, Wilmington's small-town charm, the area offers travelers outstanding bed and breakfasts plus a number of wonderful small inns. Most feature fabulous antiques and have unique, fascinating histories, decor and gardens. Some are as casual as a pajama party, while others are steeped in Victorian elegance.

Several beach bed and breakfasts invite you to enjoy the ocean breezes, dine overlooking the sea, wade in the surf and stroll on the sand. You'll find quite a different feel here — definitely easygoing and informal.

As a point of information, bed and breakfasts differ from small inns when it comes to serving food to guests. If you like a full, cooked breakfast served at a given time usually in a common dining area, a bed and breakfast is for you. On the other hand, an inn usually provides only a continental breakfast, if any at all. Some inns have kitchenette facilities so that guests may prepare their own morning meal; some have variations on the breakfast offering, but none serve a formal meal at an appointed hour. Another difference between an inn and a bed and breakfast is the location. An inn is almost always "in town" and may be associated with a pub, restaurant or have a bar on the premises; not so with a bed and breakfast, though some offer a self-service refrigerator for wine and beer or soft drinks.

Wherever you choose to stay, your hosts surely will be knowledgeable about the area and can assist you with directions and in making reservations for shows, meals, charters and golf packages.

Bed and breakfasts and inns typically do not allow pets, smoking indoors or very young children unless by prior arrangement. Most establishments accept major credit cards and personal checks, especially for making payment in advance; many charge a fee for cancellations, so be sure to ask about the policy. Also note that often they require a full weekend lodging, especially during the Azalea Festival in April and Riverfest in October (see our Annual Events chapter for information on these events).

Wilmington

15th Street Bed & Breakfast
$$-$$$$ • 111 N. 15th St., Wilmington
• (910) 763-2136, (877) 506-3974

For a truly outstanding bed and breakfast experience, you must be a guest at this delightful inn featuring gourmet dining along with warm

Price Code

Since prices are subject to change without notice, we provide only price guidelines based on per-night rates during the summer (high season). Guidelines do not reflect the 7 percent state/county and and 1 to 6 percent room occupancy tax (taxes may vary by municipality or county). Some establishments offer lower rates during the off-season, but always confirm rates and necessary amenities before reserving. It may behoove you to inquire about corporate discounts even if they are not mentioned in our descriptions.

$ $75 or less
$$ $76 to $120
$$$ $121 to $150
$$$$ $151 and more

hospitality and an ambience that's hard to match. As soon as you enter, you feel welcome and at home. Large, open, bright rooms in gold, persimmon, apricot, wine, green, yellow and white with oriental rugs accenting gorgeous hardwood floors, high ceilings, abundant contemporary art and elegant window treatments greet you at every turn. Though the architecture and decor are quite formal, the inn's tone is relaxed, intimate and uplifting.

Absolutely delightful for singles or couples and especially appealing to families, 15th Street Bed & Breakfast even permits pets upon approval. A great two-room suite arrangement complete with private stairway, hall and bath, is the perfect answer for combining family togetherness with privacy. Each of the four colorful guest rooms has a television/VCR, phone, clock radio, and private bath with period fixtures.

Located in a quiet residential area neighborhood adjacent to Wilmington's Historic District, 15th Street Bed & Breakfast is within walking distance of museums, art galleries and other cultural attractions. Ample sidewalks lend themselves to brisk morning jogs and early evening strolls, too. Area beaches are just a 15-minute drive.

Ask about seasonal special promotions with wonderful culinary delights and package rates that will make it hard to resist a weekend getaway at this incredible place. Plan a spring visit to enjoy wine and cheese in the country garden under the giant old magnolia tree with azaleas all around you. Or come in December to have hot chocolate and fresh-baked cookies in front of a cozy fire. Always you can anticipate an extraordinary brunch feast guaranteed to keep you coming back to 15th Street Bed & Breakfast time and again. They offer discounts for returning guests and artists.

219 South 5th Bed and Breakfast
$$ • 219 S. Fifth St., Wilmington
• (910) 763-5539, (800) 219-7634

The Greek Revival Deans-Maffit House (1871) offers three guest rooms of essentially country styles accented with Victorian antiques. For the cooler nights, there are gas log fireplaces in the living and dining rooms. Two of the rooms have decorative fireplaces and all have private baths. Each room features a ceiling fan, lots of antiques and individually controlled steam heating and air. The efficiency suite has its own private entrance and features a kitchenette and eating area with a mahogany table. Hot coffee and tea are delivered to the rooms each morning; wine, beer and soft drinks are available in the evenings. The back yard with its small circular goldfish pond has a nostalgic and relaxing character. Hearty, hot breakfasts are a balance of formality and familiarity, blending the use of china, antique glasses and hefty coffee mugs. Children older than 12 are welcome at the inn.

The Camellia Cottage
$$$ • 118 S. Fourth St., Wilmington
• (910) 763-9171, (866) 763-9171

Standing on a brick-paved street four blocks from the river, Camellia Cottage is a richly appointed, high-peaked Queen Anne Shingle home (built 1889) that was once the home of prominent Wilmington artist Henry J. MacMillan. Some of his work remains in the home. In

fact, artwork abounds throughout Camellia Cottage, from murals on the wrap-around piazza to hand-painted fireplace tiles. Camellia Cottage offers three spacious guest rooms and one suite, each with its own character. Queen-size, antique-style beds, private

baths and gas-fired hearths are standard. Morning coffee is provided, and beverages are available in the afternoon. Traditional Southern breakfasts are served with crystal, china and silver. The parlor is always available to guests. Winter rates and discounts for long-term stays apply.

Catherine's Inn
$$ • 410 S. Front St., Wilmington
• (910) 251-0863, (800) 476-0723

For true Southern hospitality and the feeling that you're completely at home, you'll definitely choose to stay at Catherine's Inn. From the time you come in the door, you'll relax and rid yourself of all your real-world aggravations. Catherine herself makes the choice a winner. Having raised six daughters, she's a master at delivering T.L.C., and her guests love it.

After a complete homemade breakfast of juice, pastries, quiche, waffles, sausages and other down-home cooking, sit around the dining room table with your coffee or tea and chat for awhile. Hang out with your hosts in the kitchen, read books, watch TV or just visit in one of the two Victorian double parlors, or watch river activity from the second floor screened-in porch. By all means, take advantage of lawn chairs in the large two-tiered back yard, which is just the place for a glass of wine while watching the sun set over the Cape Fear River.

Built in 1883, the Inn is an Italianate structure with wraparound front porch and five uniquely decorated guest rooms. One has an old iron sleigh bed, two feature canopy king beds and another is adorned with antique dolls; each offers a sitting area, writing desk, private bath, terrycloth robes and free local phone calls. Our favorite guest room is the Waterview room with its bay window and iron queen-size bed. Complimentary beer, wine and soda are always available in the second-floor fridge; in the evening, look for complimentary liqueurs as well. When you stay at Catherine's, you're within a five-minute stroll to fine restaurants, art galleries, antique stores, specialty shops, river cruises and carriage tours. Beautiful beaches are only a 20-minute drive away. Off-street parking is available.

Dragonfly Inn
$$ • 1914 Market St., Wilmington
• (910) 762-7025, (866) 762-7025

"Comfortable, naturally" is the motto of this casual-style bed and breakfast. With its over-sized chairs, natural decor and homemade goodies, Dragonfly Inn is indeed a home away from home. In all the bedrooms, guests will find fleece robes and slippers, homemade aromatherapy and homemade scented soaps, lotions and shampoos in the bathroom. The Spirit of the Sea room has a TV, CD player, phone and king-sized bed topped with pillows; a fireplace with gas logs adds a touch of romance. The private bath continues the ocean theme with a seashell wreath and ocean pictures. A two-bedroom suite includes the Spirit of the Forest and the Spirit of the Earth rooms, however, each room can be

BED AND BREAKFASTS AND SMALL INNS

rented separately. The Forest room includes a TV, CD player and queen-sized bed; the adjoining private bath with claw-foot tub and shower leads to the suite's private tree-top balcony. The Spirit of the Earth room, with Native-American decor, features a king-sized bed, gas fireplace, CD player, TV and phone.

The welcoming foyer, with a dragonfly stained-glass door, leads to the living room, decorated with comfortable furniture — a reclining chair that heats up and vibrates waits to sooth weary bodies after hours of shopping and touring. There are also books, games, a TV/VCR and DVD player, a gas fireplace and an antique piano. A full breakfast is served to guests in the dining room. The sitting area on the second floor offers refreshments and snacks. Hot coffee is brought to your door every morning, and homemade desserts are available in the evenings. Inquire about winter, senior, military, student and multi-day discounts.

Front Street Inn
$$-$$$$ • 215 S. Front St., Wilmington
• (910) 762-6442

Front Street Inn greets guests with a natural, understated ambiance and Bohemian charm. The Inn features original art, hand-painted 14-foot walls, maple floors and exposed brick. The 12 rooms and suites are named and decorated according to their inspirations, such as Claude Monet, Pearl Buck, Rudyard Kipling and Georgia O'Keeffe. They are beautifully appointed with every amenity a traveler would love, including private baths, terry robes, hand-milled soap, fresh flowers, wet bars, TVs, CD players and dataports with high-speed Internet access.

Some suites have large Jacuzzi tubs, multi-jet showers and fireplaces; the Hemingway Suite also has a private balcony.

The European breakfast, served buffet style all morning, offers a variety of healthful (or sinful) selections. Always you'll find coffee, fresh fruit, cold cuts, cheese, croissants, biscotti and muffins. Room service is available. The Sol y Sombra Bar, with the now-famous hand-made cork bar, offers juices, waters, sodas, beer, wine, champagne and snacks. The game room and fitness area in the lower level are wonderful for small groups, family gatherings or informal business meetings. An intimate private dining room (with catering kitchen) and porch are available for private gatherings of up to 25 people, as well.

A massage therapist and personal trainer are available. Stefany and Jay Rhodes, along with their staff, will assist you with anything from restaurant reservations to special requests (how about chocolates, flowers and champagne for an anniversary surprise?).

The Inn occupies the renovated Salvation Army building, the first in the Carolinas, built in 1923. It is up the hill from Chandler's Wharf and the Riverwalk with nice views from the second-floor balconies. Convenient off-street parking is provided. Ask about corporate and long-term rates. Children are welcome, however pets are not permitted.

Four Porches Bed & Breakfast
$$$ • 312 S. Third St., Wilmington
• (910) 342-0849

Make yourself and your pets at home in this elegantly comfortable Italianate style residence that's filled with warmth and charm. Originally built by Murdock McKay and his wife Jane McMurphy in 1837, the house was updated late in the 19th century. Current owner, Abbie Spire, has extensively remodeled the interior and added to the back of the house.

Four Porches Bed & Breakfast has three beautiful guest rooms, each has a private bath, TV/DVD, portable phone with direct line and high-speed Internet access. For a romantic getaway, the Jungle Room is a great choice. The spacious Beach Room features a king-size bed and can also accommodate a rollaway with ease. The fabulous Garden Room, located on the front of the house boasts a luxurious king bed and private porch; a fourth bedroom adjoining the oversize bathroom makes a perfect suite for families, couples or singles traveling together. An upstairs screen porch is popular for morning coffee, evening wine and

lazy hours in between. Guests with pets appreciate having a rear entrance that accesses a fenced, gated yard where Fido can get some exercise or enjoy play time.

Early risers can help themselves to coffee, fruit, juice and muffins. A full breakfast is served between 8 and 9 AM each morning in a most inviting dining area. Would you like breakfast in bed or on the porch? No problem, just let your wish be known. An ice machine and guest refrigerator stocked with soft drinks, juice and water are available for guests at all times. Smokers are welcome here, as are children and four-legged friends at no extra charge. Four Porches is within a short walking distance of the Riverwalk, Chandler's Wharf, Historic Downtown Wilmington, shopping and restaurants.

Graystone Inn
$$$-$$$$ • 100 S. Third St., Wilmington
• (910) 763-2000, (888)763-4773

This stately historic landmark is one of the city's most prestigious inns, its rich, spacious interior inviting guests to enjoy an ambience of relaxed elegance. Built in 1905-06, Graystone Inn was originally "The Bridgers Mansion." Extensive renovations during the late 1990s restored the home's turn-of-the-century magnificence and added modern-day conveniences.

The vast ground floor includes an incredible library paneled in Honduran mahogany furnished with comfortable chairs, sofa and game table; here you can relax in front of the fireplace to enjoy your morning coffee or evening glass of wine. A full-cooked breakfast is served each morning in the beautiful formal dining

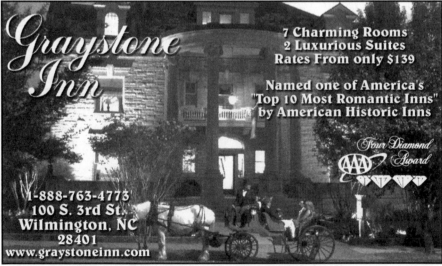

welcome to the

HOGE - WOOD HOUSE
bed & breakfast

407 SOUTH THIRD STREET
WILMINGTON, NC 28401
910-762-5299

WWW.HOGEWOODHOUSE.COM

room featuring mahogany dining tables, English floral wallpaper, fireplace and period antiques.

From the great entrance hall, a grand Renaissance-style staircase made of hand-carved oak rises three stories, culminating in the ballroom. Seven guest rooms including two large suites are on the second floor. Each room features a private bath (most with claw-foot tubs), period antiques, fine pima cotton linens, towels and robes, telephone, data port and cable TV. Five bedrooms have fireplaces. The two suites are quite large (the Bellevue Suite is 1,300 square feet and the Latimer/St. Thomas suite is 1,100 square feet). Both suites feature queen-size sleeper sofas in their sitting rooms. Room rates include a full gourmet breakfast and beverage service throughout the day. A fitness room is available for exercise buffs.

Outdoors, the garden and terraces are exquisite. Frequently used as a set for motion pictures and television, the Graystone Inn is unquestionably one of the most impressive structures in Wilmington. The Inn's location is ideal for walking to all downtown attractions and is convenient to the Riverwalk with its popular restaurants and shops.

The Graystone Inn makes a prestigious venue for weddings, receptions, reunions, birthdays, meetings and other events for up to 150 people. Choose the dining room, sitting room, entire ground floor and veranda or ballroom for your special occasion. You can depend on having a first-class experience here. Call for details.

Hoge-Wood House Bed and Breakfast
**$$-$$$ • 407 S. Third St., Wilmington
• (910) 762-5299**

Offering three upstairs guest rooms with private bathrooms and showers, TVs, VCRs, telephones and refrigerators stocked with beverages, the Hoge-Wood House is exceedingly casual. You'll find fresh flowers and art throughout the house. The downstairs parlor is cozy and inviting. The library, with its ceiling-high bookshelves, is ideal for relaxing with a good book or listening to music; it offers a supply of videos and puzzles and also houses an extensive collection of CDs, long-play records and seven-inch reel-to-reel tapes for your enjoyment. The inn's affable proprietors, Page and Larry Tootoo (pronounced toe-toe), emphasize flexibility in their service. Page is a Registered Nurse who can easily accommodate special dietary needs. Full country breakfasts are served on seasonal ceramic and china dinnerware with silverware on a classic library table. (Tip: Larry makes a great pecan waffle.) Coffee lovers will appreciate the Kona and Guatemalan coffee brewed daily.

One guest room features a queen-sized cherry sleigh bed; another a queen-sized oak mission-style bed. A third slightly smaller room has a double bed. Bicycles and fishing poles are available for guest use. The Hoge-Wood House is within walking distance of all downtown attractions and is one of the few bed and breakfast Inns in Wilmington that offers off-street parking.

The River Inn
**$$-$$$ • 314 S. Front St., Wilmington
• (910) 763-4891**

Among Wilmington's premier bed and breakfasts, The River Inn is perched on Sunset Hill directly overlooking the Cape Fear River. Owner Jenny McKinnon Wright has endowed her magnificent turreted Queen Anne home (built 1899) with unvarying elegance without forgoing comfort. Full silver-service breakfasts feature Southern-style cooking, with such homemade treats as sweet potato bread, superb quiches, French toast, special teas and coffees. Rich colors, exquisite period furnishings, including some art deco pieces, an 1860s crystal chandelier, a magnificent open staircase, original parquet floors and stained-glass windows shine throughout the house, making The River Inn an extraordinary visual experience. Also, the double back porches lure you to relax as you watch the sunset over the river. Of particular interest is the inn's convenient location within easy strolling distance of restaurants, shops or the theater.

Each of the inn's guest rooms features a private bath, antiques and wonderful paintings.

The room occupying the turret has a canopied pencil-post tester bed. Another room features a king-size bed and opens onto a porch overlooking the river. The third room has a canopied bed, fireplace and bay window. The inn's ambience is sociable, bright and never too refined for guests to congregate in the kitchen to share conversation and refreshments. Here's a place where you truly feel like a pampered guest. A splendid cat is in residence.

Rosehill Inn Bed and Breakfast
$$-$$$$ • 114 S. Third St., Wilmington
• (910) 815-0250, (800) 815-0250

The elegant Rosehill Inn provides a luxurious getaway that's as appropriate to corporate travelers as it is to honeymooners. The faithfully restored classic Greek Revival home, the Savage-Bacon House (1848), is tastefully adorned with oriental rugs, great fireplaces with beautiful mantles, fine period antiques and wall coverings. It features a magnificent pulpit staircase with quarter-sawn white oak banisters, a wraparound front porch that is ideal for relaxing and reading and large gardens with a columned pergola. While appearing quite formal, this first-class bed and breakfast inn is genuinely warm and welcoming, as are its hosts.

Possessing an interesting juxtaposition of modern-day convenience with the solidness of maturity, the Rosehill Inn's environment is fascinating and comfortable. Your eyes will not be bored as you behold a treasure trove of fascinating art, books, textures and colors, all woven into the fabric of the Inn.

Seven unique guest rooms, each with its own fireplace (non-functional), writing desk, bath-robes and private bath, are quiet and delightful. The Heritage Room boasts a New Orleans-style gate bed made from antique cast-iron fence parts. The Wedgwood Room echoes the design of the fine china of the same name. The Regency Room is decorated with a fancy iron bed and its bathroom features a whirlpool tub. The Carolina and Tea Rose rooms feature cozy bay windows. Morning coffee service is offered in the bright, inviting dining room; breakfasts include such delights as ginger pancakes with mango fool and fresh garden vegetable quiches. The Rosehill Inn is located just three blocks from the Cape Fear River with its popular Riverwalk, charming shops and excellent restaurants.

Taylor House Inn Bed & Breakfast
$$-$$$ • 14 N. Seventh St., Wilmington
• (910) 763-7581, (800) 382-9982

Taylor House Inn Bed and Breakfast is on a quiet brick-paved street just off Market Street in historic downtown Wilmington, convenient to fine dining establishments, antiques shops, galleries, clubs and the Riverwalk. You can travel the nine miles to the beach in mere minutes.

The epitome of understated elegance, the Taylor House Inn Bed & Breakfast features an interior of grandeur, replete with tall ceilings, enormous sun-filled rooms, rich oak woodwork, parquet floors, ten fireplaces and a magnificent open staircase with stained-glass windows. On the first floor, a library and a separate parlor offer ample room to rest and relax. In the formal dining room, candlelit full gourmet breakfasts are served on hand-painted china, crystal stemware and silver.

C.W. WORTH HOUSE

A Bed & Breakfast
in The Victorian Tradition

412 South 3rd Street
Wilmington, NC 28401

(910) 762-8562
1-800-340-8559

www.worthhouse.com

Upstairs, the five guest rooms in this 1905 home are carefully appointed, each with a private bath, period furnishings and in-room telephones. Upon entering your room, you will be greeted with fresh flowers, candies and crisp, freshly ironed bedding, along with period antiques, lace curtains and original artwork. Three of the private bathrooms are furnished with claw-foot soaking tubs. Two of the rooms open up to each other and serve as a suite, making it ideal for families.

Amenities include an early morning coffee service outside your door. Hot and cold drinks are available 24 hours a day, among them home-brewed mint iced tea. After long walks either at the beach or in town, a decanter of sherry awaits you in the parlor. The front porch is an ideal place to sit, relax and unwind. The Taylor House is kid-friendly, too. Inquire about corporate rates, mid-week specials and three-day off-season discount packages. Cancellations require a seven-day notice.

C. W. Worth House
$$-$$$ • 412 S. Third St., Wilmington • (910) 762-8562, (800) 340-8559

If you're looking for just the right place for a romantic interlude with your favorite person or somewhere to escape after the pressures of your 60-hour work week, Margi and Doug Erickson guarantee to provide a relaxing atmosphere for a memorable getaway. Here you'll never be imposed upon, you can be yourself and have plenty of space to do or not do whatever you choose, whether it's petting the cat, listening to music or just enjoying peace and tranquility.

Built in 1893, the fabulous C. W. Worth House is a unique example of nineteenth-century English Queen Anne style and sixteenth-century French chateaux. This turreted house has a wide front veranda and elegant interior, which includes the original paneled foyer, antiques, a formal parlor with a Victorian-era pump organ and a comfortable study. A television/VCR is available in the study and in the third-floor sitting room. The seven guest rooms are spacious, and beds are classic, including four-poster and antique queen-size. Each guest room has a private bath, comfortable sitting area, ceiling fan and telephone with dataport. Ask about the Azalea Room with its glassed-in veranda or the Hibiscus Room with its whirlpool bath and sitting area nestled in the corner turret.

Full gourmet breakfasts, served by your hosts in the formal dining room, include special blend coffee, tea, juice, muffins and fresh fruit as a first course. The entree may be goat cheese and rosemary strata, eggs Florentine, artichoke/mushroom quiche or a baked banana-pecan pancake. A nice touch for guests is a refrigerator on each floor, stocked with beverages and snacks available for guests' convenience. Outside, beautiful gardens highlighted with shade trees and brick walkways, a goldfish pond and a relaxing waterfall invite guests to linger awhile. The Worth House is a nonsmoking inn. Children age 10 and older are welcome.

If you're in Wilmington on business, staying at the C. W. Worth House is an excellent choice; here you'll find all the conveniences you'll need and a quiet environment. For the business traveler, corporate rates are available Sunday through Thursday, and a fax, copier and modem hook-ups are available.

The leisurely life requires just a few simple things.

Photo: Jay Tervo

Carolina Beach and Kure Beach

The Beacon House Inn Bed and Breakfast
$$ • 715 Carolina Beach Ave. N., Carolina Beach • (910) 458-6244, (910) 458-7322

A true beach home in every sense, The Beacon House Inn Bed and Breakfast makes you feel good the minute you walk in the front door. Everything about the place says "relax and make yourself comfortable." The fireplace in the common room, the real family kitchen, nautical appointments, warm Southern pine tongue-in-groove paneling, colorful fresh flowers, plants and personal touches give this immaculately clean house an inviting ambiance.

Bedrooms are equipped with ceiling fans and paired doors, one being louvered to take advantage of hallway breezes while still offering privacy to room occupants. Three rooms on the first floor have private baths; upstairs six bedrooms share three bathrooms. A two-bedroom/bath suite is ideal for two couples traveling together or families with a teenager. All sleeping rooms are free of TVs, telephones and smoking.

Two cozy, clean, cottages are available for rent as well. One has two bedrooms, the other three. Both have fully equipped kitchens, cable TV, phones, attractive decor, porches and a small yard area, which is perfect for families who want to bring Fido along with them on vacation.

Gourmet breakfasts that include homemade coffeecake, breads and jams, fresh fruits and egg dishes may be enjoyed by candlelight in the inviting dining area or on the upstairs balcony at 9 o'clock. Breakfast is not included in the rates for cottage guests; however, they may pay a small charge if they'd like to join the others in the main house.

The Beacon House is across the street from the ocean at a spot where the beach is always quiet and never crowded; it's close to a popular fishing pier, too. Excellent golf courses are plentiful, and historic downtown Wilmington, the N.C. Aquarium at Fort Fisher and two great state parks are just minutes away. Children and pets are welcome in the cottages.

Darlings By The Sea - Oceanfront Whirlpool Suites
$$$$ • 329 Atlantic Ave., Kure Beach • (800) 383-8111

Maureen and Kip Darling invite you to indulge yourself at their absolutely spectacular getaway place on the ocean. Celebrating a birthday or anniversary? Honeymoon? How about a "Getaway Together" long weekend where you can check in at noon on Friday and lounge around until late afternoon on Sunday? Sound good? Then this is the place for you. Catering to adults who want a luxurious, private and serene rendezvous, Darlings By The Sea is truly an extraordinary bed and breakfast experience. Each of the five fabulously appointed suites features a spacious bathroom with dual-size whirlpool, ceramic tile vanity, custom amenities and thick, soft towels imported from England.

You'll feel totally pampered the minute you open the door to your suite and find such amenities as king-size beds with Egyptian cotton triple sheets, Siberian goose down comforters, Hungarian goose down pillows and acrylic down pillows; fully mirrored walls plus yacht-quality interiors boasting Natuzzi leather from Italy and Brazilian marble entryways; plus a beautiful wood armoire, vanity and entertainment center.

Whether you're a single woman traveling on business or a totally in-love couple on a romantic holiday, Darlings By The Sea will treat you like royalty. A gourmet breakfast is discreetly delivered to your room and pre-stocked in your wet bar each night by your Evening Housekeeper, so you can arise and enjoy breakfast whenever you please — maybe you'd like to have your coffee, fruit and baked goodies on your deck while you watch the sun rise over the ocean. Then take advantage of the beach, the oceanfront fitness center with its athletic-club quality equipment, or just sit a spell in the lush Charleston-style courtyard.

Dolphin Watch Bed & Breakfast
$$-$$$$ • 910 Carolina Beach Ave. N., Carolina Beach • (910) 458-5355, (800) 846-8191

Treat yourself to a totally relaxing getaway at this cheerful, immaculate, welcoming beach cottage. Have breakfast on the covered, wrap-around porch while you watch sea oats gently sway on the sand dunes and waves lap the white sand beach. Make yourself totally at home in the family-style kitchen and comfortable living area. Settle into a cozy armchair to read for awhile or plan your day's activities. Ring the bell by the crossover when you see dolphins playing just offshore.

The only true oceanfront bed and breakfast in the greater Wilmington vicinity, Dolphin Watch offers a choice of six different types of accommodations, all with private baths. Choose a single room or a suite, full-size bed or queen-sized four-poster, first floor or second. Thoughtful touches and tasteful decorating make each room warm and inviting. In the Dolphin Suite, French doors open onto a second-story porch where you have an unbroken panorama of the sea and a perfect view of sunrise.

A private dune crossing to a quiet beach, an expansive porch full of rocking chairs facing the sea, and a gas log fireplace for cool winter evenings make Dolphin Watch Bed & Breakfast Inn a great place to hide out any time of the year. A deluxe

continental breakfast is available for two hours each morning. Early arrivals and late check-outs are possible, which is a convenient way to gain an extra day on the beach. This inn does not accept pets or children younger than 16.

Bald Head Island

Marsh Harbour Inn
$$$-$$$$ • Harbour Village, Bald Head Island • (910) 457-5002, (800) 432-7368

When you stay in Marsh Harbour Inn, conveniently located in Harbour Village, you'll be charmed by Cape Cod rockers, Shaker beds and antique wood floors that give each room a simple appeal. Many of the inn's 15 rooms have private decks overlooking Bald Head Creek or the Cape Fear River, so you can start the morning with a golden marsh sunrise or watch the sun slowly set over the marina in the evening. Rooms contain one queen-sized bed, two queen-sized beds or two twin beds. A handicapped-accessible room is also available. All rooms offer a television, telephone, coffee maker and coffee, and a private bath complete with thick linens, fine soaps and a hair dryer. Included in your stay are breakfast at the nearby River Pilot Café, afternoon snacks, use of an electric golf cart and temporary membership in the Bald Head Island Club. Other inn amenities include fax services and golf bag storage. Both children and groups are welcome, for weeks at a time or just one night. For groups, Marsh Harbour Inn also offers meal packages and meeting rooms with seating for up to 25 at a variety of rates. It's a delightful place to enjoy a corporate retreat or wedding party.

Theodosia's Bed and Breakfast
$$$-$$$$ • Harbour Village, Bald Head Isalnd • (910) 457-6563, (800) 656-1812

The island's first bed and breakfast inn, Theodosia's occupies an imposing, gabled, modern Victorian structure located at the marina. The decor and size of the 14 carefully appointed rooms are diverse, variously incorporating floral and Virgin Island motifs, king, queen and double beds, and wrought-iron and wood detailing. Everywhere there are porches or balconies offering spectacular views of the har-

INSIDERS' TIP

Often you can find fascinating books on the shelves of local inns. Some will tell stories about how folks lived here during early years, others recount the rich history of North Carolina's southern coast. Personal letters, diaries, journals and notations in the margins of old schoolbooks may be just waiting for you to find and learn from them.

So close...but a world away
Bald Head Island

Harbour Village
Post Office Box 3130
Bald Head Island
North Carolina 28461
Reservations
1(800) 656 1812
or (910) 457 6563

www.theodosias.com

5

bor, river or island marshes. All rooms have private baths (three have Jacuzzis) with soaking tubs or showers, cable TV, a VCR and telephones. The ground-floor guest room is handicapped-accessible. Two rooms occupy the adjoining Carriage House.

Innkeepers Thompson and Brandy Higgins serve complimentary full breakfasts daily at tables set for two. Meals alternate among a variety of distinctive gourmet breakfast menus. Theodosia's also features wonderful baked goods. Nightly or weekly stays include plenty of little extras, such as hors d'oeuvres served every afternoon and complimentary golf carts and bicycles (the only mechanized means of transportation permitted on Bald Head Island). Dinner at the inn is available by reservation. Guests are also welcome to a complimentary temporary membership to the Bald Head Island Country Club. A seven-day cancellation notice is requested.

INSIDERS' TIP

For first-timers, the bed-and-breakfast routine may seem a bit strange-it's not quite like a hotel, motel or condominium rental. It's more like visiting the home of a friend or relative. Generally, breakfast is served in a dining room or kitchen alcove at a specific time and it behooves you to arrive promptly, lest all the goodies get gobbled before you have your turn!

Southport-Oak Island

Lois Jane's Riverview Inn
$$ • 106 W. Bay St., Southport
• (910) 457-6701, (800) 457-1152

Owned and operated by fourth-generation descendants of the original owner, this beautifully restored 1892 home is near the old harbor pilot's tower and overlooks the mouth of the Cape Fear River. It is a quiet getaway within easy walking distance of Southport's restaurants, river walk, shops and museums. Porches on the river side of the building are ideal for rocking away the time.

Two rooms with private baths and two with a shared bath have queen-sized four-poster beds and period furnishings that have been part of the home for years. The rooms to the front of the building have beautiful river views, and one room has its own entrance to the communal upstairs porch. Full Southern-style breakfasts are served daily in the dining room, and afternoon wine and cheese are additional touches. Special breakfast arrangements can be made with advance notice. Coffee is placed in the hallway outside the guest rooms each morning, and a small refrigerator is available. Ask about the separate deluxe efficiency apartment that

is also available. Cancellations require at least a 24 hour notice for refunds.

The Brunswick Inn
$$$ • 301 E. Bay St., Southport
• (910) 457-5278

Since 1800 when it was built as the summer residence of Benjamin Smith, founder of Smithville (Southport) and tenth governor of North Carolina, this Federal-style mansion has looked out over the mouth of the Cape Fear River, The Intracoastal Waterway and the Atlantic Ocean. It served as summer residence for Governor Dudley as well. In 1856 the top two floors were rebuilt by Thomas Meares, owner of Orton Plantation around the time of the Civil War. Six years ago, Jim and Judy Clary purchased the building and went to work restoring it to its previous grandeur, including preserving the original heart pine floors, the plaster ceiling moldings, the cathedral shaped pocket doors, the Southport Bows over the door and window casings, and the nine working fireplaces. Judy chose rich, vibrant colors that set off the spacious rooms and play up the interesting architecture. In the middle of the dining room stands a huge antique table, handmade in the mountains, above which hangs a crystal chandelier dropping from the second floor ceiling, through the rotunda. This is where the full, home-cooked, gourmet breakfasts, including homemade pastries, are normally served. Some mornings, though, breakfast is served in the cozy working kitchen in front of the fireplace.

Each beautifully decorated guest room has a private bath and contains a working fireplace for which the proprietors provide a Duraflame log. A well-stocked library, a parlor and an observatory, including telescope, are all available to guests. Afternoon hors d'oeuvres and wine are served, and guests are encouraged to spend some time on the veranda watching the passing scene.

You will be welcomed by Lizzie Lou, the Sunshine Girl and sometimes Tony, the whimsical resident ghost who makes his presence known. Tony was a harpist who played at the inn when balls were common occurrences. He drowned in a boating accident off Bald Head

Island in 1882. More recently, Charles Bronson slept here. The Brunswick Inn was used in the making of several movies including *Summer Catch* with Freddie Printz, Jr. and *The Wedding* with Halle Berry.

South Brunswick Islands

Crescent Moon Inn
$-$$ • 965 Sabbath Home Rd. SW, Holden Beach • (910) 842-1190, (877) 727-1866

This modern, family-friendly bed and breakfast inn, nestled on a 1.5 acre wooded lot, is only 1.5 miles from Holden Beach. Surrounded by carefully tended flower and herb beds, it is a large, white-brick building with a rear deck shaded by tall sycamore, birch, apple and pear trees. A screened porch is available for passing lazy afternoons. The decor is attractive and casual, full of earth tones and pastels, fiber rugs, wicker and rattan. The guest rooms have peaked ceilings with beams and skylights and are furnished with king-sized, queen-sized and twin beds. Rooms are equipped with a ceiling fan, TV and VCR (a complimentary video library is available), and coffee is placed outside each room at 7:30 AM. Healthy continental breakfasts include home-baked goods to start your day. Beverages and snacks are available all day. The owners have arranged for guest parking at the beach at no additional cost. Add to this the proximity to the area's dozens of golf courses and easy access to both Wilmington and Myrtle Beach.

Heading south on U.S. Highway 17 from Wilmington, you turn left at the traffic light when you reach the intersection of U.S. 17 and N.C. Highway 211. Take the first right onto Stone Chimney Road. Continue 8 miles to Sabbath Home Road. Turn right onto Sabbath Home Road. Crescent Moon Inn will be on the left directly across from the entrance to Sea Trace development. Ask about discount rates for four or more nights. A two-night minimum is required for stays during festival weekends and holidays.

Goose Creek Bed & Breakfast
$-$$ • 1901 Egret St. SW, Ocean Isle Beach • (910) 754-5849, (800) 275-6540

Just eight minutes from the beach and situated on navigable Goose Creek, this bed and breakfast inn on the mainland side of the Intracoastal Waterway is an excellent choice. You can fish from the 90-foor pier or launch your canoe or kayak for a leisurely trek through the marshland waterways. A large, contemporary, beach-style home, it has more than 2,000 square feet of lighted outdoor decking with comfy rockers, a porch swing and hammocks. This non-smoking home has four guest rooms on the third floor. All rooms have queen-size beds and private baths. The rooms may also be configured as suites with private or shared baths.

Breakfasts are served buffet style on fine china and feature homemade breads, cinnamon rolls, coffee cakes, pastries or omelets. For a real treat, ask about the custard-baked French toast. Guests eat on the screened porch overlooking the creek.

Goose Creek Bed & Breakfast is close to more than 30 golf courses. The area features many fine restaurants, and owners Jim and Peg Grich will help you select the perfect place. This is a kid-friendly establishment and has recently been adopted by five cats. Reservations are recommended but not required.

Topsail Island Area

Bed & Breakfast at Mallard Bay
$$ • 960 Mallard Bay Rd., Hampstead • (910) 270-3363

Lodgings here include a roomy upstairs suite with a water view, four-poster bed, full private bath, sitting room with queen-size sofa bed and a TV/VCR. Laundry facilities are available at no extra cost. A full country breakfast is served on the weekends, and continental breakfast is offered on weekdays. Complimentary wine and cheese are served each afternoon. A canoe is available for a relaxing paddle in the waterway. There is a two-night minimum required. This facility is within walking distance of Harbour Village Marina, close to local golf courses and only 15 minutes from the beach, restaurants and shopping.

The Pink Palace of Topsail
$$ • 1222 S. Shore Dr., Surf City • (910) 328-5114

Treat yourself like royalty at The Pink Palace, Topsail's only oceanfront bed and breakfast. These accommodations feature a comfortable living area with all the amenities, surrounded by three rooms adorned with tropical murals on the walls. All suites have access to a screened porch and three open air decks with a hot tub on the deck extension. Enjoy relaxing in a rocker, hammock or swing. It's open from September until June; in the summer, the entire house is rented out by the week.

Weekly and Long-term Vacation Rentals

If living at the beach year round is an impossible dream, the next best thing is renting a home on or near the ocean while on vacation. The islands along North Carolina's southern coast, from Topsail in the north to the South Brunswick Islands' beach communities in the south, offer an abundance of short-term rental properties that range from modest to opulent. Choose from million-dollar homes, well-appointed condos or cheery cottages to meet your own preferences and budget. Rentals are booked primarily through agencies, and a partial list of companies is provided in this chapter.

Choosing to rent a home instead of staying in a hotel for a week or two is appealing for numerous reasons: It's usually less expensive to rent a cottage than a hotel room for a longer period of time; you can fit a bunch of family and friends into one comfortable place; and the setting is casual — you can dress the way you like and never have to worry about getting up to greet housekeeping when they tap on your door to clean.

This latter point brings up a big difference between hotels and rental properties: There's no staff on hand to wait on guests. No room service, either. A bed left unmade in the morning will stay that way unless you take care of it. Same thing for taking out the garbage, cleaning the bathrooms and doing the laundry. A vacation rental home is, simply put, your home away from home, and you're responsible for how well it runs.

Guests who don't mind the added responsibility of cooking and cleaning while on vacation will discover the special pleasures a rental home offers. There's enormous freedom in terms of scheduling the day to suit oneself. A kitchen at the beach is a bonus to cooks who appreciate the availability of fresh seafood at nearby markets. And there's an inclination for renters to make their chosen vacation home a tradition, returning year after year to a place that increasingly feels like their own home.

Accommodations and Locations

Choosing a vacation home — whether it be a house, condo or apartment — usually begins with a decision about proximity to the water. The benefits of being oceanfront include an unobstructed view of the sea, a short walk for a swim in the waves and the ability to keep an eye on the kids from the house. However, these are the most expensive rental properties. A home a block or two from the ocean can save hundreds of dollars in your vacation budget and still be a delight.

Sound-side housing is less expensive than oceanfront but more

LOOK FOR:
- Accommodations
- Locations
- Rules
- Pet Policies
- Rates
- Rental Agencies

expensive than homes in the middle of the island. If you have a boat and the house has a pier, or if you simply appreciate quiet coastal views, this can be a very exciting location that may be worth the extra cost.

Most homes are well-appointed in terms of furnishings, usually in the owner's personal tastes. Standard features include heat and air conditioning, telephone and cable TV. Some homes have stereo systems and VCRs. A condominium complex may include tennis courts, a pool and even a golf course for renter use. Dishes, pots and pans, coffeemakers and small appliances are often provided, but check with the rental agency to confirm their availability.

When renting a vacation home, you're expected to bring along or rent household or personal items, including linens, towels, paper goods, laundry detergent, beach equipment and provisions. Your rental agency often provides a detailed checklist of items you will need to bring with you. If you dread packing a lot of added equipment with luggage and personal items, consider arranging for rentals; again, ask about this service at the time of booking as some rental services require considerable advance notice.

A Few Rules

Vacation home rental involves rules and regulations that reflect the wishes of the home-owner in this kind of arrangement. A rental agency's primary allegiance is to the homeowner. The agency maintains the properties for the owners and assumes responsibility for renting the homes to reliable tenants. While some of the rules discussed in this chapter are standard for all area beaches, occasional exceptions are permitted. Please check with your rental agency for its individual list of policies.

There is an age requirement for renting most vacation homes through real estate management companies. Generally, the primary renter must be at least 21 years old, although some companies require the primary renter to be 25. An exception to this may involve marital status. If you're younger than 25 and married, you probably qualify, but companies will differ. Individual inquiry is recommended. Some companies that don't have an actual age requirement take a long, hard look at younger customers, especially in large groups. Most rental agreements forbid house parties on the premises, and that's the main reason for the age concern, especially in the quieter beach communities. Rowdiness is unappreciated on all area beaches, and a noisy party may cause you to forfeit your rental agreement without a refund. Most homes have a written maximum-occupancy regulation, and you are required to honor it. This bodes well for families seeking a peaceful location.

There is a general expectation that you'll leave the house as clean as you found it. Some rental agencies will provide cleaning service and linens for a fee if you are not particularly inclined toward domestic concerns on your getaway. If you don't clean up and haven't made arrangements for maid service, your deposit will be applied toward this work. This charge is determined by individual rental agencies according to the size of the rental property.

If cleaning services aren't part of your rental arrangement, cleaning supplies are usually already in the house because a prior vacationer bought them and left them there. It's a nice gesture on your part to do the same, even if current supplies seem ample, and it's essential for you to provide cleaning supplies if none have been left for you. Owners supply vacuum cleaners, mops and brooms. You are responsible for putting out the garbage, just like at home. Some beach towns have recycling programs, and you'll be instructed on how to participate in the event that yours does. Grilling is prohibited on all area beaches and on the decks or porches of rental properties.

Most rental homes have telephones, and you're on your honor not to use them in any way for which the owners would be charged. Some agencies place a long-distance block on the phone or deduct a fee plus the phone charge from your security deposit for long-distance calls billed to the owner. If your vacation home doesn't have a phone, most rental companies will get emergency messages to you. Of course, the proliferation of mobile phones makes this issue less important.

Pet Policies

With some notable exceptions, pets are not allowed in vacation rentals. If your four-

WEEKLY AND LONG-TERM
VACATION RENTALS

legged companion must come with you, ask your rental agent about the services of local kennels. Since your pet is not allowed on most beaches in the summer season, and the heat is hard on animals anyway, you might want to leave it at home in friendly surroundings. However, you can find some properties that will permit pets with certain restrictions. Check out our Traveling with Pets page online at www.insiders.com/wilmington for a list of companies able to help you enjoy your pet's company while you are on your vacation.

Also, please note this region has a seasonal flea problem, which more than anything else dictates this policy. Remember, it takes only two fleas to cause a flea problem in a house. If you smuggle in a pet and the guests or housekeeping staff that follow you discover fleas, be assured that your deposit will be used to pay for fumigation; flea infestation is truly a miserable occurrence! Some agencies insist on strict enforcement of the "no pet" policy and may opt to evict a tenant found with a pet on the premises.

Rates

Prices fall in a wide range from $325 to $4,800 (or more) a week, depending on your choice of accommodation, location, luxury factor and season. Bald Head Island, Wrightsville Beach and Figure Eight Island are at the high end. Topsail, Carolina Beach, Kure Beach and the Brunswick Beaches (Oak Island, Holden Beach, Ocean Isle Beach and Sunset Beach) offer a broader array of less-pricey accommodations, but also have their share of high-end properties.

Most agencies require a deposit, and there are various stipulations in the agreement that you need to be familiar with. For example, a state/county tax of 7 percent and, depending on the location, a room tax ranging from 1 to 6 percent are added to the cost. Rental rates are subject to change without notice. Winter rates may be significantly less. A deposit of 50 percent is generally required to confirm reservations. Major credit cards are usually, but not always, accepted. Check with the individual rental agency for required methods of payment. Some accept personal checks provided they arrive 30 to 60 days in advance of your arrival.

Rental Agencies

This listing of rental agencies is a sampling of the many fine companies from which you may choose. By no means do we include them all, as it would take the entire book to do so. Select the beach of your choice and contact the area's chamber of commerce for the names of other rental companies (see our Area Overviews chapter for a list of local chambers of commerce). These agencies also carry brochures about rental companies. In Wilmington, the Cape Fear Coast Convention & Visitors Bureau, (910) 341-4030, may be another helpful resource.

WEEKLY AND LONG-TERM VACATION RENTALS

Wilmington

Riverview Suites at Water Street Center
$$$ • 106 N. Water St., Wilmington
• (910) 772-9988

Riverview Suites at Water Street Center, located across the street from and operated by the Hilton, offers 65 well-appointed suites overlooking the Cape Fear River. The Riverview Suites is the only property on the Cape Fear River that offers walk-out balconies, kitchenettes and washer/dryers. The Riverview Suites is perfect for vacation and long-term corporate rentals. Come experience the best view in town!

Wrightsville Beach and Vicinity

Bryant Real Estate
1001 N. Lumina Ave., Wrightsville Beach
• (910) 256-3764, (800) 322-3764
1401 N. Lake Park Blvd., Snow's Cut Crossing, Carolina Beach • (910) 458-5658, (800) 994-5222
501 N. College Rd., Wilmington
• (910) 799-2700

Offering vacation rental homes, condos and townhomes with locations from the ocean to the sound, Bryant Real Estate has been providing quality sales, rentals and property management service in the Wilmington, Carolina, Kure and Wrightsville Beach areas for more than 50 years. For year-round rentals, call (910) 799-

2700; for Carolina/Kure Beaches, call (910) 458-5658 or (800) 994-5222; and for seasonal rentals at Wrightsville Beach, call (910) 256-3764 or (800) 322-3764.

Intracoastal Realty Corporation
605 Causeway Dr., Wrightsville Beach
• (910) 256-3780, (800) 346-2463

This company offers a great selection of properties with a mix of condominiums, featuring on-site swimming pool and tennis courts, single-family homes and old-style beach cottages on Wrightsville Beach. Intracoastal also handles long-term rentals in Wilmington and Wrightsville Beach; call (910) 509-9700, (800) 826-4428 for longterm rental information.

Station 1
95 S. Lumina Ave., Wrightsville Beach
• (910) 256-9988, (800) 635-1408

With a breathtaking view of the Atlantic Ocean from each of its 104 units, Station 1 offers weekly and monthly condominium rentals on Wrightsville Beach. This attractive complex includes 88 two- and three-bedroom condos and 16 three-bedroom townhouses. Amenities include a private tennis court, a seaside pool, laundry facilities and the use of bicycles to explore this lovely island. Each rental condo is fully furnished down to the linens and offers a spacious living/dining room, two baths, and a fully equipped kitchen with dishwasher, microwave and coffeemaker. Townhouses include all of these features but offer three baths instead of two plus a fireplace and a garage. Station 1 also has units for sale.

Figure Eight Island

Figure Eight Rentals
2413 Middle Sound Loop, Wilmington
• (910) 686-4099, (800) 470-4099

Bunnie Bachman, a 20-plus year resident of Figure Eight Island, has exclusive rentals on this unique, secluded luxury island of single family homes. Figure Eight Island is only minutes away from shopping and restaurants. Come escape to this casual yet elegant island that provides a quiet, creative, deluxe vacation for the discriminating person. They also offer their services as a personalized Buyer's Broker for those interested in purchasing a home on this fantastic island.

Figure Eight Realty
15 Bridge Rd., Wilmington
• (910) 686-4400, (800) 279-6085

This agency, which is located on Figure Eight Island, focuses on the island's neighborhood of luxury, single-family homes. Oceanfront, marsh-front and sound-front properties are available. Figure Eight Realty also offers vacation rentals on the island.

Carolina Beach and Kure Beach

Atlantic Shores Real Estate
9 S. Lake Park Blvd., Ste. A-3, Carolina Beach • (910) 458-4975, (800) 289-0028

Handling rentals on Pleasure Island only, Atlantic Shores features long-term, short-term and year-round vacation rentals for families. They specialize in upscale condominiums and private homes; most are oceanfront or ocean-view with pools.

Atlantic Towers
1615 S. Lake Park Blvd., Carolina Beach
• (910) 458-8313, (800) 232-2440

Extensively remodeled and offering attractive condominium units, including deluxe units, Atlantic Towers is situated right on the beach. The facility also includes both an outdoor pool and a heated indoor pool. Atlantic Towers offers nightly rentals and short-term and weekly rentals at discounted rates.

Bryant Real Estate
1401 N. Lake Park Blvd., Snow's Cut
Crossing, Carolina Beach • (910) 458-5658
(800) 994-5222
501 N. College Rd., Wilmington
• (910) 799-2700
1001 N. Lumina Ave., Wrightsville Beach
• (910) 256-3764, (800) 322-3764

Offering vacation rental homes, condos and townhomes with locations from the ocean to the sound, Bryant Real Estate has been providing quality sales, rental and property management service in the Wilmington, Carolina, Kure and Wrightsville Beach area for more than 50 years. On Pleasure Island, available properties extend from Carolina Beach to Fort Fisher. All rental properties are privately owned and furnished by their owners. For year-round rentals call (910) 799-2700; for Carolina/Kure Beaches, call (910) 458-5658 or (800) 994-5222.

Bullard Realty, Inc.
1404 S. Lake Park Blvd., Carolina Beach
• (910) 458-4028, (800) 327-5863

With more than 100 rentals on Carolina and Kure Beaches, Bullard Realty has the rental property for you. Choose from oceanfront, ocean-view and second-row with amenities such as indoor and outdoor pools, tennis facilities and recreation centers. Whether you want a cozy, one-bedroom condo for two or a six-bedroom, oceanfront vacation home for 17, Bullard Realty can help make your vacation dreams a reality with friendly, professional service.

Cabana De Mar Motel
31 Carolina Ave. N., Carolina Beach
• (910) 458-4456, (800) 333-8499

Cabana De Mar's 76 condominium-style suites (one to three bedrooms) are small yet pleasant, with cable TV, elevator access and daily housekeeping service. Some rooms face the ocean and have modest private balconies. Streetside suites are the best value. Laundry rooms are available, but some rooms are equipped with washer/dryers.

Coastwalk Real Estate
1025-A N. Lake Park Blvd., Carolina Beach
• (910) 458-0868, (888) 256-4804

Choose from a variety of first-class, smoke-free accommodations for your vacation pleasure, weekend getaway or seasonal stay and rest easy when you get your rental property though Coastwalk Real Estate in Carolina Beach. Whether you're looking for a luxurious oceanfront condo that sleeps eight or a cozy two-bedroom beach cottage, Coastwalk has it. Maybe you'd like to spend the winter here; you can rent TV star Linda Lavin's beautifully decorated three-bedroom, three-bath home with private gazebo, pier, screened porch, fenced yard and Jacuzzi. Coastwalk Real Estate offers great locations, exceptional properties, outstanding service and surprisingly reasonable rates. Some pet-friendly accommodations are available; call for details.

Network Real Estate
1029 N. Lake Park Blvd., Ste. 1, Carolina Beach • (910) 458-8881, (800) 830-2118

Network Real Estate offers a large selection

of vacation rentals, including oceanfront cottages and condominiums in a variety of price ranges. Amenities for most rentals include central air, major appliances, cable, outdoor decks and easy beach access. Additionally, Network's downtown Wilmington office offers new vacation rentals on the Cape Fear River across from the Battleship USS North Carolina.

Jim Ring Realty
225 Ft. Fisher Blvd., Kure Beach
• (910) 458-4300, (800) 445-1594

The nicest rentals on the beach make the nicest vacations! Let Jim Ring Realty make your vacation a pleasant, relaxing one. Rental properties are beautifully decorated and well maintained. Jim Ring Realty is a small, customer-oriented business that has been operating in Kure Beach for more than 20 years. Their goal is to deliver personal service to each client in a friendly atmosphere. Even in today's ever-changing world of technology, a firm handshake and a warm smile will not be forgotten. Let them assist you in choosing the perfect vacation property for you.

United Beach Vacations
1001 N. Lake Park Blvd., Carolina Beach
• (910) 458-9073, (800) 334-5806

This large company manages fully furnished rental units, including condominiums and single-family homes on Carolina Beach, Kure Beach and Fort Fisher. Rentals are on oceanfront, ocean-view and second-row properties. Some properties also offer amenities that include pools and tennis courts; many are in close proximity to the N.C. Aquarium at Fort Fisher.

Southport and Oak Island

Century 21 Dorothy Essey & Associates Inc., Realtors
6102 E. Oak Island Dr., Oak Island
• (910) 278-RENT, (877) 410-2121

This company offers year-round rentals and resort rentals on Oak Island, in Southport and in Boiling Spring Lakes. Properties include single-family homes, condominiums and duplexes.

Oak Island Accommodations, Inc.
300 Country Club Dr., Oak Island
• (910) 278-6011, (888) 243-8132

Oak Island Accommodations is the largest rental agency on Oak Island, offering over 400

OCEAN 1 REALTY

VACATION

4310 E. Beach Drive Oak Island, NC28465
910-278-6677 • 877-TWO RENT
or on the web at: www.ocean1.com

Ocean 1 Realty
4310 E. Beach Dr., Oak Island
• (910) 278-6677, (800) 231-4882

"Escape to Paradise" is the slogan of Ocean 1 Realty, at the same location for 25 years. The company offers houses with two to six bedrooms to accommodate family vacations or reunions. The property manager has been associated with Ocean 1 Realty since 1976. He has been a property owner since 1980 and property manager since 1995. The knowledgeable staff is waiting to help plan your next escape.

Walter Hill & Associates
6101 E. Oak Island Dr., Oak Island
• (910) 278-6659, (910) 278-5405 for reservations

Walter Hill & Associates handles single-family homes and duplexes on Oak Island for short- or long-term rentals. Most properties are oceanfront.

Bald Head Island

Bald Head Island Limited
5079 Southport Supply Rd., Southport
• (800) 432-7368

This well-established company on pristine Bald

resort rentals nightly, weekly or monthly from oceanfront to soundside. Availability and reservations can be found online 24 hours a day. Oak Island Accommodations provides pet-friendly properties, discount specials, concierge services and free brochures.

A beach walk is a dreamy way to end a day.

Photo: Jay Tervo

Head Island has 130 rental properties, primarily single-family homes, distributed throughout six island environments: maritime forest, marsh and creek, Harbour Village, golf course, West Beach and South Beach. Each rental includes round-trip ferry passage, parking on the mainland and the use of at least one four-passenger electric golf cart for transportation around the island (cars are not permitted on Bald Head Island). Guests renting through Bald Head Island Limited receive unlimited use of the business center located in the Chandler Building at Harbour Village. The company specializes in corporate retreats, weddings, family reunions and social gatherings for up to 200 people.

Bald Head Island Rentals, LCC
120 E. Moore St., Southport
• (910) 454-9419, (800) 680-8322

Bald Head Island Rentals offers a large selection of luxury resort homes, cottages, villas and suites exclusively on Bald Head Island. Their unique Five Star Guest Services program aims to ensure a dream vacation on the island, including accommodation and reservation services, concierge service, daily housekeeping or turndown service, food shopping service, in-home dining prepared by an executive chef and guest departure services.

Bald Head Island Resort Sales & Rentals
219 N. Bald Head Wynd, Bald Head Island
• (910) 457-4433, (800) 820-0545

Rentals provided by Bald Head Island Resort Sales & Rentals include oceanfront, ocean-view, forest, golf course and marsh-view sites as well as units in the villas.

the Jack Cox group
58 Dowitcher Tr., Bald Head Island
• (910) 457-4732, (888) 603-1956

The vacation rental aspect of this family-owned agency marks its fifth year in 2003. It offers a variety of rental properties that include single-family homes, cottages and condos and range from oceanfront and ocean-view to marsh, golf course and forest view.

Old Baldy Associates
1105 N. Howe St., Southport
• (910) 457-5551

Rentals available through Old Baldy Associates are located in areas that provide a creek view, golf and ocean view, ocean view, unobstructed ocean view and wooded setting as well as locations on the oceanfront.

South Brunswick Islands

Holden Beach

Brunswickland Realty
123 Ocean Blvd. W., Holden Beach
• (910) 842-6949, (800) 842-6949

In business since the 1970s, Brunswickland Realty manages single-family cottages and larger homes. Accommodations are available on the oceanfront, second row, canal side, dunes and Intracoastal Waterway.

Coastal Vacation Resorts
131 Ocean Blvd. W., Holden Beach
• (910) 842-8000, (800) 252-7000

This Holden Beach company specializes in premier vacation accommodations on peaceful

Holden Beach, including oceanfront, second row, waterway and dunes locations. Coastal takes pride in offering rentals to fit every lifestyle and budget. Bookings are available online. Call for a free brochure.

Hobbs Realty
114 Ocean Blvd. W., Holden Beach
• (910) 842-2002, (800) 655-3367

Family owned and operated, Hobbs Realty manages 200 rental properties with expertise gained from 26 years in the business. Rentals are offered from the ocean to the waterway and everywhere in between. Just cross the bridge to the island, take the first left and you will find Hobbs Realty in the second office on the left.

The Islander Villas offer spectacular floorplans featuring 4 bedroom and 4 baths. These are the best Ocean Isle Beach has to offer.
15 Causeway Dr. • Ocean Isle Beach
(910) 575-7770 • (800) 374-7361
www.oibrealty.com

Alan Holden Vacations
128 Ocean Blvd. W., Holden Beach
• (910) 842-6061, (800) 720-2200

This busy agency, the largest in the area, manages more than 325 rental properties on Holden Beach, from beach cottages and condominiums to luxury homes with private pools. Locations include oceanfront, canal and waterway, second-row and dune homes. Alan Holden will tell you "nobody knows the beach better than a Holden."

Ocean Isle Beach

Cooke Realty
1 Causeway Dr., Ocean Isle Beach
• (910) 579-3535, (800) 622-3224

This well-established island realty company offers nearly 450 rental homes, cottages and condominiums. Choose from oceanfront, second- and third-row, canal-side, West End and Island Park locations. In addition, locations are available in the condos and oceanfront homes located in the Islander Resort, with The Isles restaurant nearby.

Island Realty Inc.
109-2 Causeway Dr., Ocean Isle Beach
• (910) 579-3599, (800) 589-3599

This company offers single-family homes, cottages and condominiums exclusively on Ocean Isle Beach. These rental properties are available on oceanfront, second-row, mid-island and canal sites.

R. H. McClure Realty Inc.
24 Causeway Dr., Ocean Isle Beach
• (910) 579-3586, (800) 332-5476

R. H. McClure Realty, Inc. is a full service realty brokerage which has been established on Ocean Isle Beach for more than 20 years. A large rental inventory is offered which includes oceanfront homes and condos, mid island cottages, and deep water canal homes with individual private docks. Spring and fall discounts are available. On-line bookings are available.

Ocean Isle Beach Realty, Inc.
15 Causeway Dr., Ocean Isle Beach
• (910) 575-7770, (800) 374-7361

Ocean Isle Beach Realty handles a variety of vacation rental needs, including single-family homes, condominiums and cottages. Rentals are available on the oceanfront, interior, canal and along the Intracoastal Waterway. This versatile company also has an experienced sales staff available to help you with the purchase of any property in the area.

Sloane Realty Vacation Rentals
16 Causeway Dr., Ocean Isle Beach
• (910) 579-6216, (800) 843-6044

Sloane Realty Vacations, one of the largest and the oldest vacation rental businesses on Ocean Isle Beach, has condos and single-family homes available on the mainland and the island. Locations include oceanfront and canal views. Call for a free brochure. Winter rentals are also available. Call in September 2003 for winter rentals in 2004. Bookings are available online.

Sunset Beach

Carolina Golf and Beach Resorts
818 Colony Pl., Sunset Beach
• (910) 579-7181, (800) 222-1524

Carolina Golf and Beach Resorts provides nightly and weekly golf and accommodations packages. Accommodations include one-, two- and three-bedroom condominiums on the Oyster Bay Golf Links and beach rentals on Sunset Beach.

Sunset Properties
419 S. Sunset Blvd., Sunset Beach
• (910) 579-9900, (800) 525-0182 for reservations only

This family-owned company, founded in 1988, handles the rental of 250 vacation homes

A graceful seagull.

Photo: Jay Tervo

and duplexes exclusively on Sunset Beach. Rentals run from Saturday to Saturday during the season. A minimum stay of two nights is required in the off season. Bookings are available online.

Sunset Vacations
401 S. Sunset Blvd., Sunset Beach
• (910) 579-9000, (800) 331-6428

Sunset Vacations offers a wide assortment of attractive, single-family homes for rent throughout Sunset Beach, including oceanfront, canal, bayfront and inlet locations. They have beach homes to fit every style, location and budget, and you can book directly online. They are an experienced company with an extreme commitment to making your vacation just right.

Topsail Island

A Beach Place Realty
106 N. Topsail Dr., Surf City
• (910) 328-2522, (877) 884-2522

Fresh flowers welcome clients who rent through this new agency on Topsail Island. In addition to this special touch, renters can be assured of friendly, efficient service for all their rental needs from single family homes, duplexes and condominiums from one end of Topsail Island to the other, oceanfront or otherwise. An added benefit includes quick repair service from the agencies own construction business.

It's the little things that kids love most.

Photo: Jay Tervo

to assist vacationers or year-round renters in finding the property that meets their needs. From the ocean to the sound and mainland locations, if Jean Brown Real Estate doesn't have the property required, they will try to find it elsewhere. Friendly, professional service can always be found at this agency.

Bryson and Associates, Inc.
809 Roland Ave., Surf City
• (910) 328-2468, (800) 326-0747

Bryson and Associates have been serving the Topsail Island area for 17 years with a commitment to customer service. Prime rental properties are available on the oceanfront, second row, ocean view, soundfront, sound view and the canalfront. Queens Grant Condominiums are managed and rented through Bryson and Associates.

Century 21 Action, Inc.
518 Roland Ave., Surf City
804 Carolina Ave., Topsail Beach
200 North Shore Village, Sneads Ferry
• (910) 328-2511, (800) 255-2233

In business for 33 years, Century 21 Action has more than 300 of the best vacation rentals for you to choose from on Topsail Island. The experienced property management department also has more than 80 long-term rentals in its inventory.

Access Realty and Topsail Vacations
513 Roland Ave., Surf City
• (910) 328-4888, (800) TOPSAIL

Access Realty, under new ownership, is a full-service brokerage company with a rapidly growing property-management division, now with a full-time property manager. This company offers a variety of accommodations on Topsail Island, from oceanfront and sound-front homes to oceanfront condominiums with a pool and tennis court.

Coldwell Banker Coastline Realty
Topsail Way Shopping Center,
965 Old Folkstone Rd., Sneads Ferry
• (910) 327-7711, (800) 497-5463

This company offers oceanfront vacation rentals that include condominiums (with swim-

Jean Brown Real Estate, Inc.
522 N. New River Dr., Surf City
• (910) 328-1640, (800) 745-4480

Jean Brown Real Estate, located in the heart of Surf City, has a friendly, qualified staff ready

P.O. Box 2690
"The Fishing Village"
Surf City, NC 28445

Reservations 1-800-622-6886
E-Mail: info@islandrealestatenc.com
Internet: www.islandrealestatenc.com

ming pools and tennis courts), townhomes, single-family homes and beach cottages. Their inventory has increased to include numerous five-, six- and seven-bedroom homes. There is also a large inventory of long-term rentals.

Island Real Estate by Cathy Medlin
The Fishing Village, Roland Ave., Surf City
• (910) 328-2323, (800) 622-6886

Build sand castles and memories as you let the vacation specialists of Island Real Estate provide that perfect "beach rental" for your family. This long-time veteran of real estate sales and rentals can provide you with anything from a ten-bedroom mega-house to a six-bedroom geodesic dome to a one-two bedroom condo or townhome. If you didn't find the perfect getaway, you didn't ask the vacation team at Island Real Estate about their 180 units.

Kathy S. Parker Real Estate
1000 N.C. Hwy. 210, Sneads Ferry
• (910) 327-2219, (800) 327-2218

This full-service realty office has more than 70 long-term and vacation rental properties, primarily in the North Topsail Beach and Sneads Ferry areas. The rental specialists take pride in matching the renter with the right property. Homes or condominiums are offered for weekly, weekend or nightly rentals. This agency is open year round and offers 24-hour telephone service.

Sand Dollar Real Estate Inc.
Treasure Coast Square, 208-J N.Topsail
Dr., Surf City • (910) 328-5199,
(800) 948-4360

Specializing in Topsail Island properties, Sand Dollar offers weekly or weekend rentals from the oceanfront to the island's soundside.

Surf's up.

Photo: Jay Tervo

Rental properties include new homes and duplexes that boast up to eight bedrooms. Sand Dollar also handles property management.

Topsail Realty, Inc.
712 S. Anderson Blvd., Topsail Beach
• (910) 328-5241, (800) 526-6432

A large selection of the finest homes for vacation renters can be found at Topsail Realty. Their experienced staff takes pride in offering the best service possible to help you choose the right property. Since this is the only island agency that is exclusively a rental and property management agency, it allows the specialists to focus on providing your every vacation need. The inventory of properties includes large and small single-family homes on the oceanfront, sound-front, canal-front (often with a dock), or interior of the island, as well as attractive townhomes at Serenity Point on the southernmost tip of the island.

Treasure Realty
Treasure Plaza, Ste. R, N.C. Hwys. 210 and 172, Sneads Ferry • (910) 327-4444, (910) 327-3961, (800) 762-3961

Treasure Realty has specialized in vacation and long-term rentals in North Topsail Beach and Sneads Ferry for more than 13 years. The friendly staff has a combined 60-plus years of experience and have an extensive inventory of oceanfront homes and condominiums for you to choose from as well as sound-front and mainland selections. Treasure now features several of the largest rental homes on Topsail Island.

Ward Realty
116 S. Topsail Dr., Surf City
• (910) 328-3221, (800) 782-6216

From its variety of 160 desirable cottages and condominiums, Ward Realty's experienced staff can find just the right vacation spot for you. Whatever your choice, Ward Realty has a selection of oceanfront, sound-front and in-between locations that extend from one end of this 26-mile-long island to the other.

Can you hear the rustle of sea oats swaying in the breeze?

Photo: Jay Tervo

Camping

North Carolina's southern coast provides a myriad of camping opportunities. Campgrounds nearest the beaches are generally RV towns with ample amenities. So if you'd like to take along the kitchen sink, you may as well take your electric bug-zapper too. But, if you wear your home on your back and have the use of a small boat, leave the parking lot-style camping behind for the isolation of Masonboro Island. In the off-season, your only neighbors may be pelicans and rabbits.

Bicycle campers will find campgrounds about a day's ride apart except in the Wilmington vicinity, where campgrounds are less numerous. In any event, camping the southern coast is ideal for visitors on a budget, anglers who want to walk to the water each morning and anyone for whom recreation is re-creation.

Naturally, the highest rates at private campgrounds apply during the summer and holiday weekends. Tent sites are cheaper than RV sites. At most private grounds, weekly rates often discount the seventh day if payment is made in advance. Rentals by the month or longer are extremely limited from April to August. Some campgrounds offer camper or boat storage for a monthly fee.

As the Boy Scouts say, be prepared, especially for blistering sun, sudden electrical storms with heavy downpours, voracious marsh mosquitoes and insidious no-see-ums in summer. Temperatures in the region generally are mild, except for the occasional frost in winter. Average summer peak temperature is 88, average winter low is 36, and the overall yearly average temperature is 63. April and October average the least rainfall, about 3 inches each, while July averages the most with nearly 8 inches. However, weather patterns can be a little unpredictable, so be prepared for rain in any season. Sunscreen is essential. Hats and eye protection are wise, and insect repellent useful.

For tent camping, a waterproof tent fly is a must, and a tarp or dining fly is handy when cooking. Pack longer tent stakes or sand stakes for protection against high winds. Stay abreast of weather reports, especially during hurricane season (June 1 through November 30), and always bring a radio. A lightweight camp stove and cook set will come in handy when restaurants aren't convenient and at the many sites where fires are prohibited.

The primary creature hazards are poisonous snakes, which are prevalent in forested areas, and ticks, which have been known to carry disease. Raccoons and other small nocturnal animals are seldom more than a nuisance, although rabid animals are occasionally reported in the rural interior. Normally, the animals posing the greatest threat are human, which is why open fires and alcoholic beverages are restricted in most campgrounds. Beware of poison ivy, poison oak and poison sumac in brushwood and forests.

For hikers or cyclists carrying packs, there are two noteworthy Wilmington retail outlets for equipment. In business for more than 50 years, **Canady's Sport Center**, 3220 Wrightsville Avenue, (910) 791-6280, is an excellent outdoor outfitter with a varied inventory (closed on Sunday). Another excellent source for equipment and outdoor clothing is **Great Outdoor Provision Co**. in Hanover Center, 3501 Oleander Drive,

Wilmington, (910) 343-1648 (open seven days a week). Your other choices for field gear are **Dick's Sporting Goods**, 816 S. College Road, (910) 793-1904, and the two **Wal-Mart Super Centers**, one at 5135 Carolina Beach Road, (910) 452-0944, and the other at 5226 Sigmon Road, (910) 392-4034, which are good choices for novices and tailgate campers. In Brunswick County, **Wal-Mart Super Centers** are located in Southport at 1675 N. Howe Street, (910) 454-9909, and in Shallotte, 4540 Main Street, (910) 754-2880.

We've provided here a list of the area's nicest, most popular camping destinations. (For information on children's summer camps, refer to our Kidstuff chapter.)

Wilmington

KOA Wilmington
7415 Market St., Wilmington
• (910) 686-7705

Twenty minutes from downtown Wilmington, KOA Wilmington (formerly Camelot RV Park & Campground) is better situated for getting to all the local attractions than for getting away from it all. Given a gold rating by KOA, the tree-shaded grounds include a large swimming pool, a new children's playground, volleyball, horseshoes, a fish pond, a camp store, 107 campsites (pull-through and tent sites) and full and partial hookups. This pet-friendly lodge has clean, newly renovated restrooms, hot showers, laundry facilities and mail service. If you need a break from seeing the sites around town, there's a TV lounge and playroom with games and videos, plus access to high-speed Internet dialing. If roughing it isn't quite your style, KOA's charming heated and air-conditioned Kamping Kabins are available. A convenience store and gas station are located at the entrance to the campground. Nightly, weekly and monthly rates are available, and reservations are accepted and recommended in the high season. KOA is open year round.

Masonboro Island

Accessible only by boat, Masonboro Island is the last and largest undisturbed barrier island remaining on the southern North Carolina coast. It is the fourth component of the North Carolina National Estuarine Research Reserve (see our Higher Education and Research chapter) and deservedly so. This migrating ribbon of sand and uphill terrain, about 8 miles in length, is immediately south of Wrightsville Beach and offers campers a secluded, primitive experience in the most pristine environment on the Cape Fear coast. It is also used by anglers, bird-watchers, the occasional hunter, students and surfers (who prefer the north end). Everything you'll need must be packed in, and everything you produce should be packed out — everything!

Ninety-seven percent of Masonboro Island remains under state ownership and will always be accessible to visitors. Of the reserve's more than 5,000 acres, about 4,400 acres are tidal marsh and mud flats, so most folks land at the extreme north or south ends, on or near the sandy beaches by the inlets. Pitch camp behind the dunes only and use a cook stove; there is little or no firewood. While the North Carolina Division of Coastal Management hopes to limit its involvement with the island and preserve its traditional uses, it does prohibit polluting the island and camping on and in front of the dune ridge.

Wildlife here is remarkable and fragile. During the warm months, Masonboro Island is one of the most successful nesting areas for loggerhead turtles, a threatened species. Piping plovers, also threatened, feed at the island in winter. Keep your eyes on the marshes for river otters and, at low tide, raccoons. Gray foxes, cotton rats and tiny marsh rabbits all frequent the small maritime forest. The marshes, flats and creeks at low tide are excellent places to observe and photograph great blue and little blue herons, tricolor herons, snowy and great egrets, oystercatchers, clapper rails and many other flamboyant birds. Brown pelicans, various terns and gulls, American ospreys and shearwaters all live on Masonboro, if not permanently then at least for some part of their lives. Endangered peregrine falcons are very occasional seasonal visitors.

We recommend plenty of sun protection and insect repellent, perhaps even mosquito netting in the warm months, and trash bags always. Keep in mind that some of the island is still privately owned, not only at the north end, but also throughout the island, and all of it is fragile. The University of North Carolina at

> **INSIDERS' TIP**
> All North Carolina state parks are wildlife preserves and prohibit the removal of any plants, rocks, animals or artifacts from their sites.

The ocean brings out the best in all of us.

Photo: Jay Tervo

Wilmington's Center for Marine Science Research is conducting an ongoing survey of visitor impact on the island and a continuing study of environmental changes caused by hurricanes and other natural forces. Visitors' behavior and scientific scrutiny together will have some influence on whether Masonboro Island becomes severely restricted, so responsible usage is paramount. For more information about Masonboro Island, see the Islands section in our chapter on Attractions.

Carolina Beach

Carolina Beach State Park
Dow Rd., Carolina Beach • (910) 458-8206
Once a campsite for Paleo-Indians, Colonial explorers and Confederate troops, Carolina

Beach State Park remains a gem among camping destinations. Watersports enthusiasts are minutes from the Cape Fear River, Masonboro Sound and the Atlantic. There is a full-service marina, (910) 458-7770, with two launching ramps. Need we mention the great fishing? The park is a bird-watcher's paradise and home to lizards, snakes (mostly harmless), rare frogs, carnivorous plants (protected) and occasionally alligators, opossums, gray foxes and river otters.

Six miles of hiking trails wind through several distinct habitats, including maritime forest, pocosin (low, flat, swampy regions) and savanna. Hikers on the Sugarloaf Trail pass over tidal marsh and dunes and along three limesink ponds. Cypress Pond, the most unusual, is dominated by a dwarf cypress swamp forest.

Dense vegetation lends the campsites a fair

amount of privacy. Each site has a table and grill, and sites are available on a first-come, first-serve basis ($12 per site). Two of the 83 campsites are wheelchair accessible. Drinking water and well-kept restrooms with hot showers are close by. There is a dump station for RVs, but no hookups. Ranger-led interpretive programs deepen visitors' understanding of the region's natural bounty. Unleashed pets and possession of alcoholic beverages are prohibited.

The park is 15 miles south of Wilmington, a mile north of Carolina Beach just off U.S. 421 on Dow Road. From Wilmington, make a right at the second stoplight after crossing Snow's Cut bridge. Stop by the Visitor Center at the entrance to the park for information, hiking trail maps and brochures. (See our Sports, Fitness and Parks chapter for more information about the park.)

Southport - Oak Island

Long Beach Family Campground
5011 E. Oak Island Dr., Oak Island
• (910) 278-5737

Boasting access to both the beach and the nightlife of east Oak Island and located just minutes from historic Southport, this campground is understandably popular all year long. Few of the 185 sites enjoy any shade, but the tent areas are grassy and commonly host foraging sea birds. The campground offers a special group tenting area. Full and partial hookups are available, as are flush toilets, hot showers, sewage disposal, tables, a public phone, ice, and seasonal or permanent lease sites. Pets are welcome.

South Brunswick Islands

Ocean Aire Camp World Inc.
2614 Holden Beach Rd. SW, Supply
• (910) 842-9072

Open year round and located 2.5 miles from Holden Beach, this 133-site campground offers daily, weekly, monthly and annual rates. Amenities include 30-amp electricity, water and sewer, modern bath houses with tiled hot showers, laundry facilities, LP gas, security lights and a convenience store (open March through Octo-

ber). A large swimming pool, nine-hole putt-putt golf, pool tables, video games, volleyball, horseshoes and a children's playground provide recreation options. Monthly boat or camper storage rates are available.

Sea Mist Camping Resort
4616 Devane Rd. SW, Shallotte
• (910) 754-8916

Sea Mist's panoramic view of Shallotte Inlet and Ocean Isle Beach is enough to entice any camper, but the view is only one of the appealing amenities. Visitors love Sea Mist's pool, reputedly the largest in Brunswick County, with its shaded deck and picnic area. Volleyball, basketball, and horseshoes are among the activities available. Use of the boat ramp carries no extra charge. This Woodall-rated resort is open year round and has 250 spacious RV and tent sites with tables. Most have full hookups. The restrooms, bathhouses and coin-operated laundry facilities are clean, and the camp store is open from March 1 through December 1. Perhaps best of all, Sea Mist is only 10 minutes from the attractions of Ocean Isle Beach. Leashed pets are permitted. Daily, monthly and annual rates and storage are available. Reserve early.

Sea Mist is at the Intracoastal Waterway opposite the east end of Ocean Isle Beach. Follow the blue and white camping signs along N.C. Highway 179 to Brick Landing Road and continue to the end of the pavement. Turn left onto Devane Road.

Topsail Island

Lanier's Campground
Little Kinston Rd., Surf City
• (910) 328-9431

This large, friendly campground is on the mainland side of the Intracoastal Waterway in Surf City. Full hookups, camper/pop-up and tent sites are available, some with shade. The interior roads are paved. Campground amenities include a swimming pool, hot showers, pay phones, picnic tables, a dump station, laundry facilities, limited groceries, a bath house, an arcade and a sandwich grill with hand-dipped ice cream. New fire rings have been added to the sites this year. Horseshoes, beach Bingo on Friday nights and Saturday afternoons, a children's playground, holiday activities and interdenominational church services are some of the activities at the campground. A DJ, playing a variety of music including country and popular, will provide entertainment every other weekend between Memorial day and Labor Day

Sneads Ferry

Old Ferry Marina Campground
150 Old Ferry Rd., Sneads Ferry
• **(910) 327-2258**
Old Ferry Marina Campground makes it convenient to camp and fish from the same property. A great place for a relaxing vacation, this campground is close enough to the beach for the sun worshiper. Returning campers claim they keep coming back because they enjoy the friendship of the owners, other campers and fishermen. Full hook-ups are offered on a daily, weekly, monthly or seasonal basis. Besides fishing, amenities include a bath house.

Inland

Lake Waccamaw State Park
1866 State Park Dr., Lake Waccamaw
• **(910) 646-4748**
Lake Waccamaw, named after the region's tribal natives, is the largest of the Carolina bays and is 38 miles from Wilmington in Columbus County. It wasn't until the age of aviation that thousands of the elliptical depressions known as Carolina bays were noticed dotting the Carolinas' coastal plain. All the depressions are oriented along northwest-southeast axes. Locals came to call them "bays," referring to the abundance of bay trees — red, sweet and loblolly — that flourish there.

About 400,000 Carolina bays exist, ranging in size from a fraction of an acre to Lake Waccamaw's more than 9,000 acres. Some are lakes, but most are seasonal wetlands filled with fertile peat. Their origin is still a mystery. A hypothesis that an ancient meteor shower or explosion formed them collapsed under scrutiny. A widely accepted theory is that they were formed by strong winds blowing across a sandy landscape or shallow sea during the last Ice Age.

Lake Waccamaw's shallow waters support 52 species of fish. Several species of aquatic animals living here exist nowhere else in the world.

The Visitor Center opened in January 1998 and currently houses park offices and an auditorium where nature films are shown. An addition to the center is in process, which will feature an exhibit hall with interactive displays that highlight the lake and surrounding area.

Four nature trails — Lake Trail, Sand Ridge Nature Trail, Pine Woods Trail and Loblolly Trail — and the boardwalk provide memorable glimpses of the unique and diverse plant life here. Most trails begin from the Visitor Center or the picnic area. Among the many species of plants here are the region's oldest stands of cypress trees, reindeer moss, turkey oaks and the rare Venus's flytrap.

Visitors planning to camp at Lake Waccamaw must be willing to rough it slightly. The camping area is undeveloped, with no more facilities than pit toilets, picnic tables and fire circles. Four primitive group campsites (no water) are available by reservation or on a first-come basis. Trailer camping is not allowed. Permits may be obtained at the Visitor Center, (910) 646-4748. Fees are $8 per site with $1 per person for groups of more than eight people.

The park is about 7 miles south of U.S. Highway 74/76. Highly visible signs along that route and along N.C. Highway 214 lead the way. Entrance to the park is from Bella Coola Road, which veers off State Road 1947.

Holland's Shelter Creek
8315 N.C. Hwy. 53 E., Burgaw
• **(910) 259-5743**
Holland's offers full RV hookups in a rustic setting along the river. If you don't have a recreational vehicle, Holland's also has cabins that provide the perfect balance between rustic atmosphere and comfort. Sleeping up to four persons, the cabins have heat, air conditioning and indoor plumbing. Canoe, kayak and paddleboat rentals are available for any size group from the solitary fisherman to family reunions or scout troops camping together. Holland's Shelter Creek Restaurant and general store are located on the same property to make your camping trip complete. The campground is open year-round.

CAMPING

Restaurants

Price Code

The following price code is based on the average price for two dinner entrees only. For restaurants not serving dinner, the code reflects mid-priced lunch entrees for two. Dual codes indicate that lunch and dinner prices vary significantly. The price codes do not reflect the state/county 7 percent sales tax or gratuities.

$	Less than $15
$$	$15 to $25
$$$	$26 to $40
$$$$	More than $40

A bounty of mouthwatering, fresh-catch seafood figures prominently almost everywhere you dine along North Carolina's southern coast. These coastal waters yield consistently high-quality seafood, and just about every restaurant worth its salt offers fresh daily seafood specialties that may include tuna, grouper, mahi-mahi, mackerel, triggerfish and shellfish, to name only a few. Talented local and transplanted chefs vie to create visually appealing entrees and bring innovative flair to seafood preparation. Fresh-catch entrees and specials are often available grilled, baked, broiled, blackened or fried.

This region's restaurants, particularly in the port city of Wilmington, reflect a rich international community in the choices of cuisine now available, including Thai, Indian, Chinese (including Szechuan), Greek, Italian, German, Japanese, Jamaican, Caribbean and French. Several restaurants serving Mexican food are good places to advance the perpetual quest for the perfect margarita, but by no means does the search end there.

Health-food enthusiasts are pleased by exciting vegetarian and organic meat dishes and products offered at numerous island restaurants and markets, including Lovey's Natural Foods & Cafe and Tidal Creek Foods Co-op.

Also represented throughout our coverage area are a number of major restaurant chains, both national and regional, such as Ruby Tuesday's, Perkins, T.G.I.Fridays, Applebee's, Rock-Ola Cafe, Cracker Barrel, Outback Steakhouse and, of course, the usual fast food options. Well-known pizza franchises — Domino's, Pizza Hut, Papa John's — offer delivery, and several area restaurants feature gourmet pizzas for the connoisseur.

Favorite Local Foods

Naturally, the traditional regional specialties make up the heart and soul of Southern coastal dining. The famous Calabash-style seafood is ever-present. It gets its name from the Brunswick County town to the south once heralded as the seafood capital of the world for having nearly 30 seafood restaurants within a square mile. Calabash style calls for seasoned cornmeal batter and deep frying and has become synonymous with all-you-can-eat. Calabash restaurants typically serve a huge variety of piping-hot seafood in massive quantities accompanied by creamy coleslaw and uniquely shaped, deep-fried dollops of corn bread called hush puppies.

Low-country steam-offs are buckets filled with a variety of shellfish, potatoes, corn and Old Bay seasoning. When fresh oysters are in season in the fall, oyster roasts abound. Crab meat is popular, and competition is stiff among restaurants boasting the best crab dip. Seafood chowder and chili are two other popular dishes put to the test in local competitions and cook-offs. New Year's Day dinners may include collards and black-eyed peas, symbolic of paper money and small change, to ensure prosperity in the year to come. Okra, sweet potatoes, grits, turnip greens, mustard greens and kale are also regional favorites. Hoppin' John, based on black-eyed peas and rice, is a hearty dish seen in many variations. Shrimp and grits is another favotite dish appearing in various incarnations from

Upbeat, Casual and Delicious

Pastas/Risotto

Fresh Seafood

Beef/Mixed Grill

Sandwiches/Burritos

Smoked Fish

Daily Chef's Specials

Homemade Desserts/Breads

Largest Selection of Beer

Wines by the Glass

All ABC Permits

Check our website for
daily specials:
www.tomatozrestaurant.com

**GREAT LATE NIGHT
LIVE MUSIC
(no cover)
Tuesday, Wednesday, and
Thursday nights at 10 p.m.**

Sunday: Jazz at 8 p.m.

*"Tomatoz serves up healthy fare with
delicious panache..."*
-Gale Tolan
Wilmington Morning Star

TOMATOZ
WILMINGTON N.C.
AMERICAN GRILLE
LUNCH, DINNER and SUNDAY BRUNCH

1201 S. College Road
(at the corner of South College and
Wrightsville Avenue)
Call Ahead Seating
313-0541 • 313-0543 (fax)

DISCOVER THE *NEW*
NORTH CAROLINA AQUARIUM
AT **FORT FISHER**

NOW OPEN
1-800-832-FISH
www.ncaquariums.com

THE NEW
NORTH·CAROLINA
AQUARIUMS

Lumina Station
1900 Eastwood Road • Wilmington, NC
910-256-0995
Dinner - Tuesday thru Sunday 5pm Until
Featuring Prime Cuts Of Beef, Fresh Seafood & Weekend Entertainment

restaurant to restaurant. Boiled peanuts are popular snacks, frequently available at roadside stands, and nowhere does pecan pie taste better. Iced tea flows freely, in most places by the pitcher-full, and locals prefer it very sweet.

Many North Carolinians enjoy good barbecue in all its variations — pork or beef, chopped or shredded, sweet or tangy — and the coastal regions are no exception. Many beach communities boast at least one barbecue restaurant hidden among the seafood restaurants — touting the best recipe, of course.

Planning and Pricing

Reservations are generally not required unless your party consists of six persons or more, and many restaurants throughout the region don't accept reservations at all, especially during peak season. It wasn't very long ago that waiting time at most Wilmington restaurants was negligible. With the region's growing year-round visitor season, the wait has changed substantially for many restaurants. At most popular eateries in Wilmington, expect to find waiting lists throughout the summer, during festivals and on most holidays. Some restaurants will allow you to place your name on the waiting list before your arrival. A call to the restaurant regarding their policy is recommended.

Restaurant hours are frequently reduced or curtailed in winter, although some restaurants close entirely for a month or more, especially in the beach communities. Most places serve later on Friday and Saturday nights than on weeknights, so call ahead to verify hours and reservations. You may also want to inquire about early bird specials and senior citizen discounts even if such information isn't included in our listings.

In keeping with the area's resort character and hot summers, dining here is generally very casual. While you might feel out of place wearing shorts at fancier restaurants such as The Pilot House or Chester's, casual dress is commonplace practically everywhere else. Wearing shorts or polo shirts during the summer, even at the better restaurants, may be the only practical way to end a very full day.

Most restaurants listed here accept major credit cards, and some will accept personal checks with an ID. We'll let you know which ones do not. For restaurants not included in this chapter's listings, an inquiry in advance may save some anxious moments when paying the bill.

Coffeehouses are a welcome addition to the local landscape, particularly in Wilmington, so we've listed a number of the most popular spots near the end of the chapter. Often reflecting the communities in which they thrive, these southeastern North Carolina gathering places exhibit a definite artistic and coastal flair. Local artwork receives pride of place on many cafe walls in this culturally rich region. Warm and courteous friendliness is thrown in for good measure. All offer the standard array of coffeehouse beverages, from traditional espressos, lattes, cappuccinos and

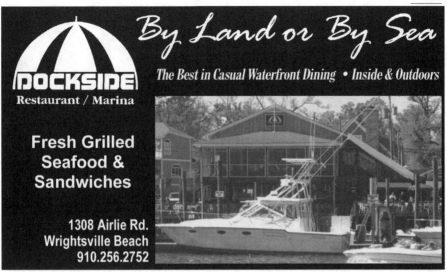
herbal teas to the cool, sweet fresh fruit smoothies, with daily specials that are exquisitely exotic. Biscotti, muffins, scones and bagels, made fresh daily on the premises or at local bakeries, are traditional fare for area cafes.

The Bakeries section at the end of this chapter lists outstanding establishments in the region. These talented and well-established bake shops also supply several local restaurants and eateries with delicious homemade breads and mouth-watering desserts.

Where To Eat

The southern coastal region, especially the Greater Wilmington area, overflows with great places to eat. A complete listing of the region's restaurants and eateries could fill an entire book. This chapter offers a sampling of what's available in each area. If your favorite restaurant isn't listed here, it may be because it's among the many fine restaurants that are impossible to miss because of reputation or location. We've made a special effort to include the more out-of-the-way places that shouldn't be missed, along with some obvious favorites. Please keep in mind that restaurants may frequently change menu items, hours of operation or close after this book goes to press. Call ahead to verify information that is important to you.

Wilmington

Alleigh's
$$-$$$ • **4925 New Centre Dr., Wilmington** • **(910) 793-0999**

Alleigh's is your best choice for excellent food at a great value. Choose from fresh sea-

food and hand-cut certified Angus beef steaks or the best ribs, burgers, sandwiches and Sunday brunch in town. This 35,000- square-foot complex has everything from live bands, an outdoor Tiki Bar & Cafe and a 31-TV Sports Bar to an intimate Jazz Bar and fun-filled Game Room. A late-night menu is available until 1 AM.

Birds Restaurant
$$ • **202 Princess St., Wilmington** • **(910) 762-1414**

This fun, family-owned and operated restaurant features "chicken with an attitude" — fast and fresh! Daily chicken specials include Tarty Chicken on Tuesday and Stinky Chicken on Wednesday. Be sure to try the house special, Birds Salad. Offering casual dining with comfortable seating in a historic downtown build-

ing, Birds welcomes large parties. You can eat in, take out or call for delivery. Birds is open for lunch and dinner Monday through Friday and for lunch on Saturday, with extended summer hours.

Chester's American Steakhouse
$$$ • Lumina Station, 1900 Eastwood Rd., Wilmington • (910) 256-0995

Sit, stay and play awhile at Chester's American Steakhouse, formerly Cafe Atlantique, featureing legendary cuisine with a warm, friendly atmosphere nestled in beautiful Lumina Station. Renowned for its prime cuts of beef, fresh local seafood and the highest quality in poultry and game, this fine restaurant is noteworthy not only for the delectable menu, but also for the eclectic wine list and superlative staff. Food critics have praised Chester's American Steakhouse for "the level of refinement found in the cuisine" and "the seamless execution of harmony among the staff." Open for lunch and dinner Tuesday through Sunday from 5 until, the menu changes seasonally, and there are daily specials. Come enjoy live music on the weekends and nightly bar specials. Reservations are recommended.

Cafe de France
$$-$$$ • 1121 Military Cutoff Rd., Wilmington • (910) 256-6600

Count on a romantic evening at Cafe de France, voted Best French cuisine by Encore for 2003.You'll enjoy a variety of crepes, fondue (Wednesdays), Morrocan meatloaf, French onion soup and more gourmet choices from the country of love. An extensive wine list gives you the perfect glass to accompany your meal. Dining beside a full-wall mural of a French village lends a feeling of being abroad. Live entertainment is offered every Sunday during brunch, so you can enjoy the sounds of Galen as you fill up on the delectable tastes of French cuisine.

Caffe Phoenix
$$ • 9 S. Front St., Wilmington • (910) 343-1395

High ceilings, original art, an interior balcony . . . what the Phoenix offers the eyes is more than complemented by a menu of consistent quality that makes it one of the most appealing dining experiences in the Cape Fear region. Situated in a historic glass-front building, the Phoenix is a favorite gathering place in downtown Wilmington. The regular menu is an eclectic blend of Italian, French, Spanish and

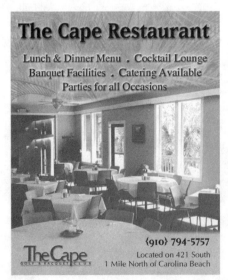

North African cuisine. Portions are generous. Dressings and sauces are all-natural and made fresh. The special seasonal offerings are always inventive and change daily. Recorded music (often classical, jazz or Brazilian) adds to the ambience. Caffe Phoenix serves lunch and dinner (with light fare in-between) every day. Mixed drinks, a selection of coffees and excellent homemade desserts are served until closing — a nice choice for a romantic nightcap. Art shows at the Phoenix occur about every four to six weeks with a party that's open to the public.

Breakfast at Caffe Phoenix's coffeehouse, available Monday through Saturday, is served continental style with muffins, breakfast bread, fresh fruit, granola and more. Sunday brunch includes their famous thick-cut French toast, egg dishes and selections borrowed from the lunch menu plus a selection of featured specials that change weekly. Specialty champagne cocktails and Bloody Marys are another Sunday brunch highlight.

The Cape Golf and Racquet Club Restaurant
$$-$$$ • 535 The Cape Boulevard, Wilmington • (910) 799-3110

Under new management, this unusual golf club restaurant looks over the beautiful golf course at The Cape. If you're in the sports bar, you may have to get Chef Mike Day to turn off one of the many cooking shows he enjoys. Every other Friday evening, Mike offers an international menu, including Greek, Chinese and Cajun cooking. The BBQ ribs with smoked jalapeno sauce and cilantro are not to be missed. A formal banquet room is available for large parties. The restaurant is open daily for lunch and on Sunday for brunch and lunch.

Caprice Bistro
$$ • 10 Market St., Wilmington • (910) 815-0810

The setting is perfect. Historic downtown Wilmington's riverfront is within view, bricked streets lead to quaint boutiques, and a period horse-drawn carriage passes by regularly. Though lace curtains adorn the windows and white tablecloths drape the tables, Caprice Bistro's atmosphere is one of friendly, casual ease and, for those who have never experienced it, a glimpse of the charm and cuisine of an authentic continental bistro. The hearty menu is traditional bistro fare and is served in generous portions at affordable prices. Your choices

D E L U X E

114 Market Street
Downtown Wilmington
910•251•0333

Reservations Strongly Suggested
Valet Parking Available

include a bounty of appetizers, entrees and classic desserts. Prepared with fresh ingredients and innovative style, this cuisine offers a full continental spectrum, from the homemade country pate, onion soup, steak au poivre, duck confit and profiterolles to an array of entrees featuring steak, seafood, poultry and game. The bistro's wine list offers European wines plus a good choice of American labels as well. Caprice Bistro's second floor is an intimate American-style sofa bar, perfect for relaxing with a martini or wine. The full menu or simply appetizers and dessert is available in this beautifully appointed bar. The sofa bar is smoker-friendly. (The downstairs dining room is non-smoking.) Caprice Bistro opens nightly for dinner. The sofa bar remains open until 2 AM.

Circa 1922
$$$ • 8 N. Front St., Wilmington
• (910) 762-1922

Voted Best Appetizers and Desserts 2003 by Encore magazine, Circa has become renowned for serving tapas for the past four years. Each course is marked by quality that makes this restaurant stand higher than the rest. The ahi seared tuna is purely delightful, and the crab dip is made to perfection. Gauge your appetite for generously portioned desserts. The bananas Foster will put you in a state of pure bliss, and the creme brulee is heavenly. The greatest part of Circa, aside from their appetizers, desserts and complete wine list, is the authentic 1922 atmosphere. You will expect F. Scott Fitzgerald to walk in the door before you leave. Circa opens nightly for dinner.

Deluxe Cafe
$$-$$$ • 114 Market St., Wilmington
• (910) 251-0333

Deluxe offers an aesthetically stimulating environment in a lively and casual atmosphere: eclectic decor of art deco, abstract expressionism and architectural formalism; paintings, wood sculpture and glasswork; and fresh flowers, high ceilings and clean lines. Featured artwork on exhibit at Deluxe rotates every six weeks. It's a sublime and friendly environment for enjoying excellent dinners, an astonishing list of over 300 fine wines, a respectable selection of port and one of Wilmington's superior brunches. Dinner is memorable, with innovative offerings that appeal visually while tempting the palate. Try the Cornmeal Dusted Local Grouper stacked with toasted brioche stuffed with smoked cheddar pimento cheese, a fresh garlic saute of tender spinach, finished with peppery arugula pesto. Another excellent choice is Cider Soaked Orange Pork Tenderloin with Vanilla-scented Carolina sweet potato risotto, spring greens, roasted roots, rosemary jus lie, and raspberry pear compote.

For brunch, the menu is equally attractive, with selections that include pecan French toast and applewood smoked salmon, served with melted white cheddar cheese, two poached eggs and topped with a mustard cream sauce.

After dinner, sit back with a 20-year-old tawny port, and you'll know why this cafe at the very heart of downtown is garnering a dedicated following. Deluxe is open for dinner every evening and for Sunday brunch from 10:30 AM to 2:30 PM.. Menu selections are prepared with a special emphasis on fresh local ingredients and exquisite plate presentation. The dual price code above reflects Sunday brunch and dinner, respectively.

Eddie Romanelli's
$$ • 5400 Oleander Dr., Wilmington
• (910) 799-7000

Voted Best Salad 2003 by Encore magazine, Eddie Romanelli's high-tone atmosphere is suffused with the richness of dark wood, red brick and comfortable banquette seating. The menu emphasizes American regional dishes, many with an Italian accent. Among the house specialties are an excellent crab dip and homemade 12-inch pizzas, some of which are unusual, such as the barbecued chicken pizza and Philly steak pizza. The menu offers a variety of appetizers (the pesto cheese toast is worth a try), sandwiches, salads with freshly made dressings, and Italian baked specialties. Lunch and dinner menus are essentially the same, with dinner

portions larger and served with a choice of soup or salad and a choice of potatoes or pasta. The popular bar adjoining the restaurant offers handsome sectional seating, and a late-night finger-food menu is served there. Menu and drink specials are offered every day. Eddie Romanelli's is open seven days a week.

Elijah's
$$-$$$ • Chandler's Wharf, Water St., Wilmington • (910) 343-1448

No one can say they've been to Wilmington until they've tried Elijah's crab dip. Directly on the Cape Fear River, Elijah's offers traditional Low-country fare as well as such delights as oysters Rockefeller, the mouthwatering Shrimp and Scallops Elijah and fried pecan chicken. Elijah's is two restaurants in one (thus the hyphenated price code) — the oyster bar, which includes outdoor deck seating, and the enclosed dining room, with its more formal presentation of seafood, poultry, pasta and choice beef. Nautical artwork recalls the building's former incarnation as a maritime museum. The ambience is casual, and the western exposure makes it a great place for a sundown toast. Elijah's is open seven days a week year round and serves lunch, dinner and Sunday brunch. Reservations are accepted only for parties of eight or more.

Elizabeth's Pizza
$$ • 4304 Market St., Wilmington • (910) 251-1005

Elizabeth's Pizza is top-crust in Encore's 2003 poll,

probably due to its locally owned and operated atmosphere, friendly staff and great pizza. A hand-tossed crust with all your favorite toppings is huge and always fresh. Sicilian style is available, but takes a few more minutes to cook. Elizabeth's has an extensive menu of sandwiches, pastas, strombolis, and calzones. Elizabeth's is open every day for lunch and late dinner, until midnight.

Elvaquero Restaurant
$$ • 4238 Market St., Wilmington • (910) 815-0506

Elvaquero Restaurant II
$$ • 3530 Carolina Beach Rd., Carolina Beach • (910) 395-1433

These top-rated Mexican restaurants offer the four main ingredients — great food, friendly service, varied selection and reasonable prices — for a great dining experience. Elvaquero's is known for made-from-scratch Mexican food. Fresh ingredients are key, and nothing is frozen except the margaritas. The staff is willing to accommodate in-house parties of up to 30 people, and owner Benjamin Avalos will serenade the person of honor. Elvaquero's is open for lunch and dinner.

Fathoms Bistro
$$-$$$ • Lumina Station, 1900 Eastwood Rd., Wilmington • (910) 256-1254

Dining at Fathoms, whether indoors or on the patio in Tahitian gliders, is a casual affair with an em-

INSIDERS' TIP
Have local restaurants inspired you to try your hand at recipes for coastal cuisine? Check out the regional cookbook section at local bookstores.

Advanced Orders Welcome 910.792.1447

Fish Market

Wilmington's best fish shack offers locally caught fish, shellfish, and blue crab.

email: fishmonger@marketstreetseafood.com

phasis on great food and a bright, cozy atmosphere. Local art and photography adorn the walls, and the menu features a coastal fusion cuisine highlighted by fresh-catch seafood, rotisserie and house-smoked meats, and local produce. The lunch menu features unique offerings in seafood, chicken and beef sandwiches, including the memorable Crab Melt sandwich. Heartier appetites will enjoy Fathoms' eclectic luncheon entrees. Dinner offerings include a great selection of mouthwatering appetizers, entrees and seasonal specials. Entrees feature seafood, beef, chicken, pasta and risotto, prepared with fresh herbs, vegetables and innovative sauces. With all ABC permits, Fathoms Bistro offers an eclectic wine list, including 20 pours by the glass, perfect for pairing with every meal.

If brunch is just your style, Fathoms Bistro serves an appealing array of choices that reinvent traditional fare into tradition with flair. Omelet, egg dishes and griddle offerings are prepared with a variety of the freshest ingredients — seafood, smoked meats, vegetables and herbs — in the bistro's signature style. The Guest's Creation omelet allows your taste to follow your imagination, or chose the chef's baked egg fritatta, created daily with a variety of fresh ingredients. Brunch is available every Saturday and Sunday. Lunch and dinner are served daily year round.

The Fish Market
$$ • 6826-F Market St., Wilmington
• (910) 792-1447

You're not likely to miss a yellow building with fish and shrimp painted on it but, just in case, this popular seafood retailer can be found in Ogden near Gordon Road. Offering more than the average fish market, you may select the freshest cut-to-order local fish and shellfish at reasonable prices. The Fish Market will steam, smoke or cook it for you on-premise and offers take-out service. \Just can't figure out how to cook it yourself at home? The market's knowledgeable staff love to talk about all things fishy and are willing to offer suggestions. Ask about the tasty rubs and marinades for sale, plus domestic and imported bottled beers to go.

The Forks Restaurant
$$ • 3151 S. 17th St., Wilmington
• (910) 395-5999

The Forks Restaurant, located in the new Louise Wells Cameron Art Museum, draws its name from the obvious nature of an eatery plus the location in south Wilmington and the two-day Civil War battle fought there. This 44-seat cafe features a menu offering contemporary regional Southern cuisine. Managed by the owners of downtown Wilmington's popular Caffe Phoenix, menu highlights and specials include selections incorporating the themes of visiting art exhibits. Dine in the beautifully appointed cafe or venture out to the cafe's 50-seat sculpture courtyard. Open for lunch seating Tuesday through Sunday, The Forks Restaurant also serves dinner on Friday evenings.

Front Street Brewery
$$ • 9 N. Front St., Wilmington
• (910) 251-1935

The Brewery is locally famous for its ales, lagers, stouts and seasonals, all freshly made on the premises, and for its pub-style food. The restaurant occupies the Foy-Roe Building (1883) with its original, high tin ceiling and heart-pine floors. Wrought-iron railings, historic photos, lush woodwork and a beautiful exterior facade are additional merits. Not surprisingly, The Brewery incorporates beer into signature menu item and sauces, including the cheddar ale soup, beer-battered fish and chips, Raspberry Wheat Ale dressing and Front Street Stout. Pub-style sandwiches, generously portioned salads, steaks, seafood and poultry are all matched to suit the excellent beers. The desserts should not be missed. Front Street Brewery now pours nine different handcrafted ales. Usually on tap are six Brewery standards — Roundhouse Stout, Plantation Pilsner, Dramtree Scottish Ale, Moonlight Lumina Lager, India Pale Ale and the popular Raspberry Wheat Ale (highly recommended). The Brewery is open for lunch and dinner seven days a week, with a full late-night menu.

Genki
$-$$ • University Landing, 419 S. College Rd., #26, Wilmington • (910) 796-8687

With the ever-growing popularity of sushi in the Wilmington area, it was a real coup that Genki won the Encore poll for 2003. Owned and operated by Masauki and Reiko Augiura, the key to this authentic Japanese restaurant is that every item is served fresh. The original flavors are tasted in every bite and aren't masked with heavy sauces or preservatives. Choose from tuna, eel, shrimp and California rolls and more, knowing that it's all low in calories and good for your health. You may watch Masauki make the rolls at the authentic sushi bar or sit in the aesthetically appealing dining room with a group of friends. Genki is open for lunch Tuesday through Friday and for dinner Tuesday through Sunday. Reservations are recommended.

Giorgio's Italian Restaurant
$-$$ • 5226 S. College Rd., Wilmington • (910) 790-9954

Tucked away in a small shopping center near the Monkey Junction area of S. College Road, this family-friendly Italian restaurant is a huge hit with Insiders who suggest that you come hungry (even the lunch portions are huge). Encore magazine readers recognized Giorgio's as the Best Italian Food for 2001, 2002 and 2003. The atmosphere is cozy, with a friendly wait staff bent on making your dining experience a pleasure. Naturally, the food is the centerpiece, with a bountiful selection

You'd look just as sweet upon the seat of a bicycle built for two.

Photo: Barbara McKenzie

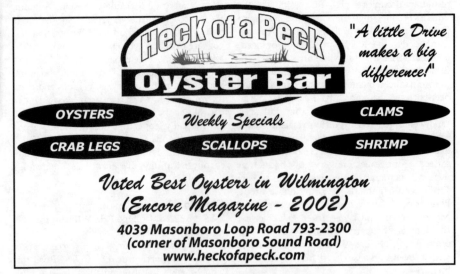

of salads, zuppas (that's soup for the uninitiated), appetizers and hearty pasta entrees with chicken, seafood, veal or sweet Italian sausage. Locals argue over their favorite dishes, but all are excellent choices. If you prefer something off the grill, try the Kansas rib eye or Roman pork tenderloin. Delicious! The lunch menu offers slightly smaller versions of some dinner items plus a selection of create-your-own pasta dishes, a gourmet's choice of calzone entrees and Giorgio's signature sandwiches. Must-try sandwiches include the Italian sausage sub, Giorgio's mufalata and the eggplant parmigiana sub. The restaurant's small lounge area with full bar service is a cozy place to wait when the dining room is full. Giorgio's opens daily for lunch and dinner. While the portions are equally hearty at lunch, the price is very reasonable, as indicated by the dual price code listed above. Takeout services and party platters are available.

Gumby's Pizza
$$ • 1414-E S. College Rd., Wilmington • (910) 313-0072

Based on the cartoon character Gumby, who has the power to go inside books and become a part of the story, this new franchise of Gumby's will have you going inside this fun restaurant for more delicious pizza. Not only does this pizza feature fresh-made dough and the finest ingredients, but there are also Pokey sticks, pepperoni rolls, stromboli, calzone, wings, mozzarella sticks, cheese fries, salads, pastas and a carry-out cheese pizza for only $3.99. Gumby's opens at 4 PM, Sunday through Thursday, and 11 AM Friday and Saturday. Extreme late-night delivery is available Sunday through Thursday until 3 AM and Friday and Saturday until 4 AM.

Harvest Moon
$$$ • 5704 Oleander Dr., Wilmington • (910) 792-0172

James Bain has been named Best Chef by Encore magazine five years in a row. The culinary genius of Harvest Moon is amazingly creative with his menu, offering the best meals with the freshest ingredients. The menu changes weekly, offering not only beef, poultry and fish, but also various game, such as veal, venison and duck. The food is outstanding, and the presentation is a true art form. Bain's reputation has grown due to his his past appearances on WECT's mid-day cooking spots. Soon he will present a new DVD, "Chapters," which reveals 50 new recipes to share with friends. Open for dinner, Harvest Moon is closed on Sunday. Dinner reservations are recommended.

Heck of a Peck Oyster Bar
$$ • 4039 Masonboro Loop Rd., Wilmington • (910) 793-2300

For steamed-oyster lovers nostalgic for the good old days of old-fashioned coastal oyster bars, Heck of a Peck is a must. Two horseshoe-shaped bars, barstool seating and casual atmosphere create a friendly and companionable setting. Staffers take the work out of your meal by shucking your order in front of you at stainless steel sinks. Voted Best Oysters 2002 by Encore magazine's annual readers' poll, the restaurant's traditional fare isn't limited to fresh steamed oysters and the fixins — warm homemade cocktail sauce, cole slaw and saltine crackers. Steamed shrimp, scallops, clams and crab legs are additional highlights. Located in southeast Wilmington at Masonboro Station, Heck of a Peck Oyster Bar is open daily for dinner.

Henry's Restaurant & Bar
$$ • Barclay Commons, 2508 Independence Blvd., Wilmington
• (910) 793-2929

Henry's is an exciting restaurant from the folks who created Eddie Romanelli's, The Oceanic and Bluewater. The cuisine is classic American fare created through high-quality, from-scratch cooking. The decor features beautifully hued stacked sandstone and hand-painted walls, a hand-painted ceiling and an awesome 100-year-old Brunswick-style tiger oak bar. Lunch possibilities range from generous salad selections (the grilled tuna and fresh spinach salad is a good choice) and cold deli sandwiches to luncheon plates (everything from roast beef and gravy to fresh catch) and hearty, two-handed sandwiches that come with your choice of a side item (12 sides to choose from). Start dinner with some of the best shrimp chowder in the region. Dinner menu highlights include hearty meal-size salads, sandwiches and generously portioned entrees, including pasta dishes, chicken, fresh seafood, prime rib and more. Insiders highly recommend Henry's awesome lump crab cake and the savory shrimp and grits. Sausage-stuffed pork chops and cashew-sesame-crusted grouper are just a few more favorites. The strawberry shortcake is made in-house and is better than Grandma's. Henry's bar offers all ABC permits with premium-pour liquors, eight draft beers and comfortable, upholstered banquettes for dining. Smoking is permitted in the bar area only.

Incredible Gourmet Pizza
$ • 3600 S. College Rd., Wilmington
• (910) 791-7080

Incredible makes the pizza most true to its name in the known universe and, in our estimation, is one of the best, most adventurous pizzas in the greater Wilmington area. The crust is not too thick, not too doughy. Twenty-one different specialty pizzas are available or you can create your own from seven sauce bases and several meats, vegetables, herbs and cheeses. Incredible's five salad choices, including Caesar, Greek and Anti Pasta, are made fresh to order in generous portions. Residential, business and hotel delivery, available within limited areas, is free. The Wilmington location is immediately east of the intersection of the 17th Street Extension, about 3 miles south of Oleander Drive. Two other locations, each under its own management, are the Eastwood Road store, (910) 256-0339, in Plaza East Shopping Center near Wrightsville Beach, and the Porters Neck location, (910) 686-7772, on N. Market Street.

Downtown Wilmington's Finest Pasta and Pizza!

Featuring Old Style Italian Cuisine & Brick Oven Designer Pizzas

Serving Lunch & Dinner
Mon-Thurs. 11-9pm Fri & Sat. 11-10pm
Sundays In Season
www.neitalianbistro.com
319 N. Front Street In The Cotton Exchange

Italian Bistro
$-$$ • 319 N. Front St., Wilmington
• (910) 762-1222

A favorite of downtown Wilmingtonians, the Italian Bistro offers old-world Italian food with a casual, old-world Italian streetscape Ernest Hemingway would have enjoyed. This James Beard award-winning eatery offer large salads, meat lasagna and ravioli. Penne is served with alfredo or the traditional marinara sauce. The pizzas are New York style with a thin crust, and the breads, including hero and focaccia, are homemade. It's located at the front of the Cotton Exchange with plenty of free parking.

Jackson's Big Oak Barbecue
$ • 920 S. Kerr Ave., Wilmington
• (910) 799-1581

A repeated winner of local magazine polls for the area's best barbecue since it opened in 1984, Jackson's is a family-run business fully deserving of the praise. The eastern Carolina-style pork barbecue is moist and tangy, the hush puppies superior, and the friendly, knowledgeable staff is as hard-working as all get-out. The fried corn sticks are a specialty that should be a given with every meal, and if you're a fan of Brunswick stew, barbecue ribs and chicken, you won't be disappointed. The dining room is rustic and familiar, a good place to greet and meet. Jackson's is open for lunch and dinner Monday through Saturday. Contact the restaurant for event planning.

Jerry's Food, Wine and Spirits
$$$ • 7220 Wrightsville Ave., Wilmington
• (910) 256-8847

For the past eight years, Jerry's has featured

executive chef Brent Williams, who honed his culinary skills at Johnson & Wales University in Charleston. Brent specializes in continental cuisine with a focus on steaks, seafood, lamb, wild game and dishes with an Oriental or southwestern flavor. Catering is available for 50 to 500 people. Open for dinner seven days a week from 6-10 PM, reservations are recommended.

Krazy's Pizza and Subs
$ • 417 S. College Rd., Wilmington • (910) 791-0598

Krazy's Pizza and Subs has been family-owned and -operated since 1986. With a loyal customer following, it offers a variety of Italian delights in a casual atmosphere with prices that won't strain your wallet. Best known for its "kreate your own" pizza, Krazy's has a wide range of toppings sure to please any palate. Or you can choose from their six specialty pizzas. Krazy's also serves up wonderful salads, including a Greek dinner salad. Don't miss their own tasty homemade Italian dressing. Not in the mood for pizza? Try the delicious homemade lasagna, veal parmigiana or the baked ziti with meat sauce, either as an entree or a la carte. Dinner entrees come with a salad and choice of bread. Appetizers, stromboli, calzone and a large selection of subs round out the menu at Krazy's. For the bambinos, a children's menu is available, plus a balloon clown provides free entertainment every Friday evening from 5:30 to 8:30 PM.

Le Catalan
$$ • 224 S. Water St., Wilmington • (910) 815-0200

This charming waterfront cafe offers good food, fine wine and a casual atmosphere along the Cape Fear River in historic downtown Wilmington. Relax and dine on the wide outdoor deck overlooking the river or the cafe's cozy atmosphere indoors with a French cafe-style menu featuring charcuterie and cheese plates, pâté, quiche, innovative salads, soup, croissants and daily specials. Le Catalan's great selection of imported and domestic wines offer both the connoisseur and the adventurous diner a tantalizing accompaniment to their meals. Daily specials and vegetarian offerings include a soup, quiche, croissant and entree of the day. But save room for Le Catalan's to-die-for chocolate mousse. The menu's wine choices rotate bi-monthly, and a great selection of bottled wines, including a muscat and sweet white wine from Le Catalan, plus port, are available in Le Catalan's wine shop. The cafe is open Tuesday through Saturday for lunch and dinner. Sundays and Mondays are reserved for private parties, receptions and special events.

Milano's
$$$ • The Forum, 1125 Military Cut-Off Rd., Wilmington • (910) 256-8870

Your first impression of Milano's is the feeling that you've been transported to a small Italian village, particularly if you're seated in the indoor courtyard area. Milano's also has additional seating off the courtyard setting plus a separate dining room perfect for private parties, wedding receptions and business functions. Black Angus steak, fresh seafood and Italian specialties are highlights of executive chef Brad Reynolds' menu, seasoned with fresh herbs and vegetables and artfully served with delicious sauces. Tempting examples are Vitello alla Picatta, sautéed veal with capers, lemon, parsley and white wine, or the Bistecca con Funghi e Grappa, a grilled five-ounce filet served with a porcini mushroom brandy sauce. Other entree choices are equally creative, featuring pasta, veal, pork and lamb. Innovative salads or an appealing array of hot or cold appetizers are a tasty start to the evening. A popular choice is the Torta di Granchio, seared jumbo lump crab cakes served with a tomato mustard cream sauce. Milano's opens for dinner nightly. The Piano Lounge opens daily at 4:30 PM, Wednesday through Saturday, offering live entertainment. Call the restaurant or check local newspapers for the schedule.

NOFO Cafe & Market
$ • The Forum, 1125 Military Cutoff Rd., Wilmington • (910) 256-5565

Whether you're dining in for lunch, enjoying a late-afternoon snack or ordering from the deli case, NOFO Cafe & Market is a delicious choice in a casual setting. Luncheon choices include two daily specials and two homemade soups in addition to the regular menu of hearty deli sandwiches, meal-size salads and homemade desserts. Can't find a sandwich to your liking? Try it "your way" from a list of deli meats and salads, cheeses, breads, condiments and side items. If you're on the go for lunch, fax your order and they'll have it waiting for you. NOFO also offers an appetizing alternative menu for special diets, corporate lunch boxes, a take-out deli counter and catering. NOFO To Go features a daily menu of supper specials that are cooked and ready to pick up. Also check out the frozen food case for meal solutions. Sunday Brunch adds egg and breakfast entrees to the cafe's regular menu. NOFO is open for dinner, Monday through Saturday, with all ABC permits.

A colorful and appealing array of specialty foods awaits you in the market area attached to the deli. You'll find shelves of gourmet foods, condiments and sauces (many from North Carolina) in addition to mouthwatering imported choco-

lates, specialty teas and coffee beans, imported and domestic wine and much more. Gift baskets are a popular feature of the market. NOFO Cafe & Market opens at 10 AM seven days a week.

Paddy's Hollow Restaurant & Pub
$$ • The Cotton Exchange, corner of Front and Walnut Sts., Wilmington
• (910) 762-4354

Tucked away in the middle courtyard of the Cotton Exchange buildings, this narrow, intimate restaurant transports you back to friendly neighborhood pubs with an Irish flavor. Seating consists of high-backed wooden booths, tables and chairs or stools at the bar, where you can have a brew and a bite while catching up with the news, both televised and local. The lunch menu offers tasty appetizers, a soup du jour and grilled seafood, chicken or steak salads. Sandwich selections, featuring seafood, shrimp, prime rib and corned beef, are hearty and include a deli pickle slice and a choice of French fries, potato salad, pasta salad or fruit. In the mood for a burger? Paddy's 6 oz. Pub-burgers, cooked to order and accompanied by a pickle and French fries, are a real treat. In the intimacy of the high-backed booths and the subdued lighting, dinner at Paddy's can be a roman-

tic affair. The dinner menu features the fresh-catch seafood prevalent in the Cape Fear area in addition to tasty beef entrees, specifically prime rib and New York strip, chicken and barbecued baby-back ribs. Check the board or ask your server for the daily lunch and dinner specials. Need some diversion? Check out Paddy's new game room. Paddy's has all ABC permits, 16 tap handles for draft beer, and bottled beer and wine. Cigar and pipe smoking are not permitted. It's open for lunch and dinner Monday through Saturday and for lunch on Sunday.

Pearl's Seafood Restaurant
$-$$ • 3500 N. Kerr Ave., Wilmington
• (910) 763-1122

As its name implies, Pearl's menu is dominated by seafood choices, including a generous selection of fresh seafood platters — shrimp, oyster, crab leg, scallop, specialty or combination platters are examples. The die-hard seafood lover who enjoys a challenge should try the huge Captain Kenny's Barge, a combination of lightly breaded or broiled fresh seafood — flounder, shrimp, oysters and scallops in addition to boiled shrimp and fried deviled crab and clam strips — choice of potato, cole slaw, a dozen hush puppies and a

RESTAURANTS

choice of clam chowder or house salad. Finish it off by yourself in an hour and you'll win a free "I Ate The Barge" T-shirt. Pearl's Platter, a lightly breaded fresh seafood combination platter and all the fixins, is another popular choice. For the land-lubber, Pearl's offers barbecue, chicken or steak platters. Nightly dinner specials may include prime rib, whole flounder or grilled fresh-catch entrees. Lunch features a daily special, soups, salads, burgers and sandwiches. Pearl's offers home-cooked meals in a family-friendly atmosphere with children's and seniors' menus. Banquets and pri-vate parties of up to 90 people can be accommo-dated. Plus, Pearl's offers off-site catering for up to 10,000 hungry folks! Open daily for lunch, Pearl's serves dinner nightly Monday through Sat-urday.

The Pilot House
$$-$$$ • Chandler's Wharf, 2 Ann St., Wilmington • (910) 343-0200

The Pilot House is among the preeminent din-ing establishments downtown. Overlooking the Cape Fear River at Chandler's Wharf, the restau-rant occupies the historic Craig House (c. 1870) and strives for innovations with high-quality Southern regional cooking. The wide-ranging din-ner menu features sautéed and chargrilled sea-food, beef and chicken, pan-seared duck, pasta and a delectable roster of appetizers. Daily lunch and dinner specials are equally tempting. Lunch selections include generous traditional and sea-food salads, innovative sandwiches and entrees. The style of service is semiformal, with linen, Wilton pewter and teamed servers, but the man-agement successfully steers for middle ground. You will see guests dressed in everything from Bermuda shorts to tuxedos. Lunch is more casual

than dinner. The wine list is carefully chosen and well-rounded. The Pilot House features additional outdoor seating, weather permitting, and serves lunch and dinner seven days a week, year round, with brunch offered on Sunday. A children's menu is available. Reservations are recommended.

Port Land Grille
$$$ • Lumina Station, 1908 Eastwood Rd., Wilmington • (910) 256-6056

Voted Best Restaurant and Waitstaff 2003 by *Encore* magazine, this five-star restaurant alone is worth a trip to the coast. Port Land Grille knows the art of fine dining. The ambiance, indoors and out, offers an appealing sense of style with over-sized tables draped with white tablecloths, black and white photographs of Old Wrightsville Beach, comfortable rooms with a view, exquisite service and, weather permitting, picturesque dining on the patio overlooking a landscaped pond at Lu-mina Station. Though the restaurant is reminis-cent of the classy supper clubs of bygone eras, the food is its key to success.

Chef Shawn Wellersdick is renowned for his ability to transform quality ingredients into a meal of layered flavors and side dishes that rival the entree in taste and creativity. An excellent ex-ample is his version of mashed sweet potatoes (the secret involves scented vanilla beans). The menu includes meal-sized appetizers, especially when coupled with one of Port Land Grille's sal-ads. A favorite is the crab cake nestled on a bed of butter beans and served with an applewood-smoked bacon vinaigrette. The popular salad choice is characterized as a simple Southern salad — a chilled iceberg lettuce wedge with crisp ba-con and bleu cheese dressing. Entrees feature fresh seafood and organically grown meats from local

ranches. Dessert is memorable, especially Port Land Grille's signature coconut cake. This wonderful confection is seven layers of cake with a lemony filling, topped with a pistachio anglaise. The restaurant's award-winning wine list is almost exclusively American selections, especially small-production boutique wines. A popular spot for drinks and dining is the beautiful, well-stocked granite bar. Seating here overlooks the action in the open theater-style kitchen. The restaurant is completely non-smoking and offers a 45-guest dining room that is perfect for private parties and corporate events. Open year-round, Port Land Grille serves dinner Monday through Saturday. Reservations are recommended, particularly on weekends, but walk-in guests are graciously accommodated.

P. T.'s Olde Fashioned Grille
$, no checks • 4544 Fountain Dr., Wilmington • (910) 392-2293

When you want a freshly grilled burger or chicken sandwich, forget the fast-food mills. Consistently voted Best Burger by Encore magazine's annual poll, P. T.'s can't be beat. Every menu item is a package deal that includes a sandwich (whopping half-pound Angus beef burgers, tender chicken breast, hot dogs, fresh roast beef, tur-

key and more), fresh-cut, spiced, skin-on French fries (or substitute a side salad) and a soft drink, refill included. Prices are low, and quality is high. You place your order by filling in an idiot-proof order form and dropping it through the window if you're eating on the outdoor deck. Order at the counter if you're eating inside. Your meal is prepared to order and ready in about 10 minutes — fast food that doesn't taste like fast food. P. T.'s also offers an alternative to beef with the lower calorie, low-fat Gardenburger. P. T.'s is west of S. College Road across from the south end of UNCW campus. Take-out orders are welcome and may be habit-forming. P. T.'s is open daily until 9 PM.

Riverboat Landing Restaurant
$$-$$$ • 2 Market St., Wilmington • (910) 762-8240

Enjoy a panoramic sunset over the USS *North Carolina* from one of the nine intimate two-seater balconies that overlook the Cape Fear River. Downtown's landmark restaurant, The Riverboat Landing is located at the foot of Market and Water Streets nestled in a building that dates to the 1800s. A newly renovated interior decor compliments the modern cuisine — an eclectic blend of Southern regional with French, Asian and Mediterranean influences. Enjoy selections from the expansive lunch menu, including traditional comfort food, as well as sandwiches from simple to sensational. Lunch is served Tuesday through Saturday. Sunday offers a special brunch menu, including the famous Eggs Chesapeake and quiche du jour. Blending a wide assortment of breakfast and lunch entrees, brunch offers selections to suit everyone's taste.

Dinner is served every night. Begin your evening with one of the unforgettable appetizers and a cocktail from the bar. Next, enjoy a great steak, such as the Salt and Pepper Seared New York Strip or the Bronzed Grouper. A member of the professional staff will be happy to assist you in pairing a wine from an award-winning wine list. Remember not to leave without sampling some legendary desserts. From Chocolate Lava Pie a la mode to Creme Brulee Napolean, they are unforgettable. For late-night diners, a lounge menu is served until 12:30 AM. Having all ABC permits, the bar makes last call at 2 AM Tuesday through Saturday and at regular dinner hours on Sunday and Monday. A children's menu is available upon request.

INSIDERS' TIP

Enjoy a panorama of the Atlantic Ocean while dining on the pier at the Oceanic Restaurant, Wrightsville Beach.

Roly Poly Rolled Sandwiches
$ • 1 S. Front St., Wilmington
• (910) 343-1311
$ • Cornerstone Center, 1616 Shipyard Blvd., Wilmington • (910) 796-0045
$ • University Landing, 419 S. College Rd.
• (910) 452-7772

Located in three convenient Wilmington locations — downtown's historic district, an active business corridor on Shipyard Boulevard and at University Landing near UNCW — Roly Poly puts the fun back into grabbing a quick bite. Their signature rolled sandwiches feature high-quality deli meats, cheeses and delicious salads topped with fresh veggies and spreads in a huge soft-flour tortilla. The large array of choices range from the traditional to the innovative, or you can get creative with the "roll your own" option. Accompany your Roly choice with a soft drink, chips or the homemade soup of the day. Need to feed a large group? Party platters, catering and box lunches are available for meetings, seminars, picnics and other special events — corporate to casual. Call either location for details. Roly Poly is open for lunch daily and offers local weekday delivery with a $15 minimum.

Rucker John's Restaurant and More
$$ • 5511 Carolina Beach Rd., Wilmington
• (910) 452-1212

Discover Rucker Johns, a local family favorite since 1992. Renowned for high quality and attention to detail, Rucker Johns' theme is casual and the service is serious. The made-from-scratch menu features an array of fresh salads, appetizers, sandwiches, burgers, hand-stretched grilled pizzas and unbeatable homemade soups. Entree choices include grilled chicken dishes, tender baby-back ribs, awesome prime rib, succulent steaks, tasty pastas and fresh seafood. Adjoining the oak-trimmed dining room is a horseshoe-shaped bar — the perfect place to enjoy live jazz on Saturday evenings or catch the big game. A second dining area is available for business luncheons and private parties. RJ's has all ABC permits and boasts a wine list with fine selections from around the world. Located in the Myrtle Grove Shopping Center at Monkey Junction, where Carolina Beach Road meets South College Road, RJ's is open for lunch and dinner seven days a week, closing late on Friday and Saturday.

Salty's
$$$ • The Forum, 1125 Military Cutoff Rd., Wilmington • (910) 256-1118

Experience the sounds and tastes of Salty's and discover why it was voted Best New Restaurant 2003 by Encore magazine. Four of the bestsellers on the menu are the Chilean sea bass, crab cakes, grouper and Salty's marinated filet — delicious! From swing and shag to fresh seafood and tender steaks, you and your friends will enjoy fabulous wines and music in a casual yet sophisticated atmosphere with a little extra pizzazz. Salty's is open from for lunch and dinner, until the last person leaves the bar.

Szechuan 132
$$ • 419 S. College Rd., Wilmington
• (910) 799-1426

Recipient of numerous awards, Szechuan 132 stands out, due in part to the personalities of the proprietor, the engaging Joseph Hou, and his staff. Much of the menu is Cantonese, but Szechuan items, such as the hot and sour soup and Szechuan pan-fried noodles, live up to their names. The house specialties feature seafood, chicken, beef, lamb, pork and duck in a tempting range of entrees, prepared from traditional

Life's short. Don't settle for ordinary sandwiches.

ROLY POLY
the original
Rolled Sandwiches

50 Tempting Choices including....

#3 Monster Veggie
jack & Swiss cheeses - lettuce - tomato - avocado - carrot - cucumber - green pepper - mushrooms - spinach - fresh dill dressing

#10 California Turkey
turkey breast - bacon - cheddar cheese - scallions - lettuce - tomato - avocado - mango chutney - ranch dressing

#12 Smokehouse Turkey
smoked turkey breast - jack cheese - bacon - avocado - scallions - lettuce - tomato - honey mustard

#15 Ranch Roast
roast beef - mild garlic cheese spread - sundried tomatoes - bacon - lettuce - tomato - ranch dressing

#18 Philly Melt
roast beef - melted jack & cheddar cheeses - onion-mushrooms - green pepper, grilled golden brown with a side of BarBQ ranch dressing

#28 Santa Fe Chicken
chicken breast strips - melted jalapeno jack cheese-onion - tomato - ranch dressing, grilled golden brown with a side of salsa

#30 Basil Cashew Chicken
white meat chicken salad - fresh basil mayo - cashews - spicy Thai sauce - avocado - lettuce - tomato

#36 Chicken Fajita
chicken breast strips - melted cheddar - onion - green pepper - tomato - fajita sauce, grilled golden brown with a side of salsa

#37 Chicken Cordon Bleu
baked ham - chicken breast strips - melted Swiss - mushrooms - tomato - basil mayo, grilled golden brown with a side of honey mustard dressing

Each Roly Poly is made with the finest quality meats, cheeses, fresh vegetables and spreads rolled up tight in a giant soft flour tortilla.

I So. Front Street Historic Downtown Wilmington 910-343-1311	Corner of Shipyard and 17th Behind Arby's and Wendy's 910-796-0045	419 S. College Rd. University Landing 910-452-7772

Check out our platters and box lunches for your next get together!

Chinese recipes from varying provinces — Szechuan, Hunan and Chung Du among them. Entrees are prepared without MSG, and the restaurant will alter spices, salt or other ingredients upon request. Those on special diets will delight in the tasty steamed vegetable, chicken or shrimp entrees, all salt-free and oil-free, with sauces served on the side. Comfortable banquettes and high-back chairs invite guests to linger, so save room for dessert, fried ice cream or mango soufflé. Szechuan 132 offers wine, beer and has all ABC permits. Take-out orders are accepted. Szechuan 132 is in the University Landing Shopping Center. Lunch and dinner are served daily, and reservations are recommended for dinner. Its sister establishment downtown, Szechuan 130, 130 N. Front Street, (910) 762-5782, offers much the same quality and service as well as a daily buffet.

Terrazzo Pizzeria/Trattoria
$$ • Landfall Center, 1319 Military Cutoff Rd., Wilmington • (910) 509-9400

For a taste of authentic Italian cuisine, New York-style, Terrazzo is a must-visit. A cozy atmosphere indoors, outdoor patio seating, friendly service and a generous menu make dining here a pleasure. Terrazzo's incredible pizza menu offers everything — a wide selection of toppings, including vegetarian, chicken, surf and turf choices, a white pizza and Terrazzo specialty pizzas. For a light snack, the large selection of tasty appetizers are a good choice. Lunch options include a daily special or generously portioned salads that, coupled with the homemade soup of the day, make a great meal. Terrazzo's subs come hot or cold and are truly awesome. The Italian Delight entree choices

feature homemade pasta dishes with fresh vegetables, meats and cheeses in delicious sauces and served with Ciabatta bread. Nightly dinner specials often include fresh local seafood. The restaurant serves beer and a huge selection of imported and domestic wines. Terrazzo is open daily, Monday through Saturday, for lunch and dinner. Come early: This eatery is a popular spot in the Wilmington-Wrightsville Beach area.

Texas Roadhouse
$$ • 230 Eastwood Rd., Wilmington • (910) 798-1770

The Texas Roadhouse story is simple — legendary food with legendary service learned from legendary people! Everything here is made from scratch. Steaks cut by hand, award-winning ribs, fresh-baked bread and delightful sides are all made from scratch with only the highest-quality ingredients. Leave room for dessert — Granny's Apple Classic, strawberry cheesecake and a Big Ol' Brownie. Texas Roadhouse is open for lunch and dinner.

Tomatoz American Grille
$$ • S. College Rd. and Wrightsville Ave., Wilmington • (910) 313-0541

Tomatoz is a great place to satisfy both the heartiest of appetites and the requirements of a health-conscious diet. The menu borrows freely from various cultures, Italy and Southwestern North America being the most prevalent influences, with a touch of Southern cuisine added for local interest. Ingredients are all natural and considered for their health value as much as for taste. Sourdough pizzas are made fresh to order with low-fat mozzarella and are available with vegetarian toppings as well as with chicken and pepperoni. Tomatoz offers an appealing range of lunch and dinner menu options, highlighted by seafood, in-house smoked fish, chicken, beef, fresh herbs and vegetables. The menu includes appetizers, sides, entree-size salads (the Oriental salad with sesame-coated tuna steak is a favorite), soups, burritos, tostadas, sandwiches and pasta. The house specialties, served after 5 PM, feature both a seafood and a beef entree of the day, shrimp or chicken stir fry and the Salmon Veracruz, prepared with capers, olives, jalapenos and tomatoes and served with rice, black beans and chile. Portions are generous, and the dressings, sauces, salsas, breads and desserts are all made fresh in the Tomatoz kitchen. In summer, light vegetable and fruit soups are added to the menu.

Sunday brunch begins at 10 AM, with a menu offering a quiche and frittata of the day, egg dishes, shrimp and grits, huevos rancheros and some of the largest omelets in town. After dinner, save room for homemade desserts (the chocolate mousse pie is heavenly) and coffee. Tomatoz offers selected ports, wine and beer. All this in a unique brick building with spacious seating and attractive decor enlivened by local artwork. Tomatoz is open daily for lunch and dinner. If you're looking for a night out during the week, the restaurant hosts live entertainment every Tuesday, Wednesday and Thursday night with Sunday evening jazz year-round. (Read more about it in the Nightlife chapter.)

Trolly Stop
$ • 121 N. Front St., Wilmington
• (910) 343-2999

Centrally located in historic downtown Wilmington, Trolly Stop was voted Best Hot Dog in 2003 by Encore magazine's readers poll and for good reason. Trolly Stop serves all-beef Sabrett hot dogs in a variety taste combinations, including the American (chili, mustard and onion), the Cape Fear (melted cheese and mayonnaise) and, naturally, the North Carolina (chili, mustard and cole slaw). Vegetarian and fat-free hot dogs are also available. Additional menu offerings are sweet Italian sausage, their unique Burger dog, a black bean salsa burrito and nachos with toppings. Enjoy Hershey's ice cream at the downtown Wilmington and Southport locations. Visit other Trolly Stop locations in Carolina Beach, 103-A Cape Fear Boulevard, (910) 458-7557; in Southport, 111 S. Howe Street, (910) 457-7017; and in Wrightsville Beach, 94 S. Lumina Avenue, (910) 256-3421. If you're heading to North Carolinas western mountains, visit their newest location at 764 King Street in Boone.

Underground Sandwich Shoppe
$ • 103 Market St., Wilmington
• (910) 763-9686

Appropriately located "underground" on the corner of Market and Front streets in downtown Wilmington, this lively sandwich shop serves a variety of classic American choices that include everything from a grilled ham and cheese or Underground club sandwich to the Rueben and Piccadilly Philly. Their BLT is one of the best in town. Can't decide? Create your own with a choice of meats, cheeses, fixings and bread. Vegetarian options are available, and Underground often features a vegan soup of the day. Salads range from the house salad to their entree-size Italian chef salad. All sand-

FINE DINING
PRIVATE PARTIES
CATERING

HARVEST MOON
5704 OLEANDER DRIVE
910.792.0172

wiches come with a soft drink or tea and chips. Try a glass of their fresh-squeezed lemonade on a hot coastal day. It's awesome! Underground also serves beer by the glass or pitcher. The atmosphere is friendly and casual, and it's a great place to bring the family. The decor's theme suggests London's Underground Mass Transit system. An eye-catching mural, painted by local artist Chappy Valente, covers one wall of the restaurant and is thought to be one of the prime pieces of public art in downtown Wilmington. Underground is open daily.

Water Street Restaurant & Sidewalk Cafe
$$ • 5 Water St., Wilmington
• (910) 343-0042

Housed in the Quince Building (1835), a former peanut warehouse on the riverfront, Water Street Restaurant can be quite romantic with its softly lit atmosphere that evokes a by-gone era in downtown Wilmington. The restaurant offers moderately priced, healthy meals all day, every day. Water Street's innovative dinner menu places emphasis on fresh-catch seafood, beef, a generous use of vegetables, delicious homemade dressings and daily soup specials (homemade, of course). Entrees include choice of Caesar or house salad and fresh-baked bread. For lunch, try the Water Greek Salad (toppings include tabouli, feta cheese, pepperoncini and sun-dried tomatoes), a black bean burrito served with rice and a small green salad, or a host of sandwiches, from the 7 oz. Water Street burger to the Oyster Po-Boy. Their Portobello mushroom sandwich is an especially good choice. Sidewalk seating is in full view of

Delicious coastal cuisine is found in every southern coast town.

Photo: Jay Tervo

the Cape Fear River, and live piano music is frequent. In fact, Water Street Restaurant is an attractive nightspot featuring live entertainment — jazz and Dixieland bands, flamenco guitar and more — Wednesday through Sunday nights. Lot parking is available for the restaurant's patrons at the corner of Dock and Water streets.

Wallace

The Mad Boar Restaurants
$-$$$ • 111 River Village Pl., Wallace
• (910) 285-8888

Just a 35-minute drive from Wilmington, the Mad Boar Restaurants encompass three distinct dining options under one roof. The Mad Boar is a casual, comfortable restaurant offering friendly service and a menu designed to please every member of the family, including appetizers, soup, salads, burgers, sandwiches and pizza. Dinner entrees feature steak, chicken and seafood. The Mad Boar is open daily for lunch and dinner. The full menu is also served in the restaurant's bar until 10 PM. Appetizers are available in the bar until its 11 PM closing. The Celtic Court banquet hall is sure to be a most appealing setting for special events and corporate functions with seating for more than 300 guests. The hall's rich atmosphere and sumptuous decor—handpainted gold leaf walls, alabaster chandeliers, hand-carved wood accent bar, lush velvet curtains—take you back in time to the splendor of Camelot. Celtic Court amenities include a bar and elevated stage. The Mad Boar restaurants are easily reached from the

southern coast and Wilmington via Interstate 40 West. Take Exit 385, then turn right.

Wrightsville Beach

Bluewater, An American Grill
$$ • 4 Marina St., Wrightsville Beach
• (910) 256-8500

Located just over the bridge on the Intracoastal Waterway, Bluewater is a sprawling two-story restaurant that offers great food with a panoramic view of the waterway that you won't want to miss. Open daily for lunch and dinner year round, Bluewater serves hearty American cuisine with a distinctly coastal flair in a tastefully nautical atmosphere. Lunch or mid-day snack choices include a dozen tasty appetizer selections (the hot crab dip is a must), numerous salad options, soups and chowder, sandwiches and generous lunch-size entrees. The coconut shrimp plate and the seafood lasagna are excellent choices, but the lump crab cake entree is incredible. Bluewater's dinner menu is equally generous in its choices and, while fresh-catch seafood is an obvious feature, the restaurant also excels with prime rib and steak entrees, chicken and barbecue baby-back ribs. Seating is available indoors on two floors, on a waterside patio downstairs and an intimate covered terrace upstairs. Enjoy live entertainment — light jazz and music with a coastal flavor — on Sunday afternoons in the high season (or as weather permits). Bluewater has all ABC permits and serves a full range of imported and domestic wine and beer.

Causeway Cafe

**$, no credit cards • 114 Causeway Dr.,
Wrightsville Beach • (910) 256-3730**

Full of character and friendly service, Causeway Cafe offers possibly the best breakfast in Wrightsville Beach. In fact, Encore magazine's annual Best Of readers' poll made it official in 2002. Traditional made-to-order egg plates are hearty and standard fare. Choose from 15 different omelets, including the Carolina Blue Crab and Beefy Vegetable as well as traditional options, made from three eggs and cheese, served with hash browns or grits. Not in the mood for eggs? The giant specialty Belgian waffles, in nine mouthwatering flavors, malted pancakes and French toast are tasty alternatives. Lunch options include daily blackboard specials, sandwiches and salads dominated by fresh seafood. Subs, burgers, steak and other sandwiches are also good choices. A child's menu is available for children younger than 10. In-season and on weekends off-season, be prepared to wait for a table. It's worth the time spent on the covered front deck, and the folks at Causeway thoughtfully provide complimentary coffee. Open seven days a week for breakfast and lunch, Causeway Cafe is located near the drawbridge beside Redix beach store.

Clarence Foster's Restaurant and Catering

**$$ • 22 N. Lumina Ave., Wrightsville
Beach • (910) 256-0224**

Clarence Foster's is a cozy and casual Wrightsville Beach restaurant located at the heart of the island. Menu offerings begin with a choice of several outstanding starters that include not-to-be-missed spinach-artichoke dip and crab dip, each served with toasted pita points. Foster's original made-fresh-daily seafood chowder is award-winning, and salad options include grilled, blackened or fried seafood or chicken. Love pasta? The chefs at Foster's allow you to create your own entree from lists of pastas, sauces, veggies, meats and cheeses. Dinner entrees feature a variety of popular signature items with steak, seafood, chicken, smoked sausage and pork. If you're in the mood for beef, the 14 oz. rib eye is a delicious and hearty meal. But if seafood is what you came to the beach for, try the Captain's Platter or one of the nightly specials. Lobster night at Foster's features a whole Maine lobster, baked potato and salad for $15.95. The Steamer Bar offers steamed seafood — shrimp, clams and oysters. A children's menu is available.

Foster's bar and lounge area is a comfortable place to meet friends, especially on Wednesday night when live comedy is featured. Wine and full bar service are also an option. Open at 4:30 PM, the restaurant's menu is served there, with a lighter bar menu available after 10 PM. Closed Monday and Tuesday, call for off-season hours. Foster's also offers catering and handles a wide range of events from "bikini to black tie." Call the restaurant for details. Free customer parking is located on the side of the restaurant.

Dockside Restaurant

**$$ • 1308 Airlie Rd., Wrightsville Beach
• (910) 256-2752**

The view of the Intracoastal Waterway alone is worth a trip to Dockside, as indicated by Encore's award of Best Outside Dining 2003. But if you're

craving delicious and well-prepared local seafood, you'll also find the dining experience to be a mouthwatering adventure. The menu, not surprisingly, is dominated by fresh seafood. Broiled or fried (lightly coated with fine cracker meal) combination platters, snow crab legs, shrimp Creole and the popular Baja tuna are just a few of the dinner options. The seafood lasagna, a Dockside favorite, is definitely worth a try. Ask your server about the day's fresh catch, and check Dockside's special board for daily soup, sandwich, wraps and chef's specials. The lunch menu, available all day, is a generous listing of soups, salads, sandwiches and house specials, including broiled or fried seafood plates, served with French fries and cole slaw. Be sure to try the homemade Key lime pie. A children's menu is available. Dockside has all ABC permits, wine and imported, domestic and draft beers. Seating is spectacular anywhere in the restaurant, but you have a choice of indoors with a view, on the outdoor deck along the ICW or outdoors under the canopy. Dockside is open daily for lunch and dinner.

King Neptune
$$ • 11 N. Lumina Ave., Wrightsville Beach • (910) 256-2525

King Neptune has been in business since 1946, outlasting hurricanes and the competition but not its appeal. From soups and chowders to steamers, platters and hearty specialties that include steaks and pizza, King Neptune focuses on seafood and does it well. Many menu items have a distinc-

tive island flair, such as the Voodoo Grouper, Curried Island Shrimp, Rasta Pasta and Jamaican Jerk Chicken. The dining room is large and bright, decorated in Caribbean colors, with local art, beach umbrellas and photographs. The children's menu is unique in that it was selected and decorated by the third and fourth grades of Wrightsville Beach Elementary School.

After dinner, the adjoining lounge is lively and offers perhaps the widest selection of rums on the Cape as well as an international selection of beers. King Neptune serves dinner seven days a week and offers senior citizen discounts. Free parking is available in the lot across the street.

Oceanic Restaurant
$$-$$$ • 703 S. Lumina Ave., Wrightsville Beach • (910) 256-5551

Few culinary experiences are as delightful as dining on the pier at the Oceanic, and Insiders know that there's nothing better, or more romantic, than a pier table in the moonlight. By day, as pelicans and sea gulls kite overhead and the surf crashes below, you could be enjoying a chilled beverage, fresh blackened tuna or some of the region's most acclaimed crab dip. Should the weather turn angry, the Oceanic's three floors of indoor seating offer breathtaking panoramic views. Off-season, the third floor, which accommodates seating for up to 78, is a sought-after location for wedding receptions, birthday parties and corporate functions. Voted Best Seafood Restaurant by Encore magazine's annual poll (a four-year running honor for

INSIDERS' TIP
Mark your calendar for Alleigh's New Year's Eve celebration, Super Bowl Party and annual Thanksgiving Day luncheon.

No matter what time of year the beach is a beautiful place.

Photo: Jay Tervo

The catch of the day.

Photo: Jay Tervo

this popular restaurant), the Oceanic offers a menu that is satisfying, delicious and dominated by fresh seafood. From entree salads, seafood platters and specialties to chicken and steaks, the menu is quite varied and includes items for kids. Entrees include a variety of extras ranging from salads, seafood gumbo and heavenly she-crab soup to hush puppies, slaw, rice pilaf, vegetables, potatoes and confetti orzo. The Super Duper Grouper, pan-seared grouper in a crust of cashew nuts and sesame seeds served over celery mashed potatoes with roasted red pepper butter, is just one of the popular selections. Nightly specials feature fresh-catch seafood that can be grilled, sauteed, blackened or prepared with Cajun spices.

Full bar service, including domestic and imported beers, is available, and the juices used in mixed drinks are all squeezed fresh daily. Those seeking the perfect margarita should definitely stop here. The Oceanic also offers a generous wine list, with most available by the glass. The maritime decor features replicas of historic newspapers, the aerial photography of Conrad Lowman and a spectacular Andy Cobb sculpture of a huge copper grouper that are attractions in themselves. Lunch and dinner are served daily. Parking is free for patrons; towing of all other cars is strictly enforced.

South Beach Grill
$$ • 100 S. Lumina Ave., Wrightsville Beach • (910) 256-4646

One of two restaurants given a four-star rating in this area, South Beach Grill offers exquisitely prepared fare in exotic coastal ambience. The decor is marked by rich colors with fresh flowers on each table and dark wood tables and armchairs. The location, immediately south of the fixed bridge near the center of the beach, is convenient and overlooks Banks Channel, which is especially nice at sunset from the patio tables outside. Most important, meals are tasty, healthy and creative, emphasizing fresh-catch seafood, poultry and beef, plus burgers, sandwiches, wraps and an array of interesting appetizers, such as crabmeat nachos served on flour tortillas or South Beach's original fried pickles served with ranch dressing. All lunches include French fries or homemade potato chips; dinner entrees include a choice of house or Caesar salad. Lunch and dinner specials are offered daily. Among the imported and domestic beer offerings is the wonderful Front Street Raspberry Wheat ale, brewed in downtown Wilmington. South Beach Grill has a children's menu and all ABC permits. Take-out orders are welcome. South Beach Grill opens for lunch and dinner daily. Reservations are accepted.

SOUTH BEACH GRILL

"★★★★-Exceptional"
Wilmington Star-News 11/02

Casual Dining • Serious Food
Open for Lunch at 11am
Nightly Dinner Specials

100 S. Lumina Ave. • All ABC Permits
Wrightsville Beach • 910-256-4646

Trolly Stop
$ • 94 S. Lumina Ave., Wrightsville Beach • (910) 256-3421

The Trolly Stop, a beach tradition since 1976 and voted 2001's Best Hot Dog by Encore magazine, offers hot dogs in a surprising array of choices. How about a Surfers Hot Dog with cheese, bacon bits and mustard? Or go Nuclear with mustard, jalapeno peppers and cheese on your dog. Want something more traditional? The North Carolina Hot Dog is as Tarheel as they come with chili, mustard and cole slaw. Trolly Stop offers all-meat, all-beef Sabrett, non-fat or vegetarian (soy) options in their "dogs." Other popular items include a black bean burrito and nachos with toppings. The Wrightsville Beach location is open daily. Their other locations are open Monday through Saturday at 111 S. Howe Street in Southport, (910) 457-7017; and 103-A Cape Fear Boulevard in Carolina Beach, (910) 458-7557 (closed off-season); and in downtown Wilmington at 121 N. Front Street, (910) 343-2999.

Carolina Beach and Kure Beach

Big Daddy's Seafood Restaurant
$$ • 202 K Ave., Kure Beach • (910) 458-8622

A Kure Beach institution for three decades, Big Daddy's serves a variety of better-quality seafood and combination platters. In addition to seafood, the restaurant offers choice steaks, prime rib and chicken every day in a family-

RESTAURANTS

oriented, casual setting. Seafood can be broiled, fried, char-grilled or steamed. Highlights of Big Daddy's menu include an inexpensive all-you-can-eat salad bar; a large selection of seafood and beef entrees; special plates for seniors and children; and the sizable Surf and Turf (filet mignon and a choice of snow crab legs or char-grilled barbecue shrimp). An after-dinner walk along the nearby beachfront or on the Kure Beach fishing pier (both are a short block away) further adds to Big Daddy's appeal. The restaurant's interior, consisting of several rooms and a total seating capacity of about 500 people, comes as a surprise; it doesn't seem that big from the outside. Rare and unusual maritime memorabilia make for entertaining distractions. Entrance to Big Daddy's is through a colorful gift shop offering novelties and taffy. Patrons frequently make secret wishes and toss coins into the fountain there. Located at the only stoplight in Kure Beach, Big Daddy's has all ABC permits and ample parking in front and across the street.

The Cottage
$$ • 1 N. Lake Park Blvd., Carolina Beach
• (910) 458-4383
The Cottage occupies a tastefully renovated 1916 beach cottage, which has been awarded historic plaques from the Federal Point Historical Society and the Wilmington Historic Foundation. The interior is modern, open and airy, preserving the several ground-level rooms as separate dining areas. An outdoor-covered deck, accompanied by a wonderful ocean breeze, makes al fresco dining a special pleasure. As a seafood grill, The Cottage features coastal cuisine at its finest. In addition to fresh -atch seafood, dinner offerings include chicken and the best in beef. The evening pasta selections feature saffron fettuccine and basil linguini, of course with seafood. The lunch menu offers delectable sandwiches, a favorite being the Carolina crab cake. Remember to save room for dessert at The Cottage, as the Berries Napoleon is fantastic and the Key lime pie is a coastal favorite. The Cottage has all ABC permits and an extensive wine list. In spring 2003 the Cottage opened a wine bar in the newly renovated upstairs area of the building. A small children's menu is available. The Cottage is open for lunch and dinner Monday through Saturday year round.

INSIDERS' TIP

You can find breakfast-all-day places, which serve meals complete with grits and biscuits, all over the southern coastal area.

Deck House Casual Dining
$$ • 205 Charlotte Ave., Carolina Beach
• (910) 458-1026
Deck House offers American, from- scratch cuisine heavily influenced by local fresh catch seafood. The exterior reflects the building's history as a church, but the decor inside is tastefully nautical. The restaurant's regular menu features a tasty variety of appetizers, soups, salads and entrees, but the nightly board specials are the draw, primarily because there are so many to choose from — 6 to 8 appetizers and 14 to 20 entrees. A mouthwatering dilemma since all are innovative and skillfully prepared from the freshest seafood and produce available. Entrees also may include chicken, pasta and steak served with a choice of salad, grouper chowder or Manhattan clam chowder and, unless entree is served over pasta, a choice of baked potato, house potato, rice pilaf, French fries or mixed vegetables. The relaxed, friendly atmosphere invites lingering over coffee and dessert. The Deck House has all ABC permits and serves beer and wine. Dinner is served nightly in-season. The restaurant is closed on Monday in the off-season. Reservations are not accepted.

Freddie's Restaurant
$$ • 111 K Ave., Kure Beach
• (910) 458-5979
Dining at Freddie's is a curiously pleasant experience. The room is cozy, almost tiny, and the seashore murals, greenery, checkered table coverings and coastal collectibles smack of Kure Beach. The service is coastal Carolina friendly with servers dressed in tuxedo vest aprons and an owner who is likely to come by and chat. The food is hearty Italian fare, well-prepared and thoroughly homemade. Barbara's famous four-layer lasagna is just like Mom's (if Mom was Italian). Nightly specials are unusual — we like the portabello mushroom parmigiana — and there's always a wide choice of meat including chops, seafood, poultry or pasta. All entrees come with a romaine salad, Italian dressing, crusty bread and a side of pasta. Tiramisu leads the dessert menu, which includes Key lime pie, ice cream cookie delight, and chocolate mousse. Freddie's is open Tuesday through Sunday nights year-round. Reservations are accepted for parties of five or more. You'll find Freddie's a few steps from the Kure Beach Pier, under an awning painted red, white and green. Naturally.

Harbor Masters Restaurant and Lounge
$$ • 315 Canal Dr., Carolina Beach
• (910) 458-7013

The view from Harbor Masters overlooks the Carolina Beach marina, making the perfect setting for this lively restaurant. The full-service menu includes seafood, beef, chicken and pasta. Among the favorites are Harbor Masters' Bourbon Street rib eye, the Hellenic shrimp scampi, broiled crab cakes and a nightly special steamed seafood platter. Appetizer choices are plentiful and range from seafood chowder to Thai wings and Potato Rags — shredded potatoes topped with crispy bacon and ranch dressing. Additional nightly specials, desserts and a children's menu are highlights. Did you spend your day fishing? A unique offering at Harbor Masters is the "You Catch 'Em, We Cook 'Em" service. Bring in your fresh catch, and the restaurant will broil, fry or blacken it, then serve it home-style with French fries, cole slaw and hush puppies. (Ask your charter captain or the restaurant's staff for details.) When crabs are in season, Harbor Masters holds a reservations-only Maryland-style Steamed Crab Night. (Call for schedule and reservations.) The restaurant has all ABC permits, beer and wine. The adjoining lounge also offers a full menu. Harbor Masters is open nightly for dinner.

The Lighthouse Restaurant
$$ • 113 K Ave., Kure Beach
• (910) 458-5608

Intimate and cozy, The Lighthouse offers a staggering amount of tasty menu choices plus five nightly special chef's suggestions and a soup and potato du jour. Lunch can be light or filling, with choices ranging from signature starters and homemade seafood chowder (their recipe won in the 2001 Pleasure Island chowder competition) or soup to plentiful salads, seafood (broiled or fried) plates and several hearty sandwiches. Selections from the raw bar and steamers portion of the menu include steamed plain or spicy shrimp, oysters and clams on the half shell, a bucket of oysters or a platter of clams. Dinner at The Lighthouse expands the lunch menu to include those items and several outstanding entrees. As with most coastal restaurants, fresh seafood is a priority here. The Lighthouse crab cakes and broiled seafood as well as the char-grilled steaks and generously portioned roasted prime rib are all local favorites. Other selections include Caribbean appetizers and entrees. The Lighthouse's award-winning team of culinary artists are led by nationally known

chef and owner Walter Harris. The restaurant's atmosphere, beautifully decorated by co-partner Debbie Pulley, enhances your dining experience. Take-out orders and catering are available. The emphasis is on casual dining at The Lighthouse, open daily for lunch and dinner from Memorial Day to Labor Day.

The attached lounge is casual and family-oriented with a dining room that seats approximately 45 guests. Tunes from the jukebox and a pool table provide amusement. The restaurant's full menu is available here, as is live entertainment on weekends. The Lighthouse has all ABC permits, beer and a fine selection of wines.

Michael's Seafood Restaurant & Catering
$$, no checks • Federal Point Shopping Center, 1018 N. Lake Park Blvd., Carolina Beach • (910) 458-7761

Winner of the 2001 Restaurant of the Year Award (Wilmington Chamber of Commerce Small Business Coalition), Michael's is a popular locals' choice. Michael's dinner menu is available all day, and fresh seafood, either steamed or broiled, is the specialty here. Nothing is fried. Alternative menu options include a good selection of steak, chicken, pasta and pork chops. Michael's updates its menu seasonally and offers lunch and nightly specials. Lunch features the award-winning Captain M's Seafood Chowder, a homemade soup of the day and a variety of sandwiches. A children's menu is available. Enjoy the indoor dining area dominated by a 700-gallon aquarium of the staff's "pets," or outdoor dining on the deck with live entertainment on the weekends. The restaurant has all ABC permits and serves imported and domestic beer and wine. Off-site catering services are also available. Michael's is open for lunch and dinner daily year-round.

Mama Mia's Italian Restaurant
$$ • 6 Lake Park Blvd., Carolina Beach
• (910) 458-9228

Lace curtains adorn the front windows of this quaint Italian restaurant in the heart of Carolina Beach. The menu offers a variety of dining choices. Dominating the menu's continental specialties are seafood, chicken and veal prepared in traditional pasta dishes and served with homemade sauces. Chicken Parmigiana, seafood lasagna, veal Marsala and shrimp scampi are a few examples. Nightly specials, often with fresh seafood, are featured. Mama Mia's also offers soups, salads, homemade pizza and a large selection of sandwiches and subs. Everything is available for take-out, and the restaurant delivers for free on Carolina Beach. A children's menu is available for children ages 12 and younger. Domestic and imported beer and wine are served. Open year-round, Mama Mia's serves dinner Sunday through Thursday and lunch and dinner on Friday and Saturday.

The SeaWitch Cafe
$$ • 227 Carolina Ave. N., Carolina Beach
• (910) 458-8682

The SeaWitch Cafe, located near Carolina Beach's oceanfront, features a menu rich in regional cuisine. Dine inside in the crisp setting or enjoy a leisurely meal on the covered wrap-around porch on the quarterdeck, which overlooks a beautifully landscaped courtyard. A bandstand in the corner of the courtyard offers an environment of wonderful entertainment showcasing some of the best bands around. This is the perfect spot for the ultimate seashore dining experience. If the same old fish recipes bore you, try the SeaWitch fish specialties, including catfish served fish-camp style, cedar plank salmon and a tuna steak with a wonderful ginger soy glaze. Fresh fish, such as yellow tail, tilapia and triggerfish, are popular choices. Seawitch also offers a variety of sandwiches, including Cajun Prime Rib, Beach Burger, Islands Classic Crab Cake and the famous half-pound Chargrilled Burger. Among the salad selections, the Roasted Almond Chicken is a favorite. Seawitch offers seafood platters, steaks, chicken, dinners for two and a variety of desserts to round out your meal. In season, the Cafe serves lunch and dinner Wednesday through Saturday. Sundays, the island's favorite brunch is served from 10 AM to 3 PM. Available for all your catering needs, the SeaWitch will host rehearsal dinners, weddings, receptions and parties for two or 200. The adjoining Tiki Bar offers a full-service bar. Call for entertainment and special event updates and off-season hours.

Trolly Stop
$ • 103-A Cape Fear Blvd., Carolina Beach
• (910) 458-7557

Voted best hot dog in Encore magazine's 2001 readers poll, Trolly Stop is centrally located in the heart of Carolina Beach and offers an all-beef Sabrett hot dog to suit almost any whim. Try the classic North Carolina dog with chili, mustard and cole slaw, the Snow's Cut (melted cheese and mayo) or the Carolina Beach (special sauce, mustard and onion). Vegetarian, all-meat and nonfat hot dogs are also available. Trolly Stop's menu includes sweet Italian sausage, their signature

Burger dog, a black bean burrito and nachos with toppings. Other Trolly Stop locations are in Wilmington, 121 N. Front Street, (910) 343-2999; Southport, 111 S. Howe Street, (910) 457-7017; and Wrightsville Beach, 94 S. Lumina Avenue, (910) 256-3421. The Carolina Beach location closes during the winter months.

Bald Head Island

The Bald Head Island Club
$$-$$$ • Bald Head Island
• (910) 457-7320

Refined yet somewhat relaxed, the Club dining room offers a warm atmosphere in which to enjoy a fine selection of seafood specialties, char-grilled steaks, pasta and fresh desserts. Regional seafood and the freshest vegetables are a hallmark of the restaurant's cuisine. The wine list is extensive and offers premium vintages. The weekly gala buffet on Saturdays, a sumptuous fixed-price feast, is a deservedly popular summer event. Set in a building reminiscent of coastal New England, the dining room is modulated by wood, carpeting and a commanding ocean view. The ambience is less formal in the Club Lounge, with a grill menu available for lunch and dinner. The lounge's bar is fully stocked, and live entertainment is a feature on Friday and Saturday nights in season.

Entry to the Club dining room and the Club Lounge require at least a temporary membership, which is included in accommodation rates for all properties leased through Bald Head Island Limited. Reservations are requested.

The Maritime Market
$ • Maritime Way, Bald Head Island
• (910) 457-7450

This is a deli and sandwich counter at the new Maritime Market grocery store. The well-prepared, variety of sandwiches, salads and hot foods provides a delightful break while shopping. Some offerings include gourmet salads, taco salad, rotisserie chicken, stuffed Cornish game hens, meat loaf, and wraps. The bright and spacious new market is located off Muscadine Wynd in the maritime forest area of the island.

River Pilot Cafe
$-$$ • Bald Head Island • (910) 457-7390

The newly remodeled River Pilot Cafe has the island's finest view of the Cape Fear River and serves breakfast, lunch and dinner in a more casual setting than the Club dining room. Nonetheless, the expanded wine list and fine linen provide an upscale tenor. The menu emphasizes Southern cuisine in its use of regional seafood, fresh vegetables, meats and daily specials. Enjoy a late-night menu and your favorite cocktail in the adjoining River Pilot Lounge. In summer, the cafe serves the island's best breakfasts. It's also a superb vantage from which to view stunning sunsets while enjoying a meal or drink. The River Pilot is open daily for breakfast, lunch and dinner.

Southport and Oak Island

Bogey's
$ - $$$ • 5908 E. Oak Island Dr.. Oak Island • (910) 278-4400

Bogey's is a bright, clean restaurant with diverse seating — high director's chairs at the bar, banquettes and tables — with room left over for dancing. Daily lunch and dinner specials add to Bogey's already full menu, featuring fresh local seafood and steak. Bogey's is open for lunch and dinner (until midnight) Monday through Saturday. Call for off-season hours.

Lighthouse Restaurant
$-$$ • 705 Ocean Dr., Oak Island • (910) 278-9238

The ocean view alone is worth a visit, but this cozy, family-friendly restaurant, located at the Yaupon Pier, serves hearty meals at a reasonable price. Breakfasts at the Lighthouse, served until noon, feature all the traditional egg plates, omelets, pancakes, side items and breakfast sandwiches. Better come hungry if the Fisherman's Special — two eggs, country ham, grits or hash browns, toast or biscuit and three pancakes — tempts you. The lunch menu offers clam chowder, fried seafood baskets and a generous selection of sandwiches and burgers. Grilled, blackened and fried seafood and meat and vegetables dominate the dinner selections, which also include a variety of appetizers, salads and pasta. Check the board for daily specials. Beer and wine are available. The Lighthouse Restaurant is open daily.

Little Bits
$ • 5902 E. Oak Island Dr., Oak Island • (910) 278-6430

In the area since 1975, Little Bits has become somewhat of a tradition. Those looking for a home-style breakfast or a light lunch whipped up before their eyes and served with a smile, found their way to Little Bits. And now they are finding their way to the new location on the main street, where the owner, Little Bit, has transformed a small building into an American-style eatery with red and white decor and successfully incorporated the elegant fans and wall hangings from her native Vietnam in the scheme. Breakfast and lunch are served daily.

Lucky Fisherman
$-$$ • 4419 Long Beach Rd. SE (NC Hwy. 133), Southport • (910) 457-9499

Family owned and operated, this lively establishment offers a huge all-you-can-eat seafood buffet Tuesday through Sunday. There are usually more than 30 hot items to choose from, including chicken and nine vegetables made from old low-country recipes. The salad and dessert bars are equally expansive. Both are included in the price of the buffet. Nightly specials keep the offerings varied. Entrees are available a la carte and include fresh fried or broiled fish and seafood, crab legs, steaks and chicken. A separate children's menu offers popular kid-size meals. Wine and beer are available. Lucky Fisherman accepts take-out orders. Reservations and special parties are welcome. The restaurant is closed from December first until February 14 each year.

The Pharmacy Restaurant & Lounge
$$$$ • 110 E. Moore St., Southport • (910) 457-5577

Nestled in the heart of historic Southport, this attractive restaurant offers the best fine dining in town. The location once housed Brunswick County's first pharmacy, dating back to 1896. Originally a wooden structure, the drugstore was replaced by the current brick version in 1905 and, although changing hands several times, operated as a pharmacy until 1975. Current owners Dan and Kelli Menna have created a charming and relaxed atmosphere conducive to fine dining with table linens, fresh flowers and candlelight. The Pharmacy menu's emphasis is placed on the freshest regional seafood, produce and greens available. Entrees also include Certified Angus beef, pork and game, often accompanied with innovative sauces and accompaniments. The domestic and imported wine list is extensive, and the restaurant's lounge has all ABC permits. Desserts, made in-house, shouldn't be missed. The Pharmacy is open for lunch Wednesday through Saturday and for dinner Wednesday through Sunday. Reservations are encouraged.

Russell's Place Restaurant
$ • 5700 E. Oak Island Dr., Oak Island • (910) 278-3070

Among Long Beach residents, Russell's Place (formerly Marge's Restaurant & Waffle House) is one of the most popular diner-style eateries for breakfast and lunch. No matter how crowded it gets, the food is served hot, fast and with a smile, and no one will rush you. Table-to-table conversation comes easily as folks dine on large omelets, flaky biscuits, pancakes and Belgian waffles for breakfast and entrees, sandwiches and burgers for lunch. Russell's Place is open daily for breakfast (served all day) and lunch. Take-out orders are welcome.

San Felipe Restaurante Mexicano
$ • 4961-9 Long Beach Rd., Southport • (910) 454-0950

For authentic Mexican cuisine in an awesome array of choices, San Felipe is hard to beat. Located in the Live Oak Village Shopping Center, San Felipe serves lunch and dinner daily in an inviting and friendly atmosphere. The decor is tastefully Mexican, and seating might be a cozy table or booths long enough to accommodate the whole family. San Felipe's made-fresh-daily traditional Mexican cuisine can be ordered in combinations or specialty entrees, with beef, chicken and seafood. The lunch-only options number over 26. Another combination list offers 30 more. The menu boasts an appealing list of appetizers, vegetarian combinations, tasty Mexican desserts and a child's plate menu for children under age 12. Locals say that San Felipe has the best margaritas, regular and flavored, in town. The restaurant also has all ABC permits and serves Mexican and domestic beer. Ask about drink and lunch specials. Take out is available.

Sandfiddler Seafood Restaurant
$$ • 1643 N. Howe St. (N.C. Hwy. 211), Southport • (910) 457-6588

With its high-pitched roof, plainly set tables and nautical decor, this large establishment offers rustic ambience and affordable low-country cuisine. Lunch specials, served with hush puppies, slaw and fries, are low-priced. Landlubbers will find plenty of landfood to choose from, including steaks and pit-cooked pork barbecue. Most of the regional seafood staples are available, including deviled crabs, fried fantail shrimp stuffed with crabmeat, and a good selection of combination platters. You can get take-out orders too. The Sandfiddler serves dinner year round and lunch every day in season except Saturday. Ask about prime rib specials on Fridays and Saturdays. Private dining facilities are available.

Thai Peppers
$$ • 115 E. Moore St., Southport • (910) 457-0095

An uncommon dining experience in the southern coastal area, Thai Peppers demands a visit. Thai foods are influenced equally by China and India, so you'll find familiar appetizers, soups and stir-fried entrees from China but also delicious Thai hybrids. You'll find such Thai specialties as satay (skewered meat), ajard (cucumber salad), tom kha gai (chicken coconut milk soup), a wide variety of stir-fries, rice and curries. Those who shy away from curry may become true believers once they sample the several varieties offered here. The fried basil leaves with meat (chicken, beef or pork), the stir-fried ginger with meat, and the green curry should not be missed. Thai food tends to be spicy, but Thai Peppers will adjust the heat of any dish to taste, avoiding pepper spice entirely if you wish. (You can always spice it yourself with the condiments on the table.) Any menu item can be prepared without meat. Excellent bargains are the lunch specials (appetizer, soup, entree and rice), which change every day. Iced Thai coffee or Thailand's Singha beer are excellent accompaniments. Founded by Voravit "Tic" Hemawong, a native of Bangkok, Thai Peppers is casual and offers sheltered outdoor seating and ample space for large parties. Meals are often served with contemporary Thai music playing in the background. It's open for lunch and dinner Monday through Saturday in-season. Call for winter hours. Take-out orders are welcome, and reservations are recommended for parties of more than five.

Trolly Stop
$ • 111 S. Howe St., Southport • (910) 457-7017

Walking through historic Southport can work up an appetite, and Trolly Stop's long list of all-beef Sabrett hot dogs is sure to appeal. Choose from the Southport (topped with special sauce, mustard and onions), the Oak Island (tomato salsa, mustard and onions), the Old Baldy (plain, of course!) and everything in between. Vegetarian, all-meat and nonfat hot dogs are additional options. Trolly Stop also serves grilled sandwiches, sweet Italian sausage, a black bean burrito and nachos with toppings. The Southport and downtown Wilmington locations also serve Hershey's ice cream.

Turtle Island Restaurant and Catering
$$-$$$ 6220 E. Oak Island Dr., Oak Island • (910) 278-4944

Turtle Island Restaurant and Catering opened in November 2001, but the managers, far from being new to the business, have a wealth of restaurant experience among them.

Playing in the ocean can work up a big appetite, and you'll find plenty to satisfy it here.

Photo: Jay Tervo

The decor is inviting, casual and tropical from the coral walls to the jungle print tablecloths to the tanks of tropical fish. A good variety of wines is available, and the menu is intriguing, including such items as Wings Over Oak Island and Hot Crab Dip for appetizers. In addition to the entree specials, the restaurant serves Calabash-style seafood, pasta and sandwiches — and with such flair! Just wait until you see the work of art that is your meal. Music on the weekends attracts diners to the wooden dance floor. (Call during the off season to inquire about entertainment.) Turtle Island is open seven days, but come early or take advantage of call-ahead seating (reservations are available only for parties of six or more).

Yacht Basin Provision Company
**$$ • 130 Yacht Basin Dr., Southport
• (910) 457-0654**

To put yourself in mind of old Key West, discover the Yacht Basin Provision company. Coastal Living magazine named it one of the country's "Top 25 Seafood Dives" in their May/June 2001 issue. The Provision Company has the best decor possible, the Southport Yacht Basin and waterfront. Sit on the open-air, covered deck that serves as a dining room. Watch the boats in the Intracoastal Waterway, the ships going out to sea, the Oak Island Lighthouse standing guard and the sun setting beyond the Oak Island bridge. Specialties of the house include great shrimp and crab cakes, conch fritters and grouper salad. Other salads and hamburgers are available as well. Open for lunch and dinner seven days a week during the season, the Provision Company has all ABC permits and is something of a nightspot. You may arrive by sea as boat slips are available. The Provision Company is open from mid-March through mid-November.

South Brunswick Islands

Archibald's Delicatessen & Rotisserie
$ • 2991 Holden Beach Rd. SW, Holden Beach • (910) 842-6888

We love the sandwiches and subs at Archibald's almost as much as the homemade desserts, and most people we meet around Holden Beach do too. The deli offers a modest menu of fine quality and value. Take the Richie's Roaster for instance — rotisserie chicken breast with provolone and garnish on a roll. Or Archie's B.L.E.S.T. — bacon, lettuce, egg salad, tomato on fresh

RESTAURANTS

honey-wheat toast. Pork ribs are another rotisserie specialty you'll want to try. You can design your own sandwich or sub or choose from a selection of excellent fresh salad plates and homemade soups. Sliced deli meats and cheeses, of a variety usually not seen outside the largest supermarket deli counters, are available to go. Many varieties of quiche are served, and fresh fruit pies are available in season. The screened-in patio is pleasant during mild weather. Archibald's serves lunch and, in high season, dinner in a comfortable, clean, casual shop, housed in a curious round building. The staff can put together party platters and complete dinners as well.

Crabby Oddwaters Restaurant and Bar
$$ • 310 Sunset Blvd., Sunset Beach • (910) 579-6372

If the food weren't so darn good, this upstairs restaurant would still be worth a visit just to read the story of how it got its "damp and crawly name" (a story told in one easy-to-remember sentence of barely more than 400 words). This is a small, handsome restaurant with an enclosed deck overlooking a creek and a beautiful stained-glass mural of a beach scene beside the front door. The tables have holes in the center where you can pitch your shucked shells, and, despite the plastic utensils, the ambience and cuisine are high quality. Local seafood of all types is the focus, featuring a raw bar, some very interesting appetizers (Ever have alligator lightly dusted in Cajun spices?), wonderful nightly specials and tasty grilled foods, including soft-shell crabs. Delicious soups, such as she-crab, shrimp bisque and clam chowder, are available. A limited choice of landfood is offered. Entrees are served with fresh seasonal vegetables, a choice of rice or the potato of the day and sweet hush puppies. Full bar service is available, as are daily drink specials. Crabby Oddwaters is above Bill's Seafood on the mainland side of the pontoon bridge and is open for dinner nightly during the high season. It's closed December 1 through February 1.

Duffer's Pub & Deli
$ • Shallotte Plaza, Main St., Shallotte • (910) 754-7229

Modestly priced and generously portioned subs (cold and hot), uncommon half-pound burgers made with Angus beef (try the blue cheese burger) and salads are Duffer's long suit. Subs and sandwiches include a side order, and the burgers come with steak fries. Specialty cold cuts include capocolla (Italian hot ham) and turkey pastrami, and salads are made fresh daily. Sandwiches are made to order, and you can even get PB&J for the kids.

Roberto's Ristorante
$$ - $$$ • 6737 Beach Dr., Ocean Isle Beach • (910) 579-4999

Family owned and operated since 1985, Roberto's offers authentic Italian-American cuisine and brick-oven baked pizza. Open for dinner year-round, the menu also features salads, homemade Italian pasta favorites, fresh seafood, veal, char-broiled steaks and nightly chef's specials. Don't miss the homemade desserts. Menu items can be packaged to take out, and a children's menu is available. Roberto's has full ABC permits. Off-season, the restaurant opens for dinner Tuesday through Saturday. From Memorial Day through the summer months, dinner is served Monday through Saturday.

Sharky's Restaurant
$ • 61 Causeway Dr., Ocean Isle Beach • (910) 579-9177

"It's feedin' time!" is the slogan at Sharky's Restaurant. Opened in 1991, Sharky's goal is to provide a family-oriented restaurant for people who enjoy good food and a relaxed atmosphere. The food at Sharky's is well-priced and can be enjoyed on the screened deck (which is handicapped accessible) overlooking the waterway where you can watch the passing boats as you dine. Or you can tie up your boat along the 150 feet of Sharky's dock — take a break from your boating and enjoy a good meal. Some customers fly into the airport, making Sharky's accessible by land, sea and air. Thoroughly casual and fun for everyone, Sharky's offers appetizers, salads, sandwiches, thin-crust pizza and dinner entrees that include steaks, pasta, seafood and daily specials. Occasionally, Sharky's hosts family-oriented holiday parties with music and plenty of food. The restaurant provides catering, free local delivery and has all ABC permits. It is open for lunch and dinner daily. For catering information, call Sandy at (910) 579-9177.

Sugar Shack
$$ • 1609 Hale Beach Rd., Ocean Isle Beach • (910) 579-3844

Don't miss this place. The house specialty is

huge steaks, marinated, slowly cooked and richly flavored. Sugar Shack features authentic Jamaican home cooking (yes, the chef is Jamaican) in a colorful, intimate setting about a mile from the beach. Amid greenery, tropical artwork and floral table coverings, recorded reggae music adds a lively island feel most days, while live music is offered on weekends. Sugar Shack specializes in its own recipe for jerk seasoning. The tangy jerk chicken, pork and beef — marinated, barbecued and served with a hot 'n' sweet sauce — anchor a small but delightful menu that also includes Stamp & Go (a traditional spicy cod fritter), Brown Stewed Fish (slowly cooked red snapper) and a curried goat so tender it literally falls off the bone. Oh, and don't forget to try the award winning baby back ribs! Nothing is too spicy for the average palate, but imported hot sauce is available if you want to hurt yourself. Some appetizers are enough for a meal, and the Jamaican Sampler is a good introduction. Other offerings include jerk chicken salads and Caesar salad, fruit dishes, homemade soups and burgers. Then top everything off with a luscious slice of Key lime pie.

Guinness Stout and Red Stripe beer are served. Take-out orders are welcome, and catering is available. Sugar Shack is one block south of Ocean Isle Beach Road, a few yards off N.C. 179. (Ocean Isle Beach Road intersects U.S. 17 about 3 miles east of Grissettown.) Sugar Shack is open nightly for dinner in summer and Tuesday through Saturday off-season. Live entertainment is featured on Saturday nights. Reservations are accepted.

Twin Lakes Restaurant
$$ • 102 Sunset Blvd., Sunset Beach
• (910) 579-6373

Many tables at Twin Lakes offer a panoramic view of the region's most picturesque watercourse and draw bridge. The restaurant stands rooted in the region's long-standing culinary tradition, having family connections to the earliest seafood days of nearby Calabash. With its tropical decor enhanced by palm trees outdoors, colorful table coverings and local art within, Twin Lakes is an attractive family restaurant that stays busy. The Twin Lakes featured menu, an astonishing 24 pages in length, includes meat and seafood specials that change nightly. Otherwise, seafood, beef, vegetables and pasta make up the bulk of a tasty and affordable menu. Entrees may be ordered fried, sauteed, grilled, broiled or blackened, and the seafood is never long out of the water. Seafood salads, stir-fry and pasta combinations are all nicely done. Ir-

resistible desserts are available as well. Twin Lakes is open nightly for dinner.

Calabash

Calabash Seafood Hut
$ • 1125 River Rd., Calabash
• (910) 579-6723

Don't be surprised to find this tiny place with a line of customers stretching around the corner. It's that popular, as much for its low, low prices as for the food, which is as good as anywhere in Calabash. The seafood platters are huge, offering combinations of Calabash-style fish, shrimp, oysters, crab and scallops. Even the biggest appetites are satisfied with the daily lunch specials. Sandwich offerings include soft-shell crab in season. Children will enjoy many items that are not even on the children's menu. All meals are served with cole slaw, french fries and hush puppies. The atmosphere is clean and bright, and everyone is friendly. The Hut also serves dinner, and it does a brisk take-out business through the street-side window. The Hut is closed Mondays. Call ahead for take-out.

The Coleman's Original Calabash Seafood Restaurant
$$ • 9931 Nance St., Calabash
• (910) 579-6875

Seafood! Everything from oyster stew and teriyaki shrimp to stuffed flounder in hollandaise and soft-shell crabs — you will find it here. But if your taste buds are set for hamburger, chicken or steak, you can indulge them here as well. Coleman's is open every day for lunch and dinner year round, so take yourself down to the foot of River Road. There you will find other restaurants, but head for the one with its name up in lights.

Ella's of Calabash
$$ • 1148 River Rd., Calabash
• (910) 579-6728

Ella's is among the stalwarts of Calabash that remain open most of the off-season, and it's been doing so since 1950. It draws patrons with good food, affordable prices and a casual, friendly atmosphere. Ella's offers a hearty lunch special that's a real bargain (choice of two kinds of seafood, plus slaw, hush puppies and fries). Steaks, chicken, oyster roasts (in season), mixed drinks and a children's menu are also available. Ella's is open daily for lunch and dinner. It is located midway between the waterfront and Beach Drive (N.C. Highway 179).

Topsail Island

Asahi
$$ • 124 N. New River Dr., Surf City
• (910) 328-1121

Asahi, complete with a sushi bar, has extensive fare normally found on a Chinese menu. This restaurant also offers Japanese choices that include appetizers and tempura entrees. There are sushi bar chef's specials, nigirisushi (ordered by the piece) and makizushi and temaki. Lunch specials include Chinese combinations, Bento box combinations, sushi, sashimi and Japanese entrees. Asahi is open daily for lunch and dinner, never closing before 10 PM. Eat in, take out or get free delivery with a minimum order of $10.

The Beach Shop and Grill
$ • 701 S. Anderson, Topsail Beach
• (910) 328-6501

Famous for their fresh-squeezed orange juice, cheeseburgers and hot dogs, The Beach Shop and Grill has a full complement of breakfast offerings and a lunch menu that also includes salads and club sandwiches. This friendly little restaurant is a favorite with local residents and vacationers. Its signature dish is crab cake, but there is also a selection of other seafood and steaks. Beer and wine are available, and you can eat in or take-out. The attached beach shop offers a full line of beach apparel and sundries. Live entertainment is offered in the Tiki Garden during the summer. You can expect to find a band playing beach music, Jimmy Buffet covers and more on selected weekend evenings. It's open for dinner only during the summer months of June, July and August.

Breezeway Restaurant
$$ • 636 Channel Blvd., Topsail Beach
• (910) 328-4302

Fresh, Southern-style seafood is the order of the day at the Breezeway, which is adjacent to the Breezeway Motel. Add that to a magnificent view of Topsail Sound, especially at sunset, and you have the makings of a wonderful dining experience. In business since 1949, the Breezeway has become a favorite with visitors and residents. Traditional fried, broiled, grilled or Cajun-spiced seafood is offered along with selections of steak and chicken. Excellent seafood lasagna and delectable hot crab dip add more choices to this outstanding menu. The chocolate pecan and Key lime pies satisfy even the most discriminating sweet-tooth. It's open nightly at 5 PM for dinner in the summer, spring and fall. A children's menu and take-out service are available, as are wine and beer.

During off hours, the dining room is available for meetings, rehearsal dinners and receptions. They offer in-house catering.

Cheri's Steakhouse
$$$ • 608 C Roland Ave., Surf City
• (910) 328-2580

Cheri's offers the largest salad bar on Topsail Island to complement its steak and chicken specialties. Tender filet mignon or New York strip with a baked potato and salad bar or Hawaiian chicken are some of the most requested favorites. Just over the swing bridge on the island side, Cheri's is situated so that diners can enjoy a delightful view of the Intracoastal Waterway. Cheri's offers a children's menu and a limited selection of mixed drinks in addition to wine and beer. It's open for dinner only.

Clamdigger Restaurant
$$ • 105 Sugar Ln., Sneads Ferry
• (910) 327-3444

There are many different dining options available at the Clamdigger. Menu items range from sandwiches, salads, pizza and pasta to beef, chicken or seafood. Adding to the choices are daily specials and a luncheon buffet on Wednesday, Friday and Sunday. An evening buffet is available on Saturday. Entertainment or special dinners may also be scheduled on a Saturday night. Breakfast at the Clamdigger is a morning routine for many local residents and businessfolk. The atmosphere is hometown friendly. It's open year round, but closed on Tuesday. A children's menu is available. Beer and wine are served.

The Crab Pot
$$ • 508 Roland Ave., Surf City
• (910) 328-5001

Low-country cuisine is the specialty of The Crab Pot. Spicy seafood gumbo, jerk chicken and much more await the casual diner looking for something different. Food can be taken away or enjoyed in the screened-in dining room/bar. A children's menu is available. The Crab Pot has all ABC permits. On selected summer evenings, you might find entertainment and shag lessons.

EM R. Wings
$ • 1016 Old Folkstone Rd., Sneads Ferry
• (910) 327-0483

Appetizers, side orders, salads and sandwiches complement the specialty of the house — buffalo wings, served mild, medium or hot. This is a fun place to enjoy casual snacking, although meal choices of ribs or steak are available. Bar seating is separate from the dining room. Take-out orders can be accommodated. EM R. Wings has all ABC permits and is open year round.

The Green Turtle
**$$-$$$ • 310 Fulchers Landing Road
Sneads Ferry • (910) 327-0262**

Exclusive, casual dining on the scenic Sneads Ferry waterfront is a good description of The Green Turtle. A fantastic She Crab soup or Stuffed Mushrooms with Crab Imperial is a great way to start a meal, followed by a mouth-watering entree of seafood, pasta or steak. Shrimp Diablo over angel hair pasta is one of the specialties as is the Chesapeake Crab Cakes. If steak is your choice The Green Turtle offers an excellent Prime Rib or filet. Be sure to leave room for dessert, one of the favorites is Turtle Cheese Cake. Changing careers after many years as an Executive Recruiter, Billy Dee, for the past eight years has earned the reputation of a fine restaurant owner and host. Many residents favor the Green Turtle for an evening out and visitors look forward to returning year after year. Open daily at 5 PM for dinner, they have all ABC permits, children's and take-out menus.

Holly Ridge Smokehouse Restaurant
**$ • 511-A U.S. Hwy. 17, Holly Ridge
• (910) 329-1708**

For breakfast, lunch or dinner, this well-known restaurant offers great home-cooked food. The specialty of the house is the slow-cooked barbecue, a favorite with eastern North Carolina barbecue lovers. The country charm is felt as soon as you approach the building. Inside, local art and crafts are offered for sale. The large breakfast biscuits melt in your mouth. A salad bar is available for one trip or a meal. On summer weekends, a country buffet is served in the large banquet room that is also available for large parties or special gatherings. Entertainment is sometimes offered, and no alcohol is served. A children's menu is available. Holly Ridge Smoke House is open year round but is closed Mondays and has reduced hours on Tuesday.

II Beauchaines
**$$$ • 831 Roland Ave., Surf City
• (910) 328-1888**

Classic food in a Southern atmosphere is what you'll find at II Beauchaines. Located just off the island on the causeway, this cozy restaurant has an menu to please every taste with seafood, chicken, pork and beef entrees. Shrimp and grits is one of the favorites, as is the Northwood's tenderloin of beef. There is an extensive list of over 32 wines to complement the meals. They offer catering (including wedding receptions), a children's menu and

mouthwatering homemade desserts. Reservations are suggested on summer weekends.

Island Delights
**$ • 312 N. New River Dr., Surf City
• (910) 328-1868**

Return to the 1950s and the days of the soda shop. Island Delights specializes in ice cream, milk shakes and sundaes as well as the expected selection of burgers and sandwiches. Vacationing families enjoy returning here year after year for their evening ice cream treats. It's closed in the winter.

Koffee Kats
**$ • 400 Roland Ave., Surf City
• (910) 328-0022**

Just a step in the door of Koffee Kats and the aroma of fresh coffee is enough to have you running to the coffee bar. Three special coffees are offered daily and might include local favorites such as Cafe Mocha or Milky Way. A complete complement of flavored frozen frappuccinos, your choice of latte, frozen or iced chais, green and black blended teas have been added to the extensive menu. For your sweet tooth, Koffee Kats offers an array of fresh pastries, including bear claws, apple muffins, scones and a selection of muffins. If pastries aren't your choice, try the variety of chocolates and pecans just waiting to be sampled. Sit and relax in the cozy nook with your treat, but be sure to browse through the shop before you leave. Koffee Kats also offers a variety of homemade pastas, sauces, jams, oils and spices.

Latitude 34 Restaurant
**$$$ • 1522 Carolina Ave., Topsail Beach
• (910) 328-3272**

Award-winning Latitude 34 Restaurant offers elegant dining in a casual atmosphere with an excellent view of Topsail Sound. Fresh fish specials are offered nightly, and regular menu items include seafood, chicken, beef and pork, all uniquely prepared. Favorites include fresh yellowfin tuna grilled with a wasabi cream sauce or shrimp and scallops sauteed with roasted red and yellow peppers and fresh vegetables served over linguini in a cilantro pesto cream sauce. The menu changes to reflect fresh seasonal cuisine that pulls influences from French, Cajun, Pacific Rim and Southwestern. Favorite appetizers include fresh oysters, lightly fried and served with an aioli dipping sauce, or French Brie, baked in a puff pastry and drizzled with an Amaretto reduction. There is always a soup of the day and a selection of salads. A children's menu is available. Latitude 34 offers a fine selection of wine and imported and domestic beers. Reservations are recommended.

Long Island Pizza
$$ • 610 N. New River Dr., Surf City
• (910) 328-3156

Long Island Pizza offers much more than pizza. The standard menu contains spaghetti and other Italian specialties, including broccoli or spinach rolls, calzones and stromboli. Daily lunch and dinner specials offer even more selections of Italian delicacies that taste like they just came from Mama's kitchen. Beer and wine are available. You can eat in, take-out or have your meals delivered to your door. It's closed from Thanksgiving until March.

Max's Pizza
$$ • 602A Roland Ave., Surf City
• (910) 328-2158

Open year round, Max's is one of the island residents' favorite choices for wintertime dining and visiting on Topsail. This casual, friendly atmosphere spills over into the summer, when visitors blend with the normal clientele to enjoy a pizza, dish of spaghetti, salad, burger or hot-oven sub. New additions to the menu include grilled chicken, lasagna, cavatini and other Italian favorites. High-backed booths hug the walls, while tables in the center of the room can be easily moved to suit the party size. Max's serves beer and wine. Take-out orders are welcome. It's closed on Wednesday during the off-season

Mollie's Restaurant
$$ • 107 N. South Shore Dr., Surf City
• (910) 328-0505

Casual dining at its best, Mollie's offers a full breakfast menu, with additional specials to make the choice of a delicious meal even more difficult. Lunchtime patrons will find great salads and sandwiches on the menu in addition to Mollie's traditional two daily luncheon specials. The crab melt sandwich, made from an old family recipe, is a once-in-a-lifetime experience. Mollie's has a full range of dinner meals, mostly fresh seafood, again with even more choices offered on the special board. Enjoy wine and imported or domestic beer with your meal. A children's menu and take-out are available. Mollie's is open year round but never on Tuesday.

Old Landing Restaurant
$$, no credit cards • 12124 N.C. Hwy. 50.,
Holly Ridge • (910) 329-1261

Old Landing is often the place families stop by on their way home from the beach to enjoy one last freshly cooked seafood meal. Generous portions, tasty cole slaw, chowder and friendly service make this place a favorite. Fried oysters are the highlight of the menu for many people. A children's menu is available. No alcohol is served in this family-style restaurant.

One Stop Seafood Restaurant
$ • 805 Roland Ave., Surf City
• (910) 328-3314

If home-style cooking is your choice, you can't miss with One Stop. Try a choice of omelet or other eggs, served with hash browns or grits with a biscuit for breakfast. Then come back for fried fish or shrimp, french fries and cole slaw for lunch. A specialty is hand-patted beef burgers. One Stop offers daily specials of meat and vegetables, all served in a old-time beach atmosphere on the waterway, where you can watch the boats go by while you eat. It is on the mainland side of the swing bridge in the same building with One Stop Bait and Tackle. If you're fortunate enough to make a big catch, and are willing to do the cleaning, One Stop will do the cooking for you for a nominal fee of $4. It's open year round.

Paliotti's at the Villa
$$$ • 790 New River Inlet Rd., North Topsail Beach • (910) 328-8501

Paliotti's is located inside the Villa Capriani resort condominium complex. An authentic Italian restaurant, Paliotti's offers a variety of fresh seafood and beef in addition to all the traditional items you would expect to find on an Italian menu. If prime rib is your choice, Paliotti's has some of the best on the island, served with a baked potato and vegetable of the day. If your choice is Italian, you can't miss the spaghetti and meatballs, lasagna or chicken parmesan with a fresh salad. Nightly dinner specials are offered. The lounge is separated from the dining rooms by the entrance hall, and the smoking and nonsmoking sections are in two different rooms. A children's menu is offered. Paliotti's has all ABC permits and is open 365 days a year.

Pirates Cove
$$ • 316 Fulchers Landing Rd., Sneads Ferry • (910) 327 3395

Adjacent to Paradise Landing Marina, Pirates Cove offers seafood and pasta combinations, steaks and daily specials that include seafood from local boats. Sit back and relax upstairs on the deck while you peel and eat fresh steamed shrimp, clams, crab claws or oysters on the half shell. It's open year round for breakfast, lunch and dinner. Full ABC permits and a children's menu are available.

Riverview Cafe
$$ • 119 Hall Point Rd., Sneads Ferry
• (910) 327-2011

The Riverview Cafe offers a longtime tradition of dinner plates heaped with your choice of fresh fried seafood, french fries, slaw and hush puppies. The waterfront location where you can watch the shrimp boats come in adds to this pleasurable experience. Visitors return year after year for a Riverview dinner, joining the locals who eat here on a regular basis. The bar is separated from the dining rooms and offers beer and wine. It's open year round.

Seahorse Cafe
$-$$ • 121 S. Topsail Dr., Surf City
• (910) 328-4331
Breakfast, lunch or dinner, you'll find it all at the Seahorse Cafe, one of the island's newest restaurants, but already famous for its delicious shrimp burger and seafood plates. For the non-seafood eater, hamburgers are a good choice. Open year round, Seahorse offers daily specials and a salad bar. Children's and senior citizens' plates are offered, as are take-outs. The only alcohol served is beer.

Sears Landing Grill & Boat Docks
$-$$ • 806 Roland Ave., Surf City
• (910) 329-1312
He's back, popular chef, Hap Alexander formerly of the Beach Shop and Grill, is opening Surf City's newest waterfront casual dining establishment. Come by boat or car, enjoy eating inside, on the porch, or order take out. Choices include fresh grilled fish of the day sandwiches, soft shelled crab, peel and eat shrimp or Hap's famous beach hotdog or hamburgers. Enjoy salads anytime, soup in the winter. Beer and Wine are available. Open from 11AM till the supper crowd is gone. Sears Landing has deep water access with boat slips available for rent by the day, week or month. Beer, soft drinks, water and ice can be purchased for your boat, trip to the beach, or to just enjoy while rocking on the porch relaxing with a view of the intracoastal waterway.

Soundside
$$$ • 209 N. New River Dr., Surf City
• (910) 328-0803
Soundside is one of Topsail Island's best selections for upscale dining in the evening. Its location on the Intracoastal Waterway, situated just right to catch those breathtaking sunsets and water views, adds to the dining experience. Serving the area since 1981, Soundside takes pride in offering a unique menu featuring local seafood blended with herbs and the perfect sauces and condiments. Appetizers, soup and featured entrees change daily. Homemade desserts at Soundside are a must. Soundside has all ABC permits. Cal for winter hours.

Subway
$ • 204 A N. New River Dr., Surf City
• (910) 328-4223
1961 U.S. Hwy. 172, Ste. 10 (Monk's Corner) Sneads Ferry • (910) 327-3252
Both of these Subway locations offer the

complete selection of subway sandwiches, soups and salads. Surf City offers a breakfast menu of deli sandwiches and croissants. They also have smoothies. Breakfast, lunch and dinner are served year round, and Subway stays open late — until 3 AM some nights. Hours are reduced during the off-seasons. The Sneads Ferry location offers the same menu, but not croissants or smoothies.

Surf City Grill
$ • 103 S. Shore Dr., Surf City
• (910) 328-4833
Just across from Bank of America, Surf City Grill offers take-out only. The Grill features a wide selection of South of the Border specialties such as tacos, taco salad and burritos along with the regular choices of burgers, hot dogs, fries and onion rings. Fried zucchini is an unusual side offering. Dave's Chili is the featured selection that's so good it has customers returning for more. All selections are freshly prepared at the time of order. Call ahead or be prepared to wait.

Hampstead Area

Carriage House Restaurant
$-$$$ • 2368 Country Club Dr., Hampstead • (910) 270-2768
The Carriage House Restaurant, part of the Belvedere Country Club, offers a fine-dining experience in the evening as well as a casual breakfast and luncheon place, often enjoyed by golfers at the country club. Jimmy and Diane Loschiavo are well known in the area for their authentic Italian

Breakfast - Lunch - Late Night

SUBWAY

eat fresh.™

Hampstead - Surf City
Sneads Ferry

XYZ PIZZA

Hampstead
(coming soon - Sneads Ferry)

meals, especially the mussels marinara with sauce "like Mama used to make." Look for the tasty signature Carriage House dishes, including the grouper sautéed in a special broth with tomatoes, olives, capers, mushrooms and spices served over pasta. In addition to the regular menu, there are both lunch and dinner specials. A specialty is the daily choice of six different hot luncheon dishes, including drink for $5. The Carriage House is open daily for breakfast and lunch. Dinner is served Thursday, Friday and Saturday nights. Children-size portions are available. A banquet room, holding 120 people is offered for special events.

Mako's Raw Bar and Grille
$$$ • 55 Scotts Hill Loop Rd., Scotts Hill • (910) 686-9042

If seafood is your choice, Mako's is the place. This new restaurant offers a wide variety of fresh seafood and a full raw bar. Oysters on the half shell, steamed shrimp, mussels, clams, crab legs, seafood salads and the daily catch are just some of the offerings. Don't overlook their special crab cakes or soups that have proven to be favorites with the customers. For the landlubber, they also have a fantastic prime rib that is slow roasted in house, sandwiches or appetizers. There are daily lunch specials and an evening special for each night, starting with steamed shrimp on Monday, flounder on Tuesday, crab legs on Wednesday, and oysters on Thursday. Full ABC permits, a children's menu and take-outs are all available.

The Pasta Grille
$$$ • 513 Country Club Dr., Hampstead • (910) 270-2425

A family tradition and ten years of experience

led Dave and Denise Nuzzi to open the Pasta Grille at Olde Pointe Golf Club. Specializing in pasta dishes as the name indicates, diners are treated to a variety of interesting dishes including angel hair pasta with Shrimp a la Rosa, Penne with Chicken in Pesto or a selection of pizzas ranging from classic to Chicken A la Rosa or grilled veggie pizza. The spinach and Greek salads are excellent choices with crisp, fresh salad fixings. Daily specials and a Sunday brunch are offered. Eat in the dining room, the bar or take-out. The Pasta Grille also has a small meeting room and a large banquet room that holds up to 120 people for special occasions. It's open seven days a week for lunch and dinner, and reservations are accepted. All ABC permits and a children's menu are available.

XYZ Pizza and Subway Food Court
$-$$ • 15010 A & B, U.S. Hwy. 17, Hampstead • (910) 270-2680

This brand-new food court is a comfortable place to enjoy a meal with family or friends. There is a shared inside seating area, with plans to soon include outside dining (where smoking will be permitted). If you don't have time to sit and relax, take out is also provided. Catering is available.

If your meal choice is Italian, XYZ Pizza has much more than pizza to offer, so don't let the name fool you. In addition to thin-crust and deep-dish pizza with a choice of toppings, the varied menu includes calzones, appetizers, salads and pasta dishes such as lasagna and desserts. Creative Chef Kurt Werner cooks up some daily surprises as well. XYZ offers no alcohol. They are open for lunch and dinner Monday through Saturday, and hours are extended during the summer season.

The Subway portion of the food court is the second largest Subway in the state. Offered is a full breakfast menu including breakfast delis, croissants, omelets and french toast. The lunch and dinner menu consist of everything Subway offers including submarine sandwiches, salads, soups, ice cream and cookies. If you have the chance, ask owners Delinda Gladstone or her son David about the 217.5-inch submarine sandwich they made for Topsail High School students. Subway is for breakfast, lunch and dinner seven days a week. Hours are extended during the summer season.

Burgaw

Holland's Shelter Creek Restaurant
$$ • 8315 N.C. Hwy. 53 E., Burgaw • (910) 259-5743

Finish off a day exploring the countryside with a meal at Holland's Shelter Creek Restaurant. Known for their fresh seafood, Holland's offers hearty platters with everything from frog legs and catfish to oysters, shrimp and deviled Crab platters. For those who prefer country cooking, Holland's offers some of the area's best barbecue and pork chops. Dine in a rustic atmosphere with a view of the river, and relax with a cup of catfish stew or shrimp Creole. Holland's has beer and wine, seniors' specials and a children's menu. They are open year-round, every day for lunch and dinner.

Coffeehouses

An interesting offspring of the traditional coffeehouse is the marriage of the cafe atmosphere and bookstores. The larger book superstores in Wilmington, *Barnes & Noble*, 322 S. College Road, and *Books-A-Million*, 3737 Oleander Drive, feature surprisingly cozy cafe settings that host cultural events, meetings and book discussion groups. *The Salt Shaker Bookstore and Cafe*, 705 S. Kerr Avenue, Wilmington, offers coffee and cafe-style food. Smaller, independent bookstores that feature the twin delights of good coffee and good books are the *Quarter Moon Bookstore*, 625-B S. Anderson Boulevard in Topsail Beach, and *Bristol Books*, 1908 Eastwood Road near Wrightsville Beach, which doesn't technically have a cafe on its premises, but allows easy access to Centro Market and Cafe through a shared door. Bristol Books also is only a brief stroll across the walkway to Lumina Station's Port City Java, home of the best chocolate milkshakes in town, hands-down!

Wilmington

General Assembly
The Cotton Exchange, 303 N. Front St., Wilmington • (910) 343-8890

Located in The Cotton Exchange, this popular coffeehouse offers yummy pastries, muffins and bagels to complement their fresh-roasted coffee, mocha shakes and specialty coffee drinks. Unique to the General Assembly is one of Wilmington's two scaled-down replicas of the Statue of Liberty. (The other is at a side entrance to Thalian Hall.). General Assembly is open daily.

Port City Java Coffee Houses & Roastery
21 N. Front St., Wilmington • (910) 762-5282
Arboretum Center, 5917 Oleander Dr., Wilmington • (910) 792-9575
Barclay Commons, 2512 Independence Blvd., Wilmington • (910) 792-0449
Porter's Neck Center, 8211 Market St., Wilmington (910) 686-1033
Lumina Station, 1900 Eastwood Rd., Wilmington • (910) 256-0993
113 N. Howe St., Southport • (910) 454-0321

Established in 1995, Wilmington's Port City Java, winner of *Encore's* Best Coffeehouse 2003, now boasts eight locations in the Wilmington-Wrightsville Beach area and one in Southport. Each is individual in decor and menu, from traditional coffeehouse fare to a luncheon menu of fresh garden salads and grilled panini (sandwich) specialties. Housing its own local roastery, Port City Java guarantees that your favorite coffee beverage is fresh daily. Try their non-java offerings, such as the Ghirardelli Hot Cocoa (a chocolate lover's dream) or the Oregon Chai Steamer, a ginger-honey spiced tea blend with steamed milk. If the heat of a coastal summer calls for something cool and refreshing, their Mocha Shake — chilled espresso, Ghirardelli chocolate and vanilla ice cream — is a popular choice. Drive-through windows are open at the Porters Neck Center and Arboretum Center locations.

Una Dolce
224 S. Water St., Ste. 1-C, Wilmington • (910) 342-9822

Una Dolce offers the perfect spot to stop for refreshment and to enjoy the city's historic waterfront. Local art in a changing range of media adorn the walls in this small and unique coffeehouse. Seating indoors is spacious. Outdoors, there are cushioned chairs on a wide deck facing the Cape Fear River and rocking chairs on the front porch overlooking Water Street. Hot, iced or frozen specialty coffee drinks and a revolving showcase with locally baked and mouthwatering desserts — pies, cakes, cheesecake — are the highlights here. Una Dolce also offers muffins, cookies, bagels and beverages, including delicious fruit smoothies and soft drinks.

INSIDERS' TIP
To avoid waiting in line at a popular restaurant, arrive before the 6:30 to 7:30 PM rush. Most are open for dinner by 5:30 PM.

The Wilmington Espresso Co.
5317 Wrightsville Ave., Wilmington
• (910) 790-5689
24 S. Front St., Wilmington
• (910) 343-1155

Wilmington Espresso Co.'s Wrightsville Avenue location is a spacious and sunny coffee bar with 1950s-style Formica-top tables and plenty of reading material such as magazines, local newspapers and books. The muffins and pastries are baked fresh daily in the shop, and all the usual specialties — espresso, cappuccino, latte, tea and fruit smoothies — are served with a smile from the friendly staff. No time to stop in on the way to work or the university? No problem. Wilmington Espresso offers a drive-through window for the coffee-lover on the run. The shop is in front of Cape Fear Memorial Hospital, near the East Entrance. The Front Street location, formerly Cape Fear Coffee & Tea, serves all of your favorite coffeehouse fare in an intimate downtown setting. Windowed tables and rocking chairs situated right outside the front door beckon you to sit and relax. Also available at this location are whole gourmet coffee beans, coffee makers and specialty teas.

Carolina Beach

Surfside Smoothies & Coffee Shop
110 N. Lake Park Blvd., Carolina Beach
• (910) 233-3480

This authentic smoothie and coffeehouse offers 32 different flavors of fruit drinks, made of pure fruit and sweetened only with fructose. You may have them additionally fortified with antioxidants, vitamins, spirulina and more. Designer coffees, frozen lattes and three frozen mocha drinks round out the beverage list. Open seasonally.

Southport/Oak Island

The Flying Pig Coffeehouse
6006 Oak Island Dr., Oak Island
• (910) 278-5929, (866) 255-6462

Have you ever drawn a picture of a flying pig with your eyes closed? Well here's you chance. Rebecca and Steve Matson, owners of The Flying Pig Coffeehouse, offer this opportunity to all their customers and the results are in a book for all to see. This bright coffeehouse, with its eclectic furniture (for sale) made by Steve, is conducive to drawing, reading, writing or just enjoying a cup of coffee. There are newspapers and books available, from The Artist's Way to If Pigs Could Fly and Other Deep Thoughts. You can relax in the lovely tea garden adjacent to the coffeehouse if your prefer. Barrows tea, Chai, smoothies and other drinks are available. Try the specialties of the house: the frozen Arctic pig or the hot Flying Pig. Ask about upcoming featured artist displays, poetry readings and weekend entertainment. The Flying Pig coffeehouse is open seven days a week for your convenience.

Children can entertain themselves for hours at the beach.

Photo: Jay Tervo

South Brunswick Islands

Cappuccino By The Sea
3331 Holden Beach Rd., Holden Beach
• (910) 842-3661

This friendly and inviting coffee shop is in a converted house on the causeway and is open year-round. Enjoying a tenth summer of business in 2003, this charming cafe features tables inside and out. Local and regional newspapers, board games and a few books are available to peruse while savoring your favorite coffee or tea beverage and snack. Try a slice of scrumptious cake. Cappuccino By The Sea also offers a line of gifts including body products, handmade mirrors and potpourri. Gift baskets, greeting cards and birthday balloons can be shipped or delivered locally. Need local info? Owner Nancy Elwell can give you the low-down on everything from attractions to minor repair referrals.

Periwinkle's Coffee Cafe
Low Country Stores, 10138 Beach Dr. SW, Calabash • (910) 575-4522

The soft comfort of Periwinkle's is evident the moment you walk in the door. You can rest your tired feet while sitting on the comfortable couch or chair complete with antimacassars on the arms. There's also seating at tables, at the coffee bar or on the old-fashioned front porch. Coffee is available in all its forms: drip, espresso, cappuccino, latte, breve, Americano, mocha, steamer and more. Hot chocolate, cider, tea, smoothies and sodas are served as well. If you're hungry, try soup or New York-style bagels and spreads. Carry the ambience with you in a bag of gourmet coffee beans (including Jamaican Me Crazy beans) in one hand and some used books in the other.

Bakeries

Wilmington

Apple Annie's Bake Shop
University Square Mall, 837 S. Kerr Ave., Wilmington • (910) 799-9023
Landfall Shopping Center, 1319 Military Cutoff Rd., Wilmington • (910) 256-6585

Boasting five generations of baking tradition, this award-winning bakery offers everything from bread to gourmet pastries. The goods are baked fresh daily on-premises with natural ingredients and no additives or preservatives.

Long, windowed pastry cases display a wide range of the day's available goodies, including cakes, pies, cheesecakes, French pastries, cookies, danish, muffins, assorted breads and rolls, cannoli, brownies and more. Wedding and special occasion cakes are their specialty. Holidays are especially festive at Apple Annie's, and they celebrate them all. Whether you want a heart-shaped Valentine's Day cake, spicy pumpkin pies for Thanksgiving or Challah bread at Rosh Hashanah, call the bakery for their holiday specials throughout the year.

Blueberry Hill Dessertery
The Forum, 1113 Military Cutoff Rd., Ste. F, Wilmington • (910) 509-0700

If your sweet tooth craves made-from-scratch confections and pastries with real butter and imported Swiss chocolate, Blueberry Hill Dessertery has something for every taste. They're famous for their Key lime pie and double fudge cookies, but the massive overhead menu board listing daily offerings includes a mouthwatering array of pies, cakes, cheesecakes and seasonal desserts. Brownies, scones, lemon bars, theme cupcakes and wedding cookies are some other featured treats. Blueberry Hill specializes in custom cakes for all occasions, including weddings, and delights in creating the unusual for your event. Billed as "Wilmington's only dessert cafe," the bakery serves Illy coffee, espresso and specialty coffee drinks to enjoy with your favorite dessert. Seating is available inside and out. Open Monday through Saturday year-round, Blueberry Hill stays open until 10 PM during the summer months.

Great Harvest Bread Co.
North 17 Shopping Center, 4302 Market St., Wilmington • (910) 763-0003

Some of the best breads in Wilmington can be found at Great Harvest. Their breads and pastries are baked fresh daily from whole wheat flour they mill themselves using no oils or preservatives. Selections vary with the season, but a typical week will feature 28 different breads plus muffins, scones, cinnamon rolls, cookies and seasonal pies. Stop by for a seasonal baking schedule that lists daily offerings. Christmas gift baskets of assorted breads are extremely popular and available from Thanksgiving to Christmas. These are great ideas for out-of-town gift-giving and are shipped from Great Harvest via UPS. At Easter, try the whimsical Honey Bunnies, a loaf of honey wheat bread made into a bunny shape. It's a delicious and fun addition to your Easter dinner menu. Limited seating is available if you'd like to enjoy coffee and a treat while making your selections. Firmly believing in the traditions of "the village bakery," Great Harvest contributes to the community in generous donations to area churches, non-profit organizations and local shelters.

Sweet & Savory Bake Shop & Cafe
1611 Pavilion Pl., Wilmington
• (910) 256-0115

One of the area's premier wholesale/retail bakeries, Sweet & Savory supplies many local restaurants with fresh-baked breads and desserts. The bakery and cafe are located near the Wrightsville Beach bridge and just east of Plaza East shopping center. Dining in the cafe (seating is situated within the bakery) provides a unique experience as you watch a working bakery in action. It comes as no surprise that the sandwich menu includes homemade breads. Sweet & Savory offers daily board specials that include two fresh fish sandwiches, two quiches, five soups (chilled soups are offered in summer) and an entree salad. Four vegetarian sandwiches and healthy, low-fat selections are included on the menu. Catering is available. The bakery is open until 7 PM Monday through Saturday.

South Brunswick Islands

The French Bake and Pastry Shop
Seaside Plaza, 7290-10 Beach Dr., Ocean Isle Beach • (910) 575-0284

Robert Van Lieden, a native of Amsterdam and previous owner of an extremely successful restaurant, Chez Robert, which was situated next to the White House in Washington, D.C., has opened this wonderful classic patisserie Francaise. If the name were not on the door, you would know the moment you enter that this is no ordinary bakery. The decor is done in the traditional French yellow and blue colors with touches of white, and on the walls are Toulouse Lautrec posters and photos of the Eiffel Tower. Your nose will tell you as well — mmmm! Just smell those muffins, turnovers, danish, rolls, croissants, eclairs, cream puffs, strudels, cheese cakes, baguettes and more. Robert bakes pies and cakes to order as well.

Nightlife

Along North Carolina's southern coastline, the term "nightlife" may have very different meanings to area natives and to visitors enjoying the sights. Plenty of residents spend summer nights away from the crowds by searching the beaches for loggerhead turtle nests and helping protect the ones they find. Others prefer the nights for offshore fishing. Many youngsters enjoy surprising ghost crabs with their flashlights as the little critters (the crabs) make their nocturnal runs on the beach. Of course, there's little more romantic or peaceful than a leisurely stroll on the beach under a Carolina moon.

If going out on the town is more your style, area nightlife is primarily concentrated in Wilmington, with its numerous restaurants, nightclubs, bars and theaters. Outlying areas, especially the South Brunswick Islands, are famous for their quiet family atmosphere, but hot spots definitely do exist at Wrightsville Beach, Carolina Beach, Surf City and on Oak Island, particularly in summer.

Stroll the Riverwalk along Water Street and Front Street in downtown Wilmington. There are plenty of exciting places along the way to pause for a toast or to hear live music. A horse-drawn carriage tour of downtown Wilmington is an exciting and informative introduction to the city too.

Billiards (see listings in this chapter) and bowling (see our Sports, Fitness and Parks chapter) are fun alternatives to the usual bar scene. Browsing our Attractions chapter will reveal more ideas — for instance, evening cruise opportunities on the Cape Fear River.

The last couple of years have brought a local resurgence of interest in jazz, blues and other musical genres, evident in the increasing number of restaurants and bars offering live music in the evenings, typically between Thursday and Sunday. Venues worth a visit for blues include The Rusty Nail, Tomatoz American Grille and Water Street Restaurant.

Wilmington's busy theater scene, with Thalian Hall as its crown jewel, offers quality entertainment year round for lovers of the performing arts. In Brunswick County, the Odell Williamson Auditorium provides another venue for live performances and dramatic productions. Fans of classical music take note of area presenters that sponsor evening concert programs year round. See our chapter on The Arts for more information on both concerts and theatrical productions.

Other live entertainment is open to the public; however, you will find some private nightclubs throughout the region. In order for an establishment to serve liquor, it must either earn the bulk of its revenue from the sale of food, or it must be a private club open only to members and their guests. Membership to most clubs is inexpensive, usually about $5 per year. At some venues, weekend visitors applying for membership should know that a three-day waiting period must elapse before you can become a full member, but it's easy to be signed in as someone's guest at the door.

What follows is a sampling and by no means the last word on the area's nightlife. At the end of the chapter is a section on movie theaters, for those whose nightlife tends toward the cinematic, and a section of a more literary persuasion.

LOOK FOR:
- Nightspots
- Movie Theaters
- Literary Pursuits

CLOSEUP:
- Beach Music, the Shag and Chicken Hicks... A True Story

VISIT US TODAY!
www.insiders.com

NIGHTLIFE

Open Daily
11AM - 2 AM

Sports Bar, Grille & Billiards

26 Pool Tables
24 Bowling Lanes
Darts Arena ★ Sports Arcade
Complete Pro Shop ★ Full Menu
Restaurant ★ 17 TV's

Marketplace Mall ★ 127 S. College Rd.
Wilmington, NC 28403
(910) 452-5455

Nightspots

Wilmington

Alleigh's
4925 New Centre Dr., Wilmington
• (910) 793-0999

With 35,000 square feet of space dedicated to great entertainment, fine food and fun, Alleigh's corners the market on nightlife. This huge complex houses four distinct restaurants, a state-of-the-art virtual reality game room, banquet facilities and live entertainment Wednesday through Sunday.

The Tiki Bar & Cafe, the newest addition to Alleigh's, is an outdoor venue designed to resemble a tropical paradise. The Tiki Bar & Cafe features an extensively landscaped pond and fountain framed with tall fronds of bamboo. Tiki Bar patrons can enjoy tropical drinks, a raw bar and a Caribbean-inspired menu Wednesday through Sunday starting at 5 PM.

The Sports Bar at Alleigh's has the unique distinction of featuring 31 TV's, including the largest TV screen (200 inches) in Wilmington. In addition, The Sports Bar is one of only three venues in Wilmington to offer NTN Trivia, a tabletop electronic trivia game that enables customers to compete with teams across the country. Live bands perform Thursday through Saturday evenings, featuring everything from beach music to rock.

The Jazz Bar at Alleigh's offers an intimate setting for a romantic dinner or a cozy venue to watch local jazz musicians perform live Thursday through Saturday evenings.

And if games entertain you, check out Alleigh's 7,200-square-foot Game Room featuring more than 120 games, including a roller coaster simulator and a 1920s Chicago-style shootout.

Alleigh's truly has something for everyone and is open Monday through Friday 11 AM to 2 AM and Saturday and Sunday 10 AM to 2 AM. A late-nite menu is offered until 1 AM.

Bluepost Billiards
15 S. Water St., Wilmington
• (910) 343-1141

Tucked away in the Jacobi Warehouse near the historic downtown Wilmington riverfront, Bluepost won Encore's coveted Best Neighborhood Bar 2003. This 5,000-square-foot billiards hall features a number of diversions — two 9-foot diamond pool tables, four valley blackcat tables, air hockey, ping pong, foosball, video games, bubble hockey and a video projector with a 10-foot screen. Worked up a thirst? They stock 50 brands of beers, including 14 on tap. Bluepost is open from 3 PM to 2 AM Monday through Friday and 2 PM to 2 AM Saturday and Sunday.

Break Time / Ten Pin Alley
127 S. College Rd., Wilmington
• (910) 395-6658

Wilmington's largest billiards parlor is also a popular bowling alley, sports bar and casual restaurant, serving sandwiches, burgers, soups, salads and more. Break Time possesses all ABC permits and has 26 top-quality pool tables, 17 televisions, 24 lanes of bowling and arcade-style diversions. Neat attire is required; no tank tops. It's open 11 AM until 2 AM, and food service is available until closing.

Marrz Theatre
15 S. Front St., Wilmington
• (910) 772-9045

Voted Best Live Music 2003 by Encore magazine, this huge 800-person venue offers live music from national and regional bands nightly, Thursday through Saturday, on one of the largest stages in any area club. A few of the national bands who recently played at Marrz include Fuel, Collective Soul and Blue Oyster Cult. Marrz has all ABC permits and offers full bar services, beer and wine but no food service. Some seating is available. The second floor houses a game room and features pool tables, Foosball and other games. The cover charge varies according to the band. Call the number listed above for prices and additional entertainment dates. Municipal parking is available directly behind the club.

Percy's Jazz Bar & Club
City Club at de Rosset, 102 S. Second St., Wilmington • (910) 343-1800

Percy's is one of the most plush nightclubs in the area and is open seven days a week with live music on Thursday, Friday and Saturday from 4 to 10 PM. Named after one of Wilmington's best-known native sons, jazz musician Percy Heath, this upscale club features authentic jazz memorabilia and enough televisions for watching that important game. Unwind after work or enjoy an evening on the town in a smoke-free environment. Outdoor seating offers a chance to bask in the wonderful weather of the Cape Fear coast. The bar menu includes favorite appetizers, entrees and desserts.

Rack 'M Pub and Billiards
415 S. College Rd., Wilmington • (910) 791-5668

Pool prices at this club-style parlor are an affordable $2 per person per hour until 7 PM. From 7 PM to closing, prices are $3 per person per hour. Rack 'M is open every day from noon until 2 AM. However, after 10 PM, you must be age 21 or older to enter. You'll find it in the rear of the University Landing shopping center near Krazy Pizza & Subs.

The Rusty Nail Blues Bar
1310 S. Fifth Ave., Wilmington • (910) 251-1888

Live blues and jazz enthusiasts don't want to miss this downtown Wilmington club's weekly line-up. Nightly featured entertainment, starting on Mondays about 8 PM, includes band practice for local amateur bands. The Blues Society of the Lower Cape Fear cuts loose on Tuesdays and the first Saturday of each month. Gary Allen's open mike is on Wednesdays. Thursdays features Georgia's Bluegrass Jam. Henry Beatty's Masters of Jazz Jam is a Sunday night highlight. Open daily at 11 AM, Sundays at noon, the club has all ABC permits, serves beer and wine, offers bar specials and provides a sandwich menu. The Rusty Nail is a private club but non-members can be signed in as guests. New members are welcome, and fees are reasonable, with sev-

eral membership options available. Call the club for details. Located between Marstellar and Greenfield streets, the club boasts its own parking lot, a rarity in downtown Wilmington.

Tomatoz American Grille
S. College Rd. and Wrightsville Ave., Wilmington • (910) 313-0541

Not only is this popular restaurant a great place to dine but it's a good place for weekly live entertainment as well. Sunday evening, live jazz begins at 8 PM. Tuesday, Wednesday and Thursday nights the action starts at 10 PM. Please call regarding the style of music. There is no cover.

Water Street Restaurant & Sidewalk Cafe
5 S. Water St., Wilmington • (910) 343-0042

Water Street's relaxed, cozy atmosphere invites you to linger with a friend or loved one late into the night, any night of the week. The decor is colorful, somewhat rustic and warm. Sidewalk seating offers a view of the riverfront, and good food is always available. Regular performers include William "Paco" Strickland on flamenco guitar, Grenaldo Frazier, bluesman Mojo Collins, and the local Dixieland Society's sextet, 30-year veterans who appear regularly on Fridays from 5 to 7:30 PM. Water Street also provides a musical venue for jazz, bluegrass and more with nightly performances, Wednesday through Sunday.

NIGHTLIFE

Wrightsville Beach

Clarence Foster's Restaurant & Catering
22 N. Lumina Ave., Wrightsville Beach
• (910) 256-0224

Clarence Foster's bar and lounge are as cozy and casual as the restaurant. The restaurant's full menu is served there or opt for lighter fare after 10 PM. Tickle your funny bone with Foster's Giggles Comedy Club featuring two nationally touring comedians on Wednesday nights at 9 PM. Admission is $5. Open at 4:30 PM, Wednesday through Sunday, the restaurant closes at 9 PM on Thursday and Sunday, and 2:30 AM on Wednesday, Friday and Saturday. Friday's highlight is karaoke and Saturday's is dancing to the sounds of a popular DJ.

King Neptune's Pirate Lounge
11 N. Lumina Ave., Wrightsville Beach
• (910) 256-2525

The Pirate Lounge in the King Neptune Restaurant is as lively as its proprietor, Bernard Carroll, who did the research to accurately identify all the pirate flags hung in the room. It's the kind of decor you might expect of someone who'd rather be sailing, and, as a salt should, Carroll places some importance on rum. His "Rum Bar" features some 19 premium rums from around the world, including Gosling's and Appleton Estate Jamaican Rum. Microbrewed and imported beers are always in stock, and an inexpensive Pub Grub menu offers plenty of quality munchies (available for take-out). The lounge is open every day and has all ABC permits.

Carolina Beach

Back Alley Lounge
110 Harper Ave., Carolina Beach
• (910) 458-9081, ext.353

A cozy indoor/outdoor space at the back of the Hotel Astor, Back Alley has a laidback atmosphere where oldies and beach music dominate. Open seven days a week, the lounge offers live entertainment. (Call for schedule, especially off-season.) Back Alley has all ABC permits with no cover or membership fees. Enter from the parking lot or through the restaurant.

Club Astor
110 Harper Ave., Carolina Beach
• (910) 458-9081

Club Astor is in the Hotel Astor on the boardwalk in Carolina Beach. Live, contemporary entertainment Tuesday through Sunday (weekends off-season) and the club's large dance floor offer an irresistible invitation to dance the night away. Open seven days a week in-season, Club Astor has all ABC permits with no cover or membership fees. Enter the club from the front of the hotel. Parking is available.

Southport-Oak Island

The Southport-Oak Island area is very much a family/fishing area. Nightlife is rather quiet: You will see long lines outside the theater in the evenings and find video stores quite busy. If your nighttime interests lie in the direction of music and entertainment, you will find a few places to go, some of which we've listed below.

Chasers Bar & Grill
502 Yaupon Dr., Oak Island
• (910) 278-1500

Chasers is a small bar with a big following. Locals like to gather there for an after-work drink. There is seating at the bar and at small tables next to it and in the room extension beyond. There are four TVs in the bar. Appreciation parties and fund-raising charity events are held throughout the year.

Concerts On The Coast
Franklin Square Park, corner of Howe and E. West Sts., Southport • (910) 253-2672, (800) 222-4790

Sponsored by the Brunswick County Parks and Recreation Department and the Southport Parks and Recreation Department, this outdoor summer concert series features a variety of live bands playing in Franklin Square Park in the heart of historic Southport. This popular event is held one night a month from 6 to 8 PM, May through September. Call for dates and schedule.

Fish Tales Restaurant & Tiki Bar
606 W. West St., Southport
• (910) 457-9222

Fish Tales Restaurant is located on the second floor of a building that sits next to the Southport Marina. The lovely view from the dining area and the deck area (which includes seating for dining as well) looks out over the marina slips to the Intracoastal Waterway and beyond. The Tiki Bar is open 11 AM until and only during the season. Outside, beside the marina under a row of young live oak trees, are tables and chairs and a small covered stage for the bands, which are featured on weekends. The Tiki Bar serves a light menu. Both the restaurant and the Tiki Bar have all ABC permits.

49th Street Station Game Room and Bar
4901 E. Oak Island Dr., Oak Island
• (910) 278-9811

If you are looking for a neighborhood bar where you can relax with a drink after work before you head home for dinner, then return later in the evening to socialize and play a game or two of pool, the Station is the one. Being a nicely refurbished old gas station, it is small, but large enough to hold the enthusiastic crowd that gathers for karaoke every Saturday night.

The Station is also known for spearheading fund drives for persons suffering as as result of catastrophes or loss of income. Be it a cookout, a float in the Christmas Parade, or a Poker run, they help those less fortunate. Hours of operation are 10 AM until, Monday through Saturday and noon until on Sunday.

Jimmy's Cafe
6302 E. Oak Island Dr., Oak Island
• (910) 201-4414

The clean lines and casual atmosphere of Jimmy's Cafe will immediately put you at ease. From 11 AM until Monday through Saturday, you can enjoy a meal prepared with all the expertise of Jimmy's 38 years of experience in the restaurant business. A variety of appetizers, salads (served with French bread), burgers, lunch sandwiches, seafood, steaks and pasta are among the offerings. Ask about fresh homemade desserts as well. And Jimmy has daily specials "for the locals to enjoy." He says, "When you leave my restaurant, you've still got your pocketbook." Live entertainment, mostly beach music, is provided Friday and Saturday nights. Jimmy's has all ABC permits and an extensive wine list with wines from California as well as Italy, Spain, Australia and Germany. The cafe also handles private parties and catering.

South Brunswick Islands

Like the Southport-Oak Island area, the South Brunswick Islands are very much family oriented. You will find lines at the video stores, and lots of people on the beach after sunset. If you are looking for live entertainment, try the following.

Concerts On The Coast
Intracoastal Waterway Stage, Jordan Blvd., Holden Beach • (910) 253-2672, (800) 222-4790

Sponsored by the Brunswick County Parks and Recreation Department and the Greater Holden Beach Merchants Association, this outdoor summer concert series is a new addition to the summer scene. These concerts feature live entertainment on the island at the Intracoastal Waterway Stage on Jordan Boulevard, located near the base of the Holden Beach bridge. Held one Thursday night each month May through September, the fun begins at 6 PM. Call for dates and schedule.

INSIDERS' TIP

Join the Cape Fear Contra Dancers, (910) 791-6646 or (910) 270-3363, and dance with the most friendly folks in town. Call for the current membership fee.

Beach Music, the Shag and Chicken Hicks ... A True Story

Carolina Beach's legendary Chicken Hicks didn't invent the shag, but he was an important cog in the wheel of shag evolution. Not only was he a mover and a shaker, he was a key factor in how real beach music changed the Boardwalk during its heyday back in the 40s.

Still a floor-cleaning shagger, Chicken has females of all ages clamoring to be his partner — besides being an awesome freestyle dancer, he's a charmer, that's for sure. Though never interested in shag competition, never a national champion (as rumor has it), never an instructor, and never a publicity seeker, Chicken Hicks is well-known from Florida to Virginia. Maybe he hasn't ever won a competitive event, but he's truly a winner when it comes to his shag dance style and charismatic personality.

According to Chicken, beach music really originated as Negro rhythm and blues - like the "60-minute Man." He got introduced to this kind of music when he was 17 or 18 years old. Born and raised in Durham, North Carolina, he took advantage of his opportunities.

At that time, the "Colored Only" Durham Armory featured top swing bands, so he'd go there on Friday nights. Not one to sit in the balcony and watch with other whites when music called him to dance, Chicken was on the dance floor. He'd dance with any partner — black or white made no difference to him — still doesn't. He says he really took to their dance style and their upbeat music.

Famous for his "camel walk," Chicken says he learned that move in five minutes at Skinny's Shoeshine Parlor in the middle of the Durham's black section. In earlier times, he liked to "hot dog" — to show off his prowess. Other dancers would just move over; they'd "clean the floor" for him. He loved it! Even today, he's called upon to give exhibitions all over the country, including the Grand National Dance Championships in Atlanta.

A natural-born dancer, he says, "The

Carolina Beach's legendary Chicken Hicks played a key role in the evolution of the shag.

Photo Courtesy: Chicken Hicks

music does my dancing for me. I feel what most other people can't feel. . . . I wish I could give people what I feel." (A lot of us pseudo-dancers wish that, too!)

When questioned about why he doesn't enter competitions, Chicken replied, "Because when you compete, you have to practice, and that's work. Competition takes the fun out of it. Dancing is for enjoyment, it shouldn't be work."

You ask: What did this guy do for Carolina Beach? I'll tell you. He brought himself, his love of dancing and a disregard for conventions of the day. A frequent summer visitor to the area, he found an environment that suited his style, so as a young adult, he spent several months a year here - just hanging out.

He went over the bridge to the "Colored Only" Seabreeze community where he found music and dance styles that brought out the best moves his feet could produce. Two of his buddies serviced jukeboxes and put records in them. Chicken convinced the pair to put some of the same tunes he'd found to his liking at Seabreeze into jukeboxes on the Boardwalk, replacing slower, more traditional dance numbers. Beach music and dancing history changed forever in a moment's time.

Of course, ham that he is, he delighted crowds everywhere on the Boardwalk when he danced, and it wasn't long before others were trying to copy him. The music, the new dance style, and Chicken Hicks were instant hits.

Reminiscing, Chicken says that the mid 40s was a magical time in Carolina Beach. The Boardwalk area was "like a movie set." People were having fun. In summer months, our strand of sand was always full of people. Open patios facing the sea had jukeboxes that beckoned young and old to come dance. He had a great time. And so did everyone else.

Chicken and his wife Lynda have shared the joys of dancing to beach music for more than 25 years. Sand is in their veins. How lucky they are. They've got plenty of shag stories to tell, too, like the time shortly after they met when Lynda was Chicken's partner for an impromptu exhibition in front of 400 people. Just think, they live right here ... a dance legend and his partner for life.

Diamond Lil's Saloon
2511-2 Seashore Rd., Holden Beach
• **(910) 842-9397**

Owner Natalie Hayney describes Diamond Lil's as a working man's saloon. The saloon is large with two pool tables, a 61-inch TV, dartboards, a number of video machines and plenty of room for dancing. Dancing? For sure, Diamond Lil's has music every weekend and sometimes during the week. They even run dance contests. Her customers, ranging in age from 25 to 65, take part in pool leagues, dart leagues, family days, football and NASCAR get togethers, all including free food.

Paradise Cafe
102 Jordan Blvd., Holden Beach
• **(910) 842-4999**

With ocean views from every seat inside or on the patio, the atmosphere at the Paradise Cafe invites you to kick back and relax Jimmy Buffet style. Open for lunch and dinner almost year round, the Paradise has daily specials to offer the freshest food available and a kids' menu to keep the little ones happy. Sit among the palm trees, tropical birds and local artwork hanging on melon-colored walls and enjoy appetizer's like Samantha's Best Ever Nachos, perhaps a Greek Salad, a deli sandwich of your own design, or a burger, pizza or hot sub. Of course, there is local seafood as well. Be sure not to leave until you have enjoyed a Paradise Sunset, the house drink. And remember, the Paradise has music on the patio week nights during the season — from country to beach music to pop.

Stars Waterfront Cafe
14 Causeway Dr., Ocean Isle Beach
• **(910) 579-7838**

Executive Chef Charles Zeran and Pastry Chef Colleen Zeran began working their magic on Stars in the middle of the high season in 2002. They moved from the Washington, D.C., area, bringing with them a wealth of talent and awards. Stars is located on the waterfront, and there is literally no seat in the house from which you cannot see the view of the salt marsh and watch the glorious sunsets. In addition to inside seating, there is a large tiered deck tastefully decorated with tropical plants. The deck is enclosed with plexiglass in the off season and contains drop-down heaters. In addition, there is a gazebo over the water where you can enjoy coffee or cognac — the perfect ending to a great evening. Live music is provided on the deck on Fridays and some Saturdays.

Topsail Island

North Topsail Beach

Paliotti's at the Villa
790 New River Inlet Rd., North Topsail Beach • (910) 328-8501

Paliotti's is not only an Italian restaurant, but also a cozy little bar inside the Villa Capriani Resort Condominium Complex. Open daily year round, this is a gathering place for area residents as well as returning condo owners. It's a place to meet, enjoy a drink and catch up on the latest Topsail happenings.

Surf City

The Brass Pelican Tavern
2112 N. New River Dr., Surf City
• (910) 328-4373

The Brass Pelican is a favorite private club for local residents and returning visitors who especially enjoy the large outdoor back deck. The membership fee is $5 and visitors can be signed in by a member. Entertainment is provided on Friday and Saturday nights with karaoke on Thursdays. Menu choices include deli sandwiches, appetizers and steamed seafood in the evening. Daily drink and food specials are offered.

The Crab Pot
508 Roland Ave., Surf City
• (910) 328-5001

This down-home establishment has a take-out window and a casual screened-in dining room and bar. It's a favorite with folks who like beach music and shagging, the dance of the beach crowd. The Crab Pot caters to this group with its "Shag Shack," featuring entertainment by local disc jockeys and popular beach bands. No one is a stranger at The Crab Pot. Vacationers look forward to a return visit year after year.

Gilligan's
Roland Ave., mainland side of Surf City
• (910) 328-4090

Next to Docksider's Gifts and Shells, Gilligan's is a private club with a membership fee of $5. Visitors for an evening can be signed in by a member. Featuring the largest dance floor in the area, Gilligan's has seasonal entertainment Wednesday through Sunday with karaoke and music for dancing. A free shuttle service is always available. It's open daily year round. All ABC permits.

Sounds Edge Bar and Bistro
211 N. New River Dr., Surf City
• (910) 328-0803

The Sounds Edge is next to and affiliated with Soundside Restaurant. In addition to the cozy indoor atmosphere and 64-inch widescreen TV, there is a great screened-in outdoor deck to enjoy drinks and food while you watch the sunset over the sound. Sounds Edge offers a full bar. Check out their entertainment schedule and special events in the local newspapers.

Surf City Wine & Cheese
602 N. New River Dr., Surf City
• (910) 328-4111

Sometimes the best nightlife on Topsail Island can be grabbing a great bottle of wine and relaxing on the deck with friends. Surf City Wine and Cheese is ready to provide you with your choice of wine, be it from their extensive variety or specially ordered. Different wines are featured weekly and new lines are continually being added. Ongoing wine tastings from April to October, advance wine ordering for vacation convenience or a 10 percent discount on a case of wine, are just some of the services offered. You will also find imported beers, an expanding variety of cheeses and wine-related gifts in this new shop.

Topsail Beach

Bingo
Assembly Building, 720 Channel Blvd.,
Topsail Beach • (910) 329-4446

Join some of the greatest folks on the island for an evening of fun. Every Thursday evening, beginning at 6:30 PM, visitors and local residents compete to see who is the first to get Bingo on a variety of games with an evening jackpot ranging from $485 to $1,000, depending on the number of players. Smokers have their own section with good ventilation assuring the smoke free area remains smoke free. Soft drinks and snacks can be purchased, coffee is free.

Sneads Ferry

Paradise Landing
318 Fulchers Rd., Sneads Ferry
• (910) 327-1317

This nightclub has a Key West theme, complete with palm trees and a fantastic patio view. Lounging on the top deck with a strawberry daiquiri or drink of your choice gives the name Paradise true meaning. Paradise Landing hosts pool tournaments on Friday nights and music by North Carolina bands on Saturday nights, with dancing on the large dance floor. Come play horseshoes on Sunday. Arrive by boat or car. Paradise Landing is open seven days a week from 9 AM to 2 AM.

Movie Theaters

There are plenty of first-run theaters in the area, but films that are foreign, controversial or "artsy" have frustratingly short runs, if they run at all. It's a paradox, considering the number of films shot in Wilmington and the high level of local interest, but the situation is improving. With some shuffling of theaters by the Carmike chain and the opening 1999 addition of four more screening rooms to its 12-screen complex off Market Street in Wilmington, the net number of screens from Wilmington to Southport jumped to 36. Another unique feature added to Carmike's now 16-screen complex is comfortable stadium seating in all screening rooms.

A valuable film resource is **Cinematique**

NIGHTLIFE

A slow walk to the beach is always worthwhile.

Photo: Jay Tervo

Did You Say (gulp!) G-g-ghosts?

Mysterious footsteps... misty apparitions... playful pranks... empty rockers rocking .... Some say the true soul of an old town is its ghosts, and the southern coast region has more specters than golfers. (We're not complaining.) Sleep in a historic house long enough—a night or two might do it—and you're likely to make an eerie acquaintance! Insiders take their ectoplasms seriously because, as the following oft-told tidbits suggest, wraiths have been a coastal way of life (and death) for a long, long time.

Bellamy's Ghostly Prank

The Bellamy Mansion, a beautiful pre-Civil War home built by Dr. John Bellamy, had scarcely been built when it was taken over by General Hawley's Federal troops during the Civil War to be used as a headquarters. After seven months of deplorable activity by the Union soldiers, the mansion was returned to the family in a shambles.

After the Bellamy family returned to the mansion, servants began to tell stories about terrifying spirits they had seen, including a skeleton in the basement. Truth be told, the servants really had seen a skeleton wandering about.

It seems that one of the Bellamy sons, William, had returned from medical school and was using a room in the basement as his office. He brought his skeleton from medical home school with him, and amused himself greatly by placing the skeleton on a coffin-lid-shaped ironing board for the servants to discover. William took great delight making the skeleton appear now and then, keeping the legend of the bony apparition alive and well.

In later years, people reported seeing an old couple in the window of an unoccupied upstairs room, and children's voices, along with a woman laughing, were reported being heard—perhaps more hijinks by the Bellamy children. Or, perhaps not ....

The Bellamy Mansion in Wilmington's Historic District is open to the public for tours. Be sure to keep your eyes and ears open. Who knows what ghosts may still be lurking?

Capt. Harper's Ghostly Rescue

Back in 1897, Captain John M. Harper, a renowned Cape Fear River skipper, found he didn't need a dark and stormy night for a convincing ghost story—but it sure didn't hurt. He used to tell this story himself.

While making the passage from Wilmington to Smithville (now Southport) through a terrible winter storm, Harper was regaled by his sole passenger, a Scot, within the ferry's pilot house. The Scot told a tale about an ancestor of his, one of three Highlanders captured by the British during the American Revolution and imprisoned nearby at colonial Brunswick Town. The three captives were condemned to die, but one of them, the passenger's ancestor, made his escape. The other two were not so lucky.

Soon after the tale was told, Capt. Harper's steamer ran hard aground on a shoal opposite the site of old Brunswick Town. There was nothing to do but wait for the tide to change and keep warm below decks. While they were there, a deckhand burst in, terrified. On deck moments before, he said, he had seen an unkempt man, dripping wet, his face contorted as if in pain. The apparition held the rail with one hand and pointed into the darkness with the other, and when the deckhand went to touch his arm, the man vanished.

Harper doubted the crewman's sobriety. But when the tide had shifted and the ship was again underway, Harper, too, witnessed the impossible. After distinctly hearing a human cry, he and his entire crew spied an old rowing barge with two emaciated men on deck, their injured legs and arms manacled and chained. Harper ordered a rope cast to them, but the barge disappeared into the darkness.

Harper continued on his course and very soon came upon a capsized ship to which two men clung for their lives in the icy, black waters. They were found in the direction in which the first apparition on deck had pointed. With the Scotsman's tale fresh in their minds, Harper's crew rescued the two survivors, the last of a riverboat's crew of seven. Evidently some ghosts, despite their own former suffering, believe in doing good deeds.

The Maco Light

Until the Atlantic Coast Railroad tore up the tracks running west through Maco, many locals living today had witnessed the strange swaying light at the old Maco crossing. President Grover Cleveland spoke about it publicly during his 1888 reelection campaign. Life magazine even reported it to the nation in 1957. The story is that of Joe Baldwin, a flagman who, one pitch-dark night in 1867, was riding a caboose that lost its coupling pin. Separated from the train, the caboose had slowed nearly to a halt when Joe spied the light of a speeding passenger train coming right at him. He stood at the back of the caboose waving a lantern in warning, but the oncoming train couldn't stop.

In the collision Joe was killed instantly, decapitated. His head was never found, but ever since then, a single swaying light could be seen over the tracks at that very spot. It was seen so frequently that trainmen routinely mounted two lights on their trains, one red and one green, so as not to be confused with the Maco Light, which hasn't been seen since the tracks were lifted. It seems Old Joe Baldwin's warnings are no longer needed.

The House on Gallows Hill

It is said that back when Wilmington barely stretched beyond what is now Third Street, the high ground just off the main road, past the old St. James burial ground, was a hanging ground. Criminals, we're told, who went to their Maker on the hill were buried nearby. But when the town outgrew its former bounds, the old gallows were dismantled and houses constructed, among them the Price-Gause House, built in 1843. Fortunately for its residents, this home's invisible guest is a playful one, occasionally mischievous but never baleful.

The ghost, who is lately called George, seems to favor phantom pipe tobacco and spectral sweet potatoes—judging by the smells that occasionally greet the living occupants, employees of an architectural firm. Other incidents? A rocker that rocks itself no matter where it's placed, clearly audible footsteps when no one's there, mysteriously clouding mirrors and, perhaps best of all, quilts yanked from beds while people lie sleeping. It's a wonder no one hears hearty laughter too.

There are many other ghostly yarns to spin about North Carolina's southern coast—the Edwardian thespians of Thalian Hall; the visitations of Samuel Jocelyn to prove he was buried alive; the phantom Confederate General William Whiting, still leading the defense of Fort Fisher. You can read the stories in books available at regional public libraries and stores:

Tar Heel Ghosts by John Harden (Chapel Hill: University of North Carolina Press, 1954)

Haunted Wilmington . . . and the Cape Fear Coast by Brooks Newton Preik (Wilmington, N.C.: Banks Channel Books, 1995)

Ghosts of the Carolinas by Nancy Roberts (Columbia: University of South Carolina Press, 1962)

Ghosts on the Battleship North Carolina by Danny Bradshaw (Wilmington: Bradshaw Publishing Co., 2002)

It's said that Wilmington's Thalian Hall is haunted.

NIGHTLIFE

of Wilmington, the series that brings acclaimed foreign and classic films to town for three-day runs every other week (sometimes more often) to historic Thalian Hall, (910) 343-3664, at the corner of Chestnut and Third streets, in downtown Wilmington. Cinematique is a bargain at $6 a ticket. It's sponsored by WHQR 91.3 FM, the local public radio station. Show times are 7:30 PM Monday through Wednesday, but schedules may change to accommodate Thalian's stage schedule. You can receive Cinematique mailings by calling (910) 343-1640 or writing to Cinematique of Wilmington, 254 N. Front Street, Wilmington, NC 28401.

Hollywood East Cinema Grill, 4402 Shipyard Boulevard, (910) 792-1084, an exciting new concept in movie theaters in Wilmington, opened in May 2001. Located at Long Leaf Shopping Center, Hollywood East offers intermediate run movies (a few weeks out of popular release) in an inviting, casual atmosphere with food and beverage service available. Hollywood East's menu consists of all the popular appetizers, sandwiches, handmade pizza, desserts and, naturally, popcorn. Beer and wine are served in addition to fountain drinks and bottled water. Prices range from $5 to $10 and the wait staff is unobtrusive during the film. The theater offers two screenings per film nightly, and seating in each of the three screening rooms is cabaret-style. The theater also accommodates private parties and sponsors corporate or sporting events. The ticket price can't be beat at $4. Ticket sales are cash only but Hollywood East accepts Visa, MC and Discover cards for food and beverage sales. Check movie schedules for Hollywood East at (910) 793-1234.

Most of the movie theaters in the region offer matinee showings every day during the summer, on holidays and weekends throughout the year at $4.50 per ticket on average. Full-price tickets typically cost between $6.50 to $7 everywhere. Discounted prices for seniors are also available at most theaters. Some area theaters now offer advance ticket sales ranging from the day of purchase to three days in advance. Since there are so few theaters outside Wilmington, we've listed all theaters together.

Carmike 16, 111 Cinema Drive, Wilmington, (910) 815-0212, is the area's newest addition and, with 16 screens, is enough of a development to require a street of its own (Cinema Drive), linking Market Street and Kerr Avenue. The new stadium seats and leg room are the most generous in town, with the least possibility of an obstructed view.

Cinema 6, 5335 Oleander Drive, Wilmington, (910) 799-6666, is less than 4 miles from Wrightsville Beach and is directly across the street from Eddie Romanelli's.

College Road Cinemas, 632 S. College Road, Wilmington, (910) 395-1780 or the movie infoline (910) 395-1790, is a six-screen complex with comfortable, high-back seats. This theater is behind Swensen's, across the street from the UNCW campus.

Cinema 4, 1020 Carolina Beach Road, Carolina Beach, (910) 458-3444, is a cozy four-screen complex in the Federal Point Plaza shopping center next to Jubilee Amusement Park. This theater is a good choice if you relish the thoughts of a night at the movies away from long lines and Wilmington's traffic.

Surf Cinemas, 4836 Long Beach Road SE, Southport, (910) 457-0320, is convenient to the entire Southport-Oak Island area, situated south of the intersection of Long Beach Road and N.C. 211 (Southport-Supply Road). Please note that children under two years of age aren't admitted to this theater.

Literary Pursuits

With a strong and supportive arts community, writers of all kinds — novelists, playwrights, poets, screenwriters, and journalists among them — flourish in the Lower Cape Fear region. Who couldn't be moved to rapturous prose by the breathtaking beauty of this coastal region or see opportunity in the overwhelming presence of the dramatic arts and the film industry. But the writing life is a solitary one, so it's no surprise that aspiring authors and poets seek out nightspots that satisfy twin desires: companionship and the need to share their work. Writers are naturally avid readers, so book discussion groups, poetry readings or a cappuccino with fellow writers are all part of the literary nightlife in coastal Carolina.

Barnes & Noble Booksellers
322 S. College Rd., Wilmington
• (910) 395-4825

The cafe at Barnes & Noble, a popular spot for both seasoned and would-be scribblers, ensures there's enough caffeine at hand to chase the muse. Past events have included family-friendly poetry readings, writers group meetings and book clubs. Check B & N's monthly schedule for these and other literary events plus local book-signings.

Bristol Books
Lumina Station Fountainside,
1908 Eastwood Rd., Wilmington
• **(910) 256-4490**

Local, regional and nationally renowned author book signings are a frequent highlight, and Bristol offers interesting (and very diverse) in-store evening book clubs. The Nonfiction Book Club meets on the second Friday of the month at 7 PM. The Final Chapter Mystery Book Club, a long-running feature of the store, meets monthly on the first Sunday at 6 PM. Devotees of Southern literature will enjoy the Sweet Tea Book Club, which meets on the last Wednesday of the month at 7 PM. Visitors are welcome to all club meetings. Call the store for a schedule of book titles to be discussed. Bristol Books is located in the expanded section of Lumina Station's shopping complex near Wrightsville Beach.

NIGHTLIFE

Shopping

If shopping is your passion, Wilmington and North Carolina's southern coast offer abundant opportunities to indulge it. The steady influx of retirees, a booming golf industry, relocating business, the resulting commercial and residential development and an active year-round tourism industry account for a wide range of shopping options, from quaint, one-of-a-kind boutiques to nationally recognized retail mega-stores.

Today, few of the region's communities remain unaffected by this retail growth. Shopping centers, both large and small, abound in and around Wilmington and the adjacent beach areas, competing with each other to provide the best and the most interesting goods and services. The current trend in shopping centers for the region often includes aesthetically pleasing architecture, landscaped grounds, sculptured art, plentiful parking and upscale shops that rival any major metropolitan area for selection and quality of goods. These multiuse commercial centers also include restaurants, office space and service providers. Near Wrightsville Beach, Lumina Station, Landfall Shopping Center and The Forum shopping centers are excellent examples of this type of center (all are described in this chapter). The number of independent shop owners has grown, and many have prospered. Southport and the beach communities now have a greater percentage of shops and businesses that remain open all year, although often with limited or shortened hours in the winter months.

It's no surprise that Wilmington, the largest city along the southern coast of North Carolina, provides the greatest variety in shopping adventures. With dozens of shopping centers, numerous art galleries and hundreds of specialty shops, you will find a wealth of treasures to choose from in domestic or imported clothing, antique and contemporary furniture, accessories, fine art and a rich selection of local artwork and crafts, traditional or estate jewelry, sought-after collectibles, an abundance of antiques and much more. Whether your tastes include the eclectic, the funky and the downright fun or have a more traditional view, you'll find what you're looking for here.

Primary business and shopping areas for the Port City include downtown Wilmington, the College Road area, Market Street, Oleander Drive, Monkey Junction and the Military Cutoff/Eastwood Road area adjacent to Wrightsville Beach, but don't hesitate to venture off onto side streets. Chances are good that you'll discover a quaint, out-of-the-way boutique or collection of shops. Wilmington also has the area's greatest concentration of superstores and discount chains, including Wal-Mart, Best Buy, Target, Office Max, PetsMart, Sam's Club, Old Navy and Stein Mart, in addition to the upscale Belk and Dillard's department stores.

As you explore the region's shopping options, you will notice that coastal North Carolinians love gourmet foods, wine, imported cheeses, hard-to-find herbs and spices, ethnic cooking and specialty bakeries. Local food markets and chain grocery stores, while not covered in this chapter, are abundant throughout the area and will stock or order new items at a customer's request.

Unfortunately, this chapter contains a mere sampling of available shopping possibilities in Wilmington and the coastal communities. An attempt to cover every store, boutique and shopping center in the region would fill an entire book. The selections in this overview describe some of the unique as well as the tried-and-true shops and have been divided into easy-to-read sections for some of the major areas of Wilmington, the Wrightsville Beach

WILMINGTON'S SHOPPING VILLAGE

BY THE BEACH

SHOP, DINE OR SIMPLY RELAX

AT WRIGHTSVILLE BEACH'S FAVORITE SHOPS AND RESTAURANTS

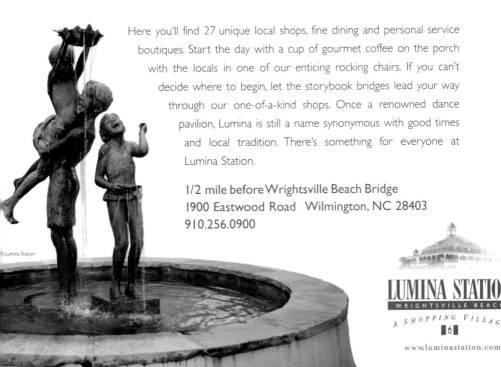

Here you'll find 27 unique local shops, fine dining and personal service boutiques. Start the day with a cup of gourmet coffee on the porch with the locals in one of our enticing rocking chairs. If you can't decide where to begin, let the storybook bridges lead your way through our one-of-a-kind shops. Once a renowned dance pavilion, Lumina is still a name synonymous with good times and local tradition. There's something for everyone at Lumina Station.

1/2 mile before Wrightsville Beach Bridge
1900 Eastwood Road   Wilmington, NC 28403
910.256.0900

Lumina Station

LUMINA STATION
WRIGHTSVILLE BEACH
A SHOPPING VILLAGE

www.luminastation.com

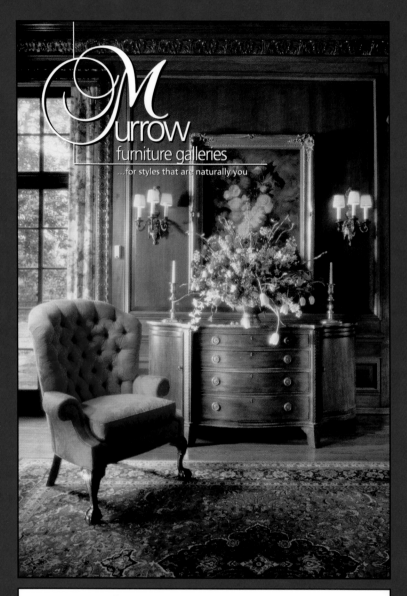

ROLEX

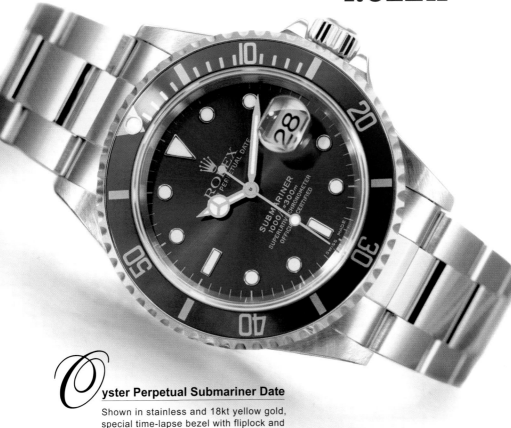

Oyster Perpetual Submariner Date

Shown in stainless and 18kt yellow gold,
special time-lapse bezel with fliplock and
extension link Oyster bracelet. Pressure-proof
to 1,000 feet. Also available in 18kt yellow gold.

REEDS®
Jewelers

WESTFIELD SHOPPINGTOWN INDEPENDENCE   910.799.6810

Rolex, ♛, Oyster Perpetual, Oyster, fliplock and Submariner are trademarks.

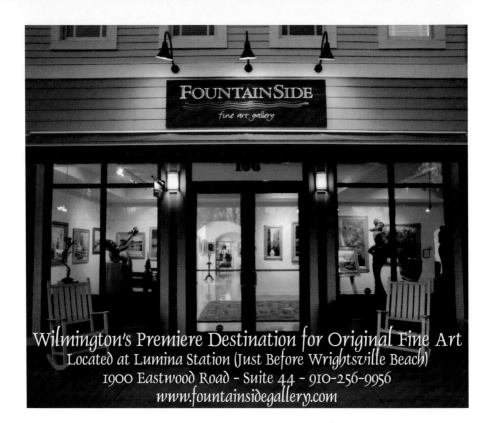

Island Passage

CLOTHING • SHOES • ELIXIR

BALD HEAD ISLAND • HISTORIC DOWNTOWN WILMINGTON • WRIGHTSVILLE BEACH

762-0484

It's Easy To Be A Fair Weather Friend...
Here at Perry's Emporium, We Dare To Be Different!
We Are Your Rainy Weather Friend.

If It Rains On Your Wedding Day
You Can Get Your Engagement Ring
Money Refunded!!

See Store For Details

PERRY'S EMPORIUM

Barklay Commons at Shipyard Blvd. & Independence Blvd. Just 1 Mi. from the Mall 392-6721 vicinity and the coastal communities of Carolina Beach, Southport-Oak Island and the South Brunswick beaches.

For the off-season visitor traveling to the beach communities, most of the stores and businesses included in this chapter offer year-round hours of operation. However, many reduce or limit these hours in the winter months so it's wise to call ahead to make sure the store will be open when you plan to visit.

General Shopping

Wilmington

Downtown

Step back in time while shopping along the streets of historic downtown Wilmington. Surrounded by the city's beautiful historic homes and museums, brick streets and serene waterfront, downtown provides a relaxed shopping experience. Rare are the shoppers who aren't tempted to slow their steps in this tranquil setting. Personal service by shop owners, an inquiry into the well-being of your family and a cozy, small-town atmosphere further add to the shopping experience. Most of the nearly 100 stores concentrated along the streets of downtown Wilmington are independently owned and reflect the interests and tastes of the owners. You won't encounter rack after rack of the same items.

Downtown offers art galleries, antiques shops, fine clothing, funky garb, traditional footwear, crazy shoes, toys, gourmet items, CDs, wine, linens, glassware, fine and costume jewelry, collectibles, books, home furnishings, scents and more. It's a great place to find interesting imports as well.

Part of the charm of this shopping district is its compact size and pleasant walkability. Park your car on the street or, if you're shopping at one of the retail/dining centers, park at no cost in their lots. Downtown is like an open-air mall with an astonishing selection of spots in which to pause and take in the beautiful scenes between purchases. Coffee shops, delicatessens, pubs, ice cream parlors, candy shops and full-service restaurants offer constant temptation to shoppers. Many downtown restaurants have outdoor seating right on the sidewalk, a setup guaranteed to lure your weary feet to pause while you gawk.

Downtown is anchored by two large centers at the northern and southern ends of the central shopping district. The Cotton Exchange is a shopping/dining/office complex at the northern end of the riverfront, and Chandler's Wharf occupies the southern end. The area between, Water Street,

Front Street and Second Street, is a busy corridor lined with restaurants, galleries, banks, services and stores. Water Street, located on downtown's riverfront, and streets that cross Front Street offer a wide variety of shopping possibilities.

Antiques buffs, surrounded by the heady sense of southern coastal history, will find it impossible to bypass downtown Wilmington's pleasing variety of antique stores. (see our section on Antiques in this chapter.)

Blackbeard's Bryde
J. W. Brooks Building, 18 S. Water St., Wilmington • (910) 815-0660

The Cape Fear region's colorful pirate history inspired the name for this intriguing boutique, but don't let the name fool you . . . this store may not be what you think it is. It has the latest and best styles with names like Dollhouse, Angie, Lucy Love, Split, Hurley and Tramp, just to mention a few, along with very unusual jewelry, including one-of-a-kind pieces. Blackbeard's Bryde has fantastic candles, soaps, 54 different incense fragrances and a gift line that may leave you with smiles and giggles. With prices you'll love, discover this local secret — you may want to visit again and again.

The Candy Bar
112 Market St., Wilmington • (910) 762-0805

Indulge your sweet tooth at this delicious downtown Wilmington candy shop. The Candy Bar offers high-quality European chocolates, Joseph Schmidt truffles, old-fashioned fudge and a large selection of regular and sugar-free candies. Wine and champagne, selected to compliment the gourmet chocolates, are featured and make a wonderful gift idea. In addition to mouthwatering confections, The Candy Bar also carries unique gifts for all ages, books and Burt's Bees personal care products. Greeting cards, complimentary gift wrapping and shipping are available.

An exciting new addition to The Candy Bar is the teddy bear creation section in the back of the shop, a Wilmington exclusive. Kids of all ages will love stuffing and dressing their very own plush animals from a choice of 20 styles and twice that number of outfits. Each bear is named by their creator and comes with a birth certificate, bow tie and cradle. Outfits are sold separately. Birthday parties (for the child, the bear or both) are available at the shop.

Chandler's Wharf Shops
2 Ann St. and 225 S. Water St., Wilmington

This center on the river has many appealing shopping opportunities. Created by Thomas

SHOPPING

SHOPPING

Henry Wright Jr. in the late 1970s, it has evolved over time as a retail/dining complex, but part of it began as a ship's chandler in the 19th century. There was a maritime museum here in the 1970s and some marine artifacts are still scattered about the grounds, including an enormous anchor and other reminders of the complex's origins. Cobblestone streets, plank walkways, attractive landscaping and a gorgeous view of the Cape Fear River are some of the features that make shopping at Chandler's Wharf Shops such a pleasant experience. The center is flourishing today with some of Wilmington's most delightful stores, and it boasts two of the city's most pleasant restaurants — The Pilot House and Elijah's (see our Restaurants chapter) — and the pleasure of dining in either one is heightened by the option of enjoying your meal on outdoor decks overlooking the river. Some of the many shops here include the shops listed below.

A Proper Garden
Chandler's Wharf Shops, 2 Ann St., Wilmington • (910) 763-7177

A Proper Garden has everything for your garden you never knew you needed until you walk in the door and find yourself wanting it all. Birdhouses, chimes, gazing globes, fountains, lawn ornaments, animal-shaped stepping stones, sundials, wind wheels and benches are just some of the items here.

A. Scott Rhodes
Chandler's Wharf Shops, 2 Ann St., Wilmington • (910) 763-6616

Located at the corner of Ann and Water streets

in historic downtown Wilmington, A. Scott Rhodes has the power to dazzle and mesmerize you with unique and one-of-a-kind jewelry. If you've decided you'd like a new look for your own jewelry, here's the place to do it. Scott has just the right artistic talents to work with you in creating new and exciting jeweled masterpieces. This charming jewelry store is an intimate, friendly, full-service shop with selections in fine diamonds, precious stones, pearls, gold, platinum, local estate jewelry and designer pieces.

Azalea Coast Gifts, Flowers and Candles
Chandler's Wharf Shops, 2 Ann St., Wilmington • (910) 815-0102

New to the Chandler's Wharf in 2002, this combination florist and specialty shop offers a tempting array of distinctive handcrafted gifts from North and South Carolina artists and craftsmen in a uniquely tasteful setting. The shop takes pride in offering "great gifts for all budgets." Some of the possibilities to savor include local photography, reproduction prints of Old Wilmington, handmade soaps, garden gifts, linens, locally made shell wreaths, handmade Charleston garden tiles, sketches of local scenes by area artists, award-winning North Carolina wines and much more. One exception to the shop's Carolinas theme is the beautiful line of handmade, hand-painted Italian ceramic art known as Cose' de Ital. The shop's florist services boasts 23 years experience in the Wilmington area and includes wedding and special events work. This fascinating shop also carries an extensive array of candles and accessories, including scented candles, hand-dipped tapers, pillars and unique candle holders as well as novelty candles. Special orders are accepted.

Gifted Gourmet
Chandler's Wharf Shops, 225 S. Water St., Wilmington • (910) 815-0977, (888) 830-3278

The Gifted Gourmet carries a mouthwatering array of gourmet treats, including chocolates, sugar-free chocolates, teas, an incredible variety of vinegars, oils, Vidalia onion vinaigrette, gourmet fruit jams and preserves, a large selection of North Carolina products and over 200 hot sauces, dips, pesto and barbecue sauces. For tasty and unique gift-giving, send a gourmet gift basket. The shop also offers free local delivery.

Rice Planter
Chandler's Wharf Shops, 225 S. Water St., Wilmington • (910) 762-2626

A charming little shop inside Chandler's

Wharf Shops, the Rice Planter features a wonderful selection of quilts by Pine Conetill and a wide variety of white cotton bed linens and sleepwear by American Canyon. The Rice Planter has a variety of vignettes: white antique furniture paired with lamps and cast iron birds; a nook that's complete with fragrant bath soap and lotions; and hard-to-find French perfumes.

Silver Cloud
Chandler's Wharf Shops, 225 S. Water St., Wilmington • (910) 762-5477

Silver Cloud claims to "cover you from head to toe" and their great selection of .925 sterling silver proves it, offering everything from traditional pieces to one-of-a-kind jewelry. The store also carries jewelry crafted by local artists. Silver hair accessories are a specialty, and Silver Cloud is the exclusive dealer for Janina custom made hair ornaments from Denmark.

Stone Heart
Chandler's Wharf Shops, 225 S. Water St., Wilmington • (910) 341-0040

In a historic warehouse across the street from the Cape Fear River, Stone Heart features works from local, national and international artists including sculpture, original design windows using stained glass paint on vintage windows, and wearable art.

Gifts of Aloha, Ltd.
Chandler's Wharf Shops, 225 S. Water St., Wilmington • (910) 251-0201

Here's the place to experience the true spirit of "Aloha." Add a touch of the tropics to your home and wardrobe or find Hawaiian-style gifts and cards for any occasion. Special arrangements can be made for deliveries direct from Hawaii to you. How about fresh pineapple, chocolate macadamia nuts and fresh flower leis?

The Cotton Exchange
321 N. Front St., Wilmington
• (910) 343-9896

The site of the largest cotton-exporting company in the world in the 19th century, this collection of eight buildings overlooking the Cape Fear River was converted into a shopping and dining center in the early 1970s. Its renovation marked the beginning of the restoration of downtown Wilmington. Shoppers can enjoy a bit of history as they stroll the mall's tri-level space, where displays of cotton bales, weighing equipment and photographs tell the story of the center's evolution and about many downtown locations. Parking is free in the large lot for visitors of the complex.

The sampling of specialty shops listed below suggest the scope of shopping possibilities at The Cotton Exchange (all stores are within the complex bounded by Water and Front streets).

Blowing In The Wind
The Cotton Exchange, 312 Nutt St., Wilmington • (910) 763-1730, (888) 691-8034

This uniquely fun shop carries a variety of kites, windsocks and flags for all occasions. If you're looking for a thrill, though, this is the place to find a full line of kite-boarding products to get you started. If your passion is puzzles,

SHOPPING

check out an area of the store called Puzzler's Paradise for a great selection of jigsaw puzzles and brain teasers for all ages and skill levels. The lighthouse puzzles are particularly beautiful.

T. S. Brown Jewelry
The Cotton Exchange, 343 N. Front St., Wilmington • (910) 762-3467

T. S. Brown specializes in gemstones and settings and also has a nice assortment of fine jewelry and costume items. Hand-crafted jewelry in original designs by 100 artists makes this a special place to look for unusual items. Stone-cutting demonstrations are frequently held — usually on Tuesday and Thursday; call for more information. Owners Tim and Sandy Brown are jewelry designers who create their own designs.

The Celtic Shop
The Cotton Exchange, 3108 Nutt St., Wilmington • (910) 763-1990

For those who love all things Celtic, this is a must-visit for fine Scottish, Irish and Welsh imports. You'll find a pleasing variety of goods, including imported Irish and Scottish clothing, Celtic music, jewelry, clan heraldry items,

books, authentic Irish breakfast tea and many other gifts ideas.

East Bank Trading Co.
The Cotton Exchange, 321 N. Front St., Wilmington • (910) 763-1047

Located in the Cotton Exchange for over 20 years, the East Bank Trading Co. continues to offer high-quality and decorative American handcrafts and pottery, especially from North Carolina crafters. You'll find a large selection of items from beautiful (and practical) pottery to hand-blown glass ornaments and stained-glass suncatchers to original, handmade jewelry.

Kringles Korner
The Cotton Exchange, 311 N. Front St., Wilmington • (910) 762-7528

This is the place to Christmas shop in downtown Wilmington. Owners Derry and Tony Witkege stock a wide variety of unique ornaments, nativities, angels and wonderful Christmas collectibles, including shell ornaments, Boyd's Bears and Seraphim Angels. Nautical and lighthouse ornaments are a specialty, and the hand-carved, hand-painted Russian ornaments are exquisite. Look for unique Wilmington ornaments while you're there; Kringles Korner carries the official

SHOPPING

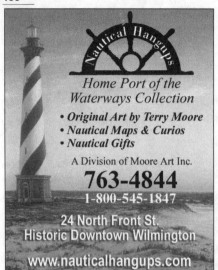

Christmas In Wilmington ornaments to benefit the Wilmington Children's Museum.

Occasions ... just write!
The Cotton Exchange, 313 N. Front St., Wilmington • (910) 343-9033

The art of a hand-written letter is alive at this charming shop, and writers of all types — professional, dabbling or social — will find just the right gift or indulgence here. Social stationery and invitations by Crane, William Arthur and Caspari are featured items. Occasions also offers fine writing instruments, including fountain and calligraphy pens, bottled ink, sealing wax, journals and desk accessories. Handmade paper is available in large sheets or letter-size sheets and envelopes in bulk. Other distinctive items include local artist Deborah Cavenaugh's prints, Blenko hand-blown glass, hand-carved hardwood letter openers and magnifying glasses, picture frames and a large selection of cards. Shipping and local delivery are available.

Two Sisters Bookery
The Cotton Exchange, 318 Nutt St., Wilmington • (910) 762-4444

This small bookstore carries a surprisingly wide range of books — contemporary novels, books of local interest, nonfiction and gift books. A writer's paradise can be found on the shelves of unique and beautiful journals. Artistic, unusual greeting cards are must-see items, and enchanting gifts of all kinds infuse the atmosphere of this cozy nook. Service is high-quality, and the staff will locate and order any available books. It's a great stop for putting literature in your beach bag before heading out to the shore.

Daughtry's Old Books
22 N. Front St., Wilmington • (910) 763-4754

In the heart of downtown Wilmington for more than 17 years, Daughtry's Old Books is a book-lover's haven. If you're searching for that long out-of-print treasure or something wonderful to read, this store is crammed from floor to ceiling with an estimated 30,000 titles, everything from the very rare to contemporary fiction. Looking for first editions? Daughtry's carries about 500.

Emily Parker
110 Market St., Wilmington • (910) 332-0329

Named for its talented owner, this charming

Fishing is great fun for everyone.

Photo: Jay Tervo

Old Wilmington City Market
119 South Water Street
Wilmington, NC 28401

ARTaTAC - Art Gallery & Coffee Shop - **910.232.9680**

Art by J.D. - Artwork - **910.763.4961**

Barouke - Gallery of Gifts & Furniture of Exotic Woods - www.barouke.com - **910.762-4999**

Bird on a Wire - Accessories for home & garden - **251.6996**

Buddy Ray's - Gifts, Antiques, Accessories, & Beanie Babies - **910.762.1912**

Captain Ken's - Sea Art, Crafts, Fine Fudge, & Taffy - **910.452.7281**

Elizabeth's Tres Chic - Ladies Clothing & More - **910.772.9004**

Fe Fi Faux - Whimsical Hand-Painted Furniture - **910.686.9119**

Four Sisters Garden - Organic Garden Supplies, Plants, Hemp, & Imports - **910.343.8500**

Glassy Chic - Fused Glass & Glass Mosaics - www.glassychic.com - **910.285.6992**

Jan Pendergrass - Cigar Box Handbags - **910.792.0227**

Kneading The Knots - Massage - **910.520.2627**

Ladybugs - A Refreshing Collection of Gifts & Accessories - **910.815.0808**

Marty K - T-Shirts & Hats - **762.9977**

Peking Gourmet - Chinese Restaurant - Free Delivery Min. $10 - **910.763.2281/763.6255**

River Muse - Exotic Gifts, Jewelry & Decor - **910.264.1990**

Ronald Williams - Artist - **910.763.6451**

Sam's Pastel Portraits - Commissioned Paintings of People, Pets & Landscapes -**910.328.0524**

Summer Sandals - Sandals- **910.791.5771**

Open Year Round

shop offers one-of-a-kind jewelry in an eclectic array of styles, from Egyptian to Victorian to extreme contemporary. Every piece is handcrafted using a variety of techniques and metals, including bronze and gold. The shop's specialty is sterling silver and semi-precious stones. A wide range of prices will suit every budget. Custom work is also available. Emily Parker is open Monday through Saturday and by appointment.

Fountaine Bridals and Formals
Austin Commons, 5202 Carolina Beach Rd., Ste. 11, Wilmington • (910) 794-9959

Fountaine Bridals and Formals, in the wedding business since 1980, provides complete bridal services to brides from all over the world. This well-established shop specializes in gown preservation and offers a bridal consulting service. Complete bridal party alterations, mothers' gowns and flower girl dresses plus an extensive selection of wedding accessories are available.

Island Passage
4 Market St., Wilmington • (910) 762-0484

Located near the waterfront at the end of Market Street, this charming boutique offers fun and stylish choices. It carries an interesting selection of women's clothing, shoes, handmade vegetable glycerin soaps and aromatherapy products, including candles, soaps and essential oils. Clothing lines include French Connection, Silver Jeans, Juicy and Michael Stars. Visit Island Passage's other location at Lumina Station I, 1908 Eastwood Road near Wrightsville Beach, (910) 256-0407; their store on Bald Head Island near the marina carries fun island resortwear, (910) 457-4944. A larger Bald Head Island location on Maritime Way has a fabulous selection of clothing, shoes and accessories for men, women and children, (910) 454-8420.

Kingoff's Jewelers
10 N. Front St., Wilmington • (910) 762-5219

A downtown jeweler since 1919, Kingoff's offers a selection of fine diamonds, colored stones, jewelry, Waterford crystal, watches and repairs. The store is the exclusive seller of the famed Old Wilmington Cup. Thomas Brown, metalsmith, created this pewter cup to celebrate the city's success in commerce and industry, and it's a favored gift among Wilmingtonians. Kingoff's also offers an exclusive Wilmington charm, depicting a dogwood blossom within a circle, available in 14K

gold or silver. There's a second Wilmington location of Kingoff's at 1409 Audubon Boulevard, (910) 799-2100.

Nautical Hangups
24 N. Front St., Wilmington • (910) 763-4844, (800) 545-1847

Dubbed the "Home Port of the Waterways Collection," Nautical Hangups showcases the unique creations of local artist Terry Moore. The Waterways Collection is a series of artistic maps depicting the coastal regions of the United States and the original maps, hand-drawn and painted in oils by Moore, are the source of these unique and highly collectible prints, note cards and other items featured in the shop. Each map includes a poem, by the artist, about the region portrayed. Look closely and you'll find a hidden, good luck rabbit in each map. Nautical Hangups also carries nautical-themed gifts and accessories to complement Moore's art.

The Old Wilmington City Market
119 S. Water St., Wilmington • (910) 763-9748

The Old Wilmington City market is a forgotten riverfront gem. This historic brick and stucco building, built in 1879, stretches a city block in width between Front and Water streets. Currently in the midst of a revival, the market is evolving from its origins as a vegetable market and its subsequent transformation into a flea market. The old-world style ar-

---

INSIDERS' TIP

A good time to buy swimwear, pool toys, beach and gift items is right at the end of "tourist season" when beach stores are clearing out merchandise before closing for the winter.

SHOPPING

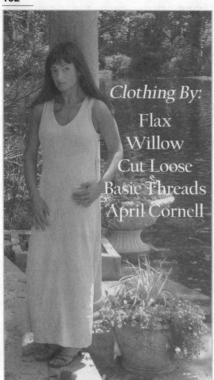

Clothing By:

Flax
Willow
Cut Loose
Basic Threads
April Cornell

cade with glass skylights is now a shopping haven featuring chic specialty shops, including women's boutiques, T-shirts, hats, jewelry, fresh-cut flowers in season, plants, gardening supplies, handmade local soaps, unique exotic woods, a coffee shop and an art gallery, imported goods and local artists. The market also features a relaxing center seating area, which is the focus of a series of ongoing events hosted by market vendors. Its' open year round, and hours vary according to season.

Rare Cargo
112 N. Front St., Wilmington
• (910) 762-7636

Describing themselves as "purveyors of stuff you could probably do without," Rare Cargo's focus is on fun for all ages. You won't want to miss their eclectic selection of fun gifts, stationery, books and cards. The shop also carries a nice collection of well-priced, trendy junior clothing as well as jewelry.

Ropa, etc.
120-B S. Front St., Wilmington
• (910) 815-0344

Are you ready for something new and exciting? Then you're invited to experience the pleasure of fine cottons and linens, which make dressing comfortable and fun. Ropa, etc. is the area's exclusive retailer for such lines as Liz and Jane, Flax, and Willow. This terrific shop also carries great makers such as Rico hand-knit sweaters, TSD, April Cornell, Habitat, Cut•Loose, Basic Threads and Naot shoes. Ropa, etc. is also known for its unique collection of jewelry from makers around the world plus great accessories to complement any outfit. Sizes range from extra small to extra large and fit a variety of shapes. Ropa, etc. has two other locations to serve you: 1121 Military Cutoff Suite D at the Forum (910) 256-8733 and 417-C North Howe Street in Southport (910) 454-8833.

Twice Baked Pottery Painting Studio
6 Market St., Wilmington
• (910) 393-9886

A great way wile away a few hours on a rainy day or after a stroll along the riverfront would be stopping in the Twice Baked Pottery Painting Studio to paint a unique pottery piece. Offering a large variety of items to choose from and more than 50 paint colors, as well as stencils, stamps and idea books, this is a fun place to forget your troubles and just get into a creative mood. Friendly staff are happy to provide assistance. Hours are Tuesday through Saturday, 11 AM to 7 PM; during the summer they're open Sundays 1 to 5 PM, too. Special rates are available for parties of seven or more - but you need to bring your own food and drinks.

Toms Drug Company
1 N. Front St., Wilmington
• (910) 762-3391

This authentic, old-style drugstore has been a landmark in downtown Wilmington since 1932. Despite a serious face-lift in 1995, the store continues to have an old-Wilmington flavor and dedication to customer service. The complete pharmacy offers citywide delivery. Have questions? Just ask Faye or any of the other friendly staff at Toms.

Oleander Drive Area

Westfield Shoppingtown Independence, the region's only enclosed shopping mall, is the dominant shopping spot along Oleander Drive. However, the area around the mall and along Oleander Drive bustles with shopping possibilities that are expanding every year. Several smaller centers offer exciting shopping opportunities.

Albert F. Rhodes Jewelers
1325 Floral Parkway, Wilmington
• (910) 313-6935

Serving Wilmington for 54 years, this family-owned and -operated jeweler is located off Oleander Drive near Westfield Shoppingtown Independence. The store specializes in a fine line of jewelry, including unique 18k gold and platinum pieces, exotic gemstones and a wide variety of diamond jewelry. It is Wilmington's only Lladro dealer. Swiss watches and distinctive giftware are another highlight. A full-service jeweler, Rhodes offers bridal services, watch and jewelry repair, appraisals and engraving with four gemologists on staff.

Audubon Village
1400 Audubon Blvd., Wilmington

A charming center worthy of mention is Audubon Village, located on a picturesque side street off of Oleander Drive. The center's businesses include **Southern Acupuncture**, (910) 799-5777, whose motto is " 5,000 years of Chinese medicine in about an hour." It offers acupuncture, smoking-cessation therapy, an herbal pharmacy and nutritional counseling by appointment. The **Michael Capristo Salon**, (910) 350-3510, is a full-service salon with 12 highly trained stylists. Call for an appointment and add a manicure and/or a pedicure to your day of beauty.

Kingoff's Jewelers, (910) 799-2100, offers

the same high caliber selection in fine jewelry and giftware found at the downtown Wilmington location at 10 N. Front Street. Kingoff's specializes in 14K, 18K and platinum jewelry and has one of the largest selections of diamond engagement rings in the area. Exclusive to Kingoff's are beautiful Wilmington charms in either gold or sterling silver. Giftware includes the famed pewter Old Wilmington Cup, Waterford crystal and more. Appraisals by Guild Gemologists and on-premise watch and jewelry repair are available.

Gallery of Oriental Rugs
4101 Oleander Dr., Wilmington
• (910) 392-2605

Entering this unique 12,000-square-foot gal-

SHOPPING

SHOPPING

lery, designed in the image of an Imperial Persian tent, is a step into the history and romance of the orient. The $10 million dollar inventory offers an unprecedented and comprehensive selection of antique and contemporary Persian and Oriental rugs. This collection includes both handmade and machine-made rugs. The store is the exclusive dealer in 17th-century Oriental rugs. Customers from all over the globe visit Gallery of Oriental Rugs for the excellent selection and unparalleled customer services. A full-service operation, the store offers tips on buying a rugs, demonstrations of rug-making on a loom, information on the history and origin of the rugs, conservation and repair services, appraisals and cleaning. The gallery also buys old rugs.

Hanover Center
3501 Oleander Dr., Wilmington

A nice complement to Westfield Shoppingtown Independence across the street, this lively strip center was completely remodeled in 2002. Wilmington's original shopping destination, it opened in 1955 — before any other strip malls — and it remains popular. Listed below are some of the merchants currently located in Hanover Center.

AAA Travel Agency, vacation and travel services plus AAA Motor Club office, (910) 763-8446. Two full-service banking centers with ATM are **Bank of America**, (910) 251-5285 and **Cooperative Bank**, (910) 343-0181. **Wild Bird Centers** offers backyard nature products, garden accessories and seed for attracting birds, (910) 343-600. **Great Clips** is a moderately priced salon providing haircuts and permanents only, (910) 362-0054. **Great Outdoor Provi-**

sion **Company** carries outdoor clothing, equipment, footwear and accessories for backpacking and paddle sports, (910) 343-1648. **Omega Sports** offers sporting gear, apparel and shoes and is also a running specialty store, (910) 762-7212.

K & W Cafeteria serves some of the best food in town for breakfast, lunch and dinner seven days a week, (910) 762-7011. **J. Michael's Philly Deli** is a great place for sandwiches and other deli fare for lunch and dinner daily, (910) 763-6466. **Temptations Foods & Cafe** is the place to go for gourmet treats, food gifts, sweets, teas and coffees, (910) 763-6662.

At **Stein Mart** you'll find upscale merchandise at discount prices, including clothing, shoes, gifts, linens and accessories, (910) 772-1533. **Sterling House** is an inviting store offering gifts, jewelry, collectibles, home accessories, Hallmark cards and fine stationery, (910) 763-3656. **Picture This** offers arts, gifts and home decor items, (910) 762-2780. **SAS Shoes** sells comfort shoes for men and women, including complete line of San Antonio Shoes with extended sizes available, (910) 772-9994. **Shoe Shak** sells fashion footwear for adults in a wide range of sizes, and they also carry accessories, (910) 772-8940. **Tiny World** is a special store carrying fine children's clothing in sizes from infant to preteen, (910) 251-8925.

Learning Express
The Courtyard, 5704 Oleander Dr., Wilmington • (910) 397-0301

This store's slogan is "Toys That Capture Imaginations." It's a great place for kids and their parents because everything in it offers educational opportunities. There's an extensive dress-up section, with everything from glittery flappers to superhero capes to cowgirl and cowboy duds. Puzzles range the complexity spectrum, and there are science kits for all age levels. The store carries books, games for all ages, yoyos (including Yomega), Brio, Playmobil, Corolle dolls, Thomas the Tank Engine, Groovy Girls, Manhattan Baby and Beanie Babies.

Learning Express carries Legos, puppets, erector sets and K'nex plus a large selection of kites for kids of all ages, from toddler to sophisticated stunt kites. In this 3,300 square feet of fun, perhaps the largest department is the art section. This popular area offers art supplies and activities to all interests, ages and skill levels from finger paints to a potter's wheel. Another sought-after feature of the store is the free personalizing offered. Items include clipboards, lap trays, beach totes, beach pails, piggy banks and more.

The store's huge Birthday Wish Bucket allows a child to select gifts for birthdays or holidays, allowing parents, grandparents and friends an easy way to shop. Other store services include a Baby Gift Registry, free gift wrapping, gift certificates, UPS shipping and a Grandparents Club that offers discounts to grandparents. Discounts are also available to teachers and other professionals who work with children. If Learning Express doesn't have a particular item, they promise to try and find it.

Oleander Oaks
5725 Oleander Dr., Wilmington

Peaceful and serene are words that come to mind at this pleasant shopping complex, despite the steady traffic along Oleander Drive. Built around majestic and ancient live oaks, the low white buildings encircle a spacious parking area and are within an easy stroll of each other. The following retail shops are a sample of what you'll find here.

The Herb Shop
Oleander Oaks, 5725 Oleander Dr., Ste. B-8, Wilmington • (910) 452-HERB (4372)

Owned and operated by a Registered Pharmacist since 1994, The Herb Shop has the right products for you. A broad range of vitamins, supplements, homeopathic remedies and herbal nutritionals are available. Numerous reputable product lines are featured as well as bulk herbs. You can also find a big variety of teas. Be sure to try some of their excellent smoothies and coffees while you're there. Free weight-control and health counseling are provided by qualified health professionals during store hours, which are Monday through Friday 10 AM to 6 PM and Saturday 10 AM to 3 PM.

The Knitting Gallery
Oleander Oaks, 5725 Oleander Dr., Ste. A-7, Wilmington • (910) 798-1441

The Knitting Gallery is a must-visit for both the novice and experienced knitter. In addition to friendly and helpful customer service, the shop specializes in a unique selection of quality yarns and all supplies for hand and machine knitting. Visit daily, Tuesday through Friday, from 2 to 4 PM for Tea Tyme. Enjoy tea and cookies in a cozy atmosphere with friendly chats and helpful knitting advice. Interested in a class? Call the shop for the current schedule. The Knitting Gallery is open Tuesday through Saturday.

Mystic Treasures
Oleander Oaks, 5725 Oleander Dr., Ste. A-5, Wilmington • (910) 395-5399

Mystic Treasures is Wilmington's exclusive dealer for Jenni K, a line of uniquely designed and individually handcrafted gold and sterling silver jewelry. This charming shop also carries gifts from around the world and home accessories.

Fine Arts Services
Oleander Oaks, 5725 Oleander Dr., Ste. E-3, Wilmington • (910) 794-8859

Lovers of old maps and botanical prints will find a treasure trove of both in this unusual and inviting shop. Most of the antique maps date prior to the early 1900s and include regional, national and world maps. This shop offers the area's largest number of antique botanical prints along with early and specialty prints and art work. Fine Arts Services also performs complete custom and conservation framing services. Conservation and restoration of antique frames is another specialty.

Solace Nail and Body Care
Bradley Square, 5629 Oleander Dr., Wilmington • (910) 790-9993

Located beside Nevada Bob's golf store in Bradley Square shopping center, Solace offers complete hair and nail services in an inviting setting. Nail services include artificial nails in addition to natural nail care and pedicures. Semi-private rooms are available. Solace is open Tuesday through Saturday by appointment and walk-ins are welcome.

Westfield Shoppingtown Independence
3500 Oleander Dr., Wilmington
• (910) 392-1776

Westfield Shoppingtown Independence, known simply as "the mall" by area residents, has more than 150 stores offering a wealth of shopping opportunities in an attractive and climate-controlled environment. Planning to "shop 'til you drop"? Strategically placed groups of upholstered chairs throughout the mall, a 400-seat food court and 15 eateries provide rest and refreshment. Sears, JCPenney, Belk and Dillard's department stores anchor this complex of trademark stores, independent shop owners and rented kiosk vendors. There are sporting goods shops, jewelry stores, software stores, numerous shoe stores, specialty gift stores, fragrance and bath shops, music stores, home furnishing stores, an impressive range of apparel boutiques for the whole family ranging from infant-size to adult plus sizes, a full-service salon, banking services and much more.

Can't decide on the perfect gift? Gift cards, redeemable in any of the mall stores or restaurants where American Express is honored, are a good choice. The customer service center, located near the food court, provides Kiddie Cruisers, wheelchairs, gift cards, complimentary gift wrap, faxing and copying services and friendly assistance. Electric wheelchairs are also available and free. A family restroom, adjacent to the food court, offers co-ed children's bathrooms, changing stations, private nursing areas and the Disney channel. Westfield Shoppingtown Independence is open daily.

Two locally owned mall stores include Fleishman's Fine Clothiers, (910) 799-4861, offering fine men's and women's clothing for all seasons or occasions, and The Gentry House, (910) 392-1338, noted for its fine men's fashions, shoes and accessories.

Reeds Jewelers
3500 Oleander Dr., Westfield
Shoppingtown Independence, Wilmington
• **(910) 799-6810**

Founded in 1946 by Bill and Roberta Zimmer, Reeds Jewelers was originally located on Front Street where it remained one of downtown Wilmington's finest stores for 56 years. Now one of the top 10 retail jewelry store chains in the United States, Reeds continues its tradition of excellence in fine jewelry at Westfield Shoppingtown Independence, next to the Belk entrance. A jeweler is on site to service your jewelry needs. Be sure to see Reeds exclusive Venus Diamond and check out brand-name product lines such as Rolex, Mikimoto, Tag Heuer, Swarovski, Omega, Scott Kay, Gucci and Tacori.

Other Wilmington Areas

Island Appliance
5946 Carolina Beach Rd., Wilmington
• **(910) 790-8580, (800) 551-3070**

This store sells and services most brands of appliances, including window air conditioners, refrigerators and freezers, washers and dryers, dishwashers, microwaves and ranges. Island Appliance also offers sales to builders. Some of its brand-name items include KitchenAid, Jenn-Air, Whirlpool, Maytag, Frigidaire, Thermador and Bosch. Low prices and free local delivery are appealing features of this appliance/service store. The knowledgeable staff at Island Appli-

ance will assist you with kitchen design, and they're a Best Brands Plus dealer.

McAllister & Solomon Books
4402 Wrightsville Ave., Wilmington
• **(910) 350-0189, (888) 617-7882**

People who love vintage, rare or just plain hard-to-find books will relish a browse through McAllister & Solomon Books, just a block off S. College Road. They stock used and rare books, a large selection of regional history books, photographs, postcards and manuscripts in this well organized and appealing bookstore. Books are bought, sold or traded with about 25,000 titles in the store at any given time. McAllister & Solomon also has access to a database of 10 million books daily through a computerized out-of-print search network. Looking for a particular title? Ask the staff about an Internet search. Specialties include local and North Carolina history, military history, world history, African Americana, genealogy, mystery fiction and literature.

New Balance Wilmington
29 Van Campen Blvd., Wilmington
• **(910) 332-2020**

This locally owned, nationally known specialty store features a full line of New Balance and Dunham footwear, New Balance performance apparel and sport bags. The friendly and knowledgeable staff will ensure you have the proper fit for your athletic needs. You will find shoe sizes ranging from 5 to 20 and widths from 2A to 6E. The store is located in the Monk's Corner Shops near the Cracker Barrel and Wal-Mart SuperCenter.

Perry's Emporium
Barclay Commons, 2520 Independence Blvd., Wilmington • **(910) 392-6721, (800) 261-5705**

Walk through the leaded-glass doors of Perry's Emporium and step back into the 1890s. Twenty-eight antique floor cases hold one of the largest collections of estate pieces in the city, in addition to more contemporary styles of fine jewelry, loose diamonds and silver flatware. An additional 14 antique wall display cases showcase jewelry, art, fine china and crystal. Celebrating over a decade of service to the area, this 5,300-square-foot store is the largest retail jeweler in Wilmington. Perry's services include two full-service master jewelers, two graduate gemologists, lapidary services, jewelry repair and a bridal service. Appraisals are available for new, used and antique jewelry.

SHOPPING

Pottery Plus
5744 Market St., Wilmington
• **(910) 791-9017**

Shopping at Pottery Plus is like having a warehouse of favorite things for your home and garden. The pallets of goods will delight the designer in you and wow your pocketbook! A favorite of the locals, this two-acre bargain paradise features wicker furniture, floral arrangements, glassware, baskets, glassware, pottery, candles, decorative lamps, outdoor furniture, fountains and statuary. . . just to mention a few. You'll love it!

Quilter's Heaven
4403 Park Ave., Wilmington
• **(910) 395-0200**

With 2,000 bolts of high-quality fabric, pattern books, batting and a complete line of quilting supplies, Quilter's Heaven is a regular stop for Insiders who quilt. The shop doubles as a Pfaff Sewing Center with sales in Pfaff sewing machines and accessories. Looking for a particular thread? Quilter's Heaven carries a variety of quilting, embroidery and specialty threads. Classes in quilting, sewing and Pfaff techniques are offered regularly, and a schedule is available by calling or stopping by the shop. Ask the friendly staff about their Embroidery Club or Pfaff Club.

Silver Jewelry Factory
814 S. College Rd., Wilmington
• **(910) 392-3625**

Located in University Square shopping center next to Dick's Clothing & Sporting Goods, the Silver Jewelry Factory offers a large selection of silver jewelry at great prices. Their inventory ranges from simple to unique designer pieces, with 70 percent of their pieces handcrafted by their own group of designers. Thousands of charms are on display, but if they don't have what you're looking for, they'll order it for you. They also provide engraving. The atmosphere is warm and friendly so feel free to come and shop at leisure. Check out their exclusive collection of handcrafted nautical jewelry by Tommy J. in 14k gold or silver, the Bounty Sword and ARMADA bracelets for men and women, authentic or replica shipwreck coins and much, much more!

Stone Garden
6955 Market St., Wilmington
• **(910) 452-1619**

Stone Garden, located at Military Cutoff and Market Street, should be your first stop when planning or beautifying your home or garden. Wander through an acre of stone or the showroom to select just the right materials for your home improvement project. Cast stone statuary, ranging from the whimsical to the unique, are prominently displayed outside. If their great selection of birdbaths, benches, planters, urns and Charleston fountains doesn't inspire you, their Secret Garden will. Hidden behind a tall fence on the grounds, this inviting water garden is a delightful haven. Don't forget to browse the gift shop's eclectic selection of garden gifts, sculpture, beautiful polished stones and geodes. Stone Garden is known to locals as a fun place to shop, and you can feel free to bring the kids. Stone Garden is open seven days per week.

Tidal Creek Cooperative Food Market
5329 Oleander Dr., Wilmington
• **(910) 799- COOP (2667)**

Since 1982, a commitment to providing the highest quality natural and organic foods, great customer service and ongoing consumer education has been central to the Tidal Creek philosophy. This member-owned cooperative food market takes pride in offering the most healthful foods and products available at the best possible prices. Their buyers look for organically produced foods from local growers, small farms and companies that share the co-op's high standards.

Among the offerings at Tidal Creek, shoppers will find fresh, natural organic foods, including produce, hormone-free dairy products, chemical-free and organic meats, local eggs, frozen prepared foods and desserts and a wide variety of packaged grocery items. Also available are organic bulk items (whole grains and flours, cereals, herbal teas, beans and pasta, natural snack foods are a few examples), health and beauty aids, aromatherapy oils, organic wines and microbrewery beers.

Having moved to a new expanded location in spring 2003, Tidal Creek has added a deli and cafe, complete with a salad bar, numerous grab-and-go sandwiches and meals, baked goods, a fresh juice bar, coffee and smoothie bar. More than just a grocery store, the co-op is the place to enjoy a delicious, healthful meal or snack and keep up with the latest in the Wilmington healthy lifestyle community. While Tidal Creek is member owned and operated, you don't have to be a member to shop there — everyone is welcome. Now located on Oleander Drive, Tidal Creek is next door to Cinema Six, across the street from Eddie Romanelli's restaurant.

Ogden-Porter's Neck-Hampstead

This section of Market Street, dormant until recent years, runs northward to Hampstead, Figure Eight Island and the Topsail Island area. Increased residential and commercial development has resulted in the growth of shopping opportunities. Listed below are a few of the more well-established shops. (Most stores in this section have Wilmington addresses.)

The Canvas Goose
7976 Market St., Wilmington
• **(910) 686-9162**

Celebrating 21 years in business in spring 2003, this quaint little shop sits in a charming, village-green-type setting. Inside you will find a wealth of collectibles and gifts, including Byers Choice Carolers, Churchill Weavers throws and Dept. 56 cottages and accessories. The Canvas Goose also offers a good variety of garden and wind sculptures, garden accessories and distinctive handcrafted items including jewelry, ceramics and glassware from primarily American artists. UPS shipping and gift wrapping are available.

Porters Neck Center
8207-8211 Market St., Wilmington

This attractive and lively shopping center contains a number of interesting shops and businesses, anchored by a Food Lion grocery store. Until recently, this area had little in the way of services and retail stores. Porters Neck Center provides the services of a U.S. Post Office branch, a bank, a hair salon, restaurants, a veterinary hospital and a small pharmacy. Retail shops include **The Everyday Gourmet**, (910) 686-9343, offering gourmet foods to go, coffee, imported and domestic wines, kitchenware and gift baskets; they also offer gourmet cooking classes. **Trade Secrets**, (910) 686-4110, is an attractive consignment boutique for children and ladies apparel and accessories. If you'd like to make your own gifts or just want to spend an afternoon being creative, check out **Stroke of Genius**, (910) 686-1602, and paint your own pottery. It's easy and fun!

Wild Birds Unlimited
7223 Market St., Wilmington
• **(910) 686-7210**

This attractive and unique store, with a motto of "We bring people and nature together," is a must-visit for bird lovers, backyard gardeners and nature enthusiasts. Choose from a large variety of specialty seeds, suet, birdhouses, birdfeeders, nature books and gifts, garden items and much more. Wild Birds Unlimited also carries a selection of Swarovski binoculars, considered the best crystal lenses on the market, Celestron spotting scopes and binoculars and Eagle Optics. Have questions? Everyone on staff is an expert, literally. Each em-

INSIDERS' TIP
For a shopping change of pace, spend the day in Southport. Stop for lunch at one of the great seafood restaurants overlooking the Waterway and the Cape Fear River. Ride the Southport-Fort Fisher Ferry. Relax on a swinging seat in the park.

SHOPPING

ployee has completed an in-depth course in ornithology through Cornell University.

The Flower Basket of Hampstead
14361 U.S. Hwy. 17 N., Hampstead
• (910) 270-4141, (877) 607-7615

A full-service florist, The Flower Basket of Hampstead offers everything from houseplants to mixed bouquets. They maintain an extensive inventory of fresh-cut flowers so if you love having beautiful floral arrangements in your home, whether for entertaining or "just because," this is the place to shop. Owner Britt Cobble's philosophy is that customer service is "zenith" and every effort is made to meet the customer's needs. Custom, wedding and funeral arrangements are available. The shop carries a selection of high-quality gifts to fit any occasion, plus a variety of plush animals, gifts made by locals, and a large inventory of unique, quality candles. Special orders and projects are no problem for Britt and his staff. The Flower Basket also offers flower-arranging seminars. Call for more information and the seminar schedule.

Wrightsville Beach

Mott's Channel Seafood
120 Short St., Wrightsville Beach
• (910) 256-3474

Since 1990, Motts has been providing fresh seafood to folks from their waterfront location at Wrightsville Beach. Whether you arrive by boat or by car, you'll find a large selection of fresh, first-quality seafood. They also offer an extensive selection of sauces and spices to help you prepare a great seafood meal. For the fisherman, they have live and frozen bait as well as ice for your catch.

Surf City Surf Shop
The Landing, 530 Causeway Dr.,
Wrightsville Beach • (910) 256-2265,
(910) 256-4353 (surf report)

In business for 25 years, Surf City describes the store as "a shop for surfers by surfers" and carries a large variety of surfboards. Whether you're into the classic boards — Hobie, Weber, Yater, Hansen and Velzy — or the newer shapes — Lost, Merrick, Rusty, HIC — Surf City has them all, as well as the clothing and accessories you'll need to hit the waves. Skateboarding gear is another feature of this lively store, with a large selection of skateboard components, including decks and wheels, clothing and accessories, including the area's largest selection of sunglasses. Into snowboarding? Surf City offers some of the best

snowboarding gear available, including boards, bindings, clothing and boots.

Sweetwater Surf Shop
10 N. Lumina Ave., Wrightsville Beach
• (910) 256-3821

Sweetwater has everything the surfer will ever need — and then some. Sharp Eye, Cannibal, DHD, JS, Action, Surf Tech, Boardworks, BIC, WRV and Glen Minami Shapes are some of the quality brands of boards it carries, along with bodyboards and skimboards. It also has repair service for the occasional unhappy landing. You'll find men's, women's and children's swimsuits and fashions, sunglasses, accessories and one of the largest selections of sandals on the beach. Check out their selection of snowboards and accessories. Sweetwater also offers snowboard repair. Rentals are available.

Wrightsville Beach Vicinity

Shopping options are limited, by design, on the largely residential Wrightsville Beach, but there's been an explosion of retail growth over the bridge on the mainland side. (All the stores in this section have a Wilmington address.)

Abigail's
The Galleria, 6766 Wrightsville Ave.,
Wilmington • (910) 256-3043,
(800) 887-1616

When locals need a wedding, birthday or housewarming gift, chances are they find it at Abigail's. Personalized customer service is a hallmark of this 14,000-square-foot store located in The Galleria near Wrightsville Beach and Landfall. Customers can choose from an impressive collection of fine gifts, garden accents, home accessories, jewelry, fine china and crystal. Product and collectible lines offered at Abigail's include Vietri, Firelight Glass, Waterford crystal and china, Arthur Court, Herend, Swarovski, Harbour Lights, Fitz and Floyd, and Virginia Metalcrafters. Don't miss the year-round Christmas and Holiday Shop to view an incredible collection of Byer's Choice Carolers, beautiful European blown-glass ornaments and unique holiday accents. Abigail's is also a Starlight Store dealer for Christopher Radko ornaments. Additional services include bridal and gift registry, free gift wrapping, custom orders and shipping via UPS or FedEx.

Abigail's Garden offers a unique shopping experience for gardeners and garden enthusiasts. Among the great selection of garden gifts and accents, this area features statuary, fountains and garden furnishings.

The Forum
1125 Military Cut-off Rd., Wilmington • (910) 256-0467

At The Forum, charming boutiques sit side by side with fine dining, sidewalk bistros and gourmet cafes. Shoppers can choose from a wide array of gifts, women's fashions, jewelry, antiques, imported furniture, handmade papers and gourmet foods.

The Forum's restaurants offer excellent fare. **Salty's**, (910) 256-1118, a delightfully casual coastal bistro, serves fresh seafood and a beach attitude. **Cafe de France**, (910) 256-6600, an authentic French creperie, is an elegant cafe featuring traditional foods from the Brittany region. More formal dining can be found at **Milano's**, (910) 256-8870, where fine Italian cuisine and a festive European environment transport visitors overseas for an evening feast. For those who prefer a casual dining experience, both the **NOFO Cafe**, (910) 256-5565, and **Wild Flour Bread Company**, (910) 256-2217, offer an array of delectable soups, salads and sandwiches. (See our Restaurants chapter.) **The Blonde Salon,** (910) 256-7468, is a contemporary salon offering a wide variety of hair care services and products. Also not to be missed is the fabulous **Ki Spa Salon** where the opportunities to rejuvenate and transform your body spirit are endless. See the spas part of our wedding planning chapter for more information.

Offering shoppers a sense of charm and graciousness, The Forum is characterized by classical architecture, warmly colored Canadian sandstone, accented with arches, columns, pediments and balustrades. The Forum's shops are unique, upscale and carry a tempting selection of goods. Those listed below are only a handful of the merchants there.

Bijoux
The Forum, 1127 Military Cutoff Rd., Wilmington • (910) 256-8655

Celebrating the revival of the handcrafted arts, Bijoux offers a unique concept to the Wilmington arts scene. This attractive shop is both a handcrafted jewelry gallery and a working studio, representing 25 different jewelers who work in sterling silver, gold, platinum and found objects. Want something tailored to your personal tastes? Owner and metalsmith Stephanie Hogan designs and cre-

ates custom pieces. This gallery's nature-inspired atmosphere also supports the work of local and national artists. If you're looking for the unique and different or a one-of-a-kind gift, Bijoux has a lot to offer in their array of handcrafted items — jewelry, pottery, glassware, wood and textiles. Active in the local arts community, Bijoux is one of five Wrightsville Beach area galleries participating in the East Side Gallery Night. Held on the second Friday every month during the summer from 5 to 9 PM, this event is an open reception introducing the galleries' new artwork.

Blue Hand Home
The Forum, 1125 Military Cutoff Rd., Wilmington • (910) 509-0088

This delightfully eclectic store's theme is "casual, chic and uncomplicated luxury." You're bound to find irresistible choices in furniture, including irreplaceable armoires, beds, dining rooms and architectural pieces. Original and reproduction pieces are inspired by old world craftsmanship in the carving, silhouette and patina. Upholstered furniture is clad in rich chenille, damask, linens or leather. Sumptuous home accessories make decorating a delight with cashmere throws, stylish lighting, unique decors, scented Votivo candles and more. At Blue Hand Home, value never goes out of fashion. Professional interior design services, from blueprint to complete decoration, are available.

Eyetech Optical Boutique
The Forum, 1113-A Military Cutoff Rd., Wilmington • (910) 509-0291

The fulfillment of a lifelong dream for owner Roxanne Armstrong, Eyetech Optical Boutique offers an environment where clients feel comfortable experimenting with eyewear as an expression of their own personal style. Her slogan, "Art for Your Face," means just that for customers because this is a place where individuality is preeminent. With a clientele that includes professionals, retirees, sports enthusiasts and fashion-forward youth, Eyetech stocks a wide range of exclusive frame collections. Lafont, Alain Mikli, Chopard and Cazal are among more than 800 frames on display; customized frames are available in hand-carved wood and genuine horn.

A 29-year optical industry veteran, Roxanne believes that collaboration between client and optician is the only way to guarantee eyewear enjoyment. Definitely not a self-serve, one-size-fits-all

SHOPPING

shop, Eyetech Optical Boutique strives to address the specific requirements of each individual.

Ikebana Design
The Forum, 1125-F Military Cutoff Rd., Wilmington • (910) 509-1383, (800) 628-9774

For 19 years, the commitment and friendliness of a dedicated staff have been the hallmark of this popular Wilmington florist. Specializing in Ikebana, European garden style baskets, vase designs and English plant gardens, Ikebana Design also offers an eclectic mix of home accents, gifts and accessories. Ikebana containers, bases, supplies and reference books are available for the novice or serious arranger.

NOFO
The Forum, 1125 Military Cutoff Rd., Wilmington • (910) 256-0467

NOFO offers an eclectic array of gifts, gardening accessories, lighting, rugs, clocks, furnishings for bed and bath, books, kitchen accessories and children's gifts. The adjacent NOFO Cafe and Market, (910) 256-5565, offers a delicious full-service cafe and aisles of gourmet foods.

Oliver
The Forum, 1125 Military Cutoff Rd., Wilmington • (910) 256-2233

High-fashion clothing and accessories from New York, Los Angeles and Europe are the focus at Oliver, offering fashionable choices in everything from jeans to lingerie to bathing suits. Their excellent jean selection is a particular highlight.

Personal Touch
The Forum, 1125 Military Cutoff Rd., Wilmington • (910) 256-8888

Personal Touch specializes in both ladies' apparel and fine designer jewelry. Clothing styles range from dressy-casual to formal. The jewelry selection, in silver, 18K and white gold, features such well-known designers as Cassis, John Hardy and Judith Jack.

Ropa, etc.
The Forum, 1121 Military Cutoff Ste. D • (910) 256-8733

Are you ready for something new and exciting? Then you're invited to experience the pleasure of fine cottons and linens, which make dressing comfortable and fun. Ropa, etc. is the area's exclusive retailer for such lines as Liz and Jane, Flax and Willow. This terrific shop also carries great makers such as Rico hand-knit sweaters, TSD, April Cornell, Habitat, Cut•Loose, Basic Threads and Naot shoes. Ropa, etc. is also known for its unique collection of jewelry from makers around the world plus great accessories to complement any outfit. Sizes range from extra small to extra large and fit a variety of shapes. Ropa, etc. has two other locations to serve you: 120-B South Front Street, Wilmington, (910) 815-0344 and 417-C North Howe Street in Southport (910) 454-8833.

The UPS Store
The Forum, 1121-C Military Cutoff Rd., Wilmington • (910) 509-0520

Delivering personalized, convenient business solutions and shipping services, The UPS Store will make your life easier and less complicated. Friendly, helpful staff lighten your work load by making black and white or color copies for you, handling faxes and providing printing services. When it comes to packaging and shipping, you've got everything you need right here. Mailboxes and postal services are offered, too. In a hurry? Drop off your holiday packages and let The UPS Store send them on their way, packed to perfection. Store hours are Monday through Friday 8 AM to 6 PM and Saturday 9 AM to 2 PM.

Landfall Shopping Center
Eastwood Rd. and Military Cutoff Rd., Wilmington

Just minutes from Wrightsville Beach, this robust center has entered the retail arena in a brisk way in the past few years. This retail, dining and service center is convenient to both downtown and Wrightsville Beach. Landfall Shopping Center offers a one-day shopping experience for all your needs from gifts to apparel to home; it offers a boutique-style Belk department store plus many other fine and specialty stores — the following are just some of them.

Aussie Island Surf Shop
Landfall Shopping Center, Eastwood Rd. and Military Cutoff Rd., Wilmington
• (910) 256-5454

Aussie Island has a mind-boggling array of clothing and equipment for surfers on sea, street and snow, including a very large selection of stylish casual sport clothing and beachwear for men and women. Aussie Island also carries a good selection of watches-regular and aquatic- and a large selection of polarized sunglasses. There are lots of surfboards on display, and this is the place to buy wakeboards, body boards, skateboards and snowboards. Ask about snowboard rentals.

JP's Lamp and Shade Shop
Landfall Shopping Center, Eastwood Rd. and Military Cutoff Rd., Wilmington
• (910) 509-1553

JP's Lamp and Shade Shop is a full-service store for your lamp and lampshade needs, offering custom-made lamps and on-premise lamp repairs in addition to extensive selections of lamps, shapes and finials. Their large collection of lampshades offer both designer and basic options in a variety of shapes and sizes. The shop is Wilmington's only lamp dealer carrying Waterford crystal lamps. JP's Lamp and Shade Shop isn't just a lamp shop. This well-appointed store also carries a nice collection of mirrors, oil

paintings and tapestries, small occasional tables, high-quality silk floral arrangements, decorative tabletop accessories, clocks, bookends and more.

The Julia
Landfall Shopping Center, Eastwood Rd. and Military Cutoff Rd., Wilmington
• (910) 256-1175,

The Julia has been offering better women's apparel in Wilmington since 1916. This veteran retailer sells upscale day and evening apparel.

The Seasoned Gourmet
Landfall Shopping Center, Eastwood Rd. and Military Cutoff Rd., Wilmington
• (910) 256-9488

An exciting store for cooks and people who enjoy entertaining, The Seasoned Gourmet is a great addition to the culinary-arts stores beginning to pepper Wilmington. There's high emphasis on cookware and cooking classes. The store sells KitchenAid mixers, cookbooks, linens, Wusthof and Henckel knives, Cuisinart, handmade Italian and Portugese ceramic oven-to-tableware, gift baskets, gourmet foods and lazy susans. It also has an impressive offering of imported cheeses. The Seasoned Gourmet's highly popular cooking classes include three 12-week courses. Each series features the shop's in-house chef and guest chefs from the region's restaurants. Contact the shop for more information and a class schedule.

Tavernay's Jewelers
Landfall Shopping Center, Eastwood Rd. and Military Cutoff Rd., Wilmington
• (910) 256-1122, (800) 430-3790

This is a second location of this well-established Wilmington business. A beautiful store, it's a fitting setting for the works of Henry Dunay, exclusively offered by Tavernay's in both Carolinas. Dunay's works have been bought by Diana Ross, Princess Di, Hillary Clinton and Elizabeth Taylor. Shoppers will also find a nice selection of estate and nautical jewelry here. Five jewelers provide extensive custom design and remounting services. The original Tavernay's is located at 4412 Wrightsville Avenue in Wilmington, (910) 799-8041.

Lumina Station
1900 Eastwood Rd., Wilmington
• (910) 256-0900

If you're shopping for local flavor, you'll find Lumina Station as satisfying as a day at the beach. Inspired by Lumina, the beloved

Wrightsville Beach dance pavilion once central to the East Coast social scene, Lumina Station is so true to its historical roots that it won *Coastal Living* magazine's first-ever award for contextual design.

Beautiful landscaping, whimsical sculptures and storybook bridges complement the heavily wooded campus, making strolling the Station a very pleasant way to pass the time. Rocking chairs — the center's signature icon — are grouped here and there under deep overhangs, providing a shady place to rest, enjoy a cappuccino, or sit back and visit with passersby.

Fortunately, the shops, restaurants and business located here are just as unique as the setting. Local merchants own and operate virtually all of the establishments. Here you'll find some truly special offerings, from art, jewelry and books to gift items, home accents and clothing for the entire family. You can pamper yourself in the day spa, work out with a personal trainer, and enjoy a fabulous meal in one of the restaurants — all without ever getting into your car.

Lumina Station cafés and restaurants provide something for everyone, from your morning coffee to fine dining. Start your day with fresh brewed coffee from Port City Java, (910) 256-0993. Centro Café, (910) 256-6144, offers salads, sandwiches, and entrees to go. Enjoy lunch or dinner at Fathoms, (910) 256-1254, which was recently voted Best Seafood restaurant for 2003 by *Wrightsville Beach Magazine*. For more formal dining, visit Chester's Steakhouse, (910) 256-0995, for great steaks, or visit The Port Land Grille, (910) 256-6056, which features progressive regional American cuisine, and has earned Best Restaurant for 2003 by *Wrightsville Beach Magazine* and *Encore*.

The following is a partial listing of the shops you'll find at Lumina Station. You'll also find friendliness and an authentic old Wrightsville Beach atmosphere. Overall, it's an experience you couldn't possibly have anywhere else.

Airlie Moon
Lumina Fountainside, 1908 Eastwood Rd., Wilmington • (910) 256-0655

Airlie Moon is an eclectic, unique gift store offering one-of-a-kind products for the bed, bath and home. Opened in 1994 as a family owned and operated gift store, Airlie Moon caters to customers seeking such items as fine bed linens, vintage furniture, exceptional glassware and handmade jewelry. Stop by to see their extraordinary gifts, perfect for any occasion or home decor. Airlie Moon also offers home design services, custom made-to-order furniture and bed linens. Free gift-wrapping is available. For Lu-

mina Station neighbors, Airlie Moon is pleased to offer personal shopping and free delivery.

Alligator Pie and Alligator Baby
Lumina Station, 1900 Eastwood Rd., Wilmington • (910) 509-1600

Alligator Pie is truly a one-of-a-kind children's boutique, offering an amazing collection of clothes, toys, gifts and furnishings for children of all ages in a friendly atmosphere and one convenient location. Whether your tastes are traditional, trendy or somewhere in between, this unique and fascinating store is likely to have what you want. In clothing, the store offers the newest and the best of American and European brands for both boys and girls from newborn to junior sizes, including Roxy, Quiksilver, Baby LuLu, Wes 'n Willy, Marsha, Catimini, One Kid, K C Parker, Three Dot and Tessuto. Their collection includes playclothes, sleepwear, special occasion wear, shoes, outerwear and accessories. Pre-teen and junior size clothes are available in their loft, which offers Buffalo, Kenzie and HardTail plus shoes and sandals, room accessories and skin care products. Naturally, Alligator Pie offers only the hottest and latest award-winning toys. Selections include crafts, puzzles, games, beach toys, Thomas the Train, Geo Mags and Groovy Girls.

The baby boutique at Alligator Pie offers almost every item you could want for a baby, including beautiful blankets, silver rattles, developmental toys, cozy sleepwear and soft lovies. Equipment offered includes Britax car seats, Peg Perego high chairs and strollers and Bjorn carriers. For expectant moms, they have a unique selection of maternity wear and skin-care products.

Bristol Books
Lumina Fountainside, 1908 Eastwood Rd., Wilmington • (910) 256-4490

Bristol Books, one of the area's most enduring independent bookstores, moved to the larger space in Lumina Fountainside in September 2000 but has managed to maintain that small, cozy hometown bookstore ambiance. The added space merely allows Bristol to expand already great selections of books, magazines, newspapers, cards frames and gifts. Other expanded areas are the Southern and regional book section and the children's section, featuring interactive games. Bristol also carries used fiction and nonfiction books in hardcover and paperback. Personal service and community involvement are hallmarks, which keeps it highly competitive in a market with several much larger bookstores. Ask about their out-of-print book search and monthly book clubs.

Embellishments

Lumina Station, 1900 Eastwood Rd.,
Wilmington • (910) 256-5263

Embellishments carries a delightful selection of options for gift-giving occasions. Choose from fine home accessories, fine stationery and unique gift ideas. The shop is also the exclusive dealer for Simon Pearce glassware in Wilmington.

Finely Finished

Lumina Station, 1900 Eastwood Rd.,
Wilmington • (910) 256-0777

Finely Finished is the ideal place to help you complete your home. They offer fine finishing touches and not-so-ordinary gifts.

Fountainside Fine Art Gallery

Lumina Station, 1900 Eastwood Rd.,
Wilmington • (910) 256-9956

Fountainside Fine Art Gallery represents local, regional and national artists. Specializing in paintings, sculpture and art glass, the gallery carries work appealing to serious collectors as well as the casual art lover. The gallery hosts shows for artists on a regular basis and also provides in-home consultation.

Harbour Club Day Spa and Salon

Lumina Fountainside, 1904 Eastwood Rd.,
Wilmington • (910) 256-5020

Here's a spa where you can relax and rejuvenate. It's a beautiful, relaxing escape from the real world. Treatment rooms are a haven of peace and tranquility — a place soothe your mind and relax your body. At Harbour Club Day Spa and Salon you'll find a team of highly trained professionals dedicated to providing you with a wide variety of personalized body treatment programs.

Among the many offerings are manicure and pedicures including nail enhancements, cosmetic application, advanced facial treatments, depilatory services, body wellness, massage therapy and hair design. Packages are available and make great gifts — especially for brides, expectant mothers and stressed-out friends.

Island Passage

Lumina Station, 1900 Eastwood Rd.,
Wilmington • (910) 256-0407

Island Passage offers a colorful palette of artistically presented attire plus accessories for all ages. It's one of Wilmington's favorites stores. Don't miss their other store at 4 Market Street in downtown Wilmington.

Jennifer's

Lumina Station, 1900 Eastwood Rd.,
Wilmington • (910) 256-6522

For a one-stop boutique-shopping experience with personalized service, you have to visit Jennifer's at Lumina Station. They offer a large selection of ladies' embellished sportswear with an amazing variety of accessories to match. You can also find gifts here..

Lumina Fitness

Lumina Fountainside, 1904 Eastwood Rd.,
Wilmington • (910) 509-9404

State-of-the-art equipment and personal training are both available at Lumina Fitness. Electronic key card access gives you the freedom to exercise whenever you want, without the crowds you'll find at larger gyms. Call Donna at the number above for more information.

Monkees & The Bamboo Hanger

Lumina Station, 1900 Eastwood Rd.,
Wilmington • (910) 256-5886

Swing into Monkees for the perfect shoes, including brand names like Stuart Weitzman and Donald Pliner. Monkees also carries accessories such as belts, scarves, purses, hosiery and jewelry. Under the same roof, The Bamboo Hanger is the contemporary clothing portion of the business, offering high-quality ladies' fashions.

R. Bryan Collections

Lumina Station, 1900 Eastwood Rd.,
Wilmington • (910) 256-9943

At R. Bryan Collections for women, expert staff can help with easy wardrobe solutions. Ask about their home wardrobe consultations, or how they can help you pack for your vacation. They have exclusive lines of comfortable sportswear, from crop pants to microfiber suiting, even have fun socks and hats!

S. Burke

Lumina Station, 1900 Eastwood Rd.,
Wilmington • (910) 256-3311

S. Burke invites you to discover a unique and beautiful selection of fine jewelry, home accessories and imaginative gifts for all occasions. Their exclusive jewelry line includes Slane & Slane, David Wysor, Honora and M.+ J Savitt. Gift wrapping is available.

The Quarter

Lumina Station, 1900 Eastwood Rd.,
Wilmington • (910) 256-6011

Lazy days along the shore, fun-filled rounds of golf, dining and dancing on balmy summer nights, that's the Coastal Carolina Lifestyle. The Quarter at Lumina Station is a shop that will help you look as good as you feel and feel as good as you look.

Carolina Beach

Shopping on Pleasure Island — Carolina Beach and Kure Beach — is concentrated in Carolina Beach, a small, family-beach community at the north end of the island. Carolina Beach offers a number of year-round specialty shops, but keep in mind that winter months mean shortened or limited hours for many retail businesses. Call ahead so you won't be disappointed by a "closed" sign.

The Book Rack
Federal Point Plaza, 1018 N. Lake Park Blvd., Carolina Beach • (910) 458-7973

The Book Rack offers approximately 12,000 titles, primarily used paperbacks and hardcover books along with new best sellers. Used paperbacks cost half of the cover price and, when you're finished, you can trade it in for a credit of half of what you paid. Used hardcover books are marked with a discounted price. Local artists and writers are given counter and wall space to display their work.

Checkered Church
800 St. Joseph St., Carolina Beach • (910) 458-0211

In a former Catholic church, this blue-and-white-checked building houses a fascinating store filled with beach-related home-accent pieces and home-decor items including pine furniture, prints, crocks, M.A. Hadley pottery, picture frames, baskets, Yankee Candles, lace curtains, weather vanes, wind chimes, bird houses and the work of many local artists. Need a unique gift idea? Nearly everything in the store can be personalized. Decorative slates and ornaments are just a few of the possibilities. Christmas items, many with a nautical theme, are available year-round. Also unique to The Checkered Church is a stunning 100 percent cotton afghan that portrays the Pleasure Island coastline and assorted wildlife found in the area. The Checkered Church truly is the little shop off the beaten path you always hope you can find.

Currents Art & Gifts
716 N. Lake Park Blvd., Ste. 1, Carolina Beach • (910) 458-2787

This bright and eclectic shop's focus is the talent of Pleasure Island and Wilmington artists. The wide range of mediums found here include pottery, stained glass, art prints, hand-crafted jewelry, art, photography, oil and acrylic canvas art, wood and more. Customer services include shipping, gift wrapping and gift certificates. If friends and family need a nudge at gift-giving occasions, Currents will keep your "wish list" on file.

Eccentric Cat
Snow's Cut Shopping Center, 1401 N. Lake Park Blvd., Carolina Beach • (910) 458-5810

Just past Snow's Cut bridge over the Intracoastal Waterway, you'll find the Eccentric Cat near the Food Lion on your right. Filled with house and garden "stuff" plus clothing and jewelry, this unique shop offers a variety of unusual items. Although they really love cats, just wait until you see their other eccentric creatures.

Fishtales
637-A Ft. Fisher Blvd. N., Kure Beach • (910) 458-7544

Unique, colorful and fun describes Fishtales, whose philosophy is providing "something for all ages." Whether you're looking for something beachy or a unique special-occasion gift, Fishtales has a lot to offer. A sampling of ideas include Mariposa serving trays and pieces, Vietri handmade ceramics, Vera Bradley Designs, garden gifts, brightly colored hand-painted housewares, Buyers' Choice Ltd. carolers, Deborah Cavanaugh prints, Beanie Babies and handmade California soaps. The shop also features a children's corner stocked with toys, games, books and gifts. Check out the pet gifts section. A large selection of sterling silver jewelry, especially charms, pins and rings, is another highlight. Fishtales offers gift certificates, gift wrapping and ample parking.

Frame Mart & Gallery
Pleasure Island Plaza, 1009 N. Lake Park Blvd., Carolina Beach • (910) 458-6116

This is a combination art gallery and frame shop. The owner, Scott Brown, offers a full line of custom framing services, including pick up and delivery. In addition, Scott offers photo and frame restoration. Bring in a treasured piece for framing or select a favorite from the varied range of work from local, regional and national artists. Framed artwork is also available for purchase, and the shop carries the Harbour Lights lighthouses. Frame Mart & Gallery is open year-round, Tuesday through Saturday, or by appointment.

Linda's
201 N. Lake Park Blvd., Carolina Beach • (910) 458-7116

Linda's, a fairly large, year-round store, has

a wide assortment of ladies sportswear, dresses for special evenings on the town, costume jewelry, scarves and other accessories. You'll find resort wear made of comfortable, machine-washable, low-maintenance material in stylish cuts and colors. "Today's fashions at yesterday's prices" is the philosophy at Linda's, and you'll enjoy the savings.

Sterling Craft Mall
101 Cape Fear Blvd., Carolina Beach
• (910) 458-4429

Set in a renovated 1920s building next to the new Courtyard by Marriott in the heart of Carolina Beach, Sterling Craft Mall features more than 90 crafters offering everything from handmade clothes and hand-carved wooden toys to pottery and stained glass. Six artists working in assorted media — oils, acrylic and watercolors — are also highlighted. Four huge cases of handcrafted sterling silver jewelry will tempt you, and the low prices are impossible to resist.

The Yankee Trader
9 S. Lake Park Blvd.,
Carolina Beach
• (910) 458-0097

Look for unusual and one-of-a-kind nautical gifts at The Yankee Trader. Bestsellers are the stoneware oil-lamp lighthouses as well as canvas Maine bags, N.C. lighthouses, authentic model ships, Lefton Lighthouses and more. Known as the island's Christmas shop, the store carries Snowbabies and North Pole Village by Department 56, Margaret Furlong angels, Boyd's Bears, limited edition Pipka Santas, Willow Tree angels, Newport collection of scrimshaw, Cape Fear throw, Mercury glass ornaments and other limited-edition collectibles. The store is closed from January 15 through March 1.

Unique Boutique
207 S. Lake Park Blvd., Carolina Beach
• (910) 458-4360

Originally built as a guest cottage for a larger home, the Unique Boutique carries one-of-a-kind ladies sample clothing at wholesale prices from boutiques in various cities around the country. Additionally, clothing, shoes, hats, jewelry, accessories and swimwear are featured.

Southport-Oak Island

The quaint charm of Southport, nestled between the Cape Fear River and the Intracoastal Water-

way, and the quiet of Oak Island's small, coastal community belie the obvious signs of growth. Recent increases in residential and commercial construction and development, plus the opening of Wal-Mart on N.C. Highway 211 between the two communities, herald a changing era for this region, and the growing number of year-round retail businesses is a reflection of this trend.

Many of the shops listed here are found within an easy walk in Southport's picturesque historic district. Leave the car parked on the street and enjoy a leisurely stroll along the town's waterfront and main thoroughfare, particularly Howe and Moore streets. You'll find gift and jewelry shops, restaurants, art galleries, clothing stores and a maritime museum. If you're interested in antiques markets, see the Southport listings in the Antiques section at the end of this chapter.

Angelwing Needle Arts
507 N. Howe St., Southport
• (910) 454-9163

Angelwing is a charming needle arts shop with a great big reputation. The shop stocks such a wide range of quality supplies, kits and accessories for needlepoint, counted thread, crewel embroidery, counted cross stitch, knitting, crochet and quilting that customers come from as far away as Raleigh to shop there. Knitting and stitching groups meet in the evenings on a regular basis to receive inspiration and moral support from each other and from the staff. Finishing services are available as well.

Blue Crab Blue
4310 Long Beach Rd., Southport
• (910) 454-8888

Wonder where the locals shop? Discover this quaint boat-builder's cottage near the Oak Island Bridge and you will find it brimming with handcrafted pottery, jewelry, stained glass, watercolors and other gift ideas. It is a treasure trove of specially commissioned, exclusive and one-of-a-kind arts all at affordable prices. Owner Barbara Donahue supports local and regional artists and selects each piece with an eye for detail and quality of craftsmanship. Pottery pieces, including raku, ceramic and coiled, range from artistic to utilitarian to whimsical. The hand-crafted jewelry is of excellent quality and design, made of sterling silver, pewter, sea glass and genuine stones. There's much more to see and, with year-round

INSIDERS' TIP

Don't miss Carolina Beach's annual Christmas "Shop 'Til You Drop" weekend event in early December. The merchants kick off the Christmas shopping season with extended hours, special sales, prize drawings and more.

hours, this friendly shop is a must-visit. In addition, every purchase leaves the shop carefully and beautifully packaged. Shipping is available via U.S. Post Office-insured mail. After-hours appointments to see the collection are welcomed.

Boat House Gifts
128 Country Club Dr., Oak Island
• (910) 278-9856

The first building you will see after you cross the bridge to Oak Island is Boat House Gifts. It is a beautiful new building with a large porch on each of its two stories. Inside, the floors are polished hardwood and wide stairs take you to the gallery on the second floor. The shop carries all kinds of beautifully displayed unique and interesting gifts, including Fenton glass, Madam Alexander dolls, lighthouses, prints, home accessories, jewelry, wind chimes and Hallmark cards. Some of its collectibles are Tom Clark's sculptural creations, Harmony Kingdom box figurines, Snowbabies and Beanie Babies.

Books 'n Stuff
4961-11 Live Oak Village Shopping Ctr.,
Long Beach Rd., Southport
• (910) 457-9017

With more than 15 years in the Oak Island-Southport area, bookstore owner Susan Warren meets the reading needs of residents and visitors alike all year long. Her store carries thousands of previously read paperbacks and hundreds of new, discounted books. Not sure what you want? Susan's extensive knowledge of books and authors will ensure that you leave with just the right one. When you're finished, trade it in for credit toward the next one. Journals, address books and book accessories are attractive recent additions to the store.

Cape Fear Jewelers
102 E. Moore St., Southport
• (910) 457-5299

Serving as Southport's jeweler since 1985, Cape Fear Jewelers boasts the largest selection of 14K gold nautical jewelry available, including the original Bald Head and Oak Island lighthouse charms. It also carries Seiko watches and American Eagle coins. The full-service store offers jewelry and watch repair and an appraisal service.

The Christmas House
104 W. Moore St., Southport
• (910) 457-5166

Catch the Christmas spirit all year long in this festively decorated Victorian-style house in the heart of Southport's historic downtown.

Choose from a delightful and reasonably priced collection of ornaments, decorations, angels, gifts, candles, stuffed animals, dolls and more. Don't miss the toy train, whose tracks are mounted above your head near the ceiling.

Heller Bookery and Coffee Bar
4956-4 Long Beach Rd., SE, Southport
• (910) 457-9653

Heller Bookery is a comfortable, soothing place, and Sheila Heller says hers is a place where people can drop in and leave their worries at the door. The decor includes soft music and comfortable seating, including a scrunchy leather chair.

Heller Bookery is a full-service book store with knowledgeable and helpful staff who provide the kind of customer service you can't get in large bookstores. You will find gifts, jigsaw puzzles, stationery, cards, CDs and magazines as well. Books can be ordered quickly, and delivery is available to Bald Head Island.

The expanded children's area contains animal rugs and pillows where the children can lie back and let the magic carpet of their books take them away. In addition to the books there are wooden doll houses, horse stables and puzzles among other things to keep the children entertained. The bookery carries an excellent selection of children's books for all ages as well as educational games, puzzles and toys.

Not to be overlooked is the small coffee bar, featuring specialty coffees and teas, fruit smoothies, hot chocolate and scrumptious homemade cakes, cookies and goodies. Decadent sweets, gourmet coffee beans and appetizers, pesto and crackers, conserve and biscotti are also available as are custom gifts and baskets. You can sit at one of the tables and work a jigsaw puzzle or play a game of Backgammon or Checkers. A poetry group and book clubs meet here and welcome new members.

Isabella Grape Boutique
319 N. Howe St., Southport
• (910) 454-0412, (866) ISABELLA

Eclectic and fine fashion for women is a hallmark of this interesting boutique. You'll also find distinctive gifts, shoes, accessories, jewelry, collectibles and more, so be sure to check every nook and cranny in every room of the shop. Don't forget to ask about the legend of Isabella Grape!

J. Huffman
600-A N. Howe St., Southport
• (910) 454-8114

At J. Huffman you can find the same quality merchandise that is available at the stores in Shallotte and Sunset Beach. Fine ladies wear includes Vera Bradley clothing, shoes, accessories, swimsuits and lingerie. A large gift selection including cards, jewelry, picture frames, decorative pillows, rugs and throws, lamps, potpourri and collectibles. J. Huffman is open Monday through Saturday.

Ropa, etc.
417-C N. Howe St., Southport
• (910) 454-8833

Are you ready for something new and exciting? Then you're invited to experience the pleasure of fine cottons and linens, which make dressing comfortable and fun. Ropa, etc. is the area's exclusive retailer for such lines as Liz and Jane, Flax, and Willow. This terrific shop also carries great makers such as Rico hand-knit sweaters, TSD, April Cornell, Habitat, Cut•Loose, Basic Threads and Naot shoes. Ropa, etc. is also known for its unique collection of jewelry from makers around the world plus great accessories to complement any outfit. Sizes range from extra small to extra large and fit a variety of shapes. Ropa, etc. has two other locations to serve you: 120-B South Front Street, Wilmington, (910) 815-0344 and 1121 Military Cutoff Suite D, (910) 256-8733.

Seaside Baskets
706 Yaupon Dr., Oak Island
• (910) 278-1444

Lynn Ingram's shop walls are decorated with paintings of sea life, and baskets of varied sizes and shapes hang from a peg board. Lynn says her shop is "an eclectic collection of stuff for joyful living," and included in that collection are fine wines and accessories, champagne, port and sherry, all of Burt's Bees personal care products, a variety of books, handmade soaps, candles and lots of gourmet food items from the Carolinas and beyond — including Gullah Gourmet food mixes, Carolina Gold Rice, coffee, tea, chocolates, biscotti, flavored nuts, snack mixes, cheese biscuits, jams and jellies and soups. What's more, you may have a cup of coffee (paid for on the honor system) or even sip a glass of wine while you shop. If you are interested in a gift basket, Lynn will put it together for you from your selections — or if you are not sure what to purchase, she will give you the personal attention of walking through the shop with you and helping you choose. If you like, you can purchase a basket and some goodies and take it to the beach for a picnic. Deliver-

ies and shipping are also available. Seaside Baskets is open Monday through Saturday.

Waterfront Gifts & Antiques
117 S. Howe St., Southport
• (910) 457-6496

When Southport Insiders need to buy a gift, Waterfront Gifts is often their first stop. This shop, near the waterfront at the end of Howe Street, is known for distinctive gifts for all occasions, including jewelry, greeting cards, distinctive accessories, antiques, wall and table top sculptures, books on local and regional history and a large selection of nautical gifts.

South Brunswick Islands

City Girl Baskets
Low Country Stores, 10138 Beach Dr. SW, Calabash • (910) 575-4522

City Girl Baskets carries North Carolina and South Carolina specialty foods along with many other gourmet choices. In addition to such items as a complete gourmet meal in a box, you will find bath and body products, cookies, cheese straws, sauces, soup mix, flavored crackers, seasonings and Carolina Seven Layer Cake. Local art work is for sale as well.

Callahan's of Calabash Nautical Gifts
9973 Beach Dr., Calabash
• (910) 579-2611, (800) 344-3816

Don't leave Calabash without a stop at Callahan's. The building is a huge sprawling structure that actually houses several departments under one roof, so plan for a long visit. Calabash Nautical Gifts, the store's namesake, has everything nautical you can imagine plus a large selection of gifts, gold and silver jewelry, homemade candy and fudge, a complete card shop and much more. St. Nick Nacks Christmas Shop, the holiday (Christmas, Easter, Halloween) collectibles area of the store, boasts nearly 3 million ornaments. If you're a collector, this is a must-stop destination. You'll find generous selections of Christopher Radko ornaments, Seraphim Classic angels, Precious Moments, Snowbabies, Department 56 Villages and others. In yet another area of this sprawling store, you'll discover Pea Landing Mercantile. This area of Callahan's features mouthwatering fudge and homemade candy, gourmet foods, cookbooks with a coastal flair and accessories for home or garden. Worn out from all this shopping? The benches on the building's covered wraparound porch are a great place to rest tired feet.

J. Huffman
Shallotte Crossing, Shallotte
• **(910) 754-9968**

J. Huffman carries a pleasing selection of ladies clothing including Vera Bradley ladies wear. Shoes, accessories, swimsuits and lingerie are available as well. Whatever the gift-giving occasion — wedding, baby, housewarming, birthday or a "just for me" present — J. Huffman is a good place to look first. Filled with great gift selections for all occasions, this attractive store also carries cards, jewelry, a large inventory of picture frames and collectibles. Visit J. Huffman at The Village at Sunset Beach, (910) 579-9998, corner of U.S. Highways 179 and 904, Sunset Beach and in Southport, (910) 454-8114, at 600-A N. Howe Street. All stores are open every day except Christmas.

Harbour Court Unique Shops
9970 Beach Dr., Calabash

Harbour Court is an attractive series of shops located directly across from Callahan's in Calabash. **Calabash Smoke Sho**p, (910) 575-7667, is for those devoted to a great cigar. Imported and domestic cigars, cigarettes, lighters and smoking accessories are all available here.

Low Country Quilting
10138-2 Beach Dr. SW, Calabash
• **(910) 575-6632**

There's more to quilting than meets they eye. Beginning in the 1920s feed sacks containing chicken feed, flour, sugar, etc. were made of printed fabric. When the sacks were empty, the fabric was used to make clothing and the left over pieces for making quilts. For years, unless one of these quilts was handed down in the family, or bought from an individual, they could not be reproduced. Now, reproduction prints can be found, and they can be found at Low Country Quilting.

Owner Cheryl Mills won Best of Show in the Tarheel Quilters Guild in 1999, First Place in the Brunswick County Extension Show in 2000, and Third place in the Horry County Museum Show in 2001. In 2002, she decided to share her expertise with others by opening Low Country Quilting. Available in this shop are approximately 500 bolts of fabric, needles, notions, self-healing cutting boards, quilt kits, and more. In addition, classes are taught including beginners classes, feed sack reproduction, 1800s

reproduction, sewing machine quilting and wool applique. Longarm quilting is available as well.

Lowell's Bookworm
3004 Holden Beach Rd. SW, Holden Beach
• **(910) 842-7380, (877) 720-7199**

L. Bookworm is a delightful place to satisfy your reading hunger. Whether you want easy beach reading or more stimulating literature, you're likely to find it here. If not, Lowell's will gladly special order it for you. They carry a good selection of new fiction, nonfiction, bestsellers, children's books, paperbacks. Used books are sold and traded; check with the store for trade-in rates. Photocopying and fax services are available. While browsing, be sure to look through the extensive regional and local history room.

Reflections Stained Glass
947 Carter Dr., Calabash • 575-3503

Patty Lewellyn started working in stained glass as a hobby more than a decade ago. She found the choice of glass and supplies was limited and dreamed of opening her own shop one day. Seven years ago she did just that, and you will find more glass and supplies in her shop than just about anywhere on the East Coast. In addition to selling pattern books, glass, grinders, cutters, copper foil, Tiffany reproduction glass, etc., Patty gives classes in the shop. She teaches an "angel" class, which takes only an hour or so to do, as well as classes in the basics, cutting and grinding, lamp making, boxes, panels and others. Classes are taught one on one by appointment. People come from as far as Murrells Inlet and Wilmington for classes and from Rocky Mount and even Virginia for purchases. Custom work and group demonstrations are available.

Sonrise Square
101 Shoreline Dr., Sunset Beach

Tucked away near the bridge at Sunset Beach on N.C. 179, this charming shopping center offers three specialty stores and an ice cream shop. **Island Breeze**, (910) 579-4125, is the place to find fashionable ladies' apparel, shoes and accessories, distinctive jewelry, select men's apparel and gifts in a friendly atmosphere. **Little Friends Children's Clothing**, (910) 579-9363, carries high-quality children's fashions, play and dress-up clothing in sizes infant to size 10 for boys and infant to size 16 for girls. **Just Lovely Gifts**, (910) 579-0809, offers solutions to your entertaining, decorating and gift-giving needs with a selection of merchandise that includes decorative picture frames, jewelry, gourmet

All the gear you need for a good time can be found in local stores.

Photo: Jay Tervo

SHOPPING

foods and treats, gifts, an assortment of instrumental CDs and silk flowers. Visit the Christmas room for a selection of ornaments, snowmen, angels and nativities or the Book Nook for Bibles and inspirational literature.

Victoria's Ragpatch
Ragpatch Row, 10164 Beach Dr. SW, Calabash • (910) 579-2015

This elegant shop is actually two boutiques at one location. The first floor is overflowing with a wide selection of upscale ladies apparel, shoes and accessories. The upstairs studio offers everything you need for entertaining or furnishing your home — linens, furniture, lamps, dinnerware, art and accessories. Step into the adjacent kitchen for tasty samples of assorted dips, soups, tea, coffee and pies. Gift baskets and gift wrapping are available. Victoria's Ragpatch has a second, smaller shop located on the Causeway at Ocean Isle Beach, (910) 579-3158.

The Village at Sunset Beach
Corner of N.C. Hwys. 179 and 904, Sunset Beach

This attractive new shopping center brings a number of amenities — a Food Lion grocery store, bank, restaurants, video store, gas station and retail stores — to the Brunswick Island communities. Specialty shops include **J. Huffman**, (910) 579-9998, a ladies' fashions and accessories boutique. **Cheney's Gifts**, (910) 579-8984, has a wonderful selection of gifts, collectibles, Yankee Candles and cards. The **Roasted Bean Beverage Co. Coffee Shop**, (910) 575-6759, large by coffee shop standards, has several private seating areas, all the goodies you expect in a coffee shop and curious art for

sale on the walls. **The Pelican Bookstore**, (910) 579-8770, is a cozy place to browse for new and used titles, gifts or books highlighting local interests. Copies, UPS shipping and a fax service are available at The Pelican.

The Yard Bird Emporium, LLC
10138 Beach Dr. SW, Calabash
• (910) 575-5455

Proprietor Mary Keefe is a storehouse of knowledge about birds and squirrels, their feeding habits and their habitats. (Hint: Never attach a bluebird house to a tree if you want them to nest in it!) Proof of her knowledge can be seen in the bluebirds feeding on the porch of her shop and flying around the buildings. In addition to all kinds of supplies such as hummingbird feeders, bird houses, squirrel feeders, field guides, bluebird nesting boxes and poles, yard ornaments, etc., The Yard Bird carries Coles Specialty Feed (Critter Munchies, Special Feeder, Cracked Corn), Droll Yankee and Duncraft products.

Topsail Island Area

A Beautiful New You Salon
332 N. New River Dr., Surf City
• (910) 328-2525

A Beautiful New You offers all the services for a complete makeover. Hairstyling by three experienced specialists, spa manicures, spa pedicures and make-up consultations are just the beginning. There are tanning beds, a massage therapist and an alpha massager to assist with weight loss and arthritis pain control. A Beautiful New You carries a complete line of spa and beauty products.

Bah Humbug!
N.C. Hwy. 50 (Roland Ave.), Surf City
• (910) 328-4422

A specialty shop that lives up to its claim of "Great Shopping for Grumps and Elves," Bah Humbug! has a year-round Christmas theme. The store is divided into small specialized areas with unique gifts for the kitchen, children, home decorating, Christmas, and more. For 2003, be sure to check out their new line of stationery and expanded assortment of wine accessories. Fabulous RHYTHM clocks and Lee Middleton dolls continue to be great gifts for the extra special people on your list. A step inside Bah Humbug! can give you a happy feeling. Call for seasonal hours.

Barefoot Child
The Fishing Village, Roland Ave., Surf City
• (910) 328-9766

Every child deserves to feel special with a gift of clothing or toys from this boutique that is filled with "Little Baby Pretty Things." Owner Cathy Medlin offers whimsical things to delight the senses of the most delightful creature — your child or grandchild. A choice of toys, picked for the sheer joy of playing, adorn the shelves. Stop by and check out their clothing, toys and other bits of stuff. Barefoot Child is open daily.

Beach Furniture Outfitters
520 New River Dr., Surf City
• (910) 328-4181

Whether you need furnishings to completely set up housekeeping or just one special accent piece, Beach Furniture Outfitters has choices for every taste and pocketbook. Its specialty is contracting to fully furnish and equip a beach home or condominium, but don't overlook the single items available to complete your decorating scheme. Free set up and delivery are offered on the island. It's open daily except Sunday.

Bert's Surf Shop
310 N. New River Dr., Surf City
• (910) 328-1010

A longtime favorite on the beach, Bert's has a full line of women's name-brand swimwear and sportswear for the whole family as well as footwear, beach T-shirts and sunglasses. It also offers a full line of sports equipment for sale, including skateboards and surfing gear. It's open seven days a week.

Carlee's
110 N. New River Dr., Surf City
• (910) 328-3407

Surf City's newest gift shop, Carlee's offers a selection of unique merchandise to delight even the most discriminating customer. You'll find a full line of specialty products to pamper yourself, including the largest selection of bath products on the island. Carlee's also features women's clothing and accessories as well as baby bath and gift items. This is a great place to shop for yourself or someone special. It's open every day.

D's Interior Designs
1961 N.C. Hwy. 172, Sneads Ferry
• (910) 327-2166

This is the place to find everything you want for your home. D's Interior Design offers furniture, unique gifts and creative interior design items, including wallpaper, fabrics for custom bedspreads and window treatments, upholstery, carpet, vinyl, laminate floor coverings, art work and accessories. D's is also an authorized Yankee Candle Dealer. It's open Monday through Saturday.

Docksider Gifts & Shells
14061 N.C. Hwy. 50, Surf City
• (910) 328-1421

This wonderful beach store, with more than 100,000 items, truly captures the feeling of being on vacation. Have that special sharks' tooth you found on the beach wired into jewelry while you browse. Pick your favorite flavor of fresh saltwater taffy. Hermit crabs, coral, windchimes, Thirstystone coasters, books, paint sets, postcards and more are displayed on the well-stocked shelves. Be sure to check out the original Topsail Island coverlet throw available in different colors. Docksider is open daily.

East Coast Sports
Village Mall, Roland Ave. Cswy., Surf City
• (910) 328-1887

East Coast Sports carries a full line of sports clothing including Columbia, Bimi Bay, Sperry Topsiders and many other name brands. In addition to clothing, you can find everything you could ever want or need for inshore or offshore fishing, including a professional staff to answer all your questions. East Coast is open year round.

The Gift Basket
702 S. Anderson Blvd., Topsail Beach
• (910) 328-7111

Serving the area since 1973, The Gift Basket is best known for its line of fine jewelry, but there is much more. At this Carin Studios dealer, you will find the latest in Tom Clark gnomes, Tim Wolfe animals and David Merch lighthouses. The Gift Basket also features an impressive line of tide and

SHOPPING

nautical clocks and precision weather instruments. The expanded shopping area upstairs offers new shopping opportunities for 2003. It's open every day but Sunday.

Island Traders
311 S. Topsail Dr., Surf City
• (910) 328-1004

Daily shipments of new merchandise assures shoppers a surprise each time they visit Island Traders. Name brand and catalog clothing at 40 to 70% below retail for guys and gals makes this shop a good place to stock up on golf, casual and school clothing. Original Tervis Tumblers and nautical license plates are also available at this shop that claims no shopper will be disappointed with the ever-changing inventory.

Island Treasures
627 S. Anderson Blvd., Topsail Beach
• (910) 328-4487

The treasures in this shop are many and varied and shoppers will wish to browse among the aisles before settling on that "something special." In the clothing department, one can choose from attractively displayed racks of fine casual clothes for women, such as the popular Cotton Connection line. While in that area,

consider the Topsail Beach embroidered T-shirts and sweatshirts, favorites for the entire family. Amble over to the surprisingly wide array of gifts that include wonderful nautical prints, lamps, flags, windsocks, a full line of sunglasses, hats, beach supplies and collectibles, including Ty. Be on the lookout for the Kids Play Corner, featuring the colorful wooden Puzzle World Train with Big City Adventure, Busy Airports, Dock 'n Discover, Dollhouses and Horse Stables. There are also many new educational puzzles and other items to amuse and intrigue the younger set. The shopper will be pleased with the personal care Island Treasures gives to their unique free gift wrap, as well as the warm welcome one always receives upon entering this shop, which is open daily.

Just A $
13741-E. N.C. Hwy. 50, Surf City
• (910) 329-0800
Northshore Village, Old Folkstone Rd.,
Sneads Ferry • (910) 327-2342

What a great addition to the Topsail area shops. With two locations to serve you, Just A $ has everything from paper and party products to cleaning supplies and pet chews; toys and office supplies to hardware and tools. Campers are excited to find necessary kitchenware items at a price that allows them to throw away purchases that won't pack up for the trip back home. Vacationers find a wonderful variety of gift and souvenirs, and Just A $ employees pride themselves on packing these treasures for travel. It is important to note that there are a few items that cost more than a dollar. It's open every day during the summer, with reduced hours off season.

Koffee Kats
Corner of Roland Ave. and N. New River Dr., Surf City • (910) 328-0022
Take time out for a specialty coffee or tea, pastry or other confection while you browse this great little shop with gourmet and health food items, chocolates and pecans, greeting and note cards, and other merchandise selected to be different than the usual beach-type offerings. It's open daily.

Mea's Jewelry and Gifts
Treasure Coast Square, 208A N. New River Dr., Surf City • (910) 328-0920
Looking for that special decorating item for your home or garden? Mea's has a selection of collectible lighthouses, accessories, flags, rugs, art candles and dishware. In addition to high-quality decorating items and specialty furniture, the store offers a wide variety of jewelry and watches, decorative beach bags, hats and other gift selections.

New Attitude/Shoreline Treasures
Surf City Food Lion Plaza, N.C. Hwy. 50, Surf City • (910) 329-1555
New Attitude is not only a beauty and tanning salon, but also a retail shop with a wide assortment of casual clothing, costume jewelry and hair products. The salon opens into Shoreline Treasures where you will find a bounty of beach items and a full line of 10K and 14K gold, sterling silver and unique gifts. The shelves are full to overflowing with the treasures. Often, even during the summer months, you will find sales on much of this delightful merchandise. It's open daily except Sundays.

Pastimes Toys and Gifts
Treasure Coast Plaza, 208D N. New River Dr., Surf City • (910) 328-2737
This quality toy store offers a wide selection of educational and fun toys to capture the imaginations of both adults and children. Whether the interest is puzzles, science, games, art and crafts or construction, the appropriate toy can be found on these well-stocked shelves. Pastimes is a great place for grandparents and parents to find the

special gift. It ranks high on the list of unique specialty shops on Topsail Island. It's open daily.

Pierside Wicker Company
205 S. Topsail Dr; Surf City • (910) 328-0203
Pierside carries a full line of rattan, indoors and all-weather wicker. Custom-made sofas are available with over 1,000 fabrics to choose from. Floor coverings, pictures, lamps and decorator pieces complement the furniture offerings. Pierside offers complete condominium packages. It's open year round.

Quarter Moon Bookstore
708 S. Anderson Blvd., Topsail Beach • (910) 328-4969, (800) 697-9134
Offering fascinating pages and gifts to enchant, Topsail Island's bookstore, Quarter Moon offers a good range of hardcover and paperback books and an excellent selection of stationery, greeting cards and note cards. The expanded gift selection includes mugs, candles, pillows, unique towels, lots of silk flowers and more. There are gifts for all occasions and many turtle-related items. A selection of smoothies, cappuccino or coffee drinks can be enjoyed in the outside seating area, or inside if you choose. It's open daily in season.

Radio Shack
1950 N.C. Hwy. 172, Ste. A., Sneads Ferry • (910) 327-1478
13741 Ocean Hwy. 50, Ste. B., Surf City • (910) 329-5000
Specializing in consumer electronics, these conveniently located Radio Shacks have the parts and pieces you may have forgotten to bring on vacation with your electronic equipment. It has a good inventory of replacement batteries, battery packs, prepaid phone cards, flashlights and alarm clocks. For rainy day or traveling activities, Radio Shack offers hand-held electronic games. They are open Monday through Saturday.

Seacoast Art Gallery
203 Greensboro Ave., Surf City • (910) 328-1112
You won't want to miss the original art works of Sandy McHugh. Her watercolors depict scenes of Topsail Island that you can take home, hang on the wall and have as a year-round reminder of your vacation. Sandy's trademark is the slogan, "Leave your footsteps behind and take a little bit of Topsail with you." You will also find unusual silver jewelry, paper weights and ceramics, mostly with a beach

theme. Look for the little pink house with the gazebo. It's open daily from June to October.

Spinnaker Surf & Sport
111 N. Shore Dr., Surf City
• (910) 328-2311

Spinnaker's is Surf City's location for surf and skate brands such as Quiksilver, Billabong, Rip Curl, Tony Hawk, Rusty, Lost, Volcom, Hurley and more. The store also has a large selection of girls' surf brand apparel, swimsuits and accessories. Spinnaker's now offers clothing and footwear for infants and toddlers. However, there is much more to be found on the three floors of this great surf shop — jewelry by Jenni K; designer eyewear such as Oakley and Dragon; shoes and sandals by DC, ES, Etnies, Roxy, Reef, Rainbow and Vans; and novelty gifts. The Spinnaker Arcade down below offers dozens of traditional games including pool tables, video games and foosball; it's a cool place out of the sun. Looking for surfboards or skateboards? Spinnaker's has a large selection.

Surf City Florist
106 N. Topsail Dr., Surf City
• (910) 328-3238

Fresh flowers for special and other memorable occasions are not all you'll find in this delightful shop. Balloons, plants and stuffed animals are available. Local flower delivery is available. Surf City Florist is open every day but Sunday.

Surf City Shopping Center Gift Shop
Corner of Roland Ave. and Topsail Dr.,
Surf City • (910) 328-0835

Bathing suits, women's casual wear and a variety of other vacation and beach items can be found here. Since this store is connected to the IGA grocery store, the merchandise in the grocery store, such as sunscreen, toiletries, magazines and paperback books, complements the items in the gift shop, allowing a great opportunity for one-stop shopping. It's open daily.

Surfside Sportswear and Gifts
314 N. New River Dr., Surf City
• (910) 328-4141

A year-round favorite with residents, Surfside offers the most complete line of women's clothing on the island. The racks are always filled with bathing suits, casual wear and party attire in a wide variety of sizes from petites to women and in styles for the young and not-so-young. Often the biggest problem is deciding which outfit to choose. In addition to clothing, Surfside offers an assortment of jewelry, glassware, decorating and

Christmas items, beach T-shirts and sweatshirts. It's open daily year round.

Terra Co. Garden Center Gift Shop
2540 N.C. Hwy. 210 E., Hampstead
• (910) 329-1290

Need a special gift for the the the gardening enthusiast? Terra Co. Gift Shop has a good selection of unique, locally made gifts for the home, lawn or garden. Plants, stepping stones, wall hangings, plant stands and hangers, paintings and decorative pieces are just some of the items displayed in this quaint little shop. This Garden Center has a wide variety of plants and shrubs. They specialize in cold weather, hardy palm trees.

The Topsail Island Trading Company
201 New River Dr., Surf City
• (910) 328-1905

Where is Capt. Ed? Looking for the famous Capt. Ed has brought a chuckle to many returning vacationers on Topsail Island. Each year, Topsail Island Trading Co. moves him somewhere different in the store and customers enjoy searching to see where he might be. After locating Capt. Ed, it's time to browse through the store, selecting from a variety of gourmet items, specialty gifts, a line of causal fine clothing for the whole family plus jewelry and accessories. But that's not all: while browsing your nose detects a delicious smell and your mouth begins to water, that's when you'll know you're in the place that makes the famous homemade fudge you've been hearing so much about. There are so many flavors it's hard to make a choice, yet it's almost impossible to leave the Trading Company without a box or bag of fudge in hand. Topsail Island Trading Co. is open daily.

Zack's
Treasure Coast Plaza, 208 N. New River
Dr., Surf City • (910) 328-5904

Home of the original "TI" euro decals, license plates, mugs and totes Zack's has found its niche in the Topsail marketplace with a selection of unique items. In addition to the TI merchandise, Zack's has the largest selection of authentic Hawaiian shirts, made in Hawaii by KoKo Island. While you're there, don't miss Zack's private label selection of old-fashioned Root Beer, Cream Soda, Ginger Beer, Black Cherry and Orange Soda. A trip to Topsail wouldn't be complete without a visit to Zack's, where you'll find something special — from bath and body products to home decor — for everyone on your gift list.

DDT-Outlet
21740 N.C. Hwy. 17 N., Hampstead
• **(910) 329-0160**

If you're looking for furniture and accessories with a beach or nautical theme, you'll find it at the DDT Outlet. With about 20,000 square feet of unique merchandise to chose from and services ranging from complete beach house and condominium packages to shipping purchases back home, shopping in this great store is a must. Be sure to have plenty of time to browse the many rooms displaying furniture, nautical gifts, wicker, barstools, pictures, yard ornaments and more. If you need help in the selection of your furniture package, Niki Miller is the expert, according to husband Tom. It's easy to see these owners take pride in their business and enjoy working with their customers. DDT is open seven days a week..

Antiques

Downtown Wilmington

Downtown Wilmington is a focal point for antiques stores that range the spectrum in size, price and quality. Antiquers can spend days exploring the possibilities. You can find many antiques stores along Front Street, and a knot of them are on nearby Castle Street. Park the car anywhere along Front Street, adjacent streets or downtown parking decks and set off on foot to discover these treasures.

To guide you through the more than 225,000 square feet of Wilmington's antiques and collectibles stores, pick up a copy of "A Guide to Greater Wilmington Antique Shops" leaflet at any of the antiques stores listed in this chapter. It was compiled by the Greater Wilmington Antique Dealers Association and contains a map with brief descriptions of about 40 shops and dealers. Unfortunately they can't all be included here, so pick up the map and venture out into the past.

About Time Antiques
30 N. Front St., Wilmington
• **(910) 762-9902**

About Time Antiques offers "a little bit of everything" in American antiques but a special feature is the selection of art glass. The shop is the exclusive dealer for Lotton art glass in the region.

Betty B's Trash To Treasure
Front Street Center, 130 N. Front St. Ste.
102, Wilmington • (910) 763-3703

If you love to stroll through antiques, collectibles and memorabilia, you'll love Betty B's.

Now in a new location, it still offers just about everything, including silver, estate and costume jewelry, small furniture, linens, dishes and glassware, books and much more.

Celestial Antiques
143 N. Front St., Wilmington
• **(910) 362-0740**

Celestial Antiques features 21 dealers with a variety of antiques, including glassware, accessories, collectibles, prints and photographs, linens and period pieces. Antique tools, shabby chic, primitives and original oil paintings and drawings are specialties, along with Oriental furniture and accessories.

Michael Moore Antiques
20 S. Front St., Wilmington
• **(910) 763-0300**

This two-story building houses Moore's collection of antique furniture, glassware and sterling silver on the bottom floor. Nine additional dealers are housed on the second floor.

Past Elegance
103 S. Front St., Wilmington
• **(910) 251-9001**

This cozy and elegant shop features late 1800s to 1970s vintage linens, lace and clothing. Owner Pauline Hopkinson provides restoration services for your fine vintage linens.

River Galleries
107 S. Front St., Wilmington
• **(910) 251-2224**

Set in the elegant Bellamy Building, River Galleries houses a wide range of antiques, including period furniture, nautical artifacts, fine art, china, crystal and silver. Appraisals are available by River Galleries owner Charles Adams, a veteran appraiser for more than 30 years in Wilmington.

The Riverside Market
208 S. Front St., Wilmington
• **(910) 763-0504**

Located in the Old Wilmington Ironworks building, The Riverside Market is a 7,000-square-foot, multi-level antiques mall with 29 vendors. Antiques buffs and collectors will find a wide and eclectic blend of items here, including primitive to period antiques, gifts, collectibles, reproductions, vintage linens and much more.

Other Areas

While the majority of the area's antiques stores are clustered in downtown Wilmington, there are many other opportunities for antiquing around the region. Listed below are some additional Wilmington, Southport and Topsail Island shops.

The Ivy Cottage
3020 & 3030 Market St., Wilmington
• (910) 815-0907, (877) 256-6441

Plan to spend a lot of time at Wilmington's premier consignment shop. With two buildings and more than 13,000 square feet of display area, these stores are filled with antiques, classic furniture and accessories, china, crystal, silver, fine jewelry and even Oriental carpets with hundreds of new items arriving daily. A wonderful place to treasure hunt, The Ivy Cottage is open seven days a week.

Just Looking
The Forum, 1121 Military Cutoff Rd., Wilmington • (910) 256-9266

This well-established antiques store carries both 18th- and 19th-century European antiques, including 19th-century pine furniture. The shop's focus is blending a mix of the old and new into today's living with original art, quality gifts and accessories featured. Design services are also available. Shopping with your canine companion? Just Looking is dog-friendly, and Addie, a Cavalier King Charles spaniel and the shop's official greeter, will enjoy the company.

The Olivia House Collections
4709 Wrightsville Ave., Wilmington
• (910) 452-9424

Is it burgundy? Eggplant? Magenta? Opinions vary wildly about the color of this charming antiques shop. Whatever your guess, you'll definitely want to step inside and browse through rooms full of treasures. Artfully arranged on two floors, the antiques, unusual gifts, mahogany period pieces, collectibles, fine old chests and high-quality accessories are reasonably priced. Olivia House also buys antiques and collectibles from individuals. Whether you're looking for fine antiques or shabby chic or you're just in the mood to browse, make sure that Olivia House is on your list for a visit. The shop is open Monday through Saturday.

The Weathered Cottage
5935 Carolina Beach Rd., Wilmington
• (910) 350-1115

Now under new ownership, The Weathered Cottage offers unique and quirky items. The shop's welcoming, laidback atmosphere invites a leisurely browse through its eclectic treasures: furniture,

The Ivy Cottage

DISTINGUISHED CONSIGNMENTS

Wilmington's Largest UPSCALE Furniture, Antiques & Home Accessories Resale Shop

Mon.-Sat. 10:00-5:00
Sun. 1:00-5:00

3020-3030 MARKET ST. **815-0907**
WWW.TWOCOTTAGES.COM

home furnishings, kitchen items, housewares, table linens, quilts, unique and glitzy jewelry and clothing and so much more. An extensive courtyard area features garden accessories, old garden tools and lawn furniture. Owner Gail Griffin offers fun and "a little bit of everything" at affordable prices at The Weathered Cottage.

Southport

Magnolia Gifts & Antiques
301 Howe St., Southport • (910) 457-4982

Visitors to this pristine shop will find a large selection of gifts, decorative accessories, jewelry and antique furniture on the first floor. An attractively arranged second floor features hand-painted furniture, glass vases and more.

Northrup Antiques Mall
111 E. Moore St., Southport
• (910) 457-9569

Antiques shoppers will delight in the 38 antiques and collectibles dealers housed under one roof in historic downtown Southport. Throughout this one-stop shopping, two-story building, shoppers will find a variety of unique gifts and the greeting cards. The possibilities for found treasures include antique furniture and accessories, sterling silver, Slow Blue and Limoges, glassware, linens, porcelain, books, Civil War artifacts and more. Don't miss the specialty candles by A. I. Root. Original Artwork by local artists is featured and sold exclusively in this shop.

Southport Antiques
105 E. Moore St., Southport
• (910) 457-1755

Quality antiques and consignments are a specialty of this store. Look for antique furniture, quilts, art, rugs, porcelain, nautical items, glass, folk art, silver, jewelry and more. Need a personal property appraisal for insurance or estate purposes? This service is available at Southport Antiques.

Topsail Island

Old Chapel Antiques
322 Sneads Ferry Rd., Sneads Ferry
• (910) 327-2060

A selection of oak, mahogany and cherry furniture and oak fireplace mantels are just some of the pieces you will find at Old Chapel Antiques. The owners, the McLaughlins, look for unusual and hard-to-find items for their shop. From Depression glass to comic books to a large collection of Hot Wheels cars and Precious Moments, you can find almost anything and everything here. It's open Wednesday through Sunday.

Watertower Gallery and Antiques
203 S. Topsail Dr., Surf City
• (910) 328-4847

Watertower Gallery and Antiques is a real treasure that combines the beauty of antiques with original art. Home to some interesting, hard-to-find antique items, such as books, jewelry, mirrors, china and glass, it is also an art studio. Jinx is the expert in the antiques department, while Trapper is the artist. In addition to his bold paintings for sale on the walls, Trapper often works on his latest creations — layering acrylics to create a masterpiece that appears alive on the canvas. Visitors have become so intrigued with the process and progression of Trapper's work that they return on a regular basis to see how the painting has changed with each new layer of color. When you visit the chamber office or the turtle hospital, be sure to enjoy Trapper's murals, his love for the area is reflected in his work. This shop is open daily.

Burgaw

Burgaw Antiqueplace
101 S. Wright Ave., Burgaw
• (910) 259-7070

If you're a serious shopper, you won't want to miss this place. There are 50 dealers located in 15,000 square feet. It's known as the largest antique mall in southeastern North Carolina. The list of items is endless, but includes dishes, glass-ware, pottery, furniture, silver, primitives and jewelry. With an antique furniture refinisher on the premises, furniture can be purchased and restored all in one place. If you wish to do your own refinishing, they also have a booth selling refinishing supplies. There are two appraisers on site that are available by appointment, or there is an appraisal fair the last Saturday of each month. Deliveries are available. To add to your shopping pleasure, try some of their fresh fudge sold on the premises. Burgaw Antiqueplace is open Monday through Saturday.

Furniture

Carolina Furniture
315 Red Cross St., Wilmington
• (910) 762-4452

This family-owned business has been a Wilmington landmark since 1922 and continues to meet the needs of area homeowners as the only full-service furniture store in the downtown area. It offers home furnishings for every room in the house, most major household appliances (refrigerators, freezers, washers, dryers, stoves), TVs and VCRs, stereos and more. The store takes pride in offering its customers reasonable, everyday prices and an affordable in-store financing plan. Customer parking, a plus in downtown Wilmington, is available.

Ecko International Furnishings
420 S. College Rd., Wilmington
• (910) 452-5442

This is a really fun place for people seeking contemporary, quality furniture on a budget. Materials and workmanship on Ecko pieces are excellent. Those undaunted by minor assembly of some of the furniture will find their efforts well-rewarded in terms of aesthetics and value.

Mangoes
619 N. Howe St., Southport
• (910) 454-8000

Step into a tropical paradise where Mango the baby elephant waits inside the door, his trunk raised in greeting. You will find beautifully hand-crafted furniture of mahogany and cane with a relaxed, West Indies feel included in the line carried by this exotic shop. Holly Rogers, shop owner, imports much of her merchandise from Egypt, India and Honduras and blends the furniture with exquisite gifts and accessories. Lamps, paintings, bookends and more, featuring monkeys, palm trees and even camels await you. The staff is available to visit your home and help you with decorating ideas.

SHOPPING

SHOPPING

The Master's Touch
Dutch Square Industrial Park, 300 Old Dairy Rd., Wilmington • (910) 799-4545

Serving the Wilmington area's furniture needs since 1978, The Master's Touch showroom, open Monday through Friday, features fine furniture from original antiques to reproduction and contemporary pieces. They are especially noted for repair and beautiful restoration services of elegant originals to simple sentimental pieces. Winning the title of "Top 125 Craftsmen in North America" by Fine Woodworking magazine, The Master's Touch is now well known for specialty carving and original designs of American art pieces being considered for the White House. For those unfamiliar with Dutch Square Industrial Park, this business area is accessible from Market Street between Martin Luther King Highway and Gordon Road, across from the Harley Davidson dealership.

McNeill Company Furniture & Mattress Center
1003 Yaupon Dr., Oak Island • (910) 278-7276

James and Martha McNeill started a used furniture business on Oak Island in 1994 in a 700-square-foot storefront. The business was very successful and they decided to add a line of mattresses. Four years ago they moved to a 7,000-square-foot storefront where they now sell new furniture, some of it at discount prices. They have quite a variety of furniture, including freestanding screens, roll-top desks and bedroom furniture in addition to living room furniture. Of course, the selection includes lamps, pictures and accessories as well. They specialize in Englander Mattresses, one of the top brands in the nation. James McNeill says you get first quality at a very good price when you shop here. Delivery is free; however, if you pick up your merchandise yourself, you receive an more substantial discount. The store is open Monday through Saturday year round.

Murrow Furniture Galleries
3514 S. College Rd., Wilmington • (910) 799-4010

On S. College Road, a few miles from the intersection with Shipyard Boulevard, is Murrow Furniture Galleries. It has 45,000 square feet in its showroom and sells hundreds of top-quality brands of furniture such as Council Craftsmen, Century, Bernhardt,

Hickory Chair, Statton, Southwood, Tropitone, Woodard, Kincaid, Maitland Smith, Baker, Bradington Young, Lane and LaBarge. Major medium- to high-end accessory lines include Howard Miller clocks and Waterford crystal. Murrow's furniture is discounted, and there's a full staff of designers in-house.

The Red Dinette
6766R Wrightsville Ave., Wilmington
• (910) 256-6700

The Red Dinette carries furnishings and home accessories with a decidedly unusual twist. Hand-painted furniture and eclectic gift items are the types of merchandise that place this store in a category all by itself. Antique and vintage rugs and fine linens are additional offerings along with lighting options — chandeliers, sconces and lamps. Services here include interior design, custom hand-painting and finishing. It's hard to place this store in terms of category because it has a fine-arts flavor in addition to being a most unusual furniture store. The Red Dinette's collection of handcrafted, one-of-a-kind jewelry, ranging in style from fine to funky, is popular.

Galleries

American Pie
113 Dock St., Wilmington
• (910) 251-2131

This is a delightful shop of contemporary American crafts and folk art. You'll discover some of the most unusual arts and crafts in the Southeast at this store. About 100 American artists are represented and their work includes handmade furniture, hand-blown glass, papier-mâché sculpture, unusual jewelry, hammered metals, ceramics, one-of-a-kind handmade books and hand-carved whistles.

The Gallery at Racine
203 Racine Dr., Wilmington
• (910) 452-2073

Located in the Racine Center for the Arts, this gallery is family-friendly and a great place for art enthusiasts of all ages. The Gallery at Racine exhibits one-of-a-kind art works by local and nationally renowned artists with an eclectic collection of art, including oils, watercolors, acrylics, sculpture, mosaic, pottery, raku, printmaking and more, in a variety of styles and price ranges. Special shows are a highlight at the gallery, and exhibits change every six to eight weeks. A sampling of the featured artists include the talented young Russian Georgie Pocheptsov, Susan Baehman, Will Scheiner, Cecil Eakins, Gwen Redfern, Donna Robertson, WenYing Ziong, Natalie Schorr, Sandra Brett, Dr. Suess, Wenzhi Zhang, Genevieve Cotter and many more. The Gallery at Racine also sponsors the Racine School of the Arts, which provides art and ceramic classes, workshops and camps for all ages and skill levels in a positive setting. Contact the gallery for more information and class schedules.

Fat Cat Gallery
5201 Oleander Dr., Wilmington
• (910) 350-2789

Expect to be enchanted by this charming little house full of artwork by talented locals. Displayed in every nook and cranny of the rooms is a wealth of styles and media, including watercolors, beautiful glass creations, art photography, handmade jewelry, pottery, quilted art and much more.

Fidler's Gallery and Framing
The Cotton Exchange, Nutt St.,
Wilmington • (910) 762-2001

Look for the bright blue awning on the Water Street side of the Cotton Exchange for this attractive gallery. The collections found here include limited-edition pieces, fine-art posters and originals from a wide range of local, regional, national and international artists. These artists include Doolittle, Mangum, Wysocki, Landry, Wyeth, Kunstler and many more. Subjects also vary greatly from florals and wildlife to land- or seascapes and the Civil War. If you're a fan of North Carolina's Bob Timberlake, be sure to see the collection here. Professional custom framing is also available. Housed within the gallery, Wrigley's Clocks offers a selection of timepieces such as wall, mantel and floor (or grandfather) clocks. Wrigley's services what it sells with authorized factory repairs as well as all other makes of clocks. They even make house calls.

Fountainside Fine Art Gallery
Lumina Station Fountainside, 1904
Eastwood Rd., Wilmington
• (910) 256-9956

Well-appointed and visually pleasing, this 3,200-square-foot gallery's focus is to showcase fine art created by local, regional and national artists in an elegant yet comfortable setting. The range of original art mediums found at Fountainside include oil paintings, pastels on paper, acrylics and bronze sculptures. The gallery also hosts artists' exhibits and receptions. Call for more information or a schedule of these events.

SHOPPING

SHOPPING

The Golden Gallery
The Cotton Exchange, 307 Front St., Wilmington • (910) 762-4651

The Golden Gallery is truly a family affair. Mary Ellen Golden's original watercolors depicting Wilmington landmarks and southeastern North Carolina scenery are well-known and sought after among visitors and residents alike. Husband John C. Golden Jr., songwriter and storyteller, is noted for his songs about coastal Carolina's legends, folklore, characters and events. Audiotapes of these ballads and songs, including the Civil War era "The Fall of Fort Fisher," are available at the gallery. His second CD, "Shipwrecks & Sea Songs II" is due out in 2003. Fine-art photography and illustrations of local landmarks are son John W. Golden's specialty, and many of his black and white and color prints are on display. Mary Ellen has been painting in watercolor since 1975 and has been in the Cotton Exchange since 1977. Her techniques and tips are featured in a video, Watercolor Can Be Easy, available for sale in the gallery.

New Elements Gallery
216 N. Front St., Wilmington
• (910) 343-8997

New Elements Gallery, a downtown Wilmington arts destination since 1985, offers changing exhibitions of fine art by local and regional artists and nationally recognized craft artists. This award-winning gallery features a wide range of contemporary and traditional works in oil, watercolor, acrylic and mixed media. Decorative and functional pieces in glass, ceramics, fiber and wood are also fea-

tured, as well as handcrafted jewelry. A sampling of the artists at New Elements Gallery include Claude Howell, Dorothy Gillespie, Bruce Bowman, Robert Irwin, Kyle Highsmith, Nancy Tuttle May, Sally Bowen Prange and Dina Wilde-Ramsing.

Racine Center for the Arts
203 Racine Dr., Wilmington
• (910) 452-2073

The Racine Center for the Arts is an exciting and unique addition to southeastern North Carolina's growing art scene. This spacious 22,000-square-foot building's two floors hosts a multitude of art forms, so whether art is your vocation or a passionate interest, there is something to inspire everyone. The first floor houses The Gallery at Racine (see the description above) and Blue Moon Showcase, an artisan/gift co-op that provides space for artists and designers of one-of-a-kind gifts and home furnishings. Open to the public, each of the 100 display areas at Blue Moon are individually stocked and maintained, providing a unique setting to exhibit work in a tasteful and protected environment. Artists in a wide variety of media are represented, including paintings, pottery, sculpture, photography, fiber art and jewelry. Additional spaces feature antiques, garden art, funky furnishings, art materials and kits, folk art and much more. Blue Moon also provides a creative play space for the little ones while you shop. Need a break? Dine in the center's lovely sculpture garden or watch an artist at work.

The second floor of the center is home to the Glory Academy of Dance Arts, (910) 452-0588, and provides classroom and studio space, including music and recital rooms for music teachers. The Racine School of the Arts multimedia art and pottery education program for kids are conducted here. For more information about Racine Center for the Arts or any of the art programs, contact the center at the number listed above.

Serenity Place Gallery
Landfall Center, 1319 Military Cutoff Rd., Wilmington • (910) 509-2820

If you love the artwork of Thomas Kinkade, the "painter of light," Serenity Place Gallery is a must see. This small but elegant gallery is filled with Kinkade's breath-taking prints and limited-edition pieces. Gift items featuring the artist's distinctive style include beautiful coffee-table books, stationery, collector's plates, calendars, music boxes and more. Serenity Place also handles Thomas Kinkade's Lamplight Village collection. Visit the gallery's second location in historic downtown Wilmington.

Spectrum Gallery
The Forum II, 1121 Military Cutoff Rd., Wilmington • (910) 256-2323, (888) 233-1444

Full of color and light, Spectrum Gallery offers an exciting collection of handcrafted jewelry, original fine art, pottery and art glass. Local and regional artists, working in a variety of media, including watercolors, oils, pastels and multimedia, are featured in an ever-changing collection of original art. The gallery's art-glass collection represents more than 30 glassblowers from the United States and Europe. However, a particular highlight of the gallery is the work of the owners, Raoul and Star Sosa. The Sosas are award-winning jewelry designers and offer stunning custom-jewelry design.

Walls Fine Art Gallery
2173 Wrightsville Ave., Wilmington • (910) 343-1703

Exhibiting fine original oil paintings in a 3,000-square-foot gallery, owners David Leadman and Nancy Marshall, painters themselves, use their more than 60 years of experience to consult with clients to help them make the best selection. They'll even simplify the selection process by bringing art to your home. Walls provides cleaning and restoration services for oil paintings, and they offer the finest hand-carved and gilded frames suitable for artwork from contemporary abstract to 12th-century icon.

Southport

ArtShak Studio and Gallery
807 N. Howe St., Southport • (910) 457-1757, (910) 457-0374

When you see the multicolored suit of armor standing on the side of the street in front of a bright blue and green building, STOP! If you don't, you will miss a most unusual art gallery. Thom Seaman, sculptor, and Linda Platt, artist, began their adventure in Southport in 1997 in a small wooden building with no heat, determined to live their dream of making a living doing what they love. They eventually graduated to the current location with 2,400 square feet of heated gallery and studio space. It's a happy space — you can feel it in the yellow room, which contains painted glassware including windows from Linda's creative hands. In the lavender room her painted furniture is

on display in all its personalities from impressionistic to funky to just cool. Don't miss the elephant table. The walls of Thom's sculpture room are covered with pegboard done in muted shades, which set off his striking metal sculptures. The sculptures are made from aluminum, brass, copper and steel, and some are finished with textures, patinas or paints. They are free-standing, wall-hung and mobiles. You can see why Thom says they have created an environment, not a business. In addition to the art in the gallery, Thom and Linda accept commissions for custom designs, including murals. Thom says, "If we design it together, you will love it forever."

Franklin Square Gallery
Howe and West Sts., behind Franklin Square Park, Southport • (910) 457-5450

Since 1979, The Franklin Square Gallery has been operated by the nonprofit Associated Artists of Southport. It is housed in an impressive historic building in the heart of Southport directly behind Franklin Square Park. The association is responsible for maintaining and operating the gallery and a pottery studio located on the grounds behind it. The City of Southport provides the buildings and maintains the exteriors. The expectation was that the artists would create and maintain an important cultural center and, indeed, they have. In addition to the workshops, classes and competitions provided by the association, the gallery features paintings and pottery of its members, the annual exhibit of the Oak Island Quilters challenge squares, the annual Brunswick County Photography Contest sponsored by the Brunswick County Parks and Recreation Department, and art work of the students of the Brunswick County Public School System. In 2002 the Associated Artists of Southport, in partnership with the North Carolina Museum of Art, participated in presenting a touring exhibition of photographs. All paintings and pottery in the gallery are available for sale to the public.

Ricky Evans Gallery
211 N. Howe St., Southport • (910) 457-1129

The Ricky Evans Gallery features his lighthouse paintings in addition to a series of paintings of historic Southport landmarks and a new coastal waterfront series. The waterfront series includes Wilmington, Southport and other coastal Carolina waterfronts. Original paintings, watercolors and limited-edition posters are available as well. He recently opened the second floor of the quaint old house, which houses the gallery, to the public. You will find paintings, pottery, stained glass, metal sculptures and more, all the work of local artists, on display and for sale. Custom picture framing is available, and the gallery is open year round. Tucked on the south side and to the rear of the gallery, Spencer Pottery is a must stop. It is a small pottery shop and working studio where classes can be scheduled as well.

Southport Art Museum
309 N. Howe St., Southport
• (910) 457-6166

Southport Art Museum is located in a charming building, within easy walking distance of restaurants and shops. The museum has art for sale and framing and exhibits on the premises. You will find a visual presentation and artifacts of the heritage of the Lower Cape Fear Indians, early explorers, pirates, Civil War years, maritime ships, lighthouses, scrimshaw, model ships, decoys and writer Robert Ruark. Admission is free.

South Brunswick Islands

The Blue Heron Gallery
The Village at Sunset Beach, Corner of N.C. Hwys.179 and 904, Sunset Beach
• (910) 575-5088

The Blue Heron is an elegant gallery that features breathtaking artwork from a variety of American artists, including talented local artists. The owners choose wisely, so be prepared to browse at length through an impressive collection of fine blown glass, pottery, sculpture, handcrafted jewelry and other visual art in a variety of media. Whether your taste is for the whimsical, traditional, modern, functional or avant garde, you can indulge it at The Blue Heron Gallery.

Coastal Metals Gallery
6709-A Beach Dr. SE, Ocean Isle Beach
• (910) 575-4085, (866) 575-4085

Step through the door of Coastal Metals Gallery into an inviting open area filled with tastefully displayed unique gifts including metal sculptures, wall hangings, numbered prints, and custom artwork. David McCune, owner and sculptor, also has a 60,000-square-foot metal fabrications facility in Fayetteville. Why? David, who has been designing for over 26 years and sometimes incorporates driftwood and other unusual finds in his work, makes art pieces that range from jewelry to 60,000-pound architectural sculptures.

Sunset River Marketplace
10283 Beach Dr. SW, Calabash
• (910) 575-5999

"A gallery of art and unique creations" is the

Pelicans are some of the most fascinating coastal birds.

Photo: Jay Tervo

way Ginny and Joe Lassiter refer to this, their retirement enterprise, which opened in 2002. And such it is. You can feel the positive energy radiating throughout the gallery as you move from display to display enchanted by what you see. You will find paintings, pottery, sculpture, jewelry, beautiful functional items and items whose function it is to be beautiful, all meticulously crafted and thoughtfully displayed by talented local artists. In addition, the marketplace provides classes and workshops in a variety of genres including painting in various media and styles, basket making, pottery and photography. Framing is done on the premises as well.

Topsail Island

Seacoast Art Gallery
203 Greensboro Ave., Surf City
• **(910) 328-1112**

Sandy McHugh is the artist in residence at this homey little gallery. Sandy's artworks depict her pleasure of returning to the beach. Many of her watercolors are local beach scenes, and her humor is evident in her sketches of beach birds with captions underneath. Stop in and visit with Sandy during the summer months only.

Topsail Art Gallery
121 S. Topsail Dr., Surf City
• **(910) 328-2138**

Topsail Art Gallery is the area's premier location offering nautical and coastal art, decor and furnishings. A wide variety of originals and reproductions from local, regional and nationally known artists are available. The area's only "Local Artisan's court" is located within the gallery and exhibits some of the finest collection of local artwork and special exhibits. An on-site frame shop can custom frame any selection. In addition to decor, the gallery offers unique gift items, wood carvings, metal works and custom house signs to accent the interior or exterior of your home. The gallery is open year round. Owners Mike and July Hendy pride themselves on their ability to fill customers' special requests.

Attractions

Known to generations of visitors for beautiful, family-friendly beaches and waterways, North Carolina's southern coast also offers a multitude of attractions that have more to do with history than geography. The rich historic legacy of Wilmington and the surrounding communities manifests itself in museums, monuments, churches, grand old residences and other structures that speak eloquently of the past. However, there is little doubt that the proximity to the sea lends a distinct resort quality to this culturally vibrant region. With the advent of a new trend in vacationing known as heritage tourism, visitors are searching for more than long days on the beach in coastal destinations. What is heritage tourism? This concept addresses the desire of modern visitors to explore sites and attractions that make history come alive and provide the ability to experience life as it was once lived in that area. Historic sites such as Thalian Hall, Brunswick Town, Fort Fisher, Penderlea Homestead and Topsail Island's Assembly Building convey specific eras and events as no textbook or commemoration can.

Downtown Wilmington's historic legacy and related attractions are integral to the identity of the Cape Fear region. This port city's historic district practically groans under the weight of its colorful past, and it is the most varied single attraction in the area, easily explored on foot, by boat, trolley or horse-drawn carriage.

By 1840, Wilmington was the largest city in North Carolina. Nicknamed the Port City by residents, it was on a par with other great Southern ports such as Charleston, Galveston and New Orleans. But when the Atlantic Coast Line Railroad company pulled out of Wilmington in the 1960s, the city went into such a rapid decline that even its skyline was flattened by the demolition of several buildings and railroad facilities on the north side of town. Downtown was nearly deserted until a core of local entrepreneurs revitalized and restored their hometown. In 1974 downtown Wilmington became the state's largest urban district listed in the National Register of Historic Places. Many of the images of Wilmington's bustling past are preserved in the North Carolina Room at the New Hanover County Public Library's main branch at 201 Chestnut Street, throughout the Cotton Exchange and at Chandler's Wharf in downtown Wilmington. Likewise, the Cape Fear Museum and the Wilmington Railroad Museum interpret the region's history in far-reaching exhibits. Combined with a variety of tour options (listed in this chapter), these places are excellent resources for interpreting what you see today or exploring the rich history preserved here.

This region is so rich in history it would be impossible to list every historical attraction in a book this size. However, preserving and sharing the rich historic bounty is such a point of pride with Insiders that visitors won't fail to notice clearly marked areas of interest as they explore the region. For example, as you travel neighboring Brunswick County to such places as Southport's Old Smithville Burial Ground, stay alert for other sites with similar stories to tell, such as Southport's old Morse Cemetery on W. West Street and the John N. Smith Cemetery on Leonard Street off Herring Drive. Memorials are so abundant you may miss the one at Bonnet's Creek (Moore Street north of downtown Southport), at the mouth of which "Gentleman Pirate" Stede Bonnet used to hide his cor-

LOOK FOR:
- **Downtown Wilmington Attractions**
- **Historic Homes and Churches**
- **Gardens**
- **Museums and Historic Sites**
- **Tours**
- **Amusement Parks**
- **Natural Attractions**
- **Islands**

CLOSE UP:
- **Dawson's Creek**

- **Cape Fear Lighthouses**

sair. (This and many other sites are on the Southport Trail, listed in this chapter.)

Naturally, many attractions are typical of the seashore: excellent fishing, fine seafood dining, the many cruise opportunities. No beach resort would be complete without water slides, go-cart tracks or batting cages, and we've got plenty of those. These amusements, as well as miniature golf, movies and bowling, are concentrated along our most heavily traveled routes. Just keep your eyes open; you can't miss them. In Wilmington, Oleander Drive east of College Road is the predominant amusement strip, having several more attractions than listed here. North of Ocean Isle Beach, Beach Drive (N.C. Highway 179/904) is another strip with its share of go-carts, miniature golf and curiosities. Around Southport, check out the rapidly expanding Long Beach Road area between Southport and Oak Island. Topsail Beach and Surf City share the limelight as Topsail Island's two centers of attractions. It would be redundant to list every enterprise — they're opening faster than we can list them, and you're bound to stumble across them as you gravitate toward each community's entertainment center.

Reasons to explore Wilmington and the southern coast don't fade with the end of summer heat and sun. The "shoulder" or off-season, with the exception of some of the smaller beach communities, has gained in vitality since the mid-1990s. Mild temperatures, reduced rates, the boom in the region's golf courses and year-round activities convince the off-season visitor that southeastern North Carolina is a great place to relax.

It would be difficult to overstate the importance of the region's gardens, for which North Carolina is rightly famous. The fact that the North Carolina Azalea Festival, in which garden tours are focal, is based in Wilmington makes a strong case for the southern coast's horticultural significance. The spectacular 100-year-old Airlie Gardens, containing 67 acres of gardens and 10 acres of lakes, is a must-see for gardening enthusiasts. Annual and perennial plantings are well-supported public works. The gardens at Orton Plantation are simply spectacular in springtime.

In this chapter we describe many of the area's prime attractions, followed by a brief section on the southern coast's islands. Wilmington's attractions are grouped into three subsections: Downtown Wilmington, Around Wilmington and Outside Wilmington. Within each section, attractions are listed alphabetically.

Information to supplement this guide can be obtained at several locations:

Cape Fear Coast Convention & Visitors Bureau, 24 N. Third Street, (910) 341-4030, in the 1892 courthouse building; the visitors information booth by the river at the foot of Market Street in Wilmington;

Public Libraries, especially New Hanover County's main branch at Third and Chestnut streets in Wilmington;

Southport Visitors' Center, 107 E. Nash Street in Southport, (910) 457-7927

Greater Topsail Area Chamber of Commerce, Treasure Coast Landing, 13775, Suite 101, N.C. Highway 50 in Surf City, (910) 329-4446 or (800) 626-2780.

Of course, all the area's chambers of commerce are helpful; see our Area Overview chapter for a list.

Downtown Wilmington

Battleship North Carolina
Cape Fear River • (910) 251-5797

Without question, the Battleship *North Carolina* is the centerpiece of the Wilmington Riverfront. A majestic symbol of this country's hard-earned naval victories, the Battleship is a "must see" attraction. Enshrined in a berth on Eagles Island across the Cape Fear River from downtown, this awesome vessel is dedicated to more than 10,000 North Carolinians of all the armed services who gave their lives during World War II.

Commissioned in 1941, the 44,800-ton warship wields nine 16-inch turreted guns and car-

ries nickel-steel hull armor 16 to 18 inches thick. It was this plating that undoubtedly helped her survive at least one direct torpedo hit in 1942. In fact, the "Immortal Showboat" is renowned for its relatively small number of casualties.

The Battleship came to its present home in 1961. It took a swarm of tugboats to maneuver the 728-foot vessel into its berth, where the river is only 500 feet wide. Predictably, the bow became stuck in the mud. When the tugs succeeded in freeing the Battleship, they failed to prevent it from slamming into Fergus's Ark, a former floating restaurant moored at the foot of Princess Street. Wilmington gained a Battleship and lost a restaurant.

You can drive to it easily enough, but using the river taxi is more fun. (See the write-up for

BELLAMY MANSION MUSEUM
of History and Design Arts

One of North Carolina's most spectacular examples of antebellum architecture, the mansion was built by free and enslaved black artisans (1859-1861) for John D. Bellamy and family. Today the museum features changing exhibitions on architectural history, historic preservation and the design arts.

Open For
TOURS
Tuesday-Saturday:
10-5pm
Sunday: 1-5pm

Tours emphasize the architectural history, construction and restoration of the house, as well as the fascinating history of its former occupants.

Located in historic downtown Wilmington, North Carolina, at the corner of Market Street and Fifth Avenue. (910) 251-3700   www.bellamymansion.org

Capt. Maffitt Sightseeing Cruise below.) You can absorb all the Battleship *North Carolina* has to offer at your own speed and see what is most interesting to you with a self-guided tour that takes you to more than nine decks. Included are the crew's quarters, galley, sick bay, gun turrets and exhibits that reveal the heart of the Battleship. More features to check out are the engine room, the plotting rooms, radio central, the Admiral's Cabin, the bridge and combat central. Don't miss the Kingfisher float plane, one of the last of its kind to survive, located on the stern of the Battleship's main deck. Plan on taking approximately two hours to enjoy the tour.

The Battleship is open every day. Hours are 8 AM to 8 PM from May 16 through September 15 and 8 AM to 5 PM from September 16 through May 15.

Tours cost $9 for those age 12 and older and $4.50 for children ages 6 through 11. Children 5 and younger get in free. The cost is $8 for senior 65 and older, retired and active-duty military personnel. Ticket sales end one hour before closing. Picnic grounds and ample RV parking adjoin the berth. Please note that only the Visitors Center and the main deck of the Battleship are wheelchair accessible. There is no extra charge for unscheduled appearances by old Charlie, the alligator who makes his home near the Battleship at the river's edge.

Bellamy Mansion Museum
503 Market St., Wilmington
• (910) 251-3700

The assertion that the Bellamy Mansion is Wilmington's premier statement of prewar opulence and wealth is impossible to contest. ("Pre-

war" here refers to the War Between the States, a.k.a. the Civil War, the War of Northern Aggression, the Late Unpleasantness.) This four-story, 22-room wooden palace completed in 1861 is a classic example of Greek Revival and Italianate architecture. Its majesty is immediately evident in 14 fluted exterior Corinthian columns. Most of the craftwork is the product of both free and enslaved African-American artisans, some of whom, it is said, were granted their freedom on the steps of this very building.

Before plans were set to renovate and restore the mansion in 1972, it hadn't been lived in since 1946. Volunteer guides are sure to point out the glassed-in portion of a wall left unrestored to illustrate the extent of a 1972 fire set by an arsonist. That event was linked to the disfavor in which the Bellamy Mansion had been held by some locals, who saw it as a symbol of slavery, which further legitimizes the mansion's value as a historic and cultural landmark. The mansion's museum exhibits embrace regional architecture, landscape architecture, preservation and decorative arts. The museum hosts multimedia traveling exhibits, workshops, films, lectures, slide shows and other activities. Ongoing and painstaking restoration qualifies Bellamy Mansion as an important work in progress. Behind the mansion, the newly rebuilt carriage house opened to the public in late spring 2001 and houses the visitors center, gift shop and mansion offices. Adjacent to the carriage house, the Bellamy Mansion slave quarters show a rare example of urban slave housing. Future renovation plans include this unique five-room, two-story brick dwelling.

Bellamy Mansion Museum is open to the

ATTRACTIONS

public Tuesday to Saturday 10 AM to 5 PM and Sunday 1 to 5 PM. Tours, both guided and self-guided, begin at the carriage house with a brief film on the mansion's history and preservation efforts. Please note that the last guided tour begins at 4 PM. Admission is $7 for adults and $3 for children ages 5 through 12. Children younger than 5 enter free of charge. Friends of the Bellamy Mansion are admitted free. Call ahead for group rate information.

Burgwin-Wright House and Garden
224 Market St., Wilmington
• (910) 762-0570

When Lord Charles Cornwallis, still in danger of a Rebel pursuit, fled to the coast after the Battle of Guilford Court House in central North Carolina in 1781, he repaired to Wilmington, then a town of 200 houses. He lodged at the gracious Georgian home of John Burgwin (pronounced "bur-GWIN"), a wealthy planter and politician, and made it his headquarters. The home, completed in 1770, is distinguished by two-story porches on two sides and seven levels of tiered gardens. The massive ballast-stone foundation remains from the previously abandoned town jail. A free-standing outbuilding houses the kitchen and a craft room and is located behind this beautifully preserved Colonial home. Monthly demonstrations of open-hearth cooking are held here on a Saturday (call for schedule).

The Burgwin-Wright House, currently owned by the National Society of the Colonial Dames of America in the State of North Carolina, is one of the great restoration/reconstruction achievements in the state, and visitors may peruse the carefully appointed rooms and period furnishings. Admission is $7 for adults, $3 for children. Children younger than 5 are admitted free. Group tours are available by appointment. The museum is open Tuesday through Saturday 10 AM to 4 PM, with the last tour at 3 PM on all days. Colonial Christmas is a special event at the house during the second weekend in December. The house is filled with music and decorated for the holiday season with greenery and fruit, while the art of open-hearth cooking is highlighted.

Cape Fear Museum
814 Market St., Wilmington
• (910) 341-4350

For an overview of the cultural and natural histories of the Cape Fear region from prehistory to the present, the Cape Fear Museum, established in 1898, stands unsurpassed. A miniature re-creation of the second battle of Fort Fisher and a remarkable scale model of the Wilmington waterfront, c. 1863, are of special interest. The Michael Jordan Discovery Gallery (which includes a popular display case housing many of the basketball star's personal items) is a long-term interactive natural history exhibit for the entire family. The Discovery Gallery includes a crawl-through beaver lodge, Pleistocene-era fossils and an entertaining Venus's-flytrap model you can feed with stuffed "bugs." Children's activities, videos, special events and acclaimed touring exhibits contribute to making the Cape Fear Museum not only one of the primary repositories of local history, but also a place where learning is fun.

The museum is open Tuesday through Saturday 9 AM to 5 PM and Sunday 1 to 5 PM. Admission is $5 for adults, $4 for seniors and students with valid ID and $1 for children ages 3 through 17. Children younger than 3 and Cape Fear Museum members are admitted free. Admission is free to all New Hanover County residents on the first Sunday of each month. Groups of 12 or more may be eligible for a discount on admission and should contact the museum for details. Cape Fear Museum is disabled accessible and offers an interesting, well-stocked gift shop for visitors.

INSIDERS' TIP
Sacred Spaces: Architecture and Religion in Historic Wilmington by Walter H. Conser Jr. is an excellent resource for studying Wilmington's historic churches.

Cape Fear Serpentarium
20 Orange St., Wilmington
• (910) 762-1669

Featuring more than 100 species of snakes, most of them poisonous, the Serpentarium boasts the largest collection of venomous snakes in the world. Owner Dean Ripa is a major breeder of the South American bushmaster, the world's longest pit viper and the rarest of venomous snakes, and he claims to be the world's first and only breeder capable of having the blackhead bushmaster reproduce in captivity. In addition to 37 bushmasters, the Serpentarium also houses gaboon vipers, king cobras, Australian taipans, a 23-foot python, black mambas, a Nile crocodile and a 6-foot monitor lizard. The Serpentarium opened in late 2002. From November through March, hours of operation are Thursday through Monday 11 AM to 5 PM; from April through October they are Wednes-

day through Monday 10:30 AM to 8 PM; hours are subject to change, so call ahead.

Capt. J. N. Maffitt Sightseeing Cruise
Riverfront Park, Foot of Market St., Wilmington • (910) 343-1611, (800) 676-0162

Named for Capt. John Newland Maffitt, one of the Confederacy's most successful blockade runners, the *Capt. Maffitt* is a converted World War II Navy launch affording 45-minute sightseeing cruises with live historical narration along the Cape Fear River. Cruises set out at 11 AM and 3 PM daily from Memorial Day to Labor Day. Off-season weekend cruises are available from May 1 to Memorial Day and from Labor Day to mid-November. Cruise tickets are $8 for adults and $4 for children ages 2 to 12. The *Capt. Maffitt* is available for charter throughout the year, and it doubles as the Battleship River Taxi during the summer. No reservations are necessary, and it runs on the quarter-hour from Wilmington's riverfront to the Battleship *North Carolina* and on the hour and half-hour for the return trip except at 11:30 AM and 3:30 PM during the sightseeing cruise times. River taxi fees are $2 per person and free for children younger than 2.

Chandler's Wharf
225 S. Water St., Wilmington • (910) 343-9896

More than 100 years ago, Chandler's Wharf was crowded with mercantile warehouses, its sheds filled with naval stores, tools, cotton and guano, and its wharves lined with merchantmen. A disastrous (and suspicious) fire in August 1874 changed the site forever. In the late 1970s, Chandler's Wharf became an Old Wilmington riverfront reconstruction site, a positive turning point for downtown revitalization.

Today, much of the flavor of the 1870s remains, and Chandler's Wharf is again a business district, or, more accurately, a shopping and dining district. Two historic homes transformed into shops stand on the cobblestone street, beside wooden sidewalks and the rails of the former waterfront railway. The original ship chandler warehouse has been converted into popular boutiques and galleries; a pictorial history of Wilmington is displayed there.

Elijah's and The Pilot House restaurants overlook the Cape Fear River, and the newly completed Riverwalk provides a delightful waterside stroll that connects Chandler's Wharf with the rest of downtown. (See our Restaurants and Shopping chapters.)

Chestnut Street United Presbyterian Church
710 N. Sixth St., Wilmington • (910) 762-1074

This tiny church, built in 1858 and originally a mission chapel of First Presbyterian Church (see below), is a remarkable example of Stick Style, or Carpenter Gothic, architecture. Its exterior details include decorative bargeboards with repeating acorn pendants, board-and-batten construction, a louvered bell tower (with carillon) and paired Gothic windows. When the congregation, then slaves, formed in 1858 under the auspices of the mother church, the chapel was surrendered by the mother church to the new, black congregation, which

ATTRACTIONS

Dawson's Creek:
Welcome to Capeside

From the first season (1997-98) of the hit TV series *Dawson's Creek*, Dawson Leery and friends — Joey, Pacey and Jen —captured the hearts of teens and young adults across the country. The show peaked great interest in the filming location, known on the show as Capeside, Massachusetts, but in  reality Wilmington and Southport, North Carolina. Even now, after the show has ended, area tourism agencies, chambers of commerce and the Wilmington Regional Film Commission continue to be inundated with calls and inquiries for information about the stars and the phenomenon called *Dawson's Creek*. Restaurant owners and merchants, particularly those whose businesses were used in filming, have grown accustomed to answering the questions of visitors checking out the filming locations. Usually with good humor and patience. After all, the show's presence created jobs, supported the local service industry and generated tourism revenue.

An overwhelming number of people love to hunt for location sites from favorite episodes of this former WB television network series. Studio tours at EUE/Screen Gems Studios, 1223 N. 23rd Street (see the Around Wilmington section in this chapter), include a look at some of the show's sets. *Dawson's Creek* often went location in the area so visitors (and locals) are likely to catch a glimpse a familiar scene from the show. Take a walking tour throughout the downtown area or drive around Wilmington and see if you recognize any of the locations.

The list below is a sampling of known *Dawson's Creek* filming locations. Can you identify the episode they appeared in?

Water Street, Downtown Wilmington
The Icehouse, 115 S. Water Street
Water Street Restaurant & Sidewalk Cafe, 5 S. Water Street
Riverfront Visitor Information Booth, corner of Water and Market streets
Island Passage, 4 Market Street
Cape Fear Riverwalk, from the foot of Market Street along Water Street
Riverfront Park

Front Street, Downtown Wilmington
Nautical Hangups, 24 N. Front Street
Reeds Jewelers, 27 N. Front Street
Paleo Sun, 35 N. Front Street

purchased the building in 1867. The congregation's many distinguished members have included the first black president of Biddle University (now Johnson C. Smith University), the publisher of Wilmington's first black newspaper, a member of the original Fisk University Jubilee Singers, the first black graduate of MIT, and North Carolina's first black physician.

First Baptist Church
411 Market St., Wilmington
• (910) 763-2471
Even having lost its stunning 197-foot, copper-sheathed steeple to Hurricane Fran in 1996, First Baptist was still Wilmington's tallest church. For years this tower, the taller of the church's two steeples, had been known to visibly sway even in an average wind. The steeple's repair was completed in early 1999.

Being literally the first Baptist church in the region, this is the mother church of many other Baptist churches in Wilmington. Its congregation dates to 1808, and construction of the red-brick building began in 1859. The church was not completed until 1870 because of the Civil War, when Confederate and Union forces in turn used the higher steeple as a lookout. Its architecture is Early English Gothic Revival with hints of Richardson Romanesque, as in its vari-colored materials and its horizontal mass re-

A hand-painted Dawson's Creek mural can be seen at EUE/Screen Gems Studios in Wilmington.

Photo: Deb Daniel

Third Street, Downtown Wilmington
Graystone Inn, 100 S. Third Street
Old New Hanover County Courthouse, 24 N. Third Street
Thalian Hall, 310 Chestnut Street (on the corner at Third Street)

Around Wilmington
University of North Carolina at Wilmington, 601 S. College Road (This is an easy one — the UNCW campus was used for exterior shots of Capeside High.)

Battleship Park, Eagle Island (across the Cape Fear River from downtown Wilmington and home of the Battleship *North Carolina*)

Airlie Gardens, Airlie Road (off Oleander Drive near Wrightsville Beach)

Greenfield Lake, 1702 Burnett Boulevard

Contact the Cape Fear Coast Convention & Visitors Bureau, (800) 222-4757, 24 N. Third Street, Wilmington, for more information and a copy of their Dawson's Creek FAQ Sheet. It has more location listings and lots of fun facts. For Southport locations, call the Southport-Oak Island Chamber of Commerce, (910) 457-6964, 4841 Long Beach Road SE in Southport.

lieved by the verticality of the spires, with their narrow, gabled vents. Inside, the pews, galleries and ceiling vents are of native heart pine.

Sunday School classes occupy an equally interesting building next door on Fifth Street, the Conoley House (1859), which exhibits such classic Italianate elements as frieze vents and brackets, and fluted wooden columns. The church offices are located in the Taylor House next door on Market Street.

First Presbyterian Church
125 S. Third St., Wilmington
• **(910) 762-6688**

Visiting clergymen held services occasionally

to Presbyterians in Wilmington in the 1700s. The First Presbyterian Church was organized in 1817. This congregation continues to have among its members some of the most influential Wilmingtonians. The Rev. Joseph R. Wilson was pastor from 1874 until 1885; his son, Thomas Woodrow Wilson, grew up to become slightly more famous. The church itself, with its finials and soaring stone spire topped with a metal rooster (a symbol of the Protestant Reformation), blends Late Gothic and Renaissance styles and is the congregation's fourth home, the previous three having succumbed to fire. During the Union occupation, the lectern Bible was stolen from the third church, which burned on New Year's Eve

1925. The stolen Bible was returned years later to become all that remains of the sanctuary.

Today, intricate tracery distinguishes fine stained-glass windows along the nave as well as the vast west window and the chancel rose. The 1928 E. M. Skinner organ, with its original pneumatic console, is used regularly. Handsomely stenciled beams, arches and trusses support a steep gabled roof. Downstairs is the Kenan Chapel, with its transverse Romanesque arches. The education building behind the sanctuary is quintessential Tudor, complete with exterior beams set in stucco, wide squared arches, casement windows with diamond panes, interior ceiling beams and eccentric compound chimneys. Having undergone major renovation in the early 1990s, First Presbyterian is an impressive sight. Its carillon can be heard daily throughout the historic district.

Ghost Walk of Old Wilmington
Market St. at the Riverfront, Wilmington
• (910) 602-6055

Visitors and locals alike enjoy this nightly walking tour of the area around downtown Wilmington. The tour meets year round by the Riverfront at the foot of Market Street. Hours are April 1 through October 31 nightly at 8:30 PM, plus Tuesday through Saturday at 6:30 PM; during November and March the tours are Tuesday through Saturday at 6:30 PM; in December, January and February, tours are Thursday through Saturday at 6:30 PM. Special Halloween times vary and you're advised to call ahead. Cost is $12 for adults, $10 for seniors, students and military, free for children ages 6 and younger.

Haunted Pub Crawl
Downtown Wilmington
• (910) 602-6055

Partake in an evening of spirited adventure on a journey to Wilmington's most wildly haunted pubs. Revel in the seamy red-light district of yore and uncover startling truths of life in an 18th-century port city. From the disreputable obsession of the merry wench, "Gallus" Meg, to the barbarous haunts of a notorious madman, this is a fun-filled night of levity and libations. Reservations are required. Tour begins at 7:30 PM, nights vary. Cost is $15 for adults.

Henrietta III
Docked at S. Water St at the foot of Dock St., Wilmington • (910) 343-1611, (800) 676-0162

This elegant, refurbished riverboat is a large three-level, paddle-free vessel with a capacity for 600 guests. In fact, the *Henrietta III* is so spacious that it can accommodate three events — wedding parties, dinner cruises, themed cruises, etc. — at once. Cruise the Cape Fear River in style on this beautiful riverboat with a variety of options that include a 90-minute narrated sightseeing cruise, narrated lunch cruise, dinner dance cruise and more. Most cruises are available from April through December, while others only go out during the summer season. Rates vary according to the type and length of the cruise. Prepaid reservations are required for cruises that include meals. The *Henrietta III* also offers special events cruises throughout the year. Contact Cape Fear Riverboats at the phone numbers above for more information on current rates, cruise schedules and special events cruises. The riverboat's elevator make all decks handicapped accessible. The boat is U.S. Coast Guard-approved.

Oakdale Cemetery
520 N. 15th St., Wilmington
• (910) 762-5682

When Nance Martin died at sea in 1857, her body was preserved seated in a chair in a large cask of rum. Six months later she was interred at Oakdale Cemetery, cask and all. Her monument and many other curious, beautiful and historic markers are to be found within the labyrinth of Oakdale Cemetery, Wilmington's first municipal burial ground, opened in 1855.

At the cemetery office, you can pick up a free map detailing some of the more interesting interments, such as the volunteer firefighter buried with the faithful dog that gave its life trying to save his master, and Mrs. Rose O'Neal Greenhow, a Confederate courier who drowned while running the blockade at Fort Fisher in 1864. Amid the profusion of monuments lies a field oddly lacking in markers — the mass grave of hundreds of victims of the 1862 yellow fever epidemic. The architecture of the monuments, the Victorian landscaping and the abundance of dogwood trees make Oakdale beautiful in every season. The cemetery is open from 8 AM to 5 PM daily. Oakdale Cemetery office hours are Monday through Friday 8:30 AM to noon and 1 to 4:30 PM. Admission is free.

The Riverwalk
Riverfront Park, along Water St., Wilmington

The heart and soul of downtown Wilmington is its riverfront. Once a bustling, gritty confusion of warehouses, docks and sheds — all suffused with the odor of turpentine — the wharf was the state's most important commercial port. Experience Wilmington's charm and historical continuity by strolling The Riverwalk, recently extended considerably, both to the north and the south. Dining, shopping and lodging establishments now line the walk, and live entertainment takes place at the small Riverfront Stage on Saturday and Sunday evenings from June to early August. Check with the visitors' information booth at the foot of Market Street for schedules.

Immediately to the north, schooners, pleasure boats and replicas of historic ships frequently visit the municipal dock. Coast Guard cutters and the occasional British naval vessel dock beyond the Federal Court House; some ships allow touring, especially during festivals. Benches, picnic tables, a fountain and snack vendors complete the scene, one of Wilmington's most popular.

Springbrook Farms Horse-Drawn Trolley & Carriage Tours
Market St. between Water and Front Sts., Wilmington • (910) 251-8889

See historic downtown Wilmington the old-fashioned way — by horse-drawn carriage or trolley. This half-hour tour in a fringed-top surrey (open-air trolley) is narrated by a knowledgeable driver wearing 19th-century garb. The personable driver offers interesting anecdotes about the historic mansions and waterfront along the way. At busy times such as Azalea Festival and Riverfest, horse-drawn tours are especially popular.

Don't miss the memorable seasonal events, including the romantic horse-drawn Valentine ride in a French evening coach, an Easter Bunny-drawn ride, the Halloween Ghost Trolley ride, or the Caroling by "Reindeer" Christmas ride. Carriage rides are also available for weddings, private parties and other special occasions. Call the number above for reservations and rates.

Seating is on a first-come, first-served basis. From April through October, tours operate Tuesday through Saturday from 10 AM to 10 PM and Sunday 11 AM to 4 PM. In November, December and March, the carriages roll Friday and Saturday 11 AM to 10 PM and Sunday 11 AM to 4 PM. During January and February, please call. Expect to pay $9 for adults and $4 for children age 11 and younger; rates are subject to change without notice, however.

St. James Episcopal Church and Burial Ground
25 S. Third St., Wilmington • (910) 763-1628

St. James is the oldest church in continuous use in Wilmington, and it wears its age well. The parish was established in 1729 at Brunswick Town across the river (also see St. Philip's Parish, below). The congregation's original Wilmington church wasn't completed until 1770. It was seized in 1781 by Tarleton's Dragoons under Cornwallis. Tarleton had the pews removed, and the church became a stable. The original church was taken down in 1839, and some of its materials were used to construct the present church, an Early Gothic Revival building with pinnacled square towers, battlements and lancet windows. The architect, Thomas U. Walter, is best known for his 1865 cast-iron dome on the U.S. Capitol. A repeat performance of pew-tossing took place during the Civil War, when occupying Federal forces used the church as a hospital. A letter written by the pastor asking President Lincoln for reparation still exists. The letter was never delivered, having been completed the day news arrived of Lincoln's assassination. Within the church hangs a celebrated painting of Christ (Ecce Homo) captured from one of the Spanish pirate ships that attacked Brunswick Town in 1748. The sanctuary also boasts a handsome wood-slat ceiling and beam-and-truss construction. Church offices are in McRae House, designed by Henry Bacon, who also designed the Lincoln memorial in Washington, D.C. and built in 1900.

The graveyard at the corner of Fourth and Market streets was in use from 1745 to 1855 and bears considerable historic importance. Here lies the patriot Cornelius Harnett, remembered for antagonizing the British by reading the Declaration of Independence aloud at the Halifax Courthouse in 1776. He died in a British prison during the war. America's first playwright, Thomas Godfrey, is also memorialized here. The cemetery once occupied grounds over which Market Street now stretches, which explains why utility workers periodically (and inadvertently) unearth human remains outside the present burial ground. This burial ground is also a favorite spot on the History-Mystery Tour in

INSIDERS' TIP
The best deal in historic Wilmington is the Passport tour ticket. Tour Bellamy Mansion Museum, the Burgwin-Wright House and the Zebulon Latimer House for $18, a $3 savings. The ticket may be purchased at any one of these locations and is good for one week after purchase.

ATTRACTIONS

October (see the Annual Events chapter for a description). Visitors are welcome to take self-guided tours of the church between 9 AM and early afternoon when services are not underway. Informative brochures are available in the vestibule.

St. Marks Episcopal Church
600 Grace St., Wilmington
• (910) 763-3212

Established in 1869, this was the first Episcopal church for blacks in eastern North Carolina, and it has conducted services uninterrupted since that time. The building (completed in 1875) is a simple Gothic Revival structure with a buttressed nave and octagonal bell tower. Visitors are welcome to enter and view the interior Monday through Friday from 1 to 6 PM. Of course, visitors are also welcome to attend worship services on Sunday. Please check local Saturday newspapers or call the church at the number listed above for the schedule.

St. Mary's Roman Catholic Church
412 Ann St., Wilmington • (910) 762-5491

Numerous historical writers have referred to this Spanish Baroque edifice (built 1908-11) as a major architectural creation, often pointing out the elaborate tiling, especially inside the dome, which embraces most of this church's cross-vaulted interior space. The plan of the brick building is based on the Greek cross, with enormous semicircular stained-glass windows in the transept vaults, arcade windows in the apse and symmetrical square towers in front. Over the main entrance, in stained glass, is an imitation of da Vinci's Last Supper. A coin given by Maria Anna Jones, the first black Catholic in North Carolina, is placed inside the cornerstone.

St. Paul's Evangelical Lutheran Church
12 N. Sixth St., corner of Sixth and Market Sts., Wilmington • (910) 762-4882

Responding to the growing number of German Lutherans in Wilmington, North Carolina's Lutheran Synod organized St. Paul's in 1858. Services began in 1861 as the Civil War broke. Construction came to a halt when the German artisans working on the building volunteered for the 18th North Carolina Regiment and became the first local unit in active duty. The building was occupied, and badly damaged, by Union troops after the fall of Fort Fisher in early 1865. Horses were stabled in the building and its wooden furnishings were used as firewood.

The completed church was dedicated in 1869, only to burn in 1894. It was promptly rebuilt. There have been several additions and renovations since. Today the building is remarkable for its blend of austere Greek Revival elements outside (such as the entablature, pediments and pilasters) and Gothic Revival (such as the slender spire, clustered interior piers and large lancet windows). Also notable are its color-patterned slate roof and copper finials and the gently arcing pew arrangement. Paneling removed during renovations in 1995-96 uncovered beautiful stenciling on the ceiling panels and ribs in the vestibule, nave and chancel.

Temple of Israel
1 S. Fourth St., Wilmington
• (910) 762-0000

The first Jewish temple in North Carolina, this unique Moorish Revival style building was erected in 1875-76 for a Reform congregation that was formed in 1872. Its two square towers are topped by small onion domes, and the paired, diamond-paned windows exhibit a mix of architrave shapes, including Romanesque, trefoil and Anglo-Saxon arches. Another notable feature is a magnificent chandelier, brought to the United States from Landau, Germany. Believed to be more than 500 years old, the chandelier was originally lighted by oil, later by candles, and finally by electricity. The Pilcher-Tracker organ, constructed in 1901 and restored in 1990, is one of only three such organs known to still be in operation. When the Front Street Methodist Episcopal Church was destroyed by fire in 1886, the Temple of Israel congregants offered their building as a substitute until a new church could be erected. The offer was accepted and the Methodists met in the Temple for a little more than two years.

Thalian Hall/City Hall
310 Chestnut St., Wilmington
• (910) 343-3664, (800) 523-2820

Since its renovation and expansion in the late 1980s, the name has been, more accurately, Thalian Hall Center for the Performing Arts. And yes, it does share the same roof with City Hall. Conceived as a combined political and cultural center, Thalian Hall was built between 1855 and 1858. During its first 75 years, the hall brought every great national performer and some surprising celebrities to its stage: Lillian Russell, Buffalo Bill Cody, John Philip Sousa, Oscar Wilde and Tom Thumb, to name a few. That tradition continues. Full-scale musicals, light opera and internationally renowned dance

Water, water everywhere!

Photo: Jay Tervo

companies are only a portion of Thalian's consistent, high-quality programming. Today the center consists of two theaters — the Main Stage and the Studio Theater — plus a ballroom (which doubles as the city council chambers). With its Corinthian columns and ornate proscenium, it's no wonder Thalian Hall is on the National Register of Historic Places. Backstage tours are offered Monday through Friday by appointment and include the main theatre, backstage, the studio theatre, ballroom, gallery and City Hall. Contact Thalian Hall's administrative offices, (910) 343-3660, to schedule a tour and for tour rates. A self-guided tour is also available from noon to 6 PM Monday through Friday and from 2 to 6 PM on Saturday and Sunday. Admission for the self-guided tour is $1.

Wilmington Adventure Walking Tour
Riverfront Park, Foot of Market St.,
Wilmington • (910) 763-1785

Lifelong Wilmington resident Bob Jenkins, the man with the straw hat and walking cane, walks fast but talks slowly, passionately and knowledgeably about his hometown. Expounding upon architectural details, family lineage and historic events, Bob whisks you through 250 years of history in about two hours. You'll see residences, churches and public buildings. Tours begin at the flagpole at the foot of Market Street at 10 AM and 2 PM daily, weather permitting, April through October. Cost is $10 for adults and $5 for children ages 6 to 12. Children younger than 6 go along for free. Although no reservations are required, it's best to call ahead, especially in summer. Off-season, November through March, group tours are by advance reservation only.

Wilmington Children's Museum
1020 Market St., Wilmington
• (910) 254-3534

The goal at this multi-faceted museum is to "stimulate children's imagination, curiosity and innate love of learning" through play. The Wilmington Children's Museum offers ample opportunity for learning and, well, it's just a fun place to visit. To learn more about what's offered, check out the Kidstuff chapter.

Wilmington National Cemetery
2011 Market St., Wilmington
• (910) 815-4877

In 1866-67, immediately after the Civil War, the United States Congress enacted legislation to create national cemeteries to honor and protect the remains of U.S. soldiers who fell in battle or died of disease.

The Wilmington National Cemetery was established in 1867 on five acres of land about a mile east of downtown. The cemetery originally contained the remains of more than 2,000 Union soldiers, many of whom died at Fort Fisher and were later interred here. More than 1,300 are unidentified; many are black, identified as U.S.C.T. (United States Colored Troops) or U.S. Col. Inf. (United States Colored Infantry). Markers with round tops indicate known burials, and stones with flat tops indicate unknowns; nearly all are government issue. Since the Civil War period, the Wilmington National Cemetery has received the remains of Americans through the Vietnam conflict. The cemetery is now closed, meaning it will not accept additional deceased soldiers. Grounds are open during daylight hours daily.

Wilmington Railroad Museum
501 Nutt St., Wilmington • (910) 763-2634

The dramatic transformation that Wilmington underwent when the Atlantic Coast Line Railroad closed its local operations in the late 1960s is clearly borne out by this museum's fine photographs and artifacts. Beyond history, the Railroad Museum is a kind of funhouse for people fascinated by trains and train culture. For the price of admission, you can climb into a real steam locomotive and clang its bell for as long as your kids will let you. Inside, volunteers will guide you to exhibits explaining why the 19th-century Wilmington & Weldon Railroad was called the "Well Done" and that the ghost of beheaded flagman Joe

Baldwin is behind the Maco Light — at least one volunteer claims to have seen it.

Ask about the museum's "Memories" book in which visitors are encouraged to share their favorite train memories; it includes entries by celebrities who have visited Wilmington. The museum building was the railroad's freight traffic office and is listed on the National Register of Historic Places. Visitors can run the model trains in the enormous railroad diorama upstairs, which is maintained by the Cape Fear Model Railroad Club (for membership information contact the museum). Downstairs, the children (both young and not so young) will enjoy the Lionel trains.

Adult programming, children's workshops and group discounts are available. The museum also invites you to conduct your birthday parties on its caboose; the rental fee includes souvenirs and a tour of the museum.

March 15 to October 14, the museum is open Monday through Saturday from 10 AM to 5 PM and Sunday from 1 to 5 PM. October 14 to March 14, it's open Monday through Saturday from 10 AM to 4 PM. The museum is closed New Year's Eve, New Year's Day, Easter Sunday, Thanksgiving, Christmas Eve and Christmas Day. Admission fees are $3.50 for adults, $2.50 for active military personnel and senior citizens and $1.50 for children ages 2 to 12. Children younger than 2 are admitted free.

Wilmington Trolley
Dock and Water Sts., Wilmington
• (910) 343-1611

Located near the *Henrietta III* at the foot of Dock Street, the Wilmington Trolley offers a 45-minute guided tour of historic downtown Wilmington over a course of about 8 miles. Available daily, April through October, the tours leave on the hour from 10 AM to 5 PM. Fees are $10 for adults and $5 for children ages 2 to 12. Call for tour availability after October.

Zebulon Latimer House
126 S. Third St., Wilmington
• (910) 762-0492

This magnificent Italianate building, built by a prosperous merchant from Connecticut, dates from 1852 and is remarkable for its original furnishings and artwork. The house boasts fine architectural details such as window cornices and wreaths in the frieze openings, all made of cast iron, and a piazza with intricate, wrought-iron tracery. Behind the building stands a rare (and possibly Wilmington's oldest) example of urban slave quarters, now a private residence. What sets the Latimer House apart from most other museums is the fact that it was continuously lived in for more than a century, until it became home to the Lower Cape Fear Historical Society in 1963. It has the look of a home where the family has just stepped out.

The Historical Society is one of the primary sources for local genealogical and historical research. For information on membership, write to 126 South Third Street, Wilmington, NC 28401. The Society's archives are housed at the Latimer House and are available to the public Monday through Friday. However, the hours vary daily, and serious researchers, history buffs or the simply curious are advised to call ahead to confirm access to the archives on the day they plan to visit.

The Latimer House is open Monday through Friday from 10 AM to 3:30 PM and Saturday noon to 5 PM. The last guided tour is conducted a half-hour before closing. Admission is $6 for adults and $3 for students. Children 5 and yougner are admitted free. Walk & Talk Tours, which encompass about 12 blocks of the historic district and last two hours, are given for $8 every Wednesday and Saturday at 10 AM.

Around Wilmington

African-American Heritage Trail
Assorted venues, Wilmington
• (910) 341-4030, (800) 222-4787

The African-American Guide Map, available from the Cape Fear Coast Convention & Visitors Bureau, 24 North Third Street, offers "an authentic African-American Experience," plus a lot of interesting information. In addition to annual events and historical biographies, the brochure features details about 17 African-American heritage sites along with an easy-to-follow map pinpointing their locations, many of which are in the downtown Historical District and easily accessible on foot. Some of the sites include Bellamy Mansion with its slave quarters, Thalian Hall, St. Mark's Episcopal Church and Wilmington National Cemetery, which has a section for African-Americans who died fighting for the Union during the Civil War.

Wilmington is "one of the most historically significant African-American cities in the United States," according to Wilmington's African-American Heritage Resource Book, published by Margaret M. Mulrooney, Ph.D. and UNC-Wilmington in 1997. This small booklet is packed full of the history and culture of African-Americans in the Cape Fear region from the earliest days of its settlement. You can find it and other resource books at the Local History Room of the New Hanover County Public Library, 201 Chestnut Street and the Curriculum Materials Center at UNCW, 601 S. College Road.

Airlie Gardens
300 Airlie Rd., Wilmington
• (910) 793-7531

Enjoy the pleasures nature has to offer, smell the roses, admire the azaleas, gaze at the camellias and stand in the shade of the 450-year-old Airlie Oak while visiting this quintessential Southern garden. Wander at your leisure along curving paths and walkways in this lush natural setting and note the bounty of flowering vines — honeysuckle, jasmine, wisteria — and the maritime forest of trees native to the region — live oaks, cedars, pines and wax myrtles. Need a rest? Benches are plentiful, so "set a spell," as they say down here in the South.

In the early 1900s, Airlie Gardens was designed in a post-Victorian European style showcasing plants for all four seasons — azaleas in spring, magnolias and live oaks in summer, camellias in the fall and winter. Statuary, pergolas and fountains grace the gardens. Bordered by Bradley Creek and salt marshes, these beautiful 67-acres support two freshwater lakes that attract swans, ducks, geese, herons, egrets and more.

From March through Mother's Day, the gardens are open Tuesday through Saturday; after Mother's Day until the end of October, they are open Thursday through Sunday. Hours of operation are 9 AM to 5 PM, except Sunday from 1 to 5 PM. Please note that the last ticket is sold at 4 PM daily and the gardens close promptly at 5 PM. Admission for New Hanover County residents (with ID) is $5 for adults, $1 for children ages 3 to 12 and $4.50 for seniors. Non-resident rates are $8 for adults, $2 for children ages 3 to 12 and $7 for seniors. New Hanover County residents are admitted free the second Saturday of each month.

EUE/Screen Gems Studios Tour
1223 N. 23rd. St., Wilmington
• (910) 343-3433

They don't call Wilmington "Hollywood East" for nothing, and Screen Gems Studios, the biggest film production facility outside of Los Angeles, is the prime reason. At the head of the entire operation is Frank Capra, Jr., filmmaker in his own right and son of the legendary film director who brought us such classics as *It's A Wonderful Life, Mr. Smith Goes To Washington, It Happened One Night* and many more.

Screen Gems offers a one-hour walking tour, featuring a variety of sights depending on the level of production activity. As activity on the lot changes, so do the tours. Regular highlights are the popular television series *Dawson's Creek*, sets, old movie sets and props in Soundstage 1, a video overview of Screen Gems' history in the studios' screening room, a question-and-answer session and more. Cameras are permitted in designated areas.

Tour hours during the summer months are Wednesday through Friday at noon; Saturday at 10 AM, noon and 2 PM; and Sundays at noon and 2 PM. Reservations aren't needed except for parties of 20 or more. Please arrive 10 minutes before the hour. Admission is $10 for adults and $5 for children younger than 12.

Greenfield Lake and Gardens
U.S. 421 S., Wilmington

In springtime the colors here are simply eye-popping. In summer the algae-covered waters and Spanish moss are reminders of the days when this was an unpopulated cypress swamp. In winter the bare tree trunks rise from the lake with starkness. Herons, egrets and ducks are regular visitors, as are hawks and cardinals. The 5-mile lake-view drive is a pleasure in any season, and there's a paved path suitable for walking, running or cycling around the entire lake. Greenfield Lake is 2 miles south of downtown Wilmington along S. Third Street. (Also see our chapter on Sports, Fitness and Parks.)

Jungle Rapids Family Fun Park
5320 Oleander Dr., Wilmington
• (910) 791-0666

This self-contained amusement mecca includes the only true water park in eastern North Carolina plus more game attractions than a family could exhaust in a week. The quarter-mile-long Grand Prix GoKart track features bridge overpasses, banked turns, timing devices and one- and two-passenger cars. Children under 56 inches tall must ride with licensed adult drivers.

The Waterpark includes six excellent slides — the Sidewinder, which is a half pike, plus the four-tube slide called the Volcanic Express. Floating the Lazy River, which encircles the water park, is great for a relaxing bask. Lifeguards are always on duty, and there are plenty of lockers, lounges, tables and umbrellas.

Also worthwhile are a wonderful wave pool, the Kiddie Splash Pool (with four kiddie slides), jungle-themed miniature golf, the adrenaline-pumping Alien Invader Laser Tag, the high-tech arcade featuring more than 100 games ranging from the classic to state-of-the-art, and the air-conditioned Kids Jungle (Wilmington's largest indoor playground, for children age 8 and younger).

Jungle Rapids caters kids' parties on site. They have on-site meeting and function rooms (the largest accommodating 200 people) and even offer off-site corporate outings and picnics for up to 5,000 people. The Big Splash Cafe and Pizzeria offers an ample menu during park hours.

The Waterpark opens Memorial Day weekend and is open daily from 11 AM to 7 PM. The Dry Park attractions are open at 10 AM; 1 PM on Sunday in-season. Call for off-season hours. Also see our Kidstuff chapter.

Louise Wells Cameron Art Museum
3201 S. 17th St., Wilmington
• (910) 395-5999

April 2002 marked the re-opening of the only art museum within 150 miles of Wilmington. Formerly the St. John's Museum of Art in downtown Wilmington, the museum was relocated into a brand-new, 42,000-square-foot facility on the corner of South 17th Street and Independence Boulevard. The Cameron Art Museum features a permanent collection focusing on North Carolina art, temporary exhibitions, a sculpture court, Civil War defensive mounds on the museum's campus, an expanded gift shop, The Forks restaurant and more. (See our Arts chapter for more information.)

Museum hours are 10 AM to 5 PM Tuesday through Thursday and Saturday; 10 AM to 8 PM Friday and 10:30 to 4 PM Sunday. Admission is $5 for adults, $8 for families and $2 for children ages 5 to 18. Children younger than 5 and museum members are admitted free. Admission is free on the first Sunday of every month.

New Hanover County Extension Service Arboretum
6206 Oleander Dr., Wilmington
• (910) 452-6393

This 7-acre teaching and learning facility is the only arboretum in southeastern North Carolina. Nature and garden enthusiasts will discover 33 gardens. The arboretum was formally opened in 1989 and is still in the midst of development. These gardens rank among the finer

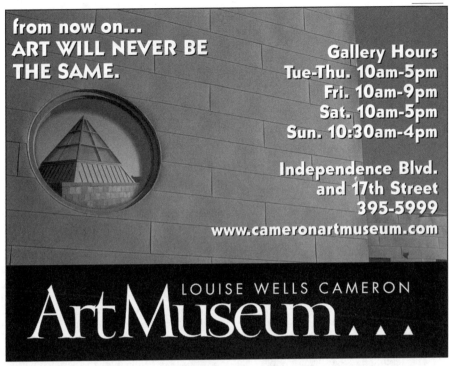
theme gardens in the area. Boardwalks and paths wind through a profusion of plants, grasses, flowers, trees, shrubs, herbs and vegetables, and there is plenty of shaded seating. Several sections, such as the Herb Garden with its variety of medicinal, culinary, fragrance and tea species, are sponsored by local garden clubs. Other themed gardens include the Rose Garden's Heritage roses, a hands-on Children's Garden and the Aquatic & Bog Gardens, some of the largest in the state. Working in cooperation with the N.C. State University Cooperative Extension, the arboretum also offers community services and educational programs on a variety of skill levels up to Master Gardener courses.

The arboretum assists commercial and private horticultural enterprises and helps residents create attractive home landscapes. This last mission is served by their plant clinic and the Garden Hotline, (910) 452-6393, where volunteer master gardeners field questions about horticulture from 9 AM to 5 PM. The arboretum also sponsors and hosts seminars, classes and workshops. Some of the programs offer certificates upon completion. Need a special gift for a gardener? Don't miss the delightful variety of gifts and gardening books (their specialty) available at The Potting Shed gift shop, (910) 452-

3470, in the Reception Center. The shop is open from 10 AM to 2 PM Monday through Friday.

Admission to the arboretum is free. Donations are welcome and much needed. Funding is primarily by area sponsors, individual and corporate, volunteers, fund-raising events and local garden clubs. Volunteer docents lead tours on request during Extension office hours from 8 AM to 5 PM Monday through Friday. Self-guided tours are permitted daily from dawn to dusk. (The gates are closed but not locked during this time.) Enter the grounds from Oleander Drive (U.S. Highway 76) immediately east of Greenville Loop Road and west of the Bradley Creek bridge. And, yes, the arboretum is available for weddings.

Outside Wilmington

Cape Fear River Circle Tour
Southport-Fort Fisher Ferry, U.S. Hwy.
421, south of Kure Beach • (910) 458-3329
(Fort Fisher), (910) 457-6942 (Southport),
(800) 368-8969

You can tour the history and culture of the Lower Cape Fear by incorporating the Southport-Fort Fisher Ferry into a circular driv-

ATTRACTIONS

ing tour that could take several hours, given the most selective stopping, or could easily last several days if you choose to explore every stop in detail.

A Circle Tour brochure is available at the ferry, the Cape Fear Coast Convention & Visitors Bureau, 24 N. Third Street, Wilmington, (910) 341-4030, and visitor information racks throughout the area; it directs you around a loop that connects Wilmington, Pleasure Island, Southport and eastern Brunswick County. Included are seven major attractions (free unless otherwise noted): Battleship NORTH CAROLINA (fee), Orton Plantation Gardens (fee), Brunswick Town/Fort Anderson, Southport Maritime Museum (fee), CP&L's Brunswick Nuclear Plant, North Carolina Aquarium (fee) and Fort Fisher Civil War Museum. Total time for driving is about two hours, which includes about 30 minutes riding the ferry. The brochure provides information on the attractions and ferry schedule.

Poplar Grove Plantation
10200 U.S. Hwy. 17, Wilmington
• (910) 686-9518 Ext. 26

This 1850 Greek Revival house and the 628-acre plantation were supported by as many as 64 slaves prior to the Civil War. Today, costumed guides lead visitors through this lovingly restored mansion and recount the plantation's colorful history. Skills important to daily 19th-century life, such as weaving, smithery and basketry, are frequently demonstrated, and visitors are invited to walk the estate's grounds and view the plantation's outbuildings, including a tenant house, an outdoor kitchen and more.

Poplar Grove, dedicated to preserving the plantation's heritage, maintains a busy schedule of classes and demonstrations throughout the year. In addition, Insiders highly recommend annual events that include Halloween hayrides, a Medieval Festival, an Antique Fair, an Herb and Garden Fair, Arts in These Parts, and a Christmas Open House. Check out the Annual Events chapter for detailed descriptions or call the Poplar Grove plantation offices, (910) 686-9518, Ext. 26.

Listed on the National Register of Historic Places, Poplar Grove Plantation is 9 miles outside Wilmington on U.S. 17 at the Pender County line. A gift shop, playground, picnic area, restaurant, wedding and party facilities are located on the grounds. Poplar Grove Plantation is open to the public Monday through Saturday 9 AM to 5 PM and Sunday noon to 5 PM. Please note that the last guided tour of the plantation house is 4 PM daily. Fees for the guided house tour are $7 for adults ($5 each for groups of 15 or more), $6 for seniors, $3 for students ages 6 to 15 and free for children 5 and younger. Poplar Grove closes for Easter, Thanksgiving and the week of Christmas until the first Monday in February. Parking is plentiful, and access to the estate's grounds and outbuildings are free.

Wrightsville Beach

Wrightsville Beach Scenic Cruises
Waynick Blvd., Wrightsville Beach
• (910) 350-2628

In the warm season, a cruise aboard the 40-foot pontoon vessel along the calm Intracoastal Waterway affords a fine view of the landscape and wildlife of the tidal environment. Nature excursions to Masonboro Island are guided by a marine biologist, one-hour harbor cruises, shuttles to Masonboro Island and sunset cruises are highlights. Walk-ons are accepted, but reservations are required for the narrated nature excursions. Call for in-season cruise and excursion schedules and off-season charters and small-group excursions.

Wrightsville Beach Museum of History
303 W. Salisbury St., Wrightsville Beach
• (910) 256-256

The Wrightsville Beach Museum is housed in the Myers cottage, one of the oldest cottages on the beach (built in 1907). The museum opened its doors in May 1995. The museum presents beach history and lifestyles through permanent exhibits featuring a scale model of the oldest built-up section of the beach, photos, furniture, artifacts, a slide show and recorded oral histories, plus rotating exhibits on loggerhead turtles, surfing, the Civil War, shipwrecks, hurricanes and beach nightlife at such bygone attractions as the Lumina Pavilion. The museum is open Tuesday through Friday 10 AM to 4 PM, Saturday noon to 5 PM and Sunday 1 to 5 PM . Admission is $3. Children younger than 12 are admitted free with an adult. Upon crossing the drawbridge, bear left at the "Welcome to Wrightsville Beach" sign; the museum is on the right near the volleyball courts beyond the fire station.

Carolina Beach and Kure Beach

Fort Fisher-Southport Ferry
U.S. Hwy. 421, south of Kure Beach
• (910) 457-6942

More than transportation, this half-hour crossing is a journey into the natural and social history of the Cape Fear River. You'll have excellent views of Federal Point, Zeke's Island and The Rocks from the upper deck. On the Southport side, you'll spot historic Price's Creek Lighthouse at the mouth of the inlet. The crew is knowledgeable, and the cabin is air-conditioned. When traveling between Southport and New Hanover County, timing your trip to the ferry schedule makes getting there half the fun. (See our Getting Around chapter for schedules.)

One-way fees are $1 for pedestrians, $2 for cyclists, $5 for motorcycles and vehicles less than 20 feet in length, $10 for vehicles or combinations up to 40 feet long and $15 for vehicles from 40 to 65 feet. The ferry can be part of a wide-ranging, self-directed car-and-foot Circle Tour that includes seven attractions and museums in Wilmington, Southport and Pleasure Island. See our listing for the Cape Fear River Circle Tour in the Outside Wilmington section of this chapter.

Fort Fisher State Historic Site
U.S. Hwy. 421, south of Kure Beach
• (910) 458-5538

Fort Fisher was the last major Confederate stronghold to fall to Union forces during the War Between the States. It was the linchpin of the Confederate Army's Cape Fear Defense System, which included forts Caswell, Anderson and Johnston and a series of smaller batteries. Largely due to the tenacity of its defenders, the port of Wilmington was never entirely sealed by the Union blockade until January 1865. The Union bombardment of Fort Fisher was the heaviest naval demonstration in history up to that time. During the war, the fort, which stretched for 1.5 miles, was the largest and strongest earthen fort in the Confederacy.

Today, the Department of Cultural Resources operates and maintains the remains of Fort Fisher as a State Historic Site. The property boasts scenic easements of both the Cape Fear River and the Atlantic Ocean. A quarter-mile tour trail surrounds the archaeological remains of the Confederate fort. Exterior exhibits, a reconstructed palisade fence and a partially restored gun emplacement enhance historic interpretation.

The tour trail encircles the Western Bastion, including the partially restored Shepherd's Battery, which boasts a fully functional reproduction of a rifled and banded 32-pounder cannon. This huge gun is the only one in the nation said to be fired on a regular basis. On the north side of the fort, re-created palisades will be of interest to Civil War buffs. Because Fort Fisher is an archeological site, metal detectors are prohibited.

Following your visit to the fort, walk across U.S. Route 421 to the Cove, where you'll find a live oak-lined area overlooking the ocean; it's a great place for a relaxing stroll by the ocean. Swimming here is discouraged because of dangerous currents and underwater hazards. However, miles of unspoiled beaches are available immediately to the south at Fort Fisher State Recreation Area, complete with bathhouse showers, visitors center and concession stand. (See Sports, Fitness and Parks.)

Highlights of the Fort Fisher Historic Site's renovated visitors center include an upgraded theater, an enlarged gift shop, disabled-accessible restrooms, a free 15-minute audiovisual program chronicling the history of the fort, a museum and a state-of-the-art 16-foot fiber optic map. An eight-minute narrative accompanying the map narrates the final Battle of Fort Fisher. Civil War enthusiasts will especially enjoy the expanded exhibits, dioramas, artifacts and an informative audio program. The surrounding grounds, including The Cove and earthworks, are open to the public and are available for tour daily.

The site, about 19 miles south of Wilmington, was once commonly known as Federal Point. The ferry from Southport is an excellent and time-saving way to get there from Brunswick County. Summer visitors center hours are April 1 to October 31 Monday through Saturday 9 AM to 5 PM and Sunday 1 to 5 PM; winter hours, November 1 to March 31, are Tuesday through Saturday 10 AM to 4 PM (closed Sunday and Monday). For more information, guided tour schedules or to inquire about group tours, call the phone number above. Admission is free but donations are appreciated.

North Carolina Aquarium at Fort Fisher
900 Loggerhead Rd., Kure Beach
• (910) 458-8257

The North Carolina Aquarium at Fort Fisher reopened in March 2002 after being closed for two years for renovation and expansion. Located on the ocean, east of U.S. 421 and south of Kure Beach, (about 20 miles south of Wilmington), the Aquarium is now three times

The Three Cape Fear Lighthouses

The first lighthouses built on North Carolina's southern coast were a series of beacons installed along the 25-mile stretch from the mouth of the Cape Fear River to Wilmington. Lighthouses like Campbell Island Light, Orton's Point Light, Upper Jetty Light and the lightship at Horseshoe Shoal have all disappeared. Price Creek Lighthouse is the only one of this original series that stands today.

Price Creek Lighthouse

Price Creek Lighthouse, erected in 1849, was the last lighthouse built in the original series. Originally there were two beacons standing next to each other at this site: a 20-foot circular brick structure and a wooden structure on top of a keeper's brick house. During the Civil War, the keeper's house was used as a Confederate States Signal Station and the beacons were a means of communication between Fort Fisher and Fort Caswell. In the hands of the Confederate States Signal Corps, the beacons served military and civilian blockade runners.

The wooden tower was seriously damaged between the late 1800s and early 1900s and eventually disintegrated. The brick beacon still stands, though it was damaged during the Civil War when the Confederate forces damaged or destroyed all beacons to prevent Union forces from safely navigating the river.

The Price Creek Lighthouse is located on private property on the west bank of the Cape Fear River, about two miles above Southport. It can be seen clearly in the distance from aboard the deck of the Southport/Fort Fisher Ferry while in the mouth of the Southport Harbor. At this writing, Price Creek Lighthouse cannot be toured, but some discussion about making it available to the public has been held in the past year or so.

Bald Head Island Lighthouse

The 1817 Bald Head Island Lighthouse, known as "Old Baldy", was not the first beacon to stand on Bald Head Island. The first was the 1795 Bald Head Island Light Station — actually the first lighthouse structure built in North Carolina. The first light station, however, was built too close to the water, was plagued with erosion problems and was torn down by 1810.

In 1817 the 109-foot-tall Old Baldy was built of bricks coated with cement on the outside. Inside it has a ground floor of brick and a stone floor in the lantern room while the rest of the floors are Carolina yellow pine. It still has the original 12" by 14" double glazed windows from Boston.

Because of the limited range of its lens, the Bald Head Island Lighthouse was not useful for warning ships away from Frying Pan Shoals. In 1854 Congress voted to place a lightship on the shoals. When the Cape Fear Lighthouse, a 150-foot steel skeleton structure, was built on the shoals in 1903, Old Baldy was downgraded to a low-intensity non-blinking light.

The Bald Head Island Lighthouse was discontinued in 1935, but from 1941 to 1958 the structure housed a radio beacon to guide ships in low visibility. With the construction of the Oak Island Lighthouse in 1958, the Cape Fear Lighthouse was dismantled and the radio beacon was removed from Old Baldy.

On self-guided tours of Old Baldy, which is now an historic site, you can climb all the way to the top. A small climbing fee is charged at the museum next door. Or you can arrange to participate in the Bald Head Island Historic tour by calling Jane Oakley at (910) 457-7481.

Oak Island Lighthouse

Constructed in 1958, the present Oak Island Lighthouse was one of the last lighthouses built in America and is the last manually operated lighthouse in the world. It was not the first beacon on Oak Island. As in the case of the Price Creek Lighthouse, there were originally two beacons on Oak Island, part of the series of navigational lights designed to guide ships to the harbors of Brunswick Town and Wilmington.

The original beacons were meant to be situated to allow approaching ships to line them up to help with navigation, but they were not properly placed. Both lights were destroyed during the Civil War. They were rebuilt in 1879, but the front beacon was seriously damaged by a hurricane in 1893, and their use was discontinued the following year.

The present lighthouse is 153 feet high with an 8-inch thick reinforced concrete base anchored with 24 pipe pilings filled with concrete to 67 feet below ground. This design allows the tower to sway about three inches in a 100 mile per hour wind. The tower itself is concrete with color compounds mixed into it to keep it from ever needing painting.

The 11-foot-tall aluminum lantern on top arrived by water from Portsmouth, Virginia, and was put into place by two Marine helicopters. The 4,000-watt, aerobeam lights can be seen 24 miles out to sea. A second bank of lights is used as backup. With 2,500,000 candlepower, it is one of the most powerful lighthouses in the world. Its characteristic flash pattern is four flashes every ten seconds.

Members of the U.S. Coast Guard act as light keepers and climb the 120 narrow metal steps to the platform and a 14-rung metal ladder to the lantern room for weekly inspections. A metal box attached to a shelf with a pulley is used to haul tools, lamps and other supplies to the top of the tower. From the base of the tower, the light is switched on each evening 30 minutes before sunset and off each morning 30 minutes after sunrise. The Oak Island Lighthouse is located on Coast Guard property in Caswell Beach. You can call the Coast Guard Station at (910) 278-1133 to ask about tours.

Old Baldy stands watch over Bald Head Island.

Photo: Jay Tervo

ATTRACTIONS

its original size and the largest of North Carolina's three aquariums. With its 235,000-gallon saltwater tank, fascinating displays, interactive exhibits and 20,000-square-foot conservatory, the aquarium features "The Waters of the Cape Fear" from Raven Rock State Park south of Raleigh to the Atlantic Ocean; 2,500 freshwater and saltwater creatures are on exhibit. It's open daily 9 AM to 5 PM except Christmas, New Year's and Thanksgiving days.

See our Closeup in the Kidstuff chapter for a detailed description of this exciting attraction.

Bald Head Island

Bald Head Island Historic Tour
Departure from Indigo Plantation, W. Ninth St., Southport • (910) 457-7481

This guided-tour package may be the most

convenient way for a daytripper to get to know Bald Head past and present. The two-hour tour begins with a 10 AM ferry departure and includes Old Baldy Lighthouse and Captain Charlie's Station. Put into service in 1817, Old Baldy is the state's oldest standing lighthouse, the second of three built on the island to guide ships across the Cape Fear Bar and into the river channel. The fee ($36 per adult, $31 per child 12 and younger — subject to change) includes parking at the ferry terminal, round-trip ferry ride, the island tour and lunch at the River Pilot Cafe. Diners may choose a specially prepared entree and a beverage from the chef's menu (gratuities included). Tour guests return to Southport by ferry at 2:30 PM. Reservations are required. You must arrive at the departure site by 9:30 AM for the 10 AM departure. If you prefer to linger on the island after the tour, ferries to Southport run every hour on the half-hour.

Southport-Oak Island

Environmental Overlook Trails
3033. E. Oak Island Dr., Oak Island
• (910) 278-5518

If you like wandering and looking for wildlife, these trails are for you. The Butterfly/Hummingbird Garden is located on the trail behind the recreation Center at 3003 E. Oak Island Drive. There are four platforms overlooking the path, including a talking live oak, other indigenous trees and flowers and food plants that attract butterflies and hummingbirds. A trail to the right of the Recreation Center leads into the rainforest area, where the wetlands can be viewed from the bird-watching platform and rainforest overlook. At the end of 31st Street (next to the Recreation Center) is Tidal Waves Park where you will find a picnic shelter near the floating dock, which can be used for launching canoes and kayaks. Canoe/kayak trail maps are available at the center. The Environment Crossover crosses the Davis Canal, giving an elevated view of the canal and the wetlands on either side. The trail winds through the trees to the other side of the island, and a crossover walk leads to the ocean and gives a closer view of the salt marsh. Wildlife such as snakes, deer and various birds make their appearances here.

The Town of Oak Island has also purchased land at the west end of Oak Island, where they are preserving the dunes. A wooden walkway has been constructed on which you can wander through the dunes and stop at two over-look points where you may chance to see red fox, black snakes, fiddler crabs, loggerhead sea turtles, raccoons or several species of shorebirds.

Fort Caswell
Caswell Beach Rd., Caswell Beach
• (910) 278-9501

Considered one of the strongest forts of its time, Fort Caswell originally encompassed some 2,800 acres at the east end of Oak Island. Completed in 1838, the compound consisted of earthen ramparts enclosing a roughly pentagonal brick-and-masonry fort and citadel. Caswell proved to be so effective a deterrent during the Civil War that it saw little action. Supply lines were cut after Fort Fisher fell to Union forces in January 1865, so before abandoning the fort, the Caswell garrison detonated the powder magazine, heavily damaging the citadel and surrounding earthworks. What remains of the citadel is essentially unaltered and is maintained by the Baptist Assembly of North Carolina, which owns the property. A more expansive system of batteries and a sea wall were constructed during the war-wary years from 1885 to 1902. Fort Caswell is open for self-guided visits Monday through Friday 8 AM to 5 PM and Saturday 8 AM to noon. Admission is $3.

Fort Johnston
Davis and Bay Sts., Southport
• (910) 457-7927

The first working military installation in the state, Fort Johnston was commissioned in 1754 to command the mouth of the Cape Fear River. A bevy of tradespeople, fishermen and river pilots soon followed, and so the town of Smithville was born (renamed Southport in 1887). During the Civil War, Confederate forces added Fort Johnston to their Cape Fear Defense System, which included forts Caswell, Anderson and Fisher. Fort Johnston's fortifications no longer stand, but the site is redolent with memories of those times and is one of the attractions listed on the Southport Trail (see later entry). The remaining original structures house personnel assigned to the Sunny Point Military Ocean Terminal, an ordnance depot a few miles north.

The Grove
Franklin Square Park, E. West and Howe Sts., Southport

Shaded by centuries-old live oaks and aflame with color in spring, this is a park to savor — a place in which to drink in the spirit of old Smithville. The walls and entrances that embrace The Grove were constructed of ballast stones used in ships more than 100 years ago. Set back among the oaks, stately Franklin Square Gallery, (910) 457-5450, now displaying art in several media, was once a schoolhouse and then City Hall. The park is a place to indulge in local legend by taking a drink of well water from the old pump — a draught that is sure to take you back.

Keziah Memorial Park
W. Moore and S. Lord Sts., Southport

A shady little park with a gazebo, benches and a partial view of the waterfront, Keziah Park is notable for its uncannily bent live oak. Estimated to be 800 years old, the tree is called the Indian Trail Tree after the legend that it was curved while a sapling by ancient natives who used it to blaze the approach to their preferred fishing grounds beyond. It later rooted itself a second time, completing an arch.

North Carolina Maritime Museum at Southport
116 N. Howe St., Southport
• (910) 457-0003

Read "Gentleman Pirate" Stede Bonnet's plea for clemency, delivered just before he was hanged; view treasures rescued from local shipwrecks; see a 2,000-year-old Indian canoe fragment; learn about hurricanes, sharks' teeth, shrimping nets and much more in one of the region's newest and most ambitious museums. Many of the exhibits are hands-on, and a Jeopardy-style trivia board is a favorite of history buffs of all ages. The museum boasts an extensive maritime research library and video collection and is within walking distance of Southport's restaurants and shopping. Hours are 9 AM to 5 PM Tuesday through Saturday. Admission is $2 for adults age 16 and older, $1 for seniors and free for children younger than 16. Ask about periodic special exhibits and lectures.

Old Brunswick Town State Historic Site
8884 St. Philips Rd. SE, off N.C. Hwy. 133, Southport • (910) 371-6613

At this site stood the first successful perma-

INSIDERS' TIP

When you're going to take the Southport-Fort Fisher Ferry, be sure to arrive early — at least 20 minutes — during the tourist season. The ferry is quite popular and fills quickly. Snacks and drinks are available and there's plenty of room to wander while you wait. When feeding the gulls while you're on the ferry, do so from the stern (back end); the other passengers will appreciate that, and the captain will fuss at you if you don't!

nent European settlement between Charleston and New Bern. It was founded in 1726 by Roger and Maurice Moore (who recognized an unprecedented real estate opportunity in the wake of the Tuscarora War, 1711-13), and the site served as port and political center. Russelborough, home of two royal governors, once stood nearby. In 1748 the settlement was attacked by Spanish privateers, who were soundly defeated in a surprise counterattack by the Brunswick settlers. A painting of Christ (Ecce Homo), reputedly 400 years old, was among the Spanish ship's plunder and now hangs in St. James Episcopal Church in Wilmington. At Brunswick Town in 1765, one of the first instances of armed resistance to the British crown occurred in response to the Stamp Act. In time, the upstart, upriver port of Wilmington superseded Brunswick. In 1776 the British burned Brunswick, and in 1862 Fort Anderson was built there to help defend Port Wilmington. The earthworks of Fort Anderson are 100 percent intact and one of the best examples of earthworks that exist today. Until recently, occasional church services were still held in the ruins of St. Philip's Church.

Admission to the historic site is free. Hours from April 1 through October 31 are 9 AM to 5 PM Monday through Saturday and 1 to 5 PM Sunday. From November 1 through March 31, visit between 10 AM and 4 PM Tuesday through Saturday and 1 and 4 PM Sunday. The site is closed on most major holidays and on Monday during winter months. From Wilmington, take N.C. 133 about 18 miles to Plantation Road. Signs will direct you to the site (exit left) that lies close to Orton Plantation Gardens. The site's visitors center offers a gift shop, a research library, a 14-minute slide presentation on the history of Old Brunswick Town, staff offices and handicapped accessibility.

Old Smithville Burial Ground
E. Moore and S. Rhett Sts., Southport

"The Winds and the Sea sing their requiem and shall forever more. . . ." Profoundly evocative of the harsh realities endured by Southport's long-gone seafarers, the Old Smithville Burial

ATTRACTIONS

Ground (1804) is a must-see. Obelisks dedicated to lost river pilots, monuments to entire crews and families who lived and died by the sea, and stoic elegies memorialize Southport's past as no other historic site can. Many of the names immortalized on these stones live on among descendants still living in the area.

Orton Plantation Gardens
Off N.C. Hwy. 133, Southport
• (910) 371-6851

Orton Plantation represents one of the region's oldest historically significant residences in continuous use. The family names associated with it make up the very root and fiber of Cape Fear's history. Built in 1725 by the imperious "King" Roger Moore, founder of Brunswick Town, the main residence at Orton Plantation underwent several expansions to become the archetype of old Southern elegance. It survived the ravages of the Civil War despite being used as a Union hospital after the fall of Fort Fisher. Thereafter it stood abandoned for 19 years until it was purchased and refurbished by Col. Kenneth McKenzie Murchison, CSA.

In 1904 the property passed to the Sprunt family, related to the Murchisons by marriage, and the plantation gardens began taking shape. In 1915 the family built Luola's Chapel, a Doric structure of modest grandeur available today for meetings and private weddings. The gardens, both formal and natural, are among the most beautiful in the east, consisting of ponds, fountains, statuary, footbridges and stands of cypress. The elaborately sculpted Scroll Garden overlooks former rice fields. Elsewhere are the tombs of Roger Moore and his family. The best times to visit Orton Plantation are from late winter to late spring. Camellias, azaleas, pansies, flowering trees and other ornamentals bloom in early spring; later, oleander, hydrangea, crepe myrtle, magnolia and annuals burst with color. Bring insect repellent in the summer. If you're lucky, you may catch a glimpse of Buster, the 10-foot gator who has lived in the lagoon near the house for many years. He's been known to sun himself in front of the gardens. Touring the gardens takes an easily paced hour or more.

The gardens are open every day; from March through August hours are 8 AM to 6 PM and from September through November hours are 10 AM to 5 PM. Admission is $9 for adults, $8 for seniors, $3 for children ages 6 through 16 and free for children younger than 6. Group rates are available. Orton Plantation is off N.C. 133, 18 miles south of Wilmington and 10 miles

north of Southport. Nearby are the historic sites of Brunswick Town and Fort Anderson.

Progress Energy - Brunswick Plant Visitor's Center
8520 River Rd., N.C. Hwy. 87, Southport
• (910) 457-6964

More than 30 energy-related exhibits are housed in this center. They include the production of electricity, electrical safety, alternative energy sources and energy conservation. The exhibits are open year round on Tuesday through Thursday from 9 AM until 4 PM. Tour of the exhibits is self-guided, and admission is free.

Southport Trail
Southport • (910) 457-7927

This two mile-long walking tour links 25 historic landmarks, among them the tiny Old Brunswick County Jail, Fort Johnston and the Stede Bonnet Memorial. Architectural beauty abounds along the route, revealing Queen Anne gables, Southport arch and bow, and porches trimmed in gingerbread. The free brochure describing this informal, self-guided chain of discoveries can be obtained at the Southport Visitor Center, 113 W. Moore Street (where the tour begins) Monday through Saturday from 10 AM to 5 PM in summer. Off-season, call for information at (800) 388-9635.

St. Philip's Episcopal Church
E. Moore and Dry Sts., Southport
• (910) 457-5643

Southport's oldest church in continuous use, St. Philip's is a beautiful clapboard church erected in 1843, partly through the efforts of Colonel Thomas Childs, then commander of Fort Johnston, one block east. It stands beside Southport City Hall. The first vestry (elected 1850) ushered the church into the diocese as "Old St. Philips" in memory of the original church of St. Philip in colonial Brunswick Town. Within the present church flies every flag that has flown over the parish's two incarnations since 1741, including the Spanish, English and Confederate.

The building exhibits Carpenter-style Greek Revival elements, particularly evident in the pediments and exterior wooden pilasters, as well as English Gothic details. Entrance is made through the small, square tower, with its louvered belfry, simple exterior arcading and colored-glass lancet windows. The church's side windows of diamond-paned clear glass flood the sanctuary with light, illuminating the handsome tongue-and-groove woodwork on the walls and ceiling. It's a beautiful, quiet place that remains open 24 hours a day for meditation, prayer or rest.

St. Philip's Parish
Old Brunswick Town State Historic Site, off N.C. Hwy. 133, north of Southport
• (910) 371-6613

After St. James Episcopal Church left Brunswick Town in favor of the rival port of Wilmington, the Anglican parish of St. Philip formed in 1741. In 1754 it began building a stone church at Brunswick, the seat of royal government in the colony. After struggling with finances and a destructive hurricane, the church was finally completed in 1768, only to be burned by the British in 1776 (the colony's first armed resistance to the Stamp Act occurred nearby at the royal governor's residence).

Today, all that remains of St. Philip's church, the only Colonial church in southeastern North Carolina, is a rectangular shell — 25-foot-high walls, 3 feet thick — plus several Colonial-era graves (some of which are resurfacing with time). The ruin's round-arched window ports are intact and suggest Georgian detailing, but little solid evidence exists about the building's original appearance beyond some glazing on the brick. Three entrances exist, in the west, north and south walls, and three, triptych-style windows open the east wall.

Until recently, several local congregations held periodic services within the ruins. The body of North Carolina's first royal governor (Arthur Dobbs) is reputed to have been interred at St. Philip's, as he requested, but it has never been identified. St. Philip's Episcopal Church in Southport (see previous listing) was named after the Colonial parish to perpetuate its memory. (Also see the listing for Old Brunswick Town State Historic Site.)

Trinity United Methodist Church
209 E. Nash St., Southport
• (910) 457-6633

Built c. 1890 for a total of $3,300, this church is the third to occupy this site. Today the building features two of the area's best stained-glass windows (at either side of the sanctuary); handsome, diagonally paneled walls; and a beaded ceiling (i.e., finished with narrow, half-round moldings) finished by a 15-year-old carpenter. Emblazoned across the original front-transom window is the abbreviation "M.E.C.S." (Methodist Episcopal Church, South) a remnant of the days when the church was split from its northerly brethren due to the Civil War.

The clapboard exterior includes Shingle-style detailing, a cedar-shingled roof and a gabled bell tower. Trinity Church stands at the corner of N. Atlantic Avenue, up the street from the Fire Department and across the street from the Post Office.

Waterfront Park
Bay St., foot of Howe St., Southport

At the end of Howe Street, you'll come upon this breezy little park and take in the breathtaking scene at the convergence of the Intracoastal Waterway, the Cape Fear River and the Atlantic ocean. From the swings overlooking the waterfront you can see Old Baldy Lighthouse and Oak Island Lighthouse (the brightest in the nation). Gone are the pirate ships and menhaden boats, but the procession of ferries, freighters, barges and sailboats keeps Southport's maritime tradition alive.

Stroll or cycle the Historic Riverwalk trail, an easy 0.7-mile scenic route that meanders from the City Pier, past the fisheries and the small boat harbor, and culminates at a 750-foot boardwalk with benches and handrails over the tidal marsh near Southport Marina. Leave your bike in the rack and walk on to the gazebo for an unbroken view of the Intracoastal Waterway and the ship channel. It's a restful, romantic place where the only sounds you're likely to hear are the cawing of crows and the clank of halyards.

Winds of Carolina Sailing Charters
Southport Marina, foot of W. West St., Southport • (910) 278-7249, (910) 232-3003

The Winds of Carolina offers four customized daily trips along the Oak Island shoreline aboard the 37-foot, twin-cabin sloop Stephania. The Morning Sail ($47 per person) leaves at 9:30 AM. The Afternoon Sail ($47 per person) leaves at 1 PM and lunch baskets are available for this excursion at an additional cost. The Sunset Sail ($49 per person) leaves at 5:30 PM and includes a fruit and cheese appetizer tray. The Moonlight Sail ($49 per person, four people minimum for this cruise) departs at 9 PM on the five days prior to and after a full moon. Call for sailing dates. Off-season (December, January and February) trips include the Morning Sail, departing at 10:30 AM, and the Sunset Sail at 3 PM.

All trips last three hours and are under the command of a USCG-licensed captain. Each includes narration of points of interest and his-

Wildlife is one of the main attractions on the southern coast.

tory of Oak Island, complementary beverages and fresh towels for sun worshiping on the forward decks. Guests are welcome to take the helm while under sail. Space is limited to six passengers, and reservations are required. Half-day and full-day private custom charters are available. Gift certificates are available for all occasions.

Have a honeymoon, birthday or engagement celebration coming up? Book the overnight Boat & Breakfast to sleep on the boat and have your breakfast delivered to your cabin in the morning. *Our State* magazine called *Stephania* "the Love Boat". The boat is also listed in the *Romantic Guide of Things to Do in NC* and it was featured in the May 2001 edition of *Southern Living magazine*.

South Brunswick Islands

Hurricane Fleet
Hurricane Fleet Marina, Calabash
• (843) 249-3571

The Hurricane Fleet has an array of cruise options aboard the Hurricane. Most popular is the inland waterway Adventure Cruise ($18 for adults; $15 for children 11 and younger), which brings passengers practically stem-to-stern with working shrimpers, dolphins at play, sharks and other marine life. Other cruise options include several fishing excursions — half-day (great for families and novice anglers), night, sport and Gulf Stream fishing. All fishing cruises include bait, tackle, rod and reel. Hurricane Fleet boats are U.S. Coast Guard approved. Call for cruise schedules and rates.

Ingram Planetarium
U.S. Hwy. 179 and N.C. Hwy. 904, The Village at Sunset Beach, Sunset Beach
• (910) 575-0033

The Ingram Planetarium, named for Stuart Ingram, founder of the Museum of Coastal Carolina, opened its doors and its sky-dome to the public in 2002. A state-of-the-art facility with a 40-foot dome theater, it is an accomplishment to be proud of. The planetarium features various shows including "Endless Horizon," "The Explorer's" and "The Sky Tonight," with starting times from 3 to 7 PM. A unique feature is Assisted Listening, which provides headsets for hearing-impaired persons. The Paul Dennis Science Room is used for classes, displays, meetings and birthday parties. In it are hands on displays such as the constellation puzzle and Stuart Ingram's collection of sextants along with an explanation of their use in steering by the stars at sea. The gift shop is a veritable storehouse of fun, educational gifts as well as decorative gift items.

Museum of Coastal Carolina
21 E. Second St., Ocean Isle Beach
• (910) 579-1016

Standing on the ocean floor would be a wonderful way to experience the marine environment up close. Visitors to this museum can do the next best thing — visit the Reef Room, believed to be the largest natural history diorama in the Southeast. Above you, sharks, dolphins and game fish "swim in place" while all types of crustaceans creep below. The remains of a shipwreck, dating from about 1800, rest on the "sea" bottom. Elsewhere, Civil War artifacts, tidal exhibits, a display of shark jaws, wildlife dioramas including dioramas of the Green Swamp, and many other exhibits bring the natural history of the southern coast vividly to life. Don't miss the Shell Room, where you will find more than 200 specimens of sea shells. Evening lectures are scheduled every second Tuesday September through June, excluding December. Call for information about special summer programs.

ATTRACTIONS

Admission is $4 for adults and $2 for kids younger than 12. Summer hours (Memorial Day through Labor Day) are 9 AM to 9 PM Monday and Thursday, 9 AM to 5 PM Tuesday, Wednesday, Friday and Saturday, and 1 to 5 PM Sunday. The rest of the year, hours are 10 AM to 4 PM Friday and Saturday and 1 to 4 PM Sunday. This large, sand-colored building is easy to find: After crossing the bridge onto the island, turn left onto Second Street.

Ocean Isle Beach Water Slide
3 Second St., Ocean Isle Beach
• (910) 579-9678

You can't miss the waterslides as you cruise across the causeway onto Ocean Isle Beach. From the tops of the slides you get a stunning view of the ocean and beach. The slides are open daily 10 AM to 7 PM during the summer months. Admission fees range from hourly ($6), all day until 4 PM ($10), and evening from 4 until 7 PM ($8). Lifeguards are on duty. Refreshments are available.

Topsail Island and Vicinity

Blackbeard's Lair
1891 N.C. Hwy. 50, Surf City
• (910) 328-4200

An 18-hole miniature golf course, Grand Prix raceway, bumper boats, playground, arcade and snack bar can all be enjoyed at this one location. It's open daily during the summer months, but has reduced hours in the spring and fall seasons.

Camp Lejeune Marine Corps Base Tour
Back Gate Base Entrance, N.C. Hwy. 172, Sneads Ferry • (910) 451-2148

In 1999 the U.S. Marine Corps instituted a self-guided tour of Camp Lejeune, home of East Coast "expeditionary forces in readiness." The tour was designed to take visitors from pre-Colonial America to the edge of technology on the.base that serves the largest single concentration of Marines anywhere in the world. A printed tour guide with map, directions and a complete narrative of the 25 points of interest can be picked up when you check in at any of the three base entrance gates, Camp Johnson or Camp Geiger. The tour is well-marked by large white signs and can start at any specific point of interest. Depending on how much you choose

to visit, a tour can range from one or two hours to a half or full day. The legacies of Marines past are witnessed on the tour. The Montford Point and NC Veteran's Cemeteries are located near Camp Johnson. These two sites are the final resting places for veterans and families from the Civil and Revolutionary Wars. Other points of interest include early historical spots, specific buildings, military equipment (both U.S. and captured pieces) and off-base historical locations. The tour is free, but can be closed down at any time for security purposes. For more information about the tour, call the number above.

Dorothy's Harbor Tours
636 Channel Blvd., Topsail Beach
• (910) 545-RIDE

Cruise Topsail Sound and the Intracoastal Waterway in Topsail Island's newest tour boat, Dorothy. With seating for 28 people, this craft offers regularly scheduled daytime and sunset cruises everyday from April through September bringing you a fantastic opportunity to watch dolphins frolicking, osprey's nesting and many other joys of nature. Private charters are available. Tickets, at a cost of $10. per person are available on site. Call for tour departure times. No food or drinks are available, but you can bring your own.

Karen Beasley Sea Turtle Rescue and Rehabilitation Center
822 Channel Blvd., Topsail Beach
• (910) 328-3377

While the primary purpose of this facility is the care and rehabilitation of injured sea turtles, it is open on a limited basis for the public to view and learn about this program aimed at protecting the endangered species. The center is open during the summer months on Monday, Tuesday, Thursday, Friday and Saturday from 2 to 4 PM. (Arrival close to 4 PM will not guarantee admission if there is a line of folks waiting.) There is less traffic on Monday, Tuesday and Saturday. The busiest days are Thursday and Friday. The center closes without notice for emergencies. When temperatures allow, it is open on Friday and Saturday in the spring and fall. During the later fall, winter and early spring when heating the water for the tanks is required, the center is closed to the public due to safety regulations. Due to the popularity and the limited size of this facility, arrival 15 minutes before opening is suggested. No calls for reservations are accepted. Visitors can expect to see large loggerhead turtles, green sea turtles or the rare Kemp's Ridley and learn the history and problems each has endured, plus more about their treatment and predicted release. Donations are appreciated. To learn more about the turtles, be sure to attend the Turtle Talks on Thursday afternoon, 4pm at the Surf City Fire Department

Missiles and More Museum
Assembly Building, 720 Channel Blvd., Topsail Beach

The Missiles and More Museum offers a tour through the history of the Topsail Island area. It begins with the early settlers and takes you through Blackbeard the Pirate to the time of World War II, when Topsail Island became part of the training ground for Camp Davis. It continues with artifacts from Operation Bumblebee, part of the nation's early space program, and the invention of the ramjet engines that were assembled here on the island and used to propel the Talos and Terrier rockets. Other displays include a history of each local town and the Ocean City Beach area. Video footage of Operation Bumblebee and World War II activities are shown as part of the museum tour. The museum is run by volunteers and is open April through October on Monday, Tuesday, Thursday, Friday and Saturday from 2 to 4 PM. For large groups, or to visit during the remainder of the year, call the Greater Topsail Area Chamber of Commerce and Tourism at (910) 329-4446 to schedule a private showing with a docent.

Ocean Breeze Family Fun Center
N.C. Hwy. 210, Sneads Ferry
• (910) 327-2700

Be "amazed" at this great park's newest attraction, a human maze. Test your skills and see if you can beat your family or friends time through the maze. Ocean Breeze offers affordable fun-filled activities for the whole family. Go-cart tracks, twin waterslides, an 18-hole miniature golf course, bumper boats, amusements rides, snack bar and arcade games can provide enough vacation entertainment that you'll need more than one trip. Be sure to ride the colorful Ferris wheel and catch the view from the top. Celebrate birthdays or special occasions with an organized party. Group rates are available. Summer hours are 10 AM to 10 PM Monday through Saturday and 11 AM to 10 PM on Sunday. Call for off-season hours and rates.

The Patio Playground
807 S. Anderson Blvd., Topsail Beach
• (910) 328-6491

In addition to the ever-popular miniature golf, Patio Playground has a unique attraction in its Gyrogym, where participants whirl in a 360-degree environment of multiple steel hoops, yielding the sensation of weightlessness. An arcade complete with pool tables rounds out this fun center that's especially popular with vacationing teenagers. Bicycle and beach item rentals are offered through Patio Playground. It's open daily in the summer and has reduced spring and fall hours.

Shellabrations
(910) 328-5341

Shellabrations offers private, group or individual shell-identification walks along the beaches of Topsail Island. Shelling expert Pat Crist will guide your tour in areas where the most shells can be found at a particular time, or the area of your choice. There is a charge of $5 per hour for each person, with children under age 5 coming along for free. Reservations are required.

Triple J Stables
120 Lake Haven Dr., Sneads Ferry
• (910) 327-0577

Triple J Stables is a new attraction in the Topsail Area offering trail rides and riding lessons. Guided trail rides are by appointment and should be reserved at least one day in advance. The stables are open 7 days per week. Plans are also in the works for a summer day camp.

Turtle Nest Sitting
(910) 328-1000

During the months from July to October, vacationers walking on the beach can find evidence of turtles nests with eggs that are ready to hatch. Turtle project volunteers prepare the nesting area and beach for the emerging turtles by creating runways and clearing the area of obstacles. At night, volunteers sit these nests and wait for the actual hatching. Visitors and residents are invited to join in this awe-inspiring experience, but survival of the baby turtles requires patience and willingness to follow instructions on the part of the spectators and participants.

Turtle Talks
Fire Department, 200 Wilmington Ave, Surf City • (910) 328-3377

Each Thursday afternoon at 4 PM between Memorial Day and Labor Day, an educational talk is given on the lifestyle and habits of the loggerhead turtle and how the Topsail Turtle Project is working to protect this endangered species. Questions are welcomed, and the presentation is geared to all age levels. Admission is free, and reservations are not required.

Other Islands

Masonboro Island

Evidence suggests that the first stretch of continental American coastline described by a European explorer may have been the beach now called Masonboro Island. The explorer was Giovanni da Verrazzano, the year, 1524. During the Civil War, Masonboro's beaches were visited by the destruction of three blockade runners and one Union blockader.

Before 1952 Masonboro was not an island but was attached to the mainland. In that year Carolina Beach Inlet was cut, giving Carolina Beach its boom in the tourist fishing trade and creating the last and largest undisturbed barrier island remaining on the southern North Carolina coast — 8-mile long Masonboro Island. Made up of 5,046 acres, of which 4,300 acres are tidal salt marshes and mud flats, Masonboro is now the fourth component of the North Carolina National Estuarine Research Reserve, the other three being Zeke's Island, which lies south of Federal Point in the Cape Fear River (see listing below), Currituck Banks and Rachel Carson Island, the latter two being farther north.

Most impressive is the island's profusion of wildlife, some abundant and some endangered, in an essentially natural state. Endangered loggerhead turtles successfully nest here, as do terns, gulls, ghost crabs and brown pelicans. Their neighbors include gray foxes, marsh rabbits, opossums, raccoons and river otters. Several types of heron, snowy egrets, willets, black skimmers and clapper rails forage in the creeks and mud flats at low tide. The estuarine waters teem with 44 species of fish and a multitude of shellfish, snails, sponges and worms. Its accessibility to UNCW's marine biology program, among the world's best, makes Masonboro an ideal classroom for the study of human impact on natural habitat. The island is a peaceful place where generations of locals have fished, hunted, sunbathed, swum, surfed, camped and sat back to witness nature. Small wonder Masonboro Island has always been close to locals' hearts. Accordingly, the Coastal Management Division of the North Carolina Department of Environment, Health and Natural Resources administers the island with as little intrusion as possible. Camping, hunting and other traditional activities pursued here are allowed to continue, albeit under monitoring intended to determine whether the island can withstand such impact. So far, so good.

If you don't own a boat and can't rent one for getting to Masonboro, refer to the listing for Turtle Island Ventures in the Rowing and Canoeing section of our Watersports chapter, or see the listing for the Blockade Runner Scenic Cruises in this chapter.

The efforts to preserve Masonboro Island are spearheaded by the Society for Masonboro Island Inc., (910) 256-5777, a nonprofit membership corporation. Much of the island, especially at the north end, remains with private landowners who could at any time alter the natural habitat or prohibit use by the public. The society's goal is to see the island acquired for public purposes and maintained in its undeveloped state. The society sponsors public education through a newsletter, nature walks, volunteer island cleanups and a speakers bureau. Membership in the society is inexpensive, ranging from $5 for students and $10 for individuals to $100 for donors and $250 for lifetime members. Information on Masonboro Island and barrier island habitats may also be obtained through UNCW's Center for Marine Science Research, 7205 Wrightsville Avenue, Wilmington, (910) 256-3721.

Zeke's Island

You can walk to this island reserve in the Cape Fear River and you need not walk on water. Simply drive down by the boat ramp at Federal Point (beyond the ferry terminal) and at low tide walk The Rocks, a breakwater first erected in 1873 that extends beyond Zeke's Island for just more than 3 miles. You can go by boat if keeping your feet on the tricky rocks isn't your idea of fun. This component of the North Carolina National Estuarine Research Reserve consists of Zeke's Island, North Island, No-Name Island and the Basin, the body of water enclosed by the breakwater, totaling 1,160 acres. The varied habitats include salt marshes, beaches, tidal flats and estuarine waters. Bottlenosed dolphins, red-tailed hawks, ospreys and colonies of fiddler crabs will keep you looking in every direction. Fishing, sunbathing and boating are the primary pursuits here, and hunting within regulations is allowed. Bring everything you need, pack out everything you bring, and don't forget drinking water!

Kidstuff

There's no limit to the wonderful imagination and limitless energy of kids. They want to know everything from "Why is the sky blue?" and "How come Santa's handwriting looks like yours?" to "What's for dinner?" and "What is there to do around here anyway?" Now that's one question you can easily answer. There really is no better place to raise a family than along North Carolina's beautiful coast. Living near the ocean means you'll find numerous water activities to engage in, and living in an area that cherishes history and fosters the arts offers many exciting educational activities too. Among a parent's greatest area resources for entertaining kids are the various museums, which offer classes and workshops in arts and crafts, and the North Carolina Aquarium at Fort Fisher, which also offers classes and workshops as well as outdoor activities. Opportunities for adolescents to learn boating skills, participate in gymnasium and team sports and take part in many other activities, both physical and cerebral, exist with the various parks and recreation departments throughout the area. To contact these resources, see the listings in our chapters on Watersports and Sports, Fitness and Parks. Information on child care can be found in our Schools and Child Care chapter.

For this chapter, we've tried to ferret out some of the participatory activities that are easily overlooked as well as the bare necessities of kidstuff to balance the ubiquitous consumer-oriented offerings. Keep in mind that many of the activities listed here are not strictly for kids; conversely, many attractions and activities listed in other chapters are not exclusively for adults. Be sure to comb other chapters (especially Attractions) for great kidstuff ideas. Each section in this chapter deals with a type of activity or interest: Amusements (including hobbies and toys), Animals, Arts, Birthday Parties, Eats, Exploring Nature, Farms, Holidays, Getting Physical, Getting Wet, Going Mental (for inquisitive minds) and Summer Camps.

Amusements

This section is designed for children who enjoy spending their free time engaging in a favorite hobby. From comics or baseball card collecting, video game playing, airplane building to toy shopping, you've come to the right place.

Adam's Memory Lane Comics
5751 Oleander Dr., Wilmington • (910) 392-6647

Stocking one of the area's largest inventories of comic books (new and old), collections and supplies, Adam's Memory Lane is an essential stopover for comics fans. Adam's claims to have the best collection of vintage comics in southeastern North Carolina. Also stocked are Yo-Gi-Oh! game cards, Comic Shop exclusive action figures, old toys and other oddities. You'll find the shop in the Philips' Azalea Plaza a short distance west of the Greenville Loop Road intersection. Memory Lane is open Monday through Saturday 12 to 6 PM and Sunday from 1 to 4 PM..

The Game Giant
419 S. College Rd., Unit 40, Wilmington • (910) 790-0154

Specializing in new and used video games and game systems, The

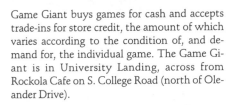
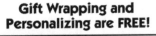
Game Giant buys games for cash and accepts trade-ins for store credit, the amount of which varies according to the condition of, and demand for, the individual game. The Game Giant is in University Landing, across from Rockola Cafe on S. College Road (north of Oleander Drive).

Hungate's Arts-Crafts & Hobbies
Westfield Shoppingtown Independence Mall, 3500 Oleander Dr., Wilmington • (910) 799-2738

Hungate's stocks an impressive inventory of art supplies, including stretched canvas. In addition to a huge assortment of model trains, planes and automobiles, the store carries rockets, toys, puzzles, novelties, miniature collectibles and books. This is a store for kids of all ages.

Learning Express
5704 Oleander Dr., Wilmington • (910) 397-0301

Learning Express, at the Courtyard on Oleander, is among those rare places that capture kids' imaginations with high-quality alternatives to the run-of-the-mill products. Interactive and entertaining, the store succeeds in making learning fun for kids from infancy through early adolescence. The staff includes education and child-development professionals with broad knowledge of the products, which translates into excellent service. Learning Express is organized in sections geared to particular interests, such as Whiz Kids (learning games and books for boys and girls), Science & Nature (including electronics and nature projects), Let's Pretend

(fantasy dress-up), Great Beginnings (for infants and toddlers) and Transit (including Thomas, Brio and Darda race tracks). This is the place to find that volcano your child needs for the diorama. Ask about professional discounts, free personalizing and Birthday Wish Buckets.

Pastimes Toys
Treasure Coast Square, 208-D N. New River Dr., Surf City • (910) 328-2737

Pastimes offers a variety of toys, most with educational value, for children of all ages and skill levels. You'll find games, books, crafts and something special for a rainy day as well as everything needed for a good time on the beach or outdoors in the sunshine. Owners Doug and Sherry Mewborn have years of experience and can assist shoppers in the selection of merchandise sure to stimulate or enhance a child's special interest.

Toys 'R' Us
4510 Oleander Dr., Wilmington • (910) 791-9067

The inevitable hunt for a child's toy may well lead you to this gargantuan chain toy store near the intersection of S. College Road.

U.S. Trolls
2305 Market St., Wilmington • (910) 251-2270

Children of all ages will enjoy troll dolls handmade by Helena, Minna and Johannes Kuuskoski. The trolls are really cute; some are furry, and all are for sale. Written description simply doesn't do this place justice. Make sure to check out this store with many unique and exciting things to

KIDSTUFF

see. There's parking in the rear of the building, with an easy exit to 23rd Street.

Animals

Despite the growing population of this region, it's not so hard to spot glimpses of nature here and there. In fact, it is not uncommon to witness hawks, ospreys and turkey vultures taking lunch breaks within Wilmington city limits. Deer are frequently sighted in outlying areas at dusk. And watching dolphins cavort mere yards offshore can be endlessly entertaining. To be truly among animals, especially of the petting or feeding-by-hand variety, also check Ashton Farm, listed in the Summer Camps section below, and Greenfield Lake, listed under Exploring Nature in this chapter and in our Attractions chapter.

Faircloth Exotic Animal Zoo
544 McKay Rd., Bolivia • (910) 253-6820

Have you ever seen Highland bulls or Watusi cows? Well, you can see them right here in eastern North Carolina, along with Texas Longhorns, Zebu cows, lions, bears, buffalo, camels, yaks, tigers, black leopards, monkeys, zebras, coatimundi and more at the privately owned and operated Faircloth Zoo. A petting zoo includes lambs and goats. The zoo is open year round from 9 AM until dusk.

Hugh MacRae Park
Oleander Dr., east of S. College Rd., Wilmington

Hugh MacRae Park is a quiet respite nestled between acres of trees right in the middle of busy Wilmington. Children love this park for the picnics, walks and many sights to see. The resident wildlife at the duck pond provides wonderful educational entertainment for children year round. Ducks march around the pond frequently, quacking as they go, especially when the park employees put out their weekly feed or when visitors offer bread. You'll often find ducks sleeping in the shade on warm afternoons. From the footbridge traversing the pond you get an excellent view of the many frogs, snapping turtles — from newborns to moss-backed elders — and fish that live beneath the water lilies. Some of the carp are of astounding size. Frogs are easiest to spot on the ground on damp mornings. Also look for spider webs, often quite large, among the bushes, but stay on the paths to avoid poison ivy. Plenty of shade trees and a gazebo invite picnicking. Be sure to bring your own beverages as there is no drinking water

available at the pond. Park restrooms and playgrounds are on the premises.

North Carolina Aquarium at Fort Fisher
900 Loggerhead Rd., Kure Beach
• (910) 458-8257

The North Carolina Aquarium at Fort Fisher reopened in March 2002 after being closed for two years for renovation and expansion. Located on the ocean, east of U.S. 421 and south of Kure Beach, (about 20 miles south of Wilmington), the Aquarium is now three times its original size and the largest of North Carolina's three aquariums.

With its 235,000-gallon saltwater tank, fascinating displays, interactive exhibits and 20,000-square-foot conservatory, the aquarium features "The Waters of the Cape Fear" from Raven Rock State Park south of Raleigh to the Atlantic Ocean. About 2,500 freshwater and saltwater creatures are on exhibit. A great new arrival in spring 2003 was a young, 30-pound green sea turtle, named for the color of its meat - not its shell; this means visitors can now see two sea turtle species instead of just one, the other being a loggerhead. Also new was a sea horse and salt marsh exhibit for the Coastal Waters gallery. The Aquarium is open daily 9 AM to 5 PM except Christmas, New Year's and Thanksgiving days. See our Attractions chapter for more information.

All three North Carolina Aquariums offer programs for people of all ages to learn more about aquatic life. The variety at the Fort Fisher facility includes everything from quickie "creature features" to half-day camps and workshops. Many activities require reservations and a nominal fee, but others are free with Aquarium admission.

Everyday visitors may encounter impromptu learning opportunities such as "smart-cart" presentations or "creature features" around the touchpool, the alligator exhibit or the moray eel cave. Videos about everything from sharks to shrimp are shown daily in the auditorium. Divers, using underwater sound equipment inside the Cape Fear Shoals tank, answer questions on a wide range of topics at least twice a day. And at 3 p.m. daily, you can watch aquarium staff feed some of the animals in their care. Educators are often present to field questions.

Surf-fishing workshops, crabbing and clamming, and salt-marsh canoeing are some of the scheduled activities that require advance sign-up and a fee. A new program called AquaCamp invites children ages 7 to 9 to participate in a special Saturday morning at the Aquarium.

Games, crafts, live animal presentations and more are all part of this three-and-a-half-hour program. Each session has a specific theme, such as sharks, reptiles, invertebrates or amphibians.

Aquarist Apprentice, another new program, lets participants join staff on a behind-the-scenes tour, help prepare animal diets and then participate in some daily care and maintenance tasks. Other programs include Breakfast with the Fishes, Aquarium Birthday Parties, Craft Classes, auditorium lecture series and more.

For advance program registration, call (910) 458-7468. Check the Aquarium website (www.ncaquariums.com) for program descriptions, fees and current schedules.

Arts

There's no better way to open a child's eyes to all the hidden beauty of the world than through the arts. Engaging in painting, music, dance and drama is also a terrific way to build a child's self-esteem and sense of community. Checking with the various parks and recreation departments in your area can be rewarding, since many of them offer art classes. Facilities hosting such activities are the Community Arts Center (see later entry), the Martin Luther King Jr. Center, 401 S. Eighth Street, (910) 341-7866, and the Derrick Davis Center in Maides Park, 1101 Manly Avenue (north of Princess Place Drive), (910) 341-7867. The latter two are administered by the Wilmington Recreation Intervention Division and offer free after-school activities that include arts and crafts. Wilmington also has an abundance of dance schools catering to young children.

Racine Center for the Arts
203 Racine Dr., Wilmington
• (910) 452-2073

A great place to enjoy the arts with your family, the Racine Center welcomes folks of all ages to visit this multi-faceted facility. Classes offering opportunities to learn pottery making, painting, printmaking, drawing, dance and other fine arts are available as are camps. All teachers are professional artists who love to teach within this warm, inviting atmosphere. Check out the wonderful galleries full of truly unique pieces at all price levels. Dine in the center's peaceful sculpture garden or check out items you'll find once in a Blue Moon.

Stages Inc. Touring Children's Theatre
808 Orange St., Wilmington
• (910) 772-1429

Stages Inc. is a non-profit touring company of professional actors who offer performances to children in grades 5 through 8. The shows are abridged versions of classical, contemporary and culturally diverse live theater. Yearly spring and fall tours consist of two show titles and cover both Carolinas, bringing the excitement of live theater to the community. Performances are about 50 minutes in length with question-and-answer sessions or study guides available upon request.

The Wilmington School of Ballet
214 Pine Grove Dr., Wilmington
• (910) 794-9590

This is Wilmington's only school dedicated exclusively to classical ballet. It emphasizes the fundamental basics of being a disciplined balle-

KIDSTUFF

rina. Ballet and modern dance classes are available for ages three to adult. Their innovative program for preschoolers (ages 3 through 5) utilizes movement props, music and imagery games to encourage learning the the joy of dance; they don't focus on the discipline of ballet until the child is mature enough. Beginning at age 6, training begins to take on more of the academic structure of a ballet class. Levels progress in a planned, sequential manner, each building on the previous level. Pre-professional training offers students the opportunity to study daily, preparing them for professional dance careers.

Serious students who take four or more dance classes a week can audition for "The Young Dancers of Wilmington," a nonprofit, in-house youth ballet company. In addition, The Wilmington School of Ballet participates in many outreach programs, including scholarships and summer camps for underprivileged youths.

The Wilmington Dance Academy
3333 Wrightsville Ave., Wilmington
• (910) 791-7660

This academy accepts children as young as 21/2 years old, who participate in creative movement classes something like a pre-dance class. "Mom and Me" classes are for ages 18 months to 21/2 years. With four teachers on staff, Wilmington Dance Academy has been operating since 1986 and teaches a variety of styles, including ballet, tap, jazz, hip hop and modern group acrobatics. A cheer team is popular for elementary through junior high students. Classes are taught Monday through Thursday.

Community Arts Center
120 S. Second St., Wilmington
• (910) 341-7860

This city-owned facility offers an annual July Arts Camp for school-age children that includes four one-week sessions of hands-on creative fun in practically every medium imaginable, such as painting, music, dance, acting and writing. Offerings change, so call for current information and register early. In addition to the Arts Camp, the Community Arts Center offers classes for children in dance, music and acting during the school year. Some adult classes are open to young adults ages 13 through 17 with permission of the instructor.

The center is managed by The Thalian Association, (910) 251-1788, the nation's oldest theater tradition. The Thalian Association Children's Theatre stages performances by young casts during the school year.

Firebird Ceramic Studio
The Forum Shopping Ctr., 1113 Military Cutoff Rd., Wilmington • (910) 509-2003

Painting your own pottery is a terrific family outing, and kids love it. Come experience the fun of creating a piece of pottery that's uniquely yours. Firebird Ceramic Studio offers a great selection of pottery, six paint lines and free instruction. You paint, they glaze and fire, and you end up with a memorable experience and a cool piece of pottery. You can bring in food and drinks. Count on having a fun, relaxing, enjoyable time.

Kindermusik of the Cape Fear Coast and MusicWorks of Wilmington
208 Treadwell St., Wilmington
• (910) 799-1656

Kindermusik is a program of music learning and movement for infants through 7-year-olds, designed to facilitate children's creative expression, listening, communication and group skills. It incorporates singing, movement, musical play and a practical approach to writing and reading the language of music. MusicWorks provides music education for grade schoolers. Instructor Janis Thomas also teaches several summer camps for infants to 12-year-olds.

The Music Loft
413 S. College Rd., Wilmington
• (910) 799-9310

The Music Loft is among the better music shops in town. It carries electronic instruments and equipment, specializing in electric guitars, bass and drums. Lessons are available. Luthier John Maertens provides expert repair of acoustic string instruments such as guitars, dulcimers and banjos. The Music Loft also has an in-house amplifier repair staff person.

Poplar Grove Plantation
10200 U.S. Hwy. 17 N., Wilmington
• (910) 686-9518

Each May, Poplar Grove Plantation and the Pender County School System sponsor "Arts in These Parts," an exhibit of student artwork. An opening day reception with refreshments is open to the public. Call for details.

Wilmington Academy of Music
1635 Wellington Ave., Wilmington
• (910) 392-1590

The Academy is a private school, founded in 1987, that offers a full range of music instruction in voice, piano, guitar, harp, violin, viola, cello, percussion, trumpet, trombone, clarinet, saxophone, flute, tuba, oboe, bagpipe and more for students of all ages. Theory, orchestration, arranging and other classes are available. Traditional Suzuki and jazz methods are offered. Weekly private lessons and monthly group lessons, recitals and master classes are offered. The school also offers the combined talents of faculty members and experienced local musicians in a variety of ensembles for weddings, receptions and special events.

Brunswick School of Dance
920 Ocean Hwy. W., Supply
• (910) 754-8281, (910) 754-6106

Housed in a remodeled country store since 1982, Brunswick School of Dance, now in its 21st year, specializes in teaching children from age 3 the basics of movement and strives to build self-esteem and confidence. Class size averages nine students. Most classes take place in the afternoon Monday through Thursday, but there are morning classes for preschoolers. Round-trip van pickup service is available. Styles taught to older students include ballet, tap, jazz, pointe and acrobatics. Adult classes include aerobics, ballroom dancing, shagging, tap and jazz. The school is convenient to most of the South Brunswick Islands.

Southport-Oak Island School of Dance
4805 Southport Supply Rd. SE (NC Hwy. 211) • (910) 454-0161

Oak Island School of dance offers a wide spectrum of styles including ballet, tap, jazz, pointe, hip-hop and creative movement. Students range in age from 3 years to adult. Dance students give a yearly dance recital in the Odell Williamson Auditorium at Brunswick Community College. Registration for classes is in August of each year.

SOLA - School of Learning and Art
216 Pine Grove Rd., Wilmington
• (910) 798-1700

SOLA offers something for creative children of all ages and abilities. Among the many wonderful programs are the following:

SOLA's Pre-School is a program for 3- to 5-year-olds offering a curriculum balanced with school preparatory academics, fine arts and developmental skills. Morning Half Day is from 8:30 AM to 12:15 PM; space is limited, so call for wait list information.

SOLA's After Pre-School Art Program is held from 12:45 PM to 3:30 PM. Drop-ins are welcome on a daily or weekly basis. This class is for 3- to 5-year-olds not registered for SOLA's morning pre-school. Students will experience a very

relaxed class, plenty of fun and exploration with pottery, paint, glue and more. Think of it as a very artsy midday pre-school.

SOLA's After-School program offers classes in drawing, painting, mixed media, pottery and music. Also available is a non-traditional after-school care program for young artists age kindergarten through 5th grade from 2:30 to 5:30 PM.

SOLA's Home School program can take care of the art and music instruction for your curriculum. Classes are designed to meet all media and cultural exposure across grade levels in a child-friendly art studio. Students are thoroughly immersed in the creative process. Parents are welcome to stay and play, too!

SOLA's Summer Camp for boys and girls puts the fun in summer camp; it features week-long sessions with age-appropriate groups and activities. Choose either Half Day Camp from 8:30 AM to 12:30 PM or Full Day Camp from 8:30 AM to 4:30 PM. Kids enjoy both indoor and outdoor activities Messy, fabulous arts and crafts are an integral part of every day. Students create pottery on the wheel and by hand, make their own T-shirts, experience paint and glue in ways they never have before while building a variety of theme-based projects. Campers play with new and old friends in a home-like workshop and backyard environment. Teachers at SOLA don't just babysit, they rock the house. Signing up is "easy as pie in the face!"

Wilmington Children's Museum
1020 Market St., Wilmington
• (910) 254-3534

Art every day! Visit the museum's art room for a variety of projects appropriate for ages 1 to 100. Using different art media, reclaimed "treasures" and items found in nature, museum staff will provide the inspiration for beautiful masterpieces. Programs vary from week to week; call for details. Toddler Time for preschoolers and adults is every Friday from 9 to 10:30 AM. This is a special time for the youngest museum visitors to enjoy art and science programs geared just for them. It's for ages 4 and younger only. The Wilmington Children's Museum hands-on exhibits and programs promote parental involvement in children's learning.

INSIDERS' TIP

Some activities for kids on rainy days: bowling, movies, skating, museum classes, library story times, the North Carolina Aquarium at Fort Fisher or one of the many other indoor attractions found in our Attractions chapter.

Birthday Parties

Gone are the days of simple birthdays with only presents and cake. Today's kids look forward to gatherings that include numerous physical activities from trampolines and gymnastics to skating and soccer. If you're looking for an extra-special place to give your child a memorable birthday party, look into these venues, offering colorful party rooms and various services. Some include the use of the arcades, games and more. And don't overlook your local bowling center; per-game prices for children younger than 12 are often discounted (see the Bowling section in our chapter on Sports, Fitness and Parks).

Coastal Tumblegym
220 Winner Ave., Carolina Beach
• (910) 458-9490, (910) 512-2686

Coastal Tumblegym hosts 90-minute birthday parties, usually on Saturday or Sunday afternoons (weekdays by special arrangement), featuring two certified professional instructors to lead the children in various physical activities. These may include mastering an obstacle course, playing on a trampoline, running relay races, working out on gymnastic equipment or traversing a 40-foot-long "Moon Walk" floor. Really popular is a 50-foot inflatable Seaweed Monster that's 12 feet high; inside is a slide and other fun stuff to climb on, over and under. Parents supply food and refreshments.

Firebird Ceramic Studio
The Forum Shopping Center, 1113 Military Cutoff Rd., Wilmington • (910) 509-2003

Both kids and parents love birthday parties at Firebird, where the birthday child receives an origi-

nal hand-painted plate (a $25 value) to be signed by all the children attending the party. With seven shelves of pottery to choose from, everyone will find something they'll enjoy painting, like dragons, fairies, dogs, horses, alligators or pretty boxes. You supply the children and Firebird supplies the instructions, paints, brushes, glazing and firing. Moms can bring a birthday cake and drinks, and Firebird will supply a colorful table, ice and balloons. The cost is $15 per child. Call for additional options.

Jelly Beans Family Skating Center
5216 Oleander Dr., Wilmington
• (910) 791-6000

Indoor roller skating can be a great way to celebrate birthdays, and Jelly Beans will provide everything you need for the party, including place settings, ice cream, refreshments, even the cake if you wish. Bonus: a host to serve and clean up afterward. Ask about other provisions, too, such as pizza (additional costs may apply). Choose among several skating sessions lasting two, three or four hours, depending on the day and time.

Jungle Rapids Family Fun Park
5320 Oleander Dr., Wilmington
• (910) 791-0666

Jungle Rapids offers several birthday packages that vary according to age and price. Choose from packages that include go-carts, laser-tag (for older children), waterpark (seasonal), a climbing wall, video games or minigolf. Packages feature play time, a party in a private room with a host, pizza and soda.

Ocean Breeze Family Fun Center
N.C. Hwy. 210, Sneads Ferry
• (910) 327-2700

Celebrate birthdays or special occasions with an organized party and special group rates. Miniature golf, go-carts and children's rides are just some of the activities to be enjoyed. Covered picnic tables provide a reserved area to open presents and celebrate with refreshments, including snow cones, popcorn, ice cream and more that is available at the center.

Putt-Putt Golf & Games
4117 Oleander Dr., Wilmington
• (910) 392-6660

Putt-Putt offers special deals for two-hour birthday parties that feature all the golf kids

can play in that time. In addition, each partygoer receives 20 tokens for video games (24 tokens for the kid of honor). Invitations, party favors, ice cream, soft drinks, a group photo, use of the party room and a special pizza deal are also included. The cost is $75 for 10 kids and $7.50 for each additional child.

Scooter's Family Skating Center
341 Shipyard Blvd., Wilmington
• (910) 791-8550

Party time at Scooter's is a great time for kids. The birthday child receives a 30-day skating pass, special announcement and a Scooter's T-shirt. The party kids get a skating pass and rental skates (note that inline skates cost $2.50). Pizza and soda are provided; all Mom needs to bring is a cake or cupcakes. The cost is $89 for up to 10 guests and $5 per additional child. Adult guests with the party are admitted free; if they wish to skate, there's a $1.50 rental fee.

Wilmington Children's Museum
1020 Market St., Wilmington
• (910) 254-3534

There are few birthday venues as educationally stimulating as the Children's Museum, where kids can pretend to be a pirate on a pirate ship, play dress-up with a variety of fun costumes, or get into any number of creative, artistic and entertaining activities with dedicated adult supervision. The Wilmington Children's Museum stimulates children's imagination, curiosity and innate love of learning. Birthday parties accommodate up to 15 children and include an art or science activity.

Wilmington Railroad Museum
501 Nutt St., Wilmington • (910) 763-2634

Conduct a birthday party on a real caboose at the Wilmington Railroad Museum. It's fun for the whole family: Thomas the Tank trains plus a hands-on play area for the younger ones, and a box car complete with hobos and a 1910 engine to climb aboard for children of all ages. While the kids are having a great time playing on the trains and going on a scavenger hunt, their parents can learn about the Atlantic Coast Line Railroad's fascinating history. Everyone will enjoy the large model train layouts and gift shop. So grab your engineer hat and railroad whistle, it's all aboard for a trainload of fun. The cost is $50 for members and $75 for non-members, which covers 10 children and 10 adults and includes a $5 gift certificate to the gift shop for the birthday child. Each child gets a paper engineer hat and a plastic whistle.

Eats

Most restaurants in our region cater to young people by offering well-priced children's menus. In addition to the usual assortment of fast food places and many chain restaurants, several local establishments are notable.

Carrabba's Italian Grill
15 Van Campen Blvd., Wilmington
• (910) 794-9094

At Carrabba's, children younger than 10 get complete activity books that include pages to color, mazes and games to play. Waitstaff give the little ones lumps of dough to make into

From the River to the Sea
It Doesn't Get Much Better Than This

Picture a six-story tall, 20,000-square-foot atrium filled with a variety of fresh water animals and hundreds of species of trees, shrubs, grasses and flowers, and not far away, a 25-foot deep, 235,000-gallon ocean water tank containing hundreds of creatures. Picture all that, and you'll have a rough idea of only a portion of what's in store for you when you visit the new North Carolina Aquarium at Fort Fisher.

The Aquarium was closed in 1999 and has re-opened in 2002 after two and a half years and over $17 million of renovation and expansion. The old aquarium, a popular tourist destination since its opening in 1976, was only about one-third the size of the new aquarium's approximately 90,000 square feet, and its largest tank was only 17,000 gallons. Today, the aquarium's exhibits total 455,000 gallons compared with the old aquarium's 77,000 gallons.

Beautifully situated on the sunny shore of the Atlantic Ocean, the North Carolina Aquarium at Fort Fisher boasts a total of 200 species and 2,500 animals, including sharks, alligators, barracuda, sea turtles, snakes, carnivorous plants, lobsters, moray eels, skates, rays, colorful reef fish, jellyfish, corals and sea cucumbers.

The Aquarium's 455,000 gallons of aquatic exhibit consists of 15 different tanks and streams plus the 235,000-gallon saltwater tank known as the Cape Fear Shoals Habitat. In addition, the Aquarium features the Rocky Outcrop Touch Tank, a pool in native coquina rock offering hands-on encounters with shoreline critters such as sea stars, horseshoe crabs, whelks, sea urchins, clams, conchs and hermit crabs—an exhibit sure to be popular with the kids.

The NC Aquarium offers exciting educational opportunities for kids of all ages.

With an overall theme of "Waters of the Cape Fear," the Aquarium showcases the aquatic animal and plant life on the Cape Fear River from just south of Raleigh as it meanders nearly 200 miles to the river's mouth, into the open ocean beyond.

Upon entering the atrium, known as the Cape Fear Conservatory, note the unique aluminum tubing and fiberglass 60 feet above, featuring sliding panels that allow natural light to enter. As you walk into the atrium, be sure to pause to examine the entrance wall explaining the "trip" you will be taking down the Cape Fear River to the sea.

The first water exhibit

continued on next page

you'll come to is Raven Rock, named for the state park where the journey to the sea begins. Featured in a series of pools and cascading water are striped bass, shortnose sturgeon, common carp and yellow perch. Farther downstream is a deep hole in the river where large predatory hunters lurk, seeking a meal. Called the Hidden Hunters, the tank features bowfin, channel catfish, chain pickerel, long-nose gar and others.

Next door, you'll find an exhibit of snakes of North Carolina, both venomous and non-venomous, including brown, red-belly, banded water snakes, cottonmouth and rat snakes, all comfortably behind glass.

Beyond the snakes, you'll come to the Town Creek exhibit featuring many small fish plus alligators and three species of turtles lounging on the river bank. Don't miss watching them underwater as they dive in for a refreshing swim.

Returning toward the center of the atrium, you'll approach the Roan Island exhibit as you pass over a wooden footbridge near a blackwater pond ringed by cypress. With water cascading over a fallen tree into a rushing stream, look through the glass behind the waterfall for the redear sunfish, pumpkinseed, bluegill, crappie and pickerel.

Over the footbridge, you will come to the Carolina Bay habitat area. Carolina Bays are shallow oval depressions found in abundance in North Carolina that are ringed by bay trees and depend on rain or underground springs for their water. These bays are home to frogs, toads salamanders and other amphibians that can survive dry periods. Near the bays, keep an eye open for the intriguing carnivorous plants—the pitcher plant, sundew and Venus's flytrap.

different shapes and then the masterpieces are taken to the kitchen for baking. By the way, both kids and parents love the Italian food, too.

Causeway Cafe
114 Causeway Dr., Wrightsville Beach
• **(910) 256-3730**

This is an extremely popular breakfast spot on Wrightsville Beach, just east of the drawbridge. The specialty pancakes and waffles are delectable and can be made in a variety of amusing shapes for children. Arrive early, especially on Sundays, and be sure to ask about the fresh fruit toppings of the day.

Chuck E Cheese's Pizza
4389 Oleander Dr., Wilmington
• **(910) 392-2531**

The ubiquitous Chuck E Cheese's has plenty of diversions to make eating a kid's least concern. A magical, fun place featuring games and rides for kids, this favorite family restaurant offers pizza, sandwiches and salad bar.

Elizabeth's Pizza
4304 Market St., Wilmington
• **(910) 251-1005**

Kids like the pizza and other Italian dishes but are fascinated by the several fish tanks that divide the room. It's open seven days a week.

Krazy's Pizza and Subs
417 S. College Rd., Wilmington
• **(910) 791-0598**

Family-owned and -operated since 1986, this restaurant has an expansive and reasonable menu featuring calzones, manicotti, a large children's menu and its famous Greek salad. There's also a video games the kids love, so be sure to bring lots of quarters. Mr. Magic often visits on Friday evenings to make balloon figures and perform a few magic tricks.

Rock-ola Cafe
418 S. College Rd., Wilmington
• **(910) 791-4288**

Rock-ola takes a tack similar to that of the famous Hard Rock Cafe, with classic rock 'n' roll and decorations, but less noise. Its menu includes several selections for children.

Sweets

No discussion of kidstuff would be complete without something for the sweet tooth. By sweets we mean not only candy but also baked goods and ice cream. As you travel the coast, you'll be tempted by all manner of strategically placed retailers who will dulcify your day. What follows here are some of the kings and queens of confectionery, the barons of bon-

bon. Read on at the risk of your waistline. Your kids will love you for it.

Wilmington

Apple Annie's Bake Shop
Outlet Mall, S. College Rd., Wilmington
• (910) 799-9023
Landfall Shopping Center, 1319 Military Cutoff Rd., Wilmington • (910) 256-6585
Two locations mean that satisfying a sweet craving will seldom take you too far out of your way. Baking everything fresh daily, Apple Annie's offers a sumptuous array of cakes, cupcakes, pies, cookies, breads and plenty more. This is one of those shops in which the air itself is intoxicating. For birthdays and other special occasions, Apple Annie's offers extraordinary custom creations. Kids cakes are out of this world! Just give them a picture, drawing, photo or other image and turn a cake into a personal statement — they can put just about any image on your cake using a computer process and a sugar laser printer. They'll also make 3-dimensional characters for the top. (Outlet Mall is a short distance south of the UNCW campus, next to Dick's Sporting Goods.)

Baskin-Robbins 31 Flavors Ice Cream and Yogurt Store
3809 Oleander Dr., Wilmington
• (910) 791-7192
Baskin-Robbins offers the typical wide variety of flavors, plus frozen yogurt, fat-free desserts and low-fat yogurt cakes. It's a great place for birthday cakes that are sure to please. Just make sure to order ahead of time.

The Candy Barrel
335 N. Front St., Wilmington
• (910) 762-3727
Situated in the Cotton Exchange downtown, The Candy Barrel features a wide assortment of taffy, fudge, jellybeans and candy by the pound, including scrumptious homemade chocolate clusters of many kinds. Come in Monday through Saturday between 10 AM and 5:30 PM to partake of sweet treats.

The Scoop Ice Cream & Sandwich Shoppe
365 N. Front St., Wilmington
• (910) 763-3566
A short walk from Wilmington's riverfront in the Cotton Exchange, "The Scoop" is just the place to grab a hot dog, sandwich or salad and milk shake for an on-the-go meal. Better yet, stay awhile and partake of such sinful creations as banana splits and peanut lovers sundaes. On those cool winter afternoons, stop in for a hot apple cider or cocoa and cookies. Especially popular in warm weather are the soda floats, including Egg Creams, Boston Coolers, Leap Frogs and Hobokens. Seating just outside the inviting shop offers an extremely pleasant shaded oasis in which to enjoy your lunch, snack or dessert in practically any season, but particularly on delicious warm days. It's a fine stopover for the weary shopper.

Swensen's
620 S. College Rd., Wilmington
• (910) 395-6740
San Francisco's contribution to great ice cream, Swensen's ranks high (some say highest) among local parlors. The Outrageous Sundaes are often too much for all but the most voracious eaters. The kids' treat called Mr. San Francisco is an ice cream creation shaped like a clown, with bubble-gum eyes and nose and a chocolate-dipped cone hat. Swensen's is a full-service restaurant and has a children's menu. A miniature train circles the ceiling of the dining room. Swensen's is a smoke-free restaurant.

Vic's Corn Popper
1616 Shipyard Blvd., Wilmington
• (910) 452-2869
343 S. College Rd., Wilmington
• (910) 794-7931
Popcorn in a sweets listing? You bet, especially if it's Vic's freshly made caramel corn. Vic's is an award-winning popcorn franchise, and you'll find more different kinds of popcorn than you may have ever seen before.

Wrightsville Beach

Kohl's Frozen Custard & Jumbo Burgers
92 S. Lumina Ave., Wrightsville Beach
6931 Market St., Wilmington
• (910) 452-2300
5658 Carolina Beach Rd., Wilmington
• (910) 350-0051
Not ice cream, but the more full-bodied custard is Kohl's claim to local fame. Whipping up homemade-style custard in vanilla and chocolate daily plus a special flavor of the day (sometimes two), Kohl's creates some mouth-watering concoctions with its custard. They also have

great cheeseburgers and hot dogs. The Wrightsville Beach store is closed during winter months.

Carolina Beach and Kure Beach

Dairy World
201 N. Fort Fisher Blvd., Kure Beach
• (910) 458-9788

This establishment, one block from the ocean, features a spacious, shady porch with plenty of bench seating, handicapped access and ample parking. Did we mention great ice cream? It's open seasonally.

Squigley's Ice Cream & Treats
208 S. Lake Park Blvd., Carolina Beach
• (910) 458-8779

With 4,050 flavors and taste sensations, this ice cream parlor offers something for everyone. They will make any flavor combination you desire, all that's required is imagination and a sweet tooth. A large board lists customers' favorite picks, such as cashews, Oreo and Butterfinger. You can also choose from ten toppings like blueberry, raspberry or peanut butter. Squigley's offers dozens of regular flavors for less daring folk. With lots of indoor and outdoor seating, Squigley's is a great choice for a tasty treat during the day or after dinner. Come get Squigled! It's open seasonally.

Southport

Lil and John's Sweetreat Ice Cream Parlor
810 N. Howe St., Southport
• (910) 457-9165

This old-fashioned ice cream parlor is a must for children of all ages. Lil and John have hand dipped 33 flavors of ice cream and made malts, shakes and ice cream sodas for 24 years. Customers are served at the long bar with barstools — reminiscent of the old ice cream bar you used to find in drug stores — or at tables and chairs sporting heart-shaped backs. Ask about their specialty — banana splits with one to ten scoops of ice cream.

South Brunswick Islands

Back Porch Ice Cream Shoppe
1572 Thomasboro Rd., Calabash
• (910) 579-1533

Back Porch, across from Callahan's Gift Shop, serves 21 hand-dipped ice cream and yogurt flavors, homemade waffle cones and plenty of other delights March through November of each year. Try the New Orleans Shaved Ice.

Topsail Island & Vicinity

Dairy Queen
Krystal Plaza Shopping Center, N.C. Hwy. 172, Sneads Ferry • (910) 327-1240
106 N. New River Dr., Surf City
• (910) 328-3112

Ice cream, cupcakes, ice cream cakes, floats, sundaes and DQ's famous blizzards make it hard to choose a favorite. If ice cream isn't your choice, hot dogs, and barbecue sandwiches are also on the menu. The Sneads Ferry Dairy Queen is open year round, Sunday to Thursday, 12 Noon to 7 PM, Saturday and Sunday 12 Noon to 9 PM. The Surf City store closes in the winter.

Exploring Nature

The most accessible, most affordable and most attractive sources of fun for kids on the southern coast are the same ones that draw adults in droves: the beaches and nearby waterways. So no matter what your kids' ages, get them down to the water, from Topsail to Calabash. Try a different beach now and then to pique their interest; there's a great difference in character from beach to beach.

Combining activities with beach visits may also be worthwhile. Driving a four-wheel-drive vehicle on the beach at the Fort Fisher State Recreation Area is a bouncy jaunt most kids love. The area offers pristine surf, calm tidal waters on the inland side suitable for toddlers, great fishing and, just minutes away, a fine Civil War museum and historic site. (See the Off-Roading section in our Sports, Fitness and Parks chapter.)

INSIDERS' TIP
Fans of model trains can get on the right track with the Cape Fear Model Railroad Club, (910) 763-2634, which meets at the Wilmington Railroad Museum, 501 Nutt Street, and welcomes novices as well as experts.

Carolina Beach State Park
Dow Rd., Carolina Beach • (910) 458-8206

In addition to all there is to do and see in this park (see our chapter on Sports, Fitness and Parks), the Sugar Loaf sand dune is one place that kids love. Running up and tumbling down is a simple pleasure, to be sure, perhaps the best kind. Elsewhere in the park, kids are challenged to locate the several carnivorous plants indigenous to the area: sun dews, pitcher plants and the famous Venus's flytrap. Be sure to instruct the children about the plants' rarity and delicacy, and leave them as you found them. You can visit the park from dawn to dusk.

Greenfield Lake and Gardens
U.S. Hwy. 421 S. (Carolina Beach Rd.), Wilmington • (910) 341-7855

Greenfield Lake and Gardens, a short drive down Third Street from downtown Wilmington, offers ideal outdoor entertainment for children. Toddlers will certainly enjoy feeding the many ducks and geese that gather at the lake shore. In fact, Greenfield Lake attracts many types of wildlife that will challenge a child's imagination and naming skills. Most youngsters love taking excursions in the paddle boats or canoes that can be rented at the dock on the north side of the lake just off Third Street. Playgrounds and picnic areas abound near the dock. Older children can enjoy a day's fishing from any of the lake's several small piers and bridges or from your own johnboat, which can be launched from the ramp on W. Lake Shore Drive, immediately east of U.S. 421. The park is open from dawn until dusk. (see our chapter on Sports, Fitness and Parks).

Oak Island Nature Center
5202 E. Yacht Dr., Oak Island • (910) 201-1392

The Oak Island Nature Center, in a beautiful setting overlooking the Intracoastal Waterway, provides binoculars so you can get an up-close look as you stroll the Talking Trees Walking Trail. The trails are marked with plaques and trees are identified with white signs. Inside the rustic building you will find exhibits and live animals including ferrets, guinea pigs, doves, rabbits, chinchilla, hedgehogs and moon crabs. Ask about special programs and classes.

Ev-Henwood Nature Preserve
6132 Rock Creek Rd. NE, Bolivia • (910) 253-6066

This 110-acre coastal forest nature preserve with its diverse variety of plants and animals is open to the public during daylight hours for hiking, research, bird-watching and nature appreciation. It contains 15 trails (about 7 miles), a picnic area and interpretive displays. It also includes several small creeks. Finding it may be a bit of a challenge, however. From U.S. Highway 17 S., exit onto Old Town Creek Road. Go to the stop sign, then turn right on Town Creek Road; go about 0.4 mile, turn left on Rock Creek Road — you'll see green and white directional signs along the way.

Farms

Ashton Farm
5645 U.S. 117 S., Burgaw • (910) 259-2431

Ashton Farm is 72 acres of historic plantation about 18 miles north of Wilmington. Owners Sally and Jim Martin provide children ages 5 through 12 with down-to-earth fun. Kids participate in farm life, sports with minimized competition and nature. Among the activities are swimming, canoeing, horseback riding, softball, hiking, crafts, animal care, rodeos and archery. (See Summer Camps later in this chapter.)

Brunswick County Center of the North Carolina Cooperative Extension Service
County Complex, Bolivia • (910) 253-2610

Educate your family by visiting a fully operational farm that specializes in beef cattle, swine and tobacco production. Or pick your own berries, tomatoes and other vegetables in season. Fresh-picked tastes so much better!

Holden Brothers Farm Market
5600 U.S. Hwy. 17 W., Shallotte • (910) 579-4500

Bring the kids to pick strawberries, sweet corn, cantaloupes, watermelons, pumpkins and other vegetables in season. The fields and market are open from April 1 through Christmas and are 3 miles south of Shallotte.

Lewis Strawberry Nursery & Farms
6517 Gordon Rd., Wilmington • (910) 452-9659

Picking berries can be almost as much fun as eating them. In late spring, peaking in May, the strawberries at Lewis' Nursery ripen into succulent concentrations of juicy, deep-red sweetness that almost defy belief. Whether you and the kids pick them yourselves or buy them by the quart, this is a treat you'll want to repeat. The Pick-Your-Own location is at Castle Hayne Road, near the

General Electric facility; it's open Monday through Saturday 8 AM to 6 PM and Sunday 1 to 6 PM.

Lewis' Gordon Road location is popular with locals for their strawberries, blueberries and blackberries, with the added attractions of homemade ice cream, potted plants and flowers for sale. Lewis Farms is open to the public only from April through mid-July, Monday through Saturday from 8 AM to 6 PM and Sunday from 1 to 6 PM. Gordon Road intersects Market Street (U.S. 17) just south of the Military Cutoff Road intersection and N. College Road near the junction with I-40.

Getting Physical

Check our chapter on Sports, Fitness and Parks for information on field and team sports for children of school age. Included in this section are physical activities that either apply specifically to young children or would otherwise fall through the cracks of the sports categories.

City of Wilmington Boxing and Physical Fitness Center
302 S. 10th St., Wilmington
• (910) 341-7837, (910) 341-7872

Administered by Wilmington Parks, Recreation and Downtown Services, the Center welcomes children ages 8 and older to participate in fitness training and professionally supervised boxing. Fitness equipment includes treadmills, stationary bicycles, stair climbers, free weights, weight machines, jump ropes, heavy bags, boxing gloves and scheduled exercise classes, all this for a facility use fee of only $40 per year for Wilmington city residents and $75 for non-residents. Hours are Monday through Friday 9 AM to 8 PM and Saturday 10 AM to 2 PM. Junior Olympic boxing is available for ages 8 to 16; call for competitive boxing information and fees.

Fit For Fun
302 S. 10th St., Wilmington
• (910) 341-4630

This program, sponsored by Wilmington Parks & Recreation Department, affords children from birth through 5 years the opportunity to play with parental involvement. The cost is $3.50 per child. Hours are Monday through Friday 9 AM to noon and 1 to 4 PM and Saturday 9 AM to noon.

Jelly Beans Family Skating Center
5216 Oleander Dr., Wilmington
• (910) 791-6000

Roller skating can be family fun at its best and perhaps simplest, and Jelly Beans appeals especially to kids and their parents. Grown-ups may appreciate the Top-40 music on Thursday nights. The rink is a clean, well-kept place with a well-stocked pro shop providing rentals, sales and repairs. Also available is a snack bar and the Stuff Shop, which sells toys and novelty items. Jelly Beans also hosts skating birthday parties and a summer day camp. Jelly Beans is near the intersection of Oleander Drive and Forest Park Road, 5 miles from downtown.

Star Skating Rink
260 Sneads Ferry Rd., Sneads Ferry
• (910) 327-2277

Star Skating offers skating Friday and Saturday nights (7 to 11 PM) and Saturday and Sunday afternoons (1:30 to 4 PM). Regular cost for evening skating is $5 and includes skates. The fee, including skates for the matinees, is $3. The charge to rent inline skates is $1 more. New this year is roller hockey on Monday evenings from 6 to 8:30 PM. The rink is available for parties on Saturday and Sunday. The snack bar sells popcorn, drinks and prepackaged sandwiches and snacks. The rink is open year round.

Topsail Beach Skating Rink
Anderson Blvd, Topsail Beach
• (910) 328-2381

Located over the Topsail Beach Post Office, this rink is open on Weekends from 7 to 10 PM in April and May. During the summer it's open nightly. The cost for admission and to rent skates is $5. Inline and traditional skates are available. Drinks and snacks are available for sale

The Martin Luther King Jr. Center
401 S. Eighth St., Wilmington
• (910) 341-7866

In the summer months, the Wilmington Recreation Intervention Division sponsors basketball for kids ages 6 to 17, divided into appropriate age groups. Other activities include field trips and games. The center has two 7-foot pool tables, bumper pool, Foosball, Ping Pong and air hockey. During the school year, the center is open Monday through Thursday for after-school homework time and games. Every second Friday the center features live entertainment in the afternoon.

Scooter's Family Skating Center
341 Shipyard Blvd., Wilmington
• (910) 791-8550

Scooter's is the current name for this classic rink, founded in 1959. Once you pass through the door, however, you walk right into the 21st

KIDSTUFF

century, complete with disco lighting show, sound system, special glow-in-the-dark carpeting and black lighting throughout the entire rink. Scooter's is a full-service roller skating center with a complete pro shop, snack bar and lots of video games to round out your night of fun. Birthday parties and fund-raising events are more than welcome.

The rink is open Wednesday 3 to 5 PM and 7 to 9 PM. On Friday night Scooter's skates from 7 to 11 PM; Saturday the rink is open from 1 to 11 PM with an all-day MegaSkate, an afternoon session from 1 to 6 PM and a night skate from 6 to 11 PM; on Sunday public skating is from 2 to 5 PM. For further information or to book a party, call the number listed above.

Getting Wet

As if the ocean weren't enough, this area offers plenty of other opportunities for kids to douse themselves, and some of them are downright thrilling, especially the water slides. One of the best is at the **Jungle Rapids Family Fun Park**, 5320 Oleander Drive, (910) 791-0666, in Wilmington. **Jubilee Park**, 1000 N. Lake Park Boulevard in Carolina Beach, (910) 458-9017, features a popular slide and the "Rain Room," a place to get nicely misted on a hot day. (Both locations are described in our Attractions chapter.) Most of these attractions are open seven days a week between Memorial and Labor days. Beyond these, kids can find places to get wet in our Watersports chapter or our Sports, Fitness and Parks chapter.

Go Fish

Captain Charlie's Kids Fishing Tournament
Southport City Pier, Waterfront Park, Southport • (910) 457-6964, (910) 457-7923

Held annually on the same weekend as the King Mackerel Tournament, the Kids Fishing Tournament fills the Southport Pier with junior anglers (up to age 16) while the senior anglers are out at sea. A joint effort of the Southport Recreation Department and the Southport Lions Club along with some retail sponsors, it is a big event for the kids, who bring their own rod and reel and bait. The first 100 kids receive a free T-shirt, and there are free hot dogs and drinks for everyone. There is a fish-bowl drawing for prizes throughout the tournament, the prize for the biggest fish is a rod and reel, and there are many other prizes

donated by merchants. Best of all, this is a catch-and-release tournament — an environmental lesson for kids.

Children's Crab Derby
Old Yacht Basin, Southport
• (910) 457-7945, (910) 457-7923

Have you ever seen a crab race? Sounds even better than a frog race, doesn't it? Bring your child (up to age 16), a small submergible basket or crab line and bait in early September and hope the tide is at its best for good crabbing! (But don't worry, a local commercial crabber usually stocks the yacht basin with some extras.) The children are divided into teams of two or three according to age. Prizes are given for the biggest crab and the most crabs caught in each age category.

Dorothy's Harbor Tours
636 Channel Blvd., Topsail Beach
• (910) 545-RIDE

Take a child on an exciting fishing adventure aboard the Dorothy, Topsail's newest cruise boat. This 2 1/2-hour educational fishing excursion offers the opportunity to catch pinfish, pigfish and various other species while learning about the various types of underwater marine life. All gear is supplied. Children younger than 7 must be accompanied by an adult. The cost is $20 per person, and available on site. Call for scheduled days. Trips are from 9 to 11:30 AM. Bring your own food and drinks (no alcohol, please).

Going Mental

Babbage's
Westfield Shoppingtown Independence Mall, 3500 Oleander Dr., Wilmington
• (910) 791-8168

Babbage's carries a fine selection of video games, CD-ROMs and computer games — many of them educational — in addition to its wide range of other computer software.

Books-A-Million
3737 Oleander Dr., Wilmington
• (910) 452-1519

This book superstore adjacent to Office Depot hosts story hours for young children every Saturday at 3:30 PM. When the children's section is otherwise quiet, kids enjoy playing on the "train-car" benches. The locomotive houses a TV that shows ongoing children's programming or videos to keep kids entertained while their parents browse nearby.

Brunswick County Library
Southport Library, 109 W. Moore St., Southport • (910) 457-6237
Leland Library, 487 Village Rd., Leland • (910) 371-9442
G.V. Barbee Branch, 818 Yaupon Dr., Oak Island • (910) 278-4283
Rourk Branch, 5068 Main St., Shallotte • (910) 754-6578

Story times, including books, music and crafts, for children ages 2 through 5 are offered at these Brunswick County public libraries at 10 AM on Monday at Southport, Tuesday at Leland, Wednesday at Oak Island and Thursday at Shallotte. Afternoon activities for school-age children from kindergarten up include special guests, speakers, stories, games and crafts and are held at 4 PM at Leland, Oak Island and Shallotte on the same days listed above. The Brunswick County Library also hosts a summer reading program for school-age children. The six-week program involves weekly meetings and activities at the branch libraries and awards incentive prizes. Be sure also to inquire about the library's weekly Preschool Music Hour, offering children the opportunity to sing, move creatively, play instruments and, in doing so — believe it or not — very possibly improve their spatial abilities and math skills. (Music really does make you smarter!) Participation in all library programs is free.

Cape Fear Astronomical Society
Wilmington • (910) 762-1033

Kids old enough to understand that those bright objects in the night sky are incredibly distant will appreciate the occasional sky observa-

It takes a lot of practice to get suntan lotion spread just right.

Photo: Jay Tervo

KIDSTUFF

tions, using members' telescopes, sponsored by the Astronomical Society to raise interest in membership. Viewing sessions are announced in the calendar of the *Wilmington Star-News*.

The public is also invited to the society's monthly meetings, which feature interesting films and presentations. Meetings take place on the first Sunday of each month (or the second, if delayed by a holiday) and are also announced in the newspaper. The society is open to everyone of any age, regardless of any astronomical knowledge, and young teenagers are among its current members.

In addition to the popular public viewing sessions, the society also undertakes periodic school talks and trips to planetariums. Membership has one prerequisite, if you could call it that: a sincere interest in astronomy and in learning more about it. Memberships cost $20 per year ($25 for families) and include the society's monthly newsletter, Cape Fear Skies, and the Astronomical League's quarterly publication, *Reflector*. Members can also get reduced subscription rates to Sky and Telescope and Astronomy magazines.

Ronnie Hawes, the club's associate vice president, teaches an astronomy class at UNCW in the Division for Public Service and Continuing Studies in the spring quarter. The class is presented in a non-technical format and is designed for anyone interested in the night sky. The society's mailing address is 305 N. 21st Street, Wilmington, NC 28405.

New Hanover County Public Library
**Main Branch, 201 Chestnut St.,
Wilmington • (910) 341-4392
Carolina Beach Branch, 300 Cape Fear
Blvd., Carolina Beach
• (910) 458-5016
Myrtle Grove Branch, 5155 S. College Rd.,
Wilmington
• (910) 452-6414
Northeast Regional Library, 1241 Military
Cutoff Rd., Wilmington • (910) 256-2173**

The Children's Rooms at these libraries are excellent resources for stimulating entertainment that isn't limited to story times. Activities are designed for children in three age groups. Toddler Time offers stories, songs and interactive finger plays just for babies ages 18 months through 3 years and their parents. Preschool Storytime may include films and is geared for ages 3 through 5. The Toddler and Preschool events are offered weekly on different days at the different library branches, giving you a choice of schedules. Book Break, offered during the summer, is a weekly storytime for children

ages 6 through 10 that offers longer stories, read-alouds, activities and films. All programs are free and open to the public.

Other library programs are cut from a wide and colorful cloth. Recurring programs include a Babysitter's Workshop, designed to teach young people ages 12 through 15 about babysitting, safety, child development, simple snacks and activities. Holiday programs include an annual selection of ghostly tales for Halloween and a Christmas crafts program that provides decorations for trimming library and family trees. Family programs may present history as related in song, African dance or readings by children's authors. Call the library's Youth Services office at the number above to inquire about schedules and registration, which may be limited for some workshops.

Fort Fisher Aquarium Outreach Program
Assembly Bldg 720 Channel Blvd, Topsail Beach • (910) 329-4446

Touch and learn about sea creatures! This popular outreach program from the North Carolina Aquarium at Fort Fisher is a one-hour presentation on invertebrates held every Wednesday afternoon during July and August from 1 to 2 PM. Children enjoy the educational experience of touching and learning about sea creatures. A donation of $5. per family is requested. The Topsail Island Historical and Cultural Arts Council sponsors this event.

Quarter Moon Book Store
708 S. Anderson Blvd., Topsail Beach • (910) 328-4969

From toddler to teenager, Quarter Moon has a great selection of books, puzzles and games. Much of the merchandise is selected for its educational value and topics to correspond with the beach and local environment.

Wilmington Children's Museum
1020 Market St., Wilmington • (910) 254-3534

The Children's Museum is a colorful, exciting space where kids up to age 12 can engage in activities that will enhance lifelong learning and creativity. Programs focus on the arts, science and technology, health and safety, mathematics, multicultural studies and the environment. In its storefront setting, the museum features a two-deck pirate ship complete with treasure maps and costumes; a fully-stocked grocery store complete with cash register and shopping carts introduces basic math concepts. Kids of all ages enjoy the theater stage where they can become different personalities using a variety of costumes and props.

Kids love to visit the "Let's Go Lego" exhibit and create a masterpiece on the mosaic wall or build a racecar to race down the indoor track. Youngsters can learn about the different properties of sand by pouring and sifting. Then they can look over a collection of 300 sand samples from around the world. Check out the purple sand!

The Art and Science classrooms always have exciting programs designed to spark a child's curiosity and innate love of learning. Explore with microscopes in the computer lab or maybe learn about what makes stars twinkle at night. The Art Studio is designed to introduce children to a multitude of arts media and methods while enhancing the capacity for learning and creativity.

The Children's Museum is entirely volunteer-driven and welcomes new participants. It is open Tuesday through Saturday from 10 AM to 5 PM; it's open on Mondays as well during June, July and August. Admission is $3.50 per person.

Holidays

The holidays are a special time for families. Be sure to check the local newspaper for details of specific events happening in the area, since the southern coastal region is known for going all out for every celebration. Christmas is filled with too many events to mention, such as the Poplar Grove Christmas Open House

Poplar Grove Historic Plantation, 10200 U.S. 17 N., (910) 686-9518 Ext.26; the Island of Lights Festival, held at various locations in Carolina Beach and Kure Beach, (910) 458-7116; and the Christmas By-The-Sea Festival in Oak Island and Southport locations, (910) 457-6964. Check these and other holiday happenings in our Annual Events chapter. Listed here are some offerings grouped by holiday. Be sure to stop by or phone the Cape Fear Coast Convention & Visitors Bureau at 24 N. Third Street in Wilmington, (910) 341-4030, (800) 222-4757, for the latest Calendar of Events; you can also access it online www.cape-fear.nc.us.

Easter

Easter Egg Hunt
Franklin Square Park, W. West and Howe Sts., Southport • (910) 457-7945
This citywide Easter egg hunt is held every year the Saturday before Easter in Franklin Square Park, where there are plenty of hiding places. Nine hundred plastic eggs with prizes inside and 10,000 candy eggs are scattered throughout the park to the delight of the participating children.

Easter Egg Hunt
Hugh MacRae Park, S. College Rd., Wilmington • (910) 395-1940
Hosted by the Wilmington Jaycees for the past 29 years, the annual Easter egg hunt is a great time for some 3,000 youngsters ages 10 and younger. Volunteers place more than 10,000 hollow plastic eggs filled with candy in "hiding places." The participating children are divided into age categories and assigned specific hunting areas. When the horn sounds on the appointed day, bedlam ensues.

Halloween

Haunted Wilmington Walking Tours and Other Fun Things
Join some of the area's most renowned local actors and ghost hunters as they lead you through old alleyways and down dark streets on a journey into the depths of Old Wilmington. Meet the poor souls who still haunt our fine city. Hear tales, both past and present. The Ghost Walk of Old Wilmington conducts a nightly walking tour throughout the year. The tour meets year round by the Riverfront at the foot of Market Street. Hours are April 1st through October 31st at 8:30 PM, plus Tuesday through Saturday at 6:30 PM; from November 1st through March 31st, the tours are Tuesday through Saturday at 6:30 PM. Special Halloween times vary. You're advised to call ahead, (910) 602-6055.

On the last Saturday and Sunday in October just before Halloween, the Bellamy Mansion, 503 Market Street, sponsors a weekend of fun ghost stories and legends and kid-friendly entertainment. You can visit many haunted, spooky homes. Tickets are $10 in advance and $12 the day of the tour. For information call (910) 251-3700.

Poplar Grove, (910) 686-9518, has more than 20 years of experience in the fine art of Halloween scariness, too. The Haunted Barn and Haunted Hayride are guaranteed to bring up some goose bumps, and all the little kids love the fun house. Professional rides and carnival games, tarot card and palm readings, colorful decorations and plenty of food are big draws, too. A costume contest,

KIDSTUFF

Take a wild ride on a waterslide.

Photo: Jay Tervo

puppet show with handmade puppets and other fun stuff make a ghostly trip to Poplar Grove a must....... fun for all ages.

The Wilmington Jaycees, (910) 395-1940, have as much fun as the kids do around Halloween. Watch the paper for dates and times to visit their famous Haunted House, which changes locations from year to year. Each room has a different theme and lots of fright-filled moments.

Kwanzaa

This seven-day African-American cultural celebration is observed yearly in the Wilmington area during the week between Christmas and New Year's Day. The word refers to the harvest's "first fruits." During the holiday, people use each day to meditate on one of the holiday's seven principles: umoja (unity), Kujichagulia (self-determination), ujima (collective work and responsibility), ujamaa (cooperative economics), nia (purpose), kuumba (creativity) and imani (faith).

Edens Institute, a nonprofit organization that promotes African-American and multicultural heritage programs, has an annual Kwanzaa celebration which features food, music, a lighting ceremony, crafts for kids, African dancing and vendors. Watch for announcements in the Friday "Currents" section of the *Wilmington Star-News*. For information, call (910) 254-0708.

Public radio WHQR 91.3 FM, broadcasts its own Kwanzaa production, "Season's Griot," created and performed by local storyteller and musician Madafo Lloyd Wilson together with other storytellers from around the country. This hour-long program is distributed nationally as a holiday special broadcast. Call for details and program times (910) 343-1640.

Christmas

Christmas Lights at Kings Grant

The Kings Grant subdivision off N.C. Highway 132 (North College Road), is a must-see for kids and adults during the weeks prior to Christmas. Each year, residents adorn their homes with an incredible array of lights and decorations, attracting caravans of people who turn off their headlights to view the spectacle in all its glory. Turn right onto Kings Drive, which is about 1.25 miles north of the Market Street overpass. Just follow the line of cars; you can't miss it!

Santa Claus at Westfield Shoppingtown Independence
3500 Oleander Dr., Wilmington
• (910) 392-1776

Santa Claus arrives at the mall every year in mid-November and remains ensconced in winter glory until his midnight ride on Christmas Eve.

Summer Camps

Summer is the main anticipation of almost any school-aged child, but it can be tiring for parents, especially those who work, to invent fun, imaginative activities for their children day after day. Summer camps are a great antidote for this problem. The southern coast offers many different camps for you and your child to choose from. Day camps and sports camps (rather than overnight camps) are the norm in the southern coastal region. For sports camps, children must own basic personal equipment, including protective gear. Team items such as bats and balls are provided. Be sure to review our chapter on Sports, Fitness and Parks as well. Day campers generally need only swim suits, towels and sneakers to get the most out of their camp experiences.

An extremely useful publication, Summer Alternatives, lists dozens of summer activities for school-age children in our area. It is distributed in late April by the New Hanover County Schools and may be obtained free by calling the Community Schools office at (910) 254-4221.

Ashton Farm Summer Day Camp
5645 U.S. 117 S., Burgaw • (910) 259-2431

Ashton Farm, established in 1975, is 72 acres of historic plantation about 18 miles north of Wilmington. Owners Sally and Jim Martin provide children ages 5 through 12 with down-to-earth fun. Kids participate in farm life, sports with minimized competition and nature. Among the activities are swimming, canoeing, horseback riding, softball, hiking, crafts, animal care, rodeos and archery and more.

One-week sessions from June to August are available (daily with permission). Discounts apply for additional weeks and/or additional children registered. The camp provides round-trip transportation to Wilmington, camper health insurance and drinks; children should pack their own lunches. Single-day camps have been added to coincide with teacher workdays.

Brigade Boys & Girls Club
2759 Vance St., Wilmington
• (910) 791-4282

Serving area children since 1896, the Brigade Boys & Girls Club is a popular place for summer activities. Between the last day of school and the first day back, kids enjoy a wide variety of games, sports competitions of all sorts, reading, arts and crafts. The regular summer program runs Monday through Friday from 10 AM to 6 PM. The Sunriser program begins at 6:30 AM. Youngsters are divided according to age groups: 6 through 11 years and 12 to 18 years. A swimming pool with certified lifeguards makes this a great place to spend a hot summer day; some swimming instruction is available.

Brunswick County Parks and Recreation Department
Planning Bldg., Government complex,
Bolivia • (910) 253-4357, (800) 222-4790

Summer sports camps in baseball, soccer and wrestling are offered at various parks in Brunswick County from June through August. Register early.

Cape Fear Museum
814 Market St., Wilmington
• (910) 341-4350

A variety of activities involving local history and nature are available to children ages 5 through 12 in half-day and full-day camps at the museum, five days a week from June through mid-August. Call weekdays between 9 AM and 5 PM for information and to register. (Also see our Attractions chapter.)

Carolina Coastal Adventures Camp
Carolina Beach • (910) 458-9111

In July Through August, week-long fun camps for kids include lessons in surfing, kayaking and fishing plus visits to the North Carolina Aquarium at Fort Fisher, hiking in the State Park and marsh exploration. When the weather doesn't cooperate, kids keep busy with games, crafts and videos with a marine science theme.

Emma Anderson Memorial Chapel Youth Program
1101 S. Anderson Blvd., Topsail Beach
• (910) 328-1619 or (910) 328-1532

This long running program by the Emma Anderson Memorial Chapel has families planning their vacation around program dates. Daytime activities for children and youth ages 6 to 19 are offered Monday through Friday during the summer months. A schedule of events is prepared weekly, and activities can include beach volleyball, fishing on the pier, miniature golf, pizza parties, a cookout, basketball, volleyball, billiards, ping pong and more. Participants can come for one day or the whole program. There is no cost to attend this program that often offers opportunities to include parents and other family members.

Girls Inc. Day Camp
1502 Castle St., Wilmington
• **(910) 763-6674**

Girls Inc. offers half-day and full-day camps in Wilmington and Burgaw from about one week after school lets out for summer break until one week before school resumes. Activities include sports, crafts, swimming, computer classes, sewing, field trips, career exploration, science projects and cooking. Guest speakers are brought in from time to time. The Wilmington camp accepts only girls from kindergarten to age 18. The Burgaw camp accepts boys and girls from kindergarten through age 15. Call for information and to register.

Jelly Beans Family Skating Center
5216 Oleander Dr., Wilmington
• **(910) 791-6000**

Jelly Beans' summer day camp, for kids ages 5 through 12, is especially convenient (and affordable) because your child can just drop in for a single day at a time. While roller skating is a natural part of regular activities, Jelly Beans concentrates heavily on outdoor and educational field trips.

North Carolina Aquarium at Fort Fisher
Kure Beach • (910) 458-8257,
(910) 458-7468

Aquarium summer camps promise learning and fun for youngsters in three age groups — 5 and 6 years old, 7 through 9 and 10 through 12. Scheduled Monday through Friday from 8:30 AM to 12:30 PM, sessions are offered in June and July. Each group of 12 campers will enjoy age-specific, fun-filled outdoor activities, including crafts and programs that help kids understand and appreciate aquatic environments.

UNCW Athletic Department
601 S. College Rd., Wilmington
• **(910) 962-3233**

UNCW sponsors day and overnight summer sports camps in baseball, basketball, swimming and diving, tennis, track, volleyball and soccer. These sessions give younger players a good foundation for the sports and emphasize fundamentals. Attendees for the "Learn To Swim" camp may be as young as 3 years old or as old as seniors in high school. Camps are also available for men's and women's basketball. Call for information early in the season, as these camps tend to be quite popular.

UNCW MarineQuest
601 S. College Rd., Wilmington
• **(910) 962-2386**

The University of North Carolina at Wilmington's Division for Public Service and Continuing Studies invites kids to become part of MarineQuest, one of the most unique marine and environmental education programs in the country. MarineQuest encompasses a wide variety of marine and education programs for ages 7 through adult. For information about Summer by the Sea Camp, Coast Trek, Oceanlab, Marine Biology Camp for Teens, Chemistry Camp, Ocean Commotion and others, call the information line at (910) 962-2386.

City of Wilmington Recreation Division Adventure Pathways Summer Camp
302 Willard St., Wilmington
• **(910) 343-4750**

For kids who truly enjoy challenging physical activities and like being on the move, the Adventure Pathways programs are just the ticket. Guaranteed not to be boring, the week-long excursions, held in June, literally go in three different directions. Sessions for boys and girls ages 10 to 14 include exploration, watersports, hiking, climbing and overnight camping. A more rigorous week-long excursion is available for boys and girls ages 14 to 17. Space is limited. Fees range from $175 to $250; registration begins at the end of February.

Wrightsville Beach Parks & Recreation Department
1 Bob Sawyer Dr., Wrightsville Beach
• **(910) 256-7925**

Summer Day Camp, Art Camp, Soccer Camp and Creative Performance Arts Camp are among the fun offerings for kids sponsored by

KIDSTUFF

Camp Tuscarora
Wilmington Family YMCA

Swimming, crafts, games, field trips, nature
hikes and more! Remember those carefree days
spent at YMCA summer camp?
Camp Tuscarora Ages 5-12
C.I.L.T. Teen Adventures Ages 13-15
2710 Market Street, Wilmington, NC 28403
(910) 251-9622

We Build strong kids, strong families, strong communities.
A United Way Agency

the Wrightsville Beach Parks & Recreation Department. How about kayaking, surfing or tennis lessons? Call for a brochure and more information.

YWCA of Wilmington
2815 S. College Rd., Wilmington
• (910) 799-6820

YWCA summer day camps for tots and juniors (from kindergarten through age 14) operate June through August on weekdays. The "Y" is open for daytime activities from 6:30 AM to 6 PM; a night care program runs from 6 PM to 12 midnight. Among the many fun things to do, kids can participate in pool swimming, roller skating, indoor and outdoor sports, arts and crafts, reading, music and games. Each grade leader has different themes, appropriate to her age group. Field trips to the beach, local attractions and other kid-friendly places are popular. Stop by to register weekdays between 8 AM and 6 PM.

Chamber Music Society of Wilmington

2003-2004 Season

McKenzie - McCallum Duo

Daedalus String Quartet

Carolina Piano Trio

Mallarmé Chamber Players

Jane Bryden & Friends

Sunday Evenings
October - April
Thalian Hall Ballroom

Ticket Info.
(910) 343-3664

The Arts

North Carolina claims a long and rich history in the arts, and the southern coastal region, especially Wilmington, nurtures that heritage with a wide range of mediums and talent in artistic expression. Seemingly removed from the large cultural centers of the country, Wilmington, with its coastal and historical ambiance, competes as a major center for the visual and performing arts. On any given day year-round the community's calendar overflows with diverse and intriguing cultural events. On occasion, Insiders lament not the lack of things to do, but the fact that they can't possibly take advantage of all the rich opportunities.

Residents of the southern coast find exciting entertainment showcased by the many established institutions devoted to the arts, including the Thalian Hall Center for the Performing Arts, Louise Wells Cameron Art Museum in Wilmington and the Odell Williamson Auditorium in Brunswick County. Touring exhibitions and artists as well as tremendously talented locals create a rich pool of talent unheard of outside the larger cultural centers. In addition to a community already rich in theatrical talent, the film industry established a working movie studio in Wilmington in 1985. It attracts film production companies and professional actors to the area on a regular basis. Often, while working on location here, many of these actors — John Travolta, Sandra Bullock, Paul Newman, Linda Lavin and Pat Hinkle, to name a few — share their expertise with local actors and thrill local audiences with performances on area stages. Some choose to stay and become a part of the working arts community.

Wilmington, especially the lively downtown area, is the hub of arts organizations and activities for the region, and it lures musicians, painters, actors, filmmakers, sculptors and dancers to the coffeehouses and cafes to discuss their crafts. Clubs and restaurants serve up a stimulating offering of live music and theater on a regular basis.

Cinematique, an ongoing showcase for "classic, foreign and notable films" is jointly sponsored by public radio station WHQR and the Thalian Hall Center for the Performing Arts. The films are screened in Thalian Hall, where the palpable history and opulence add an amazing mood to the screening. On occasion, capacity crowds have held a popular film beyond the normal Monday-through-Wednesday-night screenings.

Music is another vital part of the regional arts scene. Wilmington has its own symphony orchestra, a vibrant chamber music series, a regular concert series and dozens of ensemble groups ranging from professionals to enthusiastic amateurs.

Theater companies are plentiful and employ the talents of locals in writing, music and performance. There are several stages in town, including Thalian Hall, Kenan Auditorium and Trask Coliseum at the University of North Carolina at Wilmington, and the Scottish Rite Temple.

Touring companies regularly visit Wilmington, particularly during the Azalea Festival in the spring and Riverfest in the fall. Over the centuries, Wilmington has hosted such notables as Lillian Russell, Maurice Barrymore, Oscar Wilde and John Philip Sousa. Come closer in time and consider this diverse collection of performers: Al Hirt, Chet Atkins, Frank Sinatra, The Ciompi String Quarter, Judy Collins, Koko Taylor, Itzak Perleman, Roberta Flack, Reba McEntire, Kenny Rogers, Charlie Daniels, the Beach Boys and Ray Charles. In neighboring Brunswick County, audiences at the Odell Williamson Auditorium, located on the campus of Brunswick Community College, have thrilled to an equally impressive roster of performers, including The Tommy Dorsey Orchestra, Doc Watson, The Lettermen, Mike Cross, the Preservation Hall Jazz Band, Lee Greenwood, The Platters and The Glenn Miller Orchestra.

The visual arts occupy a prominent position in the cultural experiences of North Carolina's southern coast. In addition to several commercial art galleries, particularly in the Greater Wilmington area and Southport, the region has Louise Wells Cameron Art Museum, regarded as one of the finest small art museums in the Southeast. Local artists also find appealing venues for display in area restaurants, coffeehouses and upscale shopping centers.

North Carolina's southern coast region is a rich environment for the arts, offering a variety of opportunities for both creating and enjoying the cultural arts. This chapter lists just a sampling of the arts scene in the region.

Museums, Performance Halls and Organizations

Acme Art Inc.
711 N. 5th St., Wilmington
• **(910) 763-8010**

An avant-garde renovation of an old warehouse is the perfect home for this artist-owned and operated studio. The working environment zings electric with artists running their drills, welding with their blowtorches and dueling airbrushes on bold mats of color. The gallery space is upgraded with track lighting, and opening exhibits are warm and friendly.

Associated Artists of Southport
130 E. West St., Southport
• **(910) 278-5562, (910) 457-5450**

Housed in historic Franklin Square Gallery in Southport, this nonprofit organization provides an increasingly rich environment for the growth and development of local visual artists. It is dedicated to the cultural enrichment of the community through education and the promotion of original art. There are regularly scheduled workshops in various media by recognized artists as well as judged exhibitions and competitions, all of which are open to the public. A national juried competition and exhibit is held each July in conjunction with the N.C. Fourth of July Festival. A drawing class is held at the gallery every Thursday, year round, and is free to the public. In conjunction with Brunswick Community College, pottery classes are conducted in the pottery studio behind the gallery. In 2001 the Southport Recreation Department conducted a pottery class for exceptional children in the pottery studio. Painting and pottery classes for children of the community are conducted yearly and are partially funded by grants from the Brunswick Arts Council and Brunswick County Community Foundation.

Art in the Park is a community fun day, free to the public, sponsored by the Associated Artists, Brunswick County Parks and Recreation Department and Southport Parks and Recreation Department. Association members serve as instructors, speakers and judges for local schools and organizations. Monthly meetings are the third Monday of each month. Call for more information or a membership application.

Brunswick County Arts Council
130 E. West St., Southport
• **(910) 371-1795**

Established in 1981, this nonprofit volunteer organization is Brunswick County's primary arts information and funding source. Arts funding through the National Endowment of the Arts is channeled to this group from the North Carolina Arts Council. With money received for 2002, the Brunswick Arts Council provided financial assistance for approximately 18 local arts groups through Grassroots Arts Program grants; sponsored community events such as Art In The Park; and published a directory of Brunswick County artists and art groups called "Artists In Our Midst" as well as sponsoring the Brunswick County Arts Council Art Show. This valuable resource for local arts information is available through the organization and the Southport-Oak Island Chamber of Commerce, (910) 457-6964. Membership in the council is open to anyone interested in the arts. The range of interests include the visual arts — painting, pottery, sculpture, photography, woodworking, quilting and handwork — and the performing arts of music, drama and dance. President Victor Gerloven invites anyone who is interested to attend monthly meetings held at Brunswick Community College.

The Community Arts Center
120 S. Second St., Wilmington
• **(910) 341-7860**

The Community Arts Center, formerly the

Wilmington U.S.O., is a part of Wilmington's Parks and Recreation Department and is located in the center of historic downtown. Primarily a learning facility where anyone many go to take low-cost lessons in a full range of disciplines, the Community Arts Center also services as a rehearsal space for most of Wilmington's community theater groups. The Thalian Association community theater manages the building for the City and has offices and rehearsal space within the Center. For nominal fees, students of all ages can experience hands-on work under the direction of skilled local artists. In addition to workshops and classes, other programs include performances, concerts and fund-raisers, usually staged in the Center's Hannah Block 2nd Street Stage theater area of the facility.

Oak Island Art Guild
Oak Island • (910) 278-3000

The Oak Island Art Guild, sponsored in part by the Brunswick County Arts Council, meets the second Friday of each month at the Oak Island Recreation Center. Free workshops in watercolor, oils, acrylic, pastel, pen-and-ink, batik, colored pencil, clay, collage, tile painting, glass painting, enameling, calligraphy, portraits, abstracts and more are held monthly. Each year The Guild awards two $600 scholarships to high school seniors who are planning to major in an arts-related field. It donates arts books and videos to the local library, provides monthly art projects for residents at the Ocean Trail Nursing Home and sponsors the Labor Day Arts and Crafts Fair. In cooperation with the Parks and Recreation Department, the Guild is involved in the Silver Arts Exhibit, Arts by the Shore, the Summer Arts Camp and the Celebration of Oak Island.

Odell Williamson Auditorium
Brunswick Community College, 150 College Rd., Supply • (910) 343-0203 ext. 406

Built in 1993 by the citizens of Brunswick County for the educational and cultural enrichment of the community, this 1,500-seat state of the art facility on the campus of Brunswick Community College offers entertainment opportunities in the heart of Brunswick County. In its short history, this center for the arts has presented the talents of the North Carolina Symphony, the U.S. Marine Band, the Kingston Trio, Jerry Reed, the All American Boys Chorus, the North Carolina Shakespeare Festival, the Tommy Dorsey Orchestra, The Lettermen, Lee Greenwood, Pebo Bryson, a presentation of

The Odd Couple starring Jamie Farr and William Christopher (Klinger and Father Mulcahey from the TV show M*A*S*H) and various national touring companies performing such classics as Death of a Salesman. A recent innovation is K.I.S.S. (Kids Incredible Show Series), which presents programs especially for the little ones but loved by all. The auditorium and lobby are available for private and public rental. The auditorium has a subscription season each year. For tickets call (910) 755-7416 or (800) 754-1050 ext. 416. Look for special events planned for September 2003, the tenth anniversary of the facility.

Louise Wells Cameron Art Museum
3201 S. 17th St., Wilmington
• (910) 395-5999

An exciting new addition to the region's arts community, the Louise Wells Cameron Art Museum (formerly St. John's Museum of Art in downtown Wilmington) opened its new state-of-the-art facility on April 21, 2002. Situated on the corner of Independence Boulevard and 17th Street, this 42,000-square-foot museum was designed by renowned architect Charles Gwathmey, who characterizes the building itself as an abstract sculpture.

The Cameron Art Museum is the only American institution whose primary purpose is to collect, display, preserve and archive North Carolina art. This exceptional museum houses a stunning permanent collection of 18th-century to contemporary North Carolina art, including the works of such artists as Mary Cassatt, Minnie Evans, Claude Howell and Elisabeth Augusta Chant, in the 7,200-square-foot Permanent Collection wing. This wing, composed of 10 individual galleries, boasts much of the artwork owned by the museum itself, as well as the exhibition "From Sea to Shining Sea: American Treasures from the North Carolina Museum of Art." In addition to the permanent collection, six to eight changing exhibitions are presented each year in the Featured Exhibition wing located beneath the museum's signature pyramidal skylights. This area can be divided into as many as four individual exhibition spaces.

The Cameron Art Museum also features the Galleria, home to the museum's ceramic and decorative arts collections; a sculpture court; The Forks Restaurant; a reception hall; and the museum shop, which holds a special corner for children. Civil War buffs will enjoy the restored defensive mounds used by the Confederacy on the grounds.

wilmington concert association

2003-2004 season

OPERA VERDI EUROPA
RIGOLETTO,
BY GIUSEPPE VERDI

WEDNESDAY
OCTOBER 29, 2003

**ANTHONY AND
JOSEPH PARATORE**
PIANO DUO

SATURDAY
JANUARY 24, 2004

**PETER SCHICKELE:
PDQ BACH**
THE JEKYLL AND HYDE TOUR

SUNDAY, FEBRUARY 15, 2004

SHANGHAI QUARTET
STRING QUARTET

WEDNESDAY, MARCH 31, 2004

I MUSICI DE MONTRÉAL
DIRECTOR, YULI TUROVSKY

SUNDAY, APRIL 18, 2004

Performances at 8 p.m. at Kenan Auditorium

For single or season tickets, call **910-962-3500** or **1-800-732-3643**

Wilmington's Celebrity Roster

Wilmington and the Cape Fear area have played well-known roles throughout the nation's history, but few people are aware of the famous and talented folks who once called this area home:

CLOSE-UP

Henry Bacon, architect
David Brinkley, TV journalist
Frank Capra, Jr., motion picture filmmaker
John Cheek, operatic baritone
Charlie Daniels, country-rock musician
Sammy Davis, Sr., stage performer
Edward B. Dudley, first popularly elected governor of North Carolina
Mary Baker Eddy, founder of Christian Science Church
Nelson Eddy, singer
Minnie Evans, visionary painter
Roman Gabriel, NFL Player of the Year, 1969, L.A. Rams
Althea Gibson, tennis champion (U.S. Open 1957-58, Wimbledon 1957-58, French Open 1956)
Thomas Godfrey, first American playwright
Cornelius Harnett, patriot of the American Revolution
William Hooper, signer of the Declaration of Independence
Caterina Jarboro, operatic soprano
Michael Jordan, basketball star, Chicago Bulls
Sonny Jurgenson, NFL Hall of Famer
Charles Kuralt, TV commentator and author
Meadowlark Lemon, basketball star, Harlem Globetrotters
Sugar Ray Leonard, Olympic gold medalist boxer
Hugh Morton, preservationist, naturalist and photographer
Robert Ruark, author and safari hunter
Anna McNeill Whistler, "Whistler's Mother"
Woodrow Wilson, 28th president of the United States

Museum hours are 10 AM to 5 PM Tuesday through Thursday and on Saturday, 10 AM to 9 PM on Friday and 10:30 AM to 4 PM on Sunday. Admission is $5 for adults, $12 for families and $2 for children ages 5 to 18. Children younger than 5 and museum members are admitted free. Come on the first Sunday of each month and enjoy the museum free of charge. Restaurant seating is available Tuesday through Sunday for lunch and Friday evening for dinner.

Thalian Hall Center
for the Performing Arts
310 Chestnut St., Wilmington
• **(910) 343-3660**
Box Office: (910) 343-3664,
(800) 523-2820

Built in 1858, this majestic performance center has gone through several restorations and, at this time, offers three performance spaces. Housed within are a 752-seat main theater, the 250-seat Council Chamber and a 136-seat stu-

dio theater. With a lively local performing arts community and the addition of touring companies, at least one of the spaces is in use each evening or afternoon. More than 35 area arts and civic organizations use the facility, and more than 450 performances and screenings in music, theater, dance and film are presented each year. (See our Attractions chapter for more information.)

Wilmington Art Association
(910) 256-7475

Composed of professional and amateur visual artists and art enthusiasts, the Wilmington Art Association holds small art shows throughout the year and conducts an annual juried exhibition, the Spring Juried Art Show and Sale, usually during the Azalea Festival activities in April. The WAA also holds meetings on topics of interest, sponsors frequent workshops, critiques, educational programs and special projects, and gives two scholarships to UNC-Wilmington art students annually. Meetings are

1788-2004
*216 Years of
Community Theatre
in America*

The

association

2003-2004 SEASON
Writers' Bloc •Babes in Toyland • Deathtrap • Born Yesterday • The Music Man
Main Stage at Thalian Hall Center for the Performing Arts

*Please call the Center Box Office at (910) 343-3664
for ticket information and reservations*

For information about The Thalian Association, please call (910) 251-1788

held monthly September through June on the second Thursday evening at the Racine Center for the Arts.

Music

Azalea Coast Chorus of Sweet Adelines
(910) 791-3846
Sweet Adelines, the female counterpart of the Society for the Preservation and Encouragement of Barbershop Quartet Singing in America (see Cape Fear Chordsmen, below), promotes and preserves the art of singing four-part harmony, barbershop style. Membership is open to all women who enjoy this original American style of music.

Blues Society of the Lower Cape Fear
(910) 251-1888
Founded by a small group of blues enthusiasts in 1988, the Blues Society of the Lower Cape Fear continues to be a mainstay of Wilmington's music community and is one of the most successful music societies in eastern North Carolina. The group offers musicians of all skill levels an opportunity to participate in the society's weekly jam sessions and annual events, including an exciting blues talent competition held in October. The BSLCF also actively participates in state and local arts organizations and programs. Blues fans don't want to miss the annual Cape Fear Blues Festival held in July. (See Annual Events for more details.) The Cape Fear Bluesletter is available through membership in the society. Monthly membership meetings are held on the first Monday of the month at 7:30 PM. Musicians and blues enthusiasts can join the group's long-standing weekly jam session every Tuesday night from 8 PM until midnight (or later). BSLCF provides any professional equipment you may need, just bring your instruments. Call for meeting and jam locations.

Brunswick Concert Band
Southport • (910) 278-7908
The nonprofit Brunswick Concert Band is composed of volunteers from Brunswick, New Hanover, Pender and Horry counties who have been playing together for the past 15 years. No auditions are required, and volunteers who have at least a high-school skill level are invited to

THE ARTS

join, with the stipulation that members have their own instrument and can read music. The band plays a variety of music styles — Big Band, jazz, light classical, marches and show tunes — and conducts two formal concerts annually, a spring concert held in March or April and a Christmas concert. It also plays at a variety of festivals and events in the area, particularly the N.C. Fourth of July Celebration. Brunswick Concert Band is a member of the Association of Concert Bands. Weekly rehearsals are held on Tuesday evenings from 7 to 9 PM at the Progress Energy Visitors Center in Southport.

Cape Fear Chordsmen
(910) 799-8455

This group is Wilmington's chapter of the Society for the Preservation and Encouragement of Barber Shop Quartet Singing in America. Members practice male four-part harmony singing weekly at 7:30 PM on Tuesday evenings at the College Acres Baptist Church in Wilmington. Call for membership information and a concert schedule.

Chamber Music Society of Wilmington
Barbara McKenzie • (910) 343-1049

A long-awaited addition to the Wilmington music scene, the Chamber Music Society of Wilmington is a nonprofit presenting organization that brings world-class chamber music concerts, including Audubon String Quartet and Rossetti String Quartet, to the Thalian Hall Ballroom. Featured composers include George Crumb and Ben Johnston. Many of the artists and ensembles are North Carolinians who have gained recognition on a national and/or international level. The Society works with the New Hanover County School Board to reach young audiences with a series of children's concerts and an Instrumental Petting Zoo, where children can touch and explore the instruments. Tickets are available by subscription or individually for the five concerts in which the composer first talks with the audience about the ideas for his work. The ballroom is usually packed, so come early.

Girls Choir of Wilmington
205 Dover Rd., Wilmington • (910) 799-5073

Formed in 1997, this community-based choral

ensemble has approximately 100 girls enrolled. Girls ages 8 and older perform a variety of classical, folk, sacred, secular and popular music. The members learn teamwork, discipline, musicianship and community service through the concerts and activities.

Harmony Belles
(910) 799-5850

Formed in 1986, this local women's group sings four-part harmony a cappella. Their performances for civic organizations, churches, nursing homes, educational programs in schools and at local events emphasize their philosophy of community service. Rehearsals are Tuesday evenings from 7 to 9:30 PM. The Belle Chords, a female quartet within the group, performs in a four-part harmony, barbershop style. Call for rehearsal location and membership information.

North Carolina Jazz Festival
Wilmington Hilton Riverside, 301 N. Water St., Wilmington • (910) 763-8585

This winter weekend festival features mainstream jazz performances by national and international stars. The main event is held at the Wilmington Hilton Riverside, and a preview program is given at UNCW's Kenan Auditorium the day before. (See our Annual Events chapter.) Good luck getting tickets to the main event if you don't have a standing order for them because this is a hugely popular festival with fiercely devoted fans.

North Carolina Symphony
(910) 791-3343

This New Hanover County chapter of the state symphony sponsors five public concerts a year from September through April at UNCW's Kenan Auditorium. For tickets, call Kenan Auditorium at (910) 962-3500 or (800) 732-3643.

Sea Notes Choral Society
(910) 278-5542

This nonprofit volunteer organization is based in Southport and serves Brunswick County. Membership in the chorus, whose numbers currently exceed 100, is open to all interested singers. No auditions are required unless you are applying to be a soloist. The group rehearses every Monday evening at 7 PM at the Trinity United Methodist Church in Southport. Con-

THE ARTS

certs include a variety of music, from the Messiah to Benjamin Britten songs written in Olde English with harp accompaniment. The chorus has a new director every season with three primary concerts annually — in the spring, on the Fourth of July and at Christmas. Members are asked to pay dues of $25 per year to supplement contributions and grants. All concerts are free, though donations are gratefully accepted.

Wilmington Academy of Music
1635 Wellington Ave., Wilmington
• (910) 392-1590

The Academy is a private school, founded in 1987, that offers a full range of music instruction in voice, piano, guitar, harp, violin, viola, cello, percussion, trumpet, trombone, clarinet, saxophone, flute, tuba, oboe, bagpipe and more for students of all ages. Theory, orchestration, arranging and other classes are available. Traditional, Suzuki and jazz techniques are the methods of choice. Weekly private lessons and monthly group lessons, recitals and master classes are offered. The Academy features the combined talents of faculty members and experienced local musicians in a variety of ensembles for weddings, receptions and special events.

Wilmington Boys Choir
(910) 395-6264

This nonprofit organization, established in 1987, is a choral group for boys ages 8 and older with a repertoire of music, including classical, folk, traditional and modern. They perform in the Wilmington area throughout the year and give special holiday concerts. Past out-of-town tours have taken the group to Williamsburg, Virginia; Washington, D.C.; New York City; and Canterbury, England. Admission is by audition, and the boys practice one or two afternoons a week.

Wilmington Choral Society
(910) 790-0382

This large, well-established chorus has been a presence in Wilmington since 1950. Attracting singers from Wilmington and the surrounding areas and from a cross-section of ages and professions, the chorus prides itself on high-performance standards of classic choral selections and a wide variety of contemporary music. The group participates in three or four concerts annually. Members rehearse on Tuesdays from 7:25 to 9:30 PM at the Cape Fear Christian Church in Wilmington, and the organization is open to all interested singers. No auditions are necessary.

Wilmington Concert Association
(910) 791-7118

The Concert Association brings four or five classical music and dance concerts of national prominence to Wilmington each year at UNCW's Kenan Auditorium. The association, established in 1929, regularly enjoys subscriptions of more than 800 people each season in a house that seats 960. Performers in recent years have included the San Francisco Western Opera Theatre, Alvin Ailey Repertory Ensemble, pianist Arcadi Volodos, the Ballet du Capitole de Toulouse and the Canadian Brass. The association's mission is to bring internationally acclaimed musical artists to Wilmington. Membership is open to everyone.

Wilmington Concert Band
(910) 799-5543

A volunteer community performing organization, this band seeks musicians with a certain degree of skill. Auditions are not required, but a minimum of two years instrumental experience is expected, and members must possess their own instruments. The band performs at events and locations throughout New Hanover County throughout the summer from Memorial Day to Labor Day. Call for rehearsal dates and location.

Wilmington Symphony Orchestra
4608 Cedar Ave., Wilmington
• (910) 791-9262

Founded in 1971, Wilmington Symphony Orchestra enters its 31st year during the 2002-03 season. UNCW students and faculty members, local professional and amateur musicians from the community make up this all-volunteer symphony orchestra. Each season they present five classical concerts, matinee concerts, a chamber orchestra concert and a children's concert. The orchestra's Symphony in the Schools program allows area students to meet and interact with members and guest artists. This year, the symphony inaugurated a brand-new standing program, the Wilmington Symphony Youth Orchestra. This group draws on talented students in grades 7 through 12 and gives three concerts a year. In March, a free family concert features paired adults and students playing side by side.

Theater

Wilmington has a rich theatrical tradition that is continually expanding. Wilmington's Thalian Hall Center for the Performing Arts is home to the Thalian Association, the oldest continuous community theater in the country, dating from 1788. The theater hosts professional and amateur productions on an almost nightly basis.

Several local theatrical companies present original and popular productions at such area locations as Kenan Auditorium at the University of North Carolina at Wilmington, the Scottish Rite Temple on 17th Street, and schools and churches. Additionally, Wilmington is on the circuit for touring dance companies, symphonies and musicals.

Big Dawg Productions
(910) 772-1429

Dedicated to producing professional theater and supporting excellence in the arts, this non-profit theater company performs six shows per season at Thalian Hall Center for the Performing Arts. Other programs nurtured by the group include "The Festival of New Plays," to showcase talented North Carolinians. A K-12 company called the "The Blue Sky Project," an accredited internship program available to local high school and college students entertains youth from the public schools of New Hanover and Pender counties at Thalian Hall.

Opera House Theatre
2011 Carolina Beach Rd., Wilmington
• (910) 762-4234

A professional theater company presided over by artistic director Lou Criscuolo, this group stages seven major productions and two to three experimental works each season in Thalian Hall. Guest artists and directors are featured frequently. Auditions are open.

Stages Inc. Touring Children's Theatre
808 Orange St., Wilmington
• (910) 772-1429

Stages Inc. is a non-profit touring company of professional actors who offer performances to children in grades 5 through 8. The shows are abridged versions of classical, contemporary and culturally diverse live theater. Yearly spring and fall tours consist of two show titles and cover both Carolinas, bringing the excitement of live theater to the community. Performances are about 50 minutes in length with question and answer sessions or study guides available upon request.

Thalian Association
120 S. Second St., Wilmington
• (910) 251-1788

Tracing its theatrical roots back to 1788, the Thalian Association is a volunteer performing group, staging five full-scale productions yearly in Thalian Hall. The Thalian Association Children's Theatre (TACT) stages three productions a year in the Hannah Block 2nd Street Stage in the Community Arts Center in downtown Wilmington. Operating under the supervision of a volunteer board of directors, the Thalian Association stages a yearly fund-raising auction and seeks to involve volunteers in all its plays and activities.

Willis Richardson Players
(910) 763-1889

Established in 1974 and specializing in dramas by minority playwrights, the Willis Richardson Players perform several works per season of interest to all audiences.

Dance

The Wilmington area offers the broadest spectrum of experiences in dance classes. The following is only a sample.

Class Act Dance Company
(910) 452-4765

Class Act is a senior women's dance group that performs for local civic organizations, nursing homes, schools, churches and other community activities. Auditions for experienced dancers, 55 years and older, are held at any time. Rehearsals are held twice weekly at the New Hanover County Senior Center, Mondays from 11 AM to 1 PM and Fridays from 11:30 AM to 1 PM.

Celebrate Wilmington!
and the Walk of Fame

Mount Rushmore has its presidents, Hollywood has a star-studded sidewalk and, since 1997, Wilmington has a Walk of Fame. Located behind the Cotton Exchange shopping center in historic downtown Wilmington, the Walk of Fame Plaza was created through the efforts of Celebrate Wilmington!, which is sponsored by the University of North Carolina at Wilmington. The main goal is to celebrate Wilmington's arts community and recognize those who have enriched the Cape Fear area.

Visitors to this small plaza on Nutt Street will find a graceful arbor with flowering vines and tubs of seasonal plants at the entrance. Tall, distinctive banners bearing the Celebrate Wilmington! emblem flap overhead in a breeze from the Cape Fear River waterfront nearby. Bronze benches provide a comfortable place to rest and view the eight-pointed stars that line the walkway, bearing the names of Walk of Fame honorees.

To be chosen for this honor, candidates must satisfy a specific criteria. Inductees are those people who have lived, worked and/or enriched the Wilmington/Cape Fear region and have attained national or international recognition in one of the following fields—the arts, business, education, literature, broadcasting/television/film, journalism, sports, science, medicine, the military, politics or government.

Induction ceremonies are held twice a year, usually early spring and late fall or December. Current Walk of Fame honorees (in order and with year of induction) are:

1997 - Roman Gabriel A Wilmington native, Roman Gabriel played All-State football, baseball and basketball while at New Hanover High School and starred as a football quarterback at North Carolina State. He went on to a career in professional football as an NFL quarterback, playing for the Los Angeles Rams and the Philadelphia Eagles.

1997 - Minnie Evans A native of the Cape Fear region, Minnie Evans was a visionary artist who, without prior training, began to paint prolifically in middle age. Using whatever materials she could find, she painted vibrant and colorful pictures depicting the dreams and vision she experienced all of her life. A collection of her work hangs on permanent display in the Louise Wells Cameron Art Museum.

1998 - Hugh Morton The legacy that Hugh Morton leaves behind is as a preservationist, naturalist and photographer. He contributed much time and effort into preserving North Carolina history through his work on the Save The Battleship and Cape Hattaras Lighthouse projects. Morton is also an internationally recognized photographer whose work appeared in several well-known magazines, including Time and National Geographic.

1998 - Henry Bacon Though born in Illinois, Henry Bacon spent most of his life in Wilmington, designing the Confederate Memorial at Third and Market Streets and the estates of local families. He is most noted for his design of the Lincoln Memorial in Washington, D.C., for which he won international recognition and the highest honors of the American Institute of Architects. Bacon is buried in the Oakdale Cemetery, 520 N. 15th Street, Wilmington.

1999 - Frank Capra, Jr. Frank Capra, Jr. has been instrumental in the development of Wilmington's film industry. Internationally recognized as a filmmaker, Capra returned to Wilmington in 1996 to become president of EUE/Screen Gems Studios. His earlier visit in 1983 resulted in the filming of Dino DeLaurentiis' movie, Firestarter, on location at Orton Plantation. Since his return, Capra has been tireless in his efforts to bring film production to the Cape Fear region and strengthen communication between the industry and the community. Capra participates in Wilmington's theater arts and teaches classes in the Film Studies Program at UNC-Wilmington.

1999 - Caterina Jarboro Born Katherine Yarborough in Wilmington, Caterina attended school here until, at age 13, she journeyed to New York to study music. During her illustrious career, she achieved international fame as a soprano and paved the way for other talented African-Americans in American opera. Caterina performed in many of the world's great opera houses, including Paris, Vienna, Warsaw, Madrid, Moscow and the United States. She also thrilled Wilmington audiences on two occasions by performing at the Academy of Music (Thalian Hall) and the Williston High School auditorium.

Local celebrities are honored with a star on Wilmington's Walk of Fame.

Photo: Deb Daniel

2000 - Althea Gibson Breaking through racial barriers throughout her career, tennis legend Althea Gibson achieved several "firsts" as an African-American athlete, especially a black female athlete, and won nearly 100 professional titles. In 1958, after retiring from professional tennis competition, she made golf history as the first African-American to earn an LPGA card. Althea's connection to Wilmington dates back to her move to the city as a young girl to train with Dr. Hubert Eaton, who discovered and mentored her. She trained on Dr. Eaton's regulation-size tennis court in downtown Wilmington, living with his family and attending Williston High School.

2000 - Robert C. Ruark, Jr. Robert Ruark, born and raised in Wilmington, graduated from New Hanover High School. He later earned fame and recognition as a journalist and, eventually, as a bestselling novelist. His books include *Something of Value, Poor No More, Uhuru* and *The Honey Badger.*

2001 - David Brinkley A Wilmington native for the first twenty-one years of his life, veteran journalist and news commentator David Brinkley got his start in print news with the Wilmington Morning Star. He went on to work for the United Press and NBC radio in the 1940s before turning to an emerging new medium called television. Brinkley, one of the first journalists on television, is credited as a pioneer in the field of broadcast news.

2001 - Charlie Daniels Hit country music singer/songwriter and Grammy winner Charlie Daniels has strong roots in the Cape Fear region. Born in Wilmington in 1936, Daniels grew up on Carolina Beach Road and still has family in the area. He received an honorary degree from UNC-Wilmington in 1996. Two of Daniels' most recognized songs include The Devil Went Down to Georgia and The South's Gonna Do It Again.

2002 - Claude Howell Believing that the quality of Wilmington's light was unlike that of any other place, Claude Howell explored the effect light has upon the objects and shapes of coastal living. He helped found the art department at Wilmington College, later the University of North Carolina at Wilmington, and left many serigraphs to St. John's Museum of Art. His collection is now housed in the Louise Wells Cameron Museum of Art.

2003 - Isaac ("Ike") Bates Grainger Banking and golf made good partners for a man who excelled at both. An executive of Murchison National Bank of Wilmington, North Carolina Bank & Trust Co. of Greensboro, Grainger joined Chemical Bank of NYC (now Chase Manhattan), where he was president from 1956-60, when he reached mandatory retirement age. At the same time he was rising through the ranks of the banking world, Grainger served as chairman of the joint rules committee of the U.S. Golf Association (USGA) and the Royal and Ancient Golf Club of St. Andrews. He was president of the USGA from 1954 to 1955 and received the USGA's Bob Jones Award for distinguished sportsmanship in golf in 1988. Living to be 104, Grainger was one of the oldest veterans in New Hanover County and the oldest member of the Cape Fear Golf Club, which hosts an annual golf tournament, the Isaac B. Grainger International Match Play Championship, in his honor.

The Dance Cooperative
(910) 297-4173

The Dance Cooperative consists of six dance professionals who are bound together by one common goal, to foster a link between professional dance artists and the community. Their mission is to nurture the dance community by providing affordable classes, rehearsal space and performance opportunities to those under-served artistically, culturally and economically in the greater Wilmington area. The Dance Cooperative currently has a program of classes (drop-ins are welcome), and both an informal and formal concert series. Call Nancy at (910) 612-3706 or Erika at (910) 297-4173 for more information.

Theatre Dance Workshop
(910) 458-3302

Theatre Dance Workshop is a place where singing, dancing and acting all come together. The students are part of senior and junior companies that perform original choreography, scenes and songs from Broadway shows.

Writing

North Carolina Writers' Network
(919) 967-9540

North Carolina Writers' Network, based in Carrboro near Chapel Hill, is a vital resource for North Carolina writers. This well-established organization offers an extensive library and helps writers sharpen their skills in poetry, fiction, nonfiction, playwriting and technical writing through state-wide writer workshops. The annual themed Fall Conference, hosted in alternating North Carolina regions, is a popular event for writers of all skill levels.

North Carolina Poetry Society
(910) 686-1751

The objectives of the society are to bring together in meetings of mutual interest and fellowship the poets of North Carolina; to encourage the study, writing and publication of poetry; and to develop a public taste for the reading and appreciation of poetry. Workshops and informal meetings are conducted throughout the state regularly.

Playwrights Producing Company
(910) 799-5043

A nonprofit company supporting emerging North Carolina playwrights, this organization offers seminars and looks for scripts-in-progress, which are read by actors and critiqued by the volunteer audience. Selected productions or original plays are a highlight of monthly meetings held at the Community Arts Center in Wilmington. Membership is open. Call for meeting dates and time.

Crafts

Azalea Coast Smockers Guild
(910) 392-2696

This active group of needlewomen teaches smocking and heirloom sewing. Beginning as well as experienced smockers are welcome. Call for monthly meeting information.

Carolina Shores Quilters Guild
(910) 579-9357

Promoting awareness and education about the art of quilting, this Brunswick County guild participates in the revival of quilting as a traditional American craft and does fund-raising for local organizations. Membership is open to Carolina Shores community residents.

Embroiderers' Guild of America
(910) 686-4463

The Scotch Bonnet Chapter of the Embroiderers' Guild of America offers workshops, classes and other educational opportunities for everyone interested in the art of needlework. All skill levels and interests are welcomed to these programs, and monthly meetings are held at 10 AM on the third Monday of the months September through June.

Port City Basketmakers
Poplar Grove Plantation, 10200 U.S. Hwy. 17 N., Wilmington
• (910) 686-4868

Members of this group work to stimulate public interest in the art of basketry and to preserve the techniques of the craft. Port City Basketmakers meets the fourth Sunday of every month (except July and August) at 2:30 PM at Poplar Grove Plantation. Workshops and seminars are available, and new members, from novice to advanced weavers, are welcome.

Photography

Cape Fear Camera Club
(910) 392-2559

Founded in 1987, this club is a forum for photographic interests within the community. More than 30 members participate in education, travel, outings, workshops and friendly competition. Monthly meetings are held on the third Wednesday evening at 7:30 PM in Cameron Hall on the campus of UNCW, 601 S. College Road in Wilmington.

magnificent music!

North Carolina
Symphony

The North Carolina Symphony performs six concerts between September and May at Kenan Auditorium on the campus of UNC-Wilmington.

For information about performances of the North Carolina Symphony in Wilmington, call the Kenan Auditorium Ticket Office at 910.962.3500, 800.732.3643, M-F 10am-6pm, or visit www.ncsymphony.org.

Call: 910.962.3500   www.ncsymphony.org

Wedding Planning

"Yes, I do." These words are heard over and over again along the southern coast. The wedding industry is thriving in New Hanover, Brunswick and Pender counties with an estimated 2,700 weddings in 2002. A minister friend who officiates at local weddings testifies that Wilmington is becoming an increasingly popular place for brides and grooms to pledge their love.

Did you know that Wilmington is often called the city of churches and gardens? While couples of all ages still opt for the traditional church ceremony, a growing number plan an outdoor wedding, choosing to tie the knot on one of our beautiful beaches or in a lush garden. Exciting wedding-reception locations are abundant, from the Henrietta III Riverboat to the famous Orton Plantation and luxurious Graystone Inn.

In this chapter, we help guide you through the intricacies of planning a wedding in the Wilmington area, from applying for a license and choosing a magistrate or minister to hiring a caterer and photographer. We also provide you with information on locations, musicians, florists, formal wear, transportation and lodging. If you want someone else to handle all the necessary planning details, we suggest some superior wedding consultants. Planning a wedding can be a thrilling adventure; our goal is to make it enjoyable for you.

Making It Official

North Carolina law requires that wedding ceremonies be conducted by an ordained minister or a magistrate. A boat captain can't do the trick anymore. The state has replaced its former justice of the peace system with court-appointed magistrates. These officials may perform wedding services, but they are often severely limited as to times and places they can accommodate. A magistrate's fee for performing a ceremony is $10.

If you want to be married by a minister, most major religions are represented in Wilmington (see our Worship chapter). Many denominations do require a special counseling period, and some have specific requirements regarding re-marrying divorced persons.

A marriage license is a must. You may get the license at any county in North Carolina, but must turn it into the Register of Deeds in the county where the wedding takes place.

Courthouses are open Monday through Friday but are closed on holidays. Both parties must be present, and three forms of identification — birth certificate, Social Security card and valid driver's license or DMV picture card ID — are required in New Hanover and Brunswick counties. Pender County requires only a driver's license. If a person has been divorced for less than 60 days, the divorce decree must be recorded. No blood test, physical exam or waiting period is necessary to obtain a marriage license, which costs $50 to $60 and is payable by cash only. The license is valid for 60 days after being issued. Remember to, bring your marriage license to the wedding. The person who performs the ceremony is responsible for getting the license back to the register of deeds in the county in which you were married. After you're married, the officiant or magistrate will issue you a marriage certificate.

Local Register of Deeds

New Hanover County Register of Deeds, Vital Records, 24 N. 3rd Street, Room 103, Wilmington, (910) 341-7106

Brunswick County Register of Deeds, 75 Courthouse Drive, Bolivia, (910) 253-2690

Onslow County Register of Deeds, 109 Old Bridge Street, Jacksonville, (910) 347-3451

Pender County Register of Deeds, 300 N. Fremont Street, Burgaw, (910) 259-1225

Wedding Locations

The Wilmington area is home to literally hundreds of churches, plus four synagogues, a Muslim mosque and a Buddhist temple. Houses of worship often require that you have some affiliation if you are planning to use the facilities. Contact the person in charge and he or she will give you the specifics. Prepare to pay a fee for the use of the sanctuary as well as to compensate for services. It is customary to pay between $50 and $150 for ministerial services. See our Worship chapter or the Yellow Pages for a list of houses of worship.

Magnificent outdoor settings — pristine beaches, barrier islands, historic gardens — are a huge draw for couples who are in love with nature as well as each other. Many couples opt for an informal affair on the beach where everyone can go barefoot. Other choices include Airlie Gardens, the New Hanover County Arboretum and the historic St. Thomas Preservation Hall. If an outdoor wedding appeals to you, keep in mind that southern coast weather can be unpredictable. Always plan an indoor alternative. And remember to plan well in advance — at least a year out in many cases. You'll have a lot of competition for some locations and services.

For seaside weddings at Wrightsville or Carolina Beach, you will need to apply for a permit from the respective parks and recreation departments, especially if you want to use the Wrightsville Beach gazebo or erect a celebration tent.

Wrightsville Beach Parks and Recreation, #1 Bob Sawyer Drive, Wrightsville Beach, (910) 256-7925.

Carolina Beach Parks and Recreation, 1121 North Lake Park Boulevard, Carolina Beach, (910) 458-7416.

Read on for information on some of the area's most popular wedding locations.

Wilmington

Airlie Gardens
300 Airlie Rd., Wilmington
• (910) 793-7531

A rare gem just moments from Wrightsville Beach, the lavish landscape of historic Airlie Gardens offers 67 acres of azaleas, camellias and some of the world's most exotic plants in a setting that can accommodate up to 300 guests. The Italian pergola, which provides a natural aisle leading down to the foot of one of two man-made freshwater lakes, is the most popular place to conduct the actual ceremony. Afterwards, most couples choose the famous Airlie Oak as the site for their reception. Please make reservations at least two months in advance.

Bellamy Mansion Museum
503 Market St., Wilmington
• (910) 251-3700

Make your wedding an historic occasion with an evening event at Wilmington's beautifully restored Bellamy Mansion. This magnificent landmark provides a breathtaking backdrop for ceremonies, receptions, rehearsal dinners and wedding photography. Ornate plaster work, original brass chandeliers, marble and slate mantles and elaborate Victorian carpets provide a truly southern atmosphere. Over 5,000 square feet, including the two main floors of the house, the grounds and the porches, are all available for your guests. Your caterer may work on the basement level. Centrally located in the heart of Wilmington's downtown historic district, the mansion enjoys a large on-site parking lot. Make yourself at home and experience the comfort and beauty of this antebellum treasure.

Front Street Inn
215 S. Front St., Wilmington
• **(910) 762-6442**

A newly renovated dining room, sun porch with adjacent courtyard and catering kitchen is perfect for bridal showers, luncheons or intimate gatherings of up to 15 guests. The Sol Y Sombra Bar, which serves champagne, wine and soft drinks, is also available during this special time. Front Street Inn offers accommodations for your guests, but most importantly a lavish honeymoon suite just for the two of you. Ask for Stefany or Jenny.

The Graystone Inn
100 S. Third St. Wilmington
• **(910) 763-2000, (888) 763-4773**

The historic Graystone Inn will provide you and up to 150 guests with memories for a lifetime. Together with an atmosphere featuring turn-of-the-century grandeur, an experienced staff will take every measure to assure a memorable and lasting experience.

INSIDERS' TIP
Consider Friday or Sunday for your wedding instead of Saturday. Fees tend to be lower and some services are more available.

Henrietta III Wedding Cruise
Cape Fear Riverboats, Wilmington
• **(910) 343 1611, (800) 676 0162**

Cruise down the beautiful Cape Fear River with your sweeheart and your wedding party. Choose from several packages, including a daytime cruise from noon to 1:30 PM and a private Saturday evening cruise from 6:30 to 9:30 PM. Menu fare ranges from light hors d'oeurves to an elegant three-course dinner and includes a scrumptious tiered wedding cake and a champagne toast for all the guests.

The Pilot House
2 Ann St., Wilmington • **(910) 343-0200**

Enjoy your wedding day, rehearsal dinner, ceremony and reception at one of the most popular Cape Fear riverfront restaurants, located in the historic Craig House in Chandler's Wharf.

Serving the finest in both traditional and innovative Southern cuisine for 25 years, The Pilot House will serve you in the casual elegance of the sunny dining room or outdoors on the covered patio.

St. Thomas Preservation Hall
208 Dock St., Wilmington
• **(910) 763-4054**

Listed on the National Historic Register, St. Thomas Preservation Hall is staffed with courteous professionals who want your wedding day to run smoothly and be remembered with joy. The beautifully restored building, which dates back to 1846, is designed and fully equipped for receptions, rehearsal dinners and weddings. You can choose your own service providers, and providers have all day to set up and decorate at no extra charge. Ample parking is available. All proceeds go to help preserve part of Wilmington's history.

The Wilmingtonian
101 S. Second St., Wilmington
• **(910) 343-1800, (800) 525-0909**

The historic de Rosset House and gardens at The Wilmingtonian epitomize the architectural style of the old South, the ideal location for a sumptuous wedding. The Wilmingtonian combines Southern charm with the very best in gourmet dining and service, all in an atmosphere of elegance and refinement.

Weather permitting, plan to have both wedding and reception enhanced by the outdoor setting of the beautiful gardens. Plan B, inside the Wilmingtonian, is elegant as well.

Carolina/Kure Beach

Courtyard by Marriott
100 Charlotte St., Carolina Beach
• **(910) 458-2030 (800) 321-2211**

New in 2003, the 144 room Courtyard offers a full range of facilities and services for any size wedding. Full banquet facilities with seating for up to 250, a courteous and professional staff and the Atlantic Ocean as a dramatic backdrop make the Courtyard by Marriott the ideal setting for the perfect wedding. Why not get married right on the beach?

Bald Head Island

Theodosia's Bed and Breakfast
Harbour Village, Bald Head Island
• (910) 457-6563, (800) 656-1812
The 14 upscale guest rooms at Theodosia's and lovely rental homes on Bald Head Island are ideal places for wedding guests and honeymoons. Theodosia's can help plan your wedding ceremony and they make the most beautiful wedding cakes on the island. Catering for other special events is available as well.

The Village Chapel of Bald Head Island
105 Lighthouse Wynd, Bald Head Island
• (910) 457-1183
This is an exquisite little chapel nestled among flowers with a panoramic view of the marsh. Its cool, quiet interior is a nondenominational church. Services are held every weekend by visiting ministers. Weddings of no more than 110 guests can be held with one of the two retired ministers who live on the island officiating or you can provide your own minister. Weddings are limited to one per day and no weddings are performed during

Easter week. Remember that you will need to arrange for ferry transportation and golf cart rental for all guests as no vehicles are allowed on the island. If you think it would be fun to have a golf cart get you to the church on time, this would be one of the loveliest spots to tie the knot.

Southport and Oak Island

The Chapel at South Harbour Village
4795 Fish Factory Rd., Southport
• (910) 454-7500, (800) 454-0815
If your dream wedding takes place in a little white chapel surrounded by greenery with a whiff of salt in the air and a view of the masts of sailing boats from the arched windows, you have come to the right place. The non-denominational Chapel at South Harbour Village has this and more. The interior, with its cathedral ceiling, recessed lights and ceiling fans, is as pristine as your wedding dress. The chapel accommodates up to 120 guests in its glossy wooden pews. What's more, a wedding coordinator is available to assist you with all the details, including arranging for music and the wedding cake, recommending florists, arranging the bridal tea, rehearsal dinner and reception,

which can all be held and catered on site. The Inn at South Harbour Village can provide accommodations (see our Hotels chapter). After all, the wedding coordinator, the minister and the innkeeper are one and the same person!

Southport Community Building
Bay St., Southport • (910) 454-0522

As its name says, this is a community building that is also used for weddings and receptions. It is an absolutely lovely spot on a bluff overlooking the Cape Fear River and surrounded by ancient live oaks. The building replaced a WWII structure that burned down a few years ago. It offers a huge room with honey-colored hardwood floors, a fireplace and large windows all around. If you like, you can have the ceremony performed outside on a wooden platform and the reception indoors. The building includes a warming kitchen as well.

Ocean Crest Motel
1417 E. Beach Dr., Oak Island
• (910) 278-3333

If you are dreaming of a wedding on the beach, the folks at the Ocean Crest Motel can help that dream come true. The motel is situated on the beach and with 62 rooms and a townhouse can accommodate the wedding party and the guests as well. These friendly folks will even provide a minister for you.

South Brunswick Islands

The Islander Inn
57 W. First St., Ocean Isle Beach
• (910) 575-7000, (888) 325-4753

Dreaming of a wedding in an arbor on the beach? The Islander Inn can make that dream come true with a gorgeous view of Long Bay as the backdrop. The Isles Restaurant can cater the reception in their banquet room with food prepared with the finest of regional ingredients.

Ocean Isle Inn
37 W. First St., Ocean Isle Beach
• (910) 579-0750, (800) 352-5988

Ocean Isle Inn can help you plan your beautiful wedding by the sea. Weddings are performed on the beach or at the chapel on Ocean Isle Beach. Newly renovated deluxe accommodations as well as friendly, outgoing staff will provide you, your friends and family with memories to last a lifetime.

Silver Coast Winery
6680 Barbeque Rd., Ocean Isle Beach
• (910) 287-2800

Have you considered a winery for your wedding? A vineyard and winery set on 40 acres and surrounded by lush woods would make a beautiful spot. Or, in this particular winery, indoors may appeal to you. The barrel room and the art gallery, each beautiful in its own way, are both available for weddings. In addition to recommending caterers, the winery has oblong tables and stackable chairs for up to 140 people, 10 barrel tables, 40 stools and outdoor picnic tables.

The Sunset Inn
9 North Shore Dr., Sunset Beach
• (910) 575-1000

Weddings and/or receptions at the Sunset Inn are very special indeed. Whether you decide to marry on the beach with the ocean as a backdrop, or in the inn with its hardwood floors and soaring windows revealing the beauty of the salt marsh, you and your guests are bound to be happy with the location. This is for small weddings only; theres a limit of 100 persons. The inn even has a Honeymoon Suite complete with a Jacuzzi.

The Winds Oceanfront Inns and Suites
310 E. First St., Ocean Isle Beach
• (910) 579-6275, (800) 334-3581

The Winds offers a captivating beach setting for your wedding event. Creative honeymoon packages and catered receptions are available. Frolic in the ocean's surf, swim in the heated pool, relax in the Jacuzzi spa, explore the island on bike rides, play tennis or golf and enjoy romantic dinners for two.

Topsail Island

Assembly Building
720 Channel Blvd., Topsail Beach
• **(910) 328-0511**
Enjoy a wedding at sunset on the porch of the historic Assembly Building or get married on the beach and host your reception in this nicely decorated and equipped large building that has room for more than 100 people, a band, area to dance and a kitchen. Reservations are a must, restrictions apply and a donation is expected.

Dorothy Cruise Boat
636 Channel Blvd., Topsail Beach
• **(910) 545-RIDE**
Create a custom wedding ceremony aboard the Dorothy as you cruise the Intracoastal or choose to hold your bachelor or bachelorette party aboard the boat. Perhaps a sunset in the background is part of your dream. Capt. Dave will charter the boat for your special occasion and will work with you to make your event a very special occasion to be remembered.

St. Regis Resort
2000 New River Inlet Rd., North Topsail Beach • **(910) 328-0778**
This impressive beach resort offers wedding opportunities on the beach or in their delightful gazebo. Onslow Hall is available for smaller receptions of 75 or less people while the larger Pender Hall can accommodate up to 150. There are two bars and a dance floor in Pender Hall, tables and chairs are provided in both halls. Clients must provide for their own caterer and bartenders.

Sea Vista Motel
1521 Ocean Blvd., Topsail Beach
• **(910) 328-2171, (800) 732-8478**
An important event before every wedding is the proposal of marriage. Sea Vista managers William and Maura Johnson enjoy adding personal touches to "set the scene" for this pre-wedding time by creating a special environment on the beach, decorating the room, getting a bottle of champagne for the celebration or just helping the future bridegroom with any surprises he may have in mind. They carry this personal service forward to assist with any plans for a beach wedding or wedding celebration at the Sea Vista.

Tiffany's Motel
1502 N. New River Dr., Surf City
• **(910) 328-1397, (800) 758-3818**
Take your choice, a wedding on the elevated deck or in the delightful gathering area by the new pool, Tiffany's has a great setting for your casual, beach wedding. Motel accommodations are available for wedding guests and owners Bob and Ann Smith will go out of their way to accommodate all your wedding needs.

Topsail Motel
1195 N. Anderson Blvd., Topsail Beach
• **(910) 328-3381, (800) 726-1795**
Over the years the oceanfront Topsail Motel has gained popularity as a great place for a beach wedding and informal reception in the picnic area. They have a special honeymoon room and accommodations for wedding party and guests.

Wedding Registries

The Wilmington area offers a wide variety of stores at which the bride and groom-to-be may register for gifts. Here are some top favorites.

Belk, 3500 Oleander Drive, (910) 392-1440.

Lowe's Home Improvement, 354 S. College Road, (910) 395-8433.

Abigail's Gifts, The Galleria, Wrightsville Beach, (910) 256-3043.

Bed, Bath & Beyond #418, 352 S. College Road, (910) 784-9707.

Fisherman's Wife, 1425 Airlie Road, (910) 256-5505.

Pier 1 Imports, 3741 Oleander Drive, (910) 392-3151.

Wedding Services

Don't want to do it all yourself? Here are some professionals who are happy to help you, whether you want them to plan the whole event or just help you with some of the details.

A Carolina Wedding
6301 Single Tree Ct., Wilmington
• **(910) 686-2690**

Planning and coordinating service packages are tailored to fit your needs. You design the job description. These awesome planners become not only a part of your staff, but your support system as well. Couples call from the local area, plus all around the country — L.A., D.C. and Boston — and are well satisfied.

Coastal Carolina Ceremonies
1565 Gores Landing Rd., Ocean Isle Beach
• **(910) 755-6730**

Certified by the Federation of Christian Ministries, Marge and Tom Wilt are interfaith ministers with more than 10 years experience working with couples and helping them create a ceremony that is personal, beautiful and unforgettable. They perform contemporary and traditional weddings as a couple. To assist in the creation of your ceremony, they provide a selection of greetings, readings, vows, blessings and rituals such as the Unity Candle, the Roses Ritual and others. You can create your own ceremony being sure that it will be performed in a reverent and sensitive manner. Beach weddings are a specialty. Marge and Tom perform renewal of vows, baptisms and naming ceremonies as well.

Eventz
209 Sandybrook Rd., Wilmington
• **(910) 686-1891**

One couple said that Eventz coordinator Judy Bradley became their best friend during their wedding. She will help you choose the site, caterer, decorations, linens and anything else down to the smallest detail. Judy has a new line of pavilions that offer a very dramatic effect with suspended structures that offer more room underneath. All of her tents have columns that cover the poles in a more finished manner.

An Island Wedding
Topsail Beach • (910) 328-1962

An Island Wedding offers the wedding of your dreams. These professional wedding planners can provide personalized service for your elegant or casual wedding on Topsail Island. You can have them design a customized wedding or choose a package that can be changed or combined with other packages or a la carte items. The goal of this locally owned company is to grant your every wish and ensure an unforgettable wedding experience. Selections include everything from a beach or soundside location to a ceremony on a small cruise boat, or a reception at the historic Assembly building to an oceanfront honeymoon cottage.

Jess's Mess
122 N. U.S. Hwy. 17., Holly Ridge
• **(910) 617-1372**

From "soup to nuts" Jess's Mess offers everything to make your wedding day everything you want it to be. From traditional to casual, they offer complete packages or you can pick and choose from their services that include floral design (fresh and silk flowers), a complete line of rental equipment, decorating, musicians, photographer, videographer, limousine service, catering for everything from a pig pickin' to formal dinners, including a professional staff dressed in tuxedos. Services also include consultations and selection of a location and minister. This one-stop shopping can result in savings of up to 30 percent or more.

Reverend Michael Lewis, Minister Officiant
5018 Marathon Landing Ct., Castle Hayne
• **(910) 675-1400**

Reverend Michael Lewis feels it is a blessing to participate in your wedding. His wedding service, whether indoors or out, focuses on the extra strength that God will give your marriage. He believes that a faith perspective brings a lot more happiness down the road.

A Wedding Minister, Penelope Morningstar
4922 Marlin Ct., Wilmington
• **(910) 791-7200**

Reverend Penelope Morningstar is an interfaith minister who will help you create a beautiful ceremony and officiate your wedding at the location of your choice. Whether you are planning to be married in historic Wilmington, on our beautiful beaches or in your home, with Reverend Morningstar's help, it will be a sacred moment to treasure for a lifetime.

Florists

Flowers are the symbol of both romantic and devoted love. The Wilmington area is home to an amazing showcase of artistic florists who will make your most fanciful floral dream come true. Here are just a few big bloomers.

Wilmington

Embellir Florist & Gifts
117 Grace St., Wilmington
• (910) 763-6282

This downtown florist offers unique floral designs plus Carlson Craft engraved invitations. A true Southern flair is given to all floral arrangements from bouquets to boutonnieres.

Ikebana Design and Accessories
The Forum, 1125-S Military Cutoff Rd., Wilmington • (910) 509-1383

Master Ikebana specialists Bonnie Burney and Ruth Lees offer the most exotic wedding arrangements we've ever seen. Period! They also have gourmet trays, Oriental gifts and wedding accessories such as ring-bearer pillows and flower-girl baskets. If your preference is eclectic excellence, consult with these ladies or any of their professional staff.

Riverside Florist
114 Dock St., Wilmington
• (910) 763-5558, (800) 858-6426

A perfect wedding day deserves perfect flowers. With more than 25 years experience, Riverside Florist is happy to provide all your floral needs.

Something Special
1319 Military Cutoff Rd., Wilmington
• (910) 256-0020

Located at Landfall Shopping Center, this staff has serviced every denomination in the Wilmington area. From traditional to casual, they will suit your floral needs.

NC's southern coast is a great place to get married.

Photo: Matt McGraw

Sophia V. West Florist, Inc.
8086 Market St., Wilmington
• (910) 686-0496

For your free yet very personal consultation, have your date, time, dress colors and favorite flowers in mind. It helps to leave the planning a little open-ended for that last minute flower that might be just perfect for the wedding bouquet. Plant rentals are available.

Will Rehder Florist
1106 39th St., Wilmington
• (910) 452-9333

Founded in 1872, Will Rehder Florist is North Carolina's oldest florist. They offer premium-quality flowers from The World Wide Market and an unconditional guarantee with excellent personal service.

Southport

Brunswicktown Florist
4857 Long Beach Rd., Southport
• (910) 457-1144

Brunswicktown Florist offers free bridal consultations by appointment. Experience in weddings on the beach, at Orton Plantation, on Bald Head Island and in Wilmington is proof of the flexibility of this florist. Owner Katherine Bailey works on every wedding serviced through her shop. She can accommodate any style of wedding and is especially talented in custom designs.

INSIDERS' TIP

A few churches, including the Unitarian Universalist Fellowship of Wilmington and Unity Christ Church, are willing to rent their sanctuaries for most interdenominational services, whether you are a member of that congregation or not.

Southport Florist
313 N. Howe St., Southport
• (910) 457-5177

Located near downtown Southport, Southport Florist can fill all your basic floral needs to help the planning of your wedding run smoothly. Floral decorations in the church and reception hall as well as bouquets for the bride and her attendants, boutonnieres for the groom, best man and ushers, and corsages for the mothers and grandmothers are all beautifully done. Owner Marvin Floyd especially enjoys the creative freedom of working for a client who leaves the arrangements up to him.

Wine & Roses
8864 River Rd. SE, Southport
• (910) 457-4428

In addition to floral decorations for the church and reception hall and the traditional flowers for the members of the wedding party, Wine & Roses offers a variety of invitations from which to choose. They can refer you to services such as photography, video operators and wedding cake bakers as well.

South Brunswick Islands

Calabash Florist, Inc.
10009 Beach Dr., Calabash
• (910) 579-7837, (888) 566-1497

The folks at Calabash Florist can provide you with floral decorations in a church or indoor reception area as well as an outdoor setting such as a garden. They are willing to work with any budget and can provide invitations, guest books, engraved knives, and rental of candelabra and arches.

Coastal Florists & Gifts
4635 Main St., Shallotte • (910) 754-6200

As well as creating floral decorations any way you want them, these talented people can refer you to the best place to have your wedding cake made, and where you might find a director to help you put all the details together and make your wedding a smooth-running event.

Daisies N' Rainbows
Town Square Ctr., 9958 Beach Dr., Calabash • (910) 575-9000, (800) 309-5497

Daisies N' Rainbows offers free, full-service wedding consultations. Available through this shop are rentals of tuxedos, spiral candelabra, arched candelabra, tables and chairs, tents, kneeling benches, champagne fountains, and even a Rent-a-Wedding in silk! In this case all the floral decorations, bouquets, boutonnieres, corsages, etc. are handmade and designed in silk. Invitations and coastal weddings are available as well.

Expressions Florist & Gift Shoppe
2920 Holden Beach Rd., Holden Beach
• (910) 842-9717

Housed in a 100-year-old building, this shop advertises "Designs of Distinction." The owner, Barbara Gray, offers free wedding consultation offering suggestions and tips to make things run smoothly and beautifully. She can custom design your flowers to the style of your wedding dress, making for a unique and beautiful look while working within your budget. She also makes flowers for wedding cakes. Rentals available include spiral candelabra, seven branch candelabra and arches.

Shallotte Florist
4517 N. Main St., Shallotte
• (910) 754-4848, (800) 754-4618
Providing full wedding service, Shallotte Florist has been serving "our" community for 48 years. Phyllis uses the freshest flowers available and can decorate in any theme you desire including Oriental and tropical.

Topsail Island Area

Floral Expressions by the Sea
892 N.C. Hwy. 210, Sneads Ferry
• (910) 327-0010
This full-service florist lists among its services a large bridal selection, including customized bouquets, a complete inventory of rental equipment, set-up and decorating. They deliver and are experts in beach weddings.

The Flower Basket of Hampstead
14361 U.S. Hwy. 17, Hampstead
• (910) 270-4141, (910) 270-4141
A full service florist, The Flower Basket of Hampstead offers everything from houseplants to mixed bouquets. They maintain an extensive inventory of fresh-cut flowers so if you love having beautiful floral arrangements in your home, whether for entertaining or "just because," this is the place to shop. See also our writeup in the shopping chapter.

Surf City Florist
106 N. Topsail Dr., Surf City
• (910) 328-3238
Scheduled or last minute, Surf City Florist is ready to provide beautiful, fresh flowers for your wedding. They offer full wedding services, including rental of candelabras and other special equipment.

Bridal Shops and Formal Wear

Whether you opt for a highly formal church wedding or something more casual, the Wilmington area offers literally hundreds of stores from which to choose your wedding finery.

Brides of Wilmington
St. James Village, 4510 Fountain Dr.,
Wilmington • (910) 395-6983
The world's most beautiful gowns, plus personal service with attention to every detail, are found here. Every member of the wedding party is sure to be pleased, including the bride, bridesmaids, mother of the bride and the flower girl. Tuxedo rentals are available for the men.

Cape Fear Formal Wear
218 N. Third St., Wilmington
• (910) 762-8206
Independence Mall, Wilmington
• (910) 452-1106
Oscar de la Renta, Lord West, Andrew Fezza, Ralph Lauren, Calvin Klein — if you're looking for the best in men's formal wear, you've found it.

Elegant Brides
5424 Oleander Dr., Ste. 9, Wilmington
• (910) 796-0602
Here you will find custom designs and alterations with prices to fit everyone's budget. A wide selection of accessory pieces, invitations and references to other wedding services are sure to please.

Fountaine Bridal
5202 Carolina Beach Rd., Ste. 11,
Wilmington • (910) 794-9959
Showcasing Anjolique bridal gowns, Fountaine Bridal offers full bridal consulting, custom-made flower girl dresses, and outside (dresses bought from other shops) alterations.

Jeffrey's
120-9 Shallotte Crossing, Shallotte
• (910) 755-5333
Jeffrey's is a men's wear shop carrying a full line of dress and casual wear as well as being a tuxedo headquarters. They have a full line of tuxedos including Oscar de la Renta, After Six, Lord West, Andrew Fezza, Geoffrey Beene, Claiborne, Chaps Ralph Lauren and Perry Ellis. Dress shoes can also be purchased. Having a large wedding? Jeffrey's offers a free groom's tux and a 1/2 price ring bearer's suit with the rental of six to nine tuxedos. With the rental of ten or more, the ring bearer's suit is also free.

Merle Norman Cosmetics
4961 Long Beach Rd. SE, Southport
• (910) 457-9009
Merle Norman Cosmetics carries a full line of tuxedos. From Perry Ellis to Chaps Ralph

Lauren to After Six, you can outfit the groom, groomsmen and even the ring bearer elegantly. Ask about specials. Merle Norman Cosmetics offers makeovers as well to help the bride, her attendants and the mothers look their best. In fact, you may want to shop for dresses and accessories in their boutique.

Music

Music sets the mood of a wedding, adding to the beauty and enjoyment of the reception. The Wilmington area abounds with musicians to please any ear. Here are a few varied choices for your special day.

A Harp for All Seasons
Carmen Coles
209 NE 56th St., Oak Island
• (910) 278-4028

Carmen's repertoire of 85 pieces range from classical to pop and include Jewish, Celtic and sacred music. She has played from Bald Head to Whiteville and performs as a soloist or with flute or violin.

Celebrations DJ Service - Disc Jockey
Robert Clemmons
125 N. Hampton Rd., Wilmington
• (910) 395-1060

Robert is one of the locals' favorite DJs. He spins your best-loved tunes and provides wonderful lighting and sound.

Key Productions
1027 Captain Adkins Dr., Southport
• (910) 457-5232

Jim Minett has been providing music for over 20 years. His professional music production company will customize service for your event. He provides live music, serves as a DJ/ Master of Ceremonies for prerecorded music, or performs a combination of both using the highest-quality equipment. Karaoke is also available upon request.

Maura Kropke, Violinist
117 Nun St., Wilmington • (910) 254-0758

With 12 years experience playing for wedding parties, Maura plays from pre-ceremony through the reception. She likes classical and the standards and loves jazz. Maura enjoys the "releasing butterflies" serenade.

INSIDERS' TIP

Sometimes you can rent your wedding-day accessories, such as candelabra, arches, kneeling benches, tents, tables, chairs and even tuxedos, from your florist.

Mid Atlantic Productions - Disc Jockey Gerry White
116 Bradley Creek Point Rd., Wilmington
• (910) 256-9880

Gerry played 53 receptions in 2002. Popular guy! His Saturdays are often pretty well booked, so reserve early or opt for Fridays and Sundays, when the rates are less expensive.

Port City Pipes and Drums
Pipe Major Andrew Services
4210 Lake Ave., Apt. 123, Wilmington
• (910) 232-5678

Pipe Major Services played for the Queen of England and he will play for you! "Highland Cathedral" is a favorite, but he will play whatever you like. Expect upbeat, happy music for your reception.

Shoresound Productions
2049 Gilbert Rd. SE, Bolivia
• (910) 253-7515

Shoresound Productions is a family affair. Tommy, Teresa and daughter Kimberly provide entertainment for birthday parties, class reunions, company parties and other events as well as for rehearsal parties and wedding receptions. A unique combination of a DJ and live band is one entertainment service offered. The compact disc collection consists of classical, Big Band, jazz, beach, rhythm and blues, top 40, classic country, contemporary country, reggae, rap, classic rock, new r&b and more.

Reception Facilities and Caterers

"A jug of wine, a loaf of bread and thee beside me..." Reception facilities in the Wilmington area offer as many choices as the mind can imagine. Options include choosing a location, such as a hotel or restaurant that will provide the food and beverages, or engaging a caterer. Our Restaurants chapter lists a number of excellent places to host either a rehearsal dinner or a full-blown reception.

If you'd prefer to host the reception in Wilmington's Historic District or in a romantic oceanfront house facing one of the many beaches, a caterer can provide all services while you enjoy the company of your guests. The caterer will also clean afterwards. Expect to spend $20 to $50 per guest, depending upon your choice of menu and type of bar service.

Grouper Nancy's
501 Nutt St., Wilmington
- **(910) 251-8009**

This riverfront restaurant will cater to 200 wedding guests in house or up to 1,000 at other locations. Specializing in the freshest seafood and the most flavorful steaks, head chef Mark Moore aims to please and is delighted to customize your reception. Together with his professional staff, he's catered at such historic locations as Thalian Hall, Graystone Inn, Bellamy Mansion and Airlie Gardens.

Henrietta III Wedding Cruise
Cape Fear Riverboats
Wilmington • (910) 343-1611,
(800) 676-0162

Cruise down the beautiful Cape Fear River with your sweetheart and wedding party. Choose from several packages, including a daytime cruise from noon to 1:30 PM and a private Saturday evening cruise from 6:30 to 9:30 PM. Menu fare ranges from light hors d'oeuvres to an elegant three-course dinner and includes a scrumptious tiered wedding cake and bubbling champagne toast for all guests.

JC's Catering
212 N.C. Hwy. 210, Holly Ridge
- **(910) 347-7566**

From a formal sit-down dinner with china and silver to one of their famous pig-pickins on paper plates, JC's Catering has it all. Chose from seafood, steak or JC's delicious barbecue with salads, vegetables and/or heavy hors d' oeuvres. A minimum of 50 meals is required for JC's to travel to the location of your choice with everything needed to feed the wedding reception guests.

Jerry Rouse Catering
7220 Wrightsville Ave., Wilmington
- **(910) 256-8847**

All your catering needs for 50 to 500 wedding guests will be coordinated. A professional staff offers 28 years of professional experience and will happily assist you in selecting the most appropriate menu. For your convenience, a complete list of wedding services is offered, such as tent set-up, shrimparoos and music, to assure that your special day is memorable in every way.

RIVERBOAT LANDING RESTAURANT

Making Each Event Personal To You.

On-Premise Catering for up to 110 Guests
Off-Premise Catering for up to 500 Guests

2 Market St · Downtown Wilmington · 763-7227

King Neptune Restaurant
11 N. Lumina Ave., Wrightsville Beach
- **(910) 256-2525**

King Neptune offers fabulous Caribbean seafood in a unique island atmosphere just steps away from the ocean dunes of Wrightsville Beach. Private banquet rooms for up to 35 guests are great for rehearsal dinners and small receptions. If you want to reserve the whole restaurant, the staff can accommodate up to 125 people.

Mad Boar Restaurant
111 River Village Pl., Wallace
- **(910) 285-8888**

The Celtic Court banquet hall of this 21,000-square-foot multi-purpose facility offers a trip back to nobler times when lords and ladies gathered in grand ballrooms, feasting on food and drink and dancing supreme. Rich in historical feel and magnificent tradition, the Celtic Court offers a unique atmosphere with seating for more than 300 guests. The banquet hall comes complete with luminous alabaster chandeliers, a hand-carved wood accent bar, hand-painted gold leaf walls and an elevated stage wrapped in exquisite velvet curtains. Offering world-class cuisine, the Court is the perfect place for your rehearsal dinner or wedding reception.

Milano's
The Forum, 1124 Military Cutoff Rd.,
Wilmington • (910) 256-8870

Elegantly appointed, Milano's offers two beautiful private rooms, as well as a casual indoor courtyard for a wedding reception unlike any other. After dining on such old-world specialties as fresh seafood, steaks, chops and homemade pasta, dance the night away at Club Milano's, which features live entertainment from across the southeast. Milano's was voted Best Restaurant Atmosphere in the 2002 *Encore* Readers Poll and Most Romantic Restaurant by *Wrightsville Beach Magazine*.

Paliotti's at the Villa
790 New River Inlet Rd., North Topsail Beach • (910) 328-8501 (910) 329-2971

The Villa Capriani provides a delightful setting for a beach wedding or a ceremony on the upper or cabana deck. Following the wedding, Paliotti's, the on-premises restaurant, is the perfect place to hold a reception. They offer everything from hors d' oeuvres to a buffet or sit-down dinner for up to 100 people. Some of the more popular meal choices are prime rib, chicken picata or stuffed flounder. Dee, the wedding specialist, will help with your choice of a band or DJ, decorations for the reception and accommodations. She cautions that accommodations at the Villa can be difficult or impossible during the summer season unless reservations are made well in advance. Paliotti's has all ABC permits and will provide bar service.

Pasta Grill
513 Country Club Dr., Hampstead • (910) 270-2425

Part of the Olde Point Golf and Country Club Complex, the Pasta Grill offers outstanding food and drink for any and all wedding functions. There are three separate rooms, ranging from the intimate grill to the Osprey Room, which can seat up to 150 people. The Pasta Grill provides an excellent venue for engagement parties, bridal showers, luncheons, rehearsal dinners and wedding receptions. The quaint gazebo overlooking the clubhouse pond is the perfect spot for romantic toasts and photo opportunities.

Riverboat Landing
2 Market St., Wilmington • (910) 763-7227

Many marriage proposals have taken place from this fine restaurant's nine two-seater balconies that overlook the Cape Fear River. Owner Steve Kohlstedt said multiple family weddings result from the restaurants consistent high quality in both food and service. One couple who enjoyed a romantic balcony dinner, came back to renew their vows on their tenth wedding anniversary. The next year, they had a reception for one of their daughters. And the following year, a rehearsal dinner was held for another family member! In 18 years of business, the Riverboat Landing restaurant has hosted 1,000 wedding rehearsal dinners and an equal number of wedding receptions. The restaurant offers in-house catering to 110 people in its private banquet room and off-site catering to a maximum of 500. Catering services are fully customized with offerings of the finest seafood and steaks, hors d'oeuvres and buffets.

Sugar Shack
1609 Hale Beach Rd., Ocean Isle Beach • (910) 579-3844

The Sugar Shack, famous for its huge steaks, marinated and slow cooked, and its Jamaican home cooking, will make your wedding dinner and/or reception famous for years to come. These folks are willing to please as well, catering in-house, off-site, indoors, outdoors, full-service or supplying just the food — whatever your heart desires. They will definitely add to the ambience and appeal to the taste of the most discriminating guest.

> **INSIDERS' TIP**
> Don't leave the ordering of flowers until the last minute. Florists need time to arrange for the freshest and loveliest flowers for your day.

Turtle Island Restaurant and Catering
6220 E. Oak Island Dr., Oak Island • (910) 278-4944

The folks at Turtle Island are happy to work with you in planning the menu and in presenting their luscious food in a way that makes it candy for the eyes. They will cater your wedding reception or rehearsal dinner on-site or off-site to meet your highest expectations. Trust your wedding cake to them and you can't lose.

Photography

Al Patterson Photography
7092 Old Oak Rd. NW, Ash • (910) 287-7107

Award-winning photographer Al Patterson has been taking photographs for more than 30 years. You can find his work on the Visitor's Guide of the Brunswick County telephone directory and the cover of the South Brunswick Islands Chamber of Commerce brochure. He has wedding packages available on location or in the studio. Digital video recording is available as well. Al and his wife, Sue, have wedding invitations, stationary, place cards, programs, thank-you notes and provide complete wedding services, including accommodations, cakes and catering, florists, entertainment, limo services, tuxedo rentals, party rentals and wedding locations.

Arrow Ross Photography
711-A N. Fifth St., Wilmington
• (910) 762-2243

Photographing people is Arrow's specialty. Weddings offer an opportunity to capture the spirit of the moment in a telling photograph. Using his skills as a photojournalist, Arrow is able to anticipate and capture real moments that make memorable photographs.

Boswell Photography II
1014 W. Dolphin St., Oak Island
• (910) 278-7957

Mike Boswell has been a professional photographer for 27 years. Though his studio is traditional, using classical poses and settings, he intersperses these with candid photos and photojournalism shots for the wedding album. He views his work as recording family history and works with his customers to make that record reflect their part in the history. Mike works with black and white and/or color film and does restoration of old photos as well.

Calabash Photography Studio
9962 Beach Dr., Calabash • (910) 579-2093

The folks at Calabash Photography Studio take black and white and color photos in traditional, candid and photojournalism poses and offer you packages that include the wedding album. They will travel from the church to the reception hall in order to cover the whole event. They take wedding photos on the beach. A special service available is the posting of your wedding photos on their website, which allows your relatives and friends who live at a distance to share in the joy.

Matt McGraw Photography
417 Mosswood Ct., Wilmington
• (910) 686-8583

Matt's experience in photojournalism and full-service portrait photography allows him to click the essence of emotion in a single moment. He listens, inquires and adapts to the surroundings of the wedding party, recording the wedding celebration as it happens and telling a story that will last a lifetime.

Ocean View Photography
756 E. Ocean Rd., Holly Ridge
• (910) 329-0620

Environmental photography has been Denis Lemay's expertise for the past 30 years, making him a natural as a beach wedding photographer. He will work locally or travel up or down the N.C. coast. While beach weddings make up a large percentage of this business, Ocean View is also known for on location photography of families, large groups and events. Photography at local plantations is also a specialty of this N.Y.I.-certified, award-winning photographer

Videography

Lifetime Video Productions
110 Tara Dr., Wilmington
• (910) 392-8163, (910) 297-1522

Peter Burno believes in giving his wedding clients the service they desire, both during and after the wedding celebration. With 20 years experience, Peter knows how to be unobtrusive in capturing the spirit of the moment. He has the equipment for full DVD coverage and can even video your photo album and set it to music.

Mari Kittredge Video Productions
4930 Pine St., Wilmington
• (910) 452-7239

Mari's artistry redefines the wedding video. She has a timeless approach to recording your special day, and the results are flowing, personal and intimate. Capturing loving exchanges between family members is her forte.

Coventry Films
4577 Holly Tree Rd., Wilmington
• (910) 297-4147

Coventry Films is a full-service company that provides complete videography packages for weddings. Coventry is unique in that three distinct packages are offered, ranging from basic ceremony coverage to a comprehensive, behind-the-scenes documentary. Each package includes two-camera coverage, no time limit, no travel fee, professional editing and three copies mailed anywhere in the United States. And thanks to zoom lenses, lapel microphones and battery packs (no cables), Coventry's presence is completely unobtrusive.

Blanchard Productions, Inc.
4922 Northeaster Dr., Wilmington
• (910) 392-4211

If you want it done right, Michael Blanchard's upscale videography is for you. Screen Gem Studios will affirm the high quality of his work.

Wedding Cakes

One of our favorite sayings comes from Ann Willard, who makes the best pound cakes (and the best Ikebana arrangements) in Wilmington: "I don't have a sweet tooth. I have a whole mouthful of them!" If you have as many sweet teeth as we do, you'll be happy for the dozen or more bakeries that make fantastic cakes in this coastal area. Here are a few of our favorites.

Apple Annie's
Outlet Mall, College Rd., Wilmington
• (910) 799-9023
Landfall Shopping Center, Eastwood Rd.
and Military Cutoff Rd., Wilmington
• (910) 256-6585

Apple Annie's wedding cakes are customized to delight your palate. Each tier is like a torte with four layers of cake and three layers of filling. Representations of your favorite photograph or scene can be drawn on any sheet cake via the computer with incredible likeness.

Barb's Midtown Deli
4346 Long Beach Rd., Southport
• (910) 457-4600

Barb's Midtown Deli is known in the area for its bakery products, and when it comes to wedding cakes, they are extremely helpful. You can bring in a picture of a cake you like, choose one out of several books available in the deli, or custom design your own. In any case, you will receive a delicious and beautiful result. Barb's also provide hors d'oeuvres catering.

Blueberry Hill Dessertery
The Forum, 1113 Military Cutoff Rd.,
Wilmington • (910) 509-0700

Pastry cream laced with strawberries, Bailey's Irish Cream, Grand Marnier, chocolate mousse — you name the ingredients and Blueberry Hill will fill the bill. Each tier of the cake can be a different flavor, with pound cake the favorite and chocolate, carrot and Italian cream as close runner-ups. John Travolta gave Blueberry Hill a big thumbs up when he was shooting his last film in Wilmington.

The French Bake and Pastry Shop
Seaside Plaza 7290-10 Beach Dr., Ocean
Isle Beach • (910) 575-0284

Robert Van Lieden, a native of Amsterdam and retired from, Chez Robert, his very own famous restaurant in Washington, DC, now owns and runs this French Patisserie. He will bake custom designed wedding cakes, using his own scrumptious ingredients, that will delight you and all your guests.

Sweet & Savory Cafe and Bake Shop
1611 Pavilion Pl., Wilmington
• (910) 256-0115

Apprenticed under the best pastry chefs in Savannah, Kim Herring decorates her wedding cakes with an exquisite butter cream frosting. Nothing comes out of a can. Luscious rolled fondant and edible flowers are intertwined to please your eyes and taste buds. Kim, husband Dave and a very experienced and attractive staff will cater for 50 to 500 people.

Wildflour Cakes and Pastries
559 Riverwood Dr., Bolivia
• (910) 754-9115

We are very lucky to have Anne Ohlson in our area. Anne is a graduate of the Culinary Institute. While there, she was selected as a top 10 student chef and had the honor of assisting Julia Child and other great chefs at the annual Food and Wine Classic in Aspen, Colorado. Anne says, "The (wedding) cake is the showpiece, an expression of the tone and theme of the event." Anne will work with you to design your cake exactly as you want it. She has sketches, pictures and a portfolio of her favorite cakes. She suggests considering fresh fruit, chocolate shells or sugared flowers as decoration. She will deliver the cake and set it up as well. Wildflour Cakes and Pastries provides appetizers and reception foods such as cinnamon rolls, chocolate dipped strawberries, tarts, chocolate mousse cups, cream cheese puffs, cookie baskets and brownies.

Day Spas

Ahhh! Brides, mothers of brides and even grooms deserve time to relax and be pampered before the wedding. Day spa packages also make great gifts for members of the wedding party. Here are a few favorite places to help you take a deep breath after all the wedding planning is completed.

Wilmington

Harbour Club
**Lumina Station, 1904 Eastwood Rd.,
Ste. 101, Wilmington • (910) 256-5020**

With facials, therapeutic massage, manicures, pedicures, La Stone therapy and more, this day spa will definitely lift your spirits. Among many different packages, Harbour Club offers both a Girl's Day Out and a Guy's Day Out.

Head to Toe Day Spa
**1928-B Eastwood Rd., Wilmington
• (910) 256-3370**

Serenity and service walk hand in hand at this quality spa. Facials with chemical peels or micro-dermabrasion, waxing, acupuncture, complete hair care and makeup are just a few treats in store for you.

Ki Spa and Salon
**1125 Military Cutoff Rd., Wilmington
• (910) 509-0410**

Ki, the ancient Japanese word for energy is incorporated in all spa treatments, which include massage, nails, waxing, wellness packages, hair-styling, and body, facial and specialty treatments. Natural products are combined with pure aromatherapy and healing techniques to promote total body renewal. Specialized treatments are created to rejuvenate and transform your spirit and help you achieve the ultimate in healing and total body awareness..

Southport

Oceanic Salon & Day Spa
**4961 Long Beach Rd., Southport
• (910) 454-8800**

With services available at the Southport address and on Bald Head Island, this versatile spa provides any service you can think of, including custom cuts, color, perms, manicures, pedicures, nails, facials, micro-dermabrasion, chemical peels, oxygen facial treatments, body wraps, massage therapy, hot stone massage, hair removal and tanning. Among their many packages is "Here Comes the Bride," a five-hour experience that provides the Essential Basic Facial, Salt Glow Body Mask including a Back Body Work session, paraffin manicure, therapeutic pedicure and an eyebrow

Start a new life together at the beach.

Photo: Matt McGraw

and bikini wax. This service is recommended the week before your wedding day. For the groom — a "Just for Him" package.

Totally You Day Spa
5083 Southport-Supply Rd. SE, Southport
• (910) 457-0502

Services available at this full-service spa include haircuts, permanents, highlights, facials, basic and spa manicures, basic and spa pedicures and massages. You can build your own package or choose from one of theirs. "My Treat" is a two-hour package that provides a half-hour massage, refreshing facial and a manicure. "A Little Luxury" (three hours) includes a one-hour massage, a one-hour facial and a manicure. And for the men, "The Gentleman" serves up a one-hour massage, foot therapy and a sports facial.

South Brunswick Islands

Kozo Hair Designs & Spa
349 Village Rd., Shallotte • (910) 754-9477

Kozo offers shampooing, haircuts, color, perms, straightening, hair treatments, facials, peels, make-up, waxing, manicures, pedicures, sculptured nails, massages and more. They do specialty hair designs for weddings and proms as well as a Deluxe Bridal Package and a Bridal Value Package. Why not treat yourself and your attendants before the wedding?

Spa Rituals
7247 Beach Dr. SW, Ocean Isle Beach
• (910) 575-5435

According to owner Laura Bullington, the only thing Spa Rituals doesn't do is hair. The employees in this shop spoil their customers — make them princesses for a day. Choose from the services available and customize your package for the whole wedding party.

Topsail Island

A Beautiful New You Day Spa
322 N. New River Dr., Surf City
• (910) 328-2525

A Beautiful New You wants to pamper all the members of the wedding party and family with one of the many special wedding packages, including a Bridal Bash, Bride and Mother, Grooms Special or Wedding Party Thank You. The spa is housed in its own building and provides a peaceful, cozy, friendly atmosphere.

Transportation

Want a fancy vehicle to get you to the church on time? Try one of these services. Also check the list of limousine companies in our Getting Around chapter.

Always Platinum Limousine
P.O. Box 98752, Raleigh, NC 27624
• (888) 464-9800

This company services Wilmington, Raleigh, Myrtle Beach and Jacksonville. You have your choice of a Cadillac Escalade, Navigator SUV or Lincoln stretch limousine, which holds 17 people.

Azalea Limousine Service
244 Princess St., Wilmington
• (910) 452-5888

Azalea has provided quality local service for the past three years and looks forward to serving you with your choice of a passenger shuttle bus and two 2001 Lincoln towncar limousines.

Top Hat Limousines
6304 Market St., Wilmington
• (910) 262-8889

Top Hat gives you safe and reliable service with a smile, plus your choice of three 2001 Lincoln towncar limousines. This four-year old company will pick up your guests at the Wilmington, Raleigh or Myrtle Beach airports.

The Carriage Man/Horse-Drawn Carriage
Historic Downtown Wilmington
• (910) 251-8889

Return to the antebellum era in a special French evening coach, the wedding carriage. Dressed in full tux and top hat, carriage man John Pucci will festoon both horses and coach with silver hearts and silk flowers, so you truly feel like a princess with your prince charming. Wedding ceremonies have actually been performed on the carriage from 23rd Street down to the Cape Fear River. Other horse-drawn vehicles are available as well, including a horse-drawn trolley.

Rental Equipment

L & L Tent & Party Rentals
3703 Wrightsville Ave., Wilmington
• (910) 791-4141

L & L will lighten your load by delivering, setting up and breaking down all your wedding supplies and equipment, including small and large tents, lights, heaters or fans, sound equipment and much more.

Party Suppliers & Rentals
4013 Oleander Ave, Wilmington
• (910) 791-0024, (800) 344-8368

From archways to columns, this company will satisfy your wedding needs. They offer a wide variety of linens, wedding brass, china, silver, artificial plants and just about anything you can imagine.

Coastal Tent & Party Rentals
5711 Market St., Wilmington
• (910) 791-0013

Dress up your wedding or reception tent with side walls, whether the tent is 10' by 10' or 40' by 100'. Coastal offers complete wedding supplies, including arches, columns, seating, kneeling benches, wedding brass and candelabras.

Annual Events

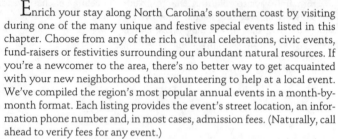

Enrich your stay along North Carolina's southern coast by visiting during one of the many unique and festive special events listed in this chapter. Choose from any of the rich cultural celebrations, civic events, fund-raisers or festivities surrounding our abundant natural resources. If you're a newcomer to the area, there's no better way to get acquainted with your new neighborhood than volunteering to help at a local event. We've compiled the region's most popular annual events in a month-by-month format. Each listing provides the event's street location, an information phone number and, in most cases, admission fees. (Naturally, call ahead to verify fees for any event.)

Need more information? Contact the appropriate chamber of commerce for assistance (see a list of chambers of commerce in our Area Overviews chapter). For events in the Greater Wilmington area, you may also contact the Cape Fear Coast Convention & Visitors Bureau, (910) 341-4030 or (800) 222-4757. Annual fishing and golf tournaments, sailing regattas and athletic events are listed in their respective chapters.

January

Model Railroad Show
American Legion Post 10, 702 Pine Grove Dr., Wilmington • (910) 270-2696

Sponsored by the Cape Fear Model Railroad Club, this annual weekend event is held in late January. In 1999 the Southeast Tourism Society voted this show one of its Top 20 Events for January and February. It's a must-see for both novice and experienced model-train enthusiasts. Expect to see displays with operating model-train layouts in three different scales (sizes), a table of goodies for sale and free clinics in model-train display techniques. The show runs for two weekend days in late January from 10 AM to 5 PM on Saturday and 10 AM to 4 PM on Sunday. Proceeds from the show help maintain and refurbish the group's awesome model-train display on the second floor of the Wilmington Railroad Museum.

Martin Luther King Jr. Day March and Commemoration
Assorted Venues., Wilmington • (910) 815-0669

Martin Luther King Jr. Day has special resonance to Wilmingtonians because (among other reasons) Dr. King was scheduled to speak here the day he was assassinated. Wilmington honors his memory on the third Monday of January with a short commemorative march from Fifth and Castle Streets to Williston Middle School, 401 S. 10th Street. A youth rally and cookout follow at Williston. Other activities include an all-day celebration at Town Hall Community Education Cultural Center with food, entertainment and speeches.

Martin Luther King Celebration
Assorted Venues, Southport • (910) 457-5144

The annual Memorial March begins at 2 PM in the parking lot of Southport Elementary School, which is located at 701 W. 9th Street.

Following the march is a program (held in the school) to launch a project entitled "Do Something." It is designed to challenge youths to perform acts of justice and kindness. The next day at 8 AM, the eighth annual roundtable breakfast is held in the Southport Community Center on Bay Street. The Walter Welsh Award is presented at the breakfast. The award was instituted to give tribute to an individual who has dedicated his life to promotion of racial harmony and understanding.

33rd Annual Greater Wilmington Antique Show
Coastline Convention Center, 501 Nutt St., Wilmington • (910) 256-5274

If you love antiques, this show's for you! Sponsored by North Carolina Junior Sorosis, the event hosts 30 antiques dealers from North Carolina and throughout the Southeast to tempt you with quality antique glass, silver, china, jewelry, Oriental rugs and more. Hallmarks of this show are the high-quality items for sale with only a limited number of exceptional reproductions permitted. Admission is $5. The hours are Friday and Saturday 10 AM to 7 PM and Sunday noon to 5 PM. Proceeds contribute to a full scholarship to UNC-Wilmington and benefit area charitable organizations. The event is held the last weekend in January.

February

North Carolina Jazz Festival
Wilmington Hilton Riverside, 301 N. Water St., Wilmington • (910) 763-8585

The performers roster of the North Carolina Jazz Festival over the years reads like a Who's Who in Dixieland and mainstream jazz: Milt Hinton, Ken Peplowski, Art Hodes, Frank Tate, Bob Wilber, Kenny Davern and Bob Rosengarden. The Friday- and Saturday-night performances, for which tickets may sell out a year in advance, enjoy a cabaret setting at the Wilmington Hilton's ballroom. A preview performance takes place on Thursday night on the main stage at UNCW's Kenan Auditorium.

How Does Your Garden Grow? Show!
Coast Line Convention Center, 501 Nutt St., Wilmington • (910) 458-6393

Get an early jump on the long North Carolina growing season by viewing what's new in landscape design and knowhow. Exhibits, lectures and demonstrations by speakers from throughout North Carolina present innovative products, designs and techniques for improving the surroundings of your home or business. Door prizes are awarded, and the show offers plenty of gift items that gardeners and landscapers would enjoy. The two-day show takes place the first weekend of February and is sponsored by the New Hanover County Extension Service Arboretum Foundation Inc., which is itself a wonderful place to visit any time of the year (see our Attractions chapter). Admission to the show costs $5. Children younger than 12 are admitted free.

Fort Anderson Civil War Encampment
Brunswick Town State Historic Site
St. Phillips Rd., Winnabow
• (910) 371-6613

In commemoration of an 1865 Civil War battle on the site, this event is interesting, entertaining and educational (but don't tell the kids!) There are programs focused on the Civil War, tours of Ft. Anderson (located at Brunswick Town State Historic Site, see our Attractions chapter) by uniformed personnel from the units bivouacked at the site, small arms demonstrations and possibly artillery demonstrations. Admission is free.

March

New Hanover County Residents' Appreciation Day
Assorted venues, Wilmington and New Hanover County • (910) 341-4030, Ext.20

This popular annual event, now in its eighth year, is a great opportunity for area residents to rediscover and savor New Hanover County attractions, including Wilmington, Wrightsville Beach and Carolina Beach locations. Best of all, this Sunday event is free! Contact the Cape Fear Coast Convention and Visitors Bureau at the number listed above for a list of participating attractions. Remember to carry proof of county residency for admission.

The Associated Artists of Southport Spring Art Show
Franklin Square Gallery, 130 E. West St., Southport • (910) 457-5450

This art show hangs in the Franklin Square Gallery for the month of March. It's a great chance to see the two- and three-dimensional artwork of the many talented artists of Southport and the surrounding area. Admission to the gallery is free, and a gift shop is on the premises.

Mardi Gras Bid For Literacy Auction
Coastline Convention Center, 501 Nutt St., Wilmington • (910) 251-0911

Mardi Gras comes to Wilmington on the second weekend in March. This annual fund-raiser is sponsored by the Cape Fear Literacy Council and has become a popular evening for auction enthusiasts. Decorated and built around a Mardi Gras theme, the auction features sales of decorated masks and strings of beads, a lavish buffet with food donated by area restaurants, a queen's cake and a silent auction. The vocal auction is the centerpiece of the evening, with all items donated from area merchants, professionals, local artists, the film community, restaurants and corporate sponsors. Past items won by lucky bidders have included cars, cruises to tropical islands, weekend getaway packages, celebrity items (a guitar signed by Reba McEntire comes to mind), signed movie scripts and film memorabilia (including Dawson's Creek items), signed local art and much more! Tickets cost $25, and the fun begins at 6 PM.

Cucalorus Film Festival
Various locations, Wilmington
• (910) 343-5995

Film buffs and aspiring filmmakers shouldn't miss this four-day cinematic festival featuring outstanding native North Carolina feature films, shorts, videos and live music. This annual juried festival also draws international films from all over the globe. The best entries chosen from each category are shown during weekend festivities so popular that local film-industry insiders — actors, filmmakers, musicians and artists — make it a point to attend every year. (In case you're wondering, a cucalorus is a filmmaker's device used on a movie set to create a dappled light effect.) Admission options from previous festivals ranged from the cost of a single feature film to a Festival Pass that includes all screenings and live entertainment. Call for current admission rates.

Poplar Grove Herb & Garden Fair
Poplar Grove Historic Plantation,
10200 U.S. Hwy. 17 N., Wilmington
• (910) 686-9518, Ext. 26

Does spring fever have you itching to get into the garden? If so, join other garden and herb enthusiasts at Poplar Grove Plantation. This annual spring event features a full day of workshops and speakers on the subject of herbs. (Pre-registration and pre-payment are recommended.) These interesting and informative classes include the art of using herbs in a variety of ways. Another highlight of the fair is a garden and plant sale featuring live herbs and herbal products, perennials, shrubs, gardening accessories and more. For reservations or information on the class schedule and fees, call the number listed above.

A Day at the Docks
Jordan Blvd., Holden Beach
• (910) 842-4820

Ever hear of a Bopple Race? Care for a free ride on a charter fishing boat? Combine these with live entertainment, crafts, free Coast Guard boat inspections, a sunset boat parade and a blessing of the boats, and you've got Holden Beach's way of welcoming the return of spring. Something of a floating festival, the event offers various entertainments at ports of call along the island; thus, the free boat rides. All the food on sale is prepared by local restaurateurs as a showcase of local fare. Sponsored by the Greater Holden Beach Merchants Association, the festivities take place on the last Saturday in March, and admission is free. (By the way, a bopple is an apple boat that is assigned a number and three randomly selected crew. The bopples are dropped from the bridge into the Intracoastal Waterway, and the one that passes the finishing line first earns its crew cash prizes.) All proceeds are channeled into community volunteer groups and community projects. And the event is fish-friendly, too; all the bopples are retrieved.

April

North Carolina Azalea Festival
Various locations, Wilmington
• (910) 794-4650

No matter what the weather, spring isn't official until the Azalea Festival in early April, signaling the opening of the season in Wilmington and the southern coast of North Carolina. This lavish annual Wednesday-through-Sunday celebration, one of the largest in the region, attracts thousands of visitors from all over the United States and Canada and features scores of musical and theatrical performances by local talent and celebrity guests, the Clyde Beatty-Cole Bros. Circus, breathtaking garden and home tours throughout historic Wilmington and Wrightsville Beach, and, naturally, a wonderland of blooming azaleas.

The Azalea Festival garden tours, an annual fund-raising event for the Cape Fear Garden Club, are available from Friday through Sunday during this festive weekend. Proceeds from this tour are returned to the community through horticultural grants and UNC-

Wilmington scholarships. Home tours are conducted on Saturday and Sunday. An admission fee is charged for both tours.

Contact the N.C. Azalea Festival office at (910) 794-4650 for admission information and a current list of featured homes and gardens. Don't miss Saturday morning's three-hour grand parade downtown, which kicks off a weekend of free outdoor entertainment on several downtown stages and a lively street fair. The fair, located along the Cape Fear River waterfront, is a beloved Wilmington tradition filled with food vendors, art and craft booths, exhibits and throngs of people.

5th Annual Oak Island Lighthouse 10K Run/Walk
Southport-Oak Island Area Chamber of Commerce, 4841 Long Beach Rd., SE, Southport • (910) 457-6964, (800) 457-6964

The route of this popular run/walk begins at the Brunswick County Airport, crosses the Oak Island Bridge, turns through tree lined streets, follows the beachfront and ends at the Oak Island Lighthouse. Awards are made to the three top runners over all and the three top runners in each age group. Come join the competition!

Medieval Festival
Poplar Grove Historic Plantation, 10200 Hwy. 17 N., Wilmington • (910) 686-9518, Ext. 26

Imagine the days of old when knights were bold and life was dangerous with dragons prowling the lands. Bring the whole family and enjoy a step back in time to medieval England. The local chapter of the Society for Creative Anachronism offers a merry old time of jousting competitions and other tournament events, dancing, demonstrations, crafts (medieval and modern), activities designed for children plus a medieval marketplace. Be lulled by bards, bagpipes and harps as the romance of knighthood comes back to existence. Call for admission fees.

Topsail Island Spring Fling
Surf City Marina, Roland Ave. Cswy., Surf City • (910) 329-4446

The first festival of the season on Topsail, Spring Fling is a celebration of the grand re-opening of the island after the quieter winter season. This event, held the last weekend in April, is a weekend full of entertainment and activities managed by the Kiwanis Club of Topsail Island in cooperation with the Chamber of Commerce and Town of Surf City. Kicking off the celebration on Saturday morning at 7 AM is the famous Kiwanis Club pancake breakfast. Arts and crafts booths, local commercial business booths, a Marine Corps display, exhibits and children's rides all begin at 10 AM on Saturday and 11 AM on Sunday, closing at 5 PM on both days.

Clowns, face-painters and a variety of local vocal and instrumental groups provide entertainment on both days. A wide range of food booths offer choices for lunch or snacking. Saturday entertainment ends with an early evening concert. On Sunday afternoon from 1 to 4 PM the headlining band performs. A beer and wine garden is open both days beginning at 1 PM and extending through the concert on Saturday night.

Surf & Turf Triathlon
Surf City Baptist Church parking lot, New River Dr. and Wilmington Ave., Surf City • (910) 329-4446

This sprint triathlon for novice or serious competitive triathletes is held in conjunction with Topsail Island Spring Fling on the last Saturday in April. It is part of the North Carolina Triathlon Series, managed by Set-up Inc. Events include a 0.5-mile ocean swim, 20K bike course and 5K run. The triathlon is a fund-raiser for the chamber of commerce and is sanctioned by the U.S. Triathlon Association. Advance registration is $45 for USAT members and $54 for non-members (on race day its $10 more). Relay teams are charged $75 and $84 respectively with a $15 charge for race-day registration. Registration can be made in advance via Set-up Inc. or on the day of the event, providing there is still room (race limit 400 participants). On-site registration and packet pick up are at the Surf City Fire Department next to the Transition Area in the parking lot of the Surf City Baptist Church.

Art in the Park
Franklin Square Park, E. West St., Southport • (910) 457-5450, (910) 253-2672, (800) 222-4790

Local and regional artists working in a vari-

INSIDERS' TIP
Check out the spookier aspects of Wilmington's colorful past with *Haunted Wilmington* by Brooks Preik. This collection of ghost stories is available at most area bookstores.

ety of media demonstrate and present their work beneath Southport's venerable live oaks. The show and sale is held on the last Saturday in April from 10 AM to 3 PM. There are games and crafts in which the children can participate, a clown or two, face-painting and a fun day for all. The event is sponsored by the Associated Artists of Southport, Partnership for Children and Brunswick County Parks and Recreation. Admission is free.

May

15th Annual Spring Concert
Brunswick Concert Band
Hatch Auditorium, Caswell Beach
• (910) 278-7908

One of two formal concerts given by the Brunswick Concert Band (see the Music section of The Arts chapter), this concert is held in the Baptist Assembly at the easternmost tip of Oak Island. The blend of ages of the individuals who make up this enthusiastic group and the blend of music, from jazz to show tunes to country to patriotic, always provides listening pleasure to the audience.

Greek Festival
St. Nicholas Greek Orthodox Church,
608 S. College Rd., Wilmington
• (910) 452-5180

The Greek Festival is a wonderful opportunity (and for some people the only opportunity) to sample homemade moussaka, baklava and other Greek delicacies. Live Greek music, cultural presentations, cooking demonstrations, souvenirs, a tour of the church and a Greek-style marketplace round out this gala weekend-long celebration. Admission is $2 for adults. Children younger than 12 get in free. Fees are charged for food. The festival opens daily at noon.

Battleship North Carolina Memorial Day Observance
Battleship North Carolina, U.S. Hwy. 421
N., Wilmington • (910) 251-5797

Memorial Day is observed aboard the monumental Battleship North Carolina with free music, guest speakers and other special events. The memorial site is near the junction of highways 17, 74, 76 and 421 and is easily accessible from either bridge serving Wilmington. A tradition since 1968, the ceremony features a high-ranking military guest speaker, all-service color guard, a gun salute by Marines, taps and a me-

morial wreath dropped into the water. The ceremony begins at 5:45 PM. See our Attractions chapter for information about touring the ship during regular hours.

Cape Fear Disabled Sportsmen's Fishing Tournament
1001 N. Lake Park Boulevard, Carolina
Beach • (910) 458-4401, (910) 617-9930,
(800) 847-5771

The Annual Cape Fear Disabled Sportsmen's Fishing Tournament sponsored by The Got-Em-On-Live-Bait-Club is held from 7 AM to 12 noon on Friday at the Kure Beach Fishing Pier. Disabled anglers from all over the state of North Carolina attend this event. Cash prizes and trophies are awarded for the first five places. This event is free to all disabled anglers and their attendants, and breakfast, snacks, drinks, fishing equipment, bait and lunch are provided. In addition, door prizes, ticket drawings and tournament T-shirts are provided. The famous Captain Jimmy Price of Southport is on hand to offer help, humor, encouragement and, of course, to autograph hats and T-shirts. The CFDST has attracted the attention of groups such as Coastal Rehab and Easter Seals. Newspapers, magazines and TV stations have provided excellent coverage, which is leading to an increasing number of participants each year.

Fabulous 50-cent Fantail Film Festival
Battleship North Carolina U.S. Hwy.
421N., Wilmington • (910) 251-5797

A popular month-long May event is the Fabulous 50-cent Fantail Film Festival. Enjoy some of Hollywood's best on the fantail of the battleship every Friday evening in June. The fun starts at 8:30 PM with an admission fee of (you guessed it!) a mere 50¢ per person. Call the number listed above for more information or the movie schedule. This weekly film festival is repeated on Friday nights in October at 7 PM.

June

Quilters By The Sea Annual Quilt Show
Coast Line Convention Center, 501 Nutt
St., Wilmington• (910) 270-0375

Quilters and quilt enthusiasts won't want to miss this annual weekend event celebrating the creative talents of regional quilters. Quilts of all types by quilters of all skill levels are featured, and competition is keen to take home coveted ribbons in a variety of categories. The show also features a merchants mart and guild booth. A raffle quilt, handmade by guild members, is another highlight. Call for admission fee.

appraise up to three items per person at a charge of $5 per item. Admission is $5. per adult, with children under 12 getting in free. A combination ticket for $10 includes a house tour featuring a quilt exhibit.

Down Home Antique Fair
Poplar Grove Plantation, 10200 U.S. Hwy 17, Wilmington • (910) 686-9518

Booths inside and outside on the plantation groves are filled with offerings of fine antiques, collectibles, china, glassware, artwork, linens and more from a variety of local and long distance vendors. A licensed appraiser is on site to

Cape Fear Shakespeare Festival
Greenfield Lake Amphitheatre in Greenfield Park, U.S. Hwy. 421 (Carolina Beach Rd.), Wilmington • (910) 392-7474

Modeled after New York City's Shakespeare in the Park festival and others around the country, the Cape Fear Shakespeare Festival debuted in 1993 and features the Bard's plays conducted

Wilmington welcomes numerous exciting events all year long.

Photo: Jay Tervo

in a newly renovated outdoor amphitheatre in Greenfield Park. Bring the whole family for an evening of fun and theater under the stars. The plays run on weekend nights throughout June, and admission is free. Shows begin near dusk at 8 PM.

July

July National Juried Art Competition and Exhibition
Franklin Square Gallery, 130 E. West St., Southport • (910) 457-5450

The exhibit gleaned from this juried competition contains only the best work submitted in art from all over the country. If you love art, this is an exhibition not to be missed. Admission to the gallery is free, and there is a gift shop on the premises.

North Carolina 4th of July Festival
Downtown Southport and Oak Island • (910) 457-5578

People come from all over the state of North Carolina (and other states as well) to participate in this old-fashioned, small-town, family celebration. The population swells and traffic is heavy, but most folks are happy to wait a bit in order to be involved in the event. There is a parade, of course, with bands and clowns and horses. There are also firemen's games, which are quite wet, plus arts and crafts vendors and food vendors. And then there are fireworks over the water. But, most importantly, there is the naturalization ceremony, in which people of varying nationalities become citizens of the USA.

Island Fireworks
Surf City Town Park, Roland Ave., Surf City • (910) 328-4131

Get the jump on your July 4th celebration with a summer concert and fireworks display at the new Surf City Town Park on the Intracoastal Waterway. Be sure to bring your blankets and lawn chairs. Fireworks begin at dark following the concert.

Fourth of July Riverfront Celebration
Along Water St., Downtown Wilmington • (910) 341-7855

Celebrate our nation's independence with food, entertainment and a street fair on the riverfront in historic downtown Wilmington. Featured entertainment performs on the main stage along Water Street. The festivities run from 5 to 10 PM, with a not-to-be-missed fireworks display scheduled at 9:05 PM (see next listing).

Battleship Blast!
On the riverfront, Downtown Wilmington • (910) 251-5797

Tens of thousands of people turn out on the Fourth of July for Wilmington's best fireworks of the year, viewing the rockets' red glare launched from the Battleship North Carolina Memorial grounds from every vantage point imaginable. The best viewing is from downtown Wilmington. Sponsored by the joint efforts of the Battleship North Carolina, the City of Wilmington, WECT and WGNI, this breathtaking show starts at 9:05 PM. It's free.

Fourth of July Fireworks
Holly Ridge Town Park, Sound Rd., Holly Ridge • (910) 329-7081

The Holly Ridge Town Park is a wonderful setting for the annual fireworks display. Children can enjoy the playground equipment while waiting for the fireworks, and the spacious grounds allow room to spread a blanket for an old-fashioned picnic supper. Bring your own picnic or purchase hot dogs and drinks at the concession stand (a fund-raiser for Holly Ridge Parks Department). Entertainment precedes the fireworks that start at approximately 9:15 PM. The location is only a short distance from Topsail Island and convenient for vacationers. Admission is free.

Baskets of Summer
Poplar Grove Historic Plantation, 10200 Hwy. 17 N., Wilmington • (910) 686-9518, ext.26

Poplar Grove Plantation holds a one-day fun-filled basketry event for all skill levels. Instructing the classes are teachers from all around the Cape Fear region. They offer morning, afternoon, and all-day classes from which to choose. Participants may select up to four basket choices in order of preference: two in the morning and two in the afternoon. For more information and to sign up for classes, please call Poplar Grove at the above number.

INSIDERS' TIP

Remember to take insect repellent and sunscreen to outdoor events.

Cape Fear Blues Festival
Assorted venues, Wilmington
• **(910) 350-8822**

Presented by The Blues Society of the Lower Cape Fear, this popular summer music festival offers local, regional and national blues musicians an opportunity to show their stuff to enthusiastic audiences. It's held in Wilmington during the last weekend in July. Events during this blues-filled weekend begin with Thursday night's kick-off at Hollywood East Cinema Grill, featuring food, drink, live blues, and blues on the big screen, followed by Friday night's not-to-be-missed Cape Fear Blues Cruise on Wilmington's riverboat, the Henrietta III, and a free Blues Musicians' Workshop on Saturday at noon. Across the Cape Fear River from downtown Wilmington, join the fun at Battleship Park, located next to the Battleship North Carolina attraction, for the festival's Saturday evening concert and the free All-Day Blues Jam at noon on Sunday. Advance tickets and all-inclusive passes to festival events are available. Due to frequent sellouts, early bookings for the Blues Cruise are highly recommended.

August

Sneads Ferry Shrimp Festival
**Community Building Field, Park Ln.,
Sneads Ferry • (910) 329-4446**

This is the longest-running festival in the Top-sail area and has been going on for more than 25 years. It celebrates the heritage of the shrimping industry in the Sneads Ferry area. Always on the second weekend in August, it is a real crowd pleaser. A parade begins on Saturday at 10 AM at the corner of Old Folkstone and Peru roads, winding through the community and ending at Fulchers Landing Road. The festival begins after the parade on Saturday and ends with an evening concert. Sunday, the grounds are open from 11 AM until 5 PM. The famous Shrimparoo dinner, consisting of mouth-watering fresh local fried shrimp, french fries, cole slaw and hush puppies, is served in the community building. Be ready to wait in line during the lunch hour. Other festival events include carnival rides, arts and crafts, food and daytime entertainment. Admission fee is $2, and the Shrimparoo dinner is $7. There is also a charge for the carnival rides.

Sneads Ferry Rotary Club King Mackerel Fishing Tournament
Sneads Ferry • (910) 329-4446

Sponsored by the Stump Sound Rotary Club, this king mackerel fishing tournament is held in conjunction with the Sneads Ferry Shrimp Festival. A Captain's Meeting is held on Friday, fishing is done on Saturday and awards are given out on Sunday.

Topsail Island Offshore Fishing Club King Mackerel Fishing Tournament
Topsail Beach • (910) 329-4446

This tournament follows the tournament in Sneads Ferry. The captain's meeting is held on Friday night, fishing on Saturday with awards on Sunday. Headquarters are the Assembly Building in Topsail Beach. For information about obtaining an application or who to contact about rules and regulations, contact the chamber of commerce at the number above.

Castles and Scoops Contest
Holiday Inn Sunspree Resort, Wrightsville Beach • (910) 254-3534

Held annually on the fourth Saturday in August, the Castles and Scoops Contest is a day full of family fun in the sun. Local businesses, families, student and civic groups and area architects are among the competitors building awesome sand sculptures for awards in five different categories, including Public Favorite. The "scoops" of the contest refers to the ice cream sundaes built by the contestants while the judges make their decisions. Proceeds from this event benefit the Wilmington Children's Museum.

Labor Day Arts & Crafts Fair
Middleton Park, E. Oak Island Dr., Oak Island • (910) 278-7560

This annual Labor Day weekend festival is a celebration of local and regional artists and craftspeople who display and sell their goods, all within sight of the ocean (or nearly so). Food is available at concession stands. The daylong fair is held from 10 AM to 5 PM and is free.

Second Annual Endless Summer Beach Blast
Carolina Beach Road and Shipyard, Wilmington Jaycees • (910) 392-0086

The Jaycees host this huge event and expect up to 4,000 people to attend. Expect entertainment like General Johnson and the Chairman of the Board, The Embers, Big John Thompson, and The Breakfast Club. A nonprofit organization, the Wilmington Jaycees support such programs and organizations as the Wilmington Interfaith Hospitality Network, The Domestic Violence Shelter, the Rape Crisis Center, Girl Scouts, Boys and Girls Homes, the Duke Cancer Center, the NC Jaycee Burn Center and the Yahweh Center. For sponsorship opportunities, contact Todd Godbey at the number above.

September

North Carolina Big Sweep
Topsail Island Beaches and Inland Waterways • (910) 328-0863

National Big Sweep, held the third Saturday of September, is an opportunity for visitors and residents alike to join in the cleaning of the beaches and inland waterways, keeping them safe for marine life and birds as well as improving the beauty of these natural resources. A free kickoff breakfast is held at the Moose Lodge, N.C. Highway 50 between Surf City and Holly Ridge at 8 AM. Instructions, supplies and assignments are given at that time. For more information contact Inez Bradt, Pender County Big Sweep chairperson, at the number above, or call the chamber of commerce.

Hampstead Spot Festival
U.S. Hwy. 17, next to Topsail High School, Hampstead • (910) 270-9642

Just a short drive down U.S. Highway 17, the Hampstead Spot Festival offers an opportunity to enjoy a dinner of spot, one of the area's best-tasting fish, along with generous helpings of cole slaw and hush puppies. This festival opens on Friday night and ends on Sunday evening. It is important to remember that the dinner is only served on Saturday and Sunday and is not available for the Friday night opening. Other events for the whole family include amusement rides, a variety show, and arts and crafts. A golf tournament in conjunction with the festival is held on Saturday. To find out more about this tournament, call the Greater Hampstead Chamber of Commerce at the number listed above.

Admission to the festival is free, but there is a charge for the golf tournament and amusement rides. For scheduled hours or more information, contact the Greater Hampstead Area Chamber of Commerce at the number above.

October

Riverfest: A River Odyssey
Various locations • (910) 452-6862

Wilmington is celebrating its 25th Riverfest, a wonderful celebration of the Cape Fear River featuring regattas, an enormous street fair with food and crafts, stage shows, live arts performances and music, an ever-popular waiter's wine race (runners carry bottles and wineglasses on trays) and a cast of thousands from all over the globe. The events are free. Riverfest is traditionally held the first weekend of October.

North Carolina Oyster Festival
Ocean Isle Beach • (910) 754-6644, (800) 426-6644

If you can find a better oyster-shucking competition, go there, but the N.C. Oyster Shucking Championship at this Oyster Festival is hard to beat. A champion oyster shucker is selected to compete in the national oyster-shucking competition with hopes of going to the international competition in Ireland. Folks love it so much there's even an amateur division. Featuring mountains of the South Brunswick Islands' favorite food, in season at this time, the festival also offers continuous live music, arts and crafts vendors, entertainment for the kids, a 5K, 10K and fun run, an oyster stew cook-off and more. Admission is $2, free for children younger than 12.

Autumn with Topsail
Assembly Building Grounds, Flake Ave. and Channel Blvd., Topsail Beach • (910) 329-4446

This fall festival is hosted by The Topsail Island Historical and Cultural Arts Council and is a fund-raiser to support the historic Assembly Building, now used as a community center. Held the third weekend in October, it opens with a Kiwanis Pancake Breakfast at 7 AM on both Saturday and Sunday mornings. A juried arts show, Taste of Topsail, beer and wine garden, horse-drawn trolley rides, children's activities and daytime entertainment are offered on both Saturday and Sunday. The Missiles and More Museum, housed in the Assembly Building, is open throughout the festival. On Saturday, activities begin at 10 AM with entertainment starting at 11 AM. On Sunday, activities begin at 11 AM and entertainment at 1 PM. A Saturday night concert at 7 PM features a professional band playing beach music. Admission is free.

Topsail Island Surf Fishing Tournament
Topsail Island Beaches and Piers , Surf City • (910) 329-4446

This is the third year for this tournament that has become a popular event on Topsail Island. There will be an Anglers' Meeting and

Festive events enrich the downtown Wilmington scene.

Photo: Jay Tervo

pig pickin' on the 17th, fishing on the 18th and awards on the 19th. For more information about the tournament or location of the anglers' meeting and pig pickin', call the number listed above.

Halloween Festival
Poplar Grove Historic Plantation, 10200 U.S. Hwy. 17, Wilmington • (910) 686-9518 Ext. 26

The Halloween Festival is Poplar Grove's spooky event for the brave and faint-hearted alike. Planners guarantee that you will get totally scared from the haunted barn and haunted hayride that goes deep into the dark, dark woods. If this isn't your taste, there is a not-so-scary hayride and haunted barn on Saturday and Sunday, along with carnival games and rides. A costume contest is offered for children of all ages (including adults).

North Carolina Festival By the Sea
Holden Beach • (910) 842-3828

Thousands of people are discovering this festival centered on a traditional Halloween carnival for the island's children. On the last Saturday in October there's a parade on the causeway and a huge outdoor festival beneath the bridge, with live music, food and more than 160 craft booths. Contests on the beach (no fee) include kite flying, sand sculpture and horseshoe toss. The fleet of feet may participate in the 1K, 5K or 10K races (for a nominal fee). Saturday night features an old-fashioned street dance with live music. Plan to carpool and arrive early. (Parking laws are relaxed for the festival.) Admission to the festival is free, and all proceeds benefit Holden Beach's volunteer groups and community projects.

Halloween History-Mystery Tour
Bellamy Mansion Museum, 503 Market St., Wilmington • (910) 251-3700

The gorgeous Bellamy Mansion takes on an eerie aspect just for Halloween and is the first stop on this popular Halloween tour on the weekend prior to trick-or-treating. The self-guided walking tour begins at the mansion and continues throughout historic downtown Wilmington from dusk until 8:30 PM. Experience the Port City's haunted and mysterious past as you visit historic homes and other venues, including a haunted cemetery. Costumed storytellers at various sites along the tour offer insights into Wilmington's rich and spooky past. Call for current ticket prices.

November

Holly Ridge Holly Fest
Holly Ridge Town Park, Sound Rd., Holly Ridge • (910) 328-7081

Get in the holiday spirit with the annual Holly Fest parade and festival the first Saturday in November. The parade, to welcome Santa Claus to town, begins at 10 AM on U.S. Highway 17 at the north end of town. It turns onto U.S. Highway 50 at the traffic light and proceeds to Hines Street and the park. Activities in the park include a variety show, entertainment, amusement rides, arts and crafts, and food concessions.

Festival of Trees
Wilmington Hilton Riverside, 301 N. Water St., Wilmington • (910) 772-5474

Festival of Trees, a benefit for the Lower Cape Fear Hospice Inc., is a dazzling display of over 120 dressed Christmas trees with a specific theme. In 2003 the theme is "A Winter Wonderland." Visit the Holiday Room, featuring holiday decorations, wreaths, ornaments, a gingerbread village and gift baskets. A weeklong pass entitles you to enter all events repeatedly. Call for the current admission fee schedule.

North Carolina Holiday Flotilla at Wrightsville Beach
Banks Channel, Wrightsville Beach • (910) 341-4030, (910) 509-1204

This floating parade of brightly lit and wildly decorated watercraft of all shapes and sizes is one of the true highlights of the holiday season. It's free and typically takes place on the last weekend of November. A fireworks display at 6 PM signals the start of this uniquely coastal celebration. A holiday fair, an arts and crafts show, a children's art show, rides, food and performing artists add to the festive atmosphere from 10 AM to 4 PM. For more information, contact the Cape Fear Coast Convention & Visitors Bureau, (800) 222-4757.

Topsail Island Holiday Boat Flotilla at Topsail Beach
Assembly Building, Topsail Beach • (910) 329-4446

Kick off the holiday season on Topsail Island with the annual boat parade beginning at dark at the new Surf City Park and increasing in number as other boaters join in at the channel in Topsail Beach. Events include a children's

art contest, food and fellowship at the Assembly building. Holiday lighting by island residents and businesses add to the festivities.

December

Christmas By-The-Sea Festival
Oak Island and Southport locations • (910) 457-6964, (800) 457-6964

A colorful holiday parade on Oak Island begins a nearly month-long celebration in the Southport-Oak Island area. Santa's arrival at the airport, home tours, band and choral concerts, and a lighted boat parade are some of the events. Contact the Southport-Oak Island Chamber of Commerce at the numbers listed above for a schedule.

Largest Living Christmas Tree
Hilton Park, near the intersection of Castle Hayne Rd. and J.E.L. Wade Dr., Wilmington • (910) 341-7855

The lighting of the world's Largest Living Christmas Tree, an enormous live oak, has been a Wilmington tradition since 1928. On a Friday evening in early December, the town turns out with Santa, the mayor, a brass band and a chorus, and the festivities begin at 5:35 PM. At 6:15 PM, the tree is lit to the sounds of music and voices raised in song, and everyone joins in. The tree remains lit nightly from 5:30 to 10 PM until New Year's Day.

Old Wilmington by Candlelight
Various locations, Wilmington • (910) 762-0492, (910) 762-2976

This is one of the most popular and atmospheric of the holiday home tours. Each year, nearly a score of Wilmington's most historic homes, churches and businesses are opened to guests for two days on the first weekend in December. Stroll into Christmases past and see how yesterday's lifestyles have been adapted to our time. The tour is self-guided. Call for more information and admission fees.

Moravian Candle Tea Covenant
Moravian Church, 4126 S. College Rd., Wilmington • (910) 799-9256

Moravian stars, beeswax candles and Moravian sugar cookies are delightful highlights of this annual event held on the first Saturday in December. Enjoy a tour of the church and demonstrations of traditional Moravian crafts, with many of the items for sale. The putz (Nativity scene) is illuminated through a special sound and light show.

Poplar Grove Christmas Open House
**Poplar Grove Historic Plantation,
10200 U.S. Hwy. 17 N., Wilmington
• (910) 686-9518 Ext.26**

Few places evoke the Southern charm of bygone days as well as Poplar Grove Plantation, especially at holiday time. Visitors easily step back in time to a Victorian Christmas. Watch traditional craftspeople demonstrate life's everyday necessities in decorated rooms of the 1850 manor house. Other highlights include a Christmas tree with all the trimmings and seasonal arts and crafts. Admission is free to this early December event. The plantation staff views the annual Open House as a Christmas gift to the community for its year-round support.

Sneads Ferry Winterfest
Community Building, Peru Rd., Sneads Ferry • (910) 329-4446

Get an early start on the holidays with the friendly folks in Sneads Ferry. Winterfest is always held the second weekend in December and begins on Friday night with a tree lighting at 7 PM. Christmas trees decorated by area clubs add to the festive decorations. Children are invited to a pancake breakfast with Santa on Saturday morning between 7 and 11 AM. You can purchase last-minute gifts at the arts and crafts show on Saturday between the hours of 9 AM and 4 PM and Sunday between the hours of noon and 4 PM. Entertainment is held throughout the festival beginning on Friday night and ending on Sunday afternoon. The entertainment schedule is posted in local newspapers. All programs are free, but there is a charge for the pancake breakfast.

Island of Lights Festival
Various locations, Carolina Beach and Kure Beach • (910) 458-7116, (910) 458-5507

The Island of Lights Festival at Pleasure Island features several weekend events, most of them free, beginning with a holiday parade on Friday night. On Saturday, an evening holiday flotilla in full seasonal regalia runs from Snow's Cut to Carolina Beach boat basin and back. The

Island of Lights Tour of Homes, held the following Saturday, features refreshments and Southern hospitality on a self-guided tour of some of Carolina and Kure Beach's most elegant homes. For more information on these events or ticket prices for the Tour of Homes, contact the number listed above.

Kwanzaa Celebration
**Various locations, Wilmington
• (910) 799-3943**

Kwanzaa is a celebration of African-American roots, culture and tradition at the end of December through January 1. A variety of events are held throughout the week of Kwanzaa, culminating in a community feast on the last day of the celebration.

And for New Year's . . .

Carolina Beach New Year's Eve Countdown Party
Kure Beach • (910) 458-7116, (910) 458-5507

Ring in the New Year with a street dance accompanied by live music (beach music, naturally!), culminating in the descent of an enormous beach ball at midnight. Top it off with fireworks, and you've got yourself a beach-style New Year's Eve to remember. Fun for the whole family, it is free and begins at 10 PM.

New Year's Eve Riverboat Cruise
Corner of Water and Dock Streets, Wilmington • (910) 343-1611, (800) 676-0162

Ring in the new year aboard the *Henrietta III* on a New Year's Eve riverboat cruise down the Cape Fear River in Wilmington. Festivities include party favors, food, a DJ and a traditional champagne toast at midnight. The cruise runs from 9 PM to 12:30 AM with boarding scheduled for 8:30 PM on Water Street, at the foot of Dock Street. Tickets are $60 per person and pre-paid reservations are required. Call the phone numbers above for more information or reservations.

A Bit of "Vegas" - Southern Style !

Casino Cruises

Sailing Twice Daily on-board the Most Elegant Casino Ship in the Carolinas.

-Where Customer Service Is Our Priority-
• Plenty of the Newest and Loosest Slots Both Reel and Video
• Live Dealer "Vegas Style" Table Games • Blackjack
Caribbean Stud Poker • Let-It-Ride • Baccarat
• Craps • Roulette

Call For Information & Reservations
Toll Free 1 (877) 250-LUCK (5825)
(843) 249 - 9811

Daytrips

Locals and visitors alike agree that Wilmington and North Carolina's southeastern coastal areas have lots to offer, with more than enough attractions, restaurants, entertainment and fun activities to satisfy just about anyone. But those with a wandering foot always want to see if the grass is greener somewhere else....

While we're definitely biased, we have to confess that traveling south to Myrtle Beach, South Carolina, or heading north to the Central Coast of North Carolina can be an interesting adventure. Strikingly different, the two places can provide long-term visitors a totally different perspective on life in the South. Even the hushpuppies and barbecue taste different. In this chapter, we've given you a snapshot of each area and what's there so you can choose a destination to fit your mood.

For complete information on these areas, pick up copies of *The Insiders' Guide to Myrtle Beach and the Grand Strand* and *The Insiders' Guide to North Carolina's Central Coast and New Bern*, or call (800) 955-1860 to order either book.

LOOK FOR:
- **Myrtle Beach**
- **Murrells Inlet**
- **Swansboro**
- **Bogue Banks**
- **Morehead City**
- **Beaufort**
- **New Bern**

Myrtle Beach, South Carolina

"Down the road a piece," as they say in the South, "y'all gonna come crosst a mighty pop'lar spot with a heap o' good eatn' and a barrel o' fun. Thet'd be Myrtle Beach, South Carolina." Those of us who live and love the Wilmington area tend to see our neighbor to the south as a bit too busy and a bit too commercial; nevertheless, we love to go there once in awhile because there's just so much going on.

The Myrtle Beach Area Chamber of Commerce reports that more than 13.7 million visitors head to the Myrtle Beach area every year, many of them from North Carolina. Year-round visitors and snowbirds are attracted to the area's abundance of lodging, dining and shopping opportunities, world-class golf courses, impressive array of live entertainment venues and profusion of attractions. The Grand Strand's subtropical climate averages a pleasant 64 degrees with about 215 sunny days per year in which to soak up some rays on the magnificent beaches.

Taking into account traffic and stops through North Myrtle Beach, a trip to where the action is will take approximately 1¾ hours from downtown Wilmington, about 69 miles following U.S. Highway 17, which is four lanes all the way. Plan on about 2½ hours to the Myrtle Beach Airport via U.S. 17 bypass around Myrtle Beach proper; it will take a little longer to Brookgreen Gardens and Murrell's Inlet.

For the daytripper, Myrtle Beach is the Strand's entertainment nerve center. For a mile on either side of the Pavilion Amusement Park (see the following Attractions section), the focus of downtown Myrtle Beach is Ocean Boulevard, a hotbed of activity. Before entering Myrtle Beach proper, the length of U.S. 17 (here called Kings Highway) is known as "Restaurant Row," where dining establishments stand shoulder to shoulder. Another rapidly growing Myrtle Beach entertainment hub is U.S. 17 Bypass near 38th Avenue, with the huge Broadway On The Beach shopping and entertainment complex as its center (see the following Entertainment section).

There are more than 1,700 full-service restaurants in Horry County,

which includes the Grand Strand and South Strand. Along with fresh-catch seafood and all the usual regional specialties, you'll find other samples of Southern fare such as chicken bog (chicken, seasoned rice and sausage), she-crab soup, alligator stew, crawfish, Calabash-style seafood and the ever-present Southern staple — hushpuppies. All-you-can-eat buffets are ubiquitous, so bring a hearty appetite.

Tourist Information

The **Myrtle Beach Area Chamber of Commerce** operates three information centers where you can pick up or order scads of information about the area: Myrtle Beach Office, 1200 N. Oak Street, Myrtle Beach, (843) 626-7444; South Strand Office, 3401 U.S. 17 S. (Business), Murrells Inlet, (843) 651-1010; and Official Grand Strand Welcome Center, 5000 U.S. 501 E. at Horry-Georgetown Technical College, Conway, (843) 626-6619. To contact the chamber for information or to request brochures, call (800) 356-3016.

Another helpful resource is the **North Myrtle Beach Chamber of Commerce**, 270 U.S. 17 N., North Myrtle Beach, (843) 281-2662; there you can find out where to go for beach music and shag dancing besides getting the inside scoop on local restaurants. Separate from Myrtle Beach, the City of North Myrtle Beach has its own treasure trove of attractions, marinas, golf and a variety of accommodations.

The **South Carolina State Welcome Center** is on U.S. 17 right at the state line, near Little River, (843) 249-1111. This is a convenient place for daytrippers from the Wilmington and Brunswick County areas to gather a wealth of brochures about the Grand Strand or other South Carolina destinations, including nearby Georgetown, Charleston and Columbia, the state capital. Many of the publications contain discount coupons that are good at dozens of Grand Strand locations. Staff members are on hand to answer questions, make suggestions and offer assistance in making hotel/motel reservations. Summer hours are daily 9 AM to 5:30 PM; winter hours are daily 9 AM to 5 PM.

Shopping

Shopping is probably tied for first place with sunshine when it comes to the Grand Strand's most popular attractions. The area is replete with shops and boutiques of every description and specialty, but it's the discount shops and factory outlet stores that are most renowned among die-hard shoppers.

Barefoot Landing, 4898 U.S. Highway 17 N. in North Myrtle Beach, (843) 272-8349 or (800) 272-2320, is one of the most popular shopping meccas in the area. The complex, which is open year 'round (although hours vary seasonally), emulates a charming seaport village atmosphere; all of it surrounds a 27-acre freshwater lake and borders the Intracoastal Waterway. With more than 75 specialty shops and factory-direct stores plus 13 waterfront restaurants, you can keep busy most of the day. After you've shopped 'til you dropped and eaten your fill, take advantage of convenient attractions that are within walking distance: the **Alabama Theatre**, (843) 272-1111 or (800) 342-2262, home of the musical group of the same name; the **House of Blues**, (843) 272-3000, a Bayou-style bistro; the **Barefoot Princess II Riverboat**, (843) 650-6600 or (800) 685-6601; and **Alligator Adventure**, (843) 361-0789, a zoo of regional and exotic reptiles, amphibians and birds (closed in winter). In summer, a carousel, simulator and several other rides for children are available.

Still in a mood to shop? More than 110 discount outlets and specialty shops await you at the **Myrtle Beach Factory Stores** on U.S. 501 W., (843) 236-5100 ext. 107; they're located about 3 miles west of the Intracoastal Waterway. Among the most popular shopping complexes, this one includes "Off Fifth," a Saks Fifth Avenue outlet, Banana Republic, Royal Doulton, Bass, Lenox, Nike, Reebok, Jones New York, Disney Character Corner, Brooks Brothers and many more name-brand stores.

New and growing rapidly is **Tanger Outlet** Center on U.S. 17 N. at the Conway Bypass, (843) 838-9830. Expected to have nearly 80 stores including apparel, hosiery and intimates, home furnishings, footwear and accessories, the complex is close to Colonial Mall and Barefoot Landing, so you can have non-stop shopping.

For those of you who remember — or have heard about — the **Waccamaw Factory Shoppes**, including Waccamaw Pottery and Waccamaw Linen, be advised that most of the stores are currently closed. This once-huge, sprawling bargain paradise is in transition with only the Pottery portion, QVC and a limited number of other shops open.

Attractions

INSIDERS' TIP

Late spring and early fall are the best times to take jaunts up and down the coast. Tourist traffic has diminished significantly, but most attractions and shops are open, eager to see your smiling faces.

The Grand Strand draws visitors by the thousands to an awesome range of attractions, including themed water parks, amusement rides, museums (both educational and just plain fun), arcades, go-cart tracks, sightseeing cruises and so much more. The listings in this section are a very small sampling of what's available so make plans to stop by or phone the visitor centers listed in Tourist Information above.

You won't want to miss the array of shops along Ocean Boulevard. Places like the Gay Dolphin gift shop and Wings beach accessories make the stopping worthwhile, not to mention a plethora of small shops filled with fun beachy stuff.

More than a mere attraction, the **Myrtle Beach Pavilion Amusement Park** on the oceanfront at Ocean Boulevard and Ninth Avenue N., (843) 448-6456, is the symbolic heart of Myrtle Beach. Open March through October, it has more than 40 fun-filled rides, more than 25 skill games, shops, an arcade, haunted house, snack concessions, an under-21 nightclub (non-alcoholic) and an on-site restaurant, all packed into an 11-acre playground. It guarantees a full day's entertainment for the whole family. Not to be missed, nor for the faint of heart, is the park's Hurricane-Category 5, reported to be the largest and wildest wooden roller coaster in South Carolina. Hours vary seasonally; the park is closed from October through mid-March.

Myrtle Waves Water Park, 3000 10th Avenue N. Extension, (843) 448-1026 or (800) 524-9283, open from mid-May to mid-September, is among the larger and more popular water parks with 30 rides on 20 acres. The NASCAR Speedpark, U.S. Hwy.17 Bypass at 21st Avenue N., (877) 626-8725, features action-packed excitement year-round for the whole family, with seven custom stock-car tracks, race simulators and racing games, plus the interactive games found in the SpeedDome. Want to see the beach from an aerial perspective? Experience the romance of aviation history with Classic Air Ventures, (843) 249-6468 or (888) 852-9226, aboard a 1940 Waco UPF-7 bi-plane. Flights originate at the Grand Strand Airport from May through October. Don't overlook the many boating, kayaking and sightseeing opportunities available on the nearby waterways, either.

Combine the excitement of a Las Vegas casino with the flair of a southern riverboat to understand the appeal of the **Southern Elegance Casino Cruise**, 4491 Waterfront Avenue in Little River. The 175-foot *Southern Elegance* is docked along the historic waterfront in Little River (about three miles north of North Myrtle Beach off U.S.17) and offers cruises daily. Two of the ship's three decks are devoted to casino entertainment — all Las Vegas style live dealer table games, video poker and more than 200 slot machines. The *Southern Elegance* also features an observation deck, food and beverage service, an elevator and a full-service lounge that is available for private parties. For more information or cruise schedules, contact the Southern Elegance Casino Cruise office at (843) 249-9811 or (877) 250-LUCK (5825).

The **Hurricane Fleet**, (910) 579-3660, (843) 249-3571 or (800) 373-2004, offers a variety of cruise opportunities designed to show off the charms of Myrtle Beach from the waterway. These tours originate from Hurricane Fleet Marina, The Waterfront at Calabash in Calabash, North Carolina. One of the most popular excursions, the Dolphin Adventure Cruise, takes passengers from inland waterways to the ocean where they can get a close-up glimpse of fishing vessels, shrimpers at work or dolphins at play. Cost for this cruise is $18 per person 12 or older and $15 per person younger than 12. Group rates are available. Call ahead for reservations or to inquire about schedules and deep-sea fishing cruises. All of the boats are U.S. Coast Guard approved. Fishing gear — bait, tackle, rods and reels — are supplied on all fishing cruises.

Entertainment

Nightlife and Myrtle Beach are practically synonymous. Live music, dancing, dinner attractions and stage shows form the core of one of the most active seaside scenes anywhere, and there are plenty of open-air bars along the boardwalk in which to relax over a drink with the sound of the surf as the backdrop.

All the fun after dark is not reserved only for adults. Non-alcoholic nightspots such as The Attic, (843) 448-6456, a club at the **Myrtle Beach Pavilion**, cater to kids younger than 21 who enjoy dancing, music and socializing.

The preeminent dinner attractions and live theaters in the area are quite touristy, and ticket prices pack a wallop, but the shows are consistently well-done and family-friendly. Reservations are recommended for all of them. The first of its kind in the area, The **Carolina Opry** at the north junction of U.S. 17 Bypass and U.S. 17 Business, (843) 913-4000 or (800) 843-6779, is one of the state's top tourist attractions. Shows offer a mix of comedy and music — standard country hits, bluegrass, gospel and medleys drawn from popular oldies — plus a special Christmas spectacular.

Legends in Concert, 301 U.S. 17 Business S. in Surfside Beach, is a Vegas-style musical extravaganza featuring impersonations of famous performers of yesterday and today. For reservations, call the box office at (843) 238-7827 or (800) 960-7469.

In the 1970s, a then-unknown group named Alabama played for tips in Myrtle Beach, earning a loyal following. Having since achieved superstardom, Alabama has made its home base the 2,000-seat **Alabama Theatre**, 4750 U.S. 17 S., (843) 272-1111 or (800) 342-2262, at Barefoot Landing in North Myrtle Beach. Introduced in 2001, the theatre features The One Show, a one-of-a-kind entertainment experience combining music, comedy and Las Vegas-style glitz. On most weekends throughout the year Alabama Theatre features touring celebrity performers such as Loretta Lynn, the Oak Ridge Boys, Eddie Miles, Louise Mandrel, Lorrie Morgan, the Platters, and naturally, Alabama in their Celebrity Concert Series.

One of the area's three dinner attractions, the **Dixie Stampede**, 8901-B U.S. 17 Business, (843) 497-9700 or (800) 433-4401, owned by Dolly Parton, is a theatrical icon of Southern culture, complete with music, horsemanship and a colorful depiction of the conflict between the North and South. The 90-minute show, held in a huge 35,000-square-foot arena, is complemented by an impressive four-course dinner. Shows are staged nightly at 6 PM (6 and 8 PM during the summer and on weekends in December).

Travel back in time at the **Medieval Times Dinner & Tournament**, 2904 Fantasy Way, for a hearty medieval feast. While you eat, chivalrous knights engaged in authentic jousting matches and hand-to-hand combat try to win your favor and the hand of a chosen Queen of Love and Beauty. The "castle," air-conditioned and wheelchair accessible, is located at the Fantasy Harbour-Waccamaw entertainment complex near Waccamaw Factory Shoppes on U.S. 501. For reservations, call (843) 236-8080 or (888) 935-6878.

One of the grandest entertainment complexes anywhere in the region is **Broadway at the Beach** on U.S. 17 Bypass at 21st Avenue N. Open year-round, this 350-acre attraction includes no fewer than nine nightclubs in **Celebrity Square**, a lively nightlife venue; the 2,700-seat **The Palace Theater**, (843) 448-0588, which is home to Spirit of the Dance, a popular Irish dance show; **Ripley's Sea Aquarium**, (843) 916-0888; the six-story movie screen housed at **IMAX Discovery Theater**, (843) 448-4629; **Pirates of the Carolinas** interactive adventure ride, (843) 918-8737; the fabulous **Butterfly Pavilion**, (843) 839-4444; 20 restaurants (including a pyramidal Hard Rock Cafe and a Planet Hollywood); a 23-acre lake featuring water-taxi tours and pedal boats; kiddie rides in **Carousel Park**; Myrtle Beach's largest movie complex (the 16-screen **Broadway Cinema**); three hotels; and enough specialty shops and boutiques to satisfy the most die-hard shoppers. For more information, call (843) 444-3200 or (800)386-4662.

Golf

When *Golf Digest* searched for the 50 Best Golf Destinations in 2000, Myrtle Beach ranked in the Top Ten. The Grand Strand has 120-plus regulation courses, some designed by the top names in the game, including Palmer, Fazio, Dye, Norman, Love and Nicklaus. Add in the mild year-round sub-tropical temperatures, a wide variety of accommodations and attractive golf packages, and the area's self-proclaimed title as the "Golf Capital of the World" is well-justified.

There are also plenty of driving ranges, par 3 courses and pro shops scattered up and down the Strand. Greens fees are lowest from November through February, and golf packages are accordingly most affordable during that time. When you tire of serious golf or just want to have fun with your family or friends, try some of the 46 miniature golf courses — many are quite creative.

The **Myrtle Beach Chamber of Commerce**, (843) 626-7444, can provide details on golf packages, or you can call (800) 571-4386 for the **Myrtle Beach Golf Connection**'s free color *Golf Vacation Planner* or **Myrtle Beach Golf Holiday**, (877) 248-2342, for their excellent free 176-page planning guide. Another good source for information is Myrtle Beach's golf magazine, On The Green, available at Chamber offices and visitors centers.

One of the longest-running annual Myrtle Beach golf highlights is the **DuPont Coolmax World Amateur Handicap Championship**, celebrating its 20th year in 2003. Dubbed "The World's Largest Amateur Tournament," this popular competition is played on 60 to 70 of the area's courses over the four-day event in late August/early September. It is the largest tournament of its kind with an incredible 5,000 players journeying from 50 states and 30 foreign countries to compete. For more information, contact the tournament office at (800) 833-8798.

Murrells Inlet, South Carolina

Growing in popularity, with a personality quite different from its big sister to the north, Murrells Inlet is well worth the extra 10- or 20- minute drive. A true old fishing village, the Inlet is known for its delectable seafood; in fact it's called the "Seafood Capital of South Carolina." Fresh grouper, flounder, clams, oysters and crabs are prepared by chefs at more than 30 restaurants along the creek.

Here you can walk among the wetlands, cruise the creek and tour the salt marsh. Rich in history, folklore and tales of pirate treasure, Murrells Inlet will captivate you. If you didn't stop to pick up tourist information before now, you can find it at the **Myrtle Beach Area Chamber of Commerce, South Strand Office**, 3401 U.S. 17 S. (Business), Murrells Inlet, (843) 651-1010. For starters, be sure to check out these places.

DAYTRIPS

Kids of all ages love the beach.

Photo: Jay Tervo

Brookgreen Gardens, U.S. Highway 17 S., 1931 Brookgreen Gardens Drive, Murrells Inlet, (843) 235-6000 or (800) 849-1931, demands a visit. Brookgreen, which is listed on the National Register of Historic Places, is located on a 300-acre section of a 9,100-acre coastal South Carolina wildlife preserve. Described by *Southern Living* magazine as "one of the South's top five gardens," Brookgreen boasts the first and largest permanent outdoor installation of American figurative sculpture. It features more than 550 works by hundreds of top-name sculptors and continues to expand in scope. Guided tours, lectures and occasional workshops and concerts are offered at this combination arboretum, aviary and outdoor museum. Brookgreen Gardens is 18 miles south of Myrtle Beach, off U.S. 17 at Pawley's Island.

The gardens are open daily from mid-March through mid-November. The rest of the year the gardens are open Tuesday through Sunday 9:30 AM to 5 PM; closed Christmas Day. Admission is $12 for adults 19 and older, $10 for seniors 65 and older, $10 for children ages 12 to 18, and free for children 12 or younger. The admission ticket is good for seven consecutive days. Free wheelchairs and strollers are available on a first-come, first-served basis. Lunch is served at the Pavilion Restaurant; refreshments are available at The Old Kitchen from 10 AM to 4 PM.

Huntington Beach State Park, U.S. Highway 17 S. (16148 Ocean Highway), (843) 237-4440, is a pristine beach, freshwater lagoon, maritime forest, nature trail and boardwalk way out in the salt marsh. It offer opportunities to observe the coast's diverse natural environment, watch tall wading birds, pelicans and raptors, glimpse alligators and commune with the wildlife. You can swim in the ocean and go crabbing, surf fishing or picnicking and camping. Huntington Beach State Park is the site of the historic Atalaya castle. The former winter home and studio of noted American sculptress Anna Hyatt Huntington and her husband Archer Milton Huntington, Atalaya is also listed as a National Historic Landmark. Park hours during Standard Time are Saturday through Thursday 6 AM to 6 PM and Friday 6 AM to 8 PM. During Daylight Savings Time, hours are Monday through Sunday 6 AM to 8 PM. Admission is $5 for adults age 16 to 64 and out-of-state seniors, $3 for children ages 6 to 15 and free for children age 5 and younger and South Carolina Seniors age 65 and older.

Head boats are available at **Captain Dick's Marina**, 4123 U.S. 17 Business (Kings Highway South) on the waterfront in Murrells Inlet, (843) 651-3676 or (866) 557-FISH (3474). Captain Dick's also offers ocean sightseeing cruises, including the Pirate Adventure Voyage and the Ocean Sightseeing Cruise plus a Saltwater Marsh Explorer Adventure. Sundown fishing trips, ocean speedboat rides, watercraft rentals and parasailing are also available.

One of the most popular dining establishments is **Drunken Jack's** on U.S. 17 Business on the waterfront in Murrells Inlet, (843) 651-2044. The restaurant features seafood "right off the boat," prepared to perfection grilled, blackened, sautéed or Southern-fried and served with their famous hush puppies and honey butter. It's open daily for dinner from 4:30 to 10 PM.

North Carolina's
Central Coast

Within a two-hour drive north by northeast up the Ocean Highway (U.S. Highway 17) from Wilmington are a multitude of daytrip possibilities. The Central Coast area (Bogue Banks, Morehead City and quaint Beaufort), also known as the Crystal Coast, and nearby historic New Bern, as well as the waters that surround and connect them, promise delightful opportunities.

The Crystal Coast area shares much in common with the Cape Fear Coast. Both boast beautiful waters, miles of oceanside communities, great restaurants and, of course, deep historical roots. However, they are different enough to make visiting each of them a unique experience.

Boaters visiting this area will be charmed by its amenities. Most marinas are just a short stroll from shopping, dining, historic sites and services. A fast powerboat can reach the area from Wilmington in several hours. Although some people make this a daytrip on the water, you'll have more time to enjoy the local attractions if you drive.

By car, simply head up U.S. Highway 17 until it intersects N.C. Highway 24 in Jacksonville. Go east on N.C. 24 toward Beaufort. It is a trip of less than 100 miles from Wilmington, and there are many views of North Carolina's waters and coastal communities along the way.

An interesting shortcut passes through the U.S. Marine base at **Camp Lejeune**. If you care to try it, veer off U.S. 17 onto N.C. Highway 172 at Folkstone, heading toward Sneads Ferry. People who have never been on a military base will find this an unusual environment, with tank-crossing signs and trucks filled with Marines training in artillery practice. Be prepared to stop for questioning by a sentry at the gate. After crossing the base, go east on N.C. Highway 24. From time to time the base portion of N.C. 172 may be closed because of troop movements or maneuvers taking place; if so, simply return the way you came and turn right on N.C. 210 to rejoin U.S. 17.

To take a self-guided tour of Camp Lejeune, obtain a visitor's pass and tour book at the base Visitor Center, located at the main gate on N.C. 24 in Jacksonville, (252) 451-2148. This is a great way to become familiar with the base, its history and environment. The tour consists of 25 points of interest marked by large, white, numbered signs that coincide with site numbers in the tour book. The tour takes you from pre-Colonial America to the cutting edge of technology.

Crystal Coast tourist information, maps and brochures are available at the **Crystal Coast Tourism Development Authority's Visitors Center**, 3409 Arendell Street, Morehead City, (252) 726-8148 or (800) 786-6962.

Swansboro

Swansboro, a historic coastal town that dates back to around 1730, is a pleasant stopover after about an hour and a half of car travel from Wilmington. Situated on the White Oak River and the Intracoastal Waterway, this lovely little town is surrounded by water on three sides.

Swansboro has a particularly charming downtown historic area lined with antiques shops, boutiques, art galleries and restaurants. Look for signs leading to the district just off N.C. 24. The area is concentrated within three blocks on the shores of the White Oak River. Parking is free, the merchants are friendly, and there are several quaint and interesting shops, including **Russell's Old Tyme Shoppe**, (910) 326-3790; **Noah's Ark**, (910) 326-5679; **White Oak Gallery/Silver Thimble Gift Shoppe**, (910) 326-8558; **Sunshine and Silks**, (910) 326-5735; **Gray Dolphin**, (910) 326-4958; **The Brass Binnacle**, (910) 326-2448; and **Through the Looking Glass,** (910) 326-3128.

The historic district is a great stopover for lunch or dinner. **Captain Charlie's Seafood Paradise**, 106 Front Street, (910) 326-4303, is a memorable place to enjoy some of North Carolina's best fried seafood. It serves dinner only. For breakfast or lunch, check out **Yana's Ye Olde Drug Store**, 119 Front Street, (910) 326-3891, where you can enjoy omelets, pancakes, old-fashioned milk shakes, made-to-order burgers and homemade onion rings in a '50s atmosphere. **Gourmet Cafe**, 108 West Corbett Avenue, (910) 326-7114, has an extensive wine list and offers tasty lunch and dinner options. Lunch choices include salads, build-your-own sandwiches and homemade desserts. Dinner specialties include seafood, beef and veal. **White Oak River Bistro**, 206 West Corbett Avenue, (910) 326-1696, features Mediterranean food. **G. Whitaker's Deli and Coffee Shop**, 105A Church Street, (910) 326-6771, offers gourmet meats; open for lunch only.

Bogue Banks

Back on N.C. 24, travel another 10 minutes to the intersection with N.C. Highway 58. A right turn is the western entrance to Bogue Banks, a barrier island separated from the mainland by Bogue Sound. You can choose to continue straight on N.C. Highway 51 or cross the bridge to take a parallel route on the barrier island. The bridge is worth the detour because its high arc gives motorists a dramatic view of the Intracoastal Waterway.

The beach communities along approximately 30 miles of the island are widely varied in tone. Emerald Isle, Indian Beach and Salter Path offer an astonishing diversity of neighborhoods, ranging from expensive beach homes and condominiums to fishing trailers. There are also a few attractions for the kids, including miniature golf, waterslides and bumper boats.

Pine Knoll Shores is an exclusive residential area of windswept live oaks and kudzu with attractive single-family homes and condominiums as well as hotels and the occasional restaurant. This beach also offers the **North Carolina Aquarium at Pine Knoll Shores**, (910) 247-4003, a lively, 35,000-square-foot facility that includes the Living Shipwreck, interactive exhibits, a touch tank and auditorium. Salt-marsh explorations and nature trails are accessible outside the building.

At the eastern end of the island is **Atlantic Beach**, a smorgasbord of beach amenities that includes an amusement park with a Ferris wheel, a fishing pier, shopping opportunities, boat rentals, fast food places, full-service restaurants and motels. The Atlantic Beach Circle, the town's center, has been sold to be developed with two hotels, condominiums and community areas. Evidence of this identity change should be visible during summer 2003.

Just beyond Atlantic Beach on the eastern tip of Bogue Banks is **Fort Macon**, (252) 726-3775, an old Civil War fort and 385-acre state park. The old fort has been totally restored to the Civil War period and is open for tours, either guided or on your own. Take a picnic and make a day of it. Visitors have access to picnic tables, outdoor grills, shelters, restrooms and drinking water in addition to the nature trails, abundant plant life and beachfront.

Morehead City

Cross over the bridge at the eastern end of Bogue Banks and enter Morehead City, home to the North Carolina State Port Authority — something Wilmington and the Crystal Coast have in common — and a multitude of restaurants specializing in fresh seafood. The undisputed traditional leader of dining in Morehead City is the **Sanitary Fish Market & Restaurant**, 501 Evans Street, (252) 247-3111. The restaurant seats 600 diners and serves fresh broiled or fried seafood, homemade chowders and Tar Heel hushpuppies that truly melt in your mouth.

Capt. Bill's Waterfront Restaurant, 701 Evans Street, (252) 726-2166, is open for lunch and dinner and serves fresh-catch seafood with traditional hushpuppies, cole slaw, chowders and fresh pies. **Finz Grill of Morehead**, 105 S. Seventh Street, (252) 726-5502, occupies the former headquarters of the Morehead Gulf Oil Company. Open for lunch and dinner, it features fresh local seafood as the specialty of the house. Dine outside on nice days and enjoy the view from a second-story deck.

Morehead City offers a wide variety of shopping opportunities but none are more charming than the waterfront area facing Bogue Sound. Stroll along Evans Street and enjoy some of the shops that tempt you. **Dee Gee's Gifts and Books**, (252) 726-3314, is a waterfront tradition that offers a large selection of books, including local and regional titles. Also check out the selection of gifts, cards and nautical charts. Looking for just the right gift for a special someone (including yourself)? **The Sea Pony,** (252) 726-6070, is the place to find pottery, clothing, fine jewelry, pictures and English antiques from Easter through Thanksgiving. The House of Duncan, (252) 240-0982, will charm you with its selection of handmade crafts, potpourri, Yankee candles and exquisite children's clothing. Be sure to ask about the "surprise box," a unique creation that is signed and numbered by the artist (and the shop's owner), C. Duncan Lewis.

Beaufort

Just a few miles from Morehead City is the magical town of Beaufort. Beaufort is so gorgeous it seems more like a postcard than a real place. This little laid-back coastal community nestles up to international waters and is a gateway from the Atlantic Ocean to America's waterways. Taylor's Creek, the body of water in front of the town's quaint commercial district, is filled with sailcraft and powerboats from all over the world. Just up Taylor's Creek you can catch sight of a menhaden fishing fleet. Beyond that is Core Sound and a view of Harkers Island, home to some of this country's earliest shipbuilders.

Beaufort boasts a very unusual view: wild horses on Carrot Island across from the waterfront. The horses are stocky, furry steeds that pretty much care for themselves on their little windswept island. In a world where horses are rarely seen running free, this is a stirring sight. If you want a closer look, ask about boat tours that depart from the Beaufort docks. The island chain across from the Beaufort Waterfront is the **Rachel Carson Estuarine Research Reserve**. Free guided tours are offered each month from April to August. Inquire at the North Carolina Maritime Museum about tour times. One catch: You have to provide your own water transportation to get to the island. If you use the ferry service, expect to pay up to $8 ($4 for kids) for a round-trip journey, but remember the island tour is free.

A fascinating history lesson awaits you when you visit the **Old Burying Ground**, where

Don't miss a view of the southern coast from the water.

Photo: Jay Tervo

there are more than 200 markers pre-dating the Civil War. Stories are told about a British officer buried standing up and the girl who died at sea and was preserved in a rum barrel until he father could get her home. Admission is free, but guided tours are available at $5 for adults and $3 for children.

The sheer beauty of the scenery at the Beaufort waterfront is enough to lull a visitor into sitting in a pleasant trance for a long time, but there is also the allure of nearby shops and attractions. Within an easy walk are stores, many appealing restaurants and the **North Carolina Maritime Museum**, 315 Front Street, (252) 728-7317, an 18,000-square-foot building that pays tribute to North Carolina's coastal heritage, natural resources and maritime history. The museum boasts the **Harvey W. Smith Watercraft Center** just across the street, a facility where students and craftsmen build wooden boats in traditional North Carolina design and welcome visitors to take a peek at boats-in-progress. As you stroll downtown, don't miss the **Beaufort Historic Site**, (252) 728-5225 or (800) 575-7483, enclosed by white picket fences in the 100 block of Turner Street. These authentically restored buildings and the costumed guides offer a fascinating glimpse of coastal Carolina living in the 18th and 19th centuries. Site tour and visitor information, special exhibits and historic artifacts are available on the grounds at the **Safrit Historical Visitor Center**, 128 Turner Street.

Shoppers will enjoy a variety of stores along the waterfront. The **Rocking Chair Book Store**, 400 Front Street, (252) 728-2671, has a fine selection of books for children and adults. **Scuttlebutt Nautical Books and Bounty**, 433 Front Street, (252) 728-7765, sells a large selection of books about the sea and boating. NOAA charts, cruising guides and chart books make this a must-stop for passing boaters. **La Vaughn's Pottery**, 517 Front Street, (252) 728-5353, is a show-stopper for shoppers interested in an extensive line of ceramics crafted by regional and local artists. **The General Store**, 515 Front Street, (252) 728-7707, has hand-dipped ice cream for your summer daytripping pleasure. Highlighting North Carolina artists and craftsmen, **Handscapes Gallery** in Somerset Square on Front Street, (252) 728-6805, offers pottery, jewelry, paintings, glass creations and metalwork.

While shopping, don't miss **The Old Beaufort Shop**, 128 Turner Street, (252) 728-5225. This unique shop is operated by the Beaufort Historical Association and offers one-of-a-kind items made by BHA volunteers — original photography, handmade dolls, books on local history and herb cuttings.

Diners will be overwhelmed with restaurant possibilities. **Beaufort Grocery Co.**, 117 Queen Street, (252) 728-3899, a lunch and dinner restaurant, offers fine dining and a full delicatessen. Breads and desserts are baked daily. **Front Street Grill At Stillwater** on the Beaufort waterfront at 300 Front Street, (252) 728-4956, has a reputation as an interesting restaurant that uses unusual spices in fresh presentations of seafood, chicken, pasta and homemade soups.

Spouter Inn, 218 Front Street, (252) 728-5190, is a charming spot where diners can enjoy a memorable clam chowder, creative seafood specialties and a great view thanks to its waterfront

DAYTRIPS

location. **Clawson's Emporium Restaurant**, 429 Front Street, (252) 728-2133, long a dining fixture on the Beaufort waterfront, serves wonderful all-American fare. Its coffee bar, known as Fishtowne Java, serves high-octane caffeine drinks.

New Bern

The small city of New Bern lies along North Carolina's largest river, the Neuse. The Neuse River is one of the state's premier sailing areas because of the width and depth of the water. You'd have to try really hard to run aground in a sailboat in the Neuse. Car travelers will appreciate the lovely view of the river and will certainly enjoy the many opportunities to shop, dine and stay overnight in historic New Bern, which was settled by the Swiss in 1710. Reach it by car from Beaufort by taking U.S. 70 W. into New Bern. If traveling from Wilmington, take U.S. 17 N.

You may be interested to know that New Bern is the place where Pepsi Cola was invented. This uniquely historic town was the site of the first public school in North Carolina, the first meeting of the North Carolina Legislature, the state's first bank and the state's first press.

The major tourist attraction in New Bern is **Tryon Palace Historic Sites and Gardens**, 610 Pollock Street, (252) 514-4900 or (800) 767-1560. Built in 1770 for Colonial governor William Tryon, the palace burned in 1798 but was reconstructed in the 1950s according to the original architectural plans. The palace is furnished with rare English and American antiques dating from the late 18th century. These pieces were selected based on an inventory of Gov. Tryon's possessions made two years after he left New Bern to become governor of the colony of New York. Tryon Palace and its many historic sites — the John Wright Stanly House and Dixon-Stevenson House — are open year round, with the exception of major holidays, and include tours, historical dramas and crafts demonstrations. For information, call or write Tryon Palace Historic Sites and Gardens, 610 Pollock Street, New Bern, NC 28563.

The **New Bern Historical Society**, 513 Broad Street, (252) 638-8558, offers tours of the 1790 Attmore-Oliver House, which features a fascinating collection of 18th- and 19th-century furnishings, New Bern artifacts and Civil War relics. Entrance to the building is located at 510 Pollock Street. Discover three centuries of history in a 1½ hour narrated Trolley Tour of historic downtown New Bern; for information call (252) 637-7316 or (800) 849-7316. The New Bern Civic Theatre, 414 Pollock Street, (252) 633-0567, presents a wide variety of live attractions year round. The Bank of the Arts, 317 Middle Street, (252) 638-2577, showcases an eclectic variety of artistic endeavors.

The **New Bern Fireman's Museum**, 408 Hancock Street, (252) 636-4087, is another interesting stop. The museum features an impressive collection of early firefighting equipment and rare photographs. Children of all ages will delight in **A Day at the Farm**, 183 Woodrow McCoy Road, (252) 514-9494, a historic New Bern dairy farm that features live animals, duck ponds, milking equipment, antiques, hay rides and more. For other attractions and expert touring advice, drop by the **Craven County Convention & Visitors Information Center** at 203 S. Front Street or call (252) 637-9400 or (800) 437-5767. Ask for the "New Bern Heritage Tour Map," the "African-American Heritage Guide" or the "Governor's Walk" brochure.

Once you've toured to your satisfaction, it's time to eat. For a small town, New Bern has an abundance of outstanding restaurants across the full spectrum of prices. **The Chelsea**, 335 Middle Street, (252) 637-5469, offers varied, unique dining experiences in a restored 1912 pharmacy — downstairs seating captures a turn-of-the-century drugstore atmosphere, while the second floor is casual Victorian in flavor. Open for lunch and dinner, the eclectic menu features a wide range of international and regional cuisine.

Fred and Claire's Restaurant, 247 Craven Street, (252) 638-5426, is a great choice for dining in New Bern's historic district. Everything is made fresh daily, and the menu offers lunch options of specialty sandwiches, daily specials, quiche, soups and salads. Dinner choices range from omelets to fresh seafood. Housed in the historic Isaac Taylor House, the **Courtyard Cafe**, 228 Craven Street, (252) 636-6360, serves breakfasts on weekends and lunch and dinner all week. Alfresco dining is available in the courtyard when the weather is inviting. Latitude 35 located in the **Sheraton Grand New Bern**, 100 Middle Street, (252) 638-3585, has a great seafood buffet on Fridays. **Captain Ratty's**, 202 Middle Street, (252) 633-2088, features an exceptionally large variety of grilled, steamed or broiled seafood.

If shopping is your reason to travel, New Bern has antiques stores and gift shops galore.

Elegant Days, 236 Middle Street, is a "treasure trove of old things." **Jane Suggs Antiques**, 228 Middle Street, (252) 637-6985, carries period furniture and reproductions, silver, porcelain and glassware. Don't let the office supplies and furniture fool you, **Branch's**, 309 Pollock Street, (252) 638-5171, offers a range of fine giftware, accessories, birdfeeders, lawn ornaments and more. For the kids there's **Snapdragon Toys**, 214 Middle Street, (252) 514-6770, a shop of toys that range from educational to just plain fun. **Carolina Creations**, 321 Pollock Street, (252) 633-4369, showcases the works of local artists. **Mitchell's Hardware**, 215 Craven Street, (252) 638-4261, is a 101-year-old working hardware store that resembles an old-fashioned dry goods emporium with something for everyone.

New Bern is such a pleasant and interesting spot, it invites the daytripper back for long weekends of exploration. There are beautiful hotels and inns in the historic downtown area on the water, including the **Sheraton Grand New Bern**, (252) 638-3585 or (800) 326-3745; the **Comfort Suite Riverfront Park**, (252) 636-0022 or (800) 228-5150; the **Bridgepoint Hotel & Marina**, 101 Howell Road, (252) 636-3637; and the **New Bern House Bed and Breakfast**, 709 Broad Street, (252) 636-2250 or (800) 842-7688, which features mystery tour weekends in a restored colonial revival home. These hotels and inns are particularly convenient to all the attractions and restaurants mentioned in this brief overview.

DAYTRIPS

Sun, Sand and Sea

Insiders and returning visitors understand the appeal of North Carolina's southern coastal region. Warm, semi-tropical weather, sandy beaches, friendly people and Carolina-blue skies, combined with the lure of the sea, make this area paradise. Bathing suits, shorts, golf shirts and sandals are a must for coastal Carolina living. Is it any wonder that visitors from all over the world return year after year or choose to retire here?

Enjoy leisurely walks along the shore. Romp in the gentle waves of the ocean or cruise the area's waterways. Relish the sun's warmth and the sway of ocean breezes. Stand barefoot in the sand and witness truly magnificent sunrises and awesome sunsets. All of these activities lift the spirit and create memories for a lifetime. But as Insiders will tell you, there are some important precautions to heed while enjoying the area's bounty.

The Sun

On the southern coast of North Carolina the skies are gorgeous, but beware the sun's rays and intense heat. Dermatologists and health officials caution against prolonged exposure to direct sunlight. By all means, enjoy your days on the beach but keep in mind some tips to make your vacation safe and pleasurable, especially if you're determined to return home with a tan, not a painful and peeling sunburn.

Sun Protection

No matter what your skin type, age or previous tanning experience, always wear sunscreen with the appropriate SPF (sun protection factor) when exposed to the sun. Select one with the best protection you can find and slather it on all exposed skin. Reapply after coming out of the water. Make a daily habit of putting on sunscreen.

Skin protection is especially vital on the open beach for several reasons. Sand, water and concrete surfaces can reflect 85 percent of the sun's rays. The intensity of the sun has increased in recent years so even if you've never been sensitive to the sun before, it's wise to take steps to protect your skin from burning or sun damage. Don't be fooled by a cloudy day. Ninety percent of the sun's rays penetrate the clouds.

Children are especially vulnerable to the sun's damaging rays and require special protection. Nearly half of the damage to skin occurs in childhood and early adolescence. Dermatologists recommend using sunscreen with an SPF-15 or higher for children. Waterproof sunscreens will eliminate constant reapplications as children play in and out of the water. Protect infants with a hat, lightweight clothing, an umbrella and sunblock. Remember that while an umbrella shades the child from direct sunlight, the reflective rays of the sun are still present, making sunblock a necessity

Hats, especially the wide-brimmed variety, are not only a fashion statement in coastal Carolina, but also a great covering for sensitive facial skin and providing shade against the sun's glare. Also a must for comfort in the summer's heat is lightweight, light-colored clothing. The natural fibers of cotton and linen are preferable because of their ability to "breathe" more than synthetic fabrics. In the heat and humidity of a summer's day here, you'll appreciate the difference.

Daylight hours between 11 AM and 3 PM are considered the hottest part of the day and pose the greatest risk for skin damage from the sun. Cover up or spend those hours doing indoor activities. The area abounds in things to do and see for every interest and every member of the family. Check out what's available in other chapters in this book.

Occasionally during the summer months, weather reports will broadcast a heat index warning for the area. This indicates that the sun's heat and the atmosphere's humidity have pushed temperatures to feel hotter than the thermometer reads. These conditions are very dangerous, especially to the elderly, small children and pets. Stay indoors in air-conditioning, wear lightweight clothing and drink plenty of fluids, especially water or Gatorade. Stay cool and take the fun indoors on these days.

The Sand

Ah, the beach! There's nothing like taking a walk on a sandy beach, barefoot and gazing out into the ocean. The benefits include gentle exercise and stress relief. Not to mention the fact that sand is a natural pumice for the soles of your feet. Did you arrive with weary, calloused feet? Chances are good that they'll be a lot smoother when you leave.

Access to area beaches is free because North Carolinians are rigid in their belief that the shores belong to the people. Look for the orange and blue signs at frequent intervals along beach roads — they point out easements between homes where you can freely cross over to get to the beach. Stick to these paths, and don't walk across private property to get to the beach.

You are free to walk the length of all area beaches, including those on private islands such as Bald Head and Figure Eight (although you'll need a private boat or, in the case of Bald Head Island, a passenger ferry to get there). Oceanfront landowner's property lines stop at the high-water mark.

Here's to the sun! Here's to the sand! Here's to the sea!

SUN, SAND AND SEA

Beach Treasures

Stay alert for hidden treasures in the sand when beachcombing. After Hurricane Bonnie in August 1998, an abundance of sharks' teeth and a wider variety of shells were reported on Topsail Island beaches. When searching for sharks' teeth, look for a characteristic glint along the water's edge or in wet, course sand. These interesting artifacts are ebony in color and varied in shape. In September 1999, a treasure trove of beautiful shells washed up on the Wrightsville Beach ocean-front when Hurricane Floyd "breezed by."

Are you spending the day on Brunswick County beaches? Frequent finds there are whole sand dollars, but make sure you don't take live ones. The all-white skeletal sand dollars are the ones you want. The brown, furry ones may still be alive and should be returned to the water. In addition, if you're lucky or very observant, you may find arrowheads from ancient Native American tribes. Considering the colorful pirate history in the area, who knows what else you might find in your search?

A Day at the Beach

Beach hospitality includes public restrooms, showers and rinse-off spots located conveniently along most beaches. Restaurants that offer everything from hot dogs to prime rib to vegetarian dining are an easy walk from the sand in many places.

Parking is generally free on the street and in public lots in the off-season after Labor Day, when the meters are retired until early spring. At the peak of summer, be sure to bring a pocketful of quarters for parking at Wrightsville Beach. The meters can be filled for several hours, so you don't have to race back and forth to stay legal. Pay attention to restaurant and business lots that have signs warning against unauthorized parking. In some cases, towing is strictly enforced. Carolina Beach also has parking meters during the season and parking lots requiring dollar bills all year long.

Beach accesses are available and clearly marked. Some offer public parking, others have me-tered spaces. Please use these accesses, not someone's front yard, to reach the beach. Property owners will appreciate your consideration.

Preparations for a day at the beach should include a blanket or old quilt, a cooler packed with soft drinks, water or Gatorade, and beach apparel for the whole family. No matter what you do, grains of sand are going to creep into everything, but a blanket will at least give you protection from the warm sand. Make sure everyone has a hat, sunglasses and sturdy foot covering. Asphalt, concrete and sand above the high-water mark get very hot, making it difficult and painful to walk to and from the parking areas.

Some laws worth noting: Don't take glass containers on the beach; don't let your dog run loose until you check local ordinances (and in all cases pick up your pet's "business" so you or other people don't step in it); don't let your parking meter expire; don't take alcohol to the beach; and don't litter. Take a portable ashtray with you if you plan to smoke because, as inconsequen-tial as a butt or two may seem, millions of them cause environmental problems. Filters are not biodegradable and can harm sea life. Trash cans are placed on most beaches.

The most important rule of all: Protect the sand dunes by not disturbing the sea oats or other precious vegetation. Dunes are a vital part of the coastal environment for buffering beachfront property and slowing erosion from tropical storms and hurricanes. Dunes also provide sanctuary for fragile turtle nests. Damaging the dunes or disturbing turtle nests and beach vegetation will incur stiff fines.

Nighttime on the beach can be magical, and a quiet stroll in the moonlight is nearly irresist-ible. In the fall, your walk might kick up a strange phosphorescent phenomenon as you move across the water's edge. A night swim may tempt you as well, but be careful. Currents can push you away from your wading-in spot, and the darkness can disorient you. Remember that the law requires that swimming attire be worn while frolicking in the waves.

The Sea

The ocean and waterways of North Carolina's beautiful southern coast satisfy a wide range of interests. Whether your passion is swimming, boating, surfing, fishing or simply watching waves, the sea offers endless possibilities for exploration, education and contemplation.

A pair of binoculars is a handy aid for spotting ships at sea. As ships enter Wilmington, be sure to wave to the sailors on deck because inbound ships have probably been at sea for months and the guys seem eager for a friendly greeting.

Swimming

If swimming is your watersport or relaxation of choice, you've come to the right place. The ocean offers limitless possibilities for everyone from the wader to the long-distance swimmer. For your safety in the spring and summer, lifeguards are posted at many of the beaches in the area. If you see someone running into the water with an orange or red float in hand, it's probably a lifeguard. You can be called closer to shore if the lifeguard thinks you're getting too far out for your own safety. These trained professionals are looking out for your best interests.

Rip currents and undertows are unseen dangers lurking beneath the waves — dangers that Insiders respect. If you are swimming and are suddenly pulled in a frightening way by the currents, the most important thing to remember is to stay calm. Panic leads to exertion, which leads to dangerous fatigue. If you find yourself in a rip current, relax and let it carry you on its natural course toward the sea. Within a few minutes, it will dissipate. Then you can swim parallel to the shoreline to get out of the rip current area and back to shore. Do not try to swim straight back into shore against the rip current; you'll only tire yourself out.

A few don'ts: Don't swim in inlets because you may not be spied by a speeding boat; don't swim alone; and don't swim in the Cape Fear River at and below Wilmington unless you can tolerate the company of alligators and big ships. Although the river is not particularly wide, it is deep — 38 feet on average — and has fast currents that have to be experienced to be believed.

Surfing

Wrightsville Beach and Carolina Beach are popular places for surfing, but there are some regulations, and you should ask the lifeguard about designated surfing zones, which shift each day. (See our Watersports chapter for more information on surf zones.) You must wear a leash and will be immediately chastised if you are not attached to your board. Lifeguards are fastidious about enforcing this rule.

Tides and Weather

The tides are such an important factor in coastal communities that their comings and goings are part of the daily weather forecast. Be aware of them if you splash out to sandbars or islands at low tide. Changing tides could make the trip back to shore a daunting swim.

Storms and threatening weather are taken seriously on the coast. Get out of the water and off the beach when these often-spectacular weather events take place. Lightning on the beach means business, and you should seek immediate shelter inside a building or in your car. Small-craft advisories are to be heeded without fail.

If a hurricane watch is announced, it's a good idea to make plans to leave the area. Should the watch upgrade to a hurricane warning, area beaches are often evacuated. Emergency management professionals have their hands full in these events so avoid adding to the confusion by sightseeing on the beach. On the positive side, storms often will be simple summer showers that pass quickly. Take your cue from the lifeguards as to when it's safe to return to the water.

Boating Safety

Ready to go boating? If you trailer your own boat, there are ample public boat ramps through-

Don't get too close to that pier when surfing! Most towns have laws restricting surfing within certain distances of the pier.

Photo: Jay Tervo

out the entire area (see our Fishing chapter). If you choose to leave your boat at the water, the area's marinas offer a variety of services, including dry-dockage, wet slips and storage (see our Marinas and the Intracoastal Waterway chapter). Boating possibilities include the Cape Fear River and its adjacent branches, the Atlantic Ocean, the Intracoastal Waterway (ICW) and area lakes.

Fuel and other amenities are available on the southern coastline, generally on the Intracoastal Waterway (ICW). If you don't have a boat of your own, you can take advantage of one of the charter services for sailing craft and, of course, tour and deep-sea fishing boats that cater to all cruising needs (see our Watersports and Fishing chapters for listings).

Boaters should understand the rules of the water when operating their own boats or chartering someone else's. Many waterways, especially the ICW at Wrightsville Beach and Carolina Beach, can become heavily congested. Educate yourself on boating safety and navigation rules before going out on the waterways.

If boating is on your list of must-dos while visiting North Carolina's southeastern coastline, check with your local college, community college or chamber of commerce for information on boating-skills courses offered in your area. Locally, boating skills and seamanship courses are periodically offered through the Cape Fear Community College continuing education department, (910) 362-7170, and taught by U.S. Coast Guard Auxiliary, Wilmington Flotilla 10-06, a working volunteer unit under the supervision of the Coast Guard. These courses include the basics of boat safety and handling, radio communication, the art of navigation, rules of the water and more. For further information and class schedules, contact the community college or U.S.C.G. Flotilla 10-06 at (910) 686-9777. The classes run for seven weeks, so if your visit will be a brief one, consider taking a boating-skills course in your area before you head for the ocean. Your advanced preparation is invaluable and guarantees a safer boating adventure.

A similar course is offered by U.S.C.G. Auxiliary, Wrightsville Beach Flotilla 10-01 through the Wrightsville Beach Parks & Recreation Department. For more information and a schedule of classes, call the Wrightsville Beach Park Office at (910) 256-7925 or Donna Sauer at (910) 270-9830.

Perhaps the most important thing about boating is preparation. File a float plan; it can be as official or informal as your circumstances require. The point is that you should tell someone where you're going and when you expect to return. You are required to have one life jacket for each person on your boat, and the Coast Guard is within its rights to stop you and see that you have proper equipment. Adults may use their own judgment about wearing a life jacket; children should wear one at all times. Life jackets may not be comfortable or glamorous, but they save lives.

Carry sufficient nonalcoholic liquids, not only for the humans aboard, but also for any pets you choose to take along. Discourage your pet from drinking sea water by having fresh water available.

Carry an emergency kit that contains flares, a fire extinguisher, first aid supplies and various repair items. Make sure that the vessel is well-maintained with the following in good working order: safety equipment, protected and sealed electrical systems, and the inboard or outboard propulsion system. Understand how to use your ship-to-shore radio and practice in advance of an emergency. Channel 16/158.8 MHz is the hailing channel but, in non-emergency situations, advise the person you're contacting to another frequency to keep 16 clear. If you're going to be out after dark, turn on your running lights. The ICW is also a highway for commerce, and you want to be sure that barges know you're out there.

Boats under sail always have the right of way over powercraft. If power is your chosen method of boating, be aware of the instability your wake can create for sailboats or small boats. If you find yourself in the shipping lanes, give big ships a wide berth. Yielding the right-of-way is often necessary because big ships require at least a mile to stop.

If you're a personal watercraft fan who loves to zoom down the waterways at high speed, be aware of no-wake zones. These zones are marked with signs, so stay alert and maintain a lawful speed. Also, avoid delicate side waters where your craft may damage the nurseries of shellfish and fish.

INSIDERS' TIP

Love seashells? Check out the Shell Room at the Museum of Coastal Carolina to view hundreds of shells common (and not so common) to coastal Carolina. The Museum is located at 21 E. Second Street in Ocean Isle Beach.

Emergencies happen on the water. The Coast Guard is particular about what constitutes an emergency, and it will not immediately come to your rescue in all situations. Generally, only life- or environment-threatening situations will get its attention. Running aground in the waterway is rarely considered an emergency because if you get stuck, it is commonly understood that you can walk to shore. A sailboat with a fixed keel is virtually guaranteed to go aground at some point, and it isn't always possible to get loose without a sturdy towboat.

Marine towing companies, such as SeaTow, (910) 452-3798, will arrive if you get stuck on a sandbar and call for help on channel 16 of your radio. Believe these Insiders who have been stuck hard aground a few times: Their service is worthwhile. Yearly membership with SeaTow — the AAA of the waterway — is a good investment.

The area's waters are full of shoals, so keep an eye on your depth-sounder. If you don't have one and charts suggest shallow waters, steer clear of questionable areas. The ICW is susceptible to shoaling near inlets, and you can't rely on charts for accuracy because changes occur frequently. The markers entering the Cape Fear River from the ocean were renumbered in 1997, so be alert to the fact that these changes may not appear on current NOAA charts.

The beauty and pleasures of North Carolina's southern coast are some of the best available. Enjoy your visit and return often. Many of the Insiders you'll meet while here started out as visitors too.

SUN, SAND AND SEA

Watersports

If you're passionate about watersports or just an enthusiastic novice, North Carolina's southern coastline offers the perfect spot to hone your skills with a combination of mild weather, warm water temperatures, good water quality, and clean, uncrowded beaches. Our coastal waters are warmed by the Gulf Stream, which not only makes for long seasons for watersports, but also brings a surprising array of tropical sea life. The region's overall subtropical climate often allows watersports enthusiasts to indulge their particular passions from early spring through late fall. Add the Intracoastal Waterway, sounds, tidal marshes, rivers and their tributaries to a generous Atlantic coastline, and the opportunities for fun in the water are limited only by your sense of adventure.

Please make note of local ordinances. For example, swimming and surfing are forbidden within 100 feet of most fishing piers. Disturbing or walking on protected dunes — greatly frowned upon by all area beach communities and strictly prohibited — carries a fine that ranges from $50 to $500, depending on the municipality. Most beaches do not allow dogs on the beach at any time, especially during the summer season, while others are more accommodating in the off-season if the animals are leashed.

This chapter is divided into sections dealing with the area's most popular watersports. The overview will tell you more about each sport as it relates to the southern coastal region and any local ordinance variations. Reluctant to pack all that equipment you'll need? This chapter also lists rental agencies, shops offering watersports equipment and supplies, and related services. For example, the Boating section of this chapter includes details on safety, rentals and boaters' maps and charts.

Other chapters of this book that address water-related topics include the Fishing chapter, which also gives the locations of boat ramps, and the Sun, Sand and Sea chapter, which discusses boating safety, swimming and other activities.

LOOK FOR:

- **Personal Watercraft**
- **Canoeing**
- **Kayaking**
- **Sailing**
- **Scuba Diving**
- **Waterskiing**
- **Surfing**
- **Swimming**
- **Windsurfing**
- **Kiteboarding**
- **Beach Access**

Personal Watercraft

If you have your own water buggy, there are beach access points on Wrightsville Beach suitable for beach trailers. One of the easiest is at the foot of Causeway Drive (straight ahead from the fixed bridge), but parking is rarely available there in the high season. Another is the paved access to the left of the Oceanic Restaurant on S. Lumina Avenue, provided there are no volleyball tournaments that day. On Topsail Island access points are fewer, largely due to dune erosion. Your best bet would be the crossover near the center of Surf City. Smooth riding is also available in the Northeast Cape Fear River, accessible from the several public boat ramps listed in our Fishing chapter, but these waters are frequently busy with other boaters, anglers and swimmers in summer. Exercise courtesy and extreme caution.

All the rental craft available in our area launch into the Intracoastal Waterway. Be sure to respect the limitations set by the individual rental services. They must operate within the parameters of their permits. Wrightsville Beach, in cooperation with the local flotilla of the U.S. Coast Guard Auxiliary, occasionally offers a personal watercraft safety course at a cost of about $25. Call Donna Sauer, (910) 270-9830 for more information.

Regulations

If you own your own personal watercraft, be aware that North Carolina requires that it be registered (see the Boat Registration section below). The use of personal watercraft in certain New Hanover County waters is restricted to safeguard people, property and the environment. Note the following rules:

• Operators must be 16 years of age. Persons 13 through 15 may operate personal watercraft provided they have passed a mandatory personal watercraft safety course approved by the state, the Coast Guard Auxiliary or the National Association of State Boating Law Administrators. Two forms of identification must be carried with the 13 to 15-year-olds — a photo ID and the safety course certificate.

• Watercraft must have a self-circling capability or an engine-cutoff device attached to the operator.

• When operating in the Intracoastal Waterway from Carolina Beach Inlet north to Mason Inlet or within the sounds and channels behind Masonboro Island and Wrightsville Beach, watercraft speed is strictly limited to 5 mph within 50 feet of the marsh or shore, an angler, a person in the water, an anchored vessel, a posted waterbird sanctuary or piers or docks.

• Operators may not chase or harass wildlife unless lawfully hunting or fishing.

These restrictions have led many jetcraft operators to move into the waterways north of Wrightsville Beach, where there are currently no rules. But common sense is called for. Refrain from operating at speeds over 5 mph when in shallow water, especially at low tide; otherwise you will probably contribute to the destruction of oyster beds, plant life and other marsh wildlife. Be especially wary of watercraft larger than your own and of water-skiers, since jet craft are more maneuverable. Finally, respect the privacy of waterfront property.

Personal Watercraft Rentals

Paradise Landing
318 Fulchers Rd., Sneads Ferry
• (910) 327-2114, (910) 327 2133

Explore the New River on a Waverunner rented from Paradise Landing. Prices are $70 per hour or $35 per half hour. Other rental choices are 18 or 24 foot pontoon boats, ski boats, kayaks, canoes and Hobie Cats. Reservations are recommended.

Performance Watercraft
Wilmington • (910) 799-WAVE

Performance, a family-run business entering its ninth season in 2003, delivers jet craft (sit-down models) to Wrightsville Beach-area waterways from April through October, weather permitting. This year Performance has added pleasure and scuba charters. Reservations are not required but are strongly recommended during the peak season. Crafts are Yamaha Wave models. Rates are $45 for one-half hour, $70 for one hour, $95 for an hour and a half, $125 for two hours and $175 for three hours. Safety equipment, basic instruction by a certified instructor, tax and fuel are included in the rental fee. A credit card is required to place a deposit. Patrons must be 25 years old to rent and 16 years old to operate the craft. Travelers' checks and credit cards (MasterCard or Visa) are welcome, and group rates are available. Instruction clinics are also available upon request at no extra charge for corporate and family groups. The emphasis at Performance Watercraft is on customer service, safety, affordability and family fun.

Weekend pleasure cruises, a recent addition to the business, offer a unique 21/2-hour sightseeing adventure along the Intracoastal Waterway. Sit back and enjoy beautiful vistas aboard a 25' Cobia with Captain Shawn Nasseri. Amenities include a gourmet box lunch, snorkel gear and a disposable camera. Reservations are required, and cruises are available year-round with one day's notice. Call Performance Watercraft for more details, reservations and rates.

Boating

At times, boating in the lower Cape Fear involves competition with oceangoing vessels, shallow water or the treacherous shoals that earned the Carolina coast the moniker "Graveyard of the Atlantic." In contrast, the upper Cape Fear River, its northeast branch and the winding creeks of the coastal plain offer a genuine taste of the old Southeast to those with small boats or canoes. Tannins leached from the cypress trees keep these waters the color of coffee. Many creeks are overhung by trees, moss

and, in summer, the occasional snake. Early spring and late autumn are particularly good times to go, since they are bug-free. See our Fishing chapter for boat ramp locations.

Safety and Resources

The U.S. Coast Guard Auxiliary conducts free Courtesy Motorboat Examinations (CME). The exams are not required for boat registration. For information, call the Marine Safety Office at (910) 815-4895, then dial 0, or call the Coast Guard Auxiliary Flotilla at (910) 256-3119. You will be referred to the examining flotilla officer nearest you. Various flotillas of the local Coast Guard Auxiliary offer Safe Boating courses five times a year (autumn, winter, spring and twice in summer). Locations include the Wrightsville Beach Recreation Center (at Wrightsville Beach Park) and Cape Fear Community College in downtown Wilmington and the Hampstead campus. These courses are strongly recommended for everyone who operates a motor boat. The fee averages $35 and includes all materials. Also inquire about the America's Boating Class, available on CD/ROM and the Basic Coastal Navigation course. For information call (910) 686-4479 for Wilmington, (910) 458-4518 for Carolina Beach, (910) 270-9830 for Wrightsville Beach and (910) 270-3193 for Hampstead.

Local chapters of the nonprofit U.S. Power Squadrons (USPS), America's largest private boating association, also offer the USPS Boating Course on a regular basis in Wilmington, Wrightsville Beach, Hampstead, Southport and Shallotte. The course is free, but a $20 fee covers the cost of materials, and you need not be a USPS member to participate. For information on the USPS classes closest to you, call (800) 336-BOAT.

For ship-to-shore calling along the Cape Fear Coast, contact the Wilmington Marine Operator on channel 26 or 28. For shore-to-ship calls dial the Coast Guard Marine Safety office at (910) 772-2200. For the information line, call (910) 256-4224. To report emergencies to the Coast Guard, all initial radio calls should be made on channel 16/158.8 MHz. The Wrightsville Beach Coast Guard station's telephone number is (910) 256-3469. Local boating and watersports enthusiasts also report that cellular phone reception is remarkably clear near the shoreline.

An excellent resource for boaters of all kinds is the *North Carolina Coastal Boating Guide*, compiled by the N.C. Department of Transportation. Obtain a free copy by calling (877) DOT4YOU; ask for the Map Department.

Boat Registration

North Carolina requires that motorized craft of any size (including water-jet craft) and sail-boats 14 feet and longer be registered. The cost is $25 for three years. Renewal forms are mailed about two months prior to expiration. Titles are optional ($20). More information on boating regulations may be obtained from the **N.C. Wildlife Resources Commission Boat Registration Section**, 512 N. Salisbury Street, Raleigh, NC 27604-1188; (800) 628-3773. The following businesses and offices can provide the necessary forms and information:

Canady's Sport Center, 3220 Wrightsville Avenue, Wilmington, (910) 791-6280

Crocker's Marine, 2035 Eastwood Road, Wilmington, (910) 256-3661

N.C. Department of Motor Vehicles License Plates Office, 14689 U.S. Highway 17 S., Hampstead, (910) 270-9010

Shallotte Marine Supplies, Main Street, Shallotte, (910) 754-6962

Motorboat Rentals

If you would like to rent a power boat, note that advance reservations are essential in summer. Most proprietors require a deposit, a valid driver's license or major credit card, plus a signed waiver of liability.

Dockside Watersports
Carolina Beach Municipal Docks, Carl Winner Blvd., Carolina Beach
• **(910) 458-0220**

Dockside Watersports rents a 23-foot pontoon boat and 19-foot center-console outboards. Rentals are available any day of the week, April to October 1, from 9 or 10 AM until dusk, and off-season by appointment. Four-hour rentals begin at around $179. Reserve in advance. Major credit cards are accepted.

Entropy Rentals & Charters
Wrightsville Beach • (910) 395-2401

On the Intracoastal Waterway at Wrightsville Beach, Entropy rents its own line of Sea Mark power boats, manufactured in Rocky Point. Fully equipped center-console vessels are available by the half-day, day or week. For a nominal fee, Entropy also rents water skis and equipment. The 12-hour day rate is about $270. Most major credit cards are accepted. Entropy serves the Wrightsville Beach area and the lower Cape Fear coast. They're open year-round; call ahead for reservations and location information.

Paradise Landing
318 Fulchers Rd., Sneads Ferry
• **(910) 327-2114, (910) 327 2133**

Parasail 1,400 feet over the Atlantic Ocean. Catch the wind in a small sailboat. Make waves in a canoe, pontoon boat, 24-foot Cobia, john boat or paddle boat. Charter a six-passenger fishing boat and captain for your party or join other fishermen aboard the 38-foot head boat departing daily from Paradise Landing. All of these options are available for your day on the water. Reservations are recommended.

Canoeing

Touring the lower Cape Fear River in a canoe isn't recommended for beginners because the river is a commercial shipping channel. But for the experienced canoeist, the lower Cape Fear holds some nice surprises. Paddlers who frequent these waters have been known to gather wild rice bequeathed by the vanished rice plantations of the past. The Black River, a protected tributary of the Cape Fear River noted for its old-growth stands of bald cypress, is an excellent, scenic canoeing choice, as are several of both rivers' tributaries. And a canoe makes excellent transportation for exploring the tidal marshes and barrier islands all along our coast.

In 1997 the Town of Oak Island dedicated some 24 miles of canoe "trails" known as the Long Beach Canoe Trail System. Four trails make up the system: Lockwood Folly (4.2 miles), Montgomery Slough (7 miles), Howells Point (6.5 miles) and Davis Creek (6 miles). Conditions range from calm, protected waters to rough, exposed waters near inlets, and all are remarkably scenic, quiet and full of wildlife. For information visit or call the Oak Island Recreation Department, 3003 E. Oak Island Drive, (910) 278-5518.

Pro Canoe & Kayak Outdoors
435 Eastwood Rd., Wilmington
• **(910) 798-8822, (888) 794-4867**

This well-equipped store offers canoes, such as Dagger, Mad River and Old Town, plus canoe rentals, guided fresh- and saltwater trips and overnight camping trips. Rental fees are $45 per day, $65 for a three-day weekend and $115 for a week. All rentals include canoe, one paddle, a personal flotation device/seat and soft roof rack. Extra paddles, safety equipment and other accessories are available for rent. Pro Canoe & Kayak Outdoors, open seven days a week all year, is convenient to the protected waters on the sound side of Wrightsville Beach. Call or

stop by the store to check on monthly rental specials, trip rates and reservations.

Island Passage
Bald Head Island Marina • (910) 457-4944

An interesting area to explore by canoe or kayak is Bald Head Creek and salt marsh, the state's largest single expanse of salt marsh, on Bald Head Island. Island Passage provides half-day canoe and kayak rentals so you can explore the creek for a morning or afternoon at your own pace. Keep in mind that the creek is a tidal waterway so excursions and rentals are tide dependant and should be planned accordingly. Rental rates are $40 per canoe (suitable for up to three adults), $40 per single kayak, and $55 per double kayak. Call for the daily schedule. Reservations are suggested.

Rowing and Kayaking

Rowing along the Cape Fear River is a time-honored tradition, dating back to the early 19th century when river pilots guided large, ocean-going vessels safely through the river's waters to safe harbor in Wilmington. These sturdy, yet speedy, boats were manned with four to six rowers and a coxswain. Rowing competitions between river pilots in the port cities along the southern coast — Wilmington, Charleston and Savannah among them — and crews from visiting ships were common.

After the Civil War rowing regattas along Wilmington's riverfront became a weekly event during the warm summer months. Rowing for sport eventually diminished with the advent of motorboat racing until a group of enthusiasts revived the sport in 1989, forming the Cape Fear River Rowing Club. (See listing below.)

Today the Cape Fear and Northeast Cape Fear rivers provide both recreational and competitive rowers an opportunity to enjoy the sport. The enthusiast interested in a casual, scenic route can travel from historic Wilmington's riverfront and the Battleship North Carolina to the State Port of Wilmington and then beyond to areas surrounded by long-abandoned rice fields, inhabited by abundant wildlife, such as deer, osprey, and alligators. A rower with competition in mind will appreciate the long portions of flat water in the rivers.

Local guides report that the popularity of kayaking along North Carolina's southern coast has doubled in the last several years. Not surprising when you consider the bounty of regional waterways and seemingly endless things to see and areas to explore — tropical sea life, exotic vegetation, a variety of waterfowl, historic landmarks accessible by water, barrier islands and pristine wildlife sanctuaries. Unique opportunities for guided tours or solo exploration are plentiful due to this abundance of water — the coastline, the Intracoastal Waterway, sounds, channels, salt marshes, inland rivers and their tributaries. Several enterprises, including Kayak Carolina and Southport's The Adventure Company (see listings below), emphasize ecological responsibility and education and bring paddlers into intimate contact with wildlife and a primal silence.

All kayaking trips listed in this section are guided by experienced paddlers who bring a love of the sport and dedication to safety on each excursion. This region's paddling season is gen-

WATERSPORTS

erally nine months long — March through November — but some experienced paddlers will argue that, due to the mild climate and warm waters, kayaking can be enjoyed year-round. Along the coast and on inland rivers, the best time is from August to May, when boat traffic is down, temperatures are less humid, insects and snakes aren't a nuisance and the chances of seeing a wider variety of wildlife are increased.

INSIDERS' TIP

It Takes Three to Water-Ski ...a boat operator, an observer and a skier. The operator must pay attention to driving the boat. The observer is the operator's "eyes in the back of the head," focusing on the skier and alerting the driver when the skier goes down. The skier must wear a U.S. Coast Guard-approved life jacket while being towed.

Unlike boating, kayaking and canoeing have few rules and regulations. The one rule that applies is a requirement for one life jacket per passenger aboard a kayak or canoe. Currently, no legislation exists to force the issue, but professional kayaking guides strongly recommend wearing a life jacket as a safety precaution.

Other rules or suggestions are simply common-sense safety considerations:

• Avoid high-traffic areas. If you do paddle in a high-traffic area, make yourself known by wearing brightly colored clothing.

• Don't paddle after dark without the proper safety equipment.

• Travel in pairs, or plan your route and let someone know where you're going. Carry a cellular phone with you for emergencies and slip it into a plastic bag to stay dry. (Cell phone reception is considered good on the waterways close to shore.)

• Carry immediate safety and survival items with you — first aid kit, flashlight, pocketknife and the means to make a fire.

The Adventure Company
807-A Howe St., Southport
• (910) 454-0607, (910) 233-5119

The Adventure Company specializes in kayak tours, rentals and coastal environmental education programs. Tours are scheduled weekly and can be customized. Kayak rentals include paddles and life jacket with single kayaks renting for $30 (four hours), $45 (full day) and $140 (five days). Tandems are available for $40 (four hours), $55 (full day) and $175 (five days). In business for three years, owner Emma Thomas, a certified kayak and canoe instructor, has been kayaking for 16 years. Also available through The Adventure Company are bicycle tours of historic Southport and adventure travel to the

Bahamas and Florida. Call for details, schedule or reservations.

Cape Fear River Rowing Club
(910) 794-3160

Founded in 1989 by a group of enthusiasts, this rowing club's goal is to promote and increase interest in the sport in the Wilmington area. Anyone interested in rowing is welcome to join, and the club offers free lessons for beginners or support and advice as a novice rower advances in skill . Members have access to a range of rowing crafts, from stable recreational boats to racing shells that challenge the seasoned scullers. Their current boathouse is located at Point Harbor Marina, 1500 Point Harbor Road, on the west bank of the Northeast Cape Fear River. Three rowing clubs use the facility — the CFRRC, the UNC-Wilmington crew and the Cape Fear Academy crew — using a mix of boats from single and double, to fours and eights. CFRRC sponsors group activities including an annual tip drill exercises and group rows. Members also compete in a variety of regattas along the East Coast. For more information about the club, call the number listed above or write to Cape Fear River Rowing Club, P.O. Box 1586, Wilmington, NC 28402.

Great Outdoor Provision Co.
Hanover Center, 3501 Oleander Dr., Wilmington • (910) 343-1648

Open seven days a week, this store sells a variety of canoes and kayaks as well as paddling accessories, maps, guidebooks, backpacking and fly-fishing gear and outdoor clothes. Instructional clinics are available, and the staff at Great Outdoor Provision Co. will be happy to arrange demonstrations of the watercraft or equipment.

Kayak Carolina
Carolina Beach • (910) 458-9111

The emphasis at Kayak Carolina is a promotion of the kayaking lifestyle, nature preservation, environmental education and, of course, lots of fun. The popular two-hour guided tour, which includes a brief basic-information clinic on kayaking techniques and safety, is a good introduction to the sport. Guides are experienced instructors and trained interpretive naturalists. Cost for this tour is $39 per person, half-price for children ages 11 and younger. Other tours include day explorations of Zeke's and Masonboro Islands, nature tours, sunrise, sunset, guided camping trips and family trips. Kayak rentals are available for single kayaks, $35 for four hours and $55 for 24 hours. Tandems rent for $45 for four hours and $65 for 24 hours. Kayak Carolina also offers both ACA and BCU kayak instruction for all skill levels. Call for details.

Pro Canoe & Kayak Outdoors
435 Eastwood Rd., Wilmington
• **(910) 798-8822, (888) 794-4867**

This well-established store sells and rents a variety of sit-on-top and cockpit kayaks (and canoes), including Dagger, Necky, Old Town, Ocean Kayak, Hobie and North Carolina's own Wilderness Systems touring boats, made in High Point. Single kayak rentals run $40 per day, $70 for a three-day weekend and $115 for a week. Tandems rent for $60 per day, $80 for a three-day weekend and $130 for the week. Visa and MasterCard are accepted. All accessories and basic instruction are included in rental fees. Reservations are preferred, and rentals are available year round with the exception of sit-on-tops, which are seasonal. Pro Canoe & Kayak Outdoors also offers fresh- and saltwater kayaking trips, including such local destinations as Masonboro Island (four to five hours) and historic Fort Fisher (approximately three hours). They will also build a trip to suit your interests. Trip fees include kayak, paddling gear, basic instruction and guide services. Since safety is their primary concern, all guides are experienced paddlers with first aid and CPR certifications. Call (888) 794-4867 for the current trip rates, reservations or more information.

Salt Marsh Kayak Company
222 Old Causeway Dr., Wrightsville Beach
• **(910) 509-2989, (866) 65-KAYAK**

The only kayak shop on Wrightsville Beach, Salt Marsh Kayak Company is a full-service paddle store, offering kayak sales, rentals, tours and instruction. The company's extensive rental fleet includes recreational sit-on-top and decked boats, as well as high-performance touring kayaks. Delivery of rental boats on Wrightsville Beach is free. Guided nature tours are available throughout the year to a variety of beautiful locations, and basic to advanced level instruction is available from ACA-certified instructors.

Pleasure Island Rentals
2 N. Lake Park Blvd., Carolina Beach
• **(910) 458-4747**

Located in the heart of Carolina Beach, this watersports equipment rental company goes by the slogan, "We rent FUN stuff." Single kayak rentals range from $20 for four hours to $35 for 24 hours and $115 for a week. Tandems run $25 (four hours), $40 (24 hours) and $130 (one week). All rentals include free pick-up and delivery, paddles and life jackets. Other available rentals include an Escape sailboat, renting from $35 (four hours) to $50 (24 hours), surfboards, body boards and fins, wetsuits ($5 per day), bicycles, scooters, umbrellas and chairs. Pleasure Island Rentals opens daily from Memorial Day to Labor Day. After hours and during the off-season, call the number above for equipment rental.

Beach Fun Rentals
132 Ocean Blvd. W, Holden Beach
• **(910) 842-9600, (888) 355-4446**

Beach Fun Rentals is the only full-service vacation equipment rental company on Holden Beach. Kayaks remain their top rental item. Single kayaks, including Frenzy, Rapido, Yakboard, Yahoo, Scrambler and Scrambler XT, rent for $35 from the time you pick it up until 6 PM the same day. So come early and get more fun for your money. Tandem kayaks such as Malibu II and Cabo rent for $55 per day. Weekly rentals are available, and they run $150 (single) and $190 (tandem). Ambush, a fishing kayak, rents for $75 per day or $150 per week. Surfboards, boogie boards and more also are available. Beach Fun Rental is open daily from 9 AM to 6 PM from March 15 through November 1. (If the weather stays mild, they have been known to stay open a little later in the season.)

Boomers
Causeway Plaza, 3468 Holden Beach Rd., Holden Beach • **(910) 842-1400, (800) 287-1990**

On the causeway in Holden Beach, this general beach rental store offers rentals on single or tandem kayaks as well as boogie boards ($20 a week) and surfboards ($40 a week). Single kayaks rent for $35 per day (24 hours) and $125 for a week. Tandems are available for $50 for 24 hours and $160 for a week.

Julie's Rentals
2 Main St., Sunset Beach
• **(910) 579-1211, (888) 5791211**

Julie's is a complete beach-rental shop that rents kayaks (singles and tandems) as well as many other recreational items. Rates for singles are $35 per day and $125 for a week. Tandem kayaks are $50 per day and $160 for a week. Julie's Rentals offers a delivery and pick-up service for $20 ($10 each trip) or you can pick up your rental from the store. Other rental items include bicycles, umbrellas and beach chairs.

Herring's Outdoor Sports
701 N. New River Dr., Surf City
• (910) 328-3291
Paddle the peaceful and interesting Intracoastal Waterway or challenge the waves of the Atlantic Ocean. Whatever your choice, Herring's has the right kayak available for rent. There are single and double passenger models and the popular sit-on-top styles. You can rent by the hour, half-day, full day or week. The kayaking experts at Herring's will outfit you with all you need and provide brief instructions to ensure safety for this adventure.

Holland's Shelter Creek
8315 N.C. Hwy. 53 E., Burgaw
• (910) 259-5743
Here's your chance to enjoy a peaceful time exploring the North Cape Fear River. Canoes and kayaks are available for everyone from the solitary fisherman to families to groups. Canoes and kayaks can be rented by the half or full day. Paddleboats can be rented by the half-hour or for one or three hours.

Sailing

An event eagerly awaited by salts and lubbers alike is the Holiday Flotilla at Wrightsville Beach, held just after Thanksgiving, in which boaters (power and sail) adorn their craft in the most flamboyant seasonal decoration possible for an evening cruise through Motts and Banks channels. Prizes are awarded for the best-decorated craft, and fireworks are a festive added attraction. Check local listings for information for this event, or call the Cape Fear Coast Convention and Visitors Bureau, (910) 341-4030.

It's useful to note that anchorage in Banks Channel at Wrightsville Beach is free. The average limit seems to be 30 to 45 days before the authorities pay a visit or post a nastygram, but boaters have been known to stay longer. Find complete information on anchorage and marina services in our chapter on Marinas and the Intracoastal Waterway.

Wrightsville Beach Ocean
Racing Association, P.O. Box 113,
Wrightsville Beach, NC 28480
For serious competition for sailors and those

who just love to cruise, WBORA (wuh-BORE-ah) is the local organization of note. Founded in 1967, it is an active, nonprofit organization that promotes and sponsors sailboat cruising and racing in the Cape Fear region and elsewhere along the North Carolina coast. Its members are a decidedly fun-loving bunch. WBORA provides race and cruise schedule management and development, hosts sailing seminars, participates in community programs, assists in youth sailing and organizes social activities around sailing events.

Sailing events span the season from spring to fall, with social events sprinkled throughout the year. Among the highlights: the Bud Cup Crew Scramble Race; The Michelob Cup; The Old Baldy (Bald Head Island) Regatta; The Blockade Runner Solo Race, a year-end awards banquet; and a Spring and Fall Point Series. In 1998 WBORA began a yearly running of the Leukemia Cup Regatta. This annual charity event is nationally recognized and held in conjunction with a weekend full of activities. Boats of various types may compete in these events, with a performance handicap racing factor (PHRF) figured into the standings.

WBORA is a member of the U.S. Sailing Association, the South Atlantic Yacht Racing Association and a charter member of the North Carolina Yacht Racing Association. Membership is open to all, and dues depend on the extent of your participation. An annual handbook and frequent newsletter are published for members. WBORA does not maintain permanent offices, but information may be obtained by contacting Howard Ling at (910) 620-4660 or Guy Staat at (910) 232-2189.

Pro Canoe & Kayak Outdoors
435 Eastwood Rd., Wilmington
• (910) 798-8822, (888) 794-4867
This year Pro Canoe introduces trimarans by Windrider. They sell four different kinds, the Windrider 10, 16, 17 and the Rave. Check them out.

Sailing Instruction
and Rentals

WaterWays Sailing & Charters
2030 Eastwood Rd., Ste. 12, Wilmington
• (910) 256-4282, (800) 562-SAIL
WaterWays Sailing School is the premier sailing school in the Carolinas certified by the American Sailing Association. The ASA awarded

Jet-skiing is a favorite high-speed coastal watersport.

Photo: Jay Tervo

WaterWays its highest honor five years in a row by naming the school the 1995, 1996, 1997,1998 and 1999 School of the Year. In addition, over eight of the school's instructors have won the ASA's Outstanding Instructor award. WaterWays offers a battery of sailing courses taught entirely by USCG-licensed captains. Courses include Basic Sailing, Basic Coastal Cruising, Bareboat Charter, Coastal Navigation, Advanced Coastal Cruising and Celestial Navigation. Captained charters are also offered for local excursions. Call for information and schedule for charters and classes.

Salt Marsh Kayak Company
222 Old Causeway Dr., Wrightsville Beach • (910) 509-2989, (866) 65KAYAK

Salt Marsh Kayak Company operates an on-water rental facility, including sailing rentals at Wrightsville Beach. Located across from the Blockade Runner Hotel on Waynick Boulevard, the facility is open seven days a week during the summer. In addition sailboat instructions is available. Contact Salt Marsh Kayak Co. for more information and updates on tour and class schedules.

Southport Sail and Power Squadron
(910) 454-4479

David Pryor, who has been sailing since he was a child, recognized the need for a U.S. Power Squadron when he moved to Southport from Michigan. In January 2002, it was chartered. The Power Squadron teaches a safe-boating course free of charge (except for the cost of materials) to anyone who is interested. Members of the organization have the opportunity to take a myriad of courses related to boating and sailing, including sailing, plotting and position finding, piloting, seamanship, cruise planning, celestial navigation, marine electronics and engine maintenance. The Southport Squadron has more than 90 members, and there is quite a bit of expertise available within the membership for educational resources. The squadron provides monthly programs or activities.

WATERSPORTS

Supplies, Accessories and Repair

There are many more businesses in the area that provide good service for marine supplies and repair than are listed here, but those below come recommended.

Boater's World Discount Marine Center
University Commons Shopping Center, S. College Rd., Wilmington • (910) 452-3000

When it comes to marine supplies, accessories, gear and clothing, there's very little that Boater's World doesn't carry. And as if an inventory that's well-displayed, comprehensive and well-priced weren't enough, the staff is expert and polite. It's open seven days a week.

Masonboro Boat Yard & Marina, Inc.
609 Trails End Rd., Wilmington • (910) 791-1893

Located at ICW Marker 136 on Whiskey Creek (5 miles south of Wrightsville Beach), Masonboro Boat Yard and Marina offers dockage (for sale or rent) up to 55 feet, dry rack storage to 25 feet, complete engine and hull repairs, a full rigging service and arrangements for sail repair. Boat owners can also opt for do-it-yourself repairs at Masonboro Boat Yard.

Blackbarry Marine
4701 Long Beach Rd., Southport • (910) 457-0667

When Barry Adkins was a young man and working in a shop, he was really into his work and was always the grimiest one at the end of the day. His co-workers began calling him Black Barry and it stuck. When he opened his marine repair shop six years ago, he had difficulty coming up with a name that someone else had not already thought of, so he decided on his nickname, knowing no one else would have that! Blackbarry Marine is a full-service marine dealership for parts and repairs to outboard and inboard engines. The shop has a full line parts department at wholesale prices. Services include trailer repair, bottom painting and winterizing as well. Barry also specializes in sales of Southern Skimmer Boats, Tohatsu Outboards, Load Rite Trailers and has 63' Jon Boat packages with Yamaha outboards.

Shallotte Marine Supplies Inc.
4607 Main St., Shallotte• (910) 754-6962

Serving the southern Brunswick County area since 1968, Shallotte Marine Supplies' motto is "Service is our policy." They offer complete boat and motor repair by factory-trained mechanics, motorboat sales, marine hardware and accessories. Boat storage by the month or the year is available, and Shallotte Marine specializes in saltwater rigging.

Scuba Diving and Snorkeling

Diving the southern coastal waters offers rewarding experiences to collectors, nature-watchers and wreck divers, despite there being no true coral reefs in these latitudes. A surprising variety of tropical fish species inhabit these waters, including blue angel fish, damsel fish and moray eels as well as several varieties of sea fans, some as large as 3 feet in height. Spiny oysters, deer cowries, helmet shells, trumpet tritons and queen conchs can be found here. Among the easiest places to find tropical aquatic life is 23 Mile Rock, part of a 12-mile-long ledge running roughly perpendicular to the coast. Another 15 miles out, the Lobster Ledge, a low-lying formation 120 feet deep, is a collectors' target. There are several smaller ledges close to shore in shallower water better suited for less-experienced divers and more bottom time.

Visibility at offshore sites averages 60 feet and often approaches 100 feet, but inshore visibility is seldom better than 20 feet. The coastal waters can be dived all year long, since their temperatures range from the upper 50s in winter and low 80s in summer. However, many local charters typically end their diving season in early fall. Some charters organize destination trips after that.

Good snorkeling in the region is a matter of knowing when and where to go. Near-shore bottoms are mostly packed sand devoid of the rugged features that make for good viewing and collecting, but a good guide can lead you to rewarding areas. When the wind is right and the tide is rising, places such as the Wrightsville Beach jetty offer good viewing and visibility. The many creeks and estuaries support an abundance of life, and the shorter visibility, averaging 15 to 20 feet, is no obstacle in water so shallow.

The waters around piers in Banks Channel at Wrightsville Beach are fair but often murky, and currents are strong. Only experienced snorkelers should attempt these waters or those in local inlets, which are treacherous, and then only at stopped tides. It is neither safe nor legal to swim beneath oceanside fishing piers. When in doubt, contact a local dive shop for information.

This region of the Graveyard of the Atlantic offers unparalleled opportunities for wreck divers. From Tubbs Inlet (near Sunset Beach) to New River Inlet (North Topsail Beach), 20 of the dozens of known shipwrecks resting here are accessible and safe. Most are Confederate blockade runners, one is a tanker torpedoed by the Nazi sub U-158, and several were sunk as part of North Carolina's artificial reef program (see the Fishing chapter for more on artificial reefs). These and higher-risk wrecks can be located with the assistance of dive shops.

Wreck diving is an advanced skill. Research prior to a dive is essential in terms of the target, techniques and potential dangers, which in this region include live ammunition and explosives that may be found on World War II wrecks. Contact the proper authorities if you observe anything suspicious, and leave it alone! Under state law, all wrecks and underwater artifacts that remain unclaimed for more than 10 years are declared state property. Anyone interested in searching for artifacts should file for a permit with the North Carolina Department of Cultural Resources, 109 E. Jones Street, Raleigh, NC 27611.

Charter boats can be arranged for dive trips through all the dive shops listed here, but there are others. Also check the marinas for fishing charters that accommodate dive trips.

Many charter boats are primarily fishing boats, so if you need custom diving craft, be sure to inquire. Most dive shops can lead you to a certification class if they don't offer one themselves. Also, proof of diver's certification is required by shops or dive masters when renting equipment, booking charters or purchasing air fills.

Aquatic Safaris & Divers Emporium
5751-4 Oleander Dr., Wilmington
• (910) 392-4386

This PADI training facility is one of Wilmington's largest full-service charter services and dive shops, offering air fills, including Nitrox, and a full range of equipment for sale and rent. Dive charters are available and range from $40 to $110 per person, depending on the trip's distance. Snorkeling equipment is for sale only. The shop is certified by major manufac-

turers to perform repairs on most life-support equipment and most other equipment as well. It's open seven days a week during the summer and six days a week in the off-season.

Bottom Time Wilmington
6014 Wrightsville Ave., Wilmington
• (910) 397-0181, | (800) NITROX1

This is a SDI-TDI and PADI five-star facility and among the largest sport diving and snorkeling facilities in the region. Services include rentals, repair, sales, air (standard and Nitrox) and instruction in diving and snorkeling. Local charters and customized dive travels to warmer climes during the winter are available. The staff is fully certified. In summer, Bottom Time is open seven days a week. Its Cape Fear season closes by early November. Bottom Time closes on Tuesdays and Wednesdays during the winter months.

Cape Fear Descenders Dive Club
(910) 792-1235, (910) 845-2330

This Southport-based dive club was started as a small group of diving enthusiasts in January 1996. Monthly meetings are held year-round in Southport on the second Tuesday of each month at 7 PM. Call for the location of the meeting. Group dives, guest speakers, parties, continuing education classes, advance dive classes and a newsletter are all perks of membership. To join, members must be certified divers. Annual dues, pro-rated after July 1, are $20 for individuals and $30 for the family (spouses are not required to be certified divers).

The Dive Shop
414 Yaupon Drive. Oak Island
• (910) 279-2267, (910) 232-1190

Whatever your needs in the line of dive equipment, you can find it at The Dive Shop, a small shop with a large inventory. They sell Tusa and Mares dive equipment, wet suits, buoyancy control devices, snorkels, masks and tanks and will ship equipment anywhere in the US. Call Paul or Tom for knowledgeable assistance and friendly service.

Seaduced-N-Sea Inc.
707 Canal Dr., Carolina Beach
• (910) 458-8715

Certified Captain and Master Instructor Dennis McKee has guided dive charters in North

Carolina's coastal waters for over 15 years. McKee and his experienced crew offer dive charters to satisfy any interest — shipwrecks, ledges, rocks and spear fishing — in a new 48-foot boat. Seaduced-N-Sea also offers classes, a dive shop, on-site accommodations, gear rentals and their own pumped gases for compressed air or NITROX tank fills. With an emphasis on service, McKee claims that "everything you need to dive in North Carolina is right here". Call for more information on charter schedules, fees, classes and rentals.

Scuba South Diving Company
222 S. River Dr., Southport
• (910) 457-5201

Among the most respected diving experts in the Southport area is Wayne Strickland, who specializes in dive charters to some of the less-frequented targets off the Cape plus such well-known sites as the City of Houston, a passenger freighter that sank in 1878 and which Strickland salvaged for the Southport Maritime Museum (artifacts are on display). Strickland will arrange dives to any site along the southern coast. Trips are aboard his custom 52-foot Scuba South II. Scuba South sells and rents a full store of equipment, including wet and dry suits, and provides air fills. Nitrox is available.

Water-Skiing

The protected waters of the lower Cape Fear River, from Carolina Beach south, are the most popular for water-skiing the greater Wilmington area. These waters are convenient to public boat ramps in Carolina Beach, including those at the marina at Carolina Beach State Park and at Federal Point. Throughout most of the region, the wider channels of the Intracoastal Waterway and adjoining sounds offer water-skiing opportunities, but be alert to other boat traffic.

The relatively hushed surf along the Brunswick Islands is well-suited to skiing, yielding about 22 miles of shoreline from Ocean Isle Beach to Sunset Beach. Big Lake, in the community of Boiling Springs Lakes, 8 miles northwest of Southport on N.C. 87, is a long, narrow body of water that's excellent for water-skiing. There is a free public boat ramp off Alton Lennon Drive. Check with the rental services listed in the Motorboat Rentals section above if you need to rent a towing craft. Many, if not most, services and some boating supply shops also rent skis and equipment.

Surfing

California surfers who come to the southern coast of North Carolina agree: The surf may be less spectacular than on the West Coast, but the water is warmer and the season is longer. Conditions were considered good enough for the U.S. Amateur Surfing Championships's Mid-Atlantic Regionals to be held at Wrightsville Beach in 1996. And surfers from here are making their mark worldwide.

Wrightsville Beach's own Ben Bourgeois became the 1996 Junior Men's Amateur World Champion, having won the Quicksilver Grommet World Championship in Bali the year before. Former Men's World Champion Bill Curry is a local resident and one of six local members of the Eastern Surf Association's All-Star team (which includes his son, Chris). With surfing now part of the pantheon of Olympic events, local surfing has naturally gained further status. Surf shops throughout the region can provide information on regional surfing competitions.

The beaches running north-south — Topsail Island down to Fort Fisher — experience consistently better surf than the Brunswick beaches, with their east-west orientation. (The Brunswick beaches are fine for bodyboarding.) A favored surfing spot is Masonboro Island's north end near the jetty; however, it's not an easy place to reach, since Masonboro Inlet is an active boat channel with dangerous currents. Crossing over from the soundside (the Intracoastal Waterway) and hiking to the beach is a good idea.

Wrightsville Beach has the most stringent rules governing surfing. Between 11 AM and 4 PM during the summer, Memorial to Labor Day, surfing is restricted to surf zones, also called sounds, which are two-block segments of the beach that move south, two streets at a time, each day. Any lifeguard can tell you where the zone currently stands. Zones do not apply during the off-season. Leash laws, however, are in effect year round. Surfing within 150 feet of fishing piers is prohibited.

Wrightsville Beach Parks and Recreation Department
1 Bob Sawyer Dr., Wrightsville Beach
• (910) 256-7925

Beginner surfing lessons are conducted weekly from June through the end of August. The three-day class is for advanced ocean swimmers age 10 to adult and is limited to six students per

WATERSPORTS

INSIDERS' TIP
Early spring and late fall are the best times of year for canoeing the region's inland waterways.

In a small catamaran, you can set sail almost anywhere.

Photo: Jay Tervo

session. The course covers surfing etiquette, paddling, wave-catching, maneuvers and basic surfing principles. Cost is $36 for Wrightsville Beach residents and $54 for nonresidents. Call for more information and schedule.

The Surfrider Foundation
Cape Fear Chapter • (910) 256-0233 for infoline

Headquartered in California, the Surfrider Foundation is a nonprofit international environmental organization that works to preserve the world's beaches through direct action (primarily cleanups), conservation and education. The Cape Fear Chapter sponsors monthly cleanup and beach sweeps in association with the Wrightsville Beach Parks and Recreation Department. Open meetings are held at Wrightsville Beach Town Hall. Education and water-testing programs are also offered.

Surf Reports

Daily surf reports for Wrightsville Beach are broadcast by radio station Surf 107-FM at 7:25 AM. Reports for conditions at Wrightsville Beach are provided by Surf City Surf Shop, (910) 350-8666; Sweetwater Surf Shop, (910) 256-8184; and Star-Line, (910) 762-1996 Ext. 2213, sponsored by Hot Wax Surf Shop. Also check the local surf shops listed below.

Surfboard Rentals

There is no shortage of places to rent a stick if you don't have one of your own. Check with the surf shops listed below or these specialty watersports shops.

Wrightsville Beach Supply Co., 1 N. Lumina Avenue, Wrightsville Beach, (910) 256-8821.

Pleasure Island Rentals, 2 N. Lake Park Boulevard, Carolina Beach, (910) 458-4747.

The Cove Surf Shop, 604 N. Lake Park Boulevard, Carolina Beach, (910) 458-4671.

Beach Fun Rentals, 132 Ocean Boulevard W., Holden Beach, (910) 842-9600, (888) 355-4446

Boomer's, Causeway Plaza, 3468 Holden Beach Road, Holden Beach, (910) 842-1400, (800) 287-1990

Spinnaker Surf & Sport, 111 N. Shore Drive, Surf City, (910) 328-2311

Surf Shops

The many surf shops in the area offer a complete selection of surf gear, apparel and accessories, including wet suits and videos. You can buy a new or used board, rent one by the day and get yours repaired. Shops can lead you to local people who customize boards too. Most surf shops are the best place to find everything you'll need for skateboarding and in-line skating, including parts and accessories, as well as surfwear and skatewear, designer eyewear, shoes and sandals, jewelry and boogie boards. Most area shops are open seven days a week in season. Call ahead in the off-season.

Aussie Island Surf Shop, Landfall Shopping Center, 1319 Military Cutoff Road, Wilmington, (910) 256-5454.

Bert's Surf Shop, 5740 Oleander Drive, Wilmington, (910) 392-4501; U.S. Highway 421, Carolina Beach, (910) 458-9047; N. New River Drive, Surf City, (910) 328-1010.

WATERSPORTS

Boomer's, Causeway Plaza, 3468 Holden Beach Road, Holden Beach, (910) 842-1400, (800) 287-1990.

Hot Wax Surf Shop, 4510 Hoggard Drive, Wilmington, (910) 791-9283.

Surf City Surf Shop, 530 Causeway Drive, Wrightsville Beach, (910) 256-2265.

Sweetwater Surf Shop, 10 N. Lumina Avenue, Wrightsville Beach, (910) 256-3821.

The Cove Surf Shop, 604 N. Lake Park Boulevard, Carolina Beach, (910) 458-4671.

Local Call Surf Shop, 609 Yaupon Beach Drive, Oak Island, (910) 278-3306.

Holden Beach Surf & Scuba, 3172-4 Holden Beach Road SW, Holden Beach, (910) 842-6899

North Shore Surf Shop, 12 E. First Street, Ocean Isle Beach, (910) 579-6223

Spinnaker Surf & Sport, 111 N. Shore Dr., Surf City, (910) 328-2311

Swimming

The southern coast is blessed with clean, relatively clear, refreshing waters and a long outdoor season. Water temperatures become comfortable usually no later than the middle of spring, generally hovering in the 75- to 80-degree range by summer. Only at the end of the season do temperatures approach those of the waters farther south. Most beaches consist of fine, clean sand. Together with the shores of the Outer Banks and beaches farther north, the southern coast gives evidence that North Carolina does indeed have the finest beaches in the east.

Except during storm surges when rip currents are a danger, the surf is generally moderate. Most beach communities employ lifeguards during the summer, but the beaches are not staffed otherwise. Swimming in a few areas is hazardous, such as at the extreme east end of Ocean Isle Beach and along the Fort Fisher Historic Site, because of either strong currents or underwater debris. All hazardous areas are well-marked. See our chapter on Sun, Sand and Sea for more on beach swimming.

Check the facilities listed below if pool swimming is more to your liking.

City of Wilmington Recreation Division
302 Willard St., Wilmington
• **(910) 341-7855, (910) 341-4602**

The City of Wilmington maintains three public swimming pools: Shipp Pool at Southside Park (beside Legion Stadium), Carolina Beach

Road, (910) 341-7863; Jackson Pool at Northside Park, 750 Bess Street, (910) 341-7865; and Murphy Pool at Robert Strange Park, 410 S. Eighth Street, (910) 341-7866. All locations are handicapped accessible and equipped with a bathhouse and slide. During the summer season, beginning Saturday of Memorial Day weekend, the pools are open Monday through Saturday 1 to 6 PM. After August 4, hours are restricted to Saturdays 1 to 5 PM, until the season ends Labor Day weekend. Admission fees are 50¢ for children and $1 for adults.

The Cape Fear Chapter of the American Red Cross conducts swimming lessons Monday through Friday at the Shipp Pool (Southside Park) from 9 AM to noon. Swimming lessons are also conducted at the Jackson Pool (Northside Park) from 5 to 5:45 PM. For more information, contact the Red Cross, (910) 762-2683.

YMCA
2710 Market St., Wilmington
• **(910) 251-9622**

The YMCA boasts two indoor pools to accommodate its many members year round. Water aerobics, scuba diving and life-guarding classes are among its many offerings. Membership is required to enjoy general use of these facilities, which are open seven days a week. Classes are open to the community with discounted fees for members. Call the YMCA for current individual or family rates.

YWCA
2815 S. College Rd., Wilmington
• **(910) 799-6820**

The YWCA has excellent facilities, water aerobics, lap swimming, a swim team and swimming instruction by highly qualified staff. Instruction in lifesaving is one of its specialties. The pool is outside and is open for summer from mid-May to September. During the off-season, September through May, the pool's bubbled roof is installed, allowing year-round swimming. YWCA membership is required to enjoy the facilities.

Windsurfing

One of the best and most popular windsurfing areas is the Basin, the partially protected body of water off Federal Point at the southern end of Pleasure Island. Accessible from a public boat ramp down the road from the ferry terminal, the Basin is enclosed by the Rocks, a 3.3-mile breakwater that extends to

Zeke's Island and beyond. Motts Channel and Banks Channel on the sound side of Wrightsville Beach are popular spots, but you'll have to contend with the boat traffic. Advanced windsurfers prefer the oceanside of the jetty at the south end of Wrightsville Beach, where action is fairly guaranteed. Around Topsail Island, the choices are the Intracoastal Waterway and the ocean. The inlets north and south of the island are not well-suited to uninterrupted runs. Along Oak Island and the South Brunswick Islands, the ocean is your best bet, although limited stretches of the ICW are OK for beginners (near the Ocean Isle Beach bridge when it's not busy, for example). Shallotte Inlet and River are narrow but worth a shot.

Up-to-date information on windsurfing conditions and competitions may be available at the surf shops listed in our Surfing section.

Kiteboarding

Kiteboarding is definitely the up-and-coming watersport. Similar to windsurfing but claiming to be easier, this sport requires less wind, no boat, and allows the rider the ability to jump 20 to 40 feet off the water. The boards used are smaller in size than those used for windsurfing. There are foot straps or bindings to hold the rider on. Different sized kites are used depending on the weight of the rider and wind conditions. The most popular spots where you can find good steady winds and local riders to ride with in the Cape Fear region are the south end of Wrightsville Beach, the Fort Fisher Basin and the north end of Carolina Beach.

Beach Access

Public beach access is a state-regulated system of pedestrian right-of-ways, dune crossovers, parking lots and, at some locations, restroom and shower facilities. A few have food concessions. Parking meters are enforced at Wrightsville Beach from March through October. At Wrightsville Beach, signs indicating beach access paths are readily visible, marked with a large orange sun over blue water.

Note that most beach communities strictly prohibit glass containers and vehicles on the strand. Kure Beach also prohibits dogs and alcohol. Keep in mind that, in most communities, crossing dunes at places other than approved crossovers can earn you a minimum $50 fine and, as of 1999, the penalty for disturbing these fragile dunes can climb as high as $500 on some area beaches.

On Wrightsville Beach, public access with restrooms, metered parking and a shower are across S. Lumina Avenue from the Oceanic Restaurant and Crystal Pier near Nathan Avenue. Restrooms and a shower are at the foot of Salisbury Street near Johnny Mercer's Pier. To the north, parking is also available adjacent to the Holiday Inn Sunspree Resort and on either side of the Duneridge Resort, about 1 mile north of Salisbury Street. One of the Duneridge lots has restrooms. At the north end of Wrightsville Beach, there is parking on both sides of Shell Island Resort. On summer weekends, unless you're parking a bicycle, arrive before 10 AM or after 2 PM to find a space.

In Carolina Beach, Kure Beach and Fort Fisher, public beach access points and parking (spaces in Carolina Beach are metered) are situated at regular intervals and are clearly marked. Public restrooms and showers are available at the boardwalk and on Hamlet Avenue in Carolina Beach, at the Kure Beach Pier and at Fort Fisher State Park.

On Caswell Beach Road along eastern Oak Island, about a half-mile east of the Fort Caswell Lighthouse at Caswell Beach, the only public beach access consists of a large gravel parking lot with no facilities. The area is open 5 AM to 11 PM, and camping, the use of alcohol, firearms and fires, and cars on the strand are prohibited.

With 65 beach accesses and over 900 parking spaces (some at the beach access and some nearby), the Town of Oak Island beach is one of the most accessible beaches to owners, renters and the public alike. The Cabana at the foot of 46th Street East has handicapped access, as have most of the beach accesses.

The majority of beach accesses on 11-mile-long Holden Beach are private, but public access points abound at the east end (Avenues A through E), near Jordan Boulevard, and at Ferry Road. Several others are west of the bridge. Parking along Ocean Boulevard is prohibited. A Regional Beach Access facility with showers, restrooms and parking, open 6 AM to 11 PM, is located nearly under the bridge off Jordan Boulevard, where limited parking and covered tables are available.

On Ocean Isle Beach, access is concentrated around the center of town, near the foot of the causeway. Beach access on Sunset Beach is indicated by small white posts about 100 yards apart. There are no sidewalks and little parking. The paved parking lot adjacent to Sunset Fishing Pier is convenient to the beach and pier facilities.

Fishing

North Carolina's long strand of barrier islands lie between the ocean and shallow waters, which form estuaries, brackish swamps and mud flats that are nurseries for shrimp, crabs, finfish and shellfish. As one of the top 10 seafood-producing states, North Carolina has more than 4,000 miles of shoreline and 2.5 million acres of marine and estuarine waters. Approximately 6,000 full-time commercial fishermen and 2 million recreational anglers enjoy the state's marine resources.

The southern coast of North Carolina is an angler's paradise. As long as the weather cooperates, an angler can enjoy the hobby 12 months per year. With ocean temperatures ranging from the 70s in the Gulf Stream to the 50s near shore in the winter months, king mackerel, sea bass and tuna can be caught in the ocean, while striped bass can be caught in the rivers. During the spring, summer and fall months, sheepshead, spot, tarpon, red drum, Spanish mackerel, bluefish, whiting, trout, flounder, amberjack, striped bass, croaker, white marlin, blue marlin, sailfish, shark, wahoo and dolphin are available.

The "North Carolina Recreational Coastal Waters Guide for Sports Fishermen," listing length minimums and creel limits for various species, is online at www.ncdmf.net/recguide.htm or www.ncfisheries.net/recgide.htm, or you can call (252) 726-7021 or (800) 682-2632 (NC only). At www.ncfisheries.net/fishfind/fishfin2htm is a site identifying and describing all North Carolina fish by common name, with data and color illustrations of the species.

Since the early 1970s, the Division of Marine Fisheries has helped create artificial reefs that provide habitat for sea life. These reefs consist of old ships, railroad cars, bridge rubble, concrete and FADs (fish-attracting devices). Using the motto "We sink 'em – you fish 'em," reef architects have built 39 ocean sites and seven estuarine sites. Judging by the number of sheepshead and mackerel landed on an average day, the program seems to be paying off. Charts are available to lead you to these sites.

Fishing is quite good in the Cape Fear River, with available species including largemouth bass, sunfish, catfish, American and hickory shad and herring. Spring is the peak season for largemouths, which usually range between 1.5 to 3 pounds. Bass can be located near the mouths of the larger tributary creeks, such as Turnbull, Hammonds, Sturgeon, Livingston and upper reaches of Town Creek.

Bluegill are plentiful in the Cape Fear River and are available during the spring spawning season near locks and dams. Bluegills average one-half and three-fourths of a pound, while redear sunfish run about a pound.

Catfish fishing is excellent in the Cape Fear River, which also hosts the three largest members of the freshwater catfish family: the channel, blue and flathead, available from Lillington to the Black River. Catfish are considered non-game fish in inland waters, and have no size or creel restrictions. They can be taken by a variety of fishing methods. April, May, September and October are the best months.

American and hickory shad can be found in the lower Cape Fear River below Wilmington, and can be taken by recreational fishermen below each of the three locks and dams above Wilmington. Information on inland water limits and licenses is available at www.ncwildlife.org, or by calling (919) 733-3391

Note that fishing from most bridges in the area is restricted or prohibited because the bridges often traverse boat channels. Be sure to check the signs on bridges before casting. Small-boat owners have many fishing opportunities around the mouths of creeks and inlets, especially during incoming tides when the boat and the bait can drift in with the bait fish. Small boats should use caution at ocean inlets during outgoing tides because the currents can be strong.

If you're traveling without tackle, rental gear is fairly abundant. Among places to check are these shops in addition to some of the fishing piers listed below. Rod and Reel Shop at 3401 Holden Beach Road SW (on the mainland side of the bridge in Holden Beach), (910) 842-2034. Rod and Reel also repairs tackle. Another renting location for both onshore and offshore tackle is Seagull Bait & Tackle at 608 S. Lake Park Boulevard in Carolina Beach, (910 458-7135. Tackle shops abound along the coast, but be sure to call ahead to determine if they rent equipment.

Fishing Licenses

Licenses are not required for saltwater and hook-and-line fishing, but you must observe size and bag limits. Familiarize yourself with regulations, which are posted at most piers and marinas. Freshwater licenses are issued by the North Carolina Wildlife Resources Commission; call (888) 248-6834 for credit card purchases or purchase from one of the locations listed below. Nonresident fishing licenses for the season are $30. Three-day licenses cost $15, a license for one day is $10, and trout fishing is an additional $10. For residents, a one-day license (not including trout waters) is $5. The annual fee is $15, or an additional $10 for a comprehensive license that includes trout fishing. Licenses may be combined with a hunting license and can be obtained at somewhat higher rates.

Wilmington

Canady's Sport Center, 3220 Wrightsville Avenue, Wilmington, (910) 791-6280

Dick's Sporting Goods, 816 S. College Road, Wilmington, (910) 793-1904

Division of Marine Fisheries, North Caro-

lina D.E.N.R., 127 Cardinal Drive, Wilmington, (910) 395-3900

County Line Bait & Tackle, 6408 Castle Hayne Road, Castle Hayne, (910) 675-8940

Hudson True Value, 5601 Castle Hayne Road, Castle Hayne, (910) 675-9205

Jim's Pawn & Guns, Inc., 4212 Oleander Drive, Wilmington, (910) 799-7314

Kmart, 815 S. College Road, Wilmington, (910) 799-5360

Roy's Bait & Tackle, 3821-A U.S. Highway 421 N., Wilmington, (910) 762-8681

Wal-Mart, Monkey Junction, Wilmington, (910) 452-0944

Wal-Mart, 5226 Sigmon Road, Wilmington, (910) 392-4034

Southport

Wal-Mart, 1675 N. Howe Street, Southport, (910) 454-9909

South Brunswick Islands

Holden Beach True Value Hardware, 3008 Holden Beach Road, Holden Beach, (910) 842-5440

Island Tackle and Hardware, N.C. Highway 179 between Ocean Isle Beach and Sunset Beach, (910) 579-6116

Wal-Mart, 4540 Main Street, Shallotte, (910) 754-2880

Fishing Reports

The most up-to-date sources of fishing information are charter captains, fishing piers and tackle shops. Star-Line, a telephone service of the *Wilmington Star-News*, provides daily fish-

FISHING

ing and weather reports at (910) 762-1996 ext. 2212, and frequent detailed reports appear in the *Star-News* print editions.

Fishing Piers

Each pier in the area has its own personality. Some have become bent and bowed after years of battering by the ocean and hurricanes, some have been rebuilt time and again, and some are completely gone. Most are festooned with odd novelties and memorabilia and proudly display photographs of trophies reeled up from the sea. On busy days, expect to be rubbing elbows with other pier-fishers between Kure and Topsail. Almost all piers charge a fee for fishing permits good for a 24-hour period. Fishing generally costs about $5 per day, and king fishing costs about twice as much. Most piers offer season-fishing permits, tackle shops, snack bars, wet cleaning tables and restrooms. Strollers are usually permitted on the piers free of charge.

Wilmington

River Road Park
6300 River Rd., Wilmington
• (910) 798-7198

River Road Park, south of the State Port about 8 miles from downtown Wilmington near the end of Cathay Road, features a handicapped-accessible fishing pier on the Cape Fear River. The park features playground equipment, bathroom facilities and a shelter that can be rented for social occasions. The park is open from 8 AM to dusk.

Wrightsville Beach

Johnnie Mercer's Pier
Foot of E. Salisbury St., Wrightsville Beach
• (910) 256-2743

This magnificent structure is the first concrete pier in North Carolina able to sustain 200 mph winds. The windows are able to buffet storm gales up to 150 mph. The light poles consist of spun concrete, and even the trash receptacles are made of stone. Twenty-five feet above sea level, Johnnie Mercer maintains a year-round presence. The new arcade and restaurant offer a sunrise breakfast, lunch and dinner with indoor/outdoor seating. General fishing is $10 per person, and the service is first class.

Carolina Beach

Carolina Beach Fishing Pier
1800 Carolina Ave. N., Carolina Beach
• (910) 458-5518

Owned and operated by the Phelps family, the 700-foot Carolina Beach Fishing Pier opened in September 1998 after having been destroyed by Hurricane Fran. The pier features a snack bar, grill, upstairs lounge with ABC permits, game area and a tackle shop, which offers new equipment, rentals and bait. There is a cleaning sink on the pier. Charge for general fishing with one or two rods is $6, and there's an extra charge for king mackerel three-rod fishing. On-site parking is available.

Kure Beach

Kure Beach Pier
Ave. K, Kure Beach • (910) 458-5524

Facilities include a snack room with cold sandwiches, drinks and other goodies; a complete tackle shop; a souvenir store; and an arcade with four pool tables. Permits are good from midnight to midnight. This pier is handicapped accessible. Permit for single-rod general fishing is $5, and a king mackerel permit allowing three rods is $12. No rentals are available. No alcoholic beverages are permitted.

Southport-Oak Island

City Pier
Waterfront Park, Bay St., Southport

This small, handicapped-accessible pier near the mouth of the Cape Fear River is a municipal facility, and usage is free. It is located adjacent to Waterfront Park where amenities include a water fountain, park benches, a gazebo, swings and usually an ice cream truck during the season.

Long Beach Pier
2729 W. Beach Dr., Long Beach
• (910) 278-5962

The new Long Beach Pier is the longest pier in the state, measuring 1,056 feet. It is wider and has good handicapped access and a 35-foot-high observation deck on the seaward end. In addition, it is the only pier with reef balls — 64 to be exact. Attached to the pilings below the surface these balls act as fish-breeding habitats, an environmentally friendly and angler-friendly installation. Amenities include a grill and a motel. Guests of the motel receive free passes to the fishing pier.

Ocean Crest Pier
1411 E. Beach Dr., Oak Island
• **(910) 278-6674, (910) 278-3333**

This 1,000-foot pier near 14th Place East has a full line tackle shop where special orders are available as well. You will also find gifts for friends at home or as souvenirs for yourself. Handicapped anglers fish for free and the owners provide a community live bait tank and a shelter at the T-shaped far end that are reserved for king fishers. Season permits are available for bottom fishing and king fishing. A full service restaurant and a motel adjoin the pier.

Yaupon Pier
Foot of Womble Ave., Oak Island
• **(910) 278-9400**

Yaupon is not only the highest pier in the state (27 feet above the high-tide line), but it also boasts the state record for the largest fish caught from a pier to date — read it and weep — a 1,150-pound tiger shark caught on rod and reel. The pier is handicapped-accessible. The adjoining Lighthouse Restaurant is known for its ocean view and homemade clam chowder.

South Brunswick Islands

Holden Beach Pier
441 Ocean Blvd. W., Oak Island
• **(910) 842-6483**

Holden Beach Pier sells daily, seasonal, three-day and seven-day fishing permits and live bait. A grill and snack counter adjoin a beach gift shop. Holden Beach Pier charges spectators a fee of 50 cents for walking the pier. Handicapped access is available to the pier. The owners prohibit the use of nets and the consumption of alcoholic beverages.

Ocean Isle Pier
Foot of Causeway Dr., Ocean Isle Beach
• **(910) 579-1271**

The large game room and small grill at this pier are popular in summer. Available are supplies, fishing tackle, season passes for fishing, and fishing rod rentals. A $1 fee is charged for spectators.

Sunset Beach Pier
Foot of Sunset Blvd., Sunset Beach
• **(910) 579-6630**

The 900-foot pier is a special area for king

FISHING

Two fish on one line? Now that's a catch!

Photo: Jay Tervo

fishermen. Amenities at Sunset Beach Pier include a double sink at the cleaning table, and a snack bar, game room and ATM in the air-conditioned pier house. Bait is for sale at the pier. It is handicapped accessible and has a reputation for clean restrooms.

Topsail Island

Jolly Roger Pier
803 Ocean Blvd., Topsail Beach
• (910) 328-4616

The Jolly Roger is a pier complex with a motel, convenience store and bait and tackle shop with small restaurant facilities. This 850-foot ocean pier, at the southern end of the island, is open from March through November.

Seaview Pier
New River Inlet Rd., North Topsail Beach
• (910) 328-3171, (910) 328-3172

The island's newest pier, completed in 1999, is 1,000 feet long. On the north end of the island, the pier shop offers bait and tackle, snack foods, ice and a game room. It's open April through November

Surf City Ocean Pier
S. Shore Dr., Surf City • (910) 328-3521

This pier is in the center of downtown Surf City. Completely rebuilt in 1997, it is 937 feet long and is open from mid-March until sometime in December. Rod rentals, bait and tackle are all available. The newly expanded grill is open Mon. - Fri. 11 AM - until and Sat. 8 AM - until, offering fried chicken, hamburgers, hot

dogs or if you've had a good day fishing, they will cook your catch. Spectators are welcome to stroll the pier for a $1.00 charge. Alcohol is not allowed on this pier.

Topsail Sound Pier
1522 Carolina Blvd., Topsail Beach
• (910) 328-3641

Topsail Sound Pier offers the only soundside fishing pier on Topsail Island. The bait and tackle shop provides one-stop shopping with all types of bait, tackle, snacks, ice, limited groceries and beach supplies.

Surf Fishing

The best time for surf fishing is during high tide with an outgoing tide. There's still a tranquil, serene spot to be found in the ever-popular Wrightsville Beach area. Behind the jetty at Masonboro Inlet, on the south end of the island, you'll find an almost hidden oasis perfect for surf fishing.

For anglers looking to get away from it all, the Fort Fisher State Recreation Area is an undeveloped 4-mile stretch of beach and tidal marsh approximately 6 miles south of Carolina Beach that is accessible by four-wheel-drive vehicle only. The entrance to the area is off U.S. Highway 421 before the North Carolina Aquarium (bear left at the fork) and to the right of the beach parking lot. There is also a public beach here with changing rooms, restrooms and shower, a snack bar and a ranger contact station. Otherwise, there are no services, so bring everything you'll need and pack out everything you bring. (Also see the "Off-Roading" section in our Sports, Fitness and Parks chapter).

Another good spot, near the Carolina Beach Inlet at the north end Canal Road on Pleasure Island, is also accessible by four-wheel-drive only. A lesser-known and more restricted fishing spot on Pleasure Island lies off Dow Road. For 3 miles south of Spartanburg Avenue, foot paths enter the woods from the roadside (you may notice vehicles parked there). Foot traffic only is permitted since this is an environmentally sensitive area, which is owned by the federal government (the "No Trespassing" warnings are not enforced). The trails lead to the Cape Fear River, but the northernmost trails lead to a secluded inlet known as the Dredge Pond, where bait fish are often stirred into a frenzy by the unseen feeders. It's also a good place to picnic and relax if the mosquitoes

North Carolina Fishing:
What's Hot and When!

January: Trout, sea bass, some grouper, some snapper, bluefish, oysters, clams

February: Trout, sea bass, some grouper, some snapper, bluefish, oysters, clams

March: Grouper, sea trout, sea bass, bluefish, croaker, oysters, some snapper, some clams

April: Bluefish, channel bass, grouper, snapper, croaker, sea trout, sea mullet, some king mackerel, some oysters, some clams

May: King mackerel, bluefish, grouper, some flounder, cobia, tuna, some sharks, crabs, soft crabs, some sea mullet, dolphin

June: Blue marlin, white marlin, dolphin, wahoo, cobia, king mackerel, bluefish, tuna, summer flounder, snapper, grouper, some Spanish mackerel, crabs, soft crabs, sharks

July: Dolphin, wahoo, tuna, blue marlin, white marlin, snapper, grouper, summer flounder, bluefish, Spanish mackerel, crab, some soft crabs, some sea mullet, sharks, king mackerel, barracuda

August: Dolphin, wahoo, tuna, grouper, snapper, Spanish mackerel, bluefish, some speckled trout, some spots, some sea mullet, sharks, crabs, king mackerel, barracuda, flounder

September: Grouper, snapper, Spanish mackerel, king mackerel, spots, sharks, bluefish, some speckled trout, sea mullet, some channel bass, tuna, dolphin, wahoo, flounder

October: King mackerel, bluefish, snapper grouper, channel bass, spots, speckled trout, some flounder, sharks, some oysters, tuna dolphin amberjack, wahoo

November: King mackerel, bluefish, speckled trout, flounder, snapper, grouper, clams, some sharks, some sea mullet, drum

December: Bluefish, flounder, speckled trout, oysters, clams, sea trout, some snapper, some sea bass, some grouper

Courtesy of N.C. Department of Environment, Health & Natural Resources, Division of Marine Fisheries http://www.enr.state.nc.us/

It doesn't get any better than this!

Photo: Jay Tervo

aren't too voracious, but keep an eye open for the resident alligator, though he's never gone after a human. Yet.

If you're looking for something a bit more adventurous, try fishing The Rocks, a 3.3-mile breaker extending from Federal Point, south of the Fort Fisher Ferry terminal. The enclosed water around Zeke's Island is called the Basin, and fishing on both sides of the barrier is excellent. However, The Rocks can be very dangerous, especially at high tide when they're slippery and wet, so try entering and leaving here at low tide.

Another great spot for surf fishing can be found at The Point, at the west end of Oak Island bordering Lockwood Folly Inlet. The Town of Oak Island has built a parking lot adjacent to the beach access. You can see the eastern end of Holden Beach and the Holden Beach bridge, but you can't get there from here!

Fly-Fishing

Saltwater fly-fishing is quickly gaining in popularity, probably because it's a type of fishing that requires great skill and a fantastic love of the sport. Neophytes and aficionados of saltwater fly-fishing should take note of the following resources in the Wilmington area and in many tackle shops throughout the region.

Gottafly Guide Service
Bridge Tender Marina next to Wrightsville Beach drawbridge • (910) 350-0890

Spend the day with Capt. Lee Parsons on his Boston Whaler 23 Outrage with light tackle or fly fishing. There's Atlantic bonito in April and sailfish, Spanish or king mackerel in June

and July. Or try wreck fishing for big amberjack in August and September. You might prefer world-class fishing for false albacore at Cape Lookout in October and November.

If you like inshore fishing, try a trip on the 18-foot Polarcraft tunnel boat chasing stripers on the Roanoke River in May or flounder gigging June through September. Night fishing for lady fish or poling the flats for drum is exciting.

Rather not fish? Try an after-dinner cruise around the beach or walk on undeveloped islands. Be sure to bring your camera to record the gorgeous coastal birds along the marshes.

Intracoastal Angler
7220 Wrightsville Ave., Ste. A, Wilmington • (910) 256-4545

A complete saltwater outfitter, Intracoastal Angler at Atlantic View Center offers perhaps the most complete selection of saltwater inshore, offshore and fly-fishing equipment and accessories in the area. The store stocks top-name rod and reels as well as sportswear from Patagonia and Columbia. They also provide an expert guide service for inshore fishing adventures. The friendly, knowledgeable staff can give you assistance with all your fishing needs. Hours are Monday through Saturday 8 AM to 6 PM.

East Coast Sports
Village Mall, Roland Ave. Cswy., Surf City • (910) 328-1887

The friendly, professional staff at East Coast Sports is ready to help you select the best bait and tackle for inshore or offshore fishing. All major brands are offered in their large selection. If you need a charter, let Capt. Chris Medlin arrange one

FISHING

for you. East Coast also has a full line of sports clothing, including Columbia Sperry, Topsiders and many other name brands. East Coast is open year round.

Boat Ramps

The North Carolina Wildlife Resources Commission maintains free ramps for pleasure boaters and anglers. Parking is generally scarce in the summer months at the busier locations such as Wrightsville Beach (which now has mostly metered parking, so be prepared and carry many quarters). The ramps are identified by black-and-white, diamond-shaped Wildlife signs. For information on public boat access, call (919) 733-3391. Included here are some private ramps as well.

Wilmington

Dram Tree Park on the corner of Castle and Surry streets off Front Street in downtown Wilmington is almost beneath the Cape Fear Memorial Bridge and gives access to the Cape Fear River.

Castle Hayne

Access to the Northeast Cape Fear River is by a ramp next to the N.C. Highway 117 bridge.

Pender County

The Northeast Cape Fear River and its tributary creeks are accessible by three public ramps. A ramp that allows access to the west bank of the river from I-40 can be reached by taking N.C. Highway 53 east about 1.7 miles, then County Road 1512 to its end. A public ramp on the east bank is off County Road 1520 about 7.7 miles north of N.C. Highway 210. The intersection of N.C. 210 and Secondary Road 1520 lies about 3 miles east of I-40 (Exit 408). Holland's Shelter Creek Campground and Restaurant, (910) 259-5743, is 7.5 miles east of I-40 down N.C. 53. Canoes are for rent ($20 flat fee), and the restaurant offers a memorable glimpse of local style. The private ramp gives access to Holly Shelter Creek. (For more on

---

INSIDERS' TIP

Anglers should practice the following:

—Avoid spilling and never dump gasoline, oil or other pollutants on land or in the water.

—Never leave trash behind, including worn line, old hooks and bait, and practice recycling.

—Learn and abide by all fishing regulations and boating laws.

—Educate fellow anglers and especially new participants about fishing ethics.

—Respect private property and the rights of other anglers and outdoor recreationists.

—Save fish for tomorrow by practicing conservation and learning proper catch-and-release techniques.

For information, contact N.C. Division of Marine Fisheries (252) 264-3011; www.ncfisheries.net

---

Holland's Shelter Creek, see our chapters on Camping and Restaurants).

Wrightsville Beach

Wrightsville Beach next to the U.S. Highway 74/76 drawbridge has a public ramp accessible from either side of the main road. This access to the ICW is very busy in summer months, especially on weekends.

Pleasure Island

On Pleasure Island, there are four ramps east of U.S. 421 at Snow's Cut. Coming south, make a hairpin right turn at the south end of Snow's Cut bridge onto Bridge Barrier Road. Turn right at Spencer Farlow Road and follow it less than a half-mile to the Wildlife sign. The lot is down a short road on your left. If you're coming north from Carolina Beach, exit U.S. 421 at Lewis Road just before the bridge and take an immediate left onto Access Road. Spencer Farlow Road is less than a half-mile ahead. Another ramp is at the end of U.S. 421, south of the Fort Fisher ferry terminal and gives access to the Basin off Federal Point.

Also on Pleasure Island, Carolina Beach State Park, off Dow Road, (910) 458-8206, has four ramps, a marina, ample parking, and provides access to Snows Cut and the Cape Fear River. The ramp directly beneath the N.C. 210 high span in North Topsail Beach is generally uncrowded. It is accessible from the last turnout from the northbound side of N.C. 210 before the bridge. Access is to New River Inlet.

Brunswick Islands

At the foot of County Road 1101, accessible from N.C. Highway 133 on the mainland side of Oak Island, the public ramp gives direct access to the Intracoastal Waterway. At Sunset Harbor, east of Lockwood Folly River, a public boat ramp gives access to Lockwood Folly River and Inlet and the Intracoastal Waterway. From N.C. 211, take County Road 1112 about 6 miles south and turn right at Lockwood Folly Road. Follow to its end. At the Wildlife Boat Ramp on

Fish Factory Road, there is access to the Intracoastal Waterway.

At the Oak Island Parks and Recreation Center, 3003 Oak Island Drive, Oak Island, access is into the Davis Canal.

Boat ramps at 55th Street NE and 57th Place W offer access on the Intracoastal Waterway.

At Holden Beach, public boat ramps are under the N.C. Highway 130 bridge on the island side. Freshwater anglers may launch into the east bank of the Waccamaw River at the N.C. Highway 904 bridge at Pineway, about 5 miles north of the South Carolina border or the Boiling Spring Lakes Boat Ramp & Dock on Alton Lennon Drive.

Topsail Island

The Town of Surf City has recently opened boat ramps at their new soundside park, 517 Roland Ave (just over the swing bridge).

A ramp is also available in Topsail Beach at Topsail Sound Pier. There is a $5.00 charge that includes launch and retrieve. There is plenty of parking at the site.

Head Boats and Charters

If you're looking to fish with a group of people, you've come to the right place. From Topsail's Treasure Coast to Calabash, there are fishing vessels aplenty. Choose the large head boats (a.k.a. party boats) accommodating dozens of people or the "six-pack" charters accommodating up to six passengers. Head boats average $40 to $75 per person for full-day excursions, and walk-ons are always welcome. The boats are equipped with full galleys and air-conditioned lounges. Handicapped accessibility to most large head boats tends to be good, but varies from ship to ship and with weather conditions.

Charters offer a variety of trips, half-day or full-day, inshore or offshore, and sometimes overnight; most are available for tournaments and diving trips (reserve early). If you can't find enough friends to chip in to cover the cost, ask about split charters; many captains book them. Most charter captains prefer reservations but will accept walk-ons when possible. Charters range anywhere from $350 for half-day excursions to $1,200 for an entire day of fishing in the Gulf Stream, which from our shores can be 40 to 70 miles offshore, depending on currents and the marina from which you embark.

Certain provisions are common to all charters: first mate, onboard coolers and ice, all the bait and tackle you'll need for kings, tuna, dol-

phin, wahoo, billfish and more. With advance notice, many will arrange food packages, and some may even arrange hotel packages. Optional electric reels may be available. Although most six-pack charters are unable to bring wheelchairs aboard, crews are often very accommodating of handicapped passengers, sometimes leaving the wheelchair ashore and providing secure seating on deck, right where the action is. Call the vessel of your choice in advance for details. Remember that no one can guarantee sea conditions. If your captain decides to turn back before you've landed a smoker, rest assured he knows what he's doing. Captains reserve the right to cancel trips if conditions are unsafe for the vessel or passengers.

Carolina Beach is the Gulf Stream fishing hub

between Bald Head and Topsail islands. A large number of vessels run out of the Carolina Beach Municipal Docks at Carl Winner Street and Canal Drive. Parking is available on the marina's west, south and east sides. There is no central booking office for the charter boats, but since you should know something about what you're chartering in advance, your best bet is to simply walk the docks and eye each one. Signs and brochures there will give you all the booking information you'll need. Ticket booths for the head boats are located at the south end of the marina. Also, check the phone book's Yellow Pages under fishing guides, charters and parties.

Charters in southern Brunswick County are concentrated at the Southport Marina, Blue

Point Marina at the western tip of Oak Island, at Holden Beach and Ocean Isle Beach. Head boats dock only in Calabash and at nearby Little River, South Carolina. There are no charters running directly out of Wilmington. Look instead for charters and head boats running from Wrightsville Beach and Carolina Beach.

So many fishing vessels are available all along our coast, we've listed below only those places (marinas mostly) booking several charters from one location (check our Marinas chapter for more options). The types of vessels available at each location, six-packs or head boats, are indicated.

Wrightsville Beach

Beach Trip Charters, Wrightsville Beach, Inshore, nearshore, offshore. Two boats, three captains, (919) 880-4424, (919) 612-2724

Fortune Hunter Charters, Wrightsville Beach, Offshore, inshore, custom charters for 1 to 6 anglers, (910) 617-4160

Gotta Fly, Inc., Wrightsville Beach, Fly fishing charters, (910) 350-0890

Last Request Charters, Wrightsville Beach, Custom charters for 1 to 6 anglers; offshore fishing, (910) 686-7065, (910) 512-9899

No Regrets Charters, Wrightsville Beach, Six-pack charters, Cell (910) 352-0737, Boat (910) 515-0839

OnMyWay Charters, Wrightsville Beach, Custom charters for 1-6 anglers; offshore/inshore, (910) 256-6072

Rod-Man Charters, Wrightsville Beach, Custom charters for 1 to 4 anglers, (910) 799-6120, (910) 520-7661

Wilmington

Cape Fear Charters, Inshore custom charters for 1 to 4 anglers, (910) 452-4147

Carolina Beach

Bird Dog Charters, Carolina Beach, Six-packs, (910) 452-9395

Blue Marlin Charters, Carolina Beach, Six-packs, (910) 458-6136, (888) 566-3474

Captain Chuck's Charters, Carolina Beach, Six-packs, (910) 458-4362, (800) 288-3474

Captain John's Fishing Charters, Carolina Beach, Custom charters, (910) 458-9111

Class Action Charters, Carolina Beach, Custom charters for 1 to 6 anglers; offshore/inshore, (910) 458-3348

Fired Up Fishing Charters, Carolina Beach, Six-packs, (910) 458-5172

Fish Witch Charters, Carolina Beach, Six-packs, (910) 458-5855

Flapjack, Carolina Beach, Six-packs, (910) 458-4362, (800) 288-3474

Hooker Fishing Charters, Carolina Beach, Six-packs, (910) 313-2828, (800) 946-1616

Hot Ticket Fishing Charters, Carolina Beach, Six-packs, (910) 791-0443

Largetime Charters, Carolina Beach, Six-packs, (800) 582-5524

Lookout Charters, Carolina Beach, Custom charters for 1 to 6 anglers, Offshore/Inshore, (910) 458-1307

Musicman Charters, Inc., Carolina Beach, Six-packs, (910) 458-5482 (800) 294-5482

Reel Pleasure Charters, Carolina Beach, Six-packs, (910) 458-5627

Sea Filly & Pink Snapper, Carolina Beach, Six-packs, (910) 458-6600

Sea Trek Charters, Carolina Beach, Six-packs, (910) 458-4362, (800) 288-3474

Winner Gulf Stream Fishing & Cruise Boats, Carolina Beach, Head boats, (910) 458-FISH

Bald Head Island

Impulsive Charters, Six-packs, (910) 457-5331

Red Head Charters, Six-packs, (910) 457-9864

Southport-Oak Island

Blue Water Point Marina, Oak Island, Headboat fishing/cruises, Custom charters, up to 6 anglers, offshore, (910) 278-1230

Buccaneer Head Boat, Southport, Head boat, (910) 457-9186

Reel-M-Ocean Charters, Southport, Six-pack, (910) 278-1386, (910) 523-0541

Salty Dog Charter Boat, Southport, Six-pack, (910) 278-9834

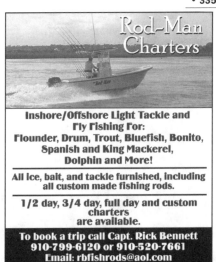

Yada Sea Charters, Southport, Six-pack, (704) 895-2566 or 352-1593

South Brunswick Islands

Fisher III Sportfishing, Holden Beach, Head boat, (910) 842-9055, (910) 233-1215

Capt'n Pete's Seafood Market, Holden Beach, Six-packs and head boats, (910) 842-6675

Intimidator Fishing Charters, Holden Beach, Six-packs and head boats, (910) 842-6200

Swag Charters, Holden Beach, Six-packs, (910) 842-4930

Bad Habit Charters, Calabash, Six-packs, (910) 287-5555

Hurricane Fleet, Calabash, Head boats, (843) 249-3571, (910) 579-3660

Red Snapper Charter Boat, Calabash, Six-pack, (910) 579-2050

Small Boys Charter, Calabash, Six-pack, (843) 446-7257 (910) 579-4220

Captain Brant's Fishing Charters, Ocean Isle Beach, Six-packs, (910) 754-4454

Rocking Robin Sportfishing, Ocean Isle Beach, Charters for 1 to 4 anglers, (910) 575-3384

Topsail Island

Vonda Kay Head Boat, 1522 Carolina Boulevard, Topsail Beach, Head boats, (910) 545-FISH, (910) 545-3474

Old Ferry Marina, Sneads Ferry (north of Topsail Island), Six-packs, (910) 327-2258

Paradise Landing, Sneads Ferry (north of Topsail Island), Six-packs and head boats, (910) 327-2114

Topsail Sound Marina & Pier, 1522 Carolina Boulevard, Topsail Beach, Six-packs and head boats, (910) 328-3641

Southern Coast Saltwater Fishing Tournaments

Tournament fishing has been luring ever-larger schools of anglers, and no wonder: The top prize can be as much as $200,000 in a single tournament. Proceeds often benefit worthwhile charities. Many contests recognize tag-and-release as part of the Governor's Cup Billfishing Conservation series. The major events are listed below. Check current listings at tackle shops, marinas and visitors centers for more detail.

May

Bald Head Island Fishing Rodeo, Bald Head Island Marina, (800) 234-1666

Seagull Spring Tournament, Seagull Bait & Tackle, Carolina Beach, (910) 458-7135

June

Flounder & Speckled Trout Tournament, Wildlife Bait & Tackle, Southport, (910) 457-9903

U.S. Open Pier Fishing Tournament, Ocean Crest and Long Beach Piers, Oak Island, (910) 457-6964

Flounder Tournament, Shallotte Point, Shallotte, (910) 794-6985

Greater Wilmington King Mackerel Tournament, Battleship North Carolina, Wilmington, (910) 617-7797 or (910) 251-5797.

Cape Fear Blue Marlin Tournament, Bridge Tender Marina, Wrightsville Beach, (910) 256-6550

July

East Coast Got-Em-On King Mackerel Classic, Carolina Beach Yacht Basin, Carolina Beach, (910) 458-2985

Jolly Mon King Mackerel Tournament, Shallotte Point, Shallotte, (910) 754-4454

Captain Eddie Haneman Sailfish Tournament, Bridge Tender Marina, Wrightsville Beach, (910) 256-6550.

August

Ladies King Mackerel Tournament, Southport Marina, Southport, (910) 278-4137

Long Bay Artificial Reef Association Club Challenge, Southport Marina, Southport, (910) 278-4137

Sneads Ferry King Mackerel Tournament, New River Marina, Sneads Ferry, (910) 327-2106, (910) 327-9691

Topsail Offshore Fishing Club King Mackerel Tournament, Topsail Beach, (910) 329-4446

King Classic King Mackerel Tournament at Holden Beach, South Brunswick Islands Chamber of Commerce, Shallotte, (910) 754-6644, (800) 426-6644

September

Flounder Tournament, Wildlife Bait & Tackle, Southport, (910) 457-9903

Wrightsville Beach King Mackerel Tournament, Bridge Tender Marina, Wrightsville Beach, (910) 256-6550

FISHING

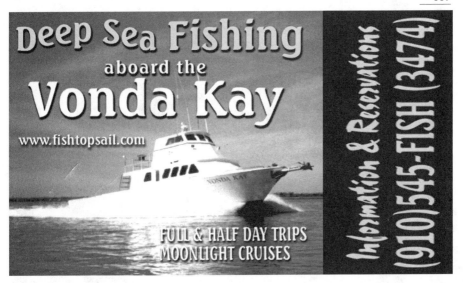

October

U.S. Open King Mackerel Tournament, Southport Marina, Southport, (910) 457-7923,(800) 457-6964

Seagull Fall Tournament, Seagull Bait & Tackle, Carolina Beach, (910) 458-7135

Topsail Island Surf Fishing Tournament, Surf City, (910) 329-4446

Fishing Clubs

Two area fishing clubs offer great opportunities to socialize, compete, swap stories and be useful as well. For fun and fellowship, or just to glean a wealth of information, check these out.

The **Cape Fear Blue Water Fishing Club** hosts a number of fishing tournaments each year, the largest being the Cape Fear Blue Water Open held in late spring. The club's main goals are to promote safe fishing and conservation of marine resources. The club also sponsors local charities. Dues are $50 a year, which entitles you to participate in all the club's social events, meetings and Billfish Points Tournament. For more information, call Rich Walter (910) 792-1616.

The popular **Got-Em-On Live Bait Club**, with a membership of nearly 250 active families, is a not-for-profit organization that supports local charities by sponsoring the annual East Coast Got-Em-On Classic, the Cape Fear Disabled Sportsmen's Tournament and the Got-Em-On Live Bait Club Scholarship Golf Tournament. Membership dues are $45 a year. For more information, call Mike Norris (910) 395-2686.

Marinas and the Intracoastal Waterway

Southeastern North Carolina's Cape Fear Coast is, simply stated, a boater's paradise. The entire length of the four-county coastal region is fronted by the Intracoastal Waterway (ICW), a series of barrier islands, numerous sounds and a variety of rivers and streams, all connecting with the Atlantic Ocean.

In addition to innumerable private and residential community boating facilities, there are well over 40 marinas and boatyards in operation, providing a full spectrum of services and supplies for the boating public. Detailed information about facilities along with a wealth of other boating information and a searchable database is available online at www.NCWaterways.com. Also invaluable to the boater is the 2003 North Carolina Boating Guide, which can be ordered by calling (877) 368-4968.

Originally developed for commercial water traffic, the Intracoastal Waterway has evolved into a route that now is used more by pleasure craft than by commercial vessels. The total waterway is about 3,000 miles in length and ranges from Boston to Key West on the Atlantic coast, and from Apalachee Bay in northwest Florida to Brownsville, Texas, on the Rio Grande River.

Authorized by Congress in 1919, the toll-free waterway is maintained by the Army Corps of Engineers to a minimum depth of 12 feet for most of its length, although 7 feet and 9 feet minimum depths will be found in some areas, and, because of shoaling, depths as little as 5 or 6 feet can be encountered in others. Generally speaking, the difficulties with minimum depth can be attributed to inadequate maintenance because of repeated budget cuts and insufficient funding for the Corps of Engineers by Congress. However, for fiscal year 2002 Congress appropriated $3 million more than the Corps' $10.9 budget request, with most of the added funds being earmarked for dredging in North and South Carolina.

The Cape Fear coastal area segment of the ICW is a bonanza for nature and wildlife lovers because so much of it traverses the sounds and marshes between the barrier islands and the mainland. Some of these areas are protected and accessible only by boat. In addition, because of the mild climate in the southern coastal region coupled with the warming effect of the Gulf Stream, boating enthusiasts can enjoy a nearly yearlong season on the waterway.

Marinas

A more than adequate number of marinas and boatyards dot the four-county Cape Fear Coast, with the vast majority being located along or adjacent to the Intracoastal Waterway or on rivers and streams connecting to the waterway. Although not a totally complete listing of all establishments available for boaters, the grouping of facilities that follows ranges from north to south and is quite representative. Facilities that are for the exclusive use of a private community or its guests are not listed. In a few instances, the address shown reflects a mailing address rather than a physical location. For maps and detailed and candid information on all these marinas, pick up a copy of native North Carolinian Claiborne Young's Cruising Guide to Coastal North Carolina. On the Internet, go to www.ncwaterways.com/marina/marina-search.asp. Most of the marinas are listed and pinpointed on the North Carolina Coastal Boating Guide Map available on the Southport-Fort Fisher Ferry, at local boating stores and by calling (877) 368-4968.

Pender County

Harbour Village Marina
101 Harbour Village Dr., Hampstead
• **(910) 270-4017**

Just off U.S. Highway 17 north of Wilmington at Belvedere Plantation, turn into Belvedere Plantation; follow the road and signs to the marina. From the water, this marina is to the north of flashing day beacon #96 and south of red marker #94. The marina has all the amenities a boater could want, including a lounge, showers, laundry facilities and transportation to restaurants. Boating guests can also enjoy swimming, tennis and golf for a fee at the country club. Contact John J. King, Harbour-Master.

Scott's Hill Marina
2570 Scott's Hill Loop Rd., Wilmington
• **(910) 686-0896**

Located north of Ogden, Scott's Hill Marina offers 62 wetslips that accommodate boats up to 38 feet. Transients are welcome to tie up here, although no fuel or restaurant is available. However, you'll find a boat ramp, restrooms, marine supplies and a repair facility.

New Hanover County

Inlet Watch Yacht Club
801 Paoli Ct., Wilmington
• **(910) 392-7106**

Just north of Snow's Cut, this exceptionally clean, well-maintained marina has fuel, a ship's store, parts and a full assortment of re-

Inlet Watch Yacht Club

• *Full Service Marina / Gas & Diesel / Ships Store*
• *Wet & Dry Slips for Sale or Lease*
• *Swimming Pool, Tennis Court, Bath House, Club House, Picnic Area*
• *Direct Ocean Access, Located on the ICW at Mile Marker 294*
• *Wet slip sizes are 25', 35' & 45'*
• *Dry slip sizes are 20', 22' 25' & 30'*

801 Paoli Court
Wilmington, NC 28409
910-392-7106
FAX: 910-392-7564

pair services. A private yacht club, Inlet Watch offers wet slips up to 45 feet and dry storage units up to 30 feet; you can either rent slips on a six-month or yearly basis or you can purchase one as an investment. Direct ocean access and first-rate service coupled with a picturesque setting and quiet, relaxing environment make Inlet Watch Yacht Club one of the area's best marine facilities. Enjoy the Club's pool and tennis court, have a picnic on the point, then watch the moon rise over the sea while sipping a cool drink in your deck chair.

To get there by land from Wilmington, take S. College Road and head toward Carolina Beach; drive through Monkey Junction, continuing straight on what will now be U.S. 421 heading south. Inlet Watch Yacht Club is on the left just before crossing the bridge over Snow's Cut into Carolina Beach.

Masonboro Boat Yard, Incorporated
609 Trails End Rd., Wilmington
• **(910) 791-1893**

This facility, which offers slips to rent or purchase, specializes in boat repairs; it has a 19-ton crane for haul-out services and allows boat owners the option of "do-it-yourself." The ship's store boasts a large inventory of diesel engine parts and a friendly staff. Masonboro Boatyard Marina has been operated by the same people since 1968 and was completely renovated in 1997, including concrete floating docks.

A three-story clubhouse includes four private showers, laundry facilities, a club room and a glorious unobstructed view of the water and Masonboro Island. You're guaranteed to find some interesting conversation among the residents.

To get there by land, travel down Oleander Drive toward Wilmington until you come to Pine Grove Drive at Hugh McRae park on the left. Take the left, stay on Pine Grove until the fork in the road, and take a right onto Masonboro Loop Road. In one and a half miles, you cross a small bridge, on your left will be Trails End Road with a sign that points out Masonboro Marina and the Trails End Steak House.

Pages Creek Marinas

Near mile 280 on the Intracoastal Waterway at Pages Creek are a group of marine facilities offering a variety of services. Those not featuring transient slips may possibly be able to accommodate transients if rental slips are open. All facilities can be reached by going north out of Wilmington on Market Street (U.S. Highway 17) and turning right onto Middle Sound Loop Road at the traffic light in Ogden.

Canady's Yacht Basin, 7624 Mason Landing Road, Wilmington, (910) 686-9116. Features: Supplies, restrooms, 72 wetslips and gas.

Johnson Marine Services, 2029 Turner Nursery Road, Wilmington, (910) 686-7565. Features: Ramp, repairs, supplies, restrooms, 60 wetslips.

Oak Winds Marina, 2127 Middle Sound Loop Road, Wilmington, (910) 686-0445. Features: Restrooms, showers, 44 wetslips, transient slips to 70 feet, 30, 50 and 100 amp power.

Carolina Yacht Yard, 2107 Middle Sound Loop Road, Wilmington, (910) 686-0004. Features: Repairs, boat haul out, supplies, restrooms, 15 wetslips, transient slips to 60 feet, 50 amp power.

Waterway Marine Service, 7618 Mason Landing Road, Wilmington, (910) 686-0284. Fea-

tures: Sailboat repairs, specializing in sailboat bottom work.

Wrightsville Beach

Boaters love Wrightsville Beach's many accommodating marinas, terrific seafood restaurants, shops and relaxed ambiance. Whatever your marine needs are, they can be met here. Facilities are available for everything from repairs to fishing gear. If you require groceries or want to do major shopping, however, you'll have to go to the mainland.

To get to Wrightsville Beach by land, take U.S. 74 and/or U.S. 76 straight to the ocean. If you're coming from downtown Wilmington, take Oleander Drive, Wrightsville Avenue or Market Street to Eastwood Road and head east.

By sea, Wrightsville Beach is approximately at mile marker 283. For exact location, check your marine charts.

Several marinas are located on Airlie Road, just before the drawbridge leading to Wrightsville Beach. Others are across the bridge on Harbour Island. For those with trailerable craft, there's a free Wildlife Access Ramp just to the north of the drawbridge.

Atlantic Marine
101 Keel St., Wrightsville Beach
• (910) 256-9911

Just past Wrightsville Marina, Motts Channel opens in the direction of the Atlantic Ocean. This marina, open seven days a week, offers repair services and is oriented to serving locals with its dry-docked, small-craft facilities. Gasoline is the only service for transients.

Bradley Creek Marina
6338 Oleander Dr., Wilmington
• (910) 350-0029

As you travel south on the ICW or take Airlie Road from Wrightsville Beach and a left onto Oleander Drive, you'll come upon the marina, just south of the bridge on Bradley Creek. Located on the western shore of the ICW, this is a large, dry-dock and wetslip facility that serves the local community and, sadly for the transient, is not a place to stop for the night. Wetslips can accommodate watercraft up to 65 feet, and dry storage is available for up to 27 feet. Slips are leased, usually by the year, or they may be purchased. Fuel is available nearby.

Bridge Tender Marina and Restaurant
1418 Airlie Rd., Wilmington
• (910) 256-6550

On the western shore, directly across from

Wrightsville Marina on Airlie Road, is a marina with a bonus: a great local seafood and steak restaurant. The marina offers all amenities, including gas and diesel fuel. One word of caution: The current is very swift here, so mind your slippage on entering and be ready with a boathook to fend off some very expensive craft docked nearby.

Dockside Marine
1306 Airlie Rd., Wilmington
• **(910) 256-3579, VHF Channel 16**
Dockside Marina is located just south of the Wrightsville Beach drawbridge at Marker 127 on the Intracoastal Waterway, (approximately Day Marker 283 coming from the south). You'll find more than 170 feet of transient dockage, fuel and power (30 and 50 amp), as well as an excellent, casual seafood restaurant. Dockside Marina is the perfect locale for an overnight stay. Call ahead for dockage reservations.

Seapath Yacht Club
330 Causeway Dr., Wrightsville Beach
• **(910) 256-3747**
On Motts Channel, just down the road from Wrightsville Marina, this well-appointed facility has some transient dockage with power, water, fuel, waste pump-out and cable TV connections. A store provides many essential supplies. Seapath is very close to Banks Channel and is the nearest approach to the Atlantic Ocean, although Bradley Creek Marina farther south is just about as close to Masonboro Inlet. You can't miss Seapath because it adjoins a high-rise condominium building that clearly marks the spot for miles.

Wrightsville Beach Marina
6 Marina St., Wrightsville Beach
• **(910) 256-6666, VHF Channel 16**
On the eastern shore of the ICW just south of the bridge, this marina is a luxurious place to dock for the night. It offers power, water, telephone service, cable TV and Internet connections, fuel and mechanical repairs. A swimming pool is even available for transients. Bluewater Restaurant overlooks the docks, welcoming famished boaters to enjoy prime rib and seafood.

Carolina Beach

Below Masonboro Sound is a stretch with no marinas. The shoreline becomes residential in character, and there is not another port until you get close to Carolina Beach.

Carolina Beach Municipal Marina
207 Canal Dr., Carolina Beach
• **(910) 458-2540**
Mooring is tight at this city marina located off the ICW at the southern end of the channel in Carolina Beach. This marina is mostly dedicated to fishing charter and party boats Transient slips are not available, but there is a designated anchorage area in the northeast corner of Myrtle Grove Sound; temporary short-term docking is available within the marina area. It's a good spot for a brief visit, particularly if you want to disembark in the heart of Carolina Beach and avail yourself of the fare at several easy-to-reach restaurants and fast-food places. Fuel is not available here.

Oceana Marina
401 Marina St., Carolina Beach
• **(910) 458-5053**
This marina lies across from Snow's Cut Landing boat launching area. It has a harbor enclosed by a breakwater and floating piers. Transients may or may not be able to find a berth for the night. The marina offers water and power connections, fuel, pump out, cable TV, showers and laundry facilities.

Carolina Beach State Park Marina
Carolina Beach State Park, Carolina Beach
• **(910) 458-7770**
At the west end of Snow's Cut, which connects the Cape Fear River with the ICW, is Carolina Beach State Park. On land, just go over the Snow's Cut Bridge on U.S. 421 S., take the first right onto Dow Road, then (about 0.2 mile) take another right onto State Park Road. The

The Cape Fear River Keeper

Bouton Baldridge works in a small office in downtown Wilmington and ponders the future of the Cape Fear River, flowing within sight of his desk. Several interns and volunteers fill the front office in a flurry of activity.

The walls are covered with maps of the river as it makes its way from Greensboro to the ocean, a journey of hundreds of miles. Newspaper articles, posters and memorabilia on the walls proudly demonstrate the accomplishments of this organization.

This is the office of Cape Fear River Watch, Inc., a local non-profit organization, and it's the workplace of two staff members, several interns, and numerous dedicated volunteers who all share one thing in common: a determination to protect the Cape Fear River. Although the office is modest, the organization's goals are ambitious.

Cape Fear River Watch, Inc. came into being in 1993 when Baldridge was struck with a notion that Wilmington's river needed protection as much as the highly publicized Neuse River to the north. Baldridge, a onetime graduate student in environmental sciences, read an article about the environmental problems in the Neuse River-unexplained fish kills, high algae levels, agricultural pollution, industrial pollution-and was heartened to note a RiverKeeper(r) had been hired by a grassroots organization in New Bern to search for the source of these and other problems.

"I read this article by Star-News reporter Kirsten Mitchell," says Baldridge, "and I found myself thinking the Cape Fear, although very different from the Neuse, also needed a RiverKeeper(r). So several of us started talking, and we got to work on it. After two years, we were able to get a grant that would allow me to do this work full time as the Cape Fear RiverKeeper(r). I felt it was important to make the needs of our river known."

The importance of the Cape Fear to Wilmington, as well as to North Carolina, is profound. "Fayetteville upstream relies on this river for 60 percent of its municipal water. Wilmington draws on it 100 percent. Many smaller communities on the way look to this river for their needs," says Baldridge. "This is a great natural resource that is in danger from over-development, hog-farm overspill, industrial pollutants, chemical spills and overuse; the problem is that nobody really knows what kind of shape it's in now compared to the past."

"No one knows what shape the River is in because there is nothing upon which to base comparisons. We really don't know what our readings should be for it to be for a healthy river," says Baldridge. "We're still learning, and the challenge is taking what we've learned and sharing it. We don't have the obvious problems of the Neuse but now is when we should start making sure we never do."

"Unfortunately, rapid residential development, hog farms and confusion over jurisdiction are causing real problems, "says Baldridge. "We have a concern with the fact that hog farms, a major contributor to increased nitrates in the water supply, are allowed to operate under relaxed legislative conditions. Then there's the concern that water quality isn't overseen by one agency. There are different rules, for example, for the Forestry Department and the Department of Water Quality. The people in charge of water quality don't have jurisdiction over what's happening on the land. The people in charge of the land issues don't have control over what's happening in the water."

There are more questions than answers about the river's health, and Baldridge notes that without serious commitment from government, it's going to be a long process to gather information, analyze it and take steps to protect the Cape Fear as well as the other rivers and streams of the state.

Raising public awareness is high on the list of goals for Cape Fear River Watch, Inc. because, unfortunately, it's like that line in Joni Mitchell's song "Big Yellow Taxi"-"You don't know what you've got 'til it's gone." That's one reason the group is involved in a storm drain awareness campaign, a wetland restoration project and a growing environmental education program. If people can be made to understand that their everyday actions contribute pollutants to the water supply that can cause environmental problems, the awareness will go a long way toward stopping abuses of the river.

"People take the Cape Fear River for granted, " says Baldridge. "We're so used to having it that we can't imagine not having it. People need to remember that Wilmington wouldn't even be here if it were not for that river."

Wilmington today depends on the river to provide not only drinking water, but also aesthetic values, recreational opportunities and an economic base.

To volunteer to protect the river or to join Cape Fear River Watch, Inc., please contact the Cape Fear RiverKeeper or the Program Coordinator at (910) 762-5606, email cfrw@ecoisp.com. Stop by the Environmental Education Headquarters at 617 Surry Street, directly under the Cape Fear Memorial Bridge.

Cape Fear River Watch sponsors Eco Tours of coastal waters.

Photo: Cape Fear River Watch

park marina offers a ramp, fuel and ample overnight dockage. If you're weary of being on a boat, you can pitch a tent and roast marshmallows over a campfire in the park. Or you can take advantage of some of the park's five great trails. The Fly Trap Trail is one of the favorites; along the trail you can look at the hungry plants known as Venus's fly traps, but don't touch! The Sugarloaf Trail follows along the Cape Fear River, providing beautiful water views as you explore nature.

Wilmington

Coming from Carolina Beach by boat, it's a 15-mile ride from Snow's Cut across the Cape Fear River into Southport and the more pro-

tected Intracoastal Waterway. This is a major shipping lane to the State Port at Wilmington, as well as the route for the Southport-Fort Fisher Ferry, so do keep a watchful eye. Before crossing over take a side trip and enter the Cape Fear River at Snow's Cut, unless you have a sailboat with mast taller than 65 feet. The Cape Fear Memorial Bridge is a bascule bridge with a clearance of 65 feet. Head north up the river for one of the most memorable trips on your cruise. You'll find increasingly improved opportunities to dock, and you can take advantage of visiting Wilmington's Historic District. "Those who miss the many attractions of this seagoing community will be less for the omission," wrote Claiborne Young in his Cruising Guide to Coastal North Carolina.

After stopping to enjoy the city's downtown, head up the Northeast Cape Fear River. You'll pass under the Isabelle Holmes Bridge, which opens on demand (the bridge tender monitors channels 13 and 18A), and you'll soon find yourself in spectacular scenery. Cruise on farther and you'll see the ruins of rice plantations from 200 years ago, with endless creeks to explore. You can cruise for miles in complete tranquility with breathtaking scenery and not see a single other boat.

Bennett Brothers Yachts
Cape Fear Marina
1701 J. E. L. Wade Dr., Wilmington
• (910) 772-9277

Just beyond the Third Street Bridge on the Northeast Cape Fear River, is Bennett Brothers Yachts, a good place to stop if you need repairs or a somewhere to tie up. Celebrating 16 years as a family business, Bennett Brothers Yachts is a full-service boatyard, custom builder and yacht brokerage. With a 70-ton Marine Travel Lift, they can haul out just about anything. Twenty-five skilled craftsmen do everything from dinghy repair to cockpit extensions. Their location at the Cape Fear Marina offers fuel and 25 slips, each with power, water, telephone, pump and cable TV connection. The dock house has clean bathrooms, showers and laundry facilities and Internet access. The slips are for sale or lease and can accommodate yachts up to 155 feet with very deep draft. The marina is massively built on a site discovered in 1663 by William Hilton, who, incidentally, chose the sight for its superb protection from foul weather.

Wilmington Marine Center
3410 River Rd., Wilmington
• (910) 395-5055

Wilmington Marine Center, located at marker 59 on the Cape Rear River between Snows Cut and historic downtown

Boating is a way of life on the southern coast.

Wilmington, is an 80-slip marina situated inside a safe, enclosed, all-weather basin. At this exceptional marine center you'll find a yacht service company with mobile and railway haulout capacity to 400 tons, a chart and ship supply company, fabricators and welders, boat builders, dock manufacturers, diesel mechanics, and a yacht brokerage and sales company that handles Rampage, Grand Banks, East Bay and Navigator yacht lines. The marina has floating docks with 110/220V electricity for yachts ranging from 20 to 120 feet. The marina, which sells diesel and unleaded gasoline seven days a week, has shipshape bath facilities on site; numerous restaurants, museums, historic sights, and entertainment venues are nearby. Friendly, professional service is the hallmark of this storm-safe marina. Beautiful sunsets are an added bonus. Wilmington Marine Center is a member of the BOATUS Cooperating Marina network.

Downtown Wilmington Waterfront

Cruising the downtown Wilmington waterfront offers a wonderful alternative to the hectic pace of the Intracoastal Waterway. Step off your boat onto one of the docks along the Riverwalk and wander into some of the appealing shops or dine in one of downtown's great restaurants. You'll be within walking distance of museums, historic residences, visitor information centers and theaters.

City of Wilmington Municipal Docks
302 Willard St., Wilmington
• (910) 520-6875

At the City of Wilmington Municipal Docks, you will find dockage within immediate proximity of Historic Downtown Wilmington. Dockage is available by reservation only. Facilities include 260 feet of floating dock space, 11 floating slips and 100 feet of usable bulkhead. Power and water are available, and boaters can take advantage of amenities offered through the Hilton Riverside and Best Western Coastline Inn. The fee for docking is $1 per foot/per day or $1.25/per foot per day with power and water hookups. Limited long term and day dockage is also available. Monitoring Channel 16 on VHF.

Bald Head Island

Bald Head Island Marina
Bald Head Island • (910) 457-7380

Bald Head Island Marina offers slips, fuel

INSIDERS' TIP

The United States Coast Guard (USCG) Boating Safety Hotline number is (800) 368-5647.

and restaurants as well as a gracious welcome to this lovely island. The marina is not reachable by road, the only way you're going to get there is by boat. Odds are you're not going to take the ferry if the marina is your destination for boating. You'll just boat right in and be delighted you did. This marina primarily serves a private, residential community where many of the homes are also vacation rentals, but it has the welcome mat out for visitors. Stop by for a rest in a beautiful setting. You'll find fuel and the opportunity for a walking adventure on this historic island or a drive in a rented golf cart to the Maritime Market for provisions.

Southport-Oak Island

South Harbor Village Transient Dock
Fish Factory Rd., Southport
• (910) 454-7486

South Harbor Village Transient Dock opened in June 2001. At 1,000 feet in length, it is the longest transient dock in North Carolina. It's a floating dock in 15 feet of water at low tide and sits at a perfect parallel to the channel, making it an easy-in, easy-out dock. Amenities include 30, 50 and 100 amp power, cable TV, gas, diesel, a pump-out station, a courtesy phone, Internet access, laundry, showers, a full-service restaurant, a deli and an 18-hole golf course on site. New in 2003 are a swimming pool and tennis courts as well as a courtesy vehicle. In addition to the transient dock, there are 128 slips. The facility is located at Mile Marker 311, one mile south of the Cape Fear River inlet.

Southport Marina Inc.
W. West Pl., Southport • (910) 457-5261

This immaculate marina is on the Southport waterfront just south of downtown. By land, take U.S. 17 from Wilmington and a left onto N.C. Highway 133 to Southport. At the intersection of N.C. Highway 211, take a left and go as far as you can without going into the water. Then take a right and drive a few blocks until the marina comes into view on the left. This marina's extensive docks welcome the cruising boater with fuel, power, transient slips, restaurants, repair service, a clubhouse and supplies. An outdoor tiki lounge invites one and all to kick back with a cocktail or soda after a hard day of boating. It is one of only about a dozen North Carolina marinas with pump-outs. This marina is owned by the federal government and leased to operators who are planning expansion in the near future.

Blue Water Point Marina Resort
W. Beach Dr. to 57th Pl., Oak Island • (910) 278-1230

Blue Water Point offers slip rentals, boat rentals, gas and diesel fuel, bait, tackle and ice. It also has deep-sea fishing charters, party boats and kayak rentals. The marina is at Intracoastal Waterway marker 33. The owners are obviously pleased to see boating visitors and are very accommodating.

South Brunswick Islands

Hughes Marina
1800 Village Point Rd., Shallotte • (910) 754-6233

Hughes Marina is available for overnight accommodations, with transient slips, fuel and shore power. However, there is a sand bar at the mouth of the Shallotte river and the current is particularly swift here, so boaters need to pay careful attention while docking. If you'd like a night ashore, the marina has a motel and restaurant on the property.

INSIDERS' TIP

Be safe on the water! Make sure you know:
- **The stability of your watercraft**
- **How to use all the equipment and safety devices on your boat**
- **The waters you will be using, tides, currents and hazards**
- **Your personal limitations and responsibilities**
- **Navigation rules and the courtesies of safe boating**

---

age, boat repair and cleaning.

Pelican Pointe Marina
2000 Sommersett Rd., Ocean Isle Beach • (910) 579-6440

This full-service marina at marker 98 on the ICW offers gas and diesel fuel, extensive dry indoor boat storage for boats up to 32 feet, and a staff of certified mechanics. A 9-ton boat forklift is available. Pelican Pointe has a ship's store complete with boat parts and supplies, beer, ice and fishing tackle. It also offers boat rentals.

Marsh Harbour Marina
10155 Beach Dr. SW, Calabash • (910) 579-3500

This large marina has 200 slips, gas and diesel fuel, shore power, water and a pump-out station. There are shoreside showers as well as showers in the marina. The marina is particularly well-sheltered for overnight dockage, and transients can berth within walking distance of Calabash restaurants.

Topsail Island

Beach House Marina
111 N. New River Dr., Surf City • (910) 328-2628

This new marina, involving property from Roland to Greensboro Ave. continues to grow. Presently completed is 192 dry storage spaces, available month to month or yearly. There are also some permanent water slips and limited docking on a daily or weekend basis for visiting boaters. Diesel fuel, gasoline and ice are available on site while boating supplies can be conveniently purchased across the street. The marina is located in downtown Surf City, close to restaurants, shopping and the beach.

Holden Beach Marina
3238 Pompano St., Holden Beach • (910) 842-5447

This marina, owned and operated by Mercer's 3 Enterprises, is located at the base of the Intracoastal Waterway bridge to Holden Beach, just a stone's throw from Oak Island. It is regarded as one of the friendliest marinas on the North Carolina coast. It has a full range of services, including fuel and transient slips. It also offers dry and wet stor-

Sports, Fitness and Parks

Except for snow skiing, rappelling and rock climbing, just about every kind of sport you could ask for is offered in the southern coastal region. In this chapter, we've included information on where to find or join most sports and recreational activities except for golf and watersports, which are in separate chapters. A section on fitness centers and descriptions of area parks with their facilities follows the sports listings. Related businesses and services are described along the way.

The *Wilmington Star-News* daily "Sports" and "Today" pages plus weekly "Currents" and "Neighbors" sections provide you with handy guides to recreation throughout the region. Also check the "Summer Camps" section in our Kidstuff chapter for information on summer sports camps for youth.

Parents should note that registration fees for youth league sports are often discounted when registering more than one child in the same league. Frequently, seniors get discounts, too. Be sure to inquire.

LOOK FOR:
• Recreation Departments
• Sports and Activities
• Fitness Centers
• Parks

Recreation Departments

Local and county parks and recreation departments organize a staggering selection of activities, including team sports for all ages. Check with them when looking into the sport of your choice. Addresses and phone numbers of the local offices are listed here.

Carolina Beach Parks and Recreation, 1121 N. Lake Park Boulevard, Carolina Beach, (910) 458-7416

City of Wilmington Parks, Recreation and Downtown Services, 302 Willard Street, Wilmington, (910) 341-7855; Athletics (910) 343-3681or 343-3682

There's nothing like a day at the park with friends.

Photo: Jay Tervo

New Hanover County Parks Department, 230 Market Place Drive, Suite 120, Wilmington, (910) 798-7181

Wrightsville Beach Parks and Recreation, 1 Bob Sawyer Drive, Wrightsville Beach, (910) 256-7925

Oak Island Parks and Recreation, 4601 E. Oak Island Drive, Oak Island, (910) 278-5518

Southport Parks and Recreation, Stevens Park, 107 E. Nash Street, Southport, (910) 457-7945

Brunswick County Parks and Recreation, Parks & Recreation Building, Government Complex, Bolivia, (910) 253-2670, (800) 222-4790

Onslow County Parks and Recreation Department, 1244 Onslow Pines Road, Jacksonville, (910) 347-5332

Sports and Recreation

Badminton

The Wilmington Athletic Club is becoming the place for a competitive game of badminton. This is not your backyard variety, so you'd better come ready for serious play. The badminton club meets every Friday night and Sunday afternoon.

Baseball and Youth Leagues

The region has several baseball youth leagues, but there are no public leagues for adults. The youth leagues offer divisions from T-ball for toddlers to baseball for teens through age 18, and some offer softball too. Registration generally takes place from early February through mid-March and carries a fee (about $50 to $90). Registrants need to present their birth certificates. The playing season begins in April. Contact one of the following organizations for specifics.

Cape Fear Optimist Club, (910) 762-7065

New Hanover County Parks Department, (910) 798-7181

Supper Optimist Club, (910) 791-5272

Wilmington Baseball Academy, (910) 798-1600

Winter Park Optimist Club, (910) 791-3566

YMCA of Wilmington (T-Ball only), (910) 251-9622

Brunswick County Parks and Recreation, (910) 253-2670, (800) 222-4790

Onslow County Parks and Recreation, (910) 347-5332

Spectator Baseball

The Wilmington Sharks
U.S. Hwy. 421 (Carolina Beach Road),
Wilmington • (910) 343-5621

One of 13 teams in the Coastal Plain League, the Wilmington Sharks debuted in 1997 and now average 1,500 fans per game. This summer league features undergraduate college players competing in 13 cities in North Carolina, South Carolina and Virginia. The level of play is said to be comparable to that of single A minor league teams. The Sharks are officially sanctioned by the NCAA and Major League Baseball and draw players from top college programs like University of North Carolina at Wilmington (UNCW), North Carolina State, University of North Carolina at Chapel Hill, East Carolina University and Clemson University. The league's 52-game regular season is capped by a best-of-three championship playoff in mid-August. The Sharks play their 27 home games, beginning around Memorial Day, at Legion Stadium Sports Complex on Carolina Beach Road, 2.3 miles south of Market Street in Wilmington. Single-ticket prices range from $3 to $6. Season tickets cost $125 for box seats, $100 for reserved seats and $80 for general admission. Besides providing great family entertainment, the Sharks staff offer affordable packages that include tickets, food coupons and even several picnic menus.

Basketball

Popular year round, but especially in the cooler months, basketball leagues are available for adults, boys and girls throughout our area. Watch the newspapers for information on registration. The following organizations have programs open to the public, just give them a call for specifics.

Carolina Beach Parks and Recreation, (910) 458-7416

City of Wilmington Parks, Recreation and Downtown Services, (910) 343-3682

YMCA of Wilmington, (910) 251-9622

Wrightsville Beach Parks and Recreation, (910) 256-7925

Brunswick County Parks and Recreation, (910) 253-4357, (800) 222-4790

Onslow County Parks and Recreation, (910) 347-5332

Wilmington Warriors
Wilmington • (910) 796-0901

This boys basketball club is for ages 10 to 17. Games are played at Laney High School, Trask Middle School and Roland Grise Middle School from March through July. Affiliated with the Amateur Athletic Union (AAU) and Youth Basketball of America (YBOA), the Warriors high school team requires tryouts, is highly competitive and travels quite a bit to tournaments in North and South Carolina. The Battle of the Beach Tournament in July attracts about 50 teams and culminates the season. Because many college recruiters scout during the spring and early summer, boys who play for the Warriors have lots of visibility and many get recognized for scholarships. Registration is $250 for all participants, regardless of age.

Bicycling

Touring most of North Carolina's southern coastal plain by bicycle can be a real pleasure. Roads tend to be lightly trafficked and flat, and most motorists have a fairly good awareness of cyclists. However, formal "bike paths" do not exist in this area. Instead, we have a system of well-marked "Share The Road" bike routes, some of which have paved bike lanes on both sides of the road that make trekking fairly easy (see the Chapter on Getting Around for information about Bike Routes).

In Wilmington bike registration is encouraged for your protection as it may help you recover your ride in the event of theft. Most bikes recovered by the police are never claimed and are auctioned off at year's end. You can register your wheels at police headquarters downtown, 115 Redcross Street, (910) 343-3600; it's free for city residents and $1 for non-residents.

New Hanover County sponsors a Bicycle Advisory Committee with members appointed by the County Commissioners. A strong supporter of bicycle advocacy, the committee works with local government groups in planning bicycle routes and developing multi-use trails.

Bicycle clubs can be an excellent way to meet other cyclists and learn about places to ride,

upcoming events and current issues. Depending on your interests, explore the Cape Fear Cyclists or the Hurricane Cycling Racing Club, both active in the Greater Wilmington area.

The Cape Fear Cyclists have regular rides throughout the year. This group is touring-oriented, with rides that often are at a casual or moderate pace. Members can obtain discounts on equipment at three local shops. More information may be obtained by calling the Two Wheeler Dealer at (910) 799-6444.

Hurricane Cycling is a racing club with membership open to men and women who are interested in learning about this exciting sport—from beginners to fitness cyclists to aspiring amateurs to race-hardened semi-pros. A sponsored member of the U.S. Cycling Federation, the club holds training rides and time trials throughout the year. For information, call the Two Wheeler Dealer at (910) 799-6444.

The New Hanover County Bicycle Advisory Committee holds an annual 20-mile "River to the Sea" bike ride in the spring. Open to experienced and recreational riders, the round-trip ride runs from the Coast Guard parking lot on Water Street downtown Wilmington along secondary roads to Wrightsville Beach. For information, contact the New Hanover County Planning Department at (910) 341-7444.

Carolina Coastal Adventures has a two-hour fun ride through and around Pleasure Island. See what life is like on the island while learning about the history, commerce and folklore that has made this island one of the area's favorite tourist destinations. Time is included for shopping and ice cream! For more information, call (910) 458-9111.

Several excellent bicycle specialty shops in our area sell new and used bicycles and provide repair services. Some businesses, particularly in beach communities, offer rentals — competitive rates are typically around $20 to $30 per day.

Chain Reaction Cycling Center
228 Eastwood Rd., Wilmington
• (910) 397-0096

Chain Reaction Cycling, in the Home Depot Shopping Center off Eastwood Road, carries a full range of mountain bikes and beach cruisers. It also sells new high-performance cycles, components, accessories and used bikes.

INSIDERS' TIP

Use of designated North Carolina game lands for purposes other than hunting, trapping and fishing is subject to the control or the landowners. Watch for signs stating any restrictions.

Come here for repairs too. The store is open Monday through Saturday.

Two Wheeler Dealer
4408 Wrightsville Ave., Wilmington
• (910) 799-6444

One of the largest bicycle shops around, Two Wheeler Dealer stocks a vast array of bicycles, including some vintage models and secondhand bikes, plus touring equipment, tricycles, bike trailers, infant seats — practically anything that rolls on spoked wheels — and accessories. Professional repair work and fitting are done on the premises. Two Wheeler is also a place to find racing information and equipment and to connect with the Cape Fear Cyclists Club.

Wrightsville Beach Supply
1 N. Lumina Ave., Wrightsville Beach
• (910) 256-8821

For fun stuff to enhance your beach vacation, here's the place to go. Among the beach chairs, umbrellas and baby joggers, you can find wet suits, surf boards, in-line skates and skateboards. Hours vary, but you can leave a phone message any time and you'll receive a prompt response.

Boomer's Bikes & More
3468-4 Holden Beach Rd., Holden Beach
• (910) 842-1400

Boomer's rents bicycles, tandems and other models (as well as many other beach items) by the hour, day and week. Boomer's also sells bikes and does repairs.

Boomer's Rentals
3468-4 Holden Beach Rd., Holden Beach
• (910) 842-1400

For all your vacation rental accessories, go to Boomer's. On the mainland, at the foot of the bridge, this shop has everything you need from beach to household items, from bikes to cribs.

Julie's Rentals
2 Main St., Sunset Beach • (910) 579-1211

Julie's is a bicycle/beach-rental shop that offers beach cruisers, adult tricycles (which are excellent for some disabled persons) and Suncycle recumbent bikes. The shop is open year-round, although you may need to call ahead in the off-season.

Bowling

Most bowling centers in our area host not only leagues, but also private parties. Some have

even added live music and dancing to their lounge entertainment, and all are family-oriented. Competitive prices average about $3.50 per game for adults on weekends. Prices on weekdays and for children 11 and younger may be lower.

Cardinal Lanes has two locations: 3907 Shipyard Boulevard, Wilmington, (910) 799-3023, and 7026 Market Street, on the south side of Ogden, (910) 686-4223.

Ten Pin Alley is at 127 S. College Road in Marketplace Mall, (910) 452-5455. They have special rates Monday through Thursday, except holidays — $1.50 for everybody until 5 PM.

Brunswick County Bowling Center, 630 Village Road, Shallotte, (910) 754-2695.

Boxing

City of Wilmington Boxing and Physical Fitness Center
302 N. S. 10th St., Wilmington
• (910) 341-7837 or (910) 341-7872

Known for its outstanding boxing program, the Center offers boxing training for both males and females ages 8 and older. In May 2002 the Center hosted the USA Junior Olympic Championship, Southeast Coast Region. Three local women participated in the American Boxing Federation Women's championships as well, with one emerging as the United States Champion; she represented our country in the second Women's World Championship in Turkey.

Additionally, the Center provides individuals and families opportunities to participate in traditional health club activities. Equipped with free weights, weight machines, treadmills, stationary bicycles and stairclimbers, the Center offers strength training, prescription exercise and cardiovascular workouts.

Classes in aerobics (including instructor training), funky jazz, kickboxing and Tae Bo are taught by certified instructors. A program geared toward the physically challenged is offered — call for details. Locker rooms and shower facilities are available. Memberships are among the best bargains in town just $40 for city residents and $75 for non-residents. Hours are Monday through Friday, 9 AM to 8 PM and Saturday 10 AM to 2 PM; the Center is closed on Sunday.

Flying

The local dearth of sizable hills, and therefore reliable updrafts, limits local aviation to powered flight. However, quite good weather conditions, large runways and pilots who fly in a radar-controlled area make Wilmington a great place to learn how to fly a plane. Why not check out the Be A Pilot Program, a non-profit organization that offers introductory flights for only $49; call (888) BE A PILOT for information.

Among the surprises of a bird's-eye view of the area is sighting the so-called "Carolina bays," enormous elliptical depressions in the earth first discovered from the air (see Lake Waccamaw State Park in our Camping chapter). Besides flying lessons, local companies offer plane rentals and sightseeing flights. See our Attractions chapter for information about air tours.

Aeronautics/Air Wilmington
**Wilmington International Airport,
1740 Airport Blvd., Wilmington
* (910) 763-4691 for Aeronautics
• (910) 763-0146 for Air Wilmington**

Aeronautics and its affiliate, Air Wilmington, can arrange for flight instruction with a private instructor and charters for companies or groups. They can also arrange for accommodations and meal delivery. A courtesy car is available with a one-hour time limit.

ISO Aero Service Inc. of Wilmington
**1410 N. Kerr Ave., Wilmington
• (910) 763-8898, (800) 526-0285**

ISO offers rentals, flight training instruction for all ratings, maintenance, sightseeing services and participates in the Be A Pilot Program. ISO has an executive facility at Wilmington International Airport next to U.S. Customs.

Football

League football beyond the scholastic realm is offered primarily by two organizing bodies, the Pop Warner program and Brunswick County Parks and Recreation. Look into registration in May or June as most teams commence practice early in August.

Coastal Pop Warner
Wilmington • (910) 798-2141

Pop Warner organizes tackle football and cheerleading teams for boys and girls age 7 through 14 in Pee Wee, Midget and Mighty Mights divisions. Flag football for 5- and 6-year-olds is offered, too. More than 1,800 youngsters in New Hanover, Pender and Brunswick counties participate in the Pop Warner program each year. Games are played at Ogden Park (see the Parks section at the end of this chapter). On Thanksgiving weekend 2002, the Mid-South Regional Playoffs for teams representing seven states will be played in Wilmington.

Wrightsville Beach Parks & Recreation
**1 Bob Sawyer Dr., Wrightsville Beach
• (910) 256-7925**

A flag football 7-on-7 adult league, sponsored by Wrightsville Beach Parks & Recreation, is offered in both spring and fall. The cost is $325 per team.

Brunswick County Parks & Recreation
**Parks & Recreation Bldg., Government complex, Bolivia • (910) 253-4357,
(800) 222-4790**

Brunswick County's coed league is open to kids ages 10 through 13. There are five football teams, each with cheerleaders (ages 8 to 13). If you're interested in becoming a referee or coach, inquire about Brunswick County's referee and coaching clinics.

Horseback Riding

Although English (hunt and saddle seat) style is favored in this region, Western is available. Most stables and riding academies offer boarding and instruction; some offer rentals and trail rides. Blacksmiths and tack shops are scarce, but the horse business in this area is thriving and bringing joy to a lot of horse lovers.

Canterbury Stables
**6021 Wrightsville Ave., Wilmington
• (910) 791-6502**

Situated on 14 1/2 acres of land, Canterbury Stables is owned and operated by Linda Shelhart, who was inducted into the United Professional Horsemen Association of the Carolinas Hall of Fame in September 2001. Shelhart trains and shows Saddlebred horses and teaches Saddle Seat Equitation. Canterbury specializes in private and group riding instruction, boarding, training and showing, but no rentals.

Castle Stables
**5513 Sidbury Rd., Castle Hayne
• (910) 675-1113**

English-style instruction is offered on a plush 30-acre spread a few minutes north of Wilmington. Castle Stables has trails, an indoor ring and two outdoor rings with jumps, one of which is lighted. Castle Stables has a therapeutic riding program for physically and/or mentally challenged individuals of all ages.

Circle K Stable
**612 Ballie Ln, Wilmington
• (910) 793-5550**

Just south of Monkey Junction off Carolina

Beach Road, the Circle K offers classes in basic English style (hunt seat), horse training and boarding. They have two show rings, one lighted, but no trails. The stable's primary focus is showing Arabians. A small on-site tack shop has feed, hay and some equipment for sale. Horses are available for instruction, but not for rent.

Dolorosa Arabians
131 Via Dolorosa, Rocky Point
• **(910) 602-3808**

Owners Jan and DeCarol Williamson have been involved in the Arabian horse industry since 1978. They are committed to breeding, raising and training horses in a way that nurtures their usefulness and adds value, so that someone will love and care for them throughout their lives.

Situated on more than 140 acres, Dolorosa Arabians boasts 150-plus stalls, two barns each with tack room, lounge, office, grooming and wash rack area. There's a spacious 80- by 220-foot covered arena, a 50-foot covered round ring with a six-horse hot walker located nearby, a 32-stall show barn with a 50-foot covered round ring, a half-mile track, an outdoor arena and turnouts. An exceptional, highly experienced staff, together with spacious, state-of-the-art breeding facilities, a laboratory and large foaling stalls equipped with cameras, are evidence of Dolorosa's excellence.

Rob Bick and Caralyn Schroter head up the training and conditioning programs. They each have extensive experience in all divisions of the Arabian show horse: English, Western, Halter, Driving, Hunter and Show Hack. They also truly enjoy the Amateur and junior rider divisions and have a gift for instilling confidence in riders of all ages that leads to superior showmanship.

Desperado Horse Farm
7214 N.C. Hwy. 210., Rocky Point
• (910) 675-0487

This horse farm offers everything from horse rentals to day or night beach rides for the horse enthusiast. Open seven days a week during daylight hours (except Sunday when they open at 2 PM), Desperado can host a special event for your church or business, provide a pony for that special birthday party, or offer trail rides, lessons, boarding or training. Reservations are required for special events and preferred for other activities. This farm is easily accessible from Wilmington on I-40, Exit 408, right on U.S. Highway 210 to Running Deer.

Hanover Stables
5901 Bizzel Ave., Castle Hayne
• **(910) 675-8923**

Offering 13 acres with 15 segregated pastures, two lighted outdoor arenas and numerous trails, Hanover Stables provides boarding service and has a full-time, on-site manager. They offer professional instruction in both Western and English (hunt seat) styles of riding, including dressage. Horses are available for sale, but not for hire.

Exceptionally family oriented, Hanover Stables holds camps for kids, birthday parties, hayrides, cookouts and trail rides on a regular basis. They have a show team and travel to many area shows. Believing that horsemanship teaches youngsters responsibility and respect for both animals and the environment, the owners and stable personnel strive to set good examples. Hanover Stables is an approved North Carolina Equine Rescue League site.

K&K Riding Stables
2619 Boonesneck Rd., Holden Beach
• **(910) 842-8002**

K&K provides English- and Western-style riding lessons, horse training and guided trail rides. Located 3 miles off Holden Beach Road, its 18 acres are laced with shady trails. The kids will love the pony rides. Horses are available for sale or rent. Boarding is available as well.

Peachtree Downs
810 Hickman Rd., Calabash
• **(910) 287-4790**

With 127 acres nearly adjacent to the South Carolina state line, Peachtree Stables is convenient to the entire southeastern corner of Brunswick County and northeastern South Carolina. The trails traverse 70 acres, much of it shady. Peachtree offers hourly trail rides, full boarding facilities, training, two outdoor riding rings and an indoor riding arena. Group and private instruction for ages 6 and up are offered in English and Western styles. They have American Quarter Horse racing from April to October. Horses are available for lease and for sale.

Sea Horse Sports
5751 Oleander Dr., Wilmington
• **(910) 791-0900**

Sea Horse Sports specializes in English riding apparel and equipment, including saddlery, boots and grooming supplies. Located 2.3 miles from College Road in Philips Plaza, the shop's hours are 10 AM to 6 PM Tuesday through Saturday.

Hunting

Among North Carolina's oldest traditions are hunting, trapping and fishing. Regulations governing these activities are designed to preserve and promote these resources so that they are abundantly available for present and future outdoor enthusiasts.

There are several game lands in the region where hunters may pursue big and small game, including dove, deer, rabbit, wild turkey and black bear. Game lands are typically leased from individual landowners and companies by North Carolina Wildlife Resources Commission, Division of Wildlife Management, 512 N. Salisbury Street, 1722 Mail Service Center, Raleigh 27699, (919) 733-7291. Some lands are owned outright by the commission. Most game lands are accessible from public roads, while some have only water access. Green diamond-shaped signs identify game lands.

The 50,120-acre Holly Shelter Game Land in Pender County is the largest local game land. It is a varied wetland of pocosins (peat-bottomed lowlands) and pine savannas threaded by winding creeks and existing in some noncontiguous parcels. It's north of Wilmington, roughly between U.S. Highway 17 west to the northeast Cape Fear River and between N.C. highways 210 and 53.

Holland's Shelter Creek, a private hunting preserve near Burgaw, offers guided or non-guided adventures on Holland's Yellow Lab Farms. The main attraction is no-limit Bobwhite Quail, Ringnecked Pheasant and Chukar Partridge. Future plans include duck hunting as well. You may hunt with your own dogs or use their kennel's bird dogs. Individuals, small groups or corporate groups are accepted, and packages including airport shuttle service, meals, lodging and bird processing are available. Call (910) 259-5743 for more information.

The Green Swamp Game Land, a 14,851-acre expanse lying in nearly one contiguous block bordered by N.C. Highway 211 in Brunswick County, is among the most isolated areas remaining in southeastern North Carolina. Foot travel only is permitted here, and it's an easy place get turned around in for a couple of days. The Nature Conservancy owns this land, and much of it, as the name suggests, is low-lying wetland and pocosin.

Lying within New Hanover County, the Sutton Lake Game Land is a 3,322-acre land leased from CP&L. It is bordered by N.C. Highway 421 and the Cape Fear River.

Roan Island is a 2,757-acre island situated in Pender County at the confluence of the Cape Fear River and the Black River — a National Scenic River that is still in relatively pristine condition. The island lies in the flood plain and has the oldest stand of bald cypress trees in the eastern United States. Partly covered by water, it supports wild turkey and black bear as well as various smaller game, including some rare and endangered species such as the shortnose sturgeon. Access to Roan Island is only by boat.

Hunting licenses are issued by the North Carolina Wildlife Resources Commission, License Section. They can be purchased specifically for big game or small game and are also available combined with fishing licenses. A wide variety of licenses is available for both residents and non-residents. Shot-term, annual and lifetime licenses can be purchased for hunting, fishing, trapping and combinations thereof.

For up-to-date details about places to hunt, seasons, fees and regulations, obtain a free copy of the current "North Carolina Inland Fishing, Hunting and Trapping Regulations Digest" wherever licenses are sold. The entire Digest is online at www.ncwildlife.com; licenses may be purchased online or by phone at (888) 248-6834. Call the License Section of the North Carolina Wildlife Resources Commission at (919) 662-4370 for more information. Licenses may also be purchased at the following locations:

County Line Bait & Tackle, 6408 Castle Hayne Road, Castle Hayne, (910) 675-8940

Hudson True Value, 5601 Castle Hayne Road, Castle Hayne, (910) 675-9205

Jim's Pawn & Gun, Inc., 4212 Oleander Drive, Wilmington, (910) 799-7314

Kmart, 815 S. College Road, Wilmington, (910) 799-5360

Roy's Bait & Tackle, 3821-A Highway 421 North, Wilmington, (910) 762-8681

Wal-Mart Super Center, 5226 Sigmon Road, Wilmington, (910) 392-4034

Wal-Mart, 5135 Carolina Beach Road at College Road, Wilmington, (910) 452-0944

Wal-Mart Super Center, 1675 Howe Street, Southport, (910) 454-9909

Hampstead Village Pharmacy, N.C. Highway 17, Hampstead, (910) 270-3411, (910) 270-3414

Holden Beach True Value, 3008 Holden Beach Road, Holden Beach, (910) 842-5440

Island Tackle & Gifts, 6855-3 Beach Drive SW, Ocean Isle Beach, (910) 579-6116

Wal-Mart, 4540 Main Street, Shallotte, (910) 754-2880

Canady's Sport Center
3220 Wrightsville Ave., Wilmington
• **(910) 791-6281**

Canady's is among the best one-stop retail

shops for hunters. Staffers are knowledgeable in rifle and bow hunting. Clothing, field gear and a good selection of binoculars are stocked. Canady's is open Monday through Saturday.

Dick's Sporting Goods
816 College Rd., Wilmington
• (910) 793-1904

All of Dick's staff in the Hunting Department are knowledgeable, active hunters and fishermen. The store carries rifle and bow hinting equipment plus knives, binoculars, clothing and other hunting supplies. The store is open seven days a week.

In-line and Roller Skating

Adults and kids alike enjoy this immensely popular activity and can be seen skating at Greenfield Lake — on the nearly 5-mile-long bike path or in the lighted skating facility, the Greenfield Grind Skate Park, (see Skateboarding in this chapter).

Inline skating is banned in Wilmington's downtown central business area and Historic District. Recreational and commuter skaters on city streets and sidewalks can be fined. So where do you go to skate? UNCW offers long stretches of wide, paved walks, including smooth, curvy stretches surrounding the lake at the university commons.

One of the best places to skate is the Loop at Wrightsville Beach. Consisting of paved walks totaling approximately 2.5 miles, the Loop runs along Wrightsville Beach Park, Causeway Drive, Lumina Avenue and Salisbury Street. There are plenty of places to stop for a cool refreshment or a dip in the ocean along the way. The Loop is busy during peak times with walkers, runners and strollers packing the pathway, so an early morning skate is just the ticket.

The No. 1 place to skate on Oak Island (outside of the Oak Island Skate Park, see Skateboarding in this chapter) consists of nearly 7 miles of municipal sidewalks along Oak Island Drive. Ramps (rather than curbs) meet every intersection. Yacht Drive, along the north side of the island, is also an excellent choice. On the south side, Dolphin Drive, just one block from the ocean, is an OK choice, but you'll have to deal with some motor traffic. Avoid Beach Drive altogether, with its heavy traffic and gravel.

Bald Head Island is a true skate haven, where the only other traffic on the smoothly paved byways is golf carts and bicycles.

The International Inline Skating Association
Wilmington • (910) 762-7004

Headquartered in Wilmington, the IISA promotes the benefits of inline skating for sport, recreation, vitality and fitness. The Association supports safety and produces educational programs, including one to certify inline skating instructors.

Jelly Beans Family Skating Center
5216 Oleander Dr., Wilmington
• (910) 791-6000

Jelly Beans hosts its own inline hockey league for ages 14 and younger. Players must provide their own equipment, which may be purchased on site. A team jersey will be provided. Jelly Beans offers instruction, practice and game time. Sessions are held in winter, spring and fall; a summer camp is offered also. The fee for each 10-week session is $75 per player. Hours vary, so please call ahead.

Kite Flying

Steady beach winds are ideal for kite flying. Of course, it pays to use common sense: Beware of power lines, piers, boat masts and homes. Stunt kites, which can fly close to the ground, may annoy some beachgoers. Fort Fisher, the north ends of Topsail Island and Carolina Beach, and the south end of Wrightsville Beach are fitting places to tie your hopes and dreams to a colorful swatch and send them aloft.

Blowing In the Wind
The Cotton Exchange, 312 Nutt St., Wilmington • (910) 763-1730

If you're a kite lover, this is your kind of store. Here you'll find kites of every shape and size, for every age and skill level. Its wide selection, from wind sleds to box kites to parafoils and beyond, will make your eyes pop. Also available are flags, windsocks and wind chimes.

Lacrosse

This rugged and almost legendary game has been gaining momentum recently in the greater Wilmington area. New Hanover County is one of the few counties in North Carolina that offers lacrosse at most public middle and high schools. UNC-Wilmington has both men's and women's lacrosse club teams open to students, faculty and staff. Play is on the campus recreation fields in fall and spring; for information call the UNCW Coordinator of Sports Clubs at (910) 962-7758.

A YMCA MEMBERSHIP
CAN DO WONDERS
FOR YOUR HEART.

Want to become a stronger person? Join the Y. Through programs like exercise classes, youth sports, and family events, you can get closer to those you love in a healthy, caring environment. Besides being a great way to lay the foundations for a healthy lifestyle, a Y membership cultivates strength, instills core values and brings balance to many lives. Think of it as an investment in the well-being of self, family and community. In doing so, your heart will be strengthened in ways you've never imagined.

Call 910-251-9622 for more information about YMCA memberships.

YMCA
We build strong kids,
strong families, strong communities.

Wilmington Family YMCA 2710 Market St. 28403

Cape Fear Academy Lacrosse Camp
3900 S. College Rd., Wilmington
• (910) 791-0287

This summer day camp for boys in grades 3 through 12 in two age divisions runs for one week in June. Three-hour sessions are directed by the academy's lacrosse coaching staff. Instruction emphasizes fundamentals, rules and team play, and the camp culminates in a round-robin tournament.

Cape Fear Lacrosse Club
Wilmington • (910) 686-1962

Men age 18 and older who are lacrosse enthusiasts may join the Cape Fear Lacrosse Club at any time; dues are $50 per year. All are welcome; experience is preferred, but not necessary. Play is on weekends at Wrightsville Beach Park in fall and spring. Players need to have their own equipment.

Marksmanship and Riflery

Jim's Pawn and Guns
4212 Oleander Dr., Wilmington
• (910) 799-7314

The largest gun shop in Wilmington carries a large display of nearly 2,500 firearms. Here you can find new and used guns, gun safes, plus an array of accessories and ammunition. Jim's is a fully licensed federal firearm dealer.

Martial Arts

Whether its the sword technique of iaido, the open-hand style of karate or the throws and take-downs of ju-jitsu that interest you, or it's self-defense, confidence, physical fitness and competition you desire, it's all available in our region. Martial arts schools are proliferating, with many offering family rates and classes.

Bushin-Kai Karate
2875 Carolina Beach Rd., Wilmington
• (910) 395-2170

Del C. Russ III teaches traditional martial arts, including Japanese sword art (iaido), aiki-kai aikido, shinbu-kai, toyama-ryo and ko-dachi. Classes are available for kids ages 6 to 13 and adults ages 14 and older. The center is open Monday through Thursday evenings and Saturday morning. Call for more information.

Champion Karate & Kickboxing Centers
127 S. College Rd. (Marketplace Mall), Wilmington • (910) 792-1131
5202 Carolina Beach Rd., Wilmington
• (910) 793-2383

Owner/instructor John Maynard was personally trained by Chuck Norris, and his studio is part of Norris's United Fighting Arts organization. Champion offers instruction in karate, kickboxing, ground defense, ju-jitsu and personal fitness for men, women and children. In October 2002 the College Road facility was the site where the third Annual Joe Lewis Fighting Systems Black Belt Research Conference was held. Co-hosted by John Maynard, the event theme was "The Educated Trainer" and included high-level instruction.

Choe's Hap Ki Do
7419-C Market St., Wilmington
• (910) 686-2678

According to historical accounts, Hap Ki Do was taught only to those selected by the royal court of Korea. Among the chosen ones, the Choe family has handed down this ancient and traditional style of martial art, along with additional special family techniques from first son to first son for nearly 2,000 years. Hap Ki Do is suitable for everyone and requires little power — it doesn't matter how strong you are, as long as you use the techniques correctly. Other benefits include mental toughness, concentration, weight control and confidence.

Grandmaster Jong Hynm Choe is a ninth-degree blackbelt in Hap Ki Do, an eighth-degree in Tae Kwon Do and an Olympic Tae Kwon Do referee; he teaches only those who, through an interview and trial course, demonstrate positive attitude, dedication, respect and sincere interest in holistic self-improvement. He specializes in teaching Hap Ki Do, the use of empty hands, with and without weapons. He also teaches women's self-defense. Students of all ages are welcome.

Iron Horse School of Traditional Tae Kwon Do
South Park Plaza, Ste. 8, Shallotte
• (910) 755-5425

Iron Horse offers classes for "Little Dragons" (ages 4-6), children, advanced children, young adults and adults. The philosophy here is to have a good time while developing discipline, a sharper focus and a positive attitude Other positive benefits include reduction of stress and improvement of health.

Leitzke's ATA Black Belt Academy
3600 S. College Rd., Wilmington
• (910) 791-0119
6841 Market St., Wilmington,
• (910) 397-7978

While all are welcome at one of Leitzke's training facilities, the emphasis here is on families and kids. Students are divided by age groups into structured programs that teach self defense and help them with their personal development. Utilizing a trademarked system for teaching children, which is different from other martial arts schools, the ATA Black Belt Academy strives to give youngsters a positive "I can do it!" attitude regardless of size, age or athletic ability.

ATA Black Belt Academy is a member of The American Taekwondo Association (ATA), which has 150,000 members and hundreds of schools. Started in 1969, the ATA has been and still is the industry leader in innovative curriculum and teaching methods. Master Leitzke is a 6th Degree Black Belt and Mrs. Leitzke is a 5th Degree Black Belt. Day and evening classes are available.

Shao-Lin Kempo Martial Arts
3512 1/2 S. Carolina Beach Rd., Wilmington
• (910) 793-1161

Stressing physical fitness, flexibility, confidence, coordination and balance, this school uses a well-rounded system with kempo, ju-jitsu, kung-fu and weapons together. Quality not quantity is the main concern here. Classes are small to enhance the learning process. The low monthly fee is $55. You'll not be asked to sign a contract or pay miscellaneous fees. Head instructor Brian Watkins is a Shihan 5th Degree Black Belt who has experience in this system since 1982; his wife Christine is an experienced instructor, too. They invite individuals ages 8 and older to become part of their family in learning.

YMCA of Wilmington
2710 Market St., Wilmington
• (910) 251-9622

The family Y offers karate and Tae Kwon Do classes with U.S. Judo Association membership included. Costs range from $25 to $40 per month, excluding other membership fees and gear.

YWCA of Wilmington
2815 S. College Rd., Wilmington
• (910) 799-6820

Adults and kids can learn basic karate techniques, history and self defense from professional instructors at the YWCA. Call for times and classes.

Off-Roading

Although most beaches in our region prohibit vehicles, there are two areas where off-road enthusiasts (especially those who fish) can indulge themselves. But driving off-road is a double-edged sword: The vehicles that access these beautiful areas also erode and damage them. Off-roaders are urged to observe regulations closely, drive responsibly and use common sense.

The Fort Fisher State Recreation Area, an undeveloped 4-mile beach strand and tidal marsh, located 5 miles south of Carolina Beach, off U.S. 421, permits four-wheel-drive vehicles. Passage onto the beach is through marked crossovers only, and vehicles must follow designated routes, avoiding dunes, vegetation and marked nesting areas. Only registered four-wheel-drive motor vehicles are allowed — no ATVs. The sand here is loose and deep. Sharp drop-offs are common. At high tide, the strand becomes very narrow and may even prevent you from turning around; also, the marshy areas tend to flood. Plan accordingly. Please, please, respect this beautiful natural area.

In Carolina Beach, at the north end of Canal Drive, an access corridor leads to an open off-roading area. Monitored by the New Hanover County Sheriff's Department, this popular stretch of beach becomes quite busy and congested during summer months. The speed limit is 15 mph and a valid driver's license is required. ATVs, trailers of any sort and motor homes are not allowed.

Racquetball

In addition to the listings here, check the Fitness Centers section in this chapter to locate those that have racquetball courts.

> **INSIDERS' TIP**
>
> Keep a close watch on the weather, especially during summer and fall. Be alert to approaching thunderstorms, strong winds and rough waters. Sudden storms are common on the coast. Have a plan so you know where to find a safe haven should you need it.

Carolina Beach Parks and Recreation
**1121 N. Lake Park Blvd., Carolina Beach
• (910) 458-7416**

For those wishing to play racquetball, the Center has one court and will furnish racquets, balls and goggles. The hours are Monday through Friday from 9 AM to 9 PM, Saturday from 10 AM to 5 PM, and Sunday from 1 to 5 PM. Persons wishing to use the facilities must be at least 16 years of age.

Wilmington Athletic Club
**2026 S. 16th St., Wilmington
• (910) 343-5950**

Here you'll find racquetball facilities of exceptional quality. Six courts, including two challenge courts, offer players the best of the best. See the entry for Wilmington Athletic Club in our Fitness section for more information.

YMCA of Wilmington
**2710 Market St., Wilmington
• (910) 251-9622**

The Y has four courts that are available to members by reservation.

Rugby

Cape Fear Rugby Club
Flytrap Downs, 21st and Chestnut Sts., Wilmington • (910) 383-0067

This club has more than 100 members and is the five-time Division II state champion. Members play and practice at the club-owned pitch (field) located at Flytrap Downs in Wilmington. British sailors like to play traditional rugby games with the Cape Fear Rugby Club whenever their ships are in our port. The club is always interested in recruiting new players and social members.

Each July, the club holds its annual Cape Fear Sevens Rugby Tournament at Ogden Park field, off Gordon Road. Considered one of the finest showcases of Sevens Rugby in the United States, the event attracts about 70 teams with more than 700 players from all over the world. In November 2002, when the Cape Fear Rugby Club again won the state championship, the entire team received "Man of the Match" honors and the coach was recognized with the "Man of the Season" award.

Running and Walking

Sure, you can run or walk just about anywhere in creation. One good place to do that includes downtown Wilmington, where you can jog over the bridges, do the hills and enjoy historic surroundings at the same time. You may want to check out some of the following prime locations or participate in one of the area's several annual racing events. Also check our Track and Field section later in this chapter.

Brunswick County Parks & Recreation Walking Club
Parks & Recreation Building, Government Plaza, Bolivia • (910) 253-2670, (800) 222-4790

Participants keep a daily log of miles walked. Rewards of a T-shirt to those who walk over 300 miles and a T-shirt and plaque for those who walk over 1,000 miles in the calendar year are given.

Greenfield Park
U.S. Hwy. 421 (Carolina Beach Rd.), Wilmington

Among the most beautiful places in Wilmington to jog or walk is the 4.5-mile loop around Greenfield Lake, south of downtown. The scenic paved path bears mile markers and follows the undulating lake shore across two wooden foot bridges (slippery when wet).

"The Loop" at Wrightsville Beach

This scenic sidewalk circuit is an approximately 2.45-mile course popular among locals. It encompasses a portion of the perimeter of Wrightsville Beach Park along Causeway Drive, plus Lumina Avenue and Salisbury Street. Bring the pooch — there's a free Dog Bar (serving only water) beside Bryant Real Estate at corner of N. Lumina and Salisbury plus two additional doggy fountains along the route. Benches and drinking water are available for people, too.

Wilmington Roadrunners Club
c/o YMCA of Wilmington, 2710 Market St., Wilmington • (910) 251-9622

The Roadrunners, based at the Y, sponsor races, picnics, fun runs and evening runs; provide information on technique and safety; and welcome entire families. Also sponsored by the club is the Cape Fear Flyers youth track organization. Membership in the Roadrunners Club includes newsletter and magazine subscriptions, discounts on gear, the opportunity to take a discounted corporate membership in the YMCA, plus other perks.

Wilmington Athletic Club
**2026 S. 16th St., Wilmington
• (910) 343-5950**

The region's largest, most complete fitness

facility, the new Wilmington Athletic Club (WAC), offers outstanding facilities and clubs for runners.

Annual Races

Races of different sorts are popular in our area — thanks to the gentle terrain and mild weather. Just a few of the regulars are listed here, but if you keep an eye on the Wilmington *Star-News* "Sports," "Today," "Neighbors" and "Currents" sections, you'll likely find a host more. Some places in Wilmington to pick up event brochures and flyers are:

Boseman's Sporting Goods, 5050 New Centre Drive, (910) 799-5990

Dick's Sporting Goods, 816 S. College Road, (910) 793-1904

Great Outdoor Provision Company, 3501 Oleander Drive, (910) 343-1648

Omega Sports, 3501 Oleander Drive, (910) 762-7217

Play It Again Sports, 3530 S. College Road, (910) 791-1572

AIDS Walk Wilmington
1821 Wrightsville Ave., Wilmington • (910) 431-9039

Annually in September, a fund-raising 11/2-mile walk benefits local not-for-profit organizations supporting our area's HIV-positive community, such as Cure AIDS of Wilmington and the HIV Care Consortium.

Battleship Half Marathon and Hardee's 5K Run
c/o YMCA of Wilmington, 2710 Market St., Wilmington • (910) 251-9622

Sponsored by Hardee's and organized by the Wilmington Roadrunners Club, this Half Marathon race (13.1 miles) is a challenging run that goes over the bridges along the waterfront, through downtown Wilmington and around Greenfield Lake. The 5K takes place at the Battleship. Both races start and finish at the Battleship. This event is held mid-November.

Buddy Walk
Down's Syndrome Connection of Wilmington • (910) 796-8968

Greenfield Park is the location for a one-mile walk in October, which is Down's Syndrome Awareness Month. This event raises money to support research, education, support and advocacy programs offered by the National Down's Syndrome Society.

Historic Wilmington Foundation 5K Run
Historic Wilmington Foundation, 702 Market St., Wilmington • (910) 762-2511

This annual event is held to benefit historic preservation in the evening of the fourth Thursday in July. In addition to the 5K run, there's a one-mile walk. Sponsors change each year. Contact the Foundation for information and registration.

Leprechaun Run
New Hanover-Pender Medical Society Alliance, Wilmington • (910) 790-5800

The Leprechaun Run consists of a 5K run and a 1-mile run/walk held at Wrightsville Beach each year on the Sunday closest to St. Patrick's Day. The 1-mile run/walk is an out-and-back course held entirely on the beach; the first half of the 5K course is on paved road and the last half on the beach. The Leprechaun Run welcomes participants of all ages.

A post-race awards party is held at the Blockade Runner Resort Hotel. For the 5K Run, cash prizes and trophies go to the 1st, 2nd, 3rd, and Masters male and female overall winners; trophies are awarded to the top three male and female winners in each of 10 age groups. For the 1-mile run/walk, trophies go to the top three male and female winners. Sponsored by the New Hanover-Pender Medical Society Alliance, the Leprechaun Run is managed and officiated by the Wilmington Roadrunners Club. Proceeds benefit local health care projects and programs.

MS Walk
National Multiple Sclerosis Society, Eastern North Carolina Chapter • (919) 834-0678, (800) FIGHTMS ext. 1, (800) 344-4867

The MS Walk in early April is a fund-raising event in which participants of all ages raise and collect pledges and walk the loop around Greenfield Lake. Incentives and prizes are awarded. Register by calling the office.

The Wilmington YMCA Tri-Span Run
c/o YMCA of Wilmington, 2710 Market St., Wilmington • (910) 251-9622

Sponsored by the YMCA of Wilmington and several area businesses, the Tri-Span 10K and 5K run takes place around the first of July. The 10K course crosses all three bridges along the Wilmington waterfront, the 5K goes through historic downtown Wilmington.

Seaside Shuffle 5K

c/o YMCA of Wilmington, 2710 Market St., Wilmington • (910) 251-9622

Organized by the Wilmington Roadrunners Club, this event benefits the United States Marine Corps Toys For Tots program. Held in Wrightsville Beach on a November afternoon, the Seaside Shuffle begins at the Blockade Runner Resort, goes to the Coast Guard Station, then returns to the hotel.

North Carolina Oyster Festival Road Race

South Brunswick Islands Chamber of Commerce • (800) 426-6644

The Oyster Fest Road Race is part of Ocean Isle Beach's North Carolina Oyster Festival, held the third weekend in October. Held on Saturday morning, this fun event is open to all ages. Three races include 10K, 5K and a 1-mile Fun Run. The race begins and ends at the pier. Call the Chamber office for more information or to register. Preregistration deadline is mid-October.

Bald Head Island Maritime Classic Road Race

Bald Head Island Management • (910) 457-7500

The Maritime Classic takes place the first Saturday in November and features a 10K and 5K footrace along some of the most scenic byways in the region, ranging through dense maritime forest, open meadow and through a manicured golf and beach community. Preregistration includes the ferry ride from Southport.

Skateboarding

Most public areas are off-limits to skateboarders and in-line skaters. That means no boarding on streets, sidewalks, parking lots, boardwalks or other tempting places. Skateboarding is permitted on the UNCW campus, where responsible boarders who respect property may ride freely. Bald Head Island allows boarding on roadways. Also, we are fortunate to have several well-designed, safe skate parks where boarding is very much alive and well. Check these out.

The Skate Barn

155 Pansy Ln., Hampstead • (910) 270-3497

This is the area's indoor skateboarding facility of note. Formerly known as the Middle School Indoor Skate Park, The Skate Barn features a 6-foot ramp, a 3-foot and a 5-foot-deep bowl and a full street course as well as an accessories shop, snack machines, video games and a Foosball table. Release forms must be signed to use the facility (parents or guardians must sign for children younger than 18). To get there, take U.S. 17 to Hampstead, turn west onto Peanut Road, then right onto unpaved Pansy Lane. The Skate Barn is open noon to 10 PM Monday through Friday; 11 AM until 1 PM for beginners on Saturday; 1 to 10 PM for everyone else; and Sunday 1 to 6 PM during the summer.

Vineyard Skate Park

4702 S. College Rd., Wilmington • (910) 397-9040

This all-steel outdoor park invites skateboarders, in-line skaters and bikers to enjoy 10,000 square feet of great fun. VSP has a 40-foot by 80-foot street course with pyramid, rails, boxes, roll over, 3-foot, 4-foot and 5-foot quarter pipes, 4-foot banks and a 6-foot mini-vert quarter pipe. Adding to the fun are a 2-foot half pipe banking onto the street course and a 48-foot-long 3-foot, 4-foot, 5-foot half pipe connecting to a 30-foot by 50-foot figure-eight bowl with a spine and roll over. New in 2002 is beginner's street course, which includes a back-to-back 2-foot ramp, two banks and a small pyramid.

Parties are welcome. Well supervised by adults with first aid and CPR training, VSP provides a safe, drug and alcohol-free environment where violence and profanity are not permitted. Helmet and liability form are required. The cost of membership is $25; initial registration is $5. Per visit fees are $3 for members and $5 for non-members.

Summer hours are Monday through Saturday 1 to 10 PM, except Wednesday, when the park is closed, and Sunday 3 to 10 PM. Winter hours are Sunday through Friday 3 to 10 PM, except Wednesday, when the park is closed, and Saturday noon to 10 PM. Call for holiday or weather-related closings.

Greenfield Grind Skate Park

Greenfield Park, U.S. Hwy. 421, Wilmington • (910) 362-8222

The City of Wilmington's lighted outdoor skate park is open to both in-line skaters and skateboarders. All use the same area, which features a banked street course, hips, rails, bowls and ledges. In the spring, the Park hosts the Grind Games where participants of all levels go head to head in several skilled categories including street, pool and best trick. Watch the paper for notices or call the Park for information about this popular event.

It's never too soon to teach a kid something new.

Photo: Jay Tervo

Entry fee is $2 for non-members; members are admitted free. Annual membership rate for New Hanover County residents is $50, all others $75. A helmet and waiver are required and skaters must be at least 7 years old; 12 and younger must have parental supervision. Skate park hours are: Mondays closed, Tuesday through Saturday noon to 10 PM and Sunday 1 to 8 PM.

Oak Island Skate Park
49th St. SE, Oak Island • (910) 278-5518

Even if you are a mere spectator sitting in the bleachers, you will enjoy watching the creativity and athletic ability displayed at this skate park designed by the youth of Oak Island. The 140-foot by 60-foot skate park contains combinations of quarter pipes, half pipe, banks, street spine, fly box, spine and pyramid none of which exceeds four feet in height. Users are required to wear protective equipment including helmet, knee and elbow pads, and wrist guards. Skate boards, inline skates and roller skates are acceptable, but must have rubber wheels and be in good working condition. Regular sessions are mainly 3 to 8 PM but sessions grouped according to age and/or skill level are also scheduled. Call the recreation center for times and fees or stop by to pick up a brochure.

Soccer

Soccer fever continues to sweep this area. Youth and adult leagues are growing in popularity, and the fields are constantly busy on weekends. Perhaps the best news for parents and players is that the investment necessary to play soccer is fairly low, generally limited to a onetime registration fee averaging $55 and shin guards that can cost less than $20. Wilmington is home to the United Soccer Leagues professional team, the Wilmington Hammerheads.

Wilmington Hammerheads
420 Raleigh St., Wilmington
• (910) 796-0076

The Pro Select League Hammerheads call Legion Sports Complex on Carolina Beach Road their home. In addition to hosting other professional soccer teams for exciting matches, the team conducts affordable, specialized clinics and camps. Individual instruction for players and coaches is available also. Clinics run year round and include spring break and summer sessions. With an average of 1,000 kids registering, it pays to sign up early. Call for information about programs and matches.

Cape Fear Soccer Association
6726 Netherlands Dr. #700, Wilmington
• **(910) 392-0306**

Boasting 205 teams and more than 3,200 players in the recreational division alone, this association, a member of the U.S. Soccer Federation, is the area's predominant soccer organization. Programs include a coed adult league. The five adult leagues include an A men's open division, an over 30 men's division, a coed B league and a C league for pick-up games. League play proceeds in two yearly cycles, fall and spring, with the year-end Hanover Cup tournament beginning in late April.

The Soccer Association offers every child and adult the opportunity to play at his or her own skill level. Teams are provided in two recreational leagues (one for youth through age 19 and one for adults), a classic league and a challenge league. Recreational League teams are open to all players without tryouts. The Youth Recreational League is a participation league in which coaches are required to play every player who constructively participates in at least one practice a week. (No scores or records are kept for the noncompetitive teams.) Recreational registration is in June and in December. Classic and Challenge league teams are formed through trials and may travel around the region and outside the state, as tournaments determine; tryouts are in May.

Professionally licensed coaches lead all teams, and all matches are refereed. Most games are held at the Hugh MacRae athletic fields (behind Hoggard High School off Shipyard Boulevard), Emma Trask Middle School fields (2900 N. College Road), and Ogden Park on Saturdays and some Sunday afternoons. The association also offers coaching clinics, uniforms, access to supplementary insurance, newsletters, tournaments, spring break and summer camps.

Pleasure Island Soccer Association (PISA)
609 Columbia Ave., Carolina Beach
• **(910) 458-6564**

A small town and a friendly recreation atmosphere make the PISA very appealing, as evidenced by rapid growth the past several years. Although membership is small — about 250 kids — enthusiasm and spirit are huge. Three coed age groups are: 5 to 6, 7 to 9, and 10 to 12. All matches are refereed by certified referees. Registration fee is only $35, which includes uniforms, awards, six to eight regular season games, a post-season tournament and a post-season party.

Soccer Stop
5725 Oleander Dr., Ste. B-5, Wilmington
• **(910) 792-1500**

The only dedicated shop of its kind in the area, Soccer Stop is co-owned and operated by a former professional player with the Wilmington Hammerheads, someone who knows soccer inside-out. Apparel, accessories, player gear and even some field equipment can all be found at Soccer Stop. Discounts apply for registered local league players. The store is in the Oleander Oaks strip mall across from Bert's Surf Shop.

YMCA of Wilmington
2710 Market St., Wilmington
• **(910) 251-9622**

The Y sponsors league games for boys and girls ages 3 through 11 during the spring and fall.

Brunswick County Parks & Recreation
Parks & Recreation Bldg., Government Complex, Bolivia • (910) 253-4357, (800) 222-4790

From September through November, Brunswick County Parks & Recreation organizes youth soccer for players ages 5 through 14 (the older players must still be in middle school). Players must furnish their own equipment.

Onslow County Parks & Recreation
1244 Onslow Pines Rd., Jacksonville
• **(910) 347-5332**

Onslow Parks & Recreation hosts a league for adults age 30 and older; play is from February to May; an adult women's soccer league (ages 18 and up) plays from August to October. Games are seven-on-seven. Teams can register for $225 and $6 per player, unlimited roster. Games are played at Hubert Bypass Park in the town of Hubert, convenient to the northern reaches of this guide's coverage.

Softball

This popular sport gives ballplayers of all ages many opportunities to join leagues or indulge in games for fun on diamonds in local parks. Except in winter, fields are often heavily scheduled for league play, especially in the evenings and on weekends. Pickup games must defer to league teams. Churches and community recreation departments frequently have solid programs as well. Here are a few organizations that sponsor softball leagues in our area.

Cape Fear Optimist Club, (910) 762-7065
Supper Optimist Club, (910) 791-5272
Winter Park Optimist Club, (910) 791-3566

City of Wilmington Parks, Recreation and Downtown Services

302 Willard St., Wilmington
• (910) 343-3682

The Recreation Division hosts 80 adult men's, women's and coed leagues, including a league for seniors, during the spring, summer and fall. Team registration for the summer/fall season is in August. Registration for the spring/summer season is in March. Play is at Empie Park and Trask Middle School. Fees range from $200 to $540 per team. Call for information and registration forms.

New Hanover County Parks Department

230 Market Place Dr., Ste. 120, Room 103, Wilmington • (910) 798-7198

Softball leagues and other groups desiring to use diamonds in the county parks need to reserve them through the Parks Department office. Also, this department maintains a list of organizations offering adult and youth softball; call them for contact information.

Wilmington Senior Softball Association

7231 Lounsberry Ct., Wilmington
• (910) 791-0852

Well-established for years in the North, senior softball made its Wilmington debut with one team in 1995. Now the local association boasts six teams with a total of almost 100 men ages 55 to 76. Spring training commences the first Tuesday in March; the season of seven-inning games runs from the first Tuesday in April through October. Doubleheaders are played on Tuesdays and Thursdays in Empie Park located at Park Avenue and Independence Boulevard in Wilmington, Ogden Park on Market Street in Ogden and Veterans Park off South College Road. Warmups start at 8:15 AM and play begins at 9. All the teams are sponsored by local businesses. Registration for the season (50 games) is $50. Worthy of note: In 2001 all three division teams won the their respective division state championships; it was the first time ever that the three teams went undefeated. For information, contact League Commissioner Phil Rose at (910) 791-0852.

Wrightsville Beach Summer Softball League

1 Bob Sawyer Dr., Wrightsville Beach
• (910) 256-7925

Wrightsville Beach Parks & Recreation organizes league play for teams of all skill levels. Registration for the summer league opens in late March or early April, and games start in May. Registration for the fall league opens in August with play beginning in September. The cost is $255 per team, plus a nominal additional fee for each player not a resident of Wrightsville Beach, up to $110 per team.

Carolina Beach Parks and Recreation

1121 N. Lake Park Blvd., Carolina Beach
• (910) 458-2977

In spring and fall, the Carolina Beach Parks and Recreation Department sponsors a men's softball league. Registration is $425 per team. Softballs are provided. Play is at Mike Chappell Park on Dow Road.

Brunswick County Parks and Recreation

Parks & Recreation Bldg., Government Complex, Bolivia • (910) 253-2670, (800) 222-4790

Brunswick County sponsors two fall adult leagues — a men's and a women's league; registration is in late July and play begins in September. Registration for the summer adult coed league is at the end of May; play starts in July. The fee is $400 per team of 20.

Softball - Girls Fastpitch

Tremendously popular in the south, fastpitch softball teams for girls up to 18 years abound, most of them travel extensively. To find teams, however, may be a bit of a challenge. Watch the local newspapers for notices, inquire at school or search online. Here are some we found that recruit area players.

Carolina BruZers, 14 and younger, Whiteville, Contact JoAnna Pridgen, (910) 642-5497.

Carolina Rockers, 14 and younger, 16 and younger, 18 and younger, Fayetteville, Contact Glen Rogers, (910) 424-1940

Coastal Breeze, 12 and younger, 14 and younger, Burgaw, Contact Tom Roper, (910) 259-9777

Hurricanes "Silver," 16 and younger, Goldsboro, Contact Trae Farthing, (910) 458-1468

Port City Cyclones, 16 and younger,

Wilmington, Contact Jeff Leeuwenburg, (910) 686-3107

Wilmington Waves, 14 and younger, Wilmington, Contact Jim Talton, (910) 395-2105

Tennis

Practically every large park and many smaller neighborhood parks have public tennis courts (see the Parks section at the end of this chapter). The legion Sports Complex on Carolina Beach road has newly refinished four lighted courts that are open until 11 PM seven days a week; no reservation required; for information call (910) 341-7855. In addition, often you can find courts at area golf clubs. Watch the local papers for tournament information.

The Wilmington Tennis League
3209 Amber Dr., Wilmington
• (910) 452-2941

With more than 1,700 players on 156 teams, the Wilmington Tennis League is one of the state's largest. A member of the Greater Wilmington Tennis Association, this USTA-affiliated league supports 10 levels of play: women's 2.5 to 4.5 and men's 3.0 to 5.0; it also runs a Senior League for players older than 50. Play runs from the end of February through May. Players must be members of the United States Tennis Association (USTA). New players should contact League Coordinator Anna Martin (910) 452-2941.

City of Wilmington Parks, Recreation and Downtown Services
302 Willard St., Wilmington
• (910) 343-3682

Mr. PeeWee tennis for ages 4 through 8 takes place May through June and July through August. Junior and adult clinics run from March through November. Play is at Empie Park. Call for more information and registration forms.

Tennis With Love
4303 Oleander Dr., Wilmington
• (910) 791-3128

If your racket needs repair or you need a new tennis outfit, stop by Tennis With Love in the Landmark Plaza across from Cape Fear Ford. This shop specializes in restringing tennis and racquetball frames and carries court clothing, shoes and accessories.

Wrightsville Beach Parks & Recreation
1 Bob Sawyer Dr., Wrightsville Beach
• (910) 256-7925

Wrightsville Beach Parks & Recreation offers private, semi-private and group tennis lessons for adults and youth (age groups 6-8, 9-12 and 13-16). Group lessons meet on Mondays and Wednesdays. Other lessons by appointment. Call for fees and hours or to schedule a lesson. A Ladies Singles Tennis Ladder for 2.5-3.0 players begins in early June; fees to join the ladder are $5 for Wrightsville Beach Residents and $7.50 for non-residents.

Squash

Wilmington Athletic Club
2026 S. 16th St., Wilmington • (910) 343-5950

This is only place to play squash in Wilmington. Need a game? The WAC game finder can locate an opponent of any level for you. Instruction is also available.

Triathlons/Adventure Races

Track and field is mostly school-related in this region, but there are a few other ways to participate. Also check the section on Running and Walking above.

Azalea Festival Triathlon
Set-Up, Inc., Wilmington • (910) 458-0299

This triathlon, sanctioned by the U.S. Triathlon Association, coincides with Wilmington's most famous annual festival, usually occurring on the second weekend in April. The event consists of a 300-yard pool swim, a 20K bike race and a 5K run. Except for some of the bike leg, the entire triathlon takes place on the UNCW campus in Wilmington. Contestants are divided into the nationally standard age and gender brackets. Registration begins January 1.

Greenfield Adventure Sprint
City of Wilmington Parks, Recreation and Downtown Services, 302 Willard St., Wilmington • (910) 343-3682

If you want a different challenge, try this one. A co-ed two-person team event, the course consists of canoeing 3 miles on Greenfield Lake, Mountain Biking (on/off road) for 16 miles, and trail running for 4 miles. In keeping with the adventure spirit, the race is run rain or shine.

Kure Beach Double Sprint Triathlon
Set-Up, Inc., Wilmington • (910) 458-0299

Here's an event tailored for overachievers.

After you get through the 400-meter ocean swim, the 1.5K run and the 10K bike legs, guess what? You get to do the entire thing all over again, in reverse-bike, run and swim. The overall distance is less than half that of an Olympic triathlon, but considering that this U.S. Triathlon Association-sanctioned race is in the heat of late June, the challenge is formidable. Contestants are divided into the nationally standard age and gender brackets. Registration begins January 1.

YMCA Triathlon
c/o YMCA of Wilmington, 2710 Market St., Wilmington • (910) 251-9622

Sponsored by the YMCA of Wilmington and the Two Wheeler Dealer, this is a sprint triathlon that takes place in Wrightsville Beach. Participants swim Banks Channel (1,500 meters), bicycle 12 miles and run a 5K (3.1 miles). This race starts in front of the Blockade Runner Resort and finishes at the park. In 2002, more than 700 people participated in this event, which is put on by Set-Up, Inc. Note: The Y has a Triathlon Club that offers coaching and training. Call for information.

Ultimate

Like any beach community worth its salt, Wilmington takes disc sports seriously. Ultimate is particularly popular in the Port City. Ultimate, which places heavy emphasis on sportsmanship and fair play is a seven-versus-seven team sport that combines throwing skill, speed and endurance. Players pass a flying disc (Frisbee) to one another until it is caught in the end zone for a goal. Having no referees, players call fouls and settle disputes themselves. Ultimate is one of the fastest growing team sports in the world.

The UNCW women's team (Seaweed) has won two National Collegiate Championships (1992 and 1996) and placed second in 2000. The UNCW men's team (Seamen) won a National Championship in 1993 and has advanced to the Nationals each of the last two seasons as the Atlantic Coast Regional Champion (2001 and 2002).

Wilmington's three current Ultimate club teams are: The Wahine (women), the Warriors (men) and HOSS (men's masters, over age 33); each advanced to the Club Nationals in Sarasota, Florida, in the fall of 2001, and HOSS did it again in 2002.

Wilmington Ultimate Frisbee Federation (WUFF)
Wilmington • (910) 794-1045

More than 100 players participate in Ultimate pick-up games that are open to anyone, and about 200 play in the WUFF Summer League, which is coed, for all ages and skill levels. Games are held at Castle Hayne Park off Parmalee Road at the end of Old Avenue, from June 1 to August 1.

In February, the City of Wilmington Parks, Recreation and Downtown Services and WUFF co-sponsor the WUFF Coed National Championships at Ogden Park; this is definitely THE single most competitive coed event of the year in ultimate Frisbee. Call Mike Gerics for information about the league, local teams and tournaments.

New Hanover Disc Club
Wilmington • (910) 793-1352

One of the world's fastest growing sports is Disc Golf, which combines the fun of Frisbee with the challenge and strategy of traditional golf. Instead of using clubs and balls, the game is played with specially designed discs that are somewhat smaller and heavier than regular flying discs and can travel very complicated paths. A Disc Golf course can have anywhere from nine to 27 holes (actually baskets on posts), though most are 18; course length is roughly one-third that of a ball golf course. Locally, Disc Golf can be played at Castle Hayne Park off Parmele Road at the end of Old Avenue — it's free and fun. Eighteen tee signs are now up and tee pads are coming soon as are benches for each hole. Call Mike Bozic for more information.

Volleyball

If you're not accustomed to playing in sand, you're in for a real workout, and if you survive, your improved agility and jumping may manifest themselves dramatically on a hard court. As you might expect, competition is fairly stiff, and local players generally take their games seriously. Sand volleyball courts are common in area parks and beaches, and anyone can use them, so enjoy!

Capt'n Bill's Backyard Grill
4240 Market St., Wilmington • (910) 762-0111

The only eight sand courts within the Wilmington city limits can be found at this popular volleyball-restaurant complex behind the North 17 Shopping Center. Year round, you can join a pickup game or register your team in one of Capt'n Bill's leagues, which are for all skill levels. Operated by the husband and wife team of John and Erin Musser, Capt'n Bill's has a friendly staff, hot food, cold drinks and 10 TV sets in its sports bar.

City of Wilmington Parks, Recreation and Downtown Services
302 Willard St., Wilmington
• **(910) 343-3682**

The City of Wilmington offers fall and spring co-ed indoor volleyball for adults. Six-person teams may register for the fall league in August and for the spring league in February; call for information and forms.

Wilmington Athletic Club
2026 S. 16th St., Wilmington
• **(910) 343-5950**

The region's largest, most complete fitness facility, the new Wilmington Athletic Club (WAC), offers outstanding facilities for volleyball enthusiasts.

Wrestling

Cape Fear Hurricanes
3118 Monticello Dr., Wilmington
• **(910) 799-7981**

One of two area teams in the East Coast Wrestling League, the Cape Fear Hurricanes offer a quality wrestling program that helps build a youngster's self-esteem, confidence and ability. Sanctioned by the AAU and USA, the Hurricanes accept wrestlers in grades K through 8 (boys and girls). The team practices two evenings a week and travels to tournaments statewide. The cost is $50 with a discounted fee of $25 for additional family members. Registration includes a T-shirt, shorts and AAU card. Call for more information and registration form.

Wilmington Warriors
454 N. Crestwood Dr., Wilmington
• **(910) 791-6209**

The Wilmington Warriors welcomes boys and girls in grades K through 8. The club's goal is to teach young people character and self-discipline through the sport of wrestling. Chartered through the Amateur Athletic Union (AAU) and part of the East Coast Wrestling League, the Warriors practice on Monday and Thursday from 6:30 to 8 PM at J. T. Hoggard High School field house, 4305 Shipyard Boule-

vard. Cost is $45 per participant, with a $5 discount for additional family members. This fee includes wrestling instruction, AAU membership, a T-shirt and sanctioned tournament entry fees. Practice begins the first Monday in December and goes through the end of February. Call for more information and registration form.

Yoga

In addition to the listings below, some fitness centers also offer classes. To find individual instructors, look for business cards and ads in local publications. Frequently, chiropractic offices, coffee shops and health food stores have yoga information available; or check the bulletin board at the Tidal Creek Food Co-op, 4406 Wrightsville Avenue, (910) 799-2667.

Wilmington Athletic Club
2026 S. 16th St., Wilmington
• **(910) 343-5950**

The Wilmington Athletic Club features a spacious yoga studio. Classes are held daily in various concentrations of yoga and are taught by top instructors.

Wilmington Yoga Center
5330 Oleander Dr., Ste. 200, Wilmington
• **(910) 350-0234**

Offering a full schedule of yoga classes conducted by experienced instructors, the Wilmington Yoga Center is located next to Cinema 6. The center offers classes throughout the day and evening for all levels; beginners and drop-ins are welcome. In addition, private classes are available for one-on-one instruction. Call for information and schedule of classes.

YMCA of Wilmington
2710 Market St., Wilmington
• **(910) 251-9622**

The Y offers regular yoga, Pilates and aerobics classes.

YWCA of Wilmington
2815 S. College Rd., Wilmington
• **(910) 799-6820**

Among the YWCA's Health and Wellness offerings, you'll find yoga classes to improve flexibility, breathing and body tone. Call for scheduled times and fees.

Wrightsville Beach Parks & Recreation
1 Bob Sawyer Dr., Wrightsville Beach
• **(910) 256-7925**

Wrightsville Beach Parks & Recreation offers year-round morning and evening classes emphasizing flexibility, alignment, conditioning and stress-reduction techniques. Gentle Yoga meets once a week for six weeks. Continuing Yoga is an advanced class that meets once a week for five weeks. Prices range from $26 to $28 for residents and $39 to $42 for non-residents. Drop-ins are welcome at $6 residents, $8 non-residents.

Fitness Centers

Many fine fitness centers along the coast offer state-of-the-art apparatus and certified instructors. Aerobics classes have become standard, as has the use of bikes, treadmills, free weights, stair-climbers and other equipment. Membership costs usually include a onetime registration fee plus a monthly fee for a required term, but some local centers cater to the short-term visitor by offering daily, weekly and monthly rates. Additional benefits at some clubs are referral rewards, travel passes that allow members to visit affiliated clubs around the country and suspension of membership for medical reasons or extended absence.

The larger, more sophisticated clubs offer a variety of amenities that may include a well-stocked pro shop, food bar or cafe serving healthy snacks and drinks, locker room facilities, nutritional supplement sales, tanning beds, spas, massages, child care and even laundry and dry-cleaning pickup/delivery.

City of Wilmington Boxing and Physical Fitness Center
302 N. S. 10th St., Wilmington
• (910) 341-7837, (910) 341-7872
The Boxing and Physical Fitness Center provides individuals and families opportunities to participate in traditional health club activities. Equipped with free weights, weight machines, treadmills, stationary bicycles and stairclimbers, the Center offers strength training, prescription exercise and cardiovascular workouts.

Classes in aerobics (including instructor training), funky jazz, kickboxing and Tae Bo are taught by certified instructors. A program geared toward the physically challenged is offered; call for details. Locker rooms and shower facilities are available. Memberships are among the best bargains in town just $40 for city residents and $75 for non-residents. Hours are Monday through Friday 9 AM to 8 PM and Saturday 10 AM to 2 PM; the center is closed on Sunday.

Carolina Beach Parks and Recreation
1121 N. Lake Park Blvd., Carolina Beach
• (910) 458-7416
Essentially a "do-it-yourself" fitness facility, the Recreation Center has a weight-training room and a cardiovascular room with limited equipment and instruction. For those wishing to play racquetball, the center has one court and will furnish racquets, balls and goggles. The hours are Monday through Friday from 9 AM to 9 PM, Saturday from 10 AM to 5 PM, and Sunday from 1 to 5 PM. Persons wishing to use the facilities must be at least 16 years of age. Also available are a basketball gym and locker and shower facilities.

Cory Everson's Aerobics & Fitness for Women
4620 Oleander Dr., Wilmington
• (910) 791-0030
Focusing exclusively on women's health, Cory Everson's offers a wide range of fitness activities. An expanded aerobics program includes sculpting, yoga and fitness evaluations. The club maintains a staff of certified personal trainers who can provide long-term personal training, though there's an additional charge. Also available are two Wolffe System tanning beds. The center is clean, nicely laid out and features state-of-the-art equipment, including Cybex and Nautilus equipment designed especially for women. Headphones may be connected through the personal E-Zone entertainment system in the cardiovascular area; these are great for listening without disturbing others. A plus is the newly renovated Kids Fun Center. Cory's has special rates for guests, corporate groups, seniors (65 and older), students and families. It's located near the southeast corner of Oleander Drive and College Road.

The Crest
a seaside fitness club
38 N. Lumina Ave., Wrightsville Beach
• (910) 509-3044
An inclusive club where you'll always feel welcome, The Crest offers the latest in cardio equipment, exercise machines and fitness expertise with seven certified personal trainers. Having a "laid back" atmosphere, this newly renovated club is open seven days a week. Pilates, yoga and kickboxing are among The Crest's group classes. Besides a good workout, you can get a massage and nutritious smoothies, juices and hot drinks. They have many types of memberships including multi-visit and daily visit punch cards. Their Phuza Juice Smoothie

SPORTS, FITNESS AND PARKS

training equipment, the Quick Fit system doesn't use weight stacks, which greatly diminishes soreness and injury.

Gold's Gym
7979 Market St., Wilmington
• **(910) 686-1766**
127 S. College Rd., Wilmington
• **(910) 392-3999**
4310 Shipyard Blvd., Wilmington
• **(910) 350-8289**
5026 Market St., Wilmington
• **(910) 794-9100**

Meticulously equipped and maintained, Gold's Gym now offers four locations. Gold's is a full-service fitness center known for its attentive staff and its array of equipment. It was voted Wilmington's most popular fitness center for six years in a local poll. Gold's is noted for personally designed exercise programs and one-on-one training by certified trainers. All locations offer the newest circuit and cardiovascular equipment available with free childcare, locker rooms with showers and dry saunas. The center at 5026 Market Street is open 24 hours, every day.

Gold's pro-shops offer sports clothing, smoothie bars and a large selection of supplements and power bars. Group exercise classes vary at each club, ranging from yoga and pilates to power punch, Body Pump, kick boxing, and senior classes. Call the Group X hotline for daily updates on all classes, (910) 792-9000. The Longleaf Mall location has Wilmington's only climbing tread wall, while Market Place Mall has Reebok Cycling. Porter's Neck and Longleaf locations both have state-of-the-art heated workout pools with group classes offered and a Guppies program for kids. Members of Gold's Gym are entitled to use these three locations in Wilmington and over 650-plus other locations worldwide.

Bar, Tanning Salon and Vitamin and Sports Supplement Store are available and open to the public.

Curves For Women
**8211 Market St.,
Wilmington**
• **(910) 686-6424**
**5725 Oleander Dr.,
Wilmington**
• **(910) 791-1115**
**5941-F Carolina Beach
Rd., Wilmington**
• **(910) 313-2466**
4381Port Loop Rd., SE, Southport
• **(910) 454-8365**
4830-B Main St., Shallotte
• **(910) 754-8607**
10195 Breach Dr. SW, Calabash
• **(910) 575-0572**

> **INSIDERS' TIP**
> Take advantage of the many environmental education programs offered by the state parks. Rangers guide you on exciting explorations where you'll learn fascinating facts as you wander nature's classroom.

Get a complete workout in just 30 minutes utilizing the Quick Fit system found only at Curves For Women. Fast, fun and proven effective, the Curves method combines strength training and cardiovascular fitness in an innovative way that's easy to master and totally self-controlled. Curves provides an exercise environment designed for women plus nutritional guidance and weight management counseling. The Quick Fit system incorporates hydraulic resistance equipment, alternating with low wooden exercise platforms and peppy music; a cue tape directs participants to change stations every 35 seconds and check their heart rate every eight minutes. In contrast to other strength

Walden's 24 Hour Fitness
**North 17 Shopping Center, 4350 Market St., Wilmington • (910) 763-7444
5621-B Carolina Beach Rd., Wilmington**
• **(910) 395-7002**

Can't sleep at night? Can't seem to fit your workouts to any fitness center's hours? One of Walden's two locations could be for you. Walden's is the area's only health club with doors open around the clock, seven days a week.

SPORTS, FITNESS AND PARKS

Walden's offers all the free weights and cardiovascular training equipment you'd expect, plus personal training and circuit training. You'll find the North 17 Shopping Center just west of Kerr Avenue. The Carolina Beach Road location is in Monkey Junction next to Taco Bell. Personal trainers are available Monday through Friday 12 to 8 PM and Saturday from 12 to 5 PM.

Wilmington Athletic Club
2026 S. 16th St., Wilmington
• (910) 343-5950

The region's largest, most complete fitness facility, the new Wilmington Athletic Club (WAC), is not only a spectacular place to work out, play, indulge yourself and improve your health status, it's a tremendous bargain. Locally owned and operated, this outstanding facility has just about everything you could want or need, from state-of-the-art Pilates and cardiovascular training equipment to a complete day spa. The Club's refurbished two-floor interior is entirely air conditioned, clean and attractive. From the locker rooms to the aerobics and yoga studio, this place is first class.

A long list of activities can be accommodated, including volleyball, basketball, racquetball, squash, badminton, swimming and running. The inviting, competition-size outdoor pool is open during warm-weather months for swim lessons, aqua aerobics classes and fun. How about trying a "road trip" using the latest indoor cycling bikes? Or maybe you'd like to tone those muscles in the expanded weight room furnished with highly advanced Cybex Eagle machines.

Personal training, VO2 max assessments, weight management, sport-specific training, senior fitness programs, social events, youth camps and massage therapy are just a few of the special features that make the Wilmington Athletic Club an all-around place for the entire family. Activity-oriented child care is available while mom or dad work out, and a terrific after-school care program is available to keep kids busy and constructively occupied.

The Wilmington Athletic Club, open to members and their guests, is affiliated with the International Health, Racquet and Sports Club Association (IHRSA) and offers reciprocity privileges through the "Passport Program;" members may use affiliated facilities around the world for free or at a discounted rate.

Coastal Tumblegym
220 Winner Ave., Carolina Beach
• (910) 458-9490

The certified instructors at Coastal Tumblegym specialize in gymnastics, tumbling, cheerleading and trampoline instruction for children ranging from preschoolers to high schoolers. Friday nights bring kids age 3 and older to open-gym sessions (a.k.a. Parents' Night Out) from 7 to 10 PM, which are open to non-members as well. Coastal Tumblegym also offers a variety of party services, including birthday parties in the gym or your home, team parties and parties for church and youth groups (also see our Kidstuff chapter). The facility's location just off U.S. 421 behind True Value (Island Tackle & Hardware) in Carolina Beach is a particular boon to those living or vacationing on Pleasure Island.

YMCA of Wilmington
2710 Market St., Wilmington
• **(910) 251-9622**

Offering a wide variety of fitness and educational activities, the YMCA of Wilmington features ample facilities, such as a large gym, two indoor pools, a Jacuzzi, four racquetball courts, free weight room, Cybex equipment and even sunbathing decks. Athletic fields, including a track, are also available. Aerobics (including water exercise), arthritis aquatics, wellness classes and massage therapy are just a few of the Y's vast offerings. League sports for youth are organized seasonally.

YWCA of Wilmington
2815 S. College Rd., Wilmington
• **(910) 799-6820**

Indoor activities include low-impact and step aerobics, toning classes, dance in many styles and karate. Programs for both kids and adults are available. The YWCA offers pre-school and kindergarten, full-service day care and after-school programs.

Wrightsville Beach Parks & Recreation
1 Bob Sawyer Dr., Wrightsville Beach
• **(910) 256-7925**

Wrightsville Beach Parks & Recreation offers low impact (age 50 and older) and tone and stretch (all ages) aerobics classes on a regular basis. Call for class times and fees ($1 to $3). Pilates classes are offered three days and one evening a week; a beginners class meets Tuesday and Thursday mornings.

Body Dimensions
5241 Main St., Shallotte • (910) 754-3808

Emphasizing the natural approach to lifelong fitness, the folks at Body Dimensions offer a full line of free weights, some aerobics classes, treadmills, stair climbers and Badger/Magnum strength systems. Visitors to the area benefit from daily, weekly, monthly and other short-term rates. The center is open every day except Sunday and is in the South Park Plaza along U.S. 17 Business (Main Street).

Brunswick County Parks & Recreation
Parks & Recreation Bldg., Government Complex, Bolivia • (910) 253-2670, (800) 222-4790

For $15 per month or $5 per drop-in, you may participate in step aerobics classes (pro-

vide your own step) twice each week at two Brunswick County locations: the Town Creek and Leland community buildings. Low-impact aerobics is also offered twice weekly at the Lockwood Folly and Waccamaw Community Buildings. Classes run from January to June and September to November. Registration is available on location, and the one-hour classes usually get underway at around 6:30 PM. Call for specific information.

Curves for Women
13775 U.S. Hwy. 50, Ste. 103., Surf City
• **(910) 329-1221**

This new, well attended physical fitness center in Surf City offers 30 minutes of training with the benefits of 90 minutes. It is a complete program, designed for women providing strength training to protect muscles and bone density as well as weight loss guidance. Starting with a counseling appointment, potential clients receive a figure analysis, have the opportunity to try the machines and assistance in setting goals and how to reach them. Owner, Julie Medin, finds Curves a great place for mothers and daughters to spend some quality, healthy time together. Curves membership has options that include travel passes allowing Topsail Island vacationers to keep up with their fitness program. Curves is open Monday to Friday 8 AM to 1 PM and 4 to 7 PM and Saturdays 8 AM to noon.

Forever Fit Fitness Center
214 Sneads Ferry Rd., Sneads Ferry
• **(910) 327-2293**

Focusing on a balanced regimen for fitness, Forever Fit offers strength training, a full line of cardio equipment, group training in step, circuit, and dance, a personal trainer on staff and AFAA-certified instructors. Water aerobics classes are offered in June, July and August. Visitors are welcome and can pay daily and weekly rates; individual memberships begin as low as $40 per month. Forever Fit is convenient to the northern Topsail Island area.

Parks

The southern costal region is rich in parks ranging from inviting walkways along the river in downtown Wilmington to the Fort Fisher State Recreation Area with seven miles of beach, wildlife reserves and visitor center. You can find neighborhood parks, beautiful gardens, hiking trails, playgrounds, athletic fields and family-friendly county facilities. Here are some places for you to explore.

New Hanover County

The New Hanover County Parks Department maintains 25 parks, three trails and two gardens. Facilities vary and may include gazebos, tennis courts, athletic areas such as soccer or baseball/softball fields, playground equipment, a Disc Golf course, an equestrian ring or picnic tables. In some cases, a fee is required. For information on specific parks or to make facility reservations, call (910) 798-7181.

Hugh MacRae Park
S. College Rd. and Oleander Dr., Wilmington

One of the oldest and best-known parks in the county, 98-acre Hugh McRae Park is well-known for its outdoor concerts and Annual Chili Cook-Off. The tranquil pond, alluring garden and picturesque gazebo are very popular for weddings, especially in spring when the azaleas are in bloom and the weather has once again turned balmy. Facilities include playground, ball fields, lighted tennis courts, equestrian ring, picnic shelters and restrooms.

Ogden Park
7069 Market St., Ogden

This 125-acre county park, located between Wilmington and Wrightsville Beach, is destined to be the flagship park of the county's north side, as Hugh MacRae Park is to the central region of the county. The park offers four baseball fields, lighted soccer/football fields, lighted tennis courts, picnic areas, restrooms, playgrounds, walking/jogging trails and a concession building. The entrance is on the west (southbound) side of Market Street, about 0.2 miles north of the intersection of Military Cutoff Road, a few minutes north of Wilmington city limits. Look for the entrance beside Mt. Ararat AME Church at Planter's Walk.

Snow's Cut Park
River Rd., near Snow's Cut Bridge

Divided into two sections along River Road, one directly beneath the bridge and the other some 100 yards west, this county park offers shady picnic grounds, sheltered tables, a gazebo and pedestrian access to Snow's Cut. It is very near Carolina Beach Family Campground. Call (910) 798-7181 to reserve the shelter.

Castle Hayne Park
Off Parmale Rd., at the end of Old Ave., Castle Hayne

Up in the far north-central part of New Hanover County, this 50-acre park is home to several sporting teams. Castle Hayne is a great family park. You'll find lighted tennis courts, soccer/football fields, playground equipment, picnic shelters, a ball field, restrooms and the area's first Disc Golf course.

Veterans Park
Carolina Beach Rd., Wilmington

Veterans Park is a unique development of educational, recreational and cultural facilities in the southern portion of New Hanover County. This 212-acre complex is home to Ashley High School, Murray Middle School, the 1,000-seat Minnie Evans Performing Arts Center and an array of athletic facilities, playgrounds and walking trails.

Wilmington

The 32 public parks maintained by the City of Wilmington differ widely. From the historic Riverwalk of downtown's Riverfront Park and the athletic fields of Empie Park to the sculpted benches of Carolina Courtyard and sunken cypress stands of Greenfield Lake, there is always a park nearby with the kind of recreation or quiet you desire. Of city parks, we list a cross-section of the larger ones. Inquiries about particular facilities at Wilmington parks should be directed to the Wilmington Parks, Recreation and Downtown Services Department office, (910) 341-7855. To reserve picnic shelters at any of the New Hanover County parks, call (910) 341-7181.

Empie Park
Park Ave. at Independence Blvd.

Empie has lighted baseball fields, picnic shelters, a playground, bike racks and a concession stand. Due to popular demand, tennis courts here could be reserved in advance ($2 for city residents with a city discount card; $4 nonresidents) by calling the Wilmington Athletics office at (910) 343-3681.

Greenfield Park
U.S. Hwy. 421 (Carolina Beach Rd.)

Greenfield Lake and its surrounding gardens are the centerpiece of Wilmington's park system and a scenic wonder that changes character from season to season. Among the city's oldest parks, it was at one time a working plantation and, later, carnival grounds. The lake attracts a wide variety of birds and contains alligators. When the azaleas bloom in early spring, the area explodes in a dazzling profusion of color. Stands of flowering magnolia, dogwood, long leaf pine and live oak — many hung with Spanish moss — line the shady 5-mile Lake Shore Drive. On the north side of the 158-acre park are lighted tennis courts, playgrounds, picnic areas, skate park, concession stand and docks where canoes and paddleboats are available for rent. A free public boat ramp is on W. Lake Shore Drive immediately east of U.S. 421. The benches at mid-span on Lions Bridge are a wonderful spot to relax on a breezy day. Open-air performances are presented in summer at the amphitheater off W. Lake Shore Drive, adjacent to the Rotary Wheel.

Legion Sports Complex
U.S. Hwy. 421 (Carolina Beach Rd.), Wilmington

Beside Greenfield Lake, approximately 1.75 miles south of the Cape Fear Memorial Bridge, the newly renovated Legion Stadium is home to New Hanover High School sports teams. Also calling the Complex home are the 2002 National Finalist Wilmington Hammerheads, a member of the Professional D-3 United Soccer League, and the Wilmington Sharks, a collegiate Coastal Plain League baseball team. The site also has lighted athletic fields, tennis courts and a swimming pool as well as plenty of parking.

Riverfront Park
Water St., Wilmington

For many locals, this park epitomizes Wilmington life. Once congested with the wharves of the state's busiest port, the newly expanded Riverwalk is now a place for quiet strolls, sightseeing, shopping, live outdoor music and dining. The sternwheeler Henrietta III docks here. You'll also find a visitors information booth. Historic sailing ships visiting town often dock here and usually offer tours.

Robert Strange Park
Eighth and Nun Sts., Wilmington

The heart of this park is its swimming pool. Other facilities include a recreation center, restrooms, a playground, picnic shelters, softball fields and lighted tennis and basketball courts.

Wrightsville Beach

Wrightsville Beach Park
Causeway Dr., Wrightsville Beach

This sprawling recreation and athletic facility is impossible to miss when traveling Causeway Drive. It spans 13 acres and includes tennis courts, basketball courts, a softball field, a football/soccer field, sand volleyball courts, playground equipment and a fitness trail. The 2.45-mile sidewalk Loop, bordering much of the park and traversing both of the island's bridges, is popular among walkers and joggers. Parking and restrooms are available.

Carolina Beach and Kure Beach

Carolina Beach State Park
Dow Rd., Carolina Beach • (910) 458-8206

This is one of the most biologically diverse parks in North Carolina and a contender for the most beautiful park in the area. Maritime forest, sandhill terrain, waterfront and sand ridges support carnivorous plants and centuries-old live oaks. Six miles of easy trails wind throughout the park. The marina offers boat ramps ($4) and 42 boat slips off the Cape Fear River. Excellent overnight camping facilities are available. The park is on Pleasure Island, 1 mile north of Carolina Beach and less than a half-mile from U.S. 421, off Dow Road. Day use is free.

Carolina Lake Park
Atlanta Ave. and U.S. Hwy. 421, Carolina Beach

Primarily a picnic site, this 11-acre park has four small gazebos, sheltered picnic tables and a playground.

Mike Chappell Park
Dow Rd., Carolina Beach

Two lighted ball fields and a football/soccer field make up the largest area of this 10-acre park, which also offers picnic tables, two tennis courts, two lighted sand volleyball courts and a playground. The park is bounded by Sumter Avenue and Clarendon Boulevard.

Fort Fisher State Recreation Area
U.S. Hwy. 421 S., Kure Beach • (910) 458-5798

Miles of white sandy beach, salt marshes, tidal creeks, mudflats and wildlife habitats make the Fort Fisher State Recreation Area a true treasure among the state's park offerings. Located on the southern tip of Pleasure Island, with the Atlantic Ocean on the east and the Cape Fear River on the west, this well-maintained park offers visitors a wide variety of pleasurable activities. Swimming, sunbathing, strolling and shelling are among the favorites for beachgoers. Fishing, hiking and birding rank high with many folks, along with boating or canoeing through shallow bays and channels. Loggerhead turtles and other endangered species make nests in the park's protected areas. Park staff offer interpretive and environmental education programs as well as surf fishing clinics; call for availability. Facilities include a Visitors Center, concession stand (10 AM to 6 PM, Memorial Day through Labor Day), restrooms and outside showers.

The Cove at Fort Fisher State Historic Site
U.S. Hwy. 421 S., Kure Beach
• (910) 458-8257

The Cove is a beautiful getaway about 6 miles south of Carolina Beach. Bordering the beach and a rocky sea wall, a grove of windswept live oaks provides shade for the picnic tables and grills. Come to fish and sunbathe but don't swim. Dangerous currents and underwater hazards make swimming extremely hazardous. Parking is available south of the area near the Fort Fisher Memorial and at the Fort Fisher State Historic Site museum across the road.

Joe Eakes Park
K Ave. at Seventh St., Kure Beach

This small park, a short walk from the beach, offers a playground, two tennis courts, volleyball and basketball courts.

Brunswick County

The six following district parks are maintained by the Brunswick County Parks & Recreation Department. All have excellent facilities, including tennis courts, ball fields, football/soccer fields, basketball courts, playgrounds and picnic shelters. Most of them also feature shuffleboard courts and horseshoe pits, plus community buildings for use by groups for such occasions as reunions, exercise classes and other events. For specific information about any of the district parks, or to reserve picnic shelters and community buildings, call (910) 253-2670. Tennis players at Ocean Isle Beach also may note the town's public courts on Third Street across from the Museum of Coastal Carolina.

Leland District Park
Village Rd., Leland

This is a 13-acre community park, situated behind the Leland Post Office. Facilities include a community building, playground and sand volleyball courts.

Lockwood District Park
N.C. Hwy. 211, a mile north of
U.S. Hwy. 17

The park is a mile north of the town of Supply. Its community building, however, is at Holden Beach. The park offers shuffleboard and horseshoes.

Northwest District Park
U.S. Hwy. 74/76, 2 miles west of the
Leland overpass

This park lies 15 minutes west of Wilmington, on the south side of the highway.

Smithville District Park
N.C. Hwy. 133, near Southport

Smithville District Park includes beach-style volleyball courts.

Shallotte District Park
Old U.S. Hwy. 17, 1 mile south of Shallotte

To find this park from U.S. 17, follow signs for U.S. 17 Business.

Town Creek District Park
U.S. Hwy. 17, near Winnabow

You can't miss this park on the east side of the road, about 15 or 20 minutes southwest of Wilmington.

E. F. Middleton Park
E. Oak Island Dr. at S.E. 47th St., Oak Island

The primary city park in Long Beach, Middleton Park offers a large playground with sand pits, swings and climbing bars, plus two tennis courts, basketball courts, a baseball field and picnic tables with some shade. The park is across the street from Town Hall and the emergency medical station.

Ev-Henwood Nature Preserve
6150 Rock Creek Rd., Town Creek
• (910) 253-6066, (910) 962-3197

This nature preserve, owned and administered by UNCW, comprises 174 acres of lush woodland with marked trails and educational displays. Among the many natural points of interest is an old tar kiln of the type once ubiquitous throughout the region. At present, only about 74 acres are open to the public. Suitable for families, the preserve is open during daylight hours seven days a week. Picnic tables and a restroom are available, and there's an onsite caretaker. Don't forget the camera and lunch. Admission is free.

Topsail Island

Stump Sound Park
N.C. Hwy. 172, Sneads Ferry

Softball fields, basketball courts, tennis courts, a children's playground and picnic shelters are available at this Onslow County Park. It opens daily at 10 AM and closes at dusk. The park is between U.S. 17 and N.C. 210, less than 1 mile from the Four Corners traffic light.

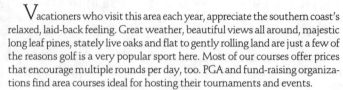

Golf

Vacationers who visit this area each year, appreciate the southern coast's relaxed, laid-back feeling. Great weather, beautiful views all around, majestic long leaf pines, stately live oaks and flat to gently rolling land are just a few of the reasons golf is a very popular sport here. Most of our courses offer prices that encourage multiple rounds per day, too. PGA and fund-raising organizations find area courses ideal for hosting their tournaments and events.

More new golf courses sprout up along the southern coast than anywhere else in North Carolina. Brunswick County alone boasts 36 courses, many located in residential golf communities. The area features challenging course designs bearing the signatures of Arnold Palmer, Rees Jones, Tom Fazio, Pete Dye, Jack Nicklaus, Dan Maples, Donald Ross, Hale Irwin, Fred Couples, Tim Cate, George Cobb and Willard Byrd, among others.

Most local courses are semiprivate, which means they're open to the public and club memberships are available. Membership, of course, offers various benefits and privileges, such as lower fees or preferred tee times. Greens fees vary according to season and location. At semiprivate courses, fees range widely, from about $20 to $100 and more, but average between $30 and $40 for 18 holes. Fees are highest at the more exclusive clubs and during the peak seasons (March 1st to May 20 and mid-September to early November). Look for special packages during non-peak times, such as three rounds at drastically reduced prices for either morning or afternoon. Discounts for seniors, corporations and groups are commonplace.

Overall, the region's courses offer an excellent balance between price and playing conditions. Many courses also offer practice ranges and club rental. Teaching pros are plentiful and eager to help you polish your game.

In this chapter we describe some of the better courses, judged by overall beauty, location and variety of challenge. We've also included a few independent driving ranges plus retail shops that offer equipment and repairs; information on golf packages and services; and some local annual tournaments. Complete listings of courses can be found at local chambers of commerce (see our Area Overviews chapter for a listings).

Courses

Wilmington

Beau Rivage Resort & Golf Club
649 Rivage Promenade, Wilmington • (910) 392-9022, (800) 628-7080

Elevations up to 72 feet and scads of bunkers (including two waste bunkers) place this course among the more dramatically landscaped in New Hanover County. It is a semiprivate par 72 course in which water hazards come into play on eight holes. Hole 4 (206 yards, par 3) is notable for its island tee box for women and a carry that is entirely over water. The course's greens, made of a genetically engineered form of bermudagrass called ultra dwarf TifEagle, are well watered and quite pleasing to golfers. Beau Rivage offers a fully-stocked golf shop, PGA instruction and club rental.

A bar and grill serving breakfast and lunch provides an attractive setting for post-round analysis. Beau Rivage is a residential development, but club memberships are available to non-residents. A 32-suite hotel adjoins the clubhouse. Formal banquet facilities with dining facilities accommodating up to 250 guests are popular for weddings, corporate retreats and family reunions.

The Cape Golf & Racquet Club
535 The Cape Blvd., Wilmington
• (910) 799-3110

A mile north of Carolina Beach, this semiprivate, meticulously landscaped, par 72 championship course sits amid 24 lakes, ponds and marshland. The bermudagrass fairways equal 6800 yards. The grounds include a driving range plus putting and chipping greens as well as a fully stocked pro shop, locker rooms with showers, a cocktail lounge, a full-service restaurant, banquet facilities and a snack bar. Club members also have access to The Cape's swimming pool and tennis courts. Greens fees range from inexpensive to moderate.

Country Club of Landfall
1550 Landfall Dr., Wilmington
• (910) 256-8411

Golfing on Landfall's two superlative courses, designed by Jack Nicklaus and Pete Dye and situated along the Intracoastal Waterway, is for members (and their guests) of Country Club of Landfall. The rewards for golfing members include challenges unparalleled on the majority of courses. The par 72 Nicklaus course has added another nine holes, giving it a total of 27. Overall, the Nicklaus course is perhaps the less forgiving of the two. It looks easier on paper than it really is, thanks largely to the many carries over marshes and water. The 6th hole, for instance, is a tough par 3 playing 190 yards from the back, with little more than marsh all the way to the ocean. Hole 8's island green is backed with a bunker with a 5-foot forward lip. Another island green is the signature hole on the Dye course. Completely waterbound, hole 2 slopes away from the sand trap that collars half its perimeter. The Dye course is a par 72. Plenty of uneven lies, marshes and pot bunkers demand that players push the envelope of their game to the utmost. Members also have access to Landfall's elaborate sports center, which has 14 tennis courts (with grass, clay and hard surfaces), a croquet course, a short-course pool and many indoor facilities such as a fitness center and dining room.

Echo Farms Golf & Country Club
4114 Echo Farms Blvd., Wilmington
• (910) 791-9318

Stands of moss-draped hardwood and some of the finest bentgrass greens in Wilmington distinguish this semiprivate course, which was rede-

signed in 1998 with a Scottish flair by European golf architect Ian Scott-Taylor. Rolling hills were added, and the bunkers are a challenge. A former dairy farm (the original farmhouse near the 17th hole is still occupied), it's now a par 72 challenge. Lakes come into play on nine holes. A driving range, practice greens, grill, bar and snack lounge are open to all. Echo Farms has developed a fine teaching facility, offering clinics and private lessons. The course is 5 miles south of downtown Wilmington off Carolina Beach Road (N.C. Highway 421).

Inland Greens
5945 Inland Greens Dr., Wilmington
• (910) 452-9900

Sharpen your short game on this public 18-hole par 3 course. For all ages and skill levels, holes average just more than 100 yards, and the greens

GOLF

GOLF

are in good condition. It's strictly a walking course, but pull-carts are available for rent. Almost midway between Wrightsville Beach and downtown Wilmington, the course is hidden off Cardinal Drive between Eastwood Road and Market Street.

Porters Neck Plantation and Country Club
8403 Vintage Club Dr., Wilmington
• (910) 686-1177

Porters Neck is an aficionado's course, aesthetically perfect and strategically challenging. Designed by Tom Fazio, this is a championship course (par 72) that emphasizes careful club selection. Impeccably maintained fairways undulate in sometimes deceptive fashion. Enormous waste bunkers and lakes abound, some of which span from tee to green (holes 11, 13, 14). Distinctive waste mounds planted with native grasses add to the course's character. Each hole presents conditions to make the most accurate golfer uncomfortable, yet leave no player unfulfilled. About 6 miles from Wilmington, this course winds through a private residential development adjacent to the Intracoastal Waterway. Public play is invited, but limited. A full-service pro shop and PGA trained staff are available. The entrance gate is a little over a mile in from the property limit on Porters Neck Road.

Wilmington Golf Course
311 S. Wallace Ave., Wilmington
• (910) 791-0558

This 1925 Donald Ross course received a face-lift in 1998, which brought it back to its original architectural design. Many sand traps and bunkers were added, making it a more challenging

course. In 2001-2002, this course was named the 7th best of 100 Public & Resort Courses in North Carolina by *Golfweek* magazine, placing it among such respected courses as Pinehurst No. 8 (ranked fifth) and Pinehurst No. 7 (ranked eighth). In its July-August issue, *Travel and Leisure* magazine voted this venerable course the No. 1 Donald Ross Course worldwide.

The course is home to the annual Wilmington City Golf Championship, which features local amateurs. Enter this par 71 facility from either Oleander Drive or Pine Grove Drive, a seven-minute drive from downtown. Compared to other local courses, the Muni, as it's called, has a relative dearth of water hazards, but the stream crossing the fairways of holes 2 (495 yards, par 5) and 12 (519 yards, par 5) is in just the wrong place for many golfers. The clubhouse and pro shop are open every day from 7 AM until sundown. The clubhouse has showers and lockers in the men's room only. Greens fees are about the cheapest you'll find, especially for city residents, and nine-hole rounds are available. This historic course is a "must-play" hidden gem within the city. Groups are limited to foursomes, and no singles or two-somes are permitted before 1:30 PM.

Wallace

River Landing Country Club
116 Paddle Wheel Dr., Wallace
• (910) 285-6693, (800) 959-3096

Home to four U.S. Open Qualifiers and the 2001 Mid-Amateur Championship, River Landing was rated one of the best courses in the state by *North Carolina Magazine*. The 27-hole layout

GOLF

combines artful landscape design and horticultural diversity with a variety of challenges from its five sets of tees. The Clyde Johnston-designed course features bentgrass greens and bermudagrass fairways and roughs. It totals more than 7000 yards from the back, with mixed elevations and carries over a variety of water hazards, including creeks, ponds and a river. The 6th, 8th, 16th and 17th holes hug the banks of the northeast Cape Fear River, while the 9th features par-resistant ravines. The signature 18th is a 402-yard, par 4 with a multi-tiered green; it's a dogleg left sloping downhill that dares you to avoid the ball-hungry bunker on the right. The elegant brick bridge there is one of many aesthetic delights. Also featured are a driving range, putting greens and snack bar. River Landing is a tranquil, private course (play is open to club members and their guests) in a golf community about 35 minutes north of Wilmington. The management welcomes corporate outings, group functions and fund-raisers. To get there from Wilmington, drive north on I-40 to Exit 385, N.C. Highway 41 East. Paddle Wheel Drive is a quarter-mile ahead on the right.

Bald Head Island

Bald Head Island Club
Bald Head Island • (910) 457-7310,
(800) 234-1666

Extremely demanding, due as much to the ocean wind as to the late George Cobb's brilliant design, this par 72 course is among the scenic gems on the East Coast. Exposed greens on its ocean side contrast sharply with interior holes where palms and maritime forest surround the holes which are separated from fairways with vir-

tually no playable rough. Four sets of tees yield course lengths up to 7040 yards. The finishing holes run alongside the ocean. The club currently hosts its own pro-am tournament, to which spectators are welcome. Bald Head Island is accessible only by ferry or private yacht, and tee times are required. A driving range and snack bar are available. Golf Getaway packages can be arranged year-round by calling (800) 432-RENT. A Day Golf Package includes parking, ferry, transfers, cart and greens fee for 18 holes.

Brunswick County

Magnolia Greens Golf Plantation
1800 Linkwood Cir., Leland
• (910) 383-0999

This magnificent 27 hole golf plantation made its opening debut to rave reviews in February of 1998. Voted the third best new golf course in North Carolina by *North Carolina Magazine*, Magnolia Greens hosted the PGA Qualifying Tour in1998 and 1999 and was recently awarded a four and one half star rating by *Golf Digest*. A Tom Jackson signature course, it provides numerous sets of tees for various skill levels, making it a challenging and yet fair course for both men and women. Senior tees are available. Lunch can be enjoyed at the 5,000-square-foot clubhouse, which features a full pro shop, bar and grill. Magnolia Greens welcomes public play and for those interested in real estate, it provides a great place to live. The course also offers East Coast Golf School. Fairway villas add to the stay-and-play golf packages.

GOLF

Southport-Oak Island

Carolina National Golf Links at Winding River Plantation
1643 Goley Hewett Rd., Bolivia
• **(910) 755-5200**

Within sight of the Lockwood Folly River, this course is Fred Couples' first design in North Carolina. Opened in 1998, it is full of dramatic elevations and bunkering nestled amid forest, scrub and wetland. Five of its 27 holes (made up of Egret 9, Heron 9, and Ibis 9) feature waste bunkers. The signature hole, Heron #5 (205-yard, par 3), features an island green set in the middle of the marsh-not the kind of place you'd want to retrieve a ball from. The toughest hole is probably Heron #7, with its right-hand approach to the green heavily fortified by timber and sand. This is a course of great beauty-one among a handful of courses certified by the Audubon Society for the designers' efforts to leave wetland habitat undisturbed-and a course of admirable challenge as well. In addition the Golf Links feature a large practice facility for warming up, including a spacious driving range and many targets. The elegant, gabled clubhouse houses the pro shop and offers a wide view of the surroundings from its high veranda. It's a great place to relax after a round with a drink or a meal from the grill. You'll find the course off Zion Hill Road, about 2.5 miles east of St. James Plantation along N.C. Highway 211 (Southport-Supply Road).

St. James Plantation - The Founders Golf Club
N.C. Hwy. 211, Southport
• **(910) 253-3008, (800) 247-4806**

Designer P.B. Dye called this his most challenging course yet. Its many carries over water hazards have been described as heroic, while its multilevel fairways, bulkheads and variety of grasses are stamped with the Dye hallmark. The final three holes play into and over a series of marshes and lakes for a spectacular finish. Five sets of tees present a variety of plays. Most greens are elevated. The Gauntlet and its companion course, the Members Club (see next entry), are 4 miles outside Southport and offer fine views of the Intracoastal Waterway. A complete practice facility and lessons are available. A restaurant and lounge are close by.

St. James Plantation - The Members Club
N.C. Hwy. 211, Southport
• **(910) 253-9500, (800) 474-9277**

Opened in 1996, this Hale Irwin-designed par 72 course utilizes the natural lay of the land to good effect, forgoing flashy, amusement-park landscaping. The course has been called user-friendly, although its proximity to the Intracoastal Waterway means winds can be deeply trying. Watch out for the 15th hole, a par 5 with lateral water hazards squeezing the fairway into a bottleneck about 200 yards down and more water in front of the green-potentially an express ticket to bogeyland. Recently, Tim Cate designed 9 holes were added to this course. The entire facility has all the amenities of the most exclusive clubs, such as practice greens and sand traps, a driving range and on-site professionals. There is a Jimmy Ballard golf school at The Members Club for all ages. The Members Club invites nonmembers to be "members for a day."

St. James Plantation - The Players
N.C. Hwy. 211, Southport
• (910) 457-0049, (800) 281-6626

Designed by Tim Cate, this 18-hole golf course is friendly and difficult. Watch out for the 6th hole, regarded as the most challenging. The course is very aesthetically pleasing, with wild flowers and heather grass in bloom all around. The course in in excellent condition year round. Construction has begun on an additional 9 holes. Private lessons and a fully stocked golf shop are on the premises. There is also a restaurant, lounge and a practice range close by. The Players is open to the public.

Oak Island Golf & Country Club
928 Caswell Beach Rd., Caswell Beach
• (910) 278-5275, (800) 278-5275

One of Brunswick County's vintage courses, this George Cobb creation is home to the Southport-Oak Island Masters Putting Tournament. It is a forgiving course (6608-yard par 72) that can be enjoyed by players of varying skills. Its wide bermudagrass fairways are relatively short, lined with live oaks and tall pines and not overly fortified with water hazards. But that ocean wind! The clubhouse is less than 200 yards from the Atlantic, and sea breezes can frustrate the best players. Hole 9 may send you to Duffers Pub and Grill early. Even so, the bermudagrass greens, driving range, putting green and swimming pool make this course quite popular.

South Brunswick Islands

Lockwood Folly Country Club
19 Clubhouse Dr., Holden Beach
• (910) 842-5666, (877) 562-9663

Lockwood Folly is a Willard Byrd–designed "hidden gem." The par 72, 18-hole course is carved in a magnificent setting from a 100-year-old private hunting preserve, bordering the Intracoastal Waterway and the Lockwood Folly River, with an ocean view. Lockwood Folly received a *Golf Digest* Four Star Award for "Places to Play" in 2000 and 2002; a Best Golf Course Community, 2002, Most Picturesque Course, 2002 (finalist) and Friendliest Golf Course Staff 2002 (finalist) by the *Myrtle Beach Golf Magazine* golfer voter poll. The course sports excellent greens, non-parallel Bermuda fairways and is always well maintained. For your convenience, you will find a well-stocked pro shop, a cafe, a practice range and a turn room. Thirty minutes south of Wilmington, Lockwood Folly is semi-private and open to the public.

Brierwood Golf Club
27 Brierwood Rd., Shallotte
• (910) 754-4660, (888) 274-3796

Brierwood was the first golf community built along the South Brunswick Islands. About 7 miles north of Ocean Isle Beach, it is a player-friendly, par 72, championship course distinguished by plenty of freshwater obstacles and surrounded by residential properties. Fourteen holes present water hazards, including part of a 3-acre lake that traverses the 10th fairway. The clubhouse includes a pro shop and the Blue Heron Bar & Grill, with its superb outdoor balcony seating above a lake. The entrance to this semiprivate course with well manicured, traditional greens is just off N.C. Highway 179 at the Shallotte town limit.

Brick Landing Plantation
1882 Goose Creek Rd., Ocean Isle Beach
• (910) 754-5545, (800) 438-3006

With 41 sand traps and 12 water holes, this handsome waterfront course was rated by *Florida Golf Week* magazine as among the top 50 distinctive golf courses in the Southeast. The Brick's fairways wind among freshwater lakes and through salt marshes, offering striking visual contrasts and championship challenges. The 18th hole finishes dramatically along the Intracoastal Waterway. The course is 6943 yards and a par 72. Amenities include a snack bar, lunch and cocktail lounge, and practice facilities. Instruction is available, as are tennis and family vacation packages and memberships.

Oyster Bay Golf Links
N.C. Hwy. 179, Sunset Beach
• (910) 579-3528, (800) 697-8372

The two signature holes at Oyster Bay Golf Links are sure to push you to excel. The par 3, 17th is one of two island greens and the par 4, 13th has water on the right which then becomes sand, This is an exceedingly challenging and imaginative public course (par 70), featuring stark elevations, deadly lakes and even a few trees smack in the middle of some fairways. Oyster Bay is one of the area's five Legends courses. It was voted Resort Course of the Year (1983) and among the top 50 public courses in the country (1990) by *Golf Digest*. The notorious 3rd hole (460 yards, par 4) presents one of the course's toughest greens. Each cart is equipped with club and ball cleaner, a cooler and ice. Beverage carts roam the course. The management enforces a dress code, and fees tend toward the medium-to-high.

GOLF

Sea Trail Golf Resort & Conference Center
211 Clubhouse Rd., Sunset Beach
• (910) 287-1100, (800) 624-6601

The Sea Trail Golf Resort features three par 72 courses-the Dan Maples, Rees Jones and Willard Byrd. All three have been given a four-star rating by *Golf Digest*. Appreciated for its attractive balance of price, friendliness and outstanding playing conditions, Sea Trail is a very popular course. The Rees Jones course was recently renovated to include L93 bentgrass greens, the bunkers have been enhanced, and more natural areas were added to the landscaping. Two restaurants, two lounges and many meeting facilities add to Sea Trail's appeal. Additional amenities include practice greens and sand traps, a driving range and on-site professionals. Two clubs, one for members and one for resort guests, offer tennis and swimming.

Calabash Golf Links
820 Thomasboro Rd., Calabash
• (910) 575-5000, (800) 841-5971

This par 72 course features large greens, soft doglegs and some lateral water hazards, but no over-water carries. Fairways are lined mostly with saplings. Greens fees are on the low end of average. Designed by Willard Byrd, the course offers four tee positions and few substantial elevations.

Carolina Shores Golf & Country Club
99 Carolina Shores Dr., Calabash
• (910) 579-2181, (800) 579-8292

Located near the shores of the historic fishing village of Calabash, Carolina shores achieved early recognition for its unique design and was rated "#1 on the Grand Strand" by Golf Course Rankings of America. One of the three courses on the new Shore Golf Tour, Carolina Shores features rolling tree lined fairways and well protected Bermuda greens. This is a shot makers dream with watery challenges and strategically placed bunkers rewarding a player for skill rather than brute strength. Under new ownership, Carolina Shores has completely renovated its clubhouse featuring a beautiful new restaurant with 11 TVs making it one of the finest 19 holes at the beach.

The Pearl Golf Links
N.C. Hwy. 179, Calabash • (910) 579-8132

These two par 72 courses, east and west, will have you wanting to play 36 straight, so start early. Architect Dan Maples endowed these links with theatrical bentgrass greens, contoured fairways and solid challenges. Course lengths are on the long side (6895 east, 7011 west), so break out the lumber and let 'er rip. A pro shop, snack bar, cocktail lounge and driving range are open year-round.

Topsail Island

Belvedere Plantation Golf & Country Club
2368 Country Club Dr., Hampstead
• (910) 270-2703

Belvedere is a narrow par 72, 18-hole course with small greens and water hazards. The length is 6059 yards with a slope of 125. Hole 3 stands out for its carry over water to an elevated green. Greens fees

GOLF

You'll find many courses on the southern coast to perfect your swing and challenge your skills.

Photo: Jay Tervo

range from $24 to $40, depending on the season and time of day. Fees include a golf cart. Reservations can be made for any time, with no restriction regarding how far in advance you can make them. Belvedere has a small pro shop, clubhouse and driving range on the premises. Belvedere offers PGA professional lessons and three- to four-day golf schools with accommodations provided. Tennis courts and a restaurant are also available on the premises.

Castle Bay
2516 Hoover Rd., Hampstead
• (910) 270-1978
Castle Bay offers authentic Scottish links with a rolling terrain and natural indigenous grasses. This par 72 course has lengths ranging from 5466 to 6713. It is in mint condition and part of an ever expanding country club that will soon house tennis courts and an Olympic size pool. Open to the public year round, seven days a week from sunup to sundown, Castle Bay is about 2 miles off U.S. 17 on Hoover Road in Hampstead. You can't miss the castle-type gates at the entrance. Rates for local residents, including cart, are $29 Monday through Thursday and $35 on Friday, Saturday and Sunday. Visitor rates are $35 Monday through Thursday and $40 on Friday, Saturday and Sunday. Off-season golfers can enjoy all day play rates and discounts are available after 1 PM during the season. Reservations can be made several months in advance. There is a pro shop and snack bar on the premises.

North Shore Country Club
N.C. Hwy. 210, Sneads Ferry
• (910) 327-2410, (800) 828-5035
North Shore is among the best-conditioned courses in the Topsail Island area with a four-star rating from *Golf Digest*. This course has 6866 yards, a 72.8 rating and a slope of 134, with water coming into play on 10 of the 18 holes. Thick Bermuda fairways and well-bunkered bentgrass greens place a premium on accurate shots. This course is quite popular with Raleigh and Triangle-area golfers, who come down to spend a day or two on the coast. The course is built on both sides of N.C. Highway 210, and an underground tunnel connects the two sides of the course. North Shore is lined with homes and tall pine trees. Golfers can sometimes be surprised and amused with alligator sightings in the course waterways.

The ninth hole is memorable for its required 250-yard tee shot — anything less is in the drink. Greens fees, including a cart, range from $37 to $55, and reservations can be made up to a year in advance with a credit card. A reservation of less than two days in advance doesn't require a credit

card. Driving range, putting green, professional lessons, club repairs and custom fitting are available. A clubhouse, bar and snack bar are on the premises with a Holiday Inn Express next door.

Olde Point Golf and Country Club
U.S. Hwy. 17 N., Hampstead
• (910) 270-2403
Olde Point is a mature, traditional course, opened in 1975 and designed by Jerry Turner. Featuring tree lined fairways, scenic ponds and lakes this 18-hole, par 72 course is 6253 yards with a slope of 120. Greens fees range from $26 to $50 depending on the season and time of day. Fees include a cart. A reserved starting time is required. The 11th hole is a long, narrow, 589-yard par 5 with a gradual dogleg right that slopes laterally downward to the right into the woods and consistently defies players' depth perception. It has been recognized by amateurs and professionals alike as one of the toughest in the area. Olde Point offers a pro shop, clubhouse, driving range, restaurant and snack bar.

Topsail Greens Golf Club
19774 U.S. Hwy. 17 N., Hampstead
• (910) 270-2883
Topsail Greens, under new ownership is undergoing a major facelift. This 18-hole, 6200-yard, par 71 course is player friendly featuring tight fairways, sand bunkers and several holes with a water hazard. The 8th hole, a 159-yard, with a par-3 is an island green playable only by a small bridge. The Greens, similar to those designed by Donald Ross, are cleverly contoured in a way that allows a miss-played shot to roll off the putting surface. Greens fees range anywhere from $20 to $35 depending on the time of day and season. Fees include a cart. Reservations are accepted. A pro shop, putting green, chipping green, and newly renovated High Five Sports Bar are on the premises. A nice porch, deck and patio area offer good places to relax and enjoy an icy cold beverage and some of the best wings in the area after an enjoyable round of golf.

Driving Ranges

Wilmington

Coastal Golf Center and Carolina Custom Discount Golf
6987 Market St., Wilmington
• (910) 791-9010
More than a driving range, Coastal is a supe-

rior one-stop facility for practicing, instruction, equipment and repairs. Stations on the lighted 257-yard driving range feature well-kept grass mats and tees. Two PGA instructors are on staff, and the pro shop offers all repair services, including shafting, refinishing and customizing. A half-mile outside Wilmington on U.S. 17 (Market Street) near the intersection with Military Cut-off Road, Carolina Custom Golf is one of seven affiliated stores based in Raleigh. It's open Monday through Saturday from 10 AM to 7 PM year around.

Valley Golf Center & Driving Range
4416 S. College Rd., Wilmington
• (910) 395-2750

Convenient to Carolina Beach and Wilmington, this large range has 40 lighted tee stations, mats and a grass hitting area as well as sand trap areas. A covered hitting area allows practice during inclement weather. The fully stocked pro shop offers repairs, accessories and instruction with PGA staff professionals. The center, which is just north of Monkey Junction, is open every day year round.

Southport-Oak Island and South Brunswick Islands

Holden Beach Driving Range
N.C. Hwy. 130, Holden Beach
• (910) 842-3717

This lighted practice facility offers lessons by Class-A PGA professionals, a small pro shop and, as any good resort-area attraction should, batting cages next door. A unique feature is that when unattended by staff, the range operates on the honor system. Payment instructions are posted beside the ball baskets.

Pro Tee Practice Range
N.C. Hwy. 179, Ocean Isle Beach
• (910) 754-4700

Two 18-station grass tee areas flank a mat area with rubber tees, all fully lighted. The pro shop stocks basic accessories, refreshments and snacks, and the management performs minor equipment repairs. Other amenities include two batting cages and a newly renovated mini golf course. Ask about the property owners' Tee Time Club Card. Pro Tee is a half-mile west of the Brick Landing Plantation Golf Course, is open daily and operates on the honor system on Christmas.

Equipment and Repairs

The Golf Shop at Dick's Sporting Goods
816 S. College Rd., Wilmington
• (910) 793-1904

One of 135 stores nationwide, Dick's has a 10,000-square-foot golf shop with a tremendous selection of golf equipment, clothing, shoes, accessories and gift items. A well-trained staff and golf pro are available to assist customers at all times. An indoor driving range is available to test those new clubs. The store is open seven days a week.

Nevada Bob's
5629 Oleander Dr., Wilmington
• (910) 799-4212

Nevada Bob's is a chain store that boasts a broad selection of new equipment and accessories and a knowledgeable staff. It has the air of a connoisseur's shop, right down to the indoor netted tee station on which to test clubs. There is also an artificial indoor putting green. Nevada Bob's is in the Bradley Square shopping center on the westbound side of Oleander. The store is open seven days a week.

Tee Smith Custom Golf Clubs
1021 S. Kerr Ave., Wilmington
• (910) 395-4008

Tee Smith has been customizing and repairing clubs commercially since 1975 and carries the approval of pro shops throughout the area. Simple repairs often have a one-day turnaround. The shop carries a full line of top-name brands and is open Monday through Saturday year round.

Golf Etc.
4956-19 Long Beach Rd., Southport
• (910) 457-1950

Owner, Alan Mattison, is especially excited about the computerized swing analysis and True Temper Shaft Lab(c) available in Golf Etc. - something you won't find for many miles around. You will find a full line of pro equipment, custom club building, reshafting and repairs available as well. In fact, everything needed for a golfing lifestyle can be purchased at Golf Etc., from golf balls, to golf bags, to indoor putting greens, to clothing and shoes, to teapots and mugs, to videos and software, books and more. Don't hesitate to shop during the broadcast of your favorite golf tournament, it's bound to be tuned in on one of the TVs in the store.

Packages and Services

The American Lung Association Golf Privilege Card offers discounts for one year on more than 700 rounds of golf at 300 courses throughout North Carolina, South Carolina and Virginia. All courses offer a reduced rate and some have unlimited play. The card, (which is really a 48-page book) costs $40; buy three and get one free. Some restrictions apply. To order, contact the American Lung Association of North Carolina, Eastern Area, P.O. Box 1407, Greenville, NC 27835, or call (252) 752-5093 or (800) 849-5949; the website is www.lungnc.org

Most travel agencies, many local hotels and vacation rental companies will assist in arranging golf packages. Coastal Golfaway, (910) 256-4576 or (800) 368-0045, books customized packages in all price ranges, from Wilmington to Pawley's Island, South Carolina, including Myrtle Beach and the Brunswick Islands/Calabash area. Be sure to click on Golf Packages in our Premier Links at the beginning of this chapter.

The Greater Topsail Area Chamber of Commerce has established a Golf Association with local area golf courses, restaurants, accommodations and activities. Information can be requested through the chamber.

Golf Tournaments

Exciting and challenging courses in beautiful settings, plus wonderful weather, set the stage for competitive golf events throughout the area. Tournaments are popular as fund-raising activities, and a number of local organizations sponsor annual events. Many local courses host their own tournaments as well. Local chambers of commerce can provide information (see our Area Overviews chapter for a listing). Major tournaments are announced in the *Wilmington Star-News* "Today" or "Sports" sections; some weekly publications, such as Encore, carry details, too.

Wilmington Golf Course, 311 South Wallace Avenue, Wilmington (910) 791-0558, sponsors an annual Men's Amateur Championship and a Women's Amateur Championship in September. These tournaments are open to golfers age 18 or older who have an established U.S.G.A. handicap. The fee for this two-day event is $50 for women and $60 for men, which includes lunch the first day.

North Shore Country Club, N.C. Highway 210, Sneads Ferry, (910) 327-2410 or (800) 828-5035, hosts two annual tournaments: the Stump Sound Rotary Golf Tournament in May and the Kiwanis Loggerhead Golf Tournament in early October. Preregistration opens about one month prior.

The Southport-Oak Island Chamber of Commerce, (910) 457-6964, (800) 457-6964 hosts the Southport-Oak Island Golf Classic in March.

In May, the South Brunswick Islands Chamber of Commerce (910) 754-6644, (800) 426-6644, hosts the South Brunswick Islands Chamber of Commerce Golf Tournament; the Southport Lions Club (910) 278-6814 hosts the Lions Club Golf Tournament; and the Master's Putting Tournament is held at the Oak Island Golf Club (910) 457- 6964, (800) 457-6964.

June brings the Brunswick Literacy Council Golf Tournament (910) 754-7323 at Carolina National in 2003 and the Southport Rotary Club Golf Tournament (910) 253-0470 and in August the county women's golf clubs, (910) 754-5726), hold the Women's Golf Club County Championship which benefits Hope Harbor Home.

Golf Associations

Golf associations are primarily connected to local courses. For example, Porters Neck Country Club (PNCC) has a Men's Golf and Ladies Golf Association that are open to members only. However, Topsail Greens Golf Club men's and women's golf associations are open to both members and non-members. Wilmington Golf Course is a municipal course, which doesn't have members, therefore, anyone can join the Men's or Women's Golf Associations. So, you need to check the courses that interest you regarding associations.

Wilmington Single Golfers
311 Sandpiper Ln., Wilmington
• (910) 270-1956

A Chapter of the American Singles Golf Association, the Wilmington organization includes unmarried men and women ages 30 and up from Pender, New Hanover and Brunswick counties. The group holds two events each month, year round — a business/social meeting the second Tuesday of the month and a golf outing usually the weekend following the meeting. Golf outings take place on some of the best courses available in the area. Four multi-chapter events of three to four days are held at the time of these holidays: New Year's, Valentine's Day, Memorial Day and Labor Day. Membership is $65 the first year and $60 for renewals, which includes national and chapter dues and newsletters.

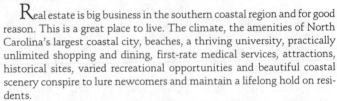

Real Estate

Real estate is big business in the southern coastal region and for good reason. This is a great place to live. The climate, the amenities of North Carolina's largest coastal city, beaches, a thriving university, practically unlimited shopping and dining, first-rate medical services, attractions, historical sites, varied recreational opportunities and beautiful coastal scenery conspire to lure newcomers and maintain a lifelong hold on residents.

Since the entire region from Topsail Island to Sunset Beach hugs the shore, land is limited to an approximately 180-degree angle. Naturally, the closer a property is to the water, the higher the price. Nevertheless, housing remains remarkably affordable throughout the southern coastal region compared to some more affluent parts of the country. There is also tremendous diversity in terms of neighborhoods, housing styles, scenery and price. The highest level, from $500,000 to beyond $3 million, consists of properties for buyers interested in waterfront and luxury homes. At the other end of the scale, there are smaller, new homes ranging from $80,000 to $130,000, just right for first-time homeowners and retirees seeking affordable housing.

Because new neighborhoods are continually sprouting in the area, we aren't even going to try describing all that are available. What follows is information about established neighborhoods, average prices (these may fluctuate according to the market) and other general facts. For specific information, contact an area Realtor (a partial list of agencies is included in this chapter) or visit sales offices in a community that appeals to you.

Neighborhoods

Downtown Wilmington

It has been said by many a native that downtown Wilmington is a separate place from the rest of the city and New Hanover County. The tone is absolutely different from any other neighborhood in the region. If you appreciate being at the crossroads of the community, downtown is the place for you. If you are looking for history and charm as well as an energetic and culturally/socially inspirational atmosphere, downtown Wilmington is definitely the place to be. It's lively, warm and relentlessly interesting.

Many of the homes date from the mid- to late 1800s and the first quarter of the 20th century. There are stunning examples of Victorian, Italianate, Renaissance, Neoclassical and Revivalist architecture. Homes in the area, small cottages and large mansions alike, feature high ceilings, hardwood floors, fascinating detail, front porches and all of the interesting characteristics one would expect of vintage homes.

The population is as eclectic as the architecture. Downtown is a very interesting melting pot of natives and newcomers. What the entire neighborhood seems to have in common is a mutual appreciation for the particular amenities of downtown: easy accessibility to cultural arts opportunities, fine dining, friendly shopping, city and county government centers, a beautiful riverfront for strolling, and a strong sense of community identity.

Topsail Island Real Estate
Sales & Rentals

At The Swing Bridge

bryson & associates, inc.

Call For Reservations

800-326-0747
910-328-2468

Book Online For 2003
www.brysontopsail.com

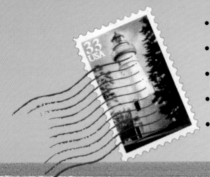

- Tom Fazio Championship Course
- Two Sparkling Swimming Pools
- Five Lighted Clay Surface Tennis Courts
- 18th Century Federal Style Clubhouse
- Gated Entrance With 24 Hour Security

Wilmington's Address
For Gracious Living

PN PORTERS NECK PLANTATION
AND COUNTRY CLUB

Relatively few homes come on the market in the more established center of the neighborhood, and the ones that do aren't available for long unless they are very large and, therefore, quite expensive. As one local Realtor put it, there is a range of everything in the way of housing and prices downtown, from larger homes in the district to small cottages with prices ranging from $70,000 to more than $1 million, depending on the location and condition. Condominiums, often housed in renovated buildings, can range from the low $100,000s and up.

Within the **Historic District** proper, many homes have been restored, but there are still handyman bargains to be had, especially in the areas outside of the district in the Historic Overlay. It takes a person with vision to redo some of the deteriorating architectural gems in these neighborhoods. The level of downtown neighborhood restoration is most stable at the river and diminishes as you head east toward the ocean at about Eighth Street.

The residential neighborhoods to the north of Market Street are generating high interest at this time and are seeing quality restoration efforts. The North Fourth Street Business District Project, a renewal effort supported in part by the City of Wilmington, business owners and residents along this corridor, promises to open new options to people who want to live downtown. To the south, the natural boundary of the neighborhood is the Cape Fear Memorial Bridge. Quality restorative development has taken place on South Second, Queen and Castle streets.

Although every type of housing style is available, the general downtown real estate market consists of single-family homes. There are also a growing number of condominiums and a few duplex developments. Some opportunities to have a rental apartment within one's own home are available.

Rental prices in the downtown area range from $800 to $1,200 a month for one-bedroom rentals. If the notion of living over a storefront or in an urban, loft-type space has appeal, ask your Realtor to show you buildings in the downtown commercial district.

Some solidly rediscovered older neighborhoods beyond downtown are the **Mansion District** and nearby **Carolina Heights** and **Carolina Place**. Both flank Market Street beyond 15th Street. These neighborhoods date from the 1920s, and architectural styles vary. In the Mansion District you can certainly purchase a mansion-style home ranging from $300,000 to $600,000, but there are also appealing cottages. Many of the larger homes started out as handyman bargains or fixer-uppers and were returned to their former elegance.

Carolina Heights and Carolina Place begin roughly at 17th Street and continue to 23rd Street. Carolina Heights is almost exclusively single-family homes with a price range from $140,000 to $250,000. In Carolina Place, the home buyer will find more diversity in architecture and price. Homes start in the $105,000 range and go up into the high $140,000s. It is widely regarded as the new frontier for not only residential investors, but also homeowners, largely thanks to its relatively new status as an Historic Registry District. It also is comfortingly close to venerable Forest Hills.

Downtown Wilmington has some beautiful homes.

Photo: Jay Tervo

Wilmington and New Hanover County

Suburbs

Forest Hills is, without dispute, a fine address. This large and very stable neighborhood was once a suburb of downtown. Today it is a conveniently located neighborhood of older homes that date from as early as the 1920s. Well-maintained lawns, large setbacks, quietness, alleys for backyard access and trash pickup, and gorgeous live oaks are the hallmarks of this neighborhood. There are ambling canopied lanes and lots of Southern-style shade. Diversity in square footage and architectural style allows for diversity in price, ranging from $190,000 to $270,000 and up. An attractive feature of this neighborhood is its proximity to shopping and services. It is minutes from the largest mall in the region.

Pine Valley, near South College Road around Longleaf Mall, is about three decades old as a development and still enjoying active home sales. It has attracted many Wilmingtonians to its quiet, pine tree-dotted blocks. A nearby golf course and clubhouse are easily accessible to people who want to live in a stable neighborhood that isn't necessarily exclusive in terms of price. Homes range from the $120,000s to $300,000.

Intracoastal Waterway Communities

On the mainland side of the Intracoastal Waterway (ICW) is the planned community of **Landfall**, 1801 Eastwood Road, (910) 256-6111. This gated community offers a pristine environment of immaculate lawns, beautiful homes, three clubhouses, two private golf courses — 27 holes designed by Jack Nicklaus and 18 holes designed by Pete Dye — a tennis facility designed by tennis legend Cliff Drysdale, an eight-lane Olympic-size swimming pool and more. Single-family homes range from $300,000 to over $3 million; home sites range from $60,000 to over $1 million. Landfall currently has 1,100 homes. The Landfall Clubhouse, a large banquet/dining/special occasions facility of 31,000 square feet, is also on the premises.

Water, sewer, recycling and waste disposal services vary tremendously, depending on where you live. Some municipalities provide some or all of these services and bill you monthly for them; others offer none. When

REAL ESTATE

INSIDERS' TIP

During an interview with a prospective real estate agent, ask such questions as:
• How long have you been in business in this area?
• Do you work full-time in the real estate market?
• Are you G.R.I., C.R.S., or A.B.R.? (There are the highest real estate degrees.)
• Make sure you are comfortable with the personality of your agent so that you will have a good rapport.

you're considering a home either for lease or purchase, you'll want to inquire at the village or city hall in that governmental jurisdiction. Even in older developed neighborhoods — but especially in beach communities and rural areas — wells and septic tanks are common and you've got to take your trash to a recycling station or dump yourself.

North of Wilmington

Demarest Landing, located on the high bluffs of Howe Creek across from Landfall, is a waterfront Middle Sound neighborhood. Although secluded, this exceptional community of 46 home sites is accessible to every convenience of suburban living, including area schools. Amenities of this well-planned community were designed to appeal to kids of all ages and include tennis, volleyball, basketball, a swimming pool, a waterfront pier and stocked boathouse, a clubhouse, 1.5 miles of sidewalks, a post office, a fountain, parks and rear service lanes for residents' garages. Endorsed by the Governor's Taskforce for Smart Growth as the "cutting edge" in Traditional Neighborhood Design, Demarest Landing is a community of great neighbors with a child-friendly atmosphere. Half-acre home sites range from $80,000 to $350,000. Established homes range from $500,000 to $1.5 million. For more information about Demarest Landing,

REAL ESTATE

contact Ray Haas at Coldwell-Banker Seacoast Realty (910) 232-2050; you may also call the Demarest Company, (910) 686-9707.

Inspired by and built adjacent to Demarest Landing, **Demarest Village** is a new Middle Sound neighborhood offering a diverse collection of residential choices that include single-family homes, townhomes and row houses. Residences in this exceptional community have unique and historic architectural features and are woven among tree-lined streets. Sidewalks surround and connect homes to the neighborhood's eight acres of open space and parks. Home sites begin at $55,000, and residences begin at $275,000 to $325,000 and more. For information about Demarest Village, contact Paula Ferebee at **Intracoastal Realty**, (910) 540-8787. You may also Contact Demarest Company, (910) 686-9707.

Porters Neck Plantation, 8204 Fazio Drive, (910) 686-7400 or (800) 423-5695, is north of Wilmington and Wrightsville Beach just off U.S. Highway 17. The setting — 650 acres of pristine, lush coastal land adjacent to the Intracoastal Waterway — is fitting for this community of extraordinary homes. The Tom Fazio-designed golf course is a key feature of the very attractive neighborhood that appeals to active people. There is a sports complex, complete with a lap pool, clay tennis courts and a fitness center. Traditional single-family homes are available in a variety of sizes and proximity to the golf course, which will determine the price, ranging from $280,000 to $450,000. Patio homes start at $230,000 for 1,800 square feet.

Figure Eight Island is a private island of upscale homes and homesites ranging from $475,000 to over $1 million; single-family home prices range from $825,000 to $3,900,000. There is a yacht club and private harbor for members. This lovely island there has no commercial development; shopping is available in nearby Ogden and Hampstead. Call your Realtor for information.

River Landing, 110 River Village Place, Wallace, (910) 285-4171 or (888) 285-4171, is just over the Duplin-Pender counties line off Interstate 40, about 35 minutes from Wilmington. It is a private, residential golf community consisting of primary residences and second homes with a wide variety of recreational facilities. Club memberships include a 27-hole championship golf course designed by Clyde Johnston, a swim and tennis center, private guest cottages, fishing and boating and walking/jogging/nature trails. The new River Club is a perfect place for a family picnic, community group or enjoying a canoe or kayak. Home sites throughout the 1,400-acre community range from the low $50,000 to $350,000 and more.

South of Wilmington

The area to the south of Wilmington is currently the fastest growing part of New Hanover county. Along College Road south of Market Street to Shipyard Boulevard, dense commercial growth has been taking place for years. However, with significantly increased residential development farther to the south down to Pleasure Island, commercial development has been following at a rapid pace. This is especially true in the **Monkey Junction/Myrtle Grove** area at the

REAL ESTATE

junction of Carolina Beach Road (U.S. Route 421) and College Road (NC Route 132), where a new Lowes and Wal-Mart Super Center have just been built, along with numerous other businesses and restaurants.

South of Monkey Junction along Carolina Beach Road, quite a few residential areas have been developed, ranging from moderately priced to upscale gated communities, interspersed with commercial establishments. The four-lane, divided highway allows easy access to any of these businesses, communities and Pleasure Island.

Just north of the Snow's Cut Bridge on River Road is the growing development of **Cypress Island**. Developed by Cypress Green Inc., (910) 790-8010, (888) 395-4770, this neighborhood consists of 1,400- to 2,000-square-foot single-family homes and 1,200- to 1,800-square-foot townhomes. Homes and lots are offered as a package deal starting at $147,500 to $194,500 for single-family homes and $99,900 to $154,500 for townhomes. The community has a 14-acre nature preserve with a nature trail that meanders beside Telfair Creek, three stocked fishing lakes, a clubhouse, a pool and tennis courts. It has a 9-hole, par 3 golf course.

Wrightsville Beach and Vicinity

Wrightsville Beach is highly residentially developed. For the most part, houses are close together, and a person who craves the mythical remote island life is not going to find it here. Development has been largely controlled, thanks to vigilance on the part of local residents and the high cost of land, so the relative density of development is palatable. In 1998 the community put building ordinances into effect that limit the size of new houses based on square footage relative to lot size.

This is a pretty beach town with a year-round population of slightly less than 3,000 residents. It's clean, there is little in the way of garishness, and the local constable does a fine job keeping order in the face of masses of visitors. A person who appreciates small-town living in a beach atmosphere with the convenience of a nearby city will adore this place. There are 5 miles of clean beach on which to jog or simply stroll. On just about any day of the year, you'll see surfers waiting for the big one to roll in.

The Wrightsville Beach real estate market is stable. If a property comes onto the market, it will often sell quickly. Many of the existing homes stay in families generation after generation. Quite a few of these properties are used only as summer homes. When homes do go on the market, the price tag is large. Expect to pay an average of $300,000 to $3 million for any single-family home, and don't be surprised by much higher prices for oceanfront property. Those homes begin at about $900,000.

Since the available land is all but exhausted in terms of development on the island and high-rises are limited to 96 feet, most of the opportunities for purchase are either replacement of older houses with new ones or, more likely, in condominiums. You could easily spend $200,000 to $1.3 million for a two-bedroom condominium on Wrightsville Beach, with those on the lower end of the range far from the beach. Condos built at the present time are typically three-bedroom, two-bath floor plans and range from $400,000 to $500,000. Custom three- to four-bedroom condominiums with 3,000 to 4,000 square feet start at $800,000 and up.

One of the newest developments near Wrightsville Beach is **The Village at Mayfaire**, a 31-acre, 208-unit residential development on Military Cutoff Road. Developed by the Charlotte-based State Street Companies, this community offers a fresh, engaging and luxurious condominium experience. Homeowners find private estate comforts beautifully composed within a handsome architectural style. Six graciously appointed floor plans are available. Two- and three-bedroom floor plans range in size from 1,260 to 2,037 square feet and include large outdoor terraces, a private garage and assigned courtyard parking.

With prices starting around $225,000, The Village at Mayfaire offers coastal-style living for a fraction of what homeowners pay for a comparable condominium at Wrightsville Beach, located 2.5 miles from the property. Amenities include a 5,525-square-foot clubhouse, 24-hour cardio center and weight-lifting area, 25-seat movie theatre and multi-media room, billiards room, conference and gaming room, junior Olympic-size pool with 75-foot lap lanes, expansive sunning deck, outdoor heated spa, gas barbecue grill area, lighted tennis courts and residents' picnic pavilion.

Perhaps The Village at Mayfaire's most distinctive amenity of all is the link to The Mayfaire Town Center. This inviting "new urbanism" community brings a vital and enchanting living, shopping and working environment, the first of its kind, to the Wilmington area. In fact, the Retail Town Center is designed to become a pivotal destination for upscale retail services. Here, residents can walk, browse and shop all day among national and local restaurants and merchants along a traditional "Main Street," with storefronts facing bustling sidewalks and public squares. For more information about The Village at Mayfaire, contact Bryan P. Williams, Director of Sales, at (910) 509-9771 or toll free at (877) 971-9771.

Carolina Beach and Kure Beach

Cross over the bridge on U.S. 421 at Snow's Cut, a U.S. Army Corps of Engineers project that connects the ICW with the Cape Fear River and the Atlantic Ocean, and you come directly into Carolina Beach. This island community represents some very interesting prospects for home ownership in the Cape Fear region.

The beach communities of Carolina Beach on the north and Kure Beach to the south are located on the land area known as Pleasure Island. Home to about 10,000 year-round residents, these friendly, family-oriented communities are often mistaken by visitors as one long island beach town referred to as Carolina Beach. This is an understandable error due to the similarities of the towns. Both have clean, wide beaches, an abundance of fishing opportunities, several nice restaurants and a growing sense of community pride that makes living here a charming prospect.

Although Carolina Beach has been a community since 1857, the whole of Pleasure island has been experiencing substantial residential growth during recent years as an affordable place to locate by or near the ocean. The assortment of ownership opportunities range from condominiums to cottages to upscale homes. There are several high-rises, many multi-story condominium buildings on the northern end, an abundance of small residences and — particularly toward the central and southern parts of the island — quite a few larger homes.

Currently, the island is experiencing considerable commercial growth, and revitalization is

well underway. A new shopping center has a Food Lion as its anchor store. Construction of an two major chain motels are scheduled for completion in early summer of 2003, both of which will positively impact downtown Carolina Beach and the Boardwalk area.

Single-family homes along Carolina Beach and Kure Beach range between $100,000 to $500,000 and up, with townhomes and condominiums priced in the mid-$50,000s to the $400,000s. Not surprisingly, oceanfront properties in both markets fall into the upper range of price quotes, $300,000 to $675,000 and up. The farther south you go on this island, the more fascinating the scenery becomes. In Fort Fisher, beautiful live oak foliage has been sculpted over the centuries by the sea breezes. At the southernmost tip of this strip of land, the Cape Fear River converges with the Atlantic Ocean near Bald Head Island.

Farther south on Pleasure Island in the village of Kure Beach, you'll find Seawatch, a residential development with homes on 101 sites ranging from oceanfront to wooded. Single-family, cottage-style homes are from 1,400 to 3,200 square feet in size and are grouped around a community pool, cabana, playground and tennis courts. A private oceanfront beachwalk features a cabana with showers, restrooms and a covered deck.

Among the Pleasure Island's notable residential developments is **Harbour Point**, (910) 458-4120, a traditional waterfront neighborhood and yacht club located on the Intracoastal Waterway at the juncture of Snow's Cut in Carolina Beach. With 90 townhomes ranging in price from $189,900 to $500,000, the properties feature tin roofs, white picket fences, pastel exteriors, romantic porches and classic styling. It's a Charleston-like community with a relaxed ambiance and quiet sophistication. Seven floor plans have been integrated into a truly unique blend of Southern architecture that combines functionality and spaciousness with just plain charm. The attractively painted interiors are graced with first-class cabinetry, oak stairs and railings, hardwood floors, quality Berber carpeting, white-on-white appliances, and cultured marble vanities in bathrooms. An extraordinary 98-slip marina that can accommodate boats up to 100 feet, a waterfront pool and clubhouse make this picture complete.

Bald Head Island

It takes 20 minutes to cross from the ferry landing at Indigo Plantation to Bald Head Island, a beautiful bit of land where there are no high-rises, no shopping malls, no crowds and no cars. Everyone travels by electric golf cart or bicycle. You'll find a clubhouse with a pool, a George Cobb–designed golf course, tennis courts, a marina and limited shopping. Opportunities for fine and casual dining range from the elegant Bald Head Island Club to the deli at the Maritime Market. There is a resort atmosphere and, to be sure, the year-round residential population count is quite low, about 175. It is largely a vacation spot where most of the homes are available for weekly rental.

Home sites range from $60,000 to more than $1.7 million. Home sales begin at $350,000 and climb upward to over $2.5 million. Single-family homes, townhouses and villas dot the island and are connected by paved golf cart paths.

Southport-Oak Island

The charming fishing village of Southport attracts not only retirees, but also families and folks who have decided to get out of the rat race. Southport's geographical location on the Cape Fear River near the Atlantic Ocean provides some lovely coastal scenery. Bald Head Island lies between Southport and the ocean. Oak Island serves as a barrier to the ocean on the south side.

Southport's quaint, historic homes date from the late 1800s and offer mostly restored, single-family residences. Houses on the waterfront are larger, and a 2,500-square-foot home may run from $370,000 to $440,000. Newer homes may cost more. Along River Drive, one can spend up to $525,000. Naturally, the farther back from the water, the lower the price. A nice finished house in Southport will average around $220,000 for 1,500 square feet. Subdivision areas are growing rapidly in and near Southport. These include Indigo Plantation, Arbor Creek, The Landing at Southport, Winding River and Marsh Creek. These neighborhoods offer a broad range of surprisingly affordable new homes in attractive settings with some very pleasant amenities.

Arbor Creek, a brief drive from historic Southport west on N.C. Highway 211, encourages potential homeowners to step back in time to a serene, friendly and more gracious era. In this charming real estate community, the traditional home styles are characterized by picket fences, window boxes and shady front porches. Manicured lawns, gazebos and walking paths add to the hometown ambience. In addition to these amenities, residents enjoy social activities in the elegant clubhouse, nature trails, a swimming pool, a putting green, tennis courts and a communal garden. Home sites range in the upper $30,000s to $70,000. Home options are available in single family or semi-custom homes, ranging from $135,000 to $275,000. Minutes away from Arbor Creek's neighborhoods are the Intracoastal Waterway and the Oak Island beaches.

Located between N.C. Hwy. 133 and Fish Factory Road where Dutchman Creek meets the Intracoastal Waterway, you will find secluded **South Harbour Village.** A PUD, it is divided into five small neighborhoods: Glen Cove, Westport, Village Green Garden Homes, Barnes Bluff and South Harbour Town Homes. Included are an 18-hole executive golf course, a small sitting park with gazebo, a full-service marina (see our Marinas chapter), a deli, several tennis courts, access to a boat ramp, a restaurant, retail shops and a nine-room inn. Also on the grounds is a non-denominational chapel, a Baptist church and a Montessori school. Planned are a clubhouse and an Olympic-size pool. Homesites range from $44,900 to $575,000 depending on size and location (golf course, wooded interior, Dutchman Creek, Intracoastal Waterway). Base prices for homes range from $149,900 to $204,900. Village Green Garden Homes range from $135,900 to 154,900. Condominiums are also available, priced from $275,000. Custom single-family homes are priced on request.

Oak Island has two beach communities: Caswell Beach and the Town of Oak Island. Both of these communities have resort rentals, but they are overwhelmingly occupied by permanent residents. Prices for single-family homes range from $90,000 to $650,000. At the center of the island, you can expect to pay from $95,000 to $200,000 for a small home. The Town of Oak Island, the biggest geographical area on the island, has oceanside properties for less than $300,000.

South Brunswick Islands

Holden Beach

The next island down the coast is Holden Beach. A remarkable bridge rises 65 feet above the mainland (at high water) and careens dizzily to the island. Some say it's a surprise attraction in itself. You get a breathtaking view of the whole island, the marshes, the ICW and the Atlantic Ocean from the top of it.

Holden Beach is another family beach. In fact, every beach from here south to the South Carolina line fits into the family-beach category. Prices for real estate are climbing rapidly. An oceanfront single-family home may cost from $300,000 to over $1 million. Second-row homes, depending on view and water access by way of a canal, begin at $250,000 and may be as high as $575,000. Duplexes, condominiums and other multi-family dwellings on the oceanfront begin at $200,000.

Ocean Isle Beach

Ocean Isle Beach is an 8-mile-long, quarter-mile-wide island that lies at the center of South Brunswick's three barrier islands. The sandy beaches face directly south, providing sunshine all day. Beach residents are accustomed to seeing the sun rise and set over the ocean. The island has a stable year-round population of about 500 residents, ensuring a sense of community. Ocean Isle Beach is an appealing residential environment of largely single-family homes that range in price from about $350,000 to over $1 million on the oceanfront to $250,000 and up in the middle of the island. Naturally, properties on the ICW side facing the mainland also fetch higher prices.

Sunset Beach

This beach may have thousands of visitors in the summer, but it is home to only about 1,800 year-round residents. It is overwhelmingly occupied by single-family dwellings, but there is a trend toward large duplexes on the oceanfront. This is because the island homes are on septic systems, and the oceanfront lots are the only ones that can accommodate two systems on one lot. Lots may range from $250,000 to $375,000 depending on location. Four finger canals, regularly dredged, escalate the cost of interior lots. Duplexes of 2,000 square feet can cost $650,000. Single-family homes may range from $350,000 to as high as $1 million.

Calabash

The town of Calabash is a fishing village with its share of world-famous restaurants that specialize in Calabash-style seafood. Calabash attracts a wide range of families and individuals who appreciate the easy pace of the area and proximity to the Myrtle Beach and Wilmington entertainment and cultural activities.

Devaun Park will be a 150-acre waterfront neighborhood built in the Traditional Neighborhood Design concept for smart growth, an increasingly popular style of neighborhood planning. Devaun Park has been endorsed by the N.C. Governor's Taskforce For Smart Growth. Situated on the high bluffs of the Calabash River, Devaun Park will offer a varied collection of residential choices that include single-family homes, row houses and more. When completed, the planned 483 residences will be surrounded by 8 miles of sidewalks that connect to 12 extraordinary parks and six exceptional neighborhoods. Recreational areas, a health club and a Town Square will be additional amenities. Now under construction, Devaun Park's first neighborhood on Whisper Park offers 60 homes overlooking the high bluff of the Calabash River. For information, contact the office at Devaun Park Pavilion, (910) 575-6500.

Carolina Shores

Carolina Shores is a golf-oriented community that attracts a high proportion of retired folks to its appealing setting. The community's approximately 800 homes, in a variety of architectural styles, average between $150,000 and $300,000. In 1993, Calabash and the development of Carolina Shores merged, but they discovered that each held differing opinions on local issues. Discussions concerning a split began. In 1999 the voting districts of "Old Calabash" and Carolina Shores, unchanged despite the merger years before, agreed to a vote to settle the matter. If either of the districts voted to become independent once again, both would agree to a split. Calabash voted for the split and, as a result, Carolina Shores incorporated into the Town of Carolina Shores.

Topsail Island

Many of the properties on Topsail Island are second homes or investment properties. However, the number of year-round residents continues to grow as more small subdivisions are built on the sound and Intracoastal Waterway, nestled in the maritime forests. The majority of these homes are occupied by retirees who enjoy the relaxed beach lifestyle. Properties most in demand are the large, oceanfront homes and other waterfront locations. The trend continues to be toward rising prices, and property purchased today will be viewed as a bargain tomorrow. You can expect to pay an average of $300,000 to $400,000 for a single-family oceanfront home. Land is limited on this barrier island, and many retirees and new families relocating to the area often choose to live on the mainland, which is still close enough to the beach to feel like they are on a lifelong vacation.

Real Estate Agencies

Any one of an abundance of area real estate agencies will be happy to assist you in your search for a new home. The agencies included here represent a fraction of the reputable companies working along the southern coast of North Carolina. Although we've grouped the agencies geographically, many of them sell properties in other communities, and some have offices in several locations throughout the area. Regardless of the office location, choose a Realtor who is knowledgeable about the areas you're interested in and with whom you feel comfortable working.

REAL ESTATE

Wilmington

ABR Realty Inc.
6209 Oleander Dr., Wilmington
• (910) 793-9803, (800) 442-6012

Sharon and Peter Kerkstra and the ABR team promise 100% buyer representation and 110% buyer satisfaction. Dedicated to serving as exclusive buyer's agents, ABR Realty will find the best property that fits your needs. Because they are looking out for your best interests, these full-time experienced brokers don't have to be concerned with listing and selling properties. They want only to assure you a positive purchase experience.

Using a team approach, ABR agents can assist you in finding exactly what you're looking for, whether it is a residential property or investment real estate in Wilmington, Wrightsville Beach, Carolina Beach, Kure Beach, Fort Fisher, Figure Eight Island, Southport, Castle Hayne, Hampstead, Brunswick County or Pender County.

This personalized service is extremely helpful for first-time home buyers, single individuals and business folks who have little time to read classifieds and homebuyer's publications or drive through neighborhoods looking for just the right house. ABR Realty will represent you only, negotiating the best price and terms and fully protecting your interests.

Bachman Realty
2411 Middle Sound Loop Rd., Wilmington
• (910) 686-4099, (800) 470-4099

Specializing in waterfront and golf properties, Bachman Realty is the ideal agency for discriminating buyers, especially for those seeking a beautiful home in one of the area's most prestigious communities, such as Landfall, Figure Eight Island and Porter's Neck. Are you interested in Turtle Hall, Masonboro Harbour, Oyster Bay or Tangle Oaks? Call founder-owner Bunnie Bachman — a true buyer's broker who takes the time to listen to each client's unique real estate needs. A Wilmington-area resident for more than 20 years, Bunnie enjoys sharing her Insider's knowledge with newcomers.

Bryant Real Estate
1001 N. Lumina Ave., Wrightsville Beach
• (910) 256-3764, (800) 322-3764
1401 N. Lake Park Blvd., Snow's Cut
Crossing, Carolina Beach • (910) 458-5658,
(800) 994-5222
501 N. College Rd., Wilmington
• (910) 799-2700

Offering vacation rental homes, condos and townhomes with locations from the ocean to the sound, Bryant Real Estate has been providing quality sales, rental and property management service in the Wilmington, Carolina Beach, Kure Beach and Wrightsville Beach areas for more than 50 years. For year-round rentals, call (910) 799-2700. Seasonal rentals are also available in Wrightsville Beach.

Century 21 Coastal Communities
3701 Wrightsville Ave., Wilmington
• (910) 395-4770, (888) 395-4770
6412 Beach Dr., Ocean Isle Beach
• (910) 579-4770, (877) 579-4777
3270 Holden Beach Rd., Holden Beach
• (910) 842-3190, (877) 752-0151

Specializing in residential and recreational

Quality craftsmanship at an affordable price.

EBCO Builders
5370 Market St.
Wilmington, NC 28405
www.ebcobuilders.com
910-799-5060

properties, Century 21 Coastal Communities has an extensive listing of fine homes and estates as well as mid-range properties. Relocation service is provided through Century 21 Relocation and Referral. This agency also offers real estate services from Wilmington to Calabash, which results in high visibility and maximum exposure. Three small offices, each staffed with highly experienced professionals, provide quality individualized service and personal attention.

Coldwell Banker Sea Coast Realty
5710 Oleander Dr., Ste. 200, Wilmington
• (910) 799-3435, (800) 522-9624
8211 Market St., Unit CC, Wilmington
• (910) 686-6855, (800) 435-7211
1430 Commonwealth Dr., Ste. 102, Wilmington
• (910) 256-1155, (800) 497-7325
1001 N. Lake Park Blvd., Carolina Beach
• (910) 458-4401, (800) 847-5771
607 North Howe Street, Southport
(910) 457-6713, (800) 346-7671
300 Country Club Rd., Oak Island
(910) 278-3311, (800) 841-4950

Coldwell Banker Sea Coast Realty is one of the dominant real estate companies in the area, with over $400 million in closed sales and 2,600 transactions in 2002. The company was named the 11th fastest growing real estate company in the U.S. by Real Trends, Inc. Having more than 175 professional Realtors, the company handles all types of residential properties, resort/vacation properties, homesites/land/acreage, as

well as commercial properties and relocation services. The company also represents an impressive list of new home communities in Wilmington, and across New Hanover, Pender and Brunswick counties. For additional information, contact one of Coldwell Banker Sea Coast's six area offices.

Demarest Company
• (910) 686-9707
The Demarest Company represents the communities of Demarest Landing and Demarest Village, as well as other prestigious planned communities in the southern coastal area. The Demarest communities offer traditional home designs reminiscent of historic Wilmington, all integrated with beautiful parks and tree-lined streets. The neighborhoods have been endorsed by the Governor's Taskforce for Smart Growth as the "cutting edge" in traditional neighhborhood design. Call the office for more information.

EXIT Homeplace Realty
311 Judges Rd., Ste. 9E, Wilmington
• (910) 452-3810, (877) 466-3400
13775 N.C. Hwy. 50, Ste 501, Surf City
• (910) 392-0900, (877) 466-3400
Capitalizing on the "most advertised word in the English language," and focusing on what you're trying to accomplish when you put your house up for sale, EXIT Homeplace Realty is part of a progressive, fast-growing, international franchise. Using a team approach to real estate sales, local offices handle all types of residential property primarily in New Hanover, Brunswick, Pender and Onslow counties.

Intracoastal Realty Corporation
Lumina Station, 1900 Eastwood Rd., Ste. 38, Wilmington • (910) 256-4503, (800) 533-1840
534 Causeway Dr., Wrightsville Beach
• (910) 256-4503, (800) 533-1840
This market leader has been in business in the area since 1974. An exclusive affiliate of Sotheby's International Realty, it is a resort and residential property specialist. This company has listings throughout the region, including historic downtown Wilmington, Wrightsville Beach and Landfall. It is a member of the RELO relocation service. The agency's New Home division represents several new home communities in the area, offering homes that range from $80,000 upwards to

INSIDERS' TIP
Always ask about the storm damage history of a potential home.

$350,000. Intracoastal also offers a vacation and long-term rental office in Wrightsville Beach at 605 Causeway Drive; for weekly vacation rentals call (910) 256-3780, (800) 346-2463; for long-term rentals call (910) 509-9700, (800) 826-4428.

Landfall Realty
1816 Mews Dr., Wilmington
• **(910) 256-6111, (800) 227-8208**

Landfall Realty deals exclusively with the fine properties in Landfall, a private gated neighborhood of single-family custom homes, villas, patio homes, townhomes, condominiums and home sites. The community boasts numerous amenities, including two championship golf courses — a Jack Nicklaus 27-hole course and the Pete Dye 18-hole course — and the Landfall Sports Center, designed by tennis legend, Cliff Drysdale. Two well-appointed clubhouses overlook Landfall's golf courses: the luxurious Landfall Clubhouse near the Nicklaus course and the Dye Clubhouse on Landfall's Pete Dye course.

Network Real Estate
1601 S. College Rd., Wilmington
• **(910) 395-4100, (800) 747-1968**
106 North Water St., Wilmington
• **(910) 772-1622, (877) 882-1622**
1029 N. Lake Park Blvd., Carolina Beach
• **(910) 458-8881, (800) 830-2118**

The sales staff at Network Real Estate takes pride in the fact that the company has helped the Greater Wilmington area with home sales, rentals and property management needs since 1982. Their motto: "We know real estate, it's our business. We know Wilmington, it's our hometown." The agency specializes in residential and single-family home sales, including Wilmington and the beaches. Network Real Estate also handles condominium sales with four new projects currently underway in the heart of historic downtown Wilmington: Water Street Center, Riverwalk, Chandler's Watch and The Masonic Temple. Rentals in downtown Wilmington are handled through their office at Water Street Center. For information about Network's vacation rentals, refer to the Weekly and Long-term Vacation Rentals chapter in this book.

Port City Properties
17 S. Second St., Wilmington
• **(910) 251-0615**

Established in 1995, Port City Properties represents residential and commercial properties throughout New Hanover, Brunswick and Pender counties. This full-service realty company covers a full geographical and price spectrum, specializing in historic downtown Wilmington and all area beach communities.

Porters Neck Plantation
8204 Fazio Dr., Wilmington
• **(910) 686-7400, (800) 423-5695,**

Porters Neck offers an extraordinary setting, with 650 acres of pristine, lush coastal land adjacent to the Intracoastal Waterway and a Tom Fazio–designed golf course. The sports complex, complete with a lap pool, clay tennis courts and a fitness center also draw active individuals to this community. Traditional single-family homes and patio homes are available in a variety of sizes. Porters Neck is north of Wilmington and Wrightsville Beach just off U.S. Highway 17. Contact the office for more information.

REAL ESTATE

REAL ESTATE

Prudential Carolina Real Estate
Relocation Services: 7040 Wrightsville Ave., Ste 100, Wilmington
• (910) 239-5799, (888) 220-4665
Sales Office: 530 Causeway Dr., Wrightsville Beach
• (910) 256-9299, (800) 562-9299
Sales Office: 1131-B Military Cutoff, Wilmington, (910) 256-0032, (800) 521-8132
Sales Office: 1025B N. Lake Park Blvd., Carolina Beach
• (910) 458-9672, (888) 313-9738
Commercial Division: 1213 Culbreth Dr., Wilmington, (910) 239-5800

This company is one of the largest real estate agencies servicing the Cape Fear Area. Residential sales include single-family homes, townhomes, condominiums, lots and developed communities, including Georgetowne, Blue Point, Saponas Point, Warlick, The Arbors at Johnson Farms, Weston, Murray Farms, Saybrook Village, The Fields at Wendover and South Point. Prudential Carolina Real Estate has a full-service Commercial Division and also specializes in corporate relocation services provided by certified relocation specialists.

Realty Executives of Wilmington
6800 Wrightsville Ave. Ste. 18, Wilmington
• (910) 256-4686, (910) 352-2000, (888) 622-6033

Dedicated to providing their clients with a level of service beyond their expectations, Sandy and Dick Beals believe that buying or selling a home is an important life transition and they work hard to ensure that it's worry free. With an experienced team of professionals, Realty Executives of Wilmington guarantees privacy and respect while delivering results. The conveniently located office is fully equipped and has an integrated network of computer and communication systems to facilitate access to all the Multiple Listing Services, public record searches and other tools that agents need in order to better serve clients.

Since its inception in Phoenix, Arizona, more than 35 years ago, Realty Executives has become one of the fastest growing franchises internationally; this is the first office in the Wilmington area.

RE/MAX Coastal Properties
2004 Eastwood Rd., and 5653 Carolina Beach Rd., Wilmington • (910) 256-8171, (800) 833-9584

Deciding to sell a home is a big step, so you'll

want to choose the best qualified person to handle your real estate needs. The company claims that no one in the world sells more real estate than RE/MAX. Averaging three times the production and more advanced industry education than other agents, RE/MAX associates are leaders in quality customer service. Customer satisfaction is reflected in their high, industry-leading rate of repeat and referral business.

Affiliation with the global RE/MAX network provides associates with multiple competitive advantages in serving real estate needs. From national television advertising to personal advertising controlled by associates, RE/MAX enjoys brand-name recognition worldwide. Belonging to a real estate network with vast market presence and market share, RE/MAX associates have the much to offer you.

Wallace

River Landing
110 River Village Pl., Wallace
• (910) 285-4171, (888) 285-4171

For the best of residential, golf-community living, look to River Landing. Just 35 minutes from Wilmington off I-40, this is a private community of primary residences and second homes with a variety of recreational facilities, including a 27-hole golf course, swim and tennis center, fishing and boating, nature trails and a club house. Contact the office at the number above for more information.

Wrightsville Beach

Bryant Real Estate
1001 N. Lumina Ave., Wrightsville Beach
• (910) 256-3764, (800) 322-3764
1401 N. Lake Park Blvd., Snow's Cut
Crossing, Carolina Beach • (910) 458-5658
(800) 994-5222
501 N. College Rd., Wilmington
• (910) 799-2700

Offering vacation rental homes, condos and townhomes with locations from the ocean to the sound, Bryant Real Estate has been providing quality sales, rental and property management service in the Wilmington, Carolina Beach, Kure Beach and Wrightsville Beach areas for more than 50 years. For year-round rentals, call (910) 799-2700. Seasonal rentals are also available in Wrightsville Beach.

REAL ESTATE

Intracoastal Realty Corporation
Lumina Station, 1900 Eastwood Rd., Ste. 38, Wilmington • (910) 256-4503, (800) 533-1840
534 Causeway Dr., Wrightsville Beach • (910) 256-4503, (800) 533-1840

This market leader has been in business in the area since 1974. An exclusive affiliate of Sotheby's International Realty, it is a resort and residential property specialist. This company has listings throughout the region, including historic downtown Wilmington, Wrightsville Beach and Landfall. It is a member of the RELO relocation service. The agency's New Home division represents several new home communities in the area, offering homes that range from $80,000 up to $350,000. Intracoastal also offers a vacation and long-term rental office in Wrightsville Beach at 605 Causeway Drive; for weekly vacation rentals call (910) 256-3780, (800) 346-2463; for long-term rentals call (910) 509-9700, (800) 826-4428.

Figure Eight Island

Bachman Realty
2411 Middle Sound Loop Rd., Wilmington • (910) 686-4099, (800) 470-4099

A Figure Eight Island resident for more than 20 years, Bunnie Bachman's specialty is that of a buyer's broker. She has the extensive knowledge needed to purchase the right waterfront home — be it oceanfront, soundfront or the Intracoastal Waterway. A part of this unique, secluded private island can be yours.

Figure Eight Realty
15 Bridge Rd., Wilmington
• (910) 686-4400, (800) 279-6085

This agency, which is located on Figure Eight Island, focuses on the island's neighborhood of luxury, single-family homes. Oceanfront, marsh-front and sound-front properties are available. Figure Eight Realty also offers vacation rentals on the island.

Carolina Beach and Kure Beach

Atlantic Shores Real Estate
9 S. Lake Park Blvd., Ste. A-3, Carolina Beach • Sales (910) 458-5878, (877) 428-5878; Rentals (910) 458-4975, (800) 289-0028

Located in the heart of Carolina Beach, Atlantic Shores Real Estate is a full-service company that lists, sells and rents residential, commercial and investment properties within Carolina Beach, Kure Beach, Wrightsville Beach and all of Wilmington. At Atlantic Shores Real Estate, special emphasis is placed on delivering personal service to clients, understanding their wants and needs, and thereby providing the professional guidance necessary to make an informed decision. The real estate professionals at Atlantic Shores Real Estate have earned their reputation for dedication, industry knowledge and individual integrity.

REAL ESTATE

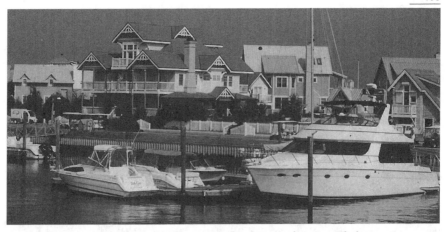

Living by the water with a boat at your door is many a homeowner's dream.

Photo: Jay Tervo

Bryant Real Estate
1001 N. Lumina Ave., Wrightsville Beach
• (910) 256-3764, (800) 322-3764
1401 N. Lake Park Blvd., Snow's Cut
Crossing, Carolina Beach • (910) 458-5658
(800) 994-5222
501 N. College Rd., Wilmington
• (910) 799-2700

Offering vacation rental homes, condos and townhomes with locations from the ocean to the sound, Bryant Real Estate has been providing quality sales, rental and property management service in the Wilmington, Carolina Beach, Kure Beach and Wrightsville Beach areas for more than 50 years. For year-round rentals, call (910) 799-2700. Seasonal rentals are also available in Wrightsville Beach.

Bullard Realty, Inc.
1404 S. Lake Park Blvd., Carolina Beach
• (910) 458-4028, (800) 327-5863

Established in 1989, Bullard Realty Inc. is a small, full-service real estate company specializing in sales and rentals on Carolina and Kure Beaches. Owner Beth Bullard and her staff can represent buyers and sellers. Bullard Realty offers the personalized service of a small company with the professionalism and technology of a larger agency. Please see the Weekly and Long-term Vacation Rentals chapter for rental information.

Network Real Estate
1029 N. Lake Park Blvd., Ste. 1, Carolina
Beach • (910) 458-8881, (800) 830-2118

This large agency's Carolina Beach office provides general real estate brokerage services for properties on Pleasure Island. Their vacation rental office is also housed at this location. Wilmington offices are located at 1601 S. College Road, (910) 395-4100, (800) 747-1968 and 106 N. Water Street, (910) 772-1622, (877) 882-1622.

Southport-Oak Island

Century 21 Dorothy Essey
and Associates Inc.
6102 E. Oak Island Dr., Oak Island
• (910) 278-3361, (877) 410-2121
113 S. Howe St., Southport
• (910) 457-4577, (877) 410-2121

This real estate company covers Southport and Oak Island as well as Boiling Spring Lakes, Bald Head Island, Caswell Beach and the South Brunswick beaches. It offers general brokerage and services for single-family homes, condominiums, duplexes, lots and commercial properties. The company has a new-home specialist on staff.

Coldwell Banker Sea Coast Realty
607 N. Howe St., Southport
• (910) 457-6713, (800) 346-7671
300 Country Club Dr., Oak Island
• (910) 278-3311, (800) 841-4950

Coldwell Banker Sea Coast Realty is a full-service real estate company dedicated to providing real estate services and products to home buyers and sellers in the New Hanover, Pender and Brunswick County areas. More than 160 highly trained sales associates offer their clients

REAL ESTATE

Coastal real estate comes in a variety of styles.

Photo: Jay Tervo

the programs, systems and best marketing tools available to achieve customer satisfaction.

the Jack Cox group
5001 O'Quinn Blvd., Ste. H, Southport
• (910) 457-6884, (888) 603-1956

From their waterfront offices at South Harbour Village just outside of Southport, the Jack Cox group handles real estate sales and rentals for a large geographic area. In addition to handling both rentals and sales on Bald Head Island, agents out of this office can help you solve your real estate needs in much of Brunswick County, including Southport, Oak Island and Shallotte. They deal extensively in both residential and commercial properties.

Ocean 1 Realty
4310 E. Beach Dr., Oak Island
• (910) 278-6753, (910) 269-3269

Ocean 1 Realty is the only real estate office located on the beach and claims to have the best sales office on Oak Island. The company specializes in oceanfront property, beach rental property and condos located on a beautiful golf course. Manager Keith Ferrell, GRI, has been brokering real estate for 26 years. His family has been building homes on Oak Island for 50 years. Answering

questions about financing, insurance and rental income is easy for this group.

Southport Realty
N.C. Hwy. 211, Southport
• (910) 457-5988, (800) 682-8846

Southport Realty handles sales at Arbor Creek, a charming real estate community a short drive from the quaint village of Southport. Home-site sales and home re-sales are offered. Home-site prices range from the upper $20,000s to the mid-$60,000s. Single-family homes and home-site packages are available, priced from $175,000 to $250,000. Southport Realty is a full-service realty organization located on site and at 114 S. Howe Street on the waterfront in Southport.

Walter Hill & Associates
6101 E. Oak Island Dr., Oak Island
• (910) 278-5469, (800) 603-5469

This company serves Southport, Oak Island's two beach communities and Brunswick County through the sale of residential and commercial properties near the water and on the mainland. The company also specializes in property management and long- or short-term beachfront rentals on Oak Island.

REAL ESTATE

Bald Head Island

Bald Head Island Limited
5079 Southport-Supply Rd., Southport
• (910) 457-7400, (800) 888-3707

Bald Head Island Limited sells single-family homes, cottages, condominiums, townhouses and home sites on Bald Head Island as well as Indigo Plantation & Marina in Southport. Properties are located along the Cape Fear River, the Atlantic Ocean, the Intracoastal Waterway, Bald Head Island creeks and marshes, the 18-hole George Cobb-designed golf course and the pristine Maritime Forest on the island. To get to Bald Head Island, you must board the Bald Head Island Ferry at Indigo Plantation & Marina in Southport for a 20-minute ride.

Bald Head Island Real Estate Sales, Inc.
1111 Howe St., Southport
• (910) 457-6463, (800) 350-7021

This real estate brokerage firm is the largest independent agency for Bald Head Island not associated with a developer. The company handles real estate on Bald Head Island, in Southport and on Oak Island, representing buyers as well as sellers.

Bald Head Island Resort Sales & Rentals
219 N. Bald Head Wynd, Bald Head Island
• (910) 457-4433, (800) 820-0545

Robin Craven has been living and selling real estate on Bald Head Island for 12 years. As an independent agent, he provides service to both buyer and seller. As a member of the Brunswick County Multiple Listing Service, he has access to all properties listed on the island to better help you discover this area.

Cape Fear Realty
120 E. Moore St., Southport
• (910) 457-1702, (800) 680-8322

Offering listings on Bald Head Island, Middle Island Plantation and on the mainland in Southport, Cape Fear Realty specializes in home re-sales, island home sites and new-home construction. The agency is a member of the Multiple Listing Service.

the Jack Cox group
58 Dowitcher Tr., Bald Head Island
• (910) 457-4732, (888) 603-1956

This family-owned and independent real estate agency opened on the island five years ago and specializes in property on exclusive Bald Head Island as well as mainland Brunswick County. They offer residential sales of single-family homes, condominiums and cottages. A recent addition is the agency's Bald Head Island vacation rental division.

Old Baldy Associates
1105 N, Howe St., Southport
• (910) 457-5551

Involved in sales for more than 24 years, Old Baldy Associates specializes in resale and rental of Bald Head Island and Middle Island Plantation property. Homesites are available overlooking the ocean and high dunes, the golf course, the maritime forest and saltwater creeks. In Middle Island Plantation, a residential-only community at the eastern end of Bald Head Island, all homesites are more than a half-acre, and amenities include a keyed beach walk, Bald Head Island Club membership, and a floating dock system for boats up to 25 feet.

The South Brunswick Islands
Holden Beach

Brunswickland Realty
123 Ocean Blvd. W., Holden Beach
• (910) 842-1300, (800) 842-6949

Brunswickland, a leading agency of property sales, is a buyer/seller agency. In addition to offering homes for sale in all locations on Holden Beach, Brunswickland offers properties on the mainland. Included are homes and lots in Lockwood Folly Country Club, bounded by the Lockwood Folly river on the east and the Intracoastal Waterway on the south.

Coastal Development and Realty
131 Ocean Blvd. W., Holden Beach
• (910) 842-4939, (800) 262-7820
900 Yaupon Dr., Oak Island
• (910) 278-6111, (888) 278-2611

Coastal Development and Realty was the No. 1 listing and selling real estate company in the multilist system in Brunswick County in 2001. Established in Brunswick County since 1985, it has offices on Holden Beach and Oak Island. Real estate sales include properties in River's Edge Golf Course and Seascape at Holden Plantation. The company offers professional services in real estate sales, vacation rentals and custom-designed home construction.

Hobbs Realty
114 Ocean Blvd. W., Holden Beach
• (910) 842-2002, (800) 655-3367

A drive across beautiful Holden Beach Bridge, a turn to the left and a stop at the second office on the left will bring you to Hobbs Realty. Situated on the island of Holden Beach close to Wilmington and Myrtle Beach, this family owned and operated business with 26 years of building experience offers resort real estate sales and new construction from the ocean to the waterway and everywhere in between. The company has an in-house relocation service as well.

Alan Holden Vacations/ RE/MAX at the Beach
128 Ocean Blvd. W., Holden Beach
• (910) 842-8686, (800) 360-0770
6900 Ocean Hwy. W., Sunset Beach
• (910) 575-7355, (888) 414-7355
6237 E. Oak Island Dr., Oak Island
• (910) 278-1950. (866) 350-7653

The Holden family bought this island from King George of England in 1756. The family has been providing rentals, sales and construction services for over seven decades. Sea Castles Inc., (910) 842-5686, the company's construction division, has an unlimited residential and commercial license.

Ocean Isle

Century 21 Coastal Communities
6412 Beach Dr., Ocean Isle Beach
• (910) 579-4770, (877) 579-4777
3270 Holden Beach Rd., Holden Beach
• (910) 842-3190, (877) 752-0151

Specializing in residential and recreational properties, Century 21 Coastal Communities has an extensive listing of fine homes and estates as well as mid-range properties. Relocation service is provided through Century 21 Relocation and Referral. This agency also offers real estate services from Wilmington to Calabash, which results in high visibility and maximum exposure. Three small offices, each staffed with highly experienced professionals, provide quality individualized service and personal attention.

Coldwell Banker -Sloane Realty Inc.
16 Causeway Dr., Ocean Isle Beach
• (910) 579-1144, (800) 237-4609
790-2 Sunset Blvd,, Sunset Beach
• (910) 579-1808, (877) 369-5777

Owned by the first permanent family to live on Ocean Isle Beach and serving the region for more than 40 years, Sloane Realty Inc. offers a wide range of new-home construction and residential re-sale options, including oceanfront living, deep-water canal homes, golf course communities and the adjacent mainland. Properties include single-family homes, condominiums and home sites.

Cooke Realty
1 Causeway Dr., Ocean Isle Beach
• (910) 579-3535, (800) 622-3224

This well-established island realty company offers complete real estate sales services as well as nearly 450 rental homes, cottages and condominiums. They offer properties on the oceanfront, second- and third-row, canal-side, West End and Island Park, as well as off the island.

Island Realty Inc.
109-2 Causeway Dr., Ocean Isle Beach
• (910) 579-3599, (800) 589-3599

Serving Ocean Isle Beach and the adjacent mainland, Island Realty Inc. offers single-family homes, condominiums and lots for sale. Property sites include beachfront, waterway and mainland locations and golf communities. Rental properties are also available.

R. H. McClure Realty, Inc.
24 Causeway Dr., Ocean Isle Beach
• (910)579-3586, (800) 332-5476

R. H. McClure Realty is a full-service realty brokerage that has been established on Ocean Isle Beach for more than 20 years. The firm specializes in residential re-sales, property management, long-term and short-term vacation rentals, and design and construction of new homes. Ralph H. McClure has been the premier builder on Ocean Isle Beach for many years. His inventory of homes and homesites include oceanfront, deep-water canal, mid-island, condos, golf course communities and mainland properties. Friendly and knowledgeable agents will provide the individual attention and personal service you deserve.

Ocean Isle Beach Realty, Inc.
15 Causeway Dr., Ocean Isle Beach
• (910) 575-7770, (800) 374-7361

This well-established real estate company has been an Ocean Isle Beach tradition since 1953, offering residential sales and vacation rentals for single-family homes, condominiums and cottages. Island locations include oceanfront, waterway, canal and interior homesites and homes. OIB Realty is the exclusive agent for the luxurious Islander Resort, located on the west end of the is-

Porches are a predominant feature of most coastal homes.

Photo: Jay Tervo

land. The Islander Resort is a master-planned development featuring four-bedroom, four-bath villas in attractive buildings with elevators. The development also features oceanfront and soundfront homes and homesites, as well as the soon-to-be completed multimillion-dollar restaurant and beach club located on the oceanfront.

Sand Dollar Realty Inc.
102 Causeway Dr., Ocean Isle Beach
• (910) 579-7038, (800) 457-7263

In business since 1985, this real estate company is a full-service brokerage and sells properties on Ocean Isle Beach and along the coast of Brunswick County. Conveniently located on the causeway on Ocean Isle Beach, Sand Dollar Realty takes pride in the fact that all of its agents are professional brokers and long-term residents of the area. It's also licensed in North Carolina and neighboring South Carolina.

Sunset Beach

Century 21 Sunset Realty
502 N. Sunset Blvd., Sunset Beach
• (910) 579-1000, (800) 451-2102

Century 21 Sunset Realty, founded in 1984, is one of the best choices in the South Brunswick Islands when it comes to a full-service real estate company. With two offices, it offers every type of real estate investment opportunity available in the area. Visit the mainland office or the beach location and discover the large list of inventory. You will also find agents equipped to help you with beach, waterway, golf course, vacant land or commercial properties.

Sunset Properties
419 S. Sunset Blvd., Sunset Beach
• (910) 579-9900, (800) 446-0218

On the island and family-owned since 1988,

this company regularly handles properties only on Sunset Beach. Single-family homes dominate this quiet residential island that attracts second-home investors, retirees and people who simply appreciate living away from it all.

Simmons Realty Inc.
4741 Main St., Shallotte
• **(910) 755-5677, (888) 683-0550**

This small real estate company has been working in sales on Sunset Beach since 1990, but broker Beth Simmons is a lifelong native of the area. The company offers general real estate services on the Brunswick Islands and the adjacent mainland. It handles single-family homes, cottages and condominium units and is a commercial brokerage. Simmons Realty is now the managing firm for Carolina Shores Resort.

ERA Bonnie Black & Associates Realty
10239 Beach Dr. SW, Calabash
• **(910) 579-4097, (800) 833-6330**

ERA Bonnie Black & Associates Realty handles residential, commercial and investment sales in Brunswick County and the Grand Strand area of Horry County. The agency is a member of the Brunswick County Board of Realtors and the Coastal Carolina Association of Realtors.

Topsail Island

A Beach Place Realty
106 N. Topsail Dr., Surf City
• **(910) 328-2522, (877) 884-2522**

After five years of experience with another agency, Laura Bageant has taken her knowledge and created her own business with some added touches. She is proud to offer virtual tours of all her properties, a way to get in the house to see what you're renting or buying. This small office of three agents is able to offer personal service to help in the selection of both residential and commercial properties on Topsail Island or the mainland.

Access Realty & Topsail Vacations
513 Roland Ave., Surf City
• **(910) 328-4888 (800) TOPSAIL**
116B South Shore Dr., Surf City
• **(910) 328-3888**

Under new ownership, Access Realty continues to be a full-service brokerage company providing friendly, personalized real estate services for buyers and sellers on Topsail Island and the adjacent mainland. The company, now expanding to a second office, handles residential, new construction and commercial sales.

Jean Brown Real Estate, Inc.
522 N. New River Dr., Surf City
• **(910) 328-1640, (800) 745-4480**

Jean Brown Real Estate, Inc. has been a top-producing island realty for many years in the Topsail and surrounding areas. Sales agents offer a wide range of experience in both residential and commercial real estate. This office consistently maintains one of the largest listing inventories of properties for sale, and is a member of both the Topsail Island and Wilmington MLS Services.

Bryson & Associates
809 Roland Ave, Surf City
• **(910) 328-2468, (800) 326-0747**

Bryson and Associates, a member of the Top-

REAL ESTATE

sail Island Multiple Listing Service, offers single-family home sales throughout the island from oceanfront and second-row to soundfront and interior. High-end, oceanfront single-family homes are their specialty. Committed to quality customer service, Bryson and Associates are also homeowner association managers.

Cape Fear Real Estate Company
785 New River Inlet Rd, North Topsail Beach • (888) 328-5599

Specializing in high-end residential and commercial property, Cape Fear Real Estate Company offers expertise in sales, leasing, building and development. The onsite construction company, Coastal Living Design and Construction, is an important piece of this "one stop shopping" opportunity. On the cutting edge of technology, this office can provide quality digital pictures of properties to be viewed on its website.

Cape Island
785 New River Inlet Rd, North Topsail Beach • (888) 328-5599

An exclusive planned community, Cape Island offers homes and homesites on a 50 acre island situated between Topsail Island and the Intracoastal Waterway. Residents enjoy a clubhouse, boat slips and ramp, dock for fishing and swimming on premises, plus easy ocean access for that daily visit to the beach. A pool will soon be added to these amenities. Nicely groomed grounds, quality landscaping and underground utilities add to the beauty and pride of ownership. A visit is a must to appreciate all Cape Island has to offer.

Century 21 Action, Inc.
518 Roland Ave., Surf City
804 Carolina Ave., Topsail Beach
200 N. Shore Village, Sneads Ferry
• (910) 328-2511, (800) 255-2233

An established business since 1969, Century 21 Action professionally markets real estate in the entire greater Topsail Island area. With 14 agents and three offices, there is always someone ready to assist with a sale or purchase anywhere on Topsail Island or on the mainland from north of Hampstead to Holly Ridge and Sneads Ferry. This company also has a large and well-managed vacation and long-term rental division.

Coldwell Banker Coastline Realty
Topsail Way Shopping Center, 965 Old Folkstone Rd., Ste. 108, Sneads Ferry
• (910) 327-7711, (800) 497-5463

This company, established in 1994 and

owned and operated by Duplin County native Bud Rivenbark, handles mostly oceanfront condominiums and soundside properties on Topsail Island and in the Sneads Ferry area. Coastline Realty offers single-family homes, townhomes and lots and is a member of the Coldwell Banker Relocation Network and is an MLS member. This company also handles commercial sales.

Exit Homeplace Realty
13775 N.C. Hwy. 50, Ste. 501,
Surf City • (910) 329-0900, (877) 466-3400

Exit Homeplace Realty was established in 1999 with one goal in mind: to give homebuyers in the Coastal Carolinas a reli-

KATHY S. PARKER REAL ESTATE

1000 Hwy 210
Sneads Ferry, NC

1(800)327-2218
910-327-2219

Visit us Online at:
www.topsailbeach.com
E-mail: kathy@topsailbeach.com

been an area builder since 1983. His full-service real estate business consists of residential and commercial sales and new construction both on Topsail Island and the surrounding areas. He is also a licensed real estate appraiser. The company's property management department handles long-term rentals.

Kathy S. Parker Real Estate
1000 N.C. Hwy. 210, Sneads Ferry
• (910) 327-2219, (800) 327-2218

Kathy S. Parker Real Estate has 20 years experience in Topsail Area Real Estate. Five real estate agents can help you sell your home or business or find your dream property or vacation home in the Jacksonville, Sneads Ferry, North Topsail Beach and Holly Ridge areas. Located close to Camp Lejeune, this agency specializes in base relocations and Veterans Administration loans.

Sand Dollar Real Estate Inc.
Treasure Coast Square, 208-J N. Topsail Dr., Surf City • (910) 328-5199, (800) 948-4360

Serving the Greater Topsail area from the oceanfront to the soundside of the island, Sand Dollar Real Estate offers assorted residential and commercial sales options, including single-family and new homes as well as duplex, condominium, townhome, business and vacant property sales.

Treasure Realty
Treasure Plaza, N.C. Hwys. 210 and 172, Sneads Ferry • (910) 327-4444, (910) 327-3961, (800)762-3961

Treasure Realty is proud to be the top-producing firm of the decade for the years 2000, 2001 and 2002 in North Topsail Beach and Sneads Ferry. Waterfront property and condominiums are their specialty. With their many years of experience, Treasure Realty's professional sales staff is ready to serve as a buyer or a seller.

Turner Real Estate
Surf City (IGA) Shopping Center, Surf City
• (910) 328-1313, (800) 326-2926

Specializing in sales of everything from single-family homes and condominiums to commercial property and building lots, Turner Real Estate has been serving all of Topsail Island since 1988. Broker-in-charge Rick Turner offers personalized service, including forwarding business calls to his home after regular business hours.

able source of information and representation in every facet of residential real estate. Using a team approach to real estate sales, the Topsail Island office handles all types of residential real estate. The company also has an office in Wilmington. The two offices together handle New Hanover, Brunswick, Pender and Onslow counties.

Harbor Real Estate
307A Roland Ave., Surf City
• (910) 328-3060

This island real estate agency has moved to a new office to better serve you. They offer residential and commercial sales anywhere between Jacksonville and Wilmington. Harbor promises to do their best to help you find a particular type home in the area you select. Appraisal services are a major part of their services.

Island Real Estate by Cathy Medlin
The Fishing Village, Roland Ave., Surf City
• (910) 328-2323, (800) 622-6886

Cathy Medlin has been selling properties on Topsail Island and the mainland in Onslow and Pender counties since 1979. She was one of the founders of the Topsail Island Board of Realtors in 1992. This company sells beach, waterway and mainland homes and lots as well as commercial buildings and property. The company also handles 180 rental properties.

Kinco Real Estate
202 S. Shore Dr., Surf City
• (910) 328-0239, (800) 513-8957

An Onslow County native, Nathan King has

Ward Realty
116 S. Topsail Dr., Surf City
• (910) 328-3221, (800) 782-6216

The original developer of Topsail Island, Ward Realty has more than 50 years of dedicated service in sales, construction, property management and rentals. Broker David Ward continues the family tradition of commitment to the buyer's interest. The rental and sales departments are strong assets and work hand-in-hand to provide a full-service, compatible real estate program.

Hampstead

Castle Bay Country Club
58 Castle Bay Dr., Hampstead
• (910) 270-1247

A dream come true for the golfing enthusiast, Castle Bay Country Club is now offering patio, town and custom-built homes, all with a golf course view. Built in the old English style, these brick homes can be purchased as built, or personalized to fit your lifestyle. Home ownership comes with a free golf membership and use of the pool and tennis, volleyball and racquetball courts. There is also a fitness center on the premises. It's a great setting for retirees and families.

Home Services

Kinetico Quality Water Systems
16126 N.C. Hwy. 17, Hampstead,
• (910) 270-1214, (800) 865-1208

Looking for a water-treatment system for your home or office? Kinetico provides NSF (National Sanitation Foundation)-approved systems for both residential and commercial use. Although they service all makes and models, Kinetico takes pride in its own patented features, such as non-electric operation, twin-tank design and demand regeneration. Its 10-year factory warranty, one of the best in the business, is definitely hard to beat. In addition, Kinetico provides high-quality drinking water through its unique under-the-counter reverse-osmosis systems and offers sales, leasing and rental options for all equipment.

Gideons Heating & Air Conditioning
98 J. H. Batts Rd., Surf City
• (910) 328-1817

Just a phone call away, Gideons Heating and Air Conditioning is ready to discuss or provide an estimate for new or replacement central heating and air conditioning units. A long-established beach business, Gideon has friendly, professional service technicians who are prepared to repair or service your present unit or install a new one. It's open daily, except Sunday. Emergency service is available.

REAL ESTATE

Retirement

Retiree-friendly pretty well characterizes the four-county area known as the Cape Fear Coast. With Historic Wilmington and New Hanover county as its focal point, the southern coast of North Carolina has been attracting retirees to its sunny, warm shores in ever-increasing numbers for years.

In North Carolina, the number of residents age 65 and older rose 20 percent in the period from 1990 to 2000, but in New Hanover County, the number of retirement-age residents grew by 36 percent during the same period. And this impressive increase does not include the many younger retirees and semi-retirees who have moved to the Cape Fear Coast to enjoy a more relaxed business climate and better quality of living.

Naturally, the mild, temperate climate of our area is a major attraction for retirees from the north, who are disenchanted with frigid winters, snow, ice, potholes and gray skies. Winter, such as it is here, is moderated considerably by the warming effect of the Atlantic Ocean and the Gulf Stream during winter months.

Although it may seem a bit odd at first, the area is also experiencing an increasing popularity with retirees moving here from Florida. Known as "Halfbacks," these new residents are usually retirees from the north who moved to Florida, became disenchanted and decided to move halfway back up, where they can enjoy moderate seasonal changes without extremes.

For those interested in gardening, the southern coastal area is in USDA growing zone 8, averages 248 or more growing days per year and has an annual rainfall of 54 inches. The heaviest rainfall months are June, July and August, and more often than not, it rains at night and is sunny during the day — Camelot right here in Dixie. Several varieties of flowers bloom all winter, and numerous shrubs and trees retain their foliage all year. The average summer high temperature is 88 degrees, the average winter low is 36 degrees and the overall average for the year is 64 degrees.

Another aspect of the Cape Fear area attracting retirees is a considerably expanded health-care system that is increasingly focused on the needs of seniors. In addition, quite a few new retirement homes are opening, and there is a strong upswing in the development of retirement communities, many of them with golf courses, tennis courts and swimming pools and offering a wide variety of housing choices.

Even though progressive and growth-oriented, the Cape Fear area still possesses elements of charm, graciousness and gentility from the old South, which, coupled with the cosmopolitan influence of retirees and new residents from all across the nation, results in a delightfully relaxed but upbeat ambiance. Also, partly due to the enormous number of activities available to them, retirees tend to feel more included living in the Cape Fear community than they would living in a large urban area where they might feel shunted aside.

Downtown Wilmington offers many activities for seniors, including horse-drawn carriage, trolley or walking tours of the Historical District, riverboat tours, art galleries, unusual stores and boutiques, Riverwalk, Battleship USS *North Carolina*, and a number of antebellum homes open for visiting, to mention just a few (see our Attractions chapter). Any

given evening will find both seniors and younger folk strolling about, shopping and dining outside, enjoying the good life.

Deciding Where To Live

Variety certainly is not lacking in homes and homesites in the four-county coastal area. Nor is variety in cost. Prices for building lots can range from as little as $20,000 to well over $1,000,000. As might be expected, oceanfront property in older exclusive communities commands the highest price, partially because there is so little of it remaining.

Generally speaking, the closer to the water, the more expensive the property. However, in the Cape Fear region, we are fortunate to have a surprisingly large amount of property that is adjacent to water of one sort or another, so the dream of living on the water is not beyond the means of all but the very wealthy. In addition to the ocean, we have sounds, which are bodies of water between the mainland and the ocean-facing barrier islands, rivers, the Intracoastal Waterway, lakes and canals. More reasonably priced housing, especially condominiums, is available on or near these waters. Often a group of homes or a condominium complex is built in conjunction with a group of boat slips or a marina.

Currently, considerable development of new residential communities is taking place on both sides of the Cape Fear River, and quite a few reasonably priced homes are available. In New Hanover County, most of the recent river development has been on the east side of River Road, and a great deal more is in the planning stages.

In Brunswick County, communities along the river are developing on both sides of N.C. Highway 133 and are working their way south toward Southport, which also has several new residential developments. Brunswick County has seen a significant housing boom in recent years and has developments all along its barrier islands and the Intracoastal Waterway. Many of these are quite popular with retirees and feature golf courses, lakes and marinas. Farther inland, very affordable housing and property can be found throughout the rural areas and small towns of Brunswick County.

To a lesser degree, much the same situation exists in Pender County in particular, and to some extent in Onslow County. Extensive development has taken place along Topsail Island and the Intracoastal Waterway behind it, and further new development is taking place along U.S. Highway 17 North. Both counties have plenty of affordable property and housing available in the towns and rural areas back from the ocean.

Within New Hanover County, construction is taking place in virtually all areas and neighborhoods. A large amount of both new and existing housing is available throughout the city and suburbs that ranges in price from very affordable to very luxurious. Downtown Wilmington, in and about the Historical District, has quite a few condos going up and a number of older historic homes are being restored, all of which are popular with retirees.

Property and housing near the ocean and sounds tends to be quite expensive, especially in and around Wrightsville Beach. However, in recent years, there has been a surge in popularity for Pleasure Island, which is bounded on the east by the Atlantic Ocean, on the west by the Cape Fear River and on the north by the Intracoastal Waterway. Consisting primarily of the towns of Carolina Beach and Kure Beach, Pleasure Island still has affordable property near the ocean, and although oceanfront property is expensive, it is considerably less so than in other locations. (See our chapter on Real Estate.)

Retirement Communities

Senior adult retirement communities — neighborhoods with congregate housing intended specifically for older occupants — offer a variety of social and recreational amenities. These communities feature single

RETIREMENT

INSIDERS' TIP

If you're headed for retirement on or near the beach, forget about all those fancy, stylish clothes you wore on weekends up north. You'll find yourself wearing shorts and a polo shirt or T-shirt about eight months of the year. When it's cool, you'll wear sweats or khakis and a long sleeve polo shirt or maybe a sweater. Two or three pairs of jogging or walking shoes and white socks are about all you'll need for footwear. You'll be pleasantly surprised to find that even business people dress in a relaxed and informal fashion.

homes or apartments providing several services, which may include meals in a central location, a pool, transportation and activities. They may or may not offer health-care services.

We have listed several of these communities. You may also contact the chamber of commerce in the area you choose for relocation (see our Area Overview chapter for a list of chambers) or one of the government agencies listed at the end of this chapter.

Alterra Clare Bridge of Wilmington
3501 Converse Dr., Wilmington
• **(910) 790-8664**

Alterra Clare Bridge is designed specifically for people with Alzheimer's disease or other memory impairments. Everything is geared to help individuals with memory problems to live the most independent and fulfilling life possible. Residents can choose from private or companion suites in a neighborhood environment. Floor plans offer helpful cues to help residents remember where they are at all times. Small living and dining rooms encourage a sense of community and help residents feel less confused as they socialize with one another. The outdoor patios and courtyards are enclosed and secured. Even pets are allowed to help the residents feel more at home. Other amenities include 24-hour staff and licensed nurse, assistance with personal care and hygiene, laundry and linen service, mealtime and feeding assistance, housekeeping, medication management, and an audio-security system. Alterra Clare Bridge also offers life-enrichment activities, memory-support programs and outings to increase self-esteem and independence.

Brightmore
2324 41st St., Wilmington
• **(910) 350-1980, (800) 556-6899**

Brightmore welcomes active retirees who wish to combine independence with a small-town atmosphere. Studio, one-bedroom, one-bedroom deluxe, two-bedroom and two-bedroom deluxe apartments are available for a monthly rental fee. Your apartment home includes a full kitchen, all utilities (except phone service and expanded cable), 24-hour security services and medical-emergency calls, housekeeping and flat linens, regularly scheduled transportation, daily choice of meals, an ice-cream parlor and recreational/exercise programs.

Brightmore is located midtown on 41st Street between the Cape Fear River and Wrightsville Beach; it is on the same campus with The Kempton at Brightmore (Assisted Living) and The Commons at Brightmore (Personal Care). Brightmore residents are priority listed for services at any of the other communities that make up their continuum of care.

Coastal Plantation
U.S. Hwy. 17 N., Hampstead
• **(888) 716-9744**

Just north of Wilmington, Coastal Plantation is a beautifully landscaped community of individually manufactured homes. Residents purchase the house and lease the land. These quality homes range in price from $56,100 to the low $100s, depending on size and options. The price includes quite a few amenities. Most homes have a utility shed, peripheral plantings, a cement driveway, all appliances, energy-efficient heating and cooling systems, a wooden deck and more. This is a community for indi-

RETIREMENT

viduals who are at least 55 years of age and appreciate independence within the context of a planned community. A clubhouse, a swimming pool, regular potluck suppers and activity groups provide social opportunities.

The Commons at Brightmore
2320 41st St., Wilmington
• (910) 392-6899

The Commons is a community where dignity, choice and individuality make the difference in personal care in all activities of daily living. Each of the spacious rooms is individually climate controlled and has ample closet space with a private bathroom and shower. Residents are encouraged to bring their own furnishings to reflect their own personal tastes. Each room is equipped with an emergency call-response system to which staff respond 24 hours a day. Cable television and private telephones are optional.

The monthly rate includes three meals a day, assistance with personal care, housekeeping and laundry, administration of physician-directed medication, utilities, and free transportation to the doctor. Residents may choose among optional services such as barber and beauty shops, physical and speech therapy. Licensed practical nurses and assistants are on call 24 hours a day. Residents enjoy a full calendar of social events and activities. The Commons also offers a 32-bed memory care unit, Paraklay Way. The Commons at Brightmore is part of the continuum of care offered at Brightmore of Wilmington.

Glenmeade Village
1518 Village Dr., Wilmington
• (910) 762-8108

Retirement living at its best! Conveniently lo-cated in a quiet, secluded setting, Glenmeade Village community offers 104 apartment homes available in four floor plans; residents select from spacious one, two, or three-bedroom units and one floor or townhouse designs. All of the tastefully decorated apartments are air-conditioned, energy-efficient and fully carpeted, with mini-blinds throughout and either a private patio or porch and storage room. Other features include ample closet space, large windows, washer/dryer (three bedroom units only), and fully equipped kitchens.

The enclosed heated pool is open year round, with aqua fitness classes offered two days a week. An inviting clubhouse provides residents a comfortable place for socializing, having a cup of coffee, reading the paper or watching cable TV. It's open every day and is the site of frequent socials and card games. A tennis court, greenhouse and laundry room are also available. Twenty-four-hour emergency maintenance service is an added plus. Small pets are accepted.

This small community is within walking distance of New Hanover Regional Medical Center, physicians' offices and other medical facilities as well as shopping. Convenient to Wilmington's riverfront, Westfield Mall, the Senior Center, golf courses and beaches, Glenmeade Village is just right for active, mature individuals age 55 or older.

The Kempton at Brightmore
2298 41st St., Wilmington
• (910) 332-6899

For assisted living, the Kempton provides a supportive environment promoting an independent lifestyle with the benefit of onsite, professionally managed services. It's designed for those individuals who may need assistance with certain everyday activities, but who do not require continued medical services.

Residents choose from a variety of studio and one-bedroom units. Each unit is equipped with a kitchenette and an emergency call system. All meals are provided along with daily maid service, flat linen service for laundry and utilities (except telephone). Staffed 24 hours a day, The Kempton offers a full social calendar, scheduled transportation, an exercise room, Country Kitchen, and an onsite beauty and barber shop. The Kempton is part of the continuum of care offered at Brightmore of Wilmington. Call for more information.

Lake Shore Commons
1402 Hospital Plaza Dr., Wilmington
• (910) 251-0067

For seniors seeking elegant, gracious retirement living in beautiful surroundings convenient to

shopping, health-care providers and medical facilities, Lake Shore Commons, owned by Holiday Retirement Corporation, is the right place. Attractive, spacious unfurnished apartments with a variety of floor plans are available in studio, one or two-bedroom styles at surprisingly affordable month-to-month rents; a lease or buy-in is never required. Within the main building, each apartment has a kitchenette, carpeting and window treatments; most feature a balcony or porch. Free laundry facilities are located on each floor. Eight cottages are equipped with full kitchens and washer/dryer. Within the main building are many comfortable, well-appointed common areas, a huge fully equipped kitchen for resident use, exercise facilities, pool table, two libraries and several multi-purpose rooms.

Peace of mind is a priority here. Resident managers are on duty 24 hours every day for assistance. Included in the monthly rent are heating/air conditioning, electricity, water, cable TV, all maintenance and repairs, weekly housekeeping (including linens and towels) and three nutritious, chef-prepared meals daily with choice of entrees. Transportation at no charge is available on a scheduled basis for residents who have appointments or shopping to do. Also part of the package are numerous organized activities, movies, tours and excursions. A unique Travel Club enables residents to free visits in other company-owned retirement communities.

Plantation Village
1200 Porters Neck Rd., Wilmington
• (910) 686-7181, (800) 334-0240 in state, (800) 334-0035 out of state

Plantation Village is a life-care retirement community on 56 acres within Porters Neck Planta-

tion. The campus has a library, bank facilities, auditorium, gym, swimming pool, woodworking shop, crafts room and many more amenities. Plantation Village is a unique retirement community in that it receives people in good health age 62 and older and offers professional, long-term nursing care services from nearby Cornelia Nixon Davis Center and Champion Assisted Living. Before nursing care is needed, residents have access to a wellness center on the campus, a 24-hour nurse on call and the visit of a doctor each week.

The Woods at Holly Tree
4610 Holly Tree Rd., Wilmington
• (910) 793-1300

The Woods at Holly Tree provides a stable and caring environment in secure, comfortable

RETIREMENT

surroundings. One all-inclusive monthly rent begins with several styles of lovely apartments and ends with a large list of amenities including three chef-prepared meals a day served in a beautiful dining room, weekly housekeeping and flat linen service, all utilities (except telephone), cable TV, free laundry facilities, social and recreational activities. The Woods at Holly Tree is an affordable residence where attention to detail and personal consideration are paramount. No lease or buy-in fee is ever required. A unique feature, the Woods at Holly Tree has two sets of resident managers on site 24 hours a day.

For the convenience of residents, scheduled transportation is available. On the premises are a beauty/barber shop, an exercise/activity room, billiard and game room, library, chapel and large-screen TV lounge as well as several cozy nooks for visiting or reading. Fire-resistant construction and structural design enhance building safety. A Travel Club enables residents to free visits in other company-owned retirement communities.

Senior Centers

The following senior centers offer a variety of exercise programs, meal services, health and wellness activities, and lots of fun things to do. Depending on the center, you can find everything from aerobics and line dancing to crafts and social events. They may offer Meals on Wheels and hot lunch programs; some offer medical transportation; others offer travel opportunities; all offer fellowship, support and friendships.

Katie B. Hines Senior Center, 308 Cape Fear Boulevard, Carolina Beach, (910) 458-6609

New Hanover County Department of Aging Senior Center, 2222 S. College Road, Wilmington, (910) 452-6400

Pender Adult Services Inc., 901 S. Walker Street, Burgaw, (910) 259-9119

Shallotte Senior Center, 5040 Main Street, Shallotte, (910) 754-8776

Southport Senior Center, 209 N. Atlantic Avenue, Southport, (910) 457-6461

Topsail Senior Center, 20959 U.S. Highway 17, Hampstead, (910) 270-0708

Employment Services

Senior AIDES Program
613 Shipyard Blvd., Ste. 100, Wilmington
• **(910) 798-3910**

This excellent program offers job counseling and training for qualified people age 55 and older

who are residents of New Hanover, Pender and Brunswick counties; applicants must meet certain income-level requirements. With grant monies from the Federal Government administered by the Cape Fear Area United Way, the AIDES program benefits individuals by providing them temporary part-time employment at local agencies in order to gain skills and work experience. The goal is to help these individuals move into permanent full-time or part-time positions.

An example would be the Senior Employment Specialists at the New Hanover County Department of Aging. Currently, an AIDES participant works 20 hours a week at the Senior Center assisting older adults to find jobs, such as sales associates in local stores, live-in companions and caregivers, or grill operators at restaurants. Potential employers make requests, which are then matched with seniors seeking jobs.

Volunteer Opportunities Just for Seniors

Although our area offers a wide range of volunteering options (see our Volunteer Opportunities chapter), there are some jobs that can be handled best by people with a lifetime of experience. Following are several organizations that would appreciate your help.

Service Corps of Retired Executives (SCORE)
69 Darlington Ave., Wilmington
• **(910) 815-4576**

A resource partner with the U.S. Small Business Administration, SCORE is dedicated to aiding in the information, growth and success of small businesses. SCORE counselors provide free, confidential counseling to help solve business problems. By volunteering your time, talent and expertise, you'll be assisting entrepreneurs who need your skills and insights. This is essentially a mentoring program. New members participate in a training program and orientation.

Senior Corps
The Senior Corps is a national service program that puts the experience and talents of seniors ages 55 and older to work getting things done in the community. Several entities come under this umbrella: Foster Grandparent Volunteers, which help children; Retired and Senior Volunteer Program (RSVP), which offers service to the community, and Senior Companion Program, which helps adults in need.

Wouldn't you just love to retire to a little place by the sea?

Photo: Jay Tervo

Retired Senior Volunteer Program (RSVP)
2222 S. College Rd., Wilmington
• (910) 452-6400

RSVP matches your interests, talents and skills with the needs of the community. This is a very flexible volunteer program. RSVP volunteers provide many different kinds of community services, such as tutoring, neighborhood watch, disaster assistance, building houses and helping organizations operate more efficiently.

Seniors Health Insurance Information Program (SHIIP)
2222 S. College Rd., Wilmington
• (910) 452-6400

An arm of RSVP, the SHIIP program utilizes volunteers who are trained by the North Carolina Department of Insurance to help people with Medicare problems and questions about supplemental (Medigap) or long-term care insurance; they also assist with medical claims paperwork and policy comparisons. Volunteer receive 24 hours of training and are schooled in counseling techniques.

Volunteer Income Tax Assistance Program (VITA)
2222 S. College Rd., Wilmington
• (910) 452-6400

Volunteers who are extensively trained assist taxpayers with special needs, including persons with disabilities, non-English speaking persons and seniors. This free service, available from the beginning of February through April 15, is very popular and greatly appreciated. Locally, VITA is sponsored by RSVP.

Foster Grandparents Program
2222 S. College Rd., Wilmington
• (910) 452-6400

Foster grandparents devote their volunteer services to children with special or exceptional needs. A one-on-one, hands-on service, it gives you the opportunity to enrich the life of a child. You could offer emotional support to child victims of abuse and neglect, tutor children who lag behind in school subjects, mentor troubled teenagers, or help care for children with physical disabilities. Foster grandparents must be age 60 or older, meet certain income eligibility guidelines and receive training. This requires a time commitment of about 20 hours per week. A modest tax-free stipend and reimbursement for some expenses is offered to offset the cost of volunteering.

Senior Net Computer Center
2222 S. College Rd., Wilmington
• (910) 452-6400

This organization needs volunteers to provide basic and advanced computer training to older adults in New Hanover County. If you're computer literate and would like to assist with

RETIREMENT

program coordination or instruction, be sure to get involved with this program.

Keep on Going

Senior Games and Silver Arts Event
2222 S. College Rd., Wilmington
• (910) 452-6400

Senior Games by the Sea, a year round health-promotion program for mature adults (55 and up), is part of a state-wide network sanctioned by North Carolina Senior Games Inc. Each spring, Senior Games by the Sea holds the local athletic and SilverArts competition. Winners at the local level can participate in the State Finals held in Raleigh each fall. In five-year incremental age groups, seniors compete in more than 20 sports, such as archery, billiards, cycling, swimming, track and field, tennis, spin casting and horseshoes. In addition, senior artisans and performers have an opportunity to showcase their talents in the SilverArts competition. Categories include visual, literary, performing and heritage arts, everything from painting, woodwork, dance and music to sculpting and crafts.

University of North Carolina at Wilmington Lifelong Learning
601 S. College Rd., Wilmington
• (910) 962-3000

UNCW's Lifelong Learning programs offer a tremendous selection of lectures, concerts, plays, educational courses, institutes and recreational activities especially geared to the retired population. You could keep busy all year long by taking advantage of the extensive offerings. Choose from Wise Women's Retreat, MarineQuest, personal growth, travel and professional development programs. Maybe you'd be more interested in Nonprofit Management, Summer Institute or the Lifelong Learning Speakers series.

Through UNCW's Adult Scholars Leadership Program, older adults learn about past and current problems in the region together with possible solutions; some subjects covered in this excellent seven-week program include history, Southern culture, health and human services,

media, government, arts and economic development. Graduates are encouraged to use what they've learned to become more actively involved in enhancing the community through volunteer and entrepreneurial service. Call for your free copy of Pathways, (910) 962-4034.

In-Home and Adult Day Care

Coastal Adult Day Care
5919 Oleander Dr., Ste. 121, Wilmington
• (910) 799-8818

A welcoming, home-like setting and heaping measures of old-fashioned tender loving care combine to make Coastal Adult Day Care a truly unique place. Here, Betty Ann and Jennifer Sanders have created an exceptionally easy, relaxed environment for their clients, many of whom suffer from memory disorders. Dedicated staff and volunteers provide stimulation by encouraging conversation, socialization and physical activity. Therapies include art, dance, music, pet, reminiscent, puppet, horticulture, field trips and other appropriate forms of recreation.

"Our family caring for your family" is their motto, and they live up to it. The center has convenient, flexible hours and a philosophy of going the extra mile for their clients. Family Focus Groups meet regularly to give family members and caregivers an opportunity to discuss therapies, treatments and home care. All work together to ensure that older adults can receive the assistance they need with activities of daily living and still retain positive feelings of dignity and self worth.

Comfort Keepers
3975-A Market St., Wilmington
• (910) 342-9200

This business offers in-home services designed for individuals or couples who are capable of handling their own physical needs, but may require assistance with functions of daily living. Available by the hour, day or week, Comfort Keepers will prepare meals, shop, help with grooming and dressing, do laundry, provide transportation, do light housekeeping, run errands, and assist with mail. From daily "check-in" phone calls to 24-hour care, Comfort Keepers can fill the bill when it comes to non-medical, in-home care.

Elderhaus at The Lake - Alper Center
1950 Amphitheater Dr., Wilmington
• **(910) 343-8209**

Family members who care for adults with limited special needs at home can rejoice! This nonprofit organization is here to help you continue your employment during weekdays and even provide some respite on Saturday so you can shop, get your hair done, relax and refresh yourself.

Offering adult day care, adult day health and weekend group respite programs, the Alper Center in Wilmington serves residents of New Hanover and Brunswick counties. Elderhaus provides qualified, professional, appropriate care, supervision and assistance for ambulatory or semi-ambulatory individuals 18 years of age or older, but primarily for seniors over the age of 60.

A variety of program services are provided in a bright, cheerful, nurturing atmosphere. Exercise, discussion groups, educational activities, arts/crafts, games and recreational therapies are built into each day's schedule; field trips, community projects and special events keep participants stimulated and active. A nurse is on site who will administer medications; assist with personal care such as feeding, ambulation and toileting; provide minor first aid and oversee individual health-care needs.

Elderhaus at Porters Neck
1013 Porters Neck Rd., Wilmington
• **(910) 686-3335**

Located on the campus of Davis Health Cen-

INSIDERS' TIP

You'll have to change that old Yankee concept about everything getting done promptly, on time and according to schedule. For example, if you call an electrician for some work and he says he'll try to get to you Tuesday afternoon, there's a good chance he might show on Tuesday, but there's just a fair chance that he might show on Wednesday or Thursday. But, rest assured, if you've got a real emergency, he'll show up almost instantly.

ter, Elderhaus at Porters Neck offers adult day care for residents of New Hanover and Pender counties. Program services are similar to those at the Alper Center, however Adult Day Health and Weekend Group Respite are not available here.

HealthMate Home Care, Inc.
3132 Wrightsville Ave., Wilmington
• **(910) 762-0050**

A licensed home-care agency, HealthMate provides nurses, medical social workers, personal-care attendants, companions and in-home aide services. Also, emergency monitoring, in-home respite care, secondary management and a medication dispensing system are available. The agency specializes in helping seniors locate affordable solutions and support services.

Government Agencies

County departments of aging offer a variety of services, including congregate and/or home-delivered meals, transportation, minor home repairs, senior center operations, in-home aides, health promotion/disease prevention, and fan/heat relief. If you're age 60 or older, ask about getting a free Senior Tar Heel Card for discounts at local businesses. For more information, contact one of the following agencies:

Brunswick County Department of Older Adults, Brunswick County Government Complex, Bolivia, (910) 253-2080

Cape Fear Council of Governments, Area Agency on Aging, 1480 Harbour Drive, Wilmington, (910) 395-4553, (800) 218-6575

New Hanover County Department of Aging, 2222 S. College Road, Wilmington, (910) 452-6400

Pender Adult Services, 901 S. Walker Street, Burgaw, (910) 259-9119

RETIREMENT

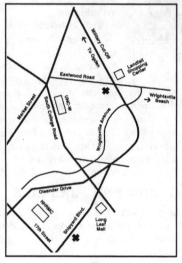

Health Care

Excellent health-care facilities and services, a result of rapid growth, increased development and a booming retirement population in North Carolina's southern coastal region, rival those in larger cities. However, that hasn't always been the case and, as recently as 20 years ago, residents sought advanced medical treatment in larger university medical centers or metropolitan hospitals. Now, in the 21st century, residents and visitors have access to more sophisticated health care and state-of-the-art technology and are no longer forced to travel inland for treatment of serious illness or injury.

In New Hanover County, more than 450 practicing physicians in a wide range of medical and surgical specialties now utilize some of the most technologically progressive facilities and equipment in the state through the New Hanover Health Network. This network, the primary source of health care in the Greater Wilmington area, comprises three formerly independent hospitals — New Hanover Regional Medical Center, Cape Fear Hospital and Pender Memorial Hospital — as well as two facilities located on the medical center's campus — Coastal Rehabilitation Hospital and The Oaks Behavorial Health Hospital. Affiliate agencies include New Hanover Regional Medical Center Emergency Medical Services, Pender Home Health, Lower Cape Fear Hospice and the New Hanover Regional Medical Center Foundation. This far-reaching partnership enlarges and enhances the region's overall health-care capabilities through upgraded and expanded facilities, more options in a range of medical and surgical specialties and improved access to health care.

Although smaller in size, Brunswick County's two hospitals — Brunswick Community Hospital and Dosher Memorial Hospital — offer a wide range of services from general medicine and round-the-clock emergency room physicians to medical/surgical specialties and community health-care affiliates. When necessary, medical care beyond the scope of their services is referred to Wilmington's larger hospitals. Residents and vacationers along the Brunswick beaches will find these smaller hospitals more convenient and an excellent source when medical attention is needed.

Hospitals

Wilmington

Cape Fear Hospital
5301 Wrightsville Ave., Wilmington • (910) 452-8100
Cape Fear Hospital is full-service community hospital with 141 licensed beds. It provides a range of services, including medical, surgical and ambulatory care, 24-hour emergency services, outpatient surgery, radiology, ultrasound, magnetic resonance imaging, laboratory facilities and a specialized orthopedic center.

The Cape Fear Orthopedic Specialty Center features trained teams of orthopedic doctors, nurses and technicians and provides the majority of orthopedic surgical services in the county. Orthopedic patients find the smaller hospital easy to navigate and benefit from convenient access to

LOOK FOR:
- **Hospitals**
- **Urgent Care**
- **Home Health Care**
- **Substance Abuse Treatment**
- **Alternative and Complementary Health Care**
- **Medical Services**
- **Massage Therapists**
- **Chiropractors**
- **Acupuncturists**
- **Adult Day Care**

rehabilitative therapy at Cape Fear or the outpatient facility at 5220 Oleander Drive, (910) 452-8104. Located near Cape Fear Hospital, this fully equipped center provides outpatient orthopedic rehabilitation, sports medicine therapy, hand therapy and pain-management therapy. Patients have access to a therapy pool and a physical and occupational therapy gym.

Total joint replacement patients can benefit from a new and innovative program called Joint Camp. Similar to an athletic training program, Joint Camp takes a team approach to pre-surgical care and post-surgical rehabilitation. Joint Camp participants recover more quickly than their traditional joint replacement surgery counterparts and benefit from the team approach to rehabilitation.

Cape Fear Hospital, a member of New Hanover Health Network, is accredited by the Joint Commission on Accreditation of Healthcare Organizations.

New Hanover Regional Medical Center
2131 S. 17th St., Wilmington
• (910) 343-7000

The largest hospital in southeastern North Carolina, New Hanover Regional Medical Center is a 628-bed teaching hospital with five intensive care units, including a neonatal intensive care unit. It also includes specialized care facilities and programs on site and at various locations throughout the region.

New Hanover Regional Medical Center is operated by a volunteer board appointed by the New Hanover County Board of Commissioners. The New Hanover Health Network (NHHN), composed of New Hanover Regional Medical Center, Cape Fear Hospital, Pender Memorial Hospital and affiliate agencies, offers high-quality care with an increasing emphasis on more critical illnesses and conditions. This health-care network is staffed by more than 4,500 employees, making it the largest employer in New Hanover County. NHHN has a medical staff of more than 450 and has more than 1,100 volunteers.

New Hanover Regional's Coastal Heart Center provides a 16-bed Coronary Care Unit, a 14-bed Cardiovascular Intensive Care Unit and some of the best physicians, surgeons and support staff in North Carolina. Services of particular importance to a community with a booming retirement population include cardiac catheterization, an electrophysiology lab, angioplasty, open-heart surgery, cardiac rehabilitation and a new cardiovascular laboratory, diagnostic testing and outpatient services.

Zimmer Cancer Center, a 30,000-square-foot facility on the medical center's grounds, consolidates all cancer services into one location. The Cancer Center's program has been designated nationally as a teaching hospital program with services that include chemotherapy, radiation therapy, gynecological oncologists specializing in cancer care for women, surgical and medical treatments, as well as participation in cancer research. A linear accelerator, used in conjunction with a CT scanner, allows technicians more accuracy in the treatment of tumors. CanSurvive, created to help people coping with cancer, meets in the center and provides individuals and their families an opportunity to share their experiences.

Designated by the state as one of the ten regional Level II trauma centers, New Hanover Regional provides mobile intensive care units through VitaLink and AirLink, which can transport the most seriously ill and injured patients from the region's community hospitals at any hour of the day or night via air or ground transportation. A paramedic, a registered nurse and an emergency medical technician are always on board.

New Hanover Regional Family Birthplace specializes in obstetrical services, offering more than two dozen rooms that combine homelike decor with sophisticated facilities to allow a family-centered birthing experience. In Women's Health Specialties, a team of perinatologists care for women with high-risk pregnancies, and the area's only board-certified reproductive endocrinologist works with women who are having difficulty conceiving. Certified nurse-midwives, working closely with physicians, provide individualized and comprehensive care to women during pregnancy and birth as well as general gynecological care throughout a woman's lifetime.

The Coastal Rehabilitation Hospital, (910) 343-7845, located on the medical center's main campus, is for patients with traumatic brain injury, spinal cord injury, neurological disorders, orthopedic conditions, stroke and other conditions that create a loss of mobility. This hospital's focus is assisting the functionally limited patient to achieve and maintain as much independence as possible through general rehabilitative programs, therapeutic equipment, a day hospital program, a therapeutic pool and Easy Street, a nationally recognized program that simulates real life environments. The Independence Rehabilitation Center, 2800 Ashton Drive, (910) 342-3270, and the Oleander Rehabilitation Center, 5220 Oleander Drive, (910) 452-8104, offer outpatient services.

PICTURE YOURSELF IN A
HEALTH CARE CAREER
ON THE CAROLINA COAST.

Why not live the best of both worlds?

A rewarding career with unlimited growth...
and a warm, wonderful coastal lifestyle most
people only dream about.

It's all here at New Hanover Health Network
in Wilmington, North Carolina. Where your
career opportunities are wide open, and
the people are welcoming, supportive
and responsive.

New Hanover offers attractive salaries,
comprehensive benefits, relocation
assistance and tuition reimbursement
for your continuing education.

And what a great place to live. Historic
Wilmington is a vibrant community, with
cultural diversity and beautiful beaches.

All things considered,
this is what quality
of life—and work—is all about.

EXCEPTIONAL PEOPLE
MAKING A DIFFERENCE.

New Hanover Health Network
WILMINGTON, NORTH CAROLINA

Equal Opportunity Employer

WARM UP TO NEW HANOVER WITH A
FREE VIDEO TOUR

Take a closer look at a rewarding career at New Hanover Health Network,
and get a taste of the good life in the captivating coastal town of Wilmington, N.
Just call us toll free at 1-877-781-2468 or visit www.nhhn.org

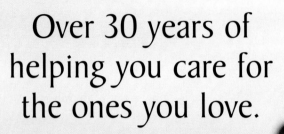
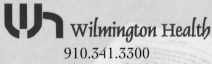

Also located on NHRMC's campus, The Oaks Behavioral Health Hospital, (910) 343-7787, offers inpatient and outpatient programs for adults. The partial hospitalization program provides outpatient treatment and counseling services. Psychiatric evaluations are available 24 hours a day.

New Hanover Regional Medical Center has the only Pediatric Unit in a six-county region. The unit is specifically designed for the needs of children. Medical equipment is hidden from view, and specially trained therapists help children cope with being in the hospital.

Other health network components provided in association with the medical center include a pulmonary rehab program, assorted clinics, including women's health and a children's AIDS clinic and the Lower Cape Fear Hospice that includes a 12-bed Hospice Care Center. Outpatient diagnostic services are available at The Medical Mall, near the hospital at 17th Street and Glen Meade Drive, makes outpatient services such as MRI, X-rays, mammography and lab tests convenient. Other outpatient diagnostic services will soon be available at The Forum near Military Cutoff in the northeast region of Wilmington. Recent additions to the hospital include a high-tech vascular operating room, an expanded emergency department and a new visitor concourse, featuring a pictorial display entitled "Healing Through Time: A History of Medicine in the Lower Cape Fear."

New Hanover Regional Medical Center, a member of New Hanover Health Network, is accredited by the Joint Commission on Accreditation of Healthcare Organizations.

Outside Wilmington

Brunswick Community Hospital
1 Medical Center Dr., off U.S. Hwy. 17, Supply • (910) 755-8121

Brunswick Community Hospital, located in central Brunswick County at Supply, is a 60-bed acute care facility with a medical staff of more than 80 physicians. The hospital has a 24-hour, physician-staffed emergency department, a wide range of medical and surgical services, a full laboratory and blood bank, a birthing center, radiology services, physical therapy, critical care units and the Chest Pain Emergency Center. Addressing the needs of Brunswick County's rapidly growing population, Brunswick Community Hospital's recent renovations include expanded services in the emergency room, surgical facilities and its imaging department. Cur-

rently, the hospital is planning a $32 million expansion and renovation of the existing facility, which includes adding 32 more beds.

Included among its comprehensive medical services are general medicine and a broad range of specialties, including family and internal medicine, obstetrics/gynecology, ophthalmology, pain management, urology, pediatrics and allergy medicine. Surgical services include general surgery, neurosurgery, vascular surgery, oral/maxillary surgery and plastic surgery. Community outreach programs include Senior Friends, (910) 755-1125, and the Safe Sitter course, (910) 755-1244. Support groups, facilitated by hospital staff members, include the Alzheimer's Support Group, (910) 755-1356, and the Diabetes Support Group, (910) 755-1013.

Brunswick Community Hospital offers the Physician Referral Service, (910) 755-1416. The hospital is accredited by the Joint Commission on Accreditation of Healthcare Organizations.

Dosher Memorial Hospital
924 N. Howe St., Southport • (910) 457-3800

Dosher Memorial Hospital is a 100-bed acute and skilled nursing care hospital that offers comprehensive medical care and extensive outpatient services. Established in 1930, this small public hospital serves the Smithville Township area, attracting patients from Oak Island, Southport, Boiling Springs Lake, Bolivia and Leland. A public facility, Dosher Memorial is focused on its community, offering outreach programs and working with local citizen organizations to promote healthy lifestyles.

The hospital has a 24-hour, physician-staffed

emergency room, respiratory therapy, nuclear medicine, CAT scanning and mammography. Medical specialties include family practice, internal medicine, gynecology, pediatrics, diagnostic imaging, cardiopulmonary services, speech, occupational and physical therapies and urology. General and comprehensive surgical services in orthopedics, urology, gynecology, ophthalmology and otolaryngology are also available. Call the Marketing and Community Services Department at (910) 454-4115 for a free Dosher Directory.

The hospital provides a valuable free publication, Safe Vacation Guide, distributed to hotels, motels, condominiums and visitor information venues in the area. It advises visitors about potential health hazards related to sunburn, dangerous aquatic life and rusty fish hooks. It also gives safety tips about avoiding alligators, snakes, snapping turtles and biting insects. The guide also offers hurricane information and a health-care reference manual that explains all services of the hospital as well as a physician guide according to specialty.

Dosher Memorial Hospital is accredited by the Joint Commission on Accreditation of Healthcare Organizations.

Pender Memorial Hospital
507 Fremont St., Burgaw • (910) 259-5451

Celebrating more than 50 years of quality health-care services to Pender County, Pender Memorial Hospital is an 43-bed general acute medical facility that provides both inpatient and outpatient services to the community. In addition to general acute medical care, the hospital's second floor houses a 43-bed skilled nursing facility. Inpatient departments include a medical/surgical unit, intensive care unit, emergency services, surgical suite, radiology department, laboratory, pharmacy, respiration therapy and rehabilitation services. Outpatient services include ambulatory surgery, laparoscopy, general and vascular surgery, orthopedics and podiatry. Rehabilitation therapists provide inpatient, outpatient and home health rehabilitation services.

Board-certified emergency physicians provide 24-hour emergency services to patients with acute medical and surgical needs. If more advanced care is needed, VitaLink or AirLink transport critically ill patients to New Hanover Regional Medical Center. A recently completed $1.3 million construction project includes an enlarged Emergency Department and a new hospital entrance, an expanded admitting and waiting area, general examination rooms and a special procedures room.

Pender Memorial, a member of the New Hanover Health Network, is accredited by the Joint Commission on Accreditation of Healthcare Organizations.

Immediate/Urgent Care

For non-surgical medical services, Wilmington and surrounding communities offer an ample number of immediate-care centers, sometimes referred to as urgent-care centers or primary-care providers. Vacationers or residents with relatively minor injuries, illnesses or conditions may prefer the convenience of visiting these centers over making an appointment to see a private doctor. Illnesses and injuries beyond the centers' capabilities are referred to area hospitals.

These are convenient places to get flu and tetanus shots or to have a limited variety of tests or physicals for school, sports or insurance purposes. Most centers have their own labs and X-ray services, and all are staffed by qualified, licensed physicians and nurses. Be advised that most of the centers operate on a first-come basis, so don't expect to be able to make an appointment. However, serious illnesses, injuries or conditions will receive first priority.

These medical service facilities are not open 24 hours a day. In many cases, they are not open seven days a week. A few medical or family practice centers offer walk-in appointments. If you need attention and choose any of these centers, you're advised to phone ahead. Listing here is for your convenience only and does not imply endorsement of any facility.

Visitors to Topsail Island are within a one-hour drive to hospitals and clinics in Wilmington. Additional public hospitals within driving range of Topsail are Onslow Memorial, (910) 577-2345, in Jacksonville, and Pender Memorial, (910) 259-5451, in Burgaw. For serious injuries and illnesses, the coastal region has ample emergency response services that can be reached by calling 911.

Wilmington

Carolina Family Urgent Care, 6927 Market Street (northeast area of Wilmington), (910) 799-1249

Doctor's Urgent Care Center, 4815 Oleander Drive, Wilmington, (910) 452-1111

ECONOMED, 1519 N. 23rd Street (north side of Wilmington), (910) 791-0075

MEDAC I Convenient Medical Care,

3710 Shipyard Boulevard (south side of Wilmington), (910) 791-0075

MEDAC II Convenient Medical Care, 1442 Military Cutoff Road (northeast area of Wilmington), (910) 256-6088

Med Care of North Carolina, 5245 S. College Road (Monkey Junction area, south of Wilmington), (910) 392-7806

Northside Medical Center, 1925-A Oleander Drive (south central area of Wilmington), (910) 251-7715

Pee Dee Clinic, 1630 Military Cutoff Road (east side of Wilmington), (910) 791-2788

Southeastern Healthcare, 2595 S. 17th Street (at Shipyard Boulevard, south central area of Wilmington)

The Downtown MedCenter, 119 Chestnut Street, (downtown Wilmington), (910) 762-5589

Outside Wilmington

Express Care, South Brunswick Island Medical Park, (off U.S. Highway 17), Shallotte, (910) 579-0800

Express Care, 25 Union School Road, Suite 3, Ocean Isle Beach, (910) 579-9955.

Coastal Immediate Care Center, 4654 Long Beach Road, Southport, (910) 457-0055

Hampstead Medical Center, 14980 U.S. Highway 17, Hampstead, (910) 270-2722

North Brunswick Family Practice, 117-H Village Road, Leland, (910) 371-0404

Penslow Medical Center, 206 N. Dyson Street, intersection of U.S. Highway 17 and N.C. Highway 50, Holly Ridge, (910) 329-7591

Seaside Medical Center, 710 Sunset Boulevard N., Suite A, Sunset Beach, (910) 575-3923

This horseshoe crab needs a little help getting back on his feet.

Photo: Jay Tervo

HEALTH CARE

Medical Services

Wilmington Health Associates
1202 Medical Center Dr., Wilmington
• (910) 341-3300

With more than 60 physicians and 350 employees, Wilmington Health Associates (WHA) is the largest multi-specialty medical practice in North Carolina. State-of-the-art facilities and highly trained specialists provide patients with a full range of medical testing, laboratory, diagnostic and treatment options. WHA's mission to continually improve the quality of medical care and services to patients is practiced as well as preached.

Comprehensive care for the entire family is provided by physicians and other health-care professionals who are dedicated, credentialed and patient-focused. Among the many exceptional medical services offered here are a travel clinic and sleep lab. Hospitalists ensure that WHA patients receive timely, appropriate care and treatment while hospitalized at New Hanover Regional Medical Center.

In addition to its main site at 1202 Medical Center Drive, WHA satellite offices are located in Carolina Beach, Porters Neck, Leland and North Chase. Off-site specialty clinics include dermatology, endocrinology, The Children's Clinic and Carolina OB-GYN.

Home Health Care

The demand for in-home care is increasing. The following list is a representative sampling of private businesses and not-for-profit agencies that offer in-home nursing care services such as certified nursing assistants, LPNs, RNs, companions and other assistance, depending upon individual need. This list is offered as a convenience and does not imply endorsement of any provider.

AssistedCare Home Health, 117 E. Village Road, Leland, (910) 332-3333, (800) 293-9389; 674 Ocean Highway W., Supply, (910) 755-9998, (800) 473-3864; 3110-1 Randall Parkway, Wilmington, (910) 763-9933, (800) 495-9998, 1620 N. Howe Street, Southport (910) 457-1140

Choice Caregivers, 107 Ridgeway Drive, Wilmington, (910) 790-3376

Eldercare Convalescent Service, 5003 Randall Parkway, Wilmington, (910) 395-5003

Home Instead Senior Care, 1804 Glen Meade Road, Wilmington, (910) 342-0455

Liberty Home Care, 2334 S. 41st Street, Wilmington, (910) 251-8111, (800) 800-0622; 1120 Ocean Highway W., Supply, (910) 754-8133

Lower Cape Fear Hospice, 725-A Wellington Avenue, Wilmington, (910) 772-5444 for administrative office, (800) 207-6908 for centralized patient referral; Hospice Care Center, 1406 Physicians Drive, Wilmington, (910) 762-9422

Pender Home Health, 507 E. Fremont Street, Burgaw, (910) 259-1224

Well Care Health Services Inc., 2715 Ashton Drive, Suite 200, Wilmington, (910) 452-1555; 118 Ocean Highway, Supply, (910) 754-9700

Substance Abuse Treatment

Numerous organizations and agencies in the area help people struggling with substance abuse. By law, mental health counselors are required to be licensed and certified by the State of North Carolina and to hold at least a master's degree from an accredited institution. So make it a point to inquire about these important credentials.

All of the following organizations are in Wilmington. For additional listings, look in the Yellow Pages section of area phone books under "Alcoholism Information & Treatment Centers" or "Drug Abuse & Addiction."

Alcoholics Anonymous, AA Referral Service and Treatment Program 24-hour Help Line, (800) 711-6375

Coastal Horizons Center Inc., 615 Shipyard Boulevard, Wilmington, (910) 343-0145

Southeastern Center for Mental Health, Developmental Disabilities and Substance Abuse, 2023 S. 17th Street, Wilmington, (910) 251-6440, (800) 293-6440

Wilmington Treatment Center, 2520 Troy Drive, Wilmington, (910) 762-2727 (in-patient facility); Local out-patient services are available at 1602 Physicians Drive, Suite 102, Wilmington, (910) 251-8100; and 4710 Main Street #4, Shallotte, (910) 754-2550

Alternative and Complementary Health Care

Acupuncture Alternative
Oleander Oaks, 5725-E Oleander Dr., Ste.2, Wilmington • (910) 392-0870

Owner/therapist Karen Vaughn describes Acupuncture Alternative's services as combined therapies to treat physical, mental, emotional and spiritual levels. She incorporates classical Chinese acupuncture, herbal therapy formulas, auricular therapy, Qi Gong and nutritional and lifestyle counseling. These elements are used to create a treatment plan as unique as the individual client. Sessions are be appointment only, Monday through Saturday.

McKay Acupuncture & Chinese Medicine
1047-C S. Kerr Ave., Wilmington
• (910) 232-5802

Leon McKay, a North Carolina native, is a master's graduate of Santa Barbara College of Oriental Medicine of Santa Barbara, California. He also has studied with master herbalists and medical doctors and has received in-depth training that combines Western medicine and Chinese herbal medicine. Using his collective knowledge and skills, he treats a variety of discomforts, such as neck, back and knee pain, migraines, sinus trouble, anxiety, colds, fatigue, PMS, insomnia, arthritis and high blood pressure. If you're looking for a holistic approach to health care and a professional practitioner who treats the entire person, Leon McKay invites you to call for a free consultation.

It's Only Natural
202 N. 13th St., Wilmington
• (910) 343-4101

An alternative medicine clinic, It's Only Natural has the philosophy of finding the source of illness and alleviating the cause rather than simply treating the symptoms. Their treatment emphasis is placed on natural medicine, focusing on diet and nutrition in conjunction with gradual lifestyle modification. Some of the services and therapies provided by the clinic include comprehensive health planning, hydrotherapy, practical nutrition planning, a wellness program, oxygen stimulation therapy, metabolic profiling, lifestyle counseling and more. Contact the clinic for more information or an appointment.

Sea of Health
Oleander Oaks, 5725-F Oleander Dr., Ste.1, Wilmington • (910) 395-4545

Sea of Health offers personal fitness training, massage therapy, La Stone therapy, yoga

and dietary counseling. Owners Kristen Ashton and Molly Hall are highly experienced in the services they offer. Kristen, a certified personal fitness trainer, holds a BS degree in Exercise Science, and Molly is a certified massage therapist and member of the American Massage Therapy Association. Sea of Health also offers yoga and nutritional counseling for type 2 diabetes, heart disease, obesity, hypertension and women's health. This center is open Monday through Friday from 9 AM to 5 PM. After 5 PM or Saturday appointments are available by special request.

Southern Acupuncture
Audubon Village, 1403 Audubon Blvd., Wilmington • (910) 799-5777

Traditional Chinese acupuncture is the focus here, treating a multitude of conditions such as back pain, headaches, carpel tunnel syndrome, TMJ, arthritis, PMS, asthma, stress and more. Treatments are quick, effective and, most important of all, painless. Southern Acupuncture also offers one of the area's most complete herbal pharmacies in Wilmington. The office is open Monday through Friday from 10 AM to 6 PM.

Chiropractors

Chiropractors are available in astonishingly high numbers in the region. A national movement toward alternative healthcare and nontraditional medical treatment of pain as well as an approach to wellness have focused attention on chiropractic care. Some well-established chiropractic offices are listed here. Check the Yellow Pages for more listings.

Wilmington
Alternative Health Care Center, 4706 Oleander Drive, Wilmington, (910) 392-3770

Back In Motion Chiropractic, 6303 Oleander Drive, Suite 104-B, Wilmington, (910) 313-1322

Friedman Chiropractic, 1033-A S. Kerr Avenue, Wilmington, (910) 350-2664

Reese Family Chiropractic, 2003 Carolina Beach Road, Wilmington, (910) 763-3611

Dr. Glenn Weckel, Chiropractic Physician, 3015 Market Street, Wilmington, (910) 762-9000; Pleasure Island Plaza, Carolina Beach, (910) 458-0804

HEALTH CARE

Outside Wilmington

Cagle Chiropractic & Acupuncture, 121 Holden Beach Road, Holden Beach, (910) 754-7737

Chirohealth Family Chiropractic, 417 N. Howe Street, Unit A, Southport, (910) 454-8100

Chiropractic Center of Shallotte, 6657 Beach Drive SW, Ocean Isle Beach, (910) 579-3502

Cypress Chiropractic PA, 814 N. Howe Street, Southport, (910) 457-1919

Family First Chiropractic, 4911 Bridgers Road, Shallotte, (910) 755-5483

Hammond Chiropractic, 717 N. Howe Street, Southport, (910) 457-9133

Island Healing Chiropractic, 6402 E. Oak Island Drive, Oak Island, (910) 278-5877

Loomis Chiropractic & Acupuncture Center, 10195-1 Beach Drive SW, Calabash, (910) 579-8891

Southeastern Chiropractic Group, 716 Ocean Highway, Shallotte, (910) 754-9000

Mead Chiropractic & Acupuncture, 14548 U.S. Hwy. 17, Hampstead, (910) 270-1515

Massage Therapy

The region also has an abundance of practitioners of massage therapy for wellness, chronic pain, strain and injuries. Every therapist or practice offers particular methods that range through Swedish, deep tissue, myofascial release, neuromuscular, craniosacral therapy, trigger point, foot reflexology, polarity, Shiatsu, acupressure, prenatal and sports. Some massage therapists work in their homes, others in offices or fitness clubs, and a few will be happy to come to your own home.

The City of Wilmington has an ordinance that requires licensed massage therapists to have a minimum of 500 hours of training at an accredited school. Therapists are also required to carry liability insurance, and North Carolina's General Assembly now recognizes massage therapy as a licensed profession throughout the state.

A local school of massage therapy offers student clinics that are open to the public: **Miller-Motte Technical College**, 606 S. College Road, Wilmington,

(910) 392-4660. Listed below is a sampling of the massage therapists available in Wilmington. Insiders does not endorse any practitioner. Check area Yellow Pages for more listings.

Harbour Club Day Spa & Salon, Lumina Station, 1904 Eastwood Road, Wilmington, (910) 256-5020

Rachel Mann Massage Therapy, Oleander Oaks, 5725-E Oleander Drive, Suite 5, Wilmington, (910) 520-2238

Janis Pulliam Massage Therapy, Oleander Oaks, 5725-E Oleander Drive, Suite 5, Wilmington, (910) 620-5765

Jacqueline Beecher, L.M.B.T. 1306, N. Kerr Office Park, 108 N. Kerr Ave. Suite A-2, Wilmington, (910) 262-7282

Barbara Dols, L.M.B.T., Still Waters Renewal Spa, 4514 Fountain Drive, Wilmington, (910) 792-0101

A Mystic Touch Nail & Massage Studio, 4711 Southport Supply Road SE, Southport, (910) 454-8663

Resort Massage & Spa Services, Village Activity Center, Sea Trail Resort & Golf Links, Sunset Beach, (910) 287-1193

Right Touch Therapy, 109-5 Causeway Drive, Ocean Isle Beach, (910) 575-3944

In-Home and Adult Day Care

When you're looking for appropriate in-home or adult day care for yourself or a loved one, check with one of these qualified, reputable organizations. Depending on the age, level of care and particular needs of the person to be enrolled, you can probably find what you need. These are NOT nursing care providers. Only Elderhaus's Alper Center offers minimal health care services on site, the others can assist with some activities of daily living, however. Adult day care facilities listed here are detailed in the Retirement chapter.

Coastal Adult Day Care
5919 Oleander Dr., Ste. 121, Wilmington
• (910) 799-8818

A relaxed, homey atmosphere where older adults can spend the day. Assistance with activities of daily living. No health care ser-

INSIDERS' TIP

The Talking Phone Book has a comprehensive section on Social and Human Services, including listings for Emergency & First Aid Resources, Food & Nutrition Services, Health Services, Pregnancy & Family Planning, Disabilities and many others. BellSouth's The Real Yellow Pages also contains similar listings in its Community Service Numbers section.

vices except for medications. Meals and snacks are provided. Coastal Adult Day Care offers a variety of therapeutic and recreational activities. Primarily weekdays, but flexible hours can be arranged, including some evening and weekend care.

Comfort Keepers
3975-A Market St., Wilmington
• **(910) 342-9200**

In-home services designed for individuals or couples who are capable of handling their own physical needs, but may require assistance with functions of daily living. Available by the hour, day or week, Comfort Keepers will prepare meals, shop, help with grooming and dressing, do laundry, provide transportation, do light housekeeping, run errands, and assist with mail. From daily "check-in" phone calls to 24-hour care, Comfort Keepers can fill the bill when it comes to non-medical in-home care.

Elderhaus at The Lake - Alper Center
1950 Amphitheater Dr., Wilmington
• **(910) 343-8209**

In addition to its regular adult day-care services, Alper Center offers limited health-care services provided by a professional nurse. Supervision, assistance and therapeutic recreation are provided for adults age 18 or older, but primarily for those older than 60, by qualified staff and volunteers. Weekend Group Respite, a program designed to give temporary relief for caregivers, is available for anyone who is over the age of 60 or has a caregiver over 60.

Elderhaus at Porters Neck
1013 Porters Neck Rd., Wilmington
• **(910) 686-3335**

Weekday care is provided for adults older than 18, although most participants are older than 60. Ambulatory and semi-ambulatory individuals receive caring supervision and socialization services. No nursing or health-care services are available here.

HealthMate Home Care, Inc.
3132 Wrightsville Ave., Wilmington
• **(910) 762-0050**

A licensed home-care agency, HealthMate provides nurses, medical social workers, personal care attendants, companion and in-home aide services. Also, emergency monitoring, in-home respite care, secondary management and a medication dispensing system are available. The agency specializes in creating affordable solutions and support services for seniors.

HEALTH CARE

Schools and Child Care

The southern North Carolina coast is served by three public school systems. New Hanover County has the largest system, as it encompasses the largest city on the state's entire coastline. Brunswick County Schools and Pender County Schools serve largely the rural populations to the southwest and north of New Hanover County.

Additionally, the region offers a growing list of independent (private) schools, both secular and religion-based, that meet a broad range of educational requirements. Home schooling has become increasingly popular, so we have included some helpful information about state and local resources.

School-age children in New Hanover County should immediately be enrolled in a public or private school. To enroll a child in the public schools, the parent or guardian must bring to the school a certified copy of the child's birth certificate along with the child's Social Security card, completed health assessment, immunization records and proof of residence. Children entering kindergarten must be 5 years old on or before October 16 of that year. Parents of students who were enrolled in a different school should bring the student's last report card and copies of standardized test reports to the new school.

Schools

Public Schools

New Hanover County School System
6410 Carolina Beach Rd., Wilmington • (910) 763-5431

The New Hanover County School System, the 10th-largest public school system in the state, serves the city of Wilmington and the county, including the beach communities of Figure Eight Island, Wrightsville Beach, Carolina Beach and Kure Beach. In 2001-02, the system served approximately 22,000 students from kindergarten through grade 12 in 36 schools.

New Hanover earned an exceptional rating on accreditation standards applied by the Southern Association of Colleges and Schools. North Carolina basic skills test scores for 2002 placed New Hanover County Schools well above the state average for grade 4 writing (54.3) percent scoring compared to 46.8 percent for the state from preliminary results), and on par with the state average for grade 7 writing (65.0 percent scoring compared to 62.9 percent for the state.) Combined SAT scores averaged 1028, compared to 998 for the state and 1020 nationally, which puts New Hanover County schools above the state and nation.

In 2001-02, 87.9 percent of the system's graduates planned to continue their education beyond high school. More than $8 million in scholarships and financial aid was awarded to 2002 graduates. The system

produced one National Morehead Scholar and one National Merit Finalist in 2002. Sixteen students were selected for enrollment in the North Carolina Governor's School, and two were selected to attend the North Carolina School of Science and Math. North Carolinas Scholars recipients, students recognized by the state for superior academic achievement, numbered 578.

The system has had the benefit of tremendous support from the business community and community volunteers. Volunteers in 2001-02 numbered 6,620 and contributed more than 227,000 documented hours of service to the system. These individuals contributed in many different ways, including tutoring, working to lower the dropout rate and offering opportunities for students to gain exposure to the corporate realm beyond the classroom. Much of the assistance from businesses comes through the Greater Wilmington Chamber of Commerce Education Foundation, a community education support organization that provides funding for mini-grants to supplement system-funded education each year.

The 2001-02 budget for New Hanover County Schools was $161 million, with 60 percent coming from the state, 34 percent from local monies and 6 percent from the federal gov-

ernment. Per-pupil expenditure was $6,740. The system is organized as kindergarten through grade 5, grades 6 through 8, and grades 9 through 12, using the middle school concept instead of junior high schools.

The school year runs from the middle of August to late May, although year-round schooling is now available at Johnson Elementary, Codington Elementary and Eaton Elementary schools. The year-round program is voluntary for students and teachers. After considerable investigation, the Board of Education found that the advantages of year-round schooling include increased learning, a reduction in stress levels for both students and teachers, more time, greater opportunity for effective enrichment and remediation, and higher motivation.

While still in high school, students in New Hanover County schools may engage in advanced studies at the University of North Carolina at Wilmington or enroll in courses at Cape Fear Community College for part of the instructional day.

In 1993, the Gregory School of Science, Mathematics and Technology opened its doors to allow elementary school students to experience a high-tech program of study that integrates science and mathematics throughout the curriculum. This was

Hands on learning is always beneficial.

Photo: Jay Tervo

the first magnet school in the system, and it has been enthusiastically received within the community. Lakeside High School is an academic alternative/school-of-choice for students in grades 9 to 12 who qualify for admittance.

There are four senior high schools in New Hanover County, and the seven middle schools that feed into these operate according to district lines, which are available for inspection at the school system office. In no case should a new resident assume his/her child will attend a neighborhood school. The county student population is 30 percent minority enrollment, and lines are periodically shifted to ensure balanced racial populations at all schools.

More than 253 courses are available to high school students, including social studies, mathematics, computer science, English, foreign languages and the full range of sciences. Students can participate in Army, Navy and Air Force JROTC Honor units as well as a broad range of extracurricular activities and programs. There are many programs in vocational education, including marine sciences and oceanography. A cultural arts curriculum includes band, orchestra, chorus, drama, art and dance.

Middle schools offer a similar, though more limited, curriculum to that of the senior high schools. Elementary schools emphasize hands-on experience in all disciplines. Elementary school students participate in a curriculum based on the use of manipulatives and inquiry to build a foundation that will support the learning of concepts in the middle grades and high school. A comprehensive program has been designed for exceptional children at all grade levels.

Basketball and football figure largely in interscholastic athletic programs. What else would you expect from the sports-minded city that produced such athletes as Michael Jordan, Meadowlark Lemon and Roman Gabriel on its public school courts and fields? Volleyball, baseball, soccer, wrestling, golf, tennis and track are also offered.

Brunswick County School System
35 Referendum Dr., N.E., Bolivia
• **(910) 253-2900**

The Brunswick County School System has a student population of more than 10,500 and operates three high schools, four middle schools and eight elementary schools. It offers an alternative high school, the Brunswick Learning Center, that provides education for students who have left the regular program or have not had success in other programs. In the fall of 1998, a 10-year building needs project was initiated to accommodate an-

ticipated rapid growth of the population. One result of this initiative is the Jesse Mae Monroe Elementary School built in Shallotte on Pea Landing Road. An instructional program has been established that stresses learning the basics while encouraging creativity and flexibility from Pre-K through grade 12. In addition to the basic K-12 instructional program, Brunswick County Schools offer a comprehensive program of instructional services for the exceptional child, vocational education, remediation and courses for the North Carolina Scholar.

The Center for Advanced Studies, a joint partnership with Brunswick Community College, encourages and offers more advanced courses in all arenas of the curriculum, including vocational coursework and AP programs. Juniors and seniors who have excelled in high school can get credit toward trades occupations. In addition to helping students pursue vocational careers, the program also is intended to expose students to college life and make them aware of higher-education options.

The system's technology plan is directed not only at students, but also at parental computer literacy. Leland Middle School, Old Fayetteville Road, Leland, (910) 371-3030, offers night courses in computer education free of charge to parents as well as students.

Pender County School System
925 Penderlea Hwy., Burgaw
• **(910) 259-2187**

The Pender County School System is among the fastest growing school systems by rate in the state. Consisting of seven elementary schools, four middle schools, three high schools and one alternative learning center, the school system's enrollment during the 2002-03 school year exceeded 6,800. With a continuing commitment to excellence, progressive leadership and community support, Pender County Schools have been rewarded with achievements to include two schools of excellence and six schools of distinction. One middle school has been recognized as a School of Excellence for three consecutive years. Other achievements include a state top 10 high school for two consecutive years and a middle school among eight national middle schools named "Schools to Watch." There is a 21st Century Community Learning Center at three school sites, an A+ School of the Arts, a year-round elementary school. Pender County offers after-school care programs at each elementary school. The staff of dedicated professionals can boast 42 national board certified teachers.

Independent (Private) Schools

The Cape Fear region's private schools offer curricula and activities for children from preschool to high school. While tuition and expenses are the responsibility of the parent or guardian, most of these schools offer financial aid or easy-pay plans. In many cases, having more than one child in a particular school allows a discount on tuition for other children within the same family. All private schools aren't listed here, but the following list suggests some alternatives to public education.

Cape Fear Academy
3900 S. College Rd., Wilmington
• **(910) 791-0287**

Cape Fear Academy is the dominant secular private school in the region. Established in 1967, this coeducational day school is open to students interested in a traditional, challenging, college-preparatory education. The program offers a developmentally appropriate curriculum within a stimulating learning environment.

The academy's mission statement, "To be a learning community sharing a commitment to respect, integrity and academic excellence," forms the framework for student life at the school as well as fostering a spirit of unity and high ideals. Close relationships with teachers are encouraged.

There are approximately 530 students in pre-kindergarten through grade 12. Pre-kindergarten and kindergarten students participate in half-day programs, with after-school care available. The Lower School comprises pre-kindergarten through grade 5. Instruction by professional faculty includes art, music, science, foreign language (Spanish), drama, computer science and physical education.

The Middle and Upper schools concentrate on college preparation in the classroom coupled with individual development through extracurricular activities. Students in grades 6 through 8 must satisfactorily complete courses in English, science, social studies, math, physical education, art, music, computer science and foreign language. At grade 9, students begin to fulfill graduation requirements within a curriculum that offers Honors and Advanced Placement courses as well. Emphasis is placed on developing study skills, organization, note-taking and test preparation.

Community service is a key component of the Middle and Upper schools programs. The Upper School student government organization has an entire branch devoted to community service. Group and individual activities are planned as students work to serve a minimum number of hours required for graduation.

Present facilities include three classroom buildings, a gymnasium and a student center. The Primary Building contains kindergarten and first-grade classrooms as well as multi-purpose commons and a teaching kitchen. The Beane Wright Student Center includes a dining hall, music and art classrooms and a fitness/weight training area. An Upper School building, Cameron Hall, which includes drama and media/technology spaces, was completed in August 2000. Along with the Bruce B. Cameron gymnasium, there are three athletic fields, tennis courts and a Lower School playground.

One hundred percent of graduates attend four-year college programs, and approximately 75 percent of those students are accepted into their first-choice college or university. The average SAT score is around 1220, which is more than 200 points higher than local, state and national averages.

To arrange for a tour, call the Admissions Office at (910) 791-0287 ext. 1015.

Chesterbrook Academy Preschool
4102 Peachtree Ave., Wilmington
• **(910) 392-4637**

In the Park Avenue area since 1983, this preschool accepts infant, toddler, and 2 and 3-year-old children into its child development, independent learning and academic programs. The school is open from 7 AM until 6 PM. Capacity is 79. Chesterbrook Academy is three-star facility that emphasizes positive discipline with an individualized, hands-on approach to learning.

Chesterbrook Academy of Wilmington
4905 College Rd., Wilmington
• **(910) 452-2330**

Wilmington's newest private school serves children in grades pre-kindergarten to sixth grade. Also available is the Paladin Program, which provides educational opportunities for attention deficit, learning disabled and dyslexic students. The emphasis here is on social, emotional and academic growth. Small class sizes, advanced learning and affordable tuition mark this school. The curriculum includes foreign language, computer instruction, art and music. Chesterbrook Academy emphasizes positive discipline with an individualized hands-on approach to learning. They also offer before- and after-school programs and a summer camp.

The Children's Schoolhouse
612 S. College Rd., Wilmington
• (910) 799-1531

Wilmington's oldest Montessori School, The Children's Schoolhouse offers classes for youngsters ages 3 to 6 years old. A small, home-like, nurturing environment fosters positive growth and development along with solid educational programming. Located within St. Matthew's Lutheran Church, the school includes a state-recognized kindergarten curriculum, high-quality instruction and lots of fun.

Owner/Director Lucy Hieronymus oversees every facet of the school's operations as well as teaching kindergarten and working with her staff of well-trained, experienced professionals; each classroom has a certified Montessori Directress. Each child gets daily individualized instruction in math and reading mixed in with a wide variety of educational activities that include such things as botany, music, art, geography, earth science, history and zoology. Although everything the child does at the school is called "work," and reflects a level of responsibility, nothing appears further from it — the kids love it!

Days and hours of attendance vary according to the child's age, level of development and parental preferences. Generally, younger children attend from 9 AM to 1 PM; kindergartners may stay until 2:30. Children bring their own snacks and lunches.

Friends School of Wilmington
350. Peiffer Ave., Wilmington
• (910) 792-1811

Friends School of Wilmington is a warm, nurturing, educational community where faculty really get to know the students and their families so that they can all work together to benefit children. Founded in 1994, Friends School of Wilmington continues a 300-year Quaker educational tradition of fostering intellectual and spiritual integrity while affirming the value of each individual.

A nurturing environment, a well-rounded, compelling academic program, developmentally appropriate curriculum and intellectual integrity combine to give students a sound educational base upon which to build their own destinies. An excellent, dedicated faculty prepare challenging, relevant, hands-on learning activities, including frequent projects, field trips and personalized growth opportunities, creating a dynamic setting for learning

By manifesting Quaker values of simplicity, community, social justice, diversity, equality, harmony and peace, Friends School of

Wilmington guides students to incorporate these values into their lives, helps them to develop an awareness of the interdependence of life that extends to the world at large, and encourages them to develop habits of respect, trust, cooperation and responsibility. Permeating the entire approach to education is the school's basic philosophy that young people who are convinced of their own value, will, in turn, seek and speak to the good in others. Accordingly, individual differences are honored, cooperation is fostered, responsibility is expected, and personal standards of excellence are developed.

The school now has two campuses spanning ages 18 months through 8th grade. Pre-

school is an established Montessori program, and the elementary school builds on this developmental approach to learning. The teacher-pupil ration is quite low (1:12). A very active Parent/Teacher Organization and a high rate of family involvement help build community and keep tuition low.

The elementary school is located in a 6,000-square-foot building at 207 Pine Grove Drive next to Winter Park Elementary School's playground. Call (910) 791-8221 for admissions information. The middle school is located on a 5-acre campus at 350 Peiffer Avenue off Oleander Drive near Greenville Loop Road. Call (910) 792-1811 for admissions information.

New Horizons Elementary School
3705 S. College Rd., Wilmington
• (910) 392-5209

At New Horizons, students in kindergarten through fifth grade learn in a highly creative, positive environment that provides ongoing opportunities for self development as well as academic growth. An unusual, home-like campus, small class size, a stimulating curriculum, plus a warm, friendly, kind and nurturing staff make this school an excellent choice.

Founded in 1983 by a group of parents and three current faculty members to provide a quality, affordable educational alternative for area children, New Horizons Elementary School's educational program stresses reading, oral and written expression, mathematics, science and social studies. Instruction in critical thinking, problem solving and study skills is integrated throughout the various subject areas. The school's challenging, innovative curriculum is

designed to help a child develop internal motivation, self-reliance and self-discipline

In keeping with the school's philosophy and mission, active parental involvement is a required. This includes monitoring a child's homework, projects, independent reading, returned classwork and evaluations. Parents are expected to serve on committees, attend school events, help with fund-raising, chaperone field trips and even assist with building maintenance.

Upon enrollment, each family becomes a voting member of New Horizons Elementary School, Inc., a non-profit organization. The governing body is a board of directors comprising parents and teachers. The professional staff oversee day-to-day operations as well as instructional, curricular and academic matters.

For more information, contact the school office. The best times are Mondays and Thursdays from 8:30 AM to 12:30 PM.

Wilmington Christian Academy
1401 N. College Rd., Wilmington
• (910) 791-4248

Situated on an 85-acre campus at the beginning of I-40, Wilmington Christian Academy is the largest private school in southeastern North Carolina. Founded in 1969, WCA is a ministry of Grace Baptist Church and provides conservative Christian education for students in kindergarten through grade 12. The school is committed to offering an academically challenging course of study in an environment that is conducive to spiritual growth with the ultimate goal of producing students who will glorify God with their lives while successfully competing in today's world. Academics, athletics and the

An Educational Oasis...
WILMINGTON CHRISTIAN ACADEMY
Your Refreshing School Alternative!

- Christian Philosophy
- Challenging Academics
- Qualified, Caring Faculty
- Biblical Teaching
- Conservative Values
- Grades K4-12

- Excellent Facilities
- Affordable Tuition
- Championship Athletics
- Fine Arts Instruction
- Serving Wilmington
  since 1969

1401 North College Road Wilmington, NC 28405
(910) 791-4248 www.wilmchristian.com

fine arts are combined to give students a well-rounded educational experience. Disciplined classrooms and a wholesome atmosphere provide an exceptional learning environment at Wilmington Christian Academy.

The elementary program emphasizes reading and math as essential elements of future academic success. Students are taught to read using a balanced phonics program; math instruction combines hands-on learning with practice drills to increase comprehension. The full curriculum includes, but is not limited to, classes in English, vocabulary, writing, math, history, science, health and Bible. All elementary students receive instruction in music, art, physical education, computer applications and library skills.

The junior high and senior high days consist of seven class periods covering five core academic subjects, one Bible class and an elective period. Students in grades 9 through 12 follow one of three academic tracks: general, college preparatory or honors. Honors and advanced courses are available in subjects such as English, advanced math, anatomy, chemistry, calculus and physics. Subject-integrated computer training gives all graduates a working knowledge of word processing, spreadsheets, graphics, Internet research, multi-media presentations and more. Resource classes are available for students with mild learning disabilities. Graduates of WCA have enrolled in major Christian and public universities throughout the United States.

The Academy's sports program includes soccer, basketball, baseball and golf for boys; volleyball, basketball, softball, tennis and cheerleading for girls. Students enjoy excellent

facilities including a well-equipped computer lab, two science labs, a media center, a gymnasium, several athletic fields and playgrounds.

Wilmington Academy of Arts & Sciences Middle School
4126 S. College Rd., Wilmington
• (910) 392-3139

Providing a high-quality, academically challenging curriculum and a learning environment free of behavioral disruptions, Wilmington Academy of Arts & Sciences (W.A.A.S.) offers students in grades 6 through 8 an exceptional educational opportunity. With class size limited to 18 and an experienced, professional faculty, the Academy strives to meet the needs of young adolescents preparing for a successful future. Teachers encourage students to reach well beyond the minimum standards, allowing them to thrive in a positive, dynamic environment.

A traditional core of subjects including language arts, literature, social studies, math and science are approached with integrated and interactive methods. Spanish, physical education, band and art are offered also. Tennis, student government, Odyssey of the Mind and MathCounts are available as extracurricular activities. Students use computers extensively and learn word processing, database management, spreadsheet design and interpretation, presentation software and Internet applications.

A parent-driven, nondenominational, not-for-profit corporation, W.A.A.S. depends on parent participation, requiring 35 volunteer hours per year from each enrolled family. Information and application materials can be received by calling the school.

South Brunswick High School's Aquaculture Program

Imagine yourself in a room surrounded by 18 display aquariums ranging in size from 55 to 200 gallons. Add to that six 500-gallon rearing tanks and four hatching troughs, and you will find yourself smack in the middle of the newly constructed Aquaculture Lab at South Brunswick High School in Southport. In addition to the laboratory, there are four half-acre ponds, a reservoir and a new classroom.

Instructor Byron Bey began the Aquaculture Program on a shoestring in 1987, raising fish in a ditch on school property. His creativity and excitement about the program along with hard work, the support of the school system, the enthusiasm of the students, a grant from the N.C. Fisheries Resource Grant Program and a great deal of community support have built the program to a level of excellence that sets a standard for the state and the nation. Testament to these facts are the awards the program has received, including the "Decade of Dominance" trophy for being awarded Best in Show in the New Hanover County Fair from 1991 through 2000. The students have bested themselves by going on and winning Best in Show in 2001 and 2002 as well. The program also won the 2000 Governor's Program of Excellence in Education Award from N.C. Governor Mike Easley.

Bey was voted the South Brunswick High School Teacher of the Year in 2001 by his peers and the Brunswick County Association of Educators. And in 2003, Bey was appointed N.C. Ambassador of Agriculture by Meg Phipps, N.C. Commissioner of Agriculture.

The South Brunswick High School Aquaculture Program participates in the Governor's Vocational Rehabilitation Program and the Governor's Job Ready Program as well. It strives to provide work experience, jobs and scholarships for as many students as possible.

Many skills are required for the day-to-day operation of the program. Using the Aquaculture Science textbook as a guide and having Bey as a leader, the students not only study the materials, but experience their practical applications as well. Bey says

2002-2003 South Brunswick Aquaculture Classes celebrate a great year.

Photo: Byron Bey

this hands-on approach is key to preparing the students for the next level. The chapters in the textbook read like a list of separate occupations, an indication of the many fields of study and the diverse occupations, from fish farming to research, that await graduates of the program: Aquatic Plants and Animals, Marketing Aquaculture, Management Practices for Fin Fish, Management Practices for Alligators, Frogs and Plants and others. Career opportunities include entrepreneurship, veterinarian, extension specialist, fisheries and wildlife instructor, fisheries biologist or technician, researcher and others.

In the third year of the program, students spend two days a week at Brunswick Community College studying college level aquaculture and the other three days at the high school doing hands-on tasks. This gives them the advantage of a smooth transition from the high school setting to a college and has sometimes been the impetus behind students furthering their education. In North Carolina, students can continue their education at Brunswick Community College and UNC Wilmington or NC State in Raleigh in fields such as Aquaculture, Mariculture or Fisheries Biology.

Ponds are essential to any aquaculture program. They allow the students live experience and training needed to survive in the field. Because the program is almost self-sustaining in that few fish are purchased and most are raised in the program, a lesson in the life cycle underlies the activities performed by the students. Eggs are gathered from the spawning pens in the ponds and transported to the hatching troughs. When they have hatched, they are moved to the rearing tanks where they are fed, tended and allowed to grow to adult size. From there they are transported back to the ponds and/or spawning pens and the cycle begins again. Sound simple? About as simple as life.

St. Mary Catholic School
412 Ann St., Wilmington • (910) 762-5491

Located downtown in the historic district, St. Mary Catholic School serves kindergarten through grade 8. The school's mission is to "ensure learning for all our students within the framework of Catholic Christian values, to help our students grow in a manner consistent with their needs, interests and abilities, and to prepare them to live in a changing world as self-directing, caring, responsible citizens."

Grades K through 5 are structured, self-contained classes. The curriculum includes math, science, social studies, computers, Spanish, music, art, physical education, religion, reading, language, (phonics in grades K through 2) and creative writing. Grades 6 through 8 have departmental teachers and students rotate to different classrooms. Classes include religion, science, social studies, math, language arts, literature, writing, computers, Spanish, music, art and physical education. St. Mary Catholic School graduates are prepared to enroll in the honors courses offered by area high schools. The school's emphasis is on preparing students to be independent learners who maintain high academic achievements and standards throughout their high school and college years.

St. Mary Catholic School, which is historically notable as the first Catholic school in North Carolina, proudly carries on its 133-year history by providing Catholic education to the children of Wilmington.

L&L Montessori School
4150 Vanessa Dr., Southport
• (910)454-7344

Montessori education is based upon the principles developed by Maria Montessori, the first woman physician to graduate in Italy. When you enter L&L Montessori School, you will see that the tables and chairs are child sized and the shelves are low so that materials are readily accessible to the students. You can see that the environment has been designed to reflect the children. The focus of the system is the development of materials, educational techniques and observations which support the natural development of children and many of the skills were designed to teach children how to become more independent. The students are taught one on one and move ahead at their own pace fulfilling contracts made with the teacher. In addition to basics, students learn zoology, botany, geology, history and even Latin. Some work is done using computers and art classes are held weekly.

Southport Christian School
8068 River Rd. SE, Southport
• (910) 457-5060

Southport Christian School describes itself as an independent, interdenominational Christian school dedicated to the spiritual and academic growth of children. Parents and clergy concerned about quality education for their children founded the school in 1996 to provide an aggressive, solid academic foundation in a nurturing, loving environment. The school is housed in an addition to the Cape Fear Alliance Church and is a permitted use of the church itself for weekly Friday chapel service. During this time pastors, puppet and mime ministries, singers, missionaries and others give a program. Growth from 24 students (Pre-K to K-5) in the first year to 92 students in 2003 speaks well for the success of the endeavor. Each class has a maximum of 16 students. The school stresses a traditional education with phonics-based reading and incremental math and is a member of the Association of Christian Schools International. In addition to basic subjects, each class is exposed to four special studies each week: art, music, physical education and Spanish. The Spanish class stresses culture as well as the language. P.E. and art classes are sometimes held outdoors in the woods surrounding the school where nature walks and exploration on the trails are included.

Special Education

Child Development Center, Inc.
3802 Princess Place Dr., Wilmington
• **(910) 343-4245**

The Child Development Center is a developmental preschool serving children from 1 to 5 years old. The center has a long history of working with children who have developmental delays and disabilities; these children are served in small classes with a highly qualified staff. The center is a United Way partner agency. Operating hours are 7:30 AM to 5:30 PM weekdays. Call for information on enrollment and openings.

Sylvan Learning Center
4900 Randall Pkwy., Bldg. A, Wilmington
• **(910) 392-6284**

Expert, individualized supplemental education programs provided by a staff of dedicated teachers at the Sylvan Learning Center can help improve academic performance. More than 900 centers in the United States, Canada and Asia offer personalized instructional services to students of all ages and skill levels. A comprehensive Skills Assessment is used to identify each student's areas of strength and weakness. Every student at Sylvan has a personalized program aimed at filling skill gaps, strengthening existing skills and acquiring new, more advanced skills, with rapid improvement and guaranteed results.

United Cerebral Palsy Developmental Center, Inc.
500 Military Cutoff Rd., Wilmington
• **(910) 392-0080**

Children from New Hanover and surrounding counties who have physical and/or other developmental delays can be referred by a parent, physician or community agency to this inclusive preschool. The United Cerebral Palsy Developmental Center is a five-star licensed center and is accredited by NAEYC. The center serves children from birth to 5 years of age who have cerebral palsy, motor delays or other developmental concerns. They also accept students without special developmental needs because the agency believes it is beneficial to bring students with and without special needs together in a quality preschool program. Educators and therapists facilitate learning through play, and promote development in areas such as gross and fine motor skills, speech and language, social, emotional, cognitive and independence skills.

Home Schooling

The State of North Carolina permits schooling outside both public and private schools for children between 7 and 16 years old whose parents/guardians prefer to administer their education. Under the auspices of the NC Division of Non-Public Education in Raleigh, home schooling requires registration, participation in annual standardized achievement testing and maintenance of immunization records. The educational program must operate on a regular schedule, excluding reasonable holidays and vacations, during at least nine calendar months a year by a person with a high school diploma or equivalency certificate; attendance records are required.

State statute defines a home school as "a non-public school in which the child receives academic instruction from the parent, legal guardian or a member of the household in which the child resides." The law also permits (no more than) two households to combine as one home school and allows the children from both households to be taught together by members of either household.

Growing consistently in popularity, homeschool enrollment in Brunswick, Pender and New Hanover counties has soared from a combined total of 86 in 1998-99, (when the state

Kids can learn something new every day.

Photo: Jay Tervo

legislation went into effect), to 1,691 in 2001-02. Statewide, the number of home schools went from 1,385 in 1998-89 to 23,909 in 2001-02, with a total enrollment of 46,909.

A family considering home instruction would begin by obtaining a Home School Information Packet from the N.C. Division of Non-Public Education, either by going to their website www.ncdnpe.org, or calling (919) 733-4276. Twenty-four-hour voicemail is available.

Support for home-schooling families is offered by North Carolinians for Home Education (NCHE). This organization was instrumental in formulating the bill that eventually was approved by the state legislature. NCHE is the state's primary advocacy group today. An excellent resource, NCHE has a full-time staff in Raleigh and can be reached at (919) 790-1100. The web address is www.nche.com; links to

support groups and other resources are available.

Several local support groups can be found in New Hanover, Pender and Brunswick counties; however, it's not always easy. First call Kathryn Iandoli, Region 11 Director for NCHE, who is also President for Christian Home Educators of Wilmington, (910) 452-9685. She can be quite helpful in directing you to other groups, most of which are centered in private homes; they tend to change leadership, and consequently phone numbers, often.

Child Care

A wide range of child-care facilities and programs is available in the greater Wilmington area. While we cannot list all of them here, we've provided a starting place. We encourage parents/guardians to visit facilities they are considering at least once and preferably several times prior to enrolling their youngsters.

After-school enrichment and youth development programs are offered by many day-care centers, schools, churches, the YMCA and YWCA, the Wrightsville Beach Parks & Recreation Department, Girls, Inc., Brigade Boys & Girls and other organizations. Check our chapters on Sports, Fitness and Parks and Kidstuff (Summer Camps, in particular). Again, a visit or two in advance is advisable.

Child Advocacy Commission
Child Care Resource and Referral
1401 S. 39th St., Wilmington
• (910) 791-1057 ext. 18

The Child Advocacy Commission Child Care Resource and Referral (CCR&R) maintains a detailed database of child-care resources in the area. As of November 2002, the Wilmington area had approximately 83 child-care centers and 120 family child-care homes listed in this database. A family child-care home can serve a maximum of five children ages infant to 13, but various stipulations may impact each situation. The CCR&R offers information and referrals at no cost, allowing parents to make informed decisions. The CCR&R provides helpful guidelines in determining which child-care situation is most appropriate for you and your family. They will provide a detailed list of questions to ask and things to look for.

The Division of Child Development licenses and regulates child-care facilities in North Carolina. Licensed child-care facilities are rated on a Star Rated License system. There are three components of the Star Rated License: Program, Education and Compliance Standards. A rating of "one star" identifies that the program meets North Carolina's minimum standards for a licensed child-care facility. Licenses with two to five stars represent higher levels of quality, with five stars signaling the highest level of quality care available. It is up to the child-care facility to apply for more than one star; it may apply for additional stars after the program has been open for at least six months. Each licensed facility must display its license.

The CCR&R encourages all parents to visit a prospective site several times in order to make the best choice possible. Complaints or concerns about a particular child-care facility should be directed to the Division of Child Development (DCD) at (800) 859-0829. A parent may also obtain a child-care facility's compliance history record by calling DCD.

The CCR&R also works to develop cooperative efforts with governmental and other community agencies to promote an awareness of children's issues. It sponsors community service activities, educational information and gives assistance to community agencies, civic groups and individuals. The CCR&R offers on-site training for child-care providers as well as parents. Check with the Child Advocacy Commission Child Care Resource and Referral Monday through Friday from 8:30 AM to 5 PM or visit the website for more information http://childadvocacywilm.org/

Below we have listed child-care facilities with four or five stars as indicated on the Child Advocacy Commission web site in November 2002 and NC Department of Health and Human Services, Division of Child Development web site in January 2003. *The Insiders' Guide* provides this information for your convenience only and does not endorse any facility.

AAI Industries Learning Center, 1206 N. 23rd Street, Wilmington, (910) 254-7384

Babies Learning Center, 705 N. Lord Street, Southport, (910) 457-9262

Brighter Day Care Center, 1409 Church Street, Wilmington, (910) 343-9651

Calabash Day Care, SR 1371 Thomasboro Road, Calabash, (910) 371-1818

Cape Fear Community College Child Development, 415 N. Second Street, Wilmington, (910) 362-7336

Child Development Center, 3802 Princess Place, Wilmington, (910) 343-4245

Children's Learning Center, 71 Darlington Avenue, Wilmington, (910) 762-7735

For Kids Only & Brunswick Academy of Total Learning, 344 Mulberry Road, Shallotte, (910) 754-7777

For Kids Only Child Development Center, Inc. After School Program, 226 Mulberry Street, Shallotte, (910) 754-3277

Grandma & Grandpa's Child Care, 705 S. Third Street, Wilmington, (910) 251-1015

Head Start of New Hanover County, 507 N. Sixth Street, Wilmington, (910) 762-4546

Imagination Station Child Development Center, SR 1349, 5103 Bridgers Road, Shallotte, (910) 754-2244

Ms. Susan's Child Care, 310 Windemere Road, Wilmington, (910) 791-8048

Park Avenue Preschool, 1306 Floral Parkway, Wilmington, (910) 791-6217

United Cerebral Palsy Development Center, 500 Military Cutoff Road, Wilmington, (910) 392-0080

SOLA - School of Learning and Art
216 Pine Grove Rd., Wilmington
• (910) 798-1700

SOLA offers something for creative children of all ages and abilities. Among the many wonderful programs are the following:

SOLA's Pre-School is a program for 3- to 5-year-olds, offering a curriculum balanced with school preparatory academics, fine arts and developmental skills. Morning Half Day is from 8:30 AM to 12:15 PM. Space is limited, so call for wait list information.

SOLA's After Pre-School Art Program is held from 12:45 to 3:30 PM. Drop-ins are welcome on a daily or weekly basis. This class is for 3- to 5-year-olds not registered for SOLA's morning pre-school. Students will experience a very relaxed class, plenty of fun and exploration with pottery, paint, glue and more. Think of it as a very artsy midday pre-school.

SOLA's After-School program offers classes in drawing, painting, mixed media, pottery and music. Also available is a non- traditional after-school care program for young artists ages kindergarten through 5th grade from 2:30 to 5:30 PM.

SOLA's Home School program can take care of the art and music instruction for your curriculum. Classes are designed to meet all media and cultural exposure across grade levels in a child-friendly art studio. Students are thoroughly immersed in the creative process. Parents are welcome to stay and play, too!

SOLA's Summer Camp for boys and girls puts the fun in summer camp; it features week-long sessions with age-appropriate groups and activities. Choose either Half Day Camp from 8:30 AM to 12:30 PM or Full Day Camp from 8:30 AM to 4:30 PM. Kids enjoy both indoor and outdoor activities. Messy, fabulous arts and crafts are an integral part of every day. Students create pottery on the wheel and by hand, make their own T-shirts, experience paint and glue in ways they never have before while building a variety of theme-based projects. Campers play with new and old friends in a home-like workshop and backyard environment. Teachers at SOLA don't just babysit, they rock the house. Signing up is "easy as pie in the face!"

Higher Education and Research

LOOK FOR:
- Universities
- Colleges
- Research Facilities

Southeastern North Carolina features some of the most outstanding universities and colleges in the state. Dating back to its beginnings, this area was famous not for its tourism, but its prosperous commercial industries. As a result, education and research play a major role in helping the southern coast continue to grow and expand to meet the needs of local businesses.

Now, as North Carolina's southern coast finds itself thrown in the limelight of popularity, more people are deciding to move here permanently, as are many new and exciting industries. Research companies such as PPD and AAI Pharma have made Wilmington their home. Major corporations reside here, such as General Electric Company and DuPont. Higher education, therefore, is working hard to meet the demands of booming industry.

The University of North Carolina at Wilmington is focusing its academics to connect student learning across four broad themes: information technology, internationalization, natural environment and regional engagement, so students graduate with a sense of civic responsibility and leadership. Cape Fear Community College and Brunswick Community College have added new buildings to meet the needs of their expanding enrollment.

The research industry also is increasing in importance and size. Not surprisingly, the major emphases of the research performed in the area are in the fields of oceanography, wetland and estuarine studies, marine biomedical and environmental physiology, and marine biotechnology and aquaculture.

Universities and Colleges

University of North Carolina at Wilmington
601 S. College Rd., Wilmington • (910) 962-3000

UNCW had a modest beginning in 1947, when the first class of 186 freshman at Wilmington College shared classroom space with New Hanover High School students. Since then, UNCW has grown tremendously both in size and reputation.

With the passage of the $3.1 billion N.C. Higher Education Facilities Bond issue in November 2000, UNCW will see the largest construction effort in its history over the next six years. With its $108 million, UNCW will build three new buildings and renovate eight existing structures. Construction is underway for a classroom building and resource center for the Watson School of Education and a 263-bed student residence hall that will showcase a new initiative whereby residents will be members of a learning community. Plans are being developed to expand and renovate the current University Union and the Burney Student Support Center to include a new 62,776-square-foot building, which will provide expanded food services, a cafe, a movie theatre, a copy center, banking services and a convenience store. This construction is being financed through student fees.

An arboretum campus situated on a 661-acre tract bordering South College Road, UNCW is a fully accredited, comprehensive level 1 university in the state's 16-campus University of North Carolina system. Through its College of Arts and Sciences, the professional schools and the graduate school, the university seeks to stimulate intellectual curiosity, imagination, rational thinking and thoughtful expression in a broad range of disciplines and professional fields. Of prime importance is the university's commitment to undergraduate teaching. The humanities, the arts, the natural and mathematical sciences, and the behavioral and social sciences make up the core of the undergraduate curriculum. Strong graduate programs complement the undergraduate curriculum.

UNCW encourages public access to its educational programs and is committed to diversity, international perspectives, community and regional service, and the integration of technology throughout the university. It strives to create a safe and secure environment in which students, faculty and staff can develop interests, skills and talents to the fullest extent. UNCW seeks to make optimum use of available resources and to celebrate, study and protect the rich heritage, the quality of life and the environment of the coastal region in which it is located.

Ranked among the top 10 public regional undergraduate universities in the South by U.S. News and World Report for the past five years, UNCW has a student body of 10,700 students, who have access to a variety of programs and the latest technological innovations and are known for their level of campus involvement and volunteer service to the community. Eighty-seven percent of 433 full-time faculty members hold doctoral or terminal degrees. The university has a total of 641 faculty and 923 staff members. The faculty to student ratio is 1 to 16.

UNCW offers four-year programs leading to the Bachelor of Arts, the Bachelor of Fine Arts in creative writing, the Bachelor of Music, the Bachelor of Science and the Bachelor of Social Work degrees. Graduate programs lead to the Master of Arts, Master of Arts in Teaching, Master of Business Administration, Master of Education, Master of Fine Arts in Creative Writing, Master of Public Administration, Master of School Administration, Master of Science, Master of Science in Nursing and Master of Science in Accountancy degrees.

A Ph.D. in marine biology, the only such degree in the state and one of only three on the East Coast, is offered in addition to a cooperative Ph.D. in marine science with N.C. State University.

Professional undergraduate programs include those offered in the Cameron School of Business, the Watson School of Education, the School of Nursing and Clinical Laboratory Science program in the College of Arts and Sciences. Pre-professional programs are offered in agriculture and forestry, allied health, health-related careers, dentistry, law, medicine, optometry, pharmacy, physical therapy, podiatry, veterinary medicine and a 2+2 program in engineering with N.C. State University.

The College of Arts and Sciences shares the university's commitment to excellence in teaching, scholarship, artistic achievement and service. It supports the university's mission by providing quality undergraduate and graduate programs taught by student-centered professional faculty who consider their scholarly practice, research and creative activities essential components of effective teaching. The college offers 40 undergraduate and 12 graduate degree programs within 18 academic departments and provides courses of study in a variety of interdepartmental programs including gerontology, environmental studies and leadership studies.

Of the nation's 1,200 business school programs, the Cameron School of Business is one of 340 to receive the Association to Advance Collegiate Schools of Business accreditation, which places it in the top one-third of business education programs in the country. There are approximately 1,730 students in the school and nearly 20 percent are considered nontraditional. An innovative dual degree program with the Centre d'Etudes Superieures Europeenes Management Mediterranee in Marseille, France, give students a unique opportunity to learn how to operate effectively in the global market.

As one of only three UNC institutions producing more than 300 teachers each year, the UNCW Watson School of Education is doing its part to address the teacher shortage in North Carolina. Through its Professional Development System, Watson School of Education faculty work closely with 95 area

INSIDERS' TIP

The area's colleges and universities provide our community with a tremendous pool of human resources, talent, energy and ability. Whether you're looking for child-care helpers, part-time office staff, interns, computer support, maintenance assistance, lawn care or what-have-you, remember that college students almost always need extra money and often are more than willing to offer their services. A good place to start would be the Student Affairs or Student Development office at UNCW.

schools and more than 1,300 public school teachers. The recipient for three national awards for partnerships, the Watson School of Education founded the first community college, business, university and K-12 partnership in the state. A new 80,000-square foot facility for the school of education is now under construction and is scheduled to open in fall 2004.

The School of Nursing, fully accredited by the National League for Nursing and approved by the North Carolina Board of Nursing, offers an undergraduate program that prepares students to practice family-centered professional nursing in a variety of current and emerging healthcare delivery systems, as well as a master's degree program for rural and urban family nurse practitioners.

UNCW's William Randall Library, (910) 962-3760, contains more than 493,000 volumes, subscribes to more than 4,280 serial titles and employs state-of-the-art electronic informational resources. The library is a partial repository for U.S. government publications and has a current inventory of 600,000 items in hard copy and microtext. Randall Library is a full repository for North Carolina documents, which are available to all users, including nonstudents. Nonstudents may obtain check-out privileges for up to four items per visit. Those under age 65 with a N.C. driver license pay $15 a year; there is no charge for people over 65 with a valid N.C. driver license.

Other instructional and research resources at UNCW include the 10-acre Bluethenthal Wildflower Preserve, the Upperman African-American Cultural Center, elaborate campus-wide computing services with wireless Internet access, and the Ev-Henwood Nature Preserve at Town Creek. Kenan Auditorium hosts theatrical, symphonic and instructional events year round.

As a part of its regional engagement, UNCW offers lifelong learning programs through the Division for Public Service and Continuing Studies. Because they respond to the interests and feedback from the region, lifelong learning activities encompass the interest and passions of youth, professionals and retirees.

MarineQuest is a popular youth program that offers marine and environmental education through the Summer Science-by-the-Sea Day Camp, Coast Trek and OceanLab. MarineQuest, based at the Center for Marine Science, also offers the Odyssey Program for adults. The Summer Lifelong Learning Society presents opportunities for intellectual, cultural and social growth through quality programs consistent with the university's outreach mission.

Featuring more than 1,000 courses, WebU is an opportunity for persons with various interests to attain educational activities from their desktops.

For those selecting intellectual stimulation along with social interactions, the Tabitha Hutaff McEachern Lifelong Learning Series features educational and entertaining programs with a catered meal. Newcomers often participate in a Living Southern program offered annually in co-sponsorship with Cape Fear Museum focusing on Southern heritage and culture.

To celebrate the arts, UNCW sponsors Celebrate Wilmington with the community. Celebrate Wilmington promotes the many cultural opportunities in the region and sponsors the Walk of Fame and Lifetime Achievement Award in the Arts.

The UNCW Executive Development Center at the Northeast Public Library offers corporate and community groups a state-of-the-art facility for professional meetings, retreats and small conferences. Located one mile west of Wrightsville Beach next to the Landfall Shopping Center, the center is designed to accommodate groups of various sizes and needs and offer high-speed wireless Internet, video conferencing, an on-site technician, convenient location and ample parking.

The UNCW Division for Public Service and Continuing Studies seeks to expand the capacity of civic engagement among all North Carolinians through two leadership programs: the Adults Scholars Leadership Program and Leadership Wilmington. Both programs provide opportunities for participants to discuss regional issues with leaders in economic development, education, government, and the business communities. The Adults Scholars Leadership Program is geared to retirees who have recently relocated to the area. The Leadership Wilmington Program attracts mid-level managers who seek to serve on regional boards and influence policy. Both programs usually conclude with a class project or presentation that alleviates some problem in the region. A recent graduating class of Leadership Wilmington identified space for and relocated a homeless shelter in New Hanover County.

Seahawk spirit is flying high on campus; 2002 was an exceptional year for athletics at UNCW. While the highlight was the men basketball team's accomplishments with the NCAA, there are other numerous reasons to be proud of Seahawk athletes — swimming, track and field, golf, and soccer. The 2001-02 men's basketball team earned the CAA title for the second time in three years and made it to the second round of the NCAA tournament by beating the much-favored USC Trojans. Unfortunately, they lost the next game in a heated contest against the Indiana Hoosiers.

HIGHER EDUCATION AND RESEARCH

The men's track and field team won the CAA title for five straight years, 1997-2001. The men's swimming team won its first CAA championship in 2002.

UNCW student athletes had the highest graduation rate among NCAA Division 1 public universities in North Carolina for the four-year class average, according to the most recent annual graduation rates report by the National Collegiate Athletic Association. UNCW paced the UNC system in four-year class averages at 74 percent, followed by UNC Asheville at 67 percent and UNC Greensboro at 53 percent.

As a member of NCAA Division 1, UNCW fields 19 varsity teams including men's and women's programs in basketball, tennis golf, track and field, cross country, swimming, diving and soccer. Other varsity programs include volleyball, softball and baseball. The Seahawk's athletic facilities include the 6,000-seat Trask Coliseum; an Olympic-sized natatorium with diving well; the 1,200-seat baseball stadium, Brooks Field; the 2,000-seat soccer stadium, the Harold Greene Track and Field Complex and Boseman Softball Field. As part of Project 2002, an 18,000-square-foot sports medicine building is planned and the expansion of Nixon Annex was completed.

UNCW's school year is divided into four sessions consisting of the standard fall and spring semesters plus two summer sessions. For information on undergraduate admissions call (910) 962-3243; for graduate studies call (910) 962-3135. For information on Public Service Programs and Continuing Studies call (910) 962-3193.

Cape Fear Community College
411 N. Front St., Wilmington
• (910) 362-7000

CFCC is one of the fastest growing community colleges in North Carolina, both in enrollment and in program offerings. Dedicated to providing workforce training through trade, technical and college transfer programs, full-time and part-time, Cape Fear Community College exerts a major educational presence in the area. It is among the state's most technologically advanced and fastest growing community colleges, serving more than 24,000 students yearly.

The main campus is located along the Cape Fear River in downtown Wilmington. A new campus located on a 140-acre site in northern Hanover County offers a growing number of courses and will continue to expand. Two satellite campuses are in Pender County: one in Burgaw, about 21 miles north of Wilmington, (910) 259-4966; the other in Hampstead, on U.S. Highway 17, (910)

270-3069. Classes are also held at area schools and community centers.

CFCC offers 50 technical and vocational fields, along with a very popular college transfer program. The college's two-year Associate in Applied Science (A.A.S.) Degrees include: Accounting, Architectural Technology, Associate Degree Nursing, Automotive Systems Technology, Business Administration, Chemical Technology, Computer Engineering Technology, Criminal Justice Technology, Dental Hygiene, Early Childhood Associate, Electrical/Electronics Technology (Instrumental Concentration), Environmental Science Technology, Heavy Equipment and Transport Technology (Marine Systems Concentration), Hotel and Restaurant Management, Information Systems, Interior Design, Landscape Gardening, Machining Technology, Marine Technology, Mechanical Engineering Technology, Mechanical Engineering Technology (Drafting and Design Concentration), Occupational Therapy Assistant, Office Systems Technology, Paralegal Technology, Radiography, and Speech and Language Pathology Assistant.

One-year diploma programs include: Air Conditioning, Heating and Refrigeration Technology, Autobody Repair, Boat Building, Carpentry, Cosmetology, Dental Assisting, early Childhood Associate, Electrical/Electronics Technology (Marine Systems Concentration), Film/Video Production, Industrial Maintenance Technology, Marine Propulsion Systems, Masonry, Medical Transcription, Pharmacy Technology, Practical Nursing and Welding Technology.

Twenty-two Certificate Programs range from six weeks to two semesters. They include many of the same areas as the diploma and degree-granting programs, but training is less comprehensive and of shorter duration. Some others are Truck Driver Training, Manicuring/Nail Technology, Real Estate and Real Estate Appraisal, Customer Service and Licensed Practical Nurse Refresher.

As part of its continuing education services, the Cape Fear Community College's Center for Business, Industry and Government offers low-cost computer classes and provides customized seminars, workshops and training programs for local companies and organizations. The community college offers a dual enrollment program to select high school students so that they can take college level classes while still in high school. The college offers free courses in high-school equivalency (GED), English as a Second Language (ESL) and adult literacy. Many other special programs and seminars are free or very reasonably priced.

CFCC maintains small and large oceangoing vessels for its quality marine technology curriculum, which is enhanced by a deep-water pier on the Cape Fear River at the Wilmington campus. One of these vessels was integral to the recovery of artifacts from the wreck of Blackbeard's flagship, Queen Anne's Revenge.

The college has a growing number of intercollegiate sports teams in men's basketball, golf and women's volleyball. Admission to all of the college's athletic events is free to the public.

Day and evening classes in semester-long cycles are available at all campuses, and financial aid is available for eligible applicants. Cape Fear Community College is one of 59 colleges in the North Carolina Community College System and is accredited by the Southern Association of Colleges and Schools. The public is always welcome to visit the campus to see all that CFCC has to offer.

Miller-Motte Technical College
606 S. College Rd., Wilmington
• (910) 392-4660, (800) 784-2110

When it was founded in 1916 by Judge Leon Motte, this school provided courtroom stenography training. Today, the college has changed its course offerings as changes in business and industry have mandated. Building on an 86-year foundation, the college is poised to educate the next generation of Americans by offering a varied, cutting-edge curriculum that include training in Microsoft Network Engineering, A+ computer repair, Massage Therapy, Medical Assisting, Surgical Technology, Business Administration, Accounting, Microcomputers and Office Administration. These programs range from nine-month certification programs to two-year Associate of Applied Science (A.A.S.) degrees. Financial Assistance is available for those who qualify, and the college offers lifetime job placement services for students.

To further enhance the skills of its graduates and in order to increase the quality of its curriculum, Miller-Motte has partnered with Microsoft in offering computer education. Miller-Motte is accredited by the Accrediting Council for Independent Colleges and Schools and falls under the jurisdiction of the University of North Carolina Board of Governors and the North Carolina Community College System.

Mt. Olive College, Wilmington Campus
1426 Commonwealth Dr., Wilmington
• (910) 256-0255, (800) 300-7478

With locations in Mount Olive, Wilmington, Goldsboro, New Bern and the Research Triangle Park, MOC has made earning a college degree more achievable than ever for adults who are at least 21 years of age. A private, liberal arts institution dedicated to the total development of its students in an environment nurtured by Christian values, the college was founded in 1951 and is sponsored by the Convention of Original Free Will Baptists.

Mount Olive College offers two Bachelor of Science degrees, one in Management and Organizational Development and the other in Criminal Justice Administration. The college has a School of Business and six academic departments, including Fine Arts, Language and Literature, Recreation and Leisure Studies, Religion, Science, Mathematics and Social Studies.

Students with 60 semester hours of college credit may complete their degrees in Management and Organizational Development or Criminal Justice Administration by attending one four-hour class per week for 55 to 59 weeks. Registration is ongoing throughout the year.

A series of curricula designed specifically for working adults is called the Heritage Program. The three-semester format provides students with the core courses needed for associate or baccalaureate programs. MOC has a tradition of student-focused, supportive programming and teaching styles. Courses are discussion-oriented, emphasizing critical thinking and research papers. Classes, which meet at night and on weekends, are limited to 20 students who proceed through the curriculum together as a group, called a cohort. Tuition includes all books and fees.

The North Carolina Independent Colleges and Universities lists Mount Olive College as the sixth most affordable private college in the state, and it is accredited by SACS the Commission on Colleges of the Southern Association of Colleges and Schools. Financial assistance is available to all qualified students.

Brunswick Community College
U.S. Hwy. 17 N., Supply • (910) 343-0203, (910) 755-7300, (800) 754-1050

BCC serves more than 1,000 curriculum students and 6,000 others in continuing education courses at its two locations: the Main Campus, located on U.S. 17 just north of U.S. 211 in Supply, about 25 miles south of Wilmington; and the Leland Center located in the Leland Industrial Park on N.C. 74/76.

Established in 1979, the college offers one and two-year certificates, diploma and associate's degree programs. These include aquaculture, various business studies, cosmetology, turfgrass management, practical nursing, medical records and an early childhood associate program.

The College Transfer program leads to an associate of arts or associate of science degree. Stu-

The University of North Carolina at Wilmington is the pride of the southern coastal region.

Photo: Jay Tervo

dents may transfer from Brunswick's two-year curricula to four-year programs at any of the 16 member universities in the UNC system. Course content, classroom instruction, textbooks, testing, grading procedures and academic support services meet university transfer standards.

BCC offers courses via the Internet; the Information Highway, which links several locations; and Telecourses, utilizing videotaped instructors and programs.

Community and continuing education courses are offered for those who wish to explore new interests or learn new skills including computer training, photography, emergency medical training, construction trades and real estate training.

Through the New and Expanding Industry Program and Small Business Center, BCC works closely with area businesses and industry to tailor curricula to meet their needs.

BCC has a fully equipped library that is open to county citizens as well as students. The library holds more than 8,000 books and periodicals and has an extensive genealogical research collection as well as an Internet research system.

BCC is widely known as an educational value for the tuition dollar. Some classes are tuition free for N.C. residents age 65 and older.

Research Facilities

UNCW Center for Marine Science
5600 Marvin K. Moss Ln., Wilmington
• (910) 962-2300

The Center for Marine Science at the University of North Carolina at Wilmington is dedicated to interdisciplinary approaches to questions in basic marine research. The mission of the center is to promote basic and applied research in the fields of oceanography, coastal and estuarine studies, marine biology, marine chemistry, marine geology, marine biotechnology and aquaculture. Faculty members conducting marine science research in the departments of Biological Sciences, Chemistry, Earth Sciences and Physics, and Physical Oceanography participate in this program.

Faculty also serve on regional, national and international research and policy advisory groups, thereby contributing to the development of agendas on marine research in the United States and the world. International interactions with labs in Europe, North and South America, Australia, New Zealand, Asia, Africa, Bermuda, the Bahamas and Caribbean, and all regions of the coastal United States augment extensive programs addressing North Carolina coastal issues. By integrating these advisory functions with research programs of the

highest quality, CMS enhances the educational experience provided by UNCW for both undergraduate and graduate students in marine science.

Located on the Intracoastal Waterway (ICW), just six miles from the main campus, the Marine Science Center has a total of 75,000 square feet of net indoor space, which includes group meeting facilities for up to 150 individuals, fully equipped research laboratories, classrooms, marine science laboratories, a greenhouse with running seawater, a radioisotope lab, computer workrooms, cold rooms, walk-in freezers, temperature-controlled rooms, fireproof data storage vault and shower/locker rooms. Core facilities include harmful algal identification and toxicology; nutrient analysis; DNA sequencing; and NMR spectroscopy.

A 900-foot pier, which can accommodate several coastal research vessels, is in place on the Intracoastal Waterway. The location of the new center provides easy access to regional marine environments such as tidal marshes/mud flats/sand flats; tidal creeks; barrier islands and tidal inlets; the Atlantic Intracoastal Waterway; near shore forests; and both highly developed and minimally developed estuarine environments. The center maintains 16 research vessels ranging in size from 13 to 65 feet and specialized equipment including a Superphantom Remotely Operated Vehicle (ROV), an ocean environmental sample (SBE-CTD), and an ADCP current profiler.

The center serves as host for the NOAA-sponsored National Undersea Research Center; an extension office for the North Carolina Sea Grant; the Marine Mammal Stranding Network; the North Carolina National Estuarine Research Reserve; and UNCW's Marine Quest Program, which is an extensive community outreach program for public schools and adult education.

North Carolina National Estuarine Research Reserve
UNCW Center for Marine Science,
5600 Marvin K. Moss Ln., Wilmington
• (910) 962-2470

The U.S. Congress created the National Estuarine Research Reserve system in 1972 to preserve undisturbed estuarine systems for research into and education about the impact of human activity on barrier beaches, adjacent estuaries and ocean waters. The reserves are outdoor classrooms and laboratories for researchers, students, naturalists and others.

The headquarters of the North Carolina National Estuarine Research Reserve (NCNERR) is housed at the UNCW Center for Marine Science Center in cooperation with the N.C. Division of Coastal Management. The NCNERR program manages four estuarine reserve sites as natural laboratories and coordinates research and education activities.

Masonboro Island and Zeke's Island are two of the four components of NCNERR, the others being Rachel Carson Reserve near Beaufort and Currituck Banks in northeastern North Carolina. Nationally threatened loggerhead sea turtles nest at Zeke's Island, Rachel Carson and Masonboro Island. Brown pelicans and ospreys are common to all four points.

With more than 5,000 protected acres, Masonboro Island is the last and largest undisturbed barrier island remaining on the southern North Carolina coast and one of the most productive estuarine systems along the coast. The Zeke's Island component of the Reserve, immediately south of Fort Fisher, includes almost 2,000 acres and actually consists of three islands — Zeke's, North Island, No-Name Island — and the Basin, the body of water enclosed by the breakwater known locally as the Rocks.

NCNERR allows traditional activities to continue, such as fishing and hunting within regulations, on Zeke's and Masonboro Island. (For further information about these islands, see our chapters on Attractions; Camping; and Sports, Fitness and Parks.)

Another reserve that has received its share of scientific scrutiny is Permuda Island. This linear 50-acre island bears substantial archaeological significance in that large tracts consist essentially of extensive shell middens created by prehistoric inhabitants over a vast span of time. Such sites are rare in the ever-shifting, acidic soils of barrier islands. Despite decades of farming, the archaeological resources survived fairly intact. The island passed into state ownership in 1986.

Of further interest is the theory that Permuda Island represents an original barrier island later eclipsed by the growth of what today is called Topsail Island. A similar theory has been posited for North Island, mentioned above, and other privately owned islands along the Pender County coast such as Hutaff and Lee islands. (The only other islands behind the barriers are dredge material islands.) Permuda Island is accessible to the public only by boat. It remains in a natural state and is managed by the North Carolina Department of Environment and Natural Resources, NCNERR and the Department of Marine Fisheries.

North Carolina State Horticultural Crops Research Station
Castle Hayne Rd., Castle Hayne
• (910) 675-2314

Another field of research important to the region is horticulture. The North Carolina Department of Agriculture and North Carolina State University run 15 horticultural research stations around the state. The station in Castle Hayne is the primary local research site. Its varied, ongoing programs concentrate on crops of local economic importance, such as blueberries, strawberries, grapes, ornamentals and cucurbits. Variety trials, breeding, insect and disease control, and herbicide tests are among the studies performed.

INSIDERS' TIP
Adults can continue their education or just have fun by taking courses or attending programs offered by UNCW's Division for Public Service and Continuing Studies. Call for information and request a copy of *Pathways*, their Lifelong Learning Catalog, (910) 962-4034 or (910) 962-3193.

The station works in limited association with the New Hanover County Extension Service arboretum, especially regarding soil studies, but primarily serves local horticulturists by making useful publications available to them through the N.C. Cooperative Extension Service.

LaQue Center for Corrosion Technology Inc.
702 Causeway Dr., Wrightsville Beach
• (910) 256-2271

LaQue (pronounced la kwee) Center for Corrosion Technology, Inc. is a corrosion testing, research and consulting services firm that has specialized in marine corrosion for more than 50 years and is internationally recognized as a pioneer and leader in the field. LaQue Center is capable of providing any and all corrosion and testing services related to marine material and machinery. Since 1935, this center has performed contract services in the areas of natural seawater testing, marine atmospheric corrosion, weathering and durability testing, cyclic corrosion cabinet testing, prototype equipment evaluations and performance, and electrochemical, mechanical and metallurgical testing. LaQue also conducts on-site corrosion monitoring; corrosion failure analyses, consulting and expert witnessing, corrosion classes and seminars, and has sponsored "The Sea Horse Institute," a marine corrosion conference. The center's natural seawater facility at Wrightsville Beach and marine atmospheric test site at Kure Beach offer various testing options.

" It's tiring and frightening. You get in a certain situation and don't know what to expect... Your heart is exploding inside of you. Do you stand here or do you run?"

Nearly 30,000 adults in the Wilmington area know what this man is talking about. For them, illiteracy is not about books and diplomas. It's driving without street signs. It's staying home instead of applying for a job. It's making excuses instead of reading to their children. It's living in fear of being exposed.

The Cape Fear Literacy Council is helping 350 adults learn to read. We rely on volunteer tutors who selflessly train each student, one-on-one. But there is more we could do. Help us tell them they don't have to run anymore.

For more information about volunteering, call the Cape Fear Literacy Council at 251-0911

Volunteer Opportunities

One of the most wonderful aspects of living in a coastal community is that the people who move here do so not out of necessity for their jobs, but because they want to live here. And when people appreciate their homes, they want to share that joy. Maybe that's why this area is filled with so many tireless volunteers.

Dedicated volunteers are always in high demand, and your willingness to serve in any capacity will most assuredly be greatly appreciated. As you'll read in this section, there's a need to suit just about anyone's interest. Involvement with good causes and organizations not only helps the community, it benefits each individual who supports them.

First Call for Help, an excellent information and referral service agency, located at 615 Shipyard Boulevard in Wilmington, (910) 397-0497, can provide information about human service organizations throughout the region. The Community Services pages of the phone books contain listings of most area human service agencies as well. Look, too, in Wilmington's *Sunday Star-News*, Section D, which has a spread called, "Community Connection;" there you'll find features about different organizations and volunteers plus an extensive list of agencies and churches needing volunteers in New Hanover, Brunswick and Pender counties.

The arts, health services, nutrition, historic preservation, environment, minority interests, business development, human relations, housing, schools and education, and special festivals make up a fraction of the volunteer possibilities in our area. The following is a condensed list of some organizations that would appreciate your involvement.

LOOK FOR:
• Human Services
• Children's Services
• The Arts
• Historic Preservation and Community Development

CLOSE UP:
• Topsail Island's Labor of Love

Human Services

American Red Cross, Cape Fear Chapter
1102 S. 16th St., Wilmington • (910) 762-2683

Volunteer positions include blood service aides, registered nurses, disaster team members, service to military case workers, health and safety class instructors and office aides. A maximum of four classes are offered each month to train volunteers for the disaster team or service to military case workers. Classes are offered in New Hanover, Brunswick, Pender and Duplin counties. This very active organization has a high community profile and is extremely responsive to people in need. It responds to emergencies both inside and beyond the region with shelter, food and funds. The simple act of giving blood is an easy way to volunteer, and this is a critical need because only 5 percent of the population donates blood. Give blood and save a life.

The Bargain Box
4213 Princess Place Dr., Wilmington • (910) 362-0603

The Bargain Box, a thrift shop, is an outreach ministry of Wilmington's

Church of the Servant, Episcopal. They encourage the recycling of quality used goods and the creative utilization of discarded merchandise. A wide variety of affordable and quality merchandise is continually offered, including a complete assortment of clothing, furniture and household items, collectibles and records, tapes and CDs, toys and games, jewelry and accessories. The Bargain Box honors all persons — the giver as well as the receiver, the volunteer as well as the shopper, the elderly and youth. All profits go back to the community for outreach/service programs, especially Good Shepherd House. The store honors emergency vouchers from area churches and social agencies. You can help in this ecumenical ministry by volunteering your time and talents, or by just by coming to the Bargain Box to shop or bring donations. Encourage your friends and family to do likewise.

INSIDERS' TIP

With so many demands on your time these days, finding a few hours to volunteer may be a challenge, but the rewards are great and well worth re-ordering your priorities.

Brunswick Family Assistance Agency
(910) 754-4766

This organization needs volunteers to help families in need of food, shelter, furniture and other necessities. It also needs help with the pantry, fund-raisers, food drives to stock the pantry and distributing clothes. The agency is in the fund-raising stages of establishing a homeless shelter. It distributes more than 500 Christmas baskets across Brunswick County and has a food pantry that distributes more than 20,000 pounds of food each year.

Brunswick County Literacy Council
282 Ocean Hwy., P.O. Box 6, Supply
• (910) 754-7323, (800) 694-7323

The Brunswick County Literacy Council promotes literacy for all ages in Brunswick County. Each year the council helps approximately 250 residents with reading, writing, math, computer and English-speaking skills, in a one-on-one confidential setting, by pairing them with volunteers who are carefully trained and matched with the students. Tutoring is free of charge, as is the training for volunteer tutors. In concert with the Brunswick Family Assistance Agency, the council runs the Family Thrift Store at Twin Creek Plaza in Shallotte, plus contributes to the Holiday Basket program with Book Share, a collection of new or almost new books for youth. In addition to tutoring, volunteers are needed for interpreting, fund-raising, publicity and other duties.

Cape Fear Area United Way
613 Shipyard Blvd., Wilmington
• (910) 798-3900

The Cape Fear Area United Way funds 60 human care programs in Brunswick, New Hanover and Pender counties in southeastern North Carolina. These programs provide food and shelter for those in need, day care and after-school care for local children, job training, family support, health services and a domestic violence shelter. The Cape Fear Area United Way also helps build a strong community through programs such as Project BUILD, a recruitment and training program for volunteers to serve on nonprofit boards; information and referral services for First Call For Help; and volunteer recruitment and training through the United Way Volunteer Center. The Cape Fear United Way needs donations of money, services and event sponsorships as well as individuals to serve on the board, volunteer for the fund-raising campaign, fund distribution teams and serve on the communication committee.

Cape Fear Hospital
5301 Wrightsville Ave., Wilmington
• (910) 452-8384

Cape Fear Hospital continues to recruit increasing numbers of volunteers to meet the growing needs of this busy facility. As the number of orthopedic surgeries increase, the volunteer requirement increases to staff the Surgical Waiting Room. The Gift Garden is a lovely place to volunteer and serve patients, visitors and staff. The main lobby reception desk uses volunteers, too. If you're interested, contact Diann Disney at the above number.

Cape Fear Literacy Council
1012 S. 17th St., Wilmington
• (910) 251-0911

The Cape Fear Literacy Council works to improve the literacy skills, which include reading, writing and math, of adults and at-risk youth. Adults in all skill levels, from the nonreader to high school level, are welcome at the Literacy Council. There is a computer literacy lab on site. The Literacy Council has a significant English as a Second Language (ESL) program, training tutors to work with students having limited or no English skills. More than 300 tutors are needed on a yearly basis to work one-on-one with adults. The council trains volunteers every month in a 12-hour workshop. Volunteers work with more than 300 students each year. The main fund-raiser ties into September's National Literacy Month with an additional fund-raiser, a festive Mardi Gras auction held in March.

Cape Fear River Watch, Inc.
617 Surry St., Wilmington
• (910) 762-5606

Cape Fear River Watch, Inc. is celebrating its 10th anniversary in 2003 of commitment to improving and protecting the water quality of the Lower Cape Fear River Basin through education, advocacy and action. Volunteers are needed to assist with many programs, including outdoor education and recreation, clean-ups, outreach, wetlands restoration, fund-raising and administrative tasks. To raise funds for its work, this organization rents bicycles and manages the paddleboat/canoe concession at Greenfield Lake. Eco-tours are available at the lake upon request.

Coastal Horizons Center
615 Shipyard Blvd., Wilmington
Crisis Line/Open House • (800) 672-2903
(24 hours)
Rape Crisis Center • (910) 392-7460
(24 hours)
Substance/Abuse Services
• (910) 343-0145

This private, nonprofit agency serving the tri-county area is for individuals who need assistance recovering from chemical dependency/substance abuse, sexual assault and other crisis situations. There is also an emergency care shelter for youths ages 8 through 17. Other programs include HIV/AIDS Outreach, pregnancy testing, criminal justice alternatives and food vouchers. Volunteers are needed to work with children at the shelter, respond to calls to assist victims at their home or in the hospital, and to answer the crisis line. A 48-hour training program is required.

Domestic Violence Shelter and Services Inc.
(910) 343-0703

This agency shelters women and children who have suffered domestic violence. Volunteers are needed for the Vintage Values resale shops, office work, transportation, children's court advocacy and direct services. They sometimes assist on-call in emergency situations. More than 1,500 women and children are assisted yearly by the shelter. The Vintage Values stores have three locations: 413 S. College Road, 609 Castle Street and 2103 Market Street. All locations need gently used clothing and re-sellable merchandise.

Elderhaus, Inc.
1950 Amphitheater Dr., Wilmington
• (910) 343-8209
1013 Porters Neck Rd., Wilmington
• (910) 686-3335

Elderhaus provides structured and stimulating daycare activities for adults, primarily the elderly, and weekend daytime respite for caregivers. Elderhaus serves persons with a variety of needs, including those with Alzheimer's disease and dementia. Volunteers are needed as program aides, activity assistants, meal servers and van assistants. Volunteer board members oversee fund-raising, public relations, educational activities and more. Elderhaus added a 7,000-square-foot center in July 1998 to serve the area's increasing need for these services; in November of that year, Elderhaus opened a second facility on the grounds of Davis Health Care Center in the Porters Neck area.

Good Shepherd House
3408 Wilshire Blvd., Wilmington
• (910) 397-2877 (shelter), (910) 397-0237
(administrative office)

This day shelter for homeless people needs volunteers to work at the front desk greeting guests, answering the phone and distributing toiletry items for the shower. Volunteers are also needed to sort clothing, distribute fresh clothing and drive the van to take clients to work or on errands. People interested in working in the kitchen are needed to set up for lunch, serve meals and clean up. People can also stop by between 8 AM and 1 PM to donate food and clothing.

Hope Harbor Home
(910) 754-5726, (910) 754-5856 24-Hour
Crisis Line

Volunteers are needed at this domestic violence shelter in Brunswick County to serve as client advocates, work on the speakers bureau and help organize and implement fund-raising activities. Also needed are people to answer the Crisis Line and work with rape victims after hours. Volunteers are needed for transportation and to help distribute and sort donated clothes at the four Hope Chest Thrift Stores.

Topsail Island's Labor of Love

The evolution of the Topsail Island Missiles and More Museum, from a community leader's dream to a museum so full of artifacts that the walls are bulging, has been a labor of love for the Topsail Island Historical Society. In the process, the museum has created a history of its own.

Betty Polzer took her dream, inspired others to join her in her efforts to preserve Topsail's history and the first museum became a reality. Appropriately housed in the southern corner of the Assembly Building, this early museum was

mostly a picture display from the beach towns and Operation Bumblebee, the early rocket-testing program conducted on Topsail Island by the government from 1946-1948. The Assembly Building was used to assemble these rockets, and Operation Bumblebee had significant historical value since the Ramjet engine, the forerunner of today's jet engine, was developed and tested as part of this program. This budding museum didn't even have operating hours, it was open only when the Assembly Building was in use.

From these humble beginnings the process that followed could be described as a metamorphosis. After the Assembly Building was designated a Historical Site on the National Register of Historic Places and its ownership acquired by the Topsail Beach Economic Development Council, the Historical Society got busy. Unfortunately, by this time, Ms. Polzer had become too ill to participate. Her successors successfully convinced the EDC that a larger area was needed for the museum. A north side portion of the building was designated museum space, and walls were built to separate it from the larger community room.

Members of the Historical Society then met with museum experts from the state and other museums to learn how to ensure the integrity of a new museum. They also sought advice on how to collect and properly display the ever-growing number of artifacts that were being donated. The name Missiles and More was chosen and help was solicited in preparing the space to house the designed displays. Many hours were spent building, painting and cleaning. Docents were trained and the first brochure for distribution to area businesses and visitors centers was created. Most impressive, this was all done by volunteers and on a budget of $600.

In the spring of 1995, the museum opened its doors to the public. The original operating hours were two hours on Saturday and Sunday during the season. Now when the ever-popular question was asked "What are those towers?" vacationers could be directed to the Missiles and More Museum to find out not only about the towers, but all about the island's colorful history. The first year, the visitor log contained over 1,500 names.

Hand in hand with the creation of the museum in the early 1990s was the research and writing of a book, *Echoes of Topsail* by David Stallman. A visitor to the island, Stallman was intrigued by the area's historical buildings, Operation Bumblebee and its link to the modern space program. Working with the Historical Society, he began an in-depth study, which led to a meeting with The Applied Physics Laboratory of Johns Hopkins University, which had guided the U.S. Navy in Operation Bumblebee. This meeting led to a real treasure: volumes of documents and other materials pertaining to Operation Bumblebee that had been stored away in the archives. Unselfishly, Johns Hopkins was willing to share these materials with the museum and they became the core exhibit.

Visitors have also had a hand in the growth and success of the museum. Many artifacts have been collected because a visitor, when looking at a display, realized

continued on next page

Topsail's Assembly Building is home to the Missles and More Museum.

Photo: Jeanne Nociti

they have pictures, uniforms and other memorabilia handed down from family members that would add another appropriate piece to the Topsail story. Some of these donated pieces helped create the Camp Davis Military exhibit. In return, on more than one occasion, a conversation between a docent and a guest has resulted in the excitement of finding a relative or friend in one of the military pictures, learning more about an early island family business or just understanding how the island used to be when grandparents first discovered this vacation paradise.

Some of the treasures now housed in the museum include video presentations, even a rare color video of actual missile firings during Operation Bumblebee, an original rocket piece that washed ashore, a complete talos rocket, an early 1700 Indian dugout canoe, found by a local resident, comprehensive histories of the beach towns and a large shell collection.

A new display that should be ready for the 2003 season is a replica of a pirate ship. The history of this most generous donation started with a visit from Betsy Caison Best, from Ohio, whose father had owned Caison's Building Supply, one of the first retail ventures in the Assembly Building during the time of private ownership.

It has been a very exciting and productive seven years according to Evelyn Bradshaw, museum director. In 2002 over 5,000 visitors, a record number, were registered at the museum. The enthusiasm generated for the museum has created such a large inventory of materials and artifacts that there isn't room to display them all. Many are stored in Ms. Bradshaw's home and other locations. Taking the next step, the Historical Society has launched a building program to expand into unused space in size almost equal to the present museum. Architects plans for the space to include room for expanded displays, an interactive media center, a research and study area and an office. Fund-raising has begun with a project completion date of 2003.

The Missiles and More Museum has come a long way in a short time. There is probably no better example of Topsail's sense of community than this labor of love.

Hospice of the Lower Cape Fear
725 Wellington Ave., Wilmington
• **(910) 772-5444**

Hospice serves the needs of clients and their families when terminal illness occurs. Volunteers are needed to visit terminally ill clients, do office work and help with fund-raising events. The Annual Festival of Trees is a major fundraiser for Hospice. Hospice also offers a 12-bed facility center that can accommodate families, patients and pets to give caregivers a respite or to treat symptoms. If interested, call the Volunteer Department, (910) 772-5473.

New Hanover Regional Medical Center
2131 S. 17th St., Wilmington
• **(910) 343-7784**

The Medical Center has many areas of volunteer involvement, and opportunities for new services are constantly evaluated. An average of 750 active volunteers give of their time and skills each year in direct patient care services. If you feel you have four or more hours per week to give to a service of your choice, call the above number.

Salvation Army
820 N. Second St., Wilmington
• **(910) 762-7354**

The Salvation Army provides shelter for the homeless and assistance for people in difficult circumstances. It needs volunteers in fund-raising activities and public relations efforts. Volunteers may serve on the Advisory Board and Ladies Auxiliary and in the shelter, which serves men, women and children. Volunteers may also work at the thrift store, the Woodlot Project, Christmas fund-raisers, the toy and food distribution center, the annual Coats for the Coatless drive and on disaster relief teams.

The shelter provides emergency housing to more than 20,000 individuals each year and has a Soup Line serving meals seven days a week between 5:30 and 6 PM for the public. This food program serves nutritious meals to more than 60,000 people each year in Bladen, Brunswick, Columbus, Pender and New Hanover counties.

Sheltered Treasures
(910) 457-1078

Sheltered Treasures accepts clothing, housewares and other donations. The sale of these items benefits Brunswick County youth who stay at the Providence Home Family Emergency Teen Shelter in Southport. Volunteers

are needed to sort and price goods, set up displays and provide customer service at the sites in Sunset Beach, Calabash, Shallotte and Southport.

Sunshine Transitional Programs
(910) 755-7248

Sunshine Transitional Programs provides housing for battered women and their families in Shallotte. Volunteers are needed to assist in Transitions, the retail shop, staffing the store, picking up furniture, and pricing and displaying items. Volunteers are also needed for program delivery and office support.

Children's Services

Public Schools

School systems offer a variety of volunteer opportunities that are essentially the same from system to system: helping in the classroom, tutoring, serving as a mentor for at-risk students, working in dropout-prevention programs, helping minority students achieve success, getting involved with the PTA/PTO. If you want to volunteer your time to the public schools, contact the Community Schools/Public Information Office in each system: New Hanover County School System, Wilmington, (910) 763-5431; Brunswick County School System, Central Office, Southport, (910) 253-2900; Pender County School System, Burgaw, (910) 259-2187.

Boy Scouts of America, Cape Fear Council
110 Longstreet Dr., Wilmington
• **(910) 395-1100**

This organization requires a tremendous number of volunteers to assist the many Boy Scouts in the Cape Fear area. Board and committee members are needed as well as a host of leaders, coaches and advisors. Volunteers are needed for the Sports Club Program, which combines traditional Scout activities with a basketball league for inner-city boys from four housing developments. They meet Saturday mornings to play basketball and participate in Boy Scout meetings.

Community Boys and Girls Club
901 Nixon St., Wilmington
• **(910) 762-1252**

The Community Boys and Girls Club is a youth development organization dedicated to promoting the health, social, educational, vocational and character development of girls and boys ages 6 to 17. Some of the club's outstanding alumni who achieved professional stardom in the NBA are Michael Jordan, Clarence Kea, Chuckie Brown, Kenny Gadison and Harlem Globetrotter legend Meadowlark Lemon. NFL athletes who participated in this program are Clyde and Jimmy Simmons. For more than 65 years the program has provided leadership and guidance to area youngsters. The club is in constant need of financial as well as volunteer support.

Family Services of the Lower Cape Fear
4014 Shipyard Blvd., Wilmington
• (910) 392-7051

This organization offers family counseling, after-school enrichment, consumer credit counseling and the Big Buddy program for the lower Cape Fear area. Volunteers are needed as office helpers, fund-raisers, board members, public relations representatives and, most of all, to be Big Buddies. The Big Buddy program provides reliable, trusted friends to boys and girls in need of positive role models and requires a minimum commitment of one year. The after-school enrichment program needs tutors and support persons to work one-on-one with the children and help with homework or activities. People with special skills or life experiences are also needed to speak to area children. Chaperones for field trips and mentors for at-risk children are welcomed too.

Guardian ad Litem
206 N. Fourth St., Wilmington
• (910) 251-2662

The Guardian ad Litem (GAL) program matches trained volunteers with children who have been indicated in abuse or/and neglect cases. Volunteers, paired with attorney advocates, make recommendations regarding the best interest of the children in order to ensure a safe, nurturing and permanent home. Volunteers collaborate with community agencies and provide written reports to the court regarding the children's needs and status. Thirty hours of pre-service training are required. This program serves more than 550 children in New Hanover and Pender counties. An urgent need for volunteers continues to exist.

Girls Inc. of Wilmington
1502 Castle St., Wilmington
• (910) 763-6674

Girls Inc. is an after-school and summer program primarily for girls ages 4 to 18. It offers programs in career and life planning, health and sexuality, leadership and community action, sports, culture, heritage, self-reliance and life skills. Volunteers are needed as tutors, group leaders and fund-raisers. Girls Inc. also needs people to assist with homework, sports, cooking, field trips and adolescent pregnancy prevention programs.

Girl Scout Council of Coastal Carolina
Wilmington • (910) 458-5164,
(800) 558-9297

The Girl Scouts need volunteers to serve in many positions. Adults serve as troop leaders, consultants, organizers, trainers, product sales coordinators (we're talking cookies here) and communicators. People with special skills and talents are also needed to share their wisdom. This council serves girls ages 5 to 18 in Brunswick, Columbus, New Hanover and Pender counties and offers leadership development through fun and rewarding programs.

Project Linus
(910) 201-1608

These Brunswick County volunteers make blankets in their homes and/or at the monthly meetings the first Tuesday of each month. The blankets can be crocheted, knitted, quilted or fleece. They are distributed to babies, children and teens who are ill or have been traumatized and are being helped in shelters, in hospitals and in foster care.

Wilmington Family YMCA
2710 Market St., Wilmington
• (910) 251-9622

If you're a real hands-on volunteer, this is certainly the place for you! Be a youth sports coach, nursery attendant, Special Olympics volunteer or a person who helps maintain the facility. The Y has a great aquatics program that offers activities for all individuals and needs volunteers for its Special Populations program for those with disabilities. How about volunteer-

INSIDERS' TIP

A Community Resources Directory is available for $10 through First Call for Help, an excellent information and referral service agency, located at 615 Shipyard Boulevard, Wilmington, (910) 397-0497.

ing for the YMCA's outreach program for at-risk children and teens?

YWCA
2815 S. College Rd., Wilmington
• **(910) 799-6820**

The YWCA needs volunteer assistance with youth, clerical and maintenance programs at three locations in the Cape Fear area. If you'd like to tutor after school, facilitate a racial dialogue group or help with a special event, call the YWCA, which serves women and their families with fitness, health, personal development, job training, counseling and childcare programs. The YWCA functions as an advocate for women's rights, diversity and the elimination of racism.

Yahweh Center Children's Village
5000 Lamb's Path Way, Wilmington
• **(910) 675-3533**

The Yahweh Center is a residential treatment and child placing agency for abused and/or neglected children less than 12 years of age. Outpatient counseling services are offered in the new children's clinic. With two buildings already occupied and five more to go, the Children's Village continues to expand its services. Volunteers are needed to help with gardening, landscaping, special projects and fundraising events. Those who work directly with children must go through a specialized training.

The Arts

Many of the organizations listed in The Arts chapter also appreciate volunteers.

Louise Wells Cameron Art Museum
3201 S. 17th St., Wilmington
• **(910) 395-6045**

This extraordinarily fine museum of visual arts needs volunteers to work in many capacities. Things are always happening at this lively center, and volunteers are needed to serve as docents and in membership, publicity, fundraising, the gift shop and much more. The museum constantly has new projects underway, such as a cookbook, art trips to other cities, film series, art sales, exhibitions, educational programs and special events. If you love the visual arts, this is a wonderful place to offer your volunteer services.

Historic Preservation and Community Development

Downtown Area Revitalization Effort, Inc. (DARE)
225 Water St., Wilmington
• **(910) 763-7349**

DARE concentrates on revitalization of the Central Business District in downtown Wilmington. Thirty-six volunteers representing a cross-section of the community serve on the Board of Directors, which is led by executive director Susi Hamilton. Thirteen are designated by other organizations, seven are elected based on their profession, and 16 serve as at-large members. This body expedites quality development of the commercial district by offering a wide range of services and detailed information to potential downtown businesses.

Habitat for Humanity, Cape Fear
1208 S. Third St., Wilmington
• **(910) 762-4744**

Thanks to former president Jimmy Carter, this organization enjoys a high profile. Call this number to find out about construction projects in progress and to volunteer your skills in a wide array of areas ranging from hands-on carpentry to office assistance to clerking in the Habitat Home Store. Donations of household goods and construction materials are also welcome at the store, which is open Tuesday through Friday from 9 AM to 5 PM and Saturday 9 AM to 1 PM. Habitat for Humanity construction volunteers work on Wednesdays and Saturdays. Volunteers are also needed to serve on committees that deal with family selection, support and public relations.

Historic Wilmington Foundation
Wilmington • (910) 762-2511

Volunteers interested in preserving the architectural heritage of the region are invited to work in these areas: public relations, membership, office work, events, education, preservation action, urban properties and gardens. There is a yearly gala, the primary fund-raiser, that relies on lots of volunteers for logistics, publicity, entertainment, food and everything else required to throw a major party and auction. The organization sponsors Home Tours during the Azalea Festival in April and a Repair Affair in spring. Maybe you'd like to help out at the Wilmington Architectural Salvage, 20 Brunswick Street, from 9 AM to 1 PM on Saturdays — that's where they sell historic architectural elements.

Lower Cape Fear Historical Society
126 S. Third St., Wilmington
• **(910) 762-0492**

Volunteers are needed for publicity, fundraising, membership drives and planning at this venerable organization, which seeks to accurately preserve the history of the area. Volunteers also work as docents and archivists in the society's home, the Latimer House. The society sponsors the annual Olde Wilmington by Candlelight Tour of Homes.

North Carolina Maritime Museum at Southport
116 N. Howe St., Southport
• **(910) 457-0003**

The North Carolina Maritime Museum at Southport displays fascinating artifacts related to the maritime history of the Cape Fear Area (see our Attractions chapter). Volunteers are needed for yard work, building exhibits, maintenance, tours and summer programs.

Smith Island Museum of History
(910) 457-7481

Run by the Old Baldy Foundation, the Smith Island Museum is a replica of the historic lightkeepers cottage. The $3 fee for touring the lighthouse is collected here, and the building houses artifacts and small items for sale. Volunteers are needed to staff the museum, to help with fund-raising and to give lectures and educational programs.

Southport Visitors Center
(910) 457-7927, (800) 388-9635

The Southport Visitors Center is a great place to stop and rest in the rockers on the porch. Inside is a fascinating wall display of the history of the area, and included in the decor are historical artifacts. There are also films shown here. The center has ongoing recruitment for volunteers to work three-hour shifts, either from 10 AM until 1 PM or 1 until 4 PM. These volunteers answer questions, provide visitors with brochures and maps of the self-guided walking tour, and sometimes sit in the rockers and shoot the breeze with folks eager to hear the old stories about the town of Southport.

VOLUNTEER OPPORTUNITES

Media

A wealth of print and broadcast media sources keep Wilmington and the surrounding coastal communities well-informed on topics of national, international and local importance. The region's large and well-established business, arts, education and film communities create a talented pool of writers, performers and media professionals. In terms of staying power, the area's dominant newspapers, magazines, radio and television stations are stable sources of information. In the print medium, visitors will also notice an abundance of tourist-oriented publications in street racks. We haven't listed all of them here, but they are generally handy guides to the area's attractions. Some of these periodicals have been around for years, while others seem to drift in one day and out the next. There's a robust business in publications on real estate; in fact, these magazines or booklets are so pervasive you can hardly go anywhere without encountering them.

Choices for radio listening are eclectic, ranging across talk, country music, urban contemporary, Top 40 and the diverse offerings of the city's own National Public Radio affiliate. Fans of each are loyal and will debate the merits of their personal preference. But one thing is clearly a given: Under Carolina-blue summer skies, few will pass up a little beach music.

Television is a somewhat limited medium without cable or satellite services, in which case a whole spectrum of channels becomes available. Public Television, broadcast from Jacksonville by way of Chapel Hill, has a strong signal.

The media resources listed below have settled into their own niches on what seems to be a permanent basis as a result of their thoroughness of coverage, accuracy, reliability and professionalism. In an ever-changing and expanding industry, these information/entertainment outlets have proven themselves over time.

LOOK FOR:
- **Newspapers**
- **Magazines**
- **Television**
- **Cable TV**
- **Radio**

Newspapers

Brunswick Beacon
208 Smith Ave., Shallotte • (910) 754-6890

A weekly community newspaper published on Thursdays, the *Beacon* has won dozens of awards during the past decade for advertising and editorial content. It covers and is distributed to all of Brunswick County, with particular emphasis on the southwestern portion of the coast. The *Beacon* is an independent, locally owned publication available through subscription, retail outlets and news racks throughout Brunswick County.

The Challenger
514 Princess St., Wilmington • (910) 762-1337, (800) 462-0738

The Challenger is a statewide, African-American-focused publication based in Wilmington, with additional distribution in Fayetteville. Published weekly on Thursday, it is a subscription-based periodical with limited news rack distribution.

Greater Wilmington Business
130 N. Front St., Ste. 105, Wilmington • (910) 343-8600

The *Greater Wilmington Business* newspaper is the region's best source for local business news and information, covering New Hanover, Brunswick, Pender and Columbus counties. Regular features of each issue include an in-depth industry spotlight, a business profile, a guest editorial, business achievement news, a calendar of events and a wealth of informative business-related articles. This monthly publication is available through subscription, at local bookstores, coffee shops and in news racks throughout the Greater Wilmington area, including New Hanover County and northern Brunswick County.

The Island Gazette
1003 Bennet Ln., Ste. F, Carolina Beach
• (910) 458-8156

Published weekly on Wednesdays since 1978, *The Island Gazette* is a well-established source of local news and real estate in southern New Hanover County, with an emphasis on Carolina Beach and Pleasure Island. Copies are available in news racks throughout the coverage area or by subscription.

The State Port Pilot
105 S. Howe St., Southport
• (910) 457-4568

Covering eastern Brunswick County in the Southport-Oak Island sphere, including Bald Head Island, Boiling Spring Lakes, St. James and Caswell Beach, this award-winning newspaper features state and community news, special event coverage, local sports, weather, feature articles and more. *The Pilot* is available by subscription or in news racks throughout its coverage area every Wednesday.

The Wilmington Journal
412 S. Seventh St., Wilmington
• (910) 762-5502

Founded in 1927 as *The Cape Fear Journal*, this weekly began as the offspring of R. S. Jervay Printers and describes itself as the voice and mirror of the African-American community in New Hanover, Brunswick, Pender, Onslow, Columbus, Jones and Craven counties. The name changed to *The Wilmington Journal* in the 1940s. It is available each Thursday at news racks throughout the city or by subscription.

Wilmington Star-News
1003 S. 17th St., Wilmington
• (910) 343-2000

The *Wilmington Star-News*, offering two editions, the daily *Wilmington Morning Star* and the weekly *Sunday Star-News*, is the only major daily paper along the southern coastal region of North Carolina. Owned by The New York Times, the *Star-News* covers national, international, state and local news. Regular features cover regional politics, community events, arts, sports, weather, real estate, the local film industry, business news and more. Supplements to the daily paper include "Neighbors", published every Wednesday for New Hanover County and every Friday for Brunswick County; "Real Estate Showcase"; "Currents", a weekly entertainment guide published on Friday; and periodic special sections on a range of topics from health care to wedding planning to hurricane preparedness. Their annual *Fact Book for New Hanover County*, published in August, contains a wealth of intriguing facts, figures and community data. Subscribers have the option to receive all editions or just the Sunday edition. Home delivery is available, and the paper can be found in news racks and stores throughout Wilmington and North Carolina's southern coast.

Magazines

Encore Magazine
255 N. Front St., Wilmington
• (910) 762-8899

Publisher Wade Wilson describes this as a "general what's happening" magazine for the Wilmington area. Arts, entertainment, local sports and essays/fiction make up this free weekly, which has published each Tuesday since 1984.

Certainly the most widely distributed free entertainment periodical in the region, *Encore*'s many highlights include festival and holiday roundups, movie and theater reviews, a dining guide, attractions, nightlife and Chuck Shepherd's syndicated "News of the Weird" column. Perhaps the most outstanding feature is a detailed calendar of weekly events.

The magazine is available at news racks practically everywhere in Wilmington, at many retail outlets elsewhere and by subscription. *Encore* co-sponsors an annual fiction contest in cooperation with the Lower Cape Fear Historical Society. In addition to the magazine, *Encore* also publishes *Directions*, a guide for students at UNCW, and *Alternatives*, a free summer and fall guide for school-age kids looking for interesting things to do. Other additions to their growing list of publications are the *Cape Fear Garden Guide* and the *Wilmington Regional Film Commission's Production Guide*.

Pelican Post
Oak Island Press, P.O. Box 1073, Oak Island • (910) 452-2773

Serving the Southport-Oak Island area since

Chris
Marshall

Kim
Fields

Bob
Townsend

5:30 am

George
Elliott

Jim
Hanchett

Frances
Weller

Bob
Bonner

5, 6 & 11 pm

WHERE NEWS COMES FIRST

www.wect.com

Eastern North Carolina has lots of interesting sites.

Photo: Jay Tervo

1993, this small regional magazine is crammed with information and interesting tidbits for visitors and locals. Regular features include a calendar of events, a listing of area attractions, a chart for daily high and low tides, the Southport-Fort Fisher Ferry schedule, an area map, plus golf tips, recipes, book reviews and more. Local authors contribute interesting stories about the area as well. *The Pelican Post* is distributed free throughout Brunswick County monthly from April through December, with a single winter issue. It is available by subscription.

Reel Carolina: Journal of Film and Video
1903 Galahad Ct., Wilmington
• (910) 233-2926

Interested in filmmaking throughout the Carolinas? This monthly magazine is your best source of information about the Wilmington film scene and movie-making in North and South Carolina. Production

Notes, Screen Gems Studios Clips and News & Notes are regular columns that highlight the latest news and technical information. Business profiles, celebrity interviews and film production feature articles fill the pages. *Reel Carolina* is available by subscription or free in racks across both Carolinas.

The Wrightsville Beach Magazine
(910) 256-4568

Available monthly, this attractive publication's focus is providing information and history about the Wrightsville Beach area and the people of this beach community. The magazine is full of interesting (and enlightening) feature articles that range from current events to history. Regular departments include the Dining Guide, FYI, Pet Scoop, Coastal Cuisine, Houses of Worship, Tides and more. Pick up a copy of this free magazine at more than 100 locations in Wrightsville Beach and the surrounding area or by subscription.

INSIDERS' TIP

Currents is the *Wilmington Star-News'* weekly, information-packed entertainment magazine. It is included in New Hanover and Brunswick County newspaper subscribers' Friday edition.

Television Stations

WECT-TV 6, NBC
322 Shipyard Blvd., Wilmington
• (910) 791-8070
    NBC-affiliated TV 6 is one of the major television stations in southeastern North Carolina. It offers full news coverage and exceptional meteorological programming.

WSFX-26, Fox
1926 Oleander Dr., Wilmington
• (910) 343-8826
    This station's strength is its Fox affiliation, featuring Fox news and entertainment programming. WSFX also carries local news.

WILM-TV 10, CBS
3333-G Wrightsville Ave., Wilmington
• (910) 798-0000
    WILM-TV is Wilmington's new CBS affiliate and broadcasts on channel 10 (channel 12 for Time-Warner Cable viewers and channel 16 for Charter Cable viewers). Regional news and major local events broadcast through the CBS Raleigh affiliate, WRAL-TV, until a Wilmington news bureau is established.

UNC-TV 39, PBS
Research Triangle Park • (800) 906-5050
    Quality national and local public television programming is the hallmark of UNC-TV. Fans of the BBC enjoy delightful offerings in drama and comedy. The station's yearly pledge drive is enthusiastically supported by southeastern North Carolinians. UNC-TV is excited about its transition to digital television, which will allow viewers to receive four channels instead of one. The other three channels are UNC-KD a full-time children's channel, UNC-NC dedicated to local happenings in NC, and UNC-ED an educational channel of high school and college courses.

WWAY-TV 3, ABC
615 N. Front St., Wilmington
• (910) 762-8581
    ABC-affiliated TV 3 is another of Wilmington's major television stations broadcasting throughout the southeastern coastal region. WWAY offers full national and regional news and complete meteorological forecasts.

Cable TV

    Cable television service is available throughout southeastern North Carolina's coastal region from two primary sources. **TimeWarner Cable**, (910) 763-4638 or (800) 222-8921, covers Wilmington and most of Brunswick County, including the South Brunswick beaches. **Charter Communications**, (910) 458-4285 or (800) 682-7814, provides service to Pleasure Island (Carolina Beach, Kure Beach and Fort Fisher) and parts of Pender County that include Topsail Island. Alternative cable providers available in Brunswick County are **Atlantic Telephone**, (910) 754-4211 or (888) 367-2862, and **Southern Cable Communications Inc.**, (800) 533-7048.

Radio Stations

Adult Contemporary and Top 40
    WGNI 102.7 FM
    WAZO 98.3 FM

Christian
    WDVV 89.7 FM
    WWIL 90.5 FM (adult contemporary Christian)
    WMYT 1180 AM (Spanish Christian)
    WWIL 1490 AM (Southern gospel)
    WLSG 1340 AM (Southern gospel)

Country
    WWQQ 101.3 FM (contemporary)
    WCCA 106.3 FM (classic country)

National Public Radio
    WHQR 91.3 FM (classical, jazz, blues, news, Radio Latino, National Public Radio and Public Radio International)

News, Talk, Sports
    WAAV 980 AM
    WMFD 630 AM
    WLTT 103.7 FM

Rock
    WFXZ 93.7FM
    WKOO 98.7 (classic rock)
    WKXB 99.9 FM (classic rock)
    WRQR 104.5 FM (classic/ contemporary rock)
    WSFM 107.5 FM (surf)

Urban Contemporary
    WMNX 97.3 FM
    WAAV 94.1 FM
    WLGX 106.7 FM

MEDIA

Commerce and Industry

The amenities of coastal living and a moderate year-round climate continually attract new residents to southeastern North Carolina. According to the Bureau of Census for 2000, these coastal counties — New Hanover, Brunswick and Pender — grew nearly 35 percent overall, surpassing the state's 21.4 percent growth rate. Population figures for the area indicate that during the ten-year period between census counts, New Hanover County (which includes Wilmington) grew more than 33 percent to 160,307. Neighboring Brunswick County's rate of growth climbed 43.5 percent for a population reaching 73,143. As a result, Brunswick County earned distinction as the fifth fastest growing North Carolina county. Pender County also experienced a large increase in population from 28,855 to 41,082 at a rate of over 42 percent.

In the last decade of the 20th century, the Lower Cape Fear region's economy remained, like the weather, moderate and relatively stable. This stability, according to local business and economic leaders, helped the area to be somewhat immune to state and national economic trends. Despite both good and bad economic periods in its history, the Greater Wilmington area hasn't experienced the excessive highs during more prosperous eras nor drastic lows during recessions as other demographically similar regions.

Now, in the dawn of the 21st century, that trend appears to continue. Although down from the dramatic 7 percent increase in 1999, overall economic growth for the three-county region is projected to rise 4.5 percent to around $7.2 billion over the course of 2003, according to UNCW economists Claude Farrell and William W. Hall Jr. Farrell and Hall noted that after "seesawing" during second and third quarter 2002, local economic activity rose dramatically during the fourth quarter of the year. The fourth-quarter growth was fueled mainly by growth in retail sales. The economists forecast relatively strong growth in the traditionally strong second and fourth quarters of 2003.

Despite a growing trend toward year-round tourism in southeastern North Carolina, the rise and fall of economic activity throughout the year, especially during the summer months, is a fact of life for coastal counties. Brunswick and Pender counties in particular experience these fluctuations in retail sales and employment to a greater degree than the more urban New Hanover County. Brunswick County traditionally reaches a maximum employment in July; not surprisingly, its low is in January, an average difference of 7 percent. Pender County, at an average rate variation of 8 percent, follows a similar pattern with an employment peak in June and the low in January. Employment in New Hanover County peaks in July with the low in January, differing on average by 6 percent.

Geography is an inevitable factor that sets Wilmington apart from the overall North Carolina economy, and it is driving new trends that are positioning Wilmington to take advantage of a new and prosperous era at the beginning of the 21st century. Its maritime environment creates opportunities for business based on what is naturally available — the sea, the river, the many beautiful views — instead of what must be manufactured. Examples include tourism, the influx of retirees drawn to the coastal amenities and the rise in championship golf courses in the area, especially in Brunswick County.

There have been, of course, significant times in history when Wilmington relied heavily on its natural resources for both manufacturing and agriculture. Early 18th-century settlers used the area's lush pine forests to foster a lumber industry that continues today. The manufacture of lumber-related by-products, such as tar, turpentine and pitch, was the dominant business in the 19th century, but this type of manufacturing has since declined.

Rice and cotton were an early source of income for the area; the downtown wharves were once the site of the largest cotton exporting operation in the world. After the War Between the States, the economy shifted away from cotton and rice plantations because the labor supply was no longer available. Railroads provided jobs for 4,000 families in the first part of the 20th century, as Wilmington became a major rail center. The Atlantic Coast Line, the evolution of the Wilmington and Weldon Railroad, was a technological marvel and the pride of the Wilmington economy at the time. Many an opulent downtown home was built on railroad dollars.

Trains moved the area's products efficiently into the inland market, and there was popular speculation that the rails would move the economy into prosperity. But in 1955, the railroad announced the closing of its corporate office and sent a considerable segment of Wilmington's population south to Jacksonville, Florida, in 1960. This was a severe economic loss that forced Wilmingtonians to ponder their destiny. Not only were good-paying jobs lost with the railroad, but service businesses all over the area lost customers.

Although manufacturing is still an economic force in the region, statistics compiled by the University of North Carolina at Wilmington's Cameron School of Business indicate that the bulk of today's employment opportunities are in the services sector. This is a broad category that includes such diverse occupations as physicians, government workers, real estate brokers, educators, service-oriented business, hotel staff and restaurant employees.

The Port

The **North Carolina State Port Authority** established a deep-water terminal at Wilmington in 1952, initiating one of the region's early forays into the service realm. The facility annually receives approximately 500 ships loaded with diverse cargoes from Europe, South America, the Far East, the Mediterranean, the Red Sea and Arabian Gulf, Africa and the Caribbean. Cargo tonnage through the Port of Wilmington for calendar year 2002 increased to 2,202,842 tons, up 6.1 percent from the 2001 2,077,819 tonnage figures.

Trade ports that do significant business through the North Carolina Port at Wilmington include Korea, Hong Kong, Italy, Taiwan, United Kingdom, Japan, Germany, Sweden, The Netherlands and Belgium. Leading imports are chemicals, metal products, forest products, general merchandise, miscellaneous forest products, woodchips, food products and tobacco. The increasingly vital international trade industry at the ports at Wilmington and Morehead City and the two inland facilities at Greensboro and Charlotte provide a living for more than 80,000 people and nearly $300 million in statewide tax revenues.

Currently of concern at the Port of Wilmington is the Wilmington Harbor Project, a plan to deepen the Cape Fear River from 38 feet to 42 feet to accommodate increasingly larger ships. This project is crucial to the future of the port in terms of servicing current customers and attracting new business. To date, approximately $129 million in federal funds and $43 million in state funds have been invested in this exciting development. The port's deepening project is slated to be completed in 2003.

Tourism

Tourism remains one of the most important industries in North Carolina's southern coastal region. With an appealing variety of attractions — beaches and waterways, breathtaking gardens, a rich arts environment, well-established cultural events, beautiful historic homes and landmarks — in moderate year-round temperatures, this industry provides a strong economic center. This translated into over $603 million in revenue for the region in 2000, according to tourism statistics from the North Carolina Department of Commerce. Travel and tourism is the state's second largest industry, and North Carolina ranks sixth in person-trip volume by state behind California, Florida, Texas, Pennsylvania and New York. Domestic travelers spent nearly $11.9 billion state-wide.

Research conducted by Travel Industry Association of America (TIA) shows that in the year 2001 domestic travelers spent approximately $301 million in New Hanover County, maintaining its rank as number eight among North Carolina's 100 counties in tourism expenditures. Brunswick County's tourism dollars totaled over $243 million, while Pender County brought in over $49 million. The economic impact is significant in terms of jobs and and payroll dollars in the three-county area. The 2000 NCDOC report for New Hanover, Brunswick and Pender counties directly attributes a total of 10,420 jobs and over $162 million in payroll as a result of tourism. Tourism-related figures are updated and released annually by the state in July. Statistics for 2001 will be available in mid-2002.

Summer is no longer the sole tourism season. Visitors Bureau officials recognize that Wilmington and the surrounding communities have moved from a three-month to a nearly year-round tourism season with the majority of visitors arriving from March through November. From January through December 2001, the Cape Fear Coast Convention and Visitors Bureau reports that a total of 51,448 visitors dropped by both downtown Wilmington visitor information locations — -the main office at 24 N. Third Street, (910) 341-4030, and the River Booth, located along the Cape Fear riverfront near the corner of Water and Market streets. The bureau's website hits have jumped dramatically from over 7 million in 2001 to more than 16 million in 2002!

There are thousands of rooms, motels and inns in the Greater Wilmington area and coastal Brunswick County. Historic downtown Wilmington and picturesque Southport offer a bounty of bed and breakfast inns. With such an abundance of accommodations at their disposal, visitors

The Riverfront is a major attraction in downtown Wilmington.

Photo: Jay Tervo

are only limited in choice by their budget or their imagination. Still, it is often difficult to find lodgings on short notice during the summer, and advance reservations for these months are highly recommended.

Other businesses that profit from a steady flow of tourists are also thriving. Visitors need a full range of services, and there are many entrepreneurs who are more than willing to provide them. Convention facilities and their attendant services represent a growing segment of the economy.

With more than 50 championship golf courses and a long mid-March through mid-November playing season, golf is another major draw to the region. Restaurants number in the hundreds and continue to proliferate at an astounding rate, with the best of them enjoying capacity dining on weekends. Special attractions and activities such as horse-and-carriage rides in the historic district, boat tours, sailing charters, a downtown Wilmington walking tour and educational tours in the historic district continue to respond to high demand.

Trade

Revenue from wholesale and retail trade remains linked strongly to tourism dollars, especially in Brunswick County, and the sales figures for 2002 indicate an upward trend in each of the three coastal counties and the City of Wilmington.

Recent years have seen the opening of such national and regional chains as The Home Depot, Office Max, Barnes & Noble, two Wal-Mart Super Centers, Target — stores Wilmingtonians never thought they would see 15 years ago. The city's retail corridor is pushing north, with extremely heavy development in the vicinity of Landfall, near Wrightsville Beach, including three large upscale shopping complexes — Landfall Shopping Center, The Forum and Lumina Station. On every corner, there seems to be a new shopping center going up, and retail stores stocking everything from beachwear and souvenirs to designer clothing and high-ticket household furnishings are everywhere.

In the last few years retail and service industry businesses have made inroads in the southern corridor from Wilmington's city limits to Carolina Beach as well. Of particular note is the recently completed Lowe's Home Improvement Superstore, the first phase of a large shopping complex in the Myrtle Grove area of South College Road. This complex features Wilmington's second Wal-Mart Superstore and borders an existing strip center, which offers several good places to eat.

While lacking the density of retail development seen in Wilmington and New Hanover County, the number of retail stores and shopping centers are increasing in Brunswick County as the trend toward year-round residents and visitors continues. The Southport-Oak Island area and Shallotte to the south both have acquired large Wal-Mart Super Stores and Lowe's Home Improvement Centers, not to mention boutiques and stores of every description. In the past two years, Shallotte has continued to grow as a retail hub for southern Brunswick County with a new shopping center and the addition of more regional and national retailers — Belk, Home Depot and Office Depot.

Office Space and Services

Because the region has a high percentage of single-staff entrepreneurs, there is a need for office space with secretarial services. Several office centers provide the individual or small company with turnkey services that include a central reception area, support staff services, use of office equipment and an opportunity to be in a professional setting. Utilities, excluding phone service, and janitorial services are included in the lease. The region also has several employee services. For additional staffing needs, look in the Yellow Pages of area phone books under Employment Agencies.

Landfall Executive Suites
1213 Culbreth Dr., Wilmington
• **(910) 256-1900, (910) 509-5008**

Located in Wilmington's hottest growth area and adjacent to Landfall Shopping Center, Landfall Executive Suites offers furnished and unfurnished office suites with long or short-term leases. These leases include a receptionist, on-site management and maintenance, security, nightly janitorial services, conference rooms, fully equipped break rooms, and utilities. With 26,000 square feet of space, it is the only center of its kind in Wilmington with offices ranging from 140 to 270 square feet. Everything an executive might need in professional support and administrative services is available at Landfall Executive Suites. A corporate identity program is also available for individuals or companies that need minimal access to an office environment.

The Cotton Exchange
321 N. Front St., Wilmington
• **(910) 343-9896**

The Cotton Exchange has offices available for individuals or small companies in a center that overlooks the Cape Fear River in Historic Downtown Wilmington. It offers unfurnished offices with both long- and short-term leases as well as a corporate identity package that includes mailboxes, phone messages and receptionist answering services for businesses not physically located at the center. Professional support services are available.

The Reserves Network
4900 Randall Pkwy., Ste. F, Wilmington
• **(910) 799-8500**

The Reserves Network combines over a decade of experience in the Wilmington market with the resources of a national agency. The agency offers total workforce solutions for the clients and applicants, providing services that include temporary placement, temporary-to-permanent placement, direct hire, payrolling and executive search and recruitment. Areas of specialization are professional, administrative, clerical support, accounting and finance, engineering, technical, sales and marketing, information technology and more.

epicdesigngroup
105 Hawthorne Dr., Wilmington
• **(910) 793-4994**

This dynamic graphic design firm takes pride in meeting the unique needs of its clients in creative and responsive ways. Services offered to the business community include logo development, corporate identity services, brochures, advertisement, packaging and signage.

Olsten Staffing Services
513 Market St., Wilmington
• **(910) 343-8763**

Olsten is part of an international company that specializes in a wide variety of temporary staffing assignments, including office services, legal support, accounting services, technical services, production/distribution/assembly and office automation.

Quality Staffing Specialists
3806 Park Ave., Wilmington
• **(910) 793-1010**

In Wilmington since November 1999, Quality Staffing Specialists is a full-service staffing agency. This agency offers temporary and temporary-to-permanent staffing in administrative, medical, legal and pharmaceutical positions as well as skilled manufacturing and trade jobs. Executive search is another aspect of the agency's services. Quality Staffing Specialists works in partnership with Phyllis Eller-Moffett, the third largest female-owned business in North Carolina's Triangle region, with a combined 60 years experience in the field.

SENC Technical Services
3142 Wrightsville Ave., Wilmington
• **(910) 251-1925**

SENC offers contract, permanent and contract-to-hire workers in technical fields such as engineering, designing/drafting, electronics, computer programming and more.

UNCW Executive Development Center
1241A Military Cutoff Rd., Wilmington
• **(910) 962-3578**

Housed in the Northeast Regional Library adjacent to the Landfall Shopping Center, this new state-of-the-art meeting facility features 8,000 square feet of first-class training space and accommodates up to 200 participants. Seven meeting rooms offer a variety of seating options — theater, classroom and boardroom styles — and include moveable tables and high-backed ergonomic executive chairs. On-site technicians are available, and the center's large list of technical equipment includes 10' by 10' motorized screens, LCD projectors, VCR/CD/DVD equipment, ELMO document cameras, Plasma TV, overhead projectors, wireless microphones, 30 laptop computers, high-speed T-1 line wireless Internet access, and more. Full-range catering is another featured service of the facility. The executive center is an extension of the University of North Carolina at Wilmington.

Youngblood Staffing
4024-A Oleander Dr., Wilmington
• **(910) 799-0103**

Serving southeastern North Carolina, Youngblood Staffing is a regional staffing ser-

Wilmington's Sister Cities

President Dwight D. Eisenhower is credited with initiating an international outreach program between the United States and foreign nations. Sister Cities International, the resulting program, began in 1956 to promote peace and understanding of other countries and other cultures by Americans. Not surprisingly, the organizations mantra is "Peace Through Understanding."

To reach its goal, the program strives to develop economic, educational and cultural exchanges, extend goodwill and expressions of cooperation to other nations and link businesses around the globe. Approximately 1,100 American cities have SCI affiliations with 1,900 corresponding cities in 120 countries.

Wilmington entered the program in September 1986, forming the Sister City Commission. This 20-member commission's mandate is to gain community participation, promote awareness and encourage exchanges in business, trade, technology, education, culture and the arts. In 2002, Wilmington has established Sister City ties with three cities — Dandong, China; Doncaster, England, and Bridgetown, Barbados.

Dandong, People's Republic of China—Wilmington and Dandong established Sister City ties in 1986 after a series of delegations and exchanges. Dandong, like Wilmington, is a port city in a highly industrialized region. The area's residents, numbering 2.4 million, work primarily in agriculture, aquaculture, electronics and textiles, not too far a stretch from Wilmington's regional economy. Benefits of the program include exchanges in business and the arts, sister schools, a Sister Port agreement and a joint sponsorship of an English teacher from Wilmington working in the Dandong teachers' college.

Doncaster, England—Wilmington acquired this second Sister City in 1989. Located north of London in South Yorkshire, Doncaster is an ancient city compared to Wilmington yet it has the railroad in common. Or, as in Wilmington's case, a rich history of it.

Sister Cities singpost at the riverfront in historic downtown Wilmington.

Photo: Deb Daniel

Doncaster, a major railway center, is also the center of England's mining industry. Lively exchanges between the two countries involve government officials, business and trade representatives, tourists and students. Sports and a sharing of the arts are additional links—the Wilmington Boys Choir, the Wheatsheaf Singers, the Doncaster Jazz Ensemble as well as school soccer teams.

Bridgetown, Barbados — Perhaps of the three, Bridgeport and Wilmington have the most in common. The long history of trade between the island and the Carolinas dates back to the 17th century and the resulting immigration is considered the source of shared social and cultural characteristics. Tourism is another shared industry. Negotiations are still in the works to formalize their Sister City agreement, but the universities of both towns have already joined forces. The University of the West Indies, Cave Hill Campus, and UNC-Wilmington have worked out a collaboration agreement for an exchange in education.

vices agency that utilizes customized staffing strategies to help companies locate and maintain a balanced and innovative work force. The agency's experienced management and staff, knowledgeable about the employment marketplace, also provide preferred employment opportunities to qualified candidates. In January 2001, the agency opened Youngblood Medical Staffing, a medical division providing clerical staff to the region's medical community.

The Film Industry

The **Wilmington Regional Film Commission**, located on the **EUE/Screen Gems Studios** lot, 1223 N. 23rd Street, Wilmington, (910) 343-3456, reports that Wilmington's film industry earned in excess of $72 million in revenue during 2001. With the largest film studio facility outside of Los Angeles, Wilmington often ranks third in filmmaking in the nation. Only New York City and Los Angeles do more film business than the Greater Wilmington area.

Since the industry's beginning in 1983, filmmaking activities in the Port City include over 300 feature film, television movie-of-the-week and mini-series productions. Six television series — *Matlock, The Young Indiana Jones Chronicles, The Road Home, American Gothic* among them — have filmed here, and numerous music videos, television commercials and still photography shoots have utilized the amenities found in the Wilmington area, the local talent and crew base and the facilities at Screen Gems Studios. *Dawson's Creek*, the popular WB television network teen series, began production on location in Wilmington in 1997 and generates an active interest in the region from its fans. Locals are no longer surprised when questioned by enthusiastic visitors in search of locations from the series.

Feature films and television movies made in the Wilmington area include *A Walk to Remember, Divine Secrets of the Ya-Ya Sisterhood, Domestic Disturbance, Black Knight, Amy & Isabelle, The Runaway, 28 Days, Muppets From Space, Freedom Song, Virus, Elmo In Grouchland, Day of the Jackal, What The Deaf Man Heard, Black Dog, Sleeping With the Enemy* and *Oprah Winfrey Presents The Wedding*. Commercials filmed here include local, regional and national companies such as SunCom, McDonnal-Douglas, Nautica, American Express, National Geographic, Mattel, Smithfield Farms, the New York Ballet, J. Crew, Kodak, Harley Davidson, Rolling Stone magazine, McDonald's, RJ Reynolds, Wachovia Bank and more.

Characterized as the largest film studio east of Hollywood, EUE/Screen Gems Studios offers a multitude of amenities to film and television production companies under the guidance of president Frank Capra Jr. The studios" lot features nine sound stages, post-production services, over 20,000 square feet of production office space, a 40-seat screening room, editing suites, sound transfer services, lighting and grip equipment rental, set construction shops and much more. In addition to the studios, production companies discover a wealth of experienced film crew professionals here. WRFC director Johnny Griffin estimates that number at 650 in the Greater Wilmington region.

Senior Services

A major industry is beginning to arise around the retirement population, thanks largely, of course, to our maritime location, which makes the climate unusually mild for our latitude. There are four discernible, although brief, seasons, an important factor for northern retirees who have grown weary of Florida's almost single season. Warm spring breezes, hot summers and occasional freezing temperatures create a more interesting yearly cycle for retirees who yearn for a little diversity. See our Retirement chapter for more about senior services.

On the state level, 12 percent of North Carolina's population is in the age 65 and older category. As of July 1, 2000, the North Carolina Department of Commerce reported 56,601 residents in the 60 years and older age bracket in the region — 29,527 in New Hanover County and Wilmington, 18,314 in Brunswick County and 8,760 in Pender County. In response and expectation, planned retirement communities, senior services, recreational opportunities aimed at retirees, and other enterprises will represent a major component of the local economy. As retirees flow into the area from more prosperous economies in the north and west, they bring their nest eggs with them, thereby giving a considerable boost to our economy. An added benefit is their contribution of skills and knowledge to area volunteer organizations.

Health Care

Health care is big business in the region. More than 450 physicians and five regional hospitals employ large numbers of medical personnel. One of the largest employers is New **Hanover Regional Medical Center**, with 4,500 employees.

Local health-care services are extensive, and many are comparable with the best state-of-the-art medical facilities and services in the nation. An example is the Zimmer Cancer Center at the New Hanover Regional Medical Center, providing complete cancer care in one facility.

The rapidly expanding seniors health-care market is a national phenomenon, but it is particularly pronounced in coastal/resort communities. In addition to extensive medical services, New Hanover, Brunswick and Pender counties offer a large — and constantly growing — number of domiciliary care facilities. See our Health Care chapter for more information about area hospitals and medical services in the three - ounty area.

Real Estate

Several factors contribute to the overall good health of the region's new-home construction and existing home sales. Among them are a 40-year record low in interest rates, the good quality of life found here, a three-year absence of hurricane activity, the overall economic climate and a positive home-price appreciation. The real estate sales business in general is phenomenal. According to the Wilmington Regional Association of Realtors, there was a 24.7 percent increase in real estate sales from 2001 to 2002. See our Real Estate chapter for more about the local market.

Manufacturing

The largest manufacturing companies in the area include **Corning Glass Works** (the Wilmington location is the largest manufacturer of optical fibers in the world); **General Electric** (aircraft engine parts, nuclear fuel components); **Progress Energy**; **International Paper Board**; **Victaulic Company of America** (steel pipe fittings, precision steel tubing) and **Rampage Sport Fishing Yachts**.

Other economically important companies include **Pharmaceutical Product Development** (clinical drug development services); **BASS** (vitamins); **Applied Analytical Industries** (pharmaceutical products), **Caterpillar Transmissions Facility** (hydrostatic transmission), and **Interroll** (conveyor components).

For a complete industrial directory, contact the **Wilmington Industrial Development, Inc.** at 1739 Hewlett Drive, (910) 763-8414. In Brunswick County, contact the **Brunswick County Economic Development Commission** office, 25 Courthouse Drive, Bolivia, (910) 253-4429, for information on the county's five industrial parks or a listing of local manufacturers.

The University

The **University of North Carolina at Wilmington**'s economic impact in southeastern North Carolina, including New Hanover, Pender, Brunswick and Columbus counties, is an impressive $400 million. The Greater Wilmington Chamber of Commerce lists the university at No. 5 of the Top 25 Employers (July 2002) in the region with 1,627 employees. Serving a student body of 10,729 as of the fall 2002 semester, the university is among the fastest-growing and most technologically advanced in the 16-campus UNC system.

Organized into the College of Arts and Sciences (including a marine biology program ranked fifth best in the world), the Cameron School of Business Administration, the Donald R. Watson School of Education, the School of Nursing and the Graduate School, the university offers 71 undergraduate programs and 24 graduate programs. See our Higher Education and Research chapter for more about education in our area.

Church of the Servant

Episcopal

4925 Oriole Dr, Wilmington NC 28403 395-0616

Church of the Servant is a Christian Community
committed to the spiritual development of the
individual so that each may become a
responsible servant in the world

MUSIC   FAMILY   GIVING   RECEIVING
CHILDREN'S PROGRAMS
SPECIAL COURSES
LIVING   LIFE   TOGETHER
DANCE GUILD
PASTORAL CARE
LITURGY   EVENSONG   SINGING
SPIRITUAL FORMATION CENTERPOINT
LEARNING   TEACHING
BARGAIN BOX
LABYRINTH

Sunday Schedule

8:30 AM Holy Eucharist

9:30 AM Religious Education

11:00 AM Holy Eucharist

Nursery 8:15-12:15

Summer Schedule

8:30 AM & 10 AM

Holy Eucharist

Nursery 8:15-11:15

Worship

Faith is a strong characteristic of southeastern North Carolina. The quest for religious freedom was one of the main reasons European settlers migrated to this area in the 18th century. The founding citizens of Wilmington brought their own beliefs with them, created spiritual homes for a broad spectrum of nationalities and eventually built stunning architectural monuments, many of which are on the National Historical Register.

The history of churches in the Cape Fear area could fill several books. Many of the region's larger churches were occupied by British or Union troops, and historical commentary about those episodes conjure up dramatic pictures. Imagine, if you will, the courtyards of downtown Wilmington churches populated by weary soldiers for so long that their camp fires permanently blackened the steeples.

From the beginning, settlers here established a religious environment of respect, support and tolerance of each other's right to observe beliefs. In the entire recorded history of Wilmington, there is no evidence of religious oppression. In fact, we find many examples of a congregation of one denomination coming to the aid of another, such as when the members of Temple Israel, the first Jewish Temple in North Carolina, freely shared their building with neighboring Methodists for two years after the Methodist church was destroyed by fire in 1886. In the aftermath of the Civil War, many white congregations offered financial and moral support to newly created black churches when black members decided the time had come to create their own houses of worship.

The grander houses of worship in downtown Wilmington date from the 18th and 19th centuries and, in addition to providing opulent settings for large congregations, figure prominently on historic tours of the area. One cannot view the Wilmington skyline without being instantly struck by the profusion of spires. The tallest and oldest, the 197-foot twin spire of First Baptist Church was toppled by Hurricane Floyd in 1999. After a full year of determination to rebuild the spire in its exact authenticity, it has been restored to its former beauty.

Visitors enjoy the fascinating history and architecture of many local churches and temples, including St. James Episcopal at the corner of S. Third and Market streets; St. Mary's Catholic on Ann Street; Temple of Israel at the corner of S. Fourth and Market streets; St. Paul's Evangelical Lutheran on Market Street; First Presbyterian on S. Third Street; and St. Stephen AME on Red Cross Street. If you want to know more about these and other historic churches, see our Attractions chapter or drop by the North Carolina Room at the New Hanover County Public Library in downtown Wilmington and ask for information.

WECT-TV published the Cape Fear Worship Directory in November 2001, and it lists 443 churches, temples and other houses of worship in New Hanover County, Brunswick County and Whiteville (Columbus County). Arranged alphabetically by city, the Directory contains church names, addresses and phone numbers. For a copy, call (910) 791-8070.

Wilmington has interdenominational, nondenominational, Full Gospel, Episcopal, Holiness, Pentecostal and AME/AME Zion houses of worship. Other religions with a presence in the area include Jewish, Roman Catholic, Jehovah's Witnesses, Greek Orthodox, Christian Science, Islam,

Pier pilings and cross ties make a geometrical form that resembles a church's nave.

Photo: Jay Tervo

Lutheran, Quaker, Unitarian, Seventh Day Adventist, Unity, Eckankar and United Methodist. Meditation groups meet in various spiritual centers. You can get specific information about spiritual organizations, services and locations via the Yellow Pages, the "Religion" page in Saturday's *Wilmington Morning-Star*, public libraries, local chambers of commerce and visitor centers.

The Thai temple rises from the coastal forests of Brunswick County in Bolivia. The Buddhist Association of North Carolina has been building this temple for many years and has relied on community donations to complete the work. It represents an important addition to the region's religious and philosophical centers. It's not easy to locate, so you'll need to call for directions, (910) 253-4526.

If you want to attend services while you're on vacation and you're wondering what to wear, here's some advice. Southern coast people don't dress up much for work and they love to wear casual clothes most of the time, but they generally dress for worship. Still, if casual clothes are all you brought, you will be welcome. People in our tourist-oriented communities are used to seeing visitors in vacation mode.

Wilmington and the southern coast area have an abundance of spiritual resources in terms of bookstores. Mainstream Christian shoppers will find Bibles, videos, tapes, music, gifts, books, cards and other religious items in these local shops: Cox Christian Bookstore, 75 S. Kerr Avenue, Wilmington, (910) 762-2272; Lemstone Books, in the Sears wing of Westfield Independence Mall on Oleander Drive, Wilmington, (910) 452-2774; Salt Shaker Bookstore and Café, 7055 S. Kerr Avenue, Wilmington, (910) 350-1753; Master's Touch, 117 Village Road, Leland, (910) 383-2800, and Eagle Christian Books and Gifts, 801 N. Howe Street, Southport.

Index of Advertisers

Index

INDEX

INDEX

INDEX

INDEX